A PRACTICAL APPROACH TO

ALTERNATIVE DISPUTE RESOLUTION

A PRACTICAL

ALTERNA DISPUTE RESOLUTION

THIRD EDITION

Susan Blake

Barrister and Associate Dean of Education, The City Law School, City University

Julie Browne

Barrister and Deputy Course Director of the BPTC, The City Law School, City University

Professor Stuart Sime

Barrister and Course Director of the BPTC, The City Law School, City University

UNIVERSITY PRESS

XFORD
UNIVERSITY PRESS

arendon Street, Oxford, OX2 6DP,
United Kingdom

sity Press is a department of the University of Oxford. University's objective of excellence in research, scholarship, by publishing worldwide. Oxford is a registered trade mark of rd University Press in the UK and in certain other countries

First edition 2011
Second edition 2012

Impression: 1

Published in the United States of America by Oxford University Press
198 Madison Avenue, New York, NY 10016, United States of America

British Library Cataloguing in Publication Data
Data available

Library of Congress Control Number: 2014940421

ISBN 978–0–19–871447–7

Printed in Great Britain by
Ashford Colour Press Ltd, Gosport, Hampshire

PREFACE

The use of Alternative Dispute Resolution, or 'ADR', continues to develop very rapidly. The implementation in April 2013 of the main proposals of the Review of Civil Litigation Costs by Sir Rupert Jackson (2009), together with ongoing judicial support for the reasonable use of ADR, effectively mean that ADR options now need to be considered at least as part of resolving any civil dispute. Government policy is to promote the use of mediation in a growing range of areas, and current proposals make it quite possible that the use of mediation may become the norm in lower value civil cases in county courts within the next few years.

The term 'ADR' does not have a fixed technical meaning, but encompasses a wide range of dispute resolution processes that may be used as alternatives to litigation in the courts. It is frequently regarded as a modern development, but parties have been negotiating settlements of disputes since time immemorial, and arbitration can be traced back to ancient Greece. Over time various ADR processes started to develop, but in recent years the importance of considering ADR when dealing with litigation in court has brought this area to the centre of civil practice. Developments since 1994 outlined in Chapter 1 (with the use of ADR gradually spreading from commercial court cases to the High Court, the County Court, and the Court of Appeal) marked a watershed in cases conducted in England and Wales. This was cemented by the introduction of the Civil Procedure Rules 1998 and the related pre-action protocols, which require parties to consider ADR before issuing proceedings and give the courts power to impose sanctions for any unreasonable failure to engage in ADR.

The Civil Justice Reforms of 2013 are aimed at seeking to reduce the overall costs of resolving civil disputes, and a key component is that there should be a serious campaign to ensure that all litigators and judges are properly informed about the benefits of ADR. As Sir Rupert Jackson has written, the aim is that no case should come to trial without the parties having undertaken some form of ADR to attempt to settle the case. Students and practitioners therefore need a rounded understanding of the full range of ADR processes that are available, combined with an appreciation of the use and possible strengths and weaknesses of each.

This book provides a full overview, focusing on the most commonly used processes, but also outlining other options to provide a complete picture. Within this range there is a key division between non-adjudicative processes, such as negotiation and mediation, which seek to assist the clients in reaching an agreement, and adjudicative processes, such as arbitration and expert determination, where a tribunal or expert agreed by the parties will come to a binding decision on the dispute.

We seek to adopt a practical approach, covering a professional level of knowledge of each process and insight into the skills required to obtain a good outcome for a client. This includes considering the range of difficulties and issues that may arise and how they may be addressed. The book also considers matters such as tactics and styles, preparation and conducting ADR processes, professional ethics issues involved in ADR, costs, the interrelation between ADR and litigation, and the enforcement of compromises and awards.

In preparing a third edition of this book we have sought to cover the wide range of developments that have taken place in the last couple of years, and to give guidance on likely developments in the near future. New cases and changes in rules up to May 2014 have also been incorporated.

The authors appreciate all the assistance and experience that have been shared with them by colleagues at the City Law School, who work constantly to enhance the training provided for those going into practice as lawyers.

Finally, we would like to thank Tom Randall and his colleagues at Oxford University Press for their assistance in publishing this book.

Susan Blake
Julie Browne
Stuart Sime
June 2014

ACKNOWLEDGEMENTS

In Chapter 14, the Annual ADR pledge statistics are reproduced by kind permission of the Ministry of Justice.

Information on the Civil Mediation Council schemes has been obtained and is provided with the kind assistance and permission of the Civil Mediation Council. The details are accurate as at May 2014; readers should refer to the CMC website at www.civilmediation.org for the most up-to-date information.

In Appendix 1, the CEDR Model Mediation Agreement is reproduced by kind permission of the Centre for Effective Dispute Resolution. This document is updated regularly; readers should consult www.cedr.com to obtain the most up-to-date version.

Every effort has been made to trace and contact copyright holders prior to publication. If notified, the publisher will undertake to rectify any errors or omissions at the earliest opportunity.

ACKNOWLEDGEMENTS

CONTENTS SUMMARY

Glossary and abbreviations	xxxv
Table of cases	xxxviii
Table of statutes	xlvii

PART I HISTORY AND RANGE OF ADR METHODS

1	Introduction	3
2	Overview of ADR options	22
3	Factors influencing the selection of an ADR option	36
4	Funding ADR procedures	52
5	Online ADR options and ODR	68
6	Professional ethics	76

PART II THE INTERPLAY BETWEEN ADR, CPR, AND LITIGATION

7	The approach of the courts to ADR	95
8	The sanctions for refusing to engage in ADR processes	125
9	Recovery of ADR costs in litigation	149

PART III NEGOTIATION AND MEDIATION

10	Overview of negotiation and mediation	159
11	Styles, strategies, and tactics in negotiation	160
12	Preparing for negotiation	174
13	The negotiation process	192
14	Mediation: general principles	215
15	Preparation for the mediation	252
16	The mediation process	268
17	Reaching a settlement	292
18	Court mediation schemes and other schemes	297
19	International mediation	319

PART IV EVALUATION, CONCILIATION, AND OMBUDSMEN

20	Conciliation	333
21	Complaints, grievances, and ombudsmen	338
22	Early neutral evaluation	346

PART V RECORDING SETTLEMENT

23 Recording settlement 355

PART VI ADJUDICATIVE ADR

24 Expert or neutral determination 377
25 Construction industry adjudication 392
26 Arbitration 408
27 Arbitral tribunals 430
28 The commercial arbitration process 439
29 International arbitration 466
30 Arbitration awards and orders 486
31 High Court jurisdiction in arbitration claims 494
32 Enforcement of settlements and awards 516

APPENDICES

APPENDIX 1 CEDR Model Mediation Agreement (13th edn) 529
APPENDIX 2 Key provisions of the Arbitration Act 1996 533

Index 573

TABLE OF CONTENTS

Glossary and abbreviations xxxv
Table of cases xxxviii
Table of statutes xlvii

PART I HISTORY AND RANGE OF ADR METHODS 1

1 INTRODUCTION 3

A BACKGROUND 3
B WHAT IS ADR? 5
C WHY IS THERE A NEED FOR ADR? 6
D THE GROWTH OF ADR OPTIONS 7
E COURT RECOGNITION OF ADR 8
F ADR AND THE REVIEW OF CIVIL LITIGATION COSTS 9
G RECENT DEVELOPMENTS 10
H THE INTERNATIONAL CONTEXT 11
I SOME ISSUES WITH REGARD TO ADR 12
J POTENTIAL ADVANTAGES OF ADR 13
Lower cost 13
Speed of settlement 13
Control of process 13
Choice of forum 14
A wider range of issues may be considered 14
Wider range of potential outcomes 14
Flexibility of process 14
Flexibility with regard to evidence 14
Confidentiality 14
Use of a problem-solving approach 15
Possible reduction of risk 15
Client satisfaction 15
K POTENTIAL DISADVANTAGES OF ADR 15
Increased expense 15
Additional delay 15
Possible reduction in outcome compared to a court judgment 15
Lack of a clear and public finding 16
Loss of potential strategic use of procedural steps 16
Loss of potential advantages of evidential rules 16
Confusion of process 16

L WEIGHING UP DISPUTE RESOLUTION OPTIONS 17
M THE PSYCHOLOGY OF DISPUTE ESCALATION 17
N ASSESSING THE SUCCESS OF ADR 18
O OVERVIEW OF REGULATORY FRAMEWORKS 19
P OVERVIEW OF TRAINING AND ACCREDITATION 20
KEY POINTS SUMMARY 21

2 OVERVIEW OF ADR OPTIONS 22

A KEY ELEMENTS OF ADR OPTIONS 23
B THE ROLE OF THE LAWYER WITH REGARD TO ADR OPTIONS 24
C NON-ADJUDICATIVE ADR OPTIONS 25
Inter-client discussion 25
Written offers 25
Negotiation 25
Mediation 28
Conciliation 30
Early neutral and/or expert evaluation 30
D ADJUDICATIVF ADR OPTIONS 31
Arbitration 31
Adjudication 33
Expert determination 33
E OTHER OPTIONS 34
Hybrids 34
Processes for dealing with grievances 34
Specialist systems 34
IT-based options 34
Dispute management systems 35
KEY POINTS SUMMARY 35

3 FACTORS INFLUENCING THE SELECTION OF AN ADR OPTION 36

A LEGAL ADVICE ON APPROPRIATE DISPUTE RESOLUTION OPTIONS 36
Overcoming possible problems in advising on ADR 36
The professional duty to give advice 37
When to give advice on ADR options 38
B ADVANCE SELECTION OF AN ADR OPTION 39
C FACTORS INFLUENCING ADR SELECTION 40
Is jurisdiction an issue? 40
Is ADR inappropriate? 41
Is a court decision creating a precedent important? 42
Is a court order necessary? 42
What is the relative cost of possible options? 43
How important is expert knowledge? 43

Is confidentiality important? 43
How much control does the client want? 43
What are the main objectives of the client? 44
Is a future relationship important? 44
What is the relevance of the chances of success? 44
Does the client want a 'day in court'? 45
Would neutral assistance be valuable? 45
What stage has the case reached? 45
How important might interim orders be? 46
Might orders relating to evidence be needed? 46
What is the attitude of the court? 46
Might enforcement be an issue? 47

D POTENTIAL CONCERNS ABOUT ADR 47
ADR can undermine litigation 47
Proposing ADR suggests a lack of faith in your case 48
ADR can undermine a lawyer's control of a case 48
ADR does not really save costs 48
ADR is a way of getting something for a weak case 48
ADR involves too much pressure to settle 49
ADR is used as a delaying tactic 49
ADR is not a robust process 49

E SECURING AGREEMENT TO ADR 49
Suggest specific benefits that ADR might offer 49
Offer information about ADR options 50
Propose a simple ADR option 50
Address any concerns that you think an opponent might have 50
Offer to pay reasonable ADR fees 50
Seek to persuade a judge to order a stay 50

F CONFIDENTIALITY IN RELATION TO ADR PROCESSES 50

G TIMING THE USE OF ADR 51

KEY POINTS SUMMARY 51

4 FUNDING ADR PROCEDURES 52

A THE FUNDING CONTEXT 52

B GENERAL CONSIDERATIONS 53
What are the main elements of expense in the case? 54
How much is at stake in the case? 54
How is the case being funded? 54
The extent to which expense has already been incurred 55
The chances of success 55
The possibility that costs may be recovered or liability for costs may shift 55

C ELEMENTS OF EXPENSE 55
Solicitor fees 56
Barrister fees 56
Evidence and information 56

Disbursements 56
Process fees 56

D WHAT ADR PROCESSES COST 56
ADR provider's fee 57
Negotiation 58
Mediation 58
Arbitration 59
Other forms of ADR 60

E EFFECTS OF THE FUNDING BASIS 60
Conditional fee agreement funding 60
Damages-based agreement 61
Insurance 61
Third-party funding 61
Legal Aid Agency funding 62

F SHIFTING THE LIABILITY FOR COSTS—PART 36 OFFERS 63

G CONSIDERATIONS FOR THE PARTIES 64

H OVERALL FINANCIAL ANALYSIS AND RISK ASSESSMENT 64

I BASIC EXAMPLE OF ADR FINANCIAL CONSIDERATIONS 66

KEY POINTS SUMMARY 67

---

5 **ONLINE ADR OPTIONS AND ODR** 68

A INTRODUCTION 68

B BACKGROUND 69

C THE MAIN BODIES CONCERNED WITH ODR 70

D THE CURRENT ROLE OF ICT IN ADR 70

E ODR SOFTWARE OPTIONS 71

F DEVELOPMENT OF ADR AND ODR WITHIN THE EU 73

G LOOKING FORWARD 74

KEY POINTS SUMMARY 75

---

6 **PROFESSIONAL ETHICS** 76

A INTRODUCTION 76

B ADVISING ABOUT ADR OPTIONS 77

C LAWYERS PROVIDING AN ADR SERVICE 78

D COMPLIANCE WITH CORE PROFESSIONAL DUTIES 79
To act within the client's instructions 79
To act at all times in the client's best interests 79
Advising on settlement 79
Conditional fee agreements (CFAs) and damages-based agreements (DBAs) 80
To be independent 80

To act with integrity 81
Fairness 81
Competence 81
Duties when advancing a client's case and drafting documents 81

E SPECIFIC DUTIES IN MEDIATION 82

F SPECIFIC DUTIES IN NEGOTIATION 82

G THE DUTY OF CONFIDENTIALITY 83
Introduction 83
The extent of the duty 84
Confidentiality in mediation 84
Confidentiality in Early Neutral Evaluation and Expert Determination 85
Confidentiality in adjudicative processes such as arbitration and adjudication 85

H LEGAL PROFESSIONAL PRIVILEGE 86

I WITHOUT PREJUDICE COMMUNICATIONS 86
Exceptions to the without prejudice communications rule 88

J PRACTICAL CONSIDERATIONS 89

K DISCLOSURE OF INFORMATION IN ADR PROCESSES 89
Non-adjudicatory ADR and expert determination 89
Adjudication and arbitration 90

L AUTHORITY TO SETTLE 90

M THE RELATIONSHIP BETWEEN BARRISTERS AND THEIR PROFESSIONAL CLIENTS IN ADR 91

KEY POINTS SUMMARY 92

PART II THE INTERPLAY BETWEEN ADR, CPR, AND LITIGATION 93

7 THE APPROACH OF THE COURTS TO ADR 95

A INTRODUCTION 95

B PRE-ACTION PROTOCOLS 97
Practice Direction — Pre-Action Conduct 97
The pre-action protocols 98
The Pre-action Protocol for Possession Claims based on Mortgage or Home Purchase Plan Arrears in Respect of Residential Property 99
The Pre-action Protocol for Construction and Engineering Disputes 99
Family proceedings 100

C THE COURT GUIDES 101
The Admiralty and Commercial Courts Guide 101
The Chancery Guide 102
The Queen's Bench Guide 104
The Technology and Construction Court Guide 104

D THE OVERRIDING OBJECTIVE AND ADR 105

E ACTIVE CASE MANAGEMENT AND ADR 105
Part 36 offers to settle 106
A more robust approach since 1 April 2013 107
Case management orders and ADR 108
F COSTS MANAGEMENT AND ADR 109
G DIRECTIONS QUESTIONNAIRES AND ADR 112
H GRANTING STAYS FOR ADR 113
I JUDICIAL ENCOURAGEMENT OF ADR 114
J THE APPROACH OF THE COURTS TO CONTRACTUAL ADR CLAUSES 116
K CAN THE COURT COMPEL THE PARTIES TO USE ADR? 120
KEY POINTS SUMMARY 123

8 THE SANCTIONS FOR REFUSING TO ENGAGE IN ADR PROCESSES 125
A INTRODUCTION 125
B THE COURT'S GENERAL POWERS TO MAKE COSTS ORDERS 126
C ADVERSE COSTS ORDERS AGAINST A PARTY WHO FAILS TO COMPLY WITH THE PRE-ACTION PROTOCOLS 127
D ADVERSE COSTS ORDERS AGAINST A PARTY WHO UNREASONABLY REFUSES TO CONSIDER ADR 128
The nature of the dispute 129
The merits of the case 129
The extent to which other settlement methods have been attempted 130
Whether the costs of ADR would be disproportionately high 137
Whether any delay in setting up and attending ADR would be prejudicial 137
Whether ADR had a reasonable prospect of success 138
E OTHER FACTORS 139
Whether an ADR order was made by the court 139
Requesting further information or evidence before using ADR 140
Both parties at fault 141
F REJECTING ADR AFTER JUDGMENT AND BEFORE THE HEARING OF AN APPEAL 142
G DELAY IN CONSENTING TO MEDIATION (OR ANOTHER ADR PROCESS) 143
H BACKING OUT OF AN AGREED ADR PROCESS 144
I UNREASONABLE CONDUCT IN THE MEDIATION 144
J IMPOSING A COSTS CAP ON SOLICITOR-CLIENT COSTS FOR FAILING TO PURSUE ADR 145
K INDEMNITY COSTS ORDERS FOR FAILING TO CONSIDER ADR 145
L WHAT PRACTICAL STEPS SHOULD BE TAKEN BY A PARTY TO AVOID SANCTIONS? 146
M HOW DOES THE COURT TREAT PRIVILEGED MATERIAL WHEN SEEKING TO IMPOSE SANCTIONS? 147
KEY POINTS SUMMARY 148

9 RECOVERY OF ADR COSTS IN LITIGATION 149

A INTRODUCTION 149

B COSTS OF INTERIM APPLICATIONS RELATING TO ADR 149

C RECOVERY OF THE COSTS OF UNSUCCESSFUL ADR PROCESSES 150
ADR processes that deal with costs 150
Costs of failed ADR as part of the costs of litigation 150
The agreement between the parties determines liability in respect of ADR costs 151
The parties make no agreement about the costs of the ADR process 152
Agreement between the parties for the costs of the ADR process to be costs in the case 153
Settlement or determination on all issues apart from costs 154

D RECOVERING THE COSTS OF AN ADR PROCESS AS DAMAGES 154

KEY POINTS SUMMARY 155

PART III NEGOTIATION AND MEDIATION 157

10 OVERVIEW OF NEGOTIATION AND MEDIATION 159

11 STYLES, STRATEGIES, AND TACTICS IN NEGOTIATION 160

A THE IMPORTANCE OF STYLE, STRATEGY, AND TACTICS 160

B STYLES 161
Co-operative 161
Competitive/confrontational 161
Choice of style 161

C STRATEGIES 161
Co-operative 162
Competitive or positional 162
Collaborative—principled or problem solving 163
Pragmatic 165
Choice of strategy 166
Interaction of strategies 167

D TACTICS 167
Tactics relating to information 168
Tactics relating to offers and demands 169
Tactics relating to structure 170
Tactics relating to presentation 171
Tactics relating to law 172

KEY POINTS SUMMARY 173

12 PREPARING FOR NEGOTIATION 174
A THE IMPORTANCE OF PREPARATION 174
B IDENTIFYING THE OBJECTIVES 174
C THE IMPORTANCE OF THE PROCEDURAL STAGE THE CASE HAS REACHED 175
The case is at a very early stage 175
The case is at a pre-action protocol stage 176
After the issue of proceedings 176
The case is being prepared for trial 177
D IDENTIFYING THE ISSUES 177
E THE RELEVANCE OF THE LEGAL CONTEXT 177
F PREPARING TO DEAL WITH FACTS AND EVIDENCE 178
The client's view of the facts and evidence 178
The opponent's view of the facts and evidence 179
Dealing with gaps and ambiguities 179
Preparing to deal with facts and information in negotiation 180
G PREPARING TO DEAL WITH FIGURES 180
H IDENTIFYING PERSUASIVE ARGUMENTS 181
Arguments based on the application of the law 182
Arguments based on facts 182
Merit-based or moral argument 182
Practical or personal arguments 183
Mixed arguments 183
I PLANNING POTENTIAL DEMANDS, OFFERS AND CONCESSIONS 183
Plan what you will seek from the other side 184
Plan how and when you will ask 184
Plan what you will offer 185
Plan how and when you will make offers 185
J LINKING CONCESSIONS 186
K IDENTIFYING THE BATNA 186
L IDENTIFYING THE WATNA 188
M CLARIFYING YOUR INSTRUCTIONS AND AUTHORITY 188
KEY POINTS SUMMARY 189

13 THE NEGOTIATION PROCESS 192
A WHEN, HOW, AND WHERE 192
B WHO 194
C COMMUNICATING EFFECTIVELY 194
Reciprocal or 'mirroring' behaviour 195
Effective presentation 195
Responding effectively 196
Questioning effectively 196
Listening effectively 196

D STRUCTURE AND AGENDA SETTING 197

E OPENING 198

Open by agreeing an agenda 198
Open with a statement or a proposal 198
Start by asking some key questions 199
Invite your opponent to open 199
Start with items that can be agreed easily 200
Start with items where your case is strong 200
Make limits on authority clear 200
Refer to privilege for discussion 201
Dealing with problems in opening 201

F SEEKING INFORMATION 201

G MAKING YOUR CASE ON THE ISSUES 203

Presenting the merits of your case 203
Addressing weaknesses in your case 203
Bringing out weaknesses in your opponent's case 204
Proposing an outcome 204
Additions to oral argument 204

H PLANNING AND TIMING CONCESSIONS, OFFERS, AND DEMANDS 205

Implementing concession plan 205
Gaining concessions 206
Making demands 206
Making concessions 207
Linking concessions 207
Making offers 208
Reaching a deal 208
Bargaining tactics 209

I MAKING PROGRESS 210

J DEALING WITH DIFFICULTIES 210

Gaps in information 210
Getting bogged down, or reaching deadlock 211
Dealing with a poorly prepared opponent 211
Dealing with a very competitive opponent 212
Frustration and emotion 212
Concern about possible inexperience 212

K REACHING A CLOSE—SETTLEMENT OR BREAKDOWN 213

Making an oral contract 213
Recording the outcome 213
No agreement is reached 214

KEY POINTS SUMMARY 214

---

14 MEDIATION: GENERAL PRINCIPLES 215

A WHAT IS MEDIATION? 215

B WHY IS MEDIATION AN EFFECTIVE ADR PROCESS? 216

C JUDICIAL ENDORSEMENT OF MEDIATION 218

D DISPUTES SUITABLE FOR MEDIATION 219

E THE ADVANTAGES OF MEDIATION 220

F DOES MEDIATION WORK? 221

G WHY DO THE PARTIES USE MEDIATION? 222

H WHAT CAN BE DONE TO MAKE A RELUCTANT PARTY ENGAGE IN MEDIATION? 223

Mediation Information Assessment Meetings 224

I THE TIMING OF MEDIATION 225

Before litigation begins 225

After litigation begins 227

J THE COSTS OF MEDIATION 227

The party's own costs of preparing for the mediation 227

The mediator's fee 228

Expenses of the mediation 228

K THE FUNDING OF MEDIATION COSTS, FEES, AND EXPENSES 229

Public funding 229

Funding under a CFA 229

L STYLES OF MEDIATION 229

Facilitative mediation 230

Evaluative mediation 231

Transformative mediation 232

M THE ROLE OF THE MEDIATOR 232

Organizing the mediation process 233

Acting as a facilitator 233

Acting as intermediary 234

Post-mediation role 234

N ACCREDITATION AND REGULATION OF MEDIATION 234

Introduction 234

Training and accreditation requirements 235

O THE CIVIL MEDIATION COUNCIL 236

The CMC Provider Accreditation Scheme 237

The CMC Individual Membership Scheme 238

The CMC Registered Workplace Mediation Organisation Scheme 238

Is further regulation required? 238

P ETHICAL CONSIDERATIONS AFFECTING MEDIATORS 240

Competence 240

Independence and neutrality 240

Impartiality 241

The mediation procedure 241

Fairness 241

Confidentiality 242

Termination of the mediation 242

Repeat instructions 242

Practice administration 242

Q THE WITHOUT PREJUDICE RULE IN MEDIATION 243
Communications that are not protected by the without prejudice rule in mediation 244
Can the mediator rely on the without prejudice rule? 246

R LEGAL ADVICE PRIVILEGE IN MEDIATION 246

S CONFIDENTIALITY IN MEDIATION 247
Example of a confidentiality clause 247
Information given to the mediator 247
Can the mediator enforce the confidentiality clause? 247
When will the court override the confidentiality provisions in the interests of justice? 248
Other exceptions to confidentiality 248

T THE MEDIATOR AS WITNESS 249
Should the law be reformed? 250

U CAN A MEDIATOR BE SUED? 250
Legal proceedings 250
Disciplinary proceedings 251

KEY POINTS SUMMARY 251

15 PREPARATION FOR THE MEDIATION 252

A INTRODUCTION 252

B SELECTING A MEDIATOR 252
The qualities required in an effective mediator 253
Factors influencing the selection of a mediator 253

C THE DURATION OF MEDIATION 255

D SELECTING A VENUE 255

E THE AGREEMENT TO MEDIATE 256

F PRE-MEDIATION MEETING/CONTACT 258

G THE ATTENDEES 258
Representatives of the parties 259
Person with authority to settle 259
Lawyers 259
Insurers 260
Interest groups 260
Experts 260
Witnesses of fact 260

H THE POSITION STATEMENTS 261
The aims in drafting the position statement 261
The content of the position statement 261
Joint position statement 263

I THE KEY SUPPORTING DOCUMENTS 263
Agreed bundle 263
Confidential bundles 264

J DISCLOSURE OF POSITION STATEMENTS AND DOCUMENTS 264
K OTHER DOCUMENTS THAT THE PARTIES MAY WISH TO BRING TO THE MEDIATION 265
L OTHER INFORMATION THAT THE MEDIATOR MAY SEEK FROM THE PARTIES BEFORE THE MEDIATION 265
M OTHER STEPS THAT NEED TO BE TAKEN TO PREPARE FOR THE MEDIATION 265
N CONCLUSION 267
KEY POINTS SUMMARY 267

16 THE MEDIATION PROCESS 268

A WHEN DOES THE MEDIATION START? 268
B THE STAGES IN MEDIATION 269
C THE OPENING STAGE 271
Introductions 271
The opening joint meeting (plenary session) 271
Opening statements by the parties 273
Witnesses and experts 275
Closing the opening joint meeting 275
Extension of the plenary session 276
The separate private meetings (or closed meetings) 276
D THE EXPLORATION/INFORMATION STAGE 277
Carrying out a 'reality test' 277
Probing the underlying issues 277
Devising options for settlement 278
E THE NEGOTIATING/BARGAINING STAGE 278
Acting as a shuttle-diplomat 279
Devising strategies to help the parties work through deadlock 279
F JOINT OPEN MEETINGS IN THE EXPLORATION OR BARGAINING STAGE 281
Joint meetings of representatives of the parties 281
Joint meetings between the lay clients 281
Joint meetings of the experts 281
G THE SETTLEMENT/CLOSING STAGE 281
If settlement is reached 281
If no settlement is reached 282
H THE CLOSING JOINT MEETING 283
I TERMINATION AND ADJOURNMENT OF THE MEDIATION 283
J THE MEDIATOR'S ROLE FOLLOWING THE CONCLUSION OF THE MEDIATION 283
K THE MAIN VARIATIONS IN THE PROCESS 284
Evaluative mediation 284
Evaluation of the merits of the case requested by both parties 284
Evaluation of one or more issues requested by one party only 285
MED-ARB 285

ARB-MED 285
Telephone mediations 286
Mediations conducted online 286

L THE ROLE OF THE ADVOCATE IN MEDIATION 287
Preparation and case analysis 287
Mediation advocacy 287
Advisory skills in mediation 288
Delivery of the opening statement at the opening joint meeting 289
The advocate's role during private closed meetings 289
Settlement 290

KEY POINTS SUMMARY 291

---

17 REACHING A SETTLEMENT 292

A REACHING AN ORAL AGREEMENT 292

B THE ROLE OF THE LAWYER 292

C CHECKING COVERAGE AND DETAIL 293

D RECORDING THE OUTCOME 294

E OPTIONS FOR RECORDING THE SETTLEMENT 295

F IF NO AGREEMENT IS REACHED 295

G CONTRACTUAL PRINCIPLES 296

H ENFORCEMENT OF SETTLEMENT AGREEMENTS 296

KEY POINTS SUMMARY 296

---

18 COURT MEDIATION SCHEMES AND OTHER SCHEMES 297

A INTRODUCTION 297

B HISTORIC SCHEMES 298
The Central London County Court Voluntary Mediation Pilot Scheme 298
The Central London County Court Compulsory Mediation Pilot Scheme 298
The National Mediation Helpline 299

C CURRENT COURT MEDIATION SCHEMES 299
The Mayor's and City of London County Court Mediation Scheme 299
The HMCTS Small Claims Mediation Scheme 300
The Court of Appeal Mediation Scheme 301
The West Midlands Family Mediation Scheme 302
County court local schemes 302

D CURRENT MEDIATION INFORMATION PILOT COURT SCHEMES 302
The Birmingham, Manchester and Central London County Courts Mediation Information Pilot Schemes 302
The Court of Appeal Mediation Pilot Scheme 303

E THE CIVIL MEDIATION ONLINE DIRECTORY 303

F JUDICIAL MEDIATION SCHEMES 304

The Court Settlement Process in the Technology and Construction Court 304
Judicial mediation in Family Cases 305
Judicial mediation in Employment Tribunals 305

G MEDIATION IN SPECIFIC CASES 306
Mediation in cases in the Commercial Court 306
Complex construction, engineering, and technology disputes 306
Family cases 307
Workplace mediation 309
Mediation in employment disputes 310
Mediation in personal injury cases 311

H MEDIATING MULTI-PARTY DISPUTES 312

I OTHER SPECIALIST MEDIATION SCHEMES 313

J OTHER MEDIATION PROCESSES 314
Project mediation 314
The mini-trial or executive tribunal 314
Consensus-building mediation in environmental disputes or disputes that involve public policy issues 315
Deal mediation 316

K RESTORATIVE JUSTICE 316

L COMMUNITY MEDIATION 316

M PRO BONO MEDIATION AND LAWWORKS 317

KEY POINTS SUMMARY 318

19 INTERNATIONAL MEDIATION 319

A INTRODUCTION 319

B THE ADVANTAGES OF MEDIATION IN INTERNATIONAL DISPUTES 320

C PREPARATION FOR MEDIATION IN INTERNATIONAL DISPUTES 320

D THE PROCESS IN INTERNATIONAL MEDIATION 321

E THE GROWTH OF MEDIATION IN EUROPE 322

F A MOVE TOWARDS HARMONIZING PRACTICES IN INTERNATIONAL MEDIATION 322

G THE EU DIRECTIVE ON MEDIATION IN CIVIL AND COMMERCIAL CASES (DIRECTIVE 2008/52/EC) 323
The objective of the Directive 323
The application of the Directive 324
Implementation of the Directive by the United Kingdom 324
The main provisions of the Directive and the implementation of these provisions by the United Kingdom 324
Application of the Directive to domestic mediations 329
Implementation of the EU Mediation Directive in other member states 329

H THE EUROPEAN CODE OF CONDUCT FOR MEDIATORS 329

I ENFORCEABILITY OF INTERNATIONAL MEDIATION SETTLEMENT AGREEMENTS 330

KEY POINTS SUMMARY 330

PART IV EVALUATION, CONCILIATION, AND OMBUDSMEN 331

20 CONCILIATION 333

A WHAT IS CONCILIATION? 333

B AN OUTLINE OF THE PROCESS 333

C ADVISORY, CONCILIATION AND ARBITRATION SERVICE 334
Mandatory Early Conciliation 334
Post-claim conciliation 334
Collective conciliation 335

D CONCILIATION IN FAMILY CASES 335
The process 335

E OTHER CONCILIATION SCHEMES 336
The Disability Conciliation Service 336
The Furniture Ombudsmen Conciliation Scheme 336

KEY POINTS SUMMARY 336

21 COMPLAINTS, GRIEVANCES, AND OMBUDSMEN 338

A INTRODUCTION 338

B COMPLAINTS AND GRIEVANCE PROCEDURES 338
Definitions 339
Complaints handling 339
Complaints against solicitors 340
Employment grievances 340
Acting for a party in a complaint 342
Decisions in complaints and grievance investigations 342
Effectiveness of complaints and grievance procedures 343

C OMBUDSMEN 343
Complaints handling by ombudsmen 343
Procedure on references to ombudsmen 344
Grounds on which ombudsmen make their decisions 344
Effect of ombudsman's decision 345

KEY POINTS SUMMARY 345

22 EARLY NEUTRAL EVALUATION 346

A WHAT IS EARLY NEUTRAL EVALUATION? 346

B AT WHAT STAGE SHOULD IT BE EMPLOYED? 346

C WHEN SHOULD IT BE USED? 347

D WHO SHOULD BE APPOINTED TO CARRY OUT THE EVALUATION? 347

E THE PROCEDURE 347

F NEUTRAL FACT FINDING 348

G JUDICIAL EVALUATION 348
Judicial evaluation in the Commercial Court 348
Judicial evaluation in the Technology and Construction Court 348
Judicial evaluation in Social Security and Child Support Tribunal ENE pilot scheme 349
Judicial evaluation in the Chancery Division 350
H EVALUATION IN PERSONAL INJURY CASES 351
KEY POINTS SUMMARY 351

PART V RECORDING SETTLEMENT 353

23 RECORDING SETTLEMENT 355
A REACHING AGREEMENT 355
B FORMS OF RECORDED OUTCOME 356
Compromise agreements 357
Full and final settlement 357
Subject to contract 357
C RECORDS MADE DURING THE ADR PROCESS 358
D WHO SHOULD PRODUCE A FORMAL RECORD? 358
E ENFORCEABLE FORMS FOR RECORDING SETTLEMENT 358
An oral contract 358
A written contract 359
An award with statutory authority 359
A court order 359
Other legal documents 359
F DRAFTING TERMS OF SETTLEMENT 359
G METHODS OF RECORDING SETTLEMENT AGREEMENTS 360
Exchange of letters 360
Contract or deed 360
Settlements where there are existing court proceedings 363
Endorsement on briefs 363
Interim order 366
Consent order 367
Tomlin order 369
Relitigating after settlement 372
H TERMS AS REGARDS COSTS 372
I INFORMING THE COURT OF SETTLEMENT 373
KEY POINTS SUMMARY 373

PART VI ADJUDICATIVE ADR 375

24 EXPERT OR NEUTRAL DETERMINATION 377
A INTRODUCTION 377

B WHEN SHOULD NEUTRAL OR EXPERT DETERMINATION BE USED? 378
Stage at which the parties may agree to expert determination 378
Cases where expert determination is particularly suitable 378

C AGREEMENT TO USE EXPERT (OR NEUTRAL) DETERMINATION 379

D THE GENERAL APPROACH OF THE COURTS TO EXPERT DETERMINATION 379
Contractual effect of expert determination clauses 379
Applications to stay court proceedings pending expert determination 379

E ADVANTAGES OF EXPERT DETERMINATION 380

F DIFFERENCES BETWEEN EXPERT DETERMINATION AND NEGOTIATION, MEDIATION, AND NEUTRAL EVALUATION 380

G SIMILARITIES WITH OTHER FORMS OF ADR 380

H SELECTION OF THE NEUTRAL OR EXPERT DETERMINER 381

I THE PROCESS 381

J CONFIDENTIAL INFORMATION 382

K THE NATURE OF THE DECISION 383

L REASONS FOR THE DECISION 383

M THE COURT IS THE FINAL DECISION MAKER AS TO WHETHER THE EXPERT HAS JURISDICTION 383

N OTHER GROUNDS FOR CHALLENGING A FINAL DECISION BY COURT PROCEEDINGS 384
Material departure from instructions 384
Fraud or collusion 385
No reasons for decision 385
Manifest error 385
An error of law 386
Failure to act lawfully or fairly 387
The decision is not intended to be final on matters of construction 387

O PROCEDURE FOR MAKING A CHALLENGE 388

P ENFORCING A DECISION 388

Q SUING THE EXPERT 389

R HOW NEUTRAL OR EXPERT DETERMINATION DIFFERS FROM ARBITRATION 389

S DISPUTES REVIEW PANELS 389

KEY POINTS SUMMARY 391

---

25 CONSTRUCTION INDUSTRY ADJUDICATION 392

A INTRODUCTION 392

B NATURE OF ADJUDICATION 393

C REQUIREMENTS 393
Construction contract 394
Dispute 394
Former requirement for written agreement 395

D EXPRESS CONTRACTUAL RIGHT TO ADJUDICATION 395
E DEFAULT PROVISIONS IN THE SCHEME FOR CONSTRUCTION CONTRACTS 396
F COMMENCEMENT OF THE ADJUDICATION 396
Notice of adjudication: the commencement of adjudication 396
Ambit of the reference 399
Nomination of adjudicator 399
Referral notice 400
G PROCEDURE BEFORE THE HEARING 403
Response to referral notice 403
Subsequent statements of case 403
Timetable for procedural steps 403
Documents, questions, and impartiality 403
Site visits 404
Related disputes 404
Confidentiality 404
H ADJUDICATOR'S DECISION 404
Inquisitorial approach 404
Hearing 404
The decision-making process 405
Communicating decision to the parties 405
Reasons, interest, and costs 405
I BINDING, BUT INTERIM EFFECT, OF DECISIONS 405
J OVERALL COST 406
K ADJUDICATION IN RESIDENTIAL BUILDING CONTRACTS 406
L COURT ENFORCEMENT OF SUM FOUND DUE ON ADJUDICATION 406
KEY POINTS SUMMARY 407

26 ARBITRATION 408
A INTRODUCTION 408
B ARBITRATION AND LITIGATION 409
C FUNDAMENTAL CONCEPTS IN ARBITRATION 409
D HISTORY OF ARBITRATION 409
E INTERPRETATION OF THE ARBITRATION ACT 1996 410
F CONTRACTUAL FOUNDATION TO ARBITRATION 410
Separability of arbitration clause 411
Mandate of the arbitral tribunal 411
G REQUIREMENTS 412
Dispute or difference 413
Arbitrable dispute 413
Agreement to arbitrate 414
The arbitration agreement 416
Dispute must come within the arbitration agreement 417

Capacity 418
Conditions precedent to arbitration 418

H OVERVIEW OF ARBITRATION PROCEDURE 419

I GENERAL PRINCIPLES AND DUTIES 419

J FAIR RESOLUTION OF DISPUTES 419
Saving costs and expedition 419
General duty of the tribunal 421
Duty to follow the rules of natural justice 421
Arbitration need not be adversarial 421

K PARTY AUTONOMY 421
Mandatory and non-mandatory provisions 421
Sources of party agreement 422

L COURT APPLICATIONS 423

M DIFFERENT TYPES OF ARBITRATION 424
Institutional arbitration 424
Ad hoc arbitration 424
Non-binding arbitration 425
Statutory arbitration 425
Consumer arbitration 425
Med-arb 425
Family arbitration 426

N MULTI-TIERED DISPUTE RESOLUTION 426

O ONE-STOP ADJUDICATION 426

P EUROPEAN CONVENTION ON HUMAN RIGHTS AND ARBITRATION 426

Q MAIN FEATURES OF ARBITRATION 427

KEY POINTS SUMMARY 428

---

27 ARBITRAL TRIBUNALS 430

A INTRODUCTION 430

B COMMENCEMENT OF ARBITRATION 430
Importance of the date of commencement of an arbitration 430
Contractual time limits 430
Limitation periods 431
Date of commencement of arbitration 431
Avoiding the consequences of failing to comply with a time limit 431

C NOTICE OF ARBITRATION 431

D APPOINTMENT OF ARBITRAL TRIBUNAL 433
Number of arbitrators 433
Appointing the arbitrators 433
Chairperson 433
Umpire 433
Judges as arbitrators 434
Failure of appointment procedure 434

E CONTRACTUAL BASIS OF THE ARBITRATORS' MANDATE 434
Qualifications of arbitrators 435
Impartiality and independence 435

F TERMS OF REFERENCE 435

G REMOVAL, RESIGNATION, AND VACANCIES 436
Removal 436
Resignation 436
Death 436
Vacancies 437

H IMMUNITIES 437
Immunity of arbitrators 437
Immunity of arbitral institutions 437

I LIABILITY FOR ARBITRATORS' FEES 437

KEY POINTS SUMMARY 438

28 THE COMMERCIAL ARBITRATION PROCESS 439

A INTRODUCTION 439

B DEFINITION OF 'COMMERCIAL' 439

C PRIVACY AND CONFIDENTIALITY 440
Privacy 440
Confidentiality 440

D RANGE OF PROCEDURAL APPROACHES IN ARBITRATION 441

E PROCEDURAL RULES GOVERNING THE ARBITRATION 441
Bespoke arbitration clause 441
Arbitral institution rules 441
Silence in institutional rules 443

F ROLE OF LEGAL REPRESENTATIVES IN ARBITRATION 443
Advice on the arbitration clause 443
Reference of a dispute to arbitration 443
Defining the issues 444
Putting together the case 444
Hearings 444

G COMMENCEMENT 445

H 'LOOK-SNIFF' ARBITRATIONS 445

I SHORT-FORM ARBITRATIONS 445

J GENERAL PROCEDURE IN COMMERCIAL ARBITRATION 446
Preliminary meeting 447
Procedural orders 447
Peremptory orders 449
Dismissal for inordinate and inexcusable delay 450
Statements of case 451

Evidence 453
Witness statements 456
Experts 456
Pre-trial hearing/conference 457
No right to an oral hearing 457
Bundles 457
Arrangements for the hearing 458
The hearing 458
The decision 460
Ex aequo et bono/amiable compositeur (equity clauses) 461
The award and appeals 461

K EXAMPLE OF ARBITRAL RULES THAT CLOSELY FOLLOW COURT PROCEDURES 461
Commencement of arbitration 461
Counter-notice 462
Appointment of tribunal 462
Procedure 462
Statements of case 462
Documents and samples 463
Directions 463
Hearings 464
Awards 464
Appeals 464

KEY POINTS SUMMARY 465

---

29 INTERNATIONAL ARBITRATION 466

A INTRODUCTION 466

B MEANING OF 'INTERNATIONAL' IN ARBITRATION 467

C ADVISING THE CLIENT 467

D SEAT 468
Designation of seat 468
Supervisory jurisdiction 469
Place of award 469

E PROBLEMS CAUSED BY DIFFERENT SYSTEMS OF LAW 469

F APPLICABLE LAW 470
Proper law of the contract 470
Law of the arbitration agreement 472
Jurisdiction Regulation (Brussels Convention) 473
Procedural law of the arbitration (curial law) 473
Law of the place of enforcement 474
Stateless arbitrations 474

G OBJECTIONS TO JURISDICTION 474
Procedures available for raising an objection to jurisdiction 474
Substantive jurisdiction 476
Time when an objection to jurisdiction should be taken 476

Reserving client's position 477
Taking a step in the arbitration 477
Kompetenz-Kompetenz 478
Anti-suit injunctions 478

H PROCEDURAL MATTERS RELEVANT TO INTERNATIONAL ARBITRATION 479
Language of the arbitration 479
Meetings and hearings 479
Privilege 479
Security for costs 480

I ICC RULES OF ARBITRATION 480
Request for arbitration 480
Answer to the request 481
ICC arbitral tribunals 481
Seat of the arbitration 481
Terms of reference 481
Procedure prior to the hearing 481
Hearings and the decision 482

J UNCITRAL MODEL LAW ON INTERNATIONAL COMMERCIAL ARBITRATION 482
Interpretation of the Model Law 482
Commencement of Model Law arbitration 483
Model Law arbitral tribunals 483
Interim measures 483
Statements of case under the Model Law 484
Subsequent procedure 484
Hearings 484

KEY POINTS SUMMARY 485

---

30 ARBITRATION AWARDS AND ORDERS 486

A INTRODUCTION 486

B PROCEDURAL ORDERS 486

C INTERIM AWARDS AND AWARDS ON DIFFERENT ISSUES 487

D SETTLEMENT 487

E MAIN AWARDS 487
Majority decisions 489
Reasons 490
Seat of the arbitration 490
Date of award 490
Place where award is made 490
Remedies 491
Notification of award 491
Binding effect 491

F AWARD OF COSTS 492

KEY POINTS SUMMARY 493

31 HIGH COURT JURISDICTION IN ARBITRATION CLAIMS 494

A INTRODUCTION 494

B ORDERS TO PREVENT PARTIES BREACHING AGREEMENTS TO ARBITRATE 495
Stay of legal proceedings 495
Taking a step in the proceedings 496
Anti-suit injunctions 496

C APPOINTMENT, REMOVAL, AND REPLACEMENT OF ARBITRATORS 497
Extending time for beginning arbitral proceedings 497
Setting aside appointment of sole arbitrator 497
Failure of the appointment procedure 497
Removal of arbitrators 497
Relief from liability after resignation of an arbitrator 498

D PROCEDURAL ORDERS TO ASSIST IN THE DETERMINATION OF ARBITRAL PROCEEDINGS 498
Powers to secure evidence etc available to tribunals 498
Court jurisdiction on procedural matters 499
Disclosure in aid of arbitration 499
Interim injunctions 500
Applications for procedural orders 500
Exclusion of section 44 501

E JUDICIAL REVIEW OF ARBITRAL PROCEEDINGS 501

F PRELIMINARY POINTS OF LAW 501
Conditions to be satisfied 502
Procedure on applications on preliminary points of law 502

G SERIOUS IRREGULARITY 502
Meaning of 'serious irregularity' 502
Substantial injustice 504
Loss of right to object 505
Powers available to deal with a serious irregularity 505

H APPEAL ON A POINT OF LAW 505
Question of law 505
No contrary agreement 506
No agreement to dispense with reasons 506
Tribunal asked to determine the point 506
Exhaustion of arbitral appeals and reviews 506
Point must arise from an award 507
Appeal must be made within 28 days 507
Agreement or permission to appeal 507
Permission of the court 507
Powers available to deal with points of law 508

I PROCEDURE IN ARBITRATION CLAIMS 508
Application or Part 8 claim 508
Time limit 509
Defendants to the arbitration claim 509

Courts having jurisdiction over arbitration claims 509
Procedure on arbitration claims 513
Hearings in arbitration claims under Part 62 513

J APPEALS TO THE COURT OF APPEAL 513

KEY POINTS SUMMARY 514

32 ENFORCEMENT OF SETTLEMENTS AND AWARDS 516

A INTRODUCTION 516

B BASIC METHODS OF ENFORCING COMPROMISE AGREEMENTS 517

C MERGER OR DISCHARGE OF ORIGINAL OBLIGATION BY COMPROMISE 517
Express term reviving old obligations in the event of non-performance 517
Compromise based on performance of the agreed terms 517
Compromise ineffective 518

D MAKING A CHOICE ON ENFORCEMENT OPTIONS 518

E ENFORCEMENT OF COMPROMISES RECORDED AS A CONTRACT 518
Enforcement by civil proceedings 518
Defences to claims for breach of compromise agreements 519
Bankruptcy and winding up 519

F CHALLENGING A SETTLEMENT RECORDED AS A CONTRACT 520

G ENFORCEMENT OF COURT ORDERS 520

H COSTS ONLY PROCEEDINGS 521

I ENFORCEMENT OF CONSTRUCTION INDUSTRY ADJUDICATION DECISIONS 522

J ARBITRATION SETTLEMENTS AND AWARDS 522
Negotiated settlements in arbitration proceedings 522
Enforcement of domestic arbitral awards 523
Recognition and enforcement of New York Convention arbitration awards 523
Grounds for refusing recognition or enforcement of a New York Convention award 524
Enforcement of Geneva Convention awards 524

KEY POINTS SUMMARY 524

APPENDICES

APPENDIX 1 CEDR Model Mediation Agreement (13th edn) 529
APPENDIX 2 Key provisions of the Arbitration Act 1996 533

Index 573

GLOSSARY AND ABBREVIATIONS

AAA	American Arbitration Association
ACAS	Advisory, Conciliation and Advisory Service in relation to employment matters
Ad hoc	An arbitration not administered by an arbitral institution
ADR	Alternative dispute resolution
Adjudication	Adjudicative dispute resolution procedure for construction industry disputes, providing a binding, speedy, but temporary decision
AICA	Association of Independent Construction Adjudicators
APCM	Assessed Professionally Competent Mediator
Arbitral institution	An organization, which may be international, professional, trade or independent, which administers arbitrations within its area of interest. They often also publish their own institutional arbitration rules
Arbitration	Adjudicative dispute resolution procedure under which the parties agree to submit their dispute to an impartial tribunal appointed by a process agreed by the parties
ATE	After the event
B2C	Business to consumer
BATNA	Best alternative to a negotiated agreement
BIOA	British and Irish Ombudsman Association
BSB	Bar Standards Board
C2C	Consumer to consumer
CA	Court of Appeal
CAMS	Court of Appeal Mediation Scheme
CEDR	Centre for Effective Dispute Resolution
CFA	Conditional Fee Agreement
CIA	Chartered Institute of Arbitrators
CIETAC	China International Economic and Trade Arbitration Commission
Claimant	Party bringing a claim, particularly in litigation and arbitrations
CMC	Civil Mediation Council
Complainant	Person making a complaint
Confidentiality	The duty not to disclose information or documents about a dispute to outsiders. In relation to dispute resolution procedures this will usually mean that disclosure will be limited to the parties, their lawyers, and the dispute resolution provider
CPD	Continuing Professional Development
CPR	Civil Procedure Rules 1998 (SI 1998/3132), the procedural governing litigation in the High Court and county courts
Court	In litigation this describes the tribunal appointed to decide the issues between the parties (typically a judge or appeal court). In arbitration a court is usually a governing body of an arbitral institution, and usually has no judicial function
CSP	Court Settlement Process
Curial law	The procedural law governing arbitral proceedings. Also known as the *lex arbitiri*

DAC	Departmental Advisory Committee on Arbitration, set up by the Department of Trade and Industry, whose reports formed the basis for the Arbitration Act 1996
DBA	Damages-based agreement
Defendant	Party responding to a claim (particularly in arbitration and litigation). Often used interchangeably with 'respondent' in arbitrations
Determiner	Expert or other person appointed to decide a matter referred to expert determination or neutral determination
DRC	Disability Rights Commission
DTJ	District Tribunals Judge
eADR	Electronic ADR
EHRC	Equality and Human Rights Commission
ENE	Early neutral evaluation
ESCP	European Small Claims Procedure
FDR	Financial dispute resolution
FHDRA	First hearing dispute resolution appointment
FMA	Family Mediators Association
FMC	Family Mediation Council
ICANN	International Corporation for the Assignment of Names and Numbers
IDAP	Independent Dispute Avoidance Panel
iDR	Internet dispute resolution
IFLA	Institute of Family Law Arbitrators
IMI	International Mediation Institute
LAA	Legal Aid Agency
LFA	Litigation funding agreement
LSC	Legal Services Commission
MIAM	Mediation information assessment meeting
MSEO	Mediation Settlement Enforcement Order
NCTDR	National Center for Technology and Dispute Resolution
NFM	National Family Mediation
NMH	National Mediation Helpline
ODR	Online dispute resolution
QOCS	Qualified One Way Costs Shifting
Redfern schedule	Four-column document giving disclosure of documents in arbitrations
Respondent	Party responding to a claim or application (particularly in arbitration and litigation). Often used interchangeably with 'defendant' in arbitrations
RIBA	Royal Institute of British Architects
RICS	Royal Institution of Chartered Surveyors
SCMA	Standing Council of Mediation Advocates
Scott schedule	Multi-column document used in construction disputes for setting out defects or disputes on an item-by-item basis, with columns for the responses of the other parties and the court or adjudicator
Seat	The jurisdiction where an arbitration is proceeding as a matter of law. Actual hearings may take place in another country without affecting the seat of the arbitration

Separability	Concept, particularly in arbitration, that an agreement to arbitrate has a life which is separate from the underlying contract
SIAC	Singapore International Arbitration Centre
SME	Small and medium enterprise
SRA	Solicitors Regulation Authority
TCC	Technology and Construction Court, a specialist court within the High Court
TeCSA	Technology and Construction Solicitors' Association
TOLATA	Trusts of Land and Appointment of Trustees Act 1996
Tomlin order	Consent order in litigation which stays a claim on terms set out in a schedule
Tribunal	Body appointed to determine a dispute. It is often used interchangeably with 'the arbitrators'. It is also used to describe the court, judge, or jury in litigation, and in relation to statutory tribunals
UNCITRAL	United Nations Commission on International Trade Law
WATNA	Worst alternative to a negotiated agreement

TABLE OF CASES

AAG Investments Ltd v BAA Airports Ltd [2010] EWHC 2844 (Comm) 88
A & E Television Networks LLC v Discovery Communications Europe Ltd [2013] EWHC 276 (Pat) 146
AB v CD Ltd [2013] EWHC 1376 (TCC) 245, 249, 257, 269, 282
Abbas (t/a AH Design) v Rotary (International) Ltd 2012 NIQB 41 380
Abbott v Long [2011] EWCA Civ 874. . . . 142
Ackerman v Ackerman [2011] EWHC 2438 (Ch) 385
ADS Aerospace Ltd v EMS Global Tracking Ltd [2012] EWHC 2904 (TCC). 41, 130, 131, 137, 138, 143
AES Ust-Kamenogorsk Hydropower Plant LLP v Ust-Kamenogorsk Hydropower Plant JSC [2013] 1 WLR 1889 478
Aird & Aird v Prime Meridian [2007] BLR 105 . . . . 88, 215, 243, 244, 247
Alassini v Telecom Italia SpA (Joined Cases C-317–320/08) [2010] 3 CMLR 17 ECJ. 122, 123
Ali Ghaith v Indesit Company UK Limited [2012] EWCA Civ 642. . . . . 140, 143
Ali Shipping Corp v Shipyard Trogir [1999] 1 WLR 314 . . . . 85, 440
Alliance Bank v Broom (1864) 2 Dr & Sm 289 357
Amec Projects Ltd v Whitefriars City Estates Ltd [2004] EWHC 393 (TCC). . . 406, 522
Andrew v Barclays Bank Plc [2012] CTLC 115 139
Andrews v Bradshaw [2000] BLR 6 498
Anon [1468] YB 8 Edw IV. 7, 409
AOOT Kalmneft v Glencore [2001] 1 Lloyd's Rep 128. 509
AP (UK) Ltd v West Midland Fire and Civil Defence Authority [2013] EWHC 385 (QB). 51, 127
Arenson v Casson Beckman Rutley and Co [1977] AC 405. 389
Arthur J S Hall & Co (a firm) v Simmons [2002] 1 AC 615 20
Ascot Commodities v Olam [2002] CLC 277 412
ASM Shipping Ltd of India v TTMI Ltd of England [2006] 1 Lloyd's Rep 375. . . 477, 503, 504
Aspect Contracts (Asbestos) Ltd v Higgins Construction plc [2014] BLR 79 406
Assimina Maritime Ltd v Pakistan National Shipping Corporation [2005] 1 All ER (Comm) 460 500
Athletic Union of Constantinople v National Basketball Association [2002] 1 WLR 2863 514
Atkinson v Castan (1991) *The Times*, 17 April 521
Aughton Ltd v MF Kent Services Ltd [1991] 57 BLR 1 416
Aveat Heating Ltd v Jerram Falkus Construction Ltd [2007] EWHC 131 (TCC) 395, 396, 405
AWG Construction Services Ltd v Rockingham Speedway Ltd [2004] EWHC 888 (TCC) 406

B v S [2011] 2 Lloyd's Rep 18 . . . . . . 419, 421
Balfour Beatty Construction Northern Ltd v Modus Corovest (Blackpool) Ltd [2008] EWHC 3029 (TCC). 118
Ballast plc v The Burrell Company [2001] BLR 529 522
Bank Mellat v Helliniki Techniki SA [1984] 1 QB 291. 474
Barclays Bank plc v Nylon Capital LLP [2011] EWCA Civ 826. . . . . 383, 384, 386
Barden v Commodities Research Unit (Holdings) Ltd [2013] EWHC 1633 (Ch) 245, 282, 291, 293
Barder v Caluori [1988] AC 20 369
Barnetson v Framlington Group Ltd [2007] 1 WLR 2443 87
Barr v Biffa Waste Services Ltd (Costs) EWHC 1107 (TCC). 145
Beauty Star Ltd v Janmohamed [2014] EWCA Civ 451 280
Belair LLC v Basel LLC [2009] EWHC 725 (Comm) 499
Bellway Homes Ltd v Seymour (Civil Engineering Contractors) Ltd [2013] EWHC 1890 (TCC). 64, 132
Berg v IML London Ltd [2002] 1 WLR 3271 88
Bernard Schulte GmbH v Nile Holdings Ltd [2004] 2 Lloyd's Rep 352 382
Berry Trade Ltd v Moussavi (No 3) [2003] EWCA Civ 715 88

Best Buy Co Inc v Worldwide Sales Corpn Espana SL [2011] EWCA Civ 618 88
Binns v Firstplus Financial Group plc [2013] EWHC 2436 (QB) 139
Birkett v James [1978] AC 297 450
Booker Belmont Wholesale Ltd v Ashford Developments Ltd (2000) LTL 18/7/2000 373
Boulos Gad Tourism and Hotels Ltd v Uniground Shipping Co Ltd (2001) LTL 21/2/2002 457
Bradford & Bingley plc v Rashid [2006] 1 WLR 2066 87
Bradford v James [2008] EWCA Civ 837 225
Braes of Doune Wind Farm (Scotland) Ltd v Alfred McAlpine Business Services Ltd [2008] 2 All ER (Comm) 493 468
Brandeis Brokers Ltd v Black [2001] 2 Lloyd's Rep 359 503
Brawley v Marczynski (Nos 1 and 2) [2003] 1 WLR 813 154
Brennan v Bolt Burden (a firm) (2003) *The Times*, 7 November 520
Brit Inns Ltd (in liquidation) v BDW Trading Ltd (Costs) [2012] EWHC 2489 (TCC) 135
British Russian Gazette and Trade Outlook Ltd v Associated Newspapers Ltd [1933] 2 KB 616 517
British Shipbuilders v VSEL Consortium plc [1997] 1 Lloyd's Rep 106 . . . . . . 385, 387
Brookes v HSBC Bank [2011] EWCA Civ 354 55
Brookfield Construction (UK) Ltd v Mott Macdonald Ltd [2010] EWHC 659 (TCC) 115
Brown v Rice [2007] EWHC (Ch) 625; [2007] EWCA Civ 625 . . . . 85, 243–6, 257, 268, 269, 283
Brownlee v Brownlee, decision of the South Gauteng High Court of South Africa 2008/25274 145
Bruce v Carpenter [2006] EWHC 3301 (Ch) 382
Buckland v Farrar & Moody [1978] 3 All ER 229 20
Burchell v Bullard [2005] BLR 330 . . . . 9, 37, 128, 130, 218

C v D [2008] Bus LR 843 469
Cable & Wireless plc v IBM United Kingdom Ltd [2002] 2 All ER (Comm) 1041 . . . 39, 118, 119, 222
Calderbank v Calderbank [1976] Fam 93 . . . 8
Campbell v Edwards [1976] 1 WLR 403 385
Cape Durasteel Ltd v Rosser & Russell Building Services Ltd [1995] 46 Con LR 75 119
Carleton (Earl of Malmesbury) v Strutt and Parker [2008] EWHC 424 (QB) 144
Carroll v Kynaston [2010] EWCA Civ 1404 120
Cetelem SA v Roust Holdings Ltd [2005] 1 WLR 3555 . . . . 500, 514
CGU International Insurance plc v Astrazeneca Insurance Co Ltd [2007] Bus LR 162 . . . . 470, 514
Chanel v FW Woolworth [1981] 1 All ER 745 358
Channel Tunnel Group Ltd v Balfour Beatty Construction Ltd [1993] AC 334 . . . . 35, 119, 379, 390
Chantrey Vellacott v The Convergence Group plc [2007] EWHC 1774 (Ch) 153
Chartbrook Ltd v Persimmon Homes Ltd [2009] 1 AC 1101 357
Chartwell Estate Agents Ltd v Fergies Properties SA [2014] EWCA Civ 506 . . 107
Checkpoint Ltd v Strathclyde Pension Fund [2003] 1 EGLR 1 . . . . . 412, 460, 490, 504
Chemistree Homecare Ltd v Abbvie Ltd [2013] EWHC 264 (Ch) 128
Choudury v Kingston Hospital NHS Trust [2006] EWHC 90057 410
Citation plc v Ellis Whittam Ltd [2012] EWHC 764 (QB) 150
City of London v Sancheti [2009] Bus LR 996 496
Clark v In Focus Asset Management & Tax Solutions Ltd [2014] EWCA Civ 118 345
Clarke v Redcar & Cleveland Borough Council [2006] IRLR 324 335
CMA CGM Marseille v Petro Broker International [2011] EWCA Civ 461 . . 523
CMA CGM SA v Beteiligungs-KG MS 'Northern Pioneer' Schiffahrtgesellschaft mbH and Co [2003] 1 WLR 1015 . . . . 507, 508
Community Care North East v Durham County Council [2012] 1 WLR 338 . . . . . 295, 371
Compagnie Europeenne de Cereals SA v Tradax Export SA [1986] 2 Lloyd's Rep 301 478
Connex South Eastern Ltd v MJ Building Services Group plc [2004] BLR 333 . . . 402
Conoco (UK) Ltd v Phillips Petroleum Co UK Ltd (unreported, 19 August 1996) 385

Cook v Wright (1861) 1 B & S 559 357
Corby Group Litigation v Corby DC [2009] EWHC 2019 (TCC). 140
Corenso (UK) Ltd v Burnden Group plc [2003] EWHC 1805 (QB) 133
Cott UK Ltd v FE Barber Ltd [1997] 3 All ER 540 . . . . 118, 379
County Personnel v Alan R Pulber [1987] 1 All ER 289 20
Courtwell Properties Ltd v Glencore PF (UK) Ltd [2014] EWHC 184 (TCC). 146
Coventry Scaffolding Co (London) Ltd v Lancsville Construction Ltd [2009] EWHC 3295 (TCC). 522
Cream Holdings Ltd v Davenport [2011] EWCA Civ 1287 382
CRM Trading Ltd v Chubb Electronic Security Ltd [2013] EWHC 3482 (QB) 111
Cruden Construction Ltd v Commission for the New Towns [1995] 2 Lloyd's Rep 387. 413
Cuflet Chartering v Carousel Shipping Ltd [2001] 1 Lloyd's Rep 707 504
Cumbria Waste Management Ltd v Baines Wilson [2008] BLR 330. 246
Cutts v Head [1984] Ch 290 . . . . 86, 88

D & C Builders v Rees [1966] 2 QB 107 . . 520
D (Minors), Re [1993] 2 All ER 693 88
Daejan Investments Ltd v Park West Club Ltd [2003] EWHC 2178 (TCC) 127
Dallah Real Estate and Tourism Co v Ministry of Religious Affairs of the Government of Pakistan [2011] 1 AC 763 . . . . . . 414, 476
Daniels v Commissioner of Police for the Metropolis [2005] EWCA Civ 1312 . . 129
Dearling v Foregate Developments (Chester) Ltd [2003] EWCA Civ 913 154
de Lasala v de Lasala [1980] AC 546 369
Delta Reclamation Ltd v Premier Waste Management Ltd [2008] EWHC 2579 (QB). 414
Demco Investments and Commercial SA v SE Banken Forsakring Holding Aktiebolag [2005] EWHC 1398 (Comm) 505
Detz v Lennig [1969] 1 AC 170 520
Deutsche Schachtbau-und Tiefbohrgesellschaft mbH v Ras Al Khaimah National Oil Co [1987] 2 All ER 769. 473
Deweer v Belgium [1980] 2 EHRR 239 . . . 12, 120, 123
DGT Steel & Cladding Ltd v Cubitt Building & Interiors Ltd [2007] BLR 371 . . . . 119, 120, 380
Dickinson v Jones Alexander & Co [1990] Fam Law 137. 20
Dolling-Baker v Merrett [1991] 1 WLR 1205 . . . . 85, 456
Donohue v Armco [2001] 1 Lloyd's Rep 425. 414
Dorchester Hotel Ltd v Vivid Interiors Ltd [2009] Bus LR 1026 405
Downing v Al Tameer Establishment [2002] 2 All ER (Comm) 545 414
Dunhill v Burgin (Nos 1 and 2) [2014] 1 WLR 933 356
Dunnett v Railtrack plc [2002] 1 WLR 2434 . . . . . 9, 131, 142, 218, 299
Durrant v Chief Constable of Avon & Somerset Constabulary [2013] EWCA Civ 1624 107
Dyson v Leeds City Council [2000] CP Rep 42 . . . . 114, 140, 145

Eagle Star Insurance Co Ltd v Yuval Insurance Co [1978] 1 Lloyd's Rep 357. 496
Econet Wireless Ltd v Vee Networks Ltd [2006] 2 Lloyd's Rep 428 . . . . . . 499, 500
Edmund Nuttall Ltd v RG Carter Ltd [2002] BLR 312 413
EDO Corporation v Ultra Electronics Ltd [2009] Bus LR 1306 500
EF Phillips and Sons Ltd v Clarke [1970] Ch 322 371
Egan v Motor Services (Bath) Ltd [2008] 1 WLR 1589 . . . . 219, 225
Egon Oldendorff v Liberia Corporation (No 2) [1996] 1 Lloyd's Rep 380 . . . . . . 469, 472
Elvanite Full Circle Ltd v Amec Earth and Environmental (UK) Ltd [2013] EWHC 1643 (TCC). 111, 146
Emmott v Michael Wilson & Partners Ltd [2009] 1 Lloyd's Rep 233 . . . . 86, 450
Epsom College v Pierse Contracting Southern Ltd (in liquidation) (Costs) [2011] EWCA Civ 1449 145
Essex CC v Premier Recycling Ltd [2007] BLR 233 506
Estor Ltd v Multifit (UK) Ltd (2009) 126 Con LR 40 . . . . 5 22
Euroption Stragetic Fund Ltd v Skandinaviska Enskilda Banken AB [2012] EWHC 749 (Comm) 130, 145
Excalibur Ventures LLC v Texas Keystone Inc [2011] EWHC 1624 (Comm). . . . 145, 478

F & C Alternative Investments (Holdings) Ltd v Barthelemy (Costs) [2012] EWCA Civ 843 135

Faida v Elliot Corporation [2012] EWCA Civ 287 . . . . 41, 219
Fairclough Homes Ltd v Summers [2012] UKSC 26 135
Farm Assist Ltd (in liquidation) v Secretary of State for the Environment, Food and Rural Affairs [2009] BLR 399 . . . . 85, 246, 248, 249
Fastrack v Morrison [2000] BLR 168 522
Fidelity Management SA v Myriad International Holdings BV [2005] EWHC 1193 (Comm) 504, 505
Fili Shipping Co Ltd v Premium Nafta Products Ltd [2007] Bus LR 1719 . . . 409, 411, 417, 426, 478
Finesse Group Ltd v Bryson Products [2013] EWHC 3273 (TCC) 52
Fiona Trust & Holding Corporation v Privalov *see* Fili Shipping Co Ltd v Premium Nafta Products Ltd
Fitzroy Robinson Ltd v Mentmore Towers Ltd [2010] EWHC 98 (TCC) 131
Flatman v Germany [2013] EWCA Civ 278 91
Fons HF v Corporal Ltd [2013] EWHC 1278 (Ch) 51
Food Corp of India v Achilles Halcoussis [1988] 2 Lloyd's Rep 56 418
Forstater v Python (Monty) Pictures Ltd [2013] EWHC 3759 (Ch) 128, 146
Fortress Value Recovery Fund I LLC v Blue Skye Special Opportunities Fund LP [2013] 1 WLR 3466 416
Fox v Foundation Piling Ltd [2011] 6 Costs LR 961 . . . . 131, 132, 136
Frost v Wake Smith & Tofields Solicitors [2013] EWCA Civ 772 290
Fulham Football Club (1987) Ltd v Richards [2012] Bus LR 606 495

Gaston, Broughton v Courtenay [2004] EWHC 600 . . . . 138, 140
Gbangola v Smith & Sherriff Ltd [1998] 3 All ER 730 421
Geogas Ltd v Trammo Gas Ltd [1991] 1 Lloyd's Rep 349 . . . . 508, 514
Glencot Development and Design Co Ltd v Ben Barrett & Son (Contractors) Ltd [2001] BLR 207 . . . . 285, 522
Glidepath Holding BV v Thompson [2005] 1 All ER (Comm) 434 499
Green v Rozen [1955] 1 WLR 741 . . . . . . 365, 367
Groundshire v VHE Construction [2001] 1 Lloyd's Rep 399 504
Guidance Investments Ltd v Guidance Hotel Investments Co BSC (Closed) [2013] EWHC 3413 (Comm) 379, 418
Guinle v Kirreh [2000] CP Rep 62 112
Guinness Peat Properties Ltd v Fitzroy Robinson Partnership [1987] 1 WLR 1027 86

Halifax Financial Services Ltd v Intuitive Systems Ltd [1999] 1 All ER 303 40
Halifax Life Ltd v Equitable Life Assurance Society [2007] 1 Lloyd's Rep 528 . . . . 85, 382, 383
Halki Shipping Corp v Sopex Oils Ltd [1998] 1 WLR 726 413
Halsey v Milton Keynes General NHS Trust [2004] 1 WLR 3002 . . . . . . 9, 12, 37, 108, 112, 120–3, 128, 129, 131, 136, 138–40, 142–4, 147, 148, 151, 218, 243, 298
Hammersmatch Properties (Welwyn) Ltd v Saint-Gobain Ceramics & Plastics Ltd [2013] EWHC 2227 (TCC) 64, 135
Harley v McDonald Harley (a Firm) (2001) *The Times*, 15 May 20
Harper v Interchange Group Ltd [2007] EWHC 1834 (Comm) 379
Harris v Manahan [1996] 4 All ER 454 . . . 369
Harrison v Bloom Camillin (1999) *The Times*, 12 November 19
Hart v Smith [2009] EWHC (TCC) 2223 406
Hashwani v Jivaj [2011] 1 WLR 1872 435
Hawk Shipping Ltd v Cron Navigation [2003] EWHC 1828 (Comm) 460
Henley v Bloom [2010] 1 WLR 1770 357
Henry v News Group Newspapers Ltd [2013] EWCA Civ 19 . . . . 10, 111
Herschel Engineering Ltd v Breen Property Ltd [2000] 70 Con LR 1 . . . . 119, 120
Hickman v Blake Lapthorn [2006] EWHC 12 (QB) 129
Hillcrest Homes Ltd v Beresford & Curbishley Ltd [2014] EWHC 280 (TCC) 418
Hinde v Hinde [1953] 1 All ER 171 367
Hirani v Hirani [2012] EWHC 1645 (Ch) 154
Hiscox v Outhwaite [1992] 1 AC 562 490
HMV UK Ltd v Propinvest Friar Ltd Partnership [2011] EWCA Civ 1708 508
Hodgkinson & Corby Ltd v Wards Mobility Services Ltd [1997] FSR 178 88
Holloway v Chancery Mead [2007] EWHC 2495 . . . . 118, 119
Homepace Ltd v Sita South East Ltd [2008] EWCA Civ 1 . . . . 386, 387

Huddersfield Banking Co Ltd v Henry Lister & Son Ltd [1895] 2 Ch 273 520
Hurst v Leeming [2002] EWHC 1051; [2003] 1 Lloyd's Rep 379 . . . . 129, 138
Hussmann (Europe) Ltd v Al Ameen Development and Trade Co [2000] 2 Lloyd's Rep 83 . . . . 472, 476, 490
Hyman v Hyman [1929] AC 601 369
Hyundai Merchant Marine Co Ltd v Americas Bulk Transport Ltd [2013] EWHC 470 (Comm) 417

Igloo Regeneration (General Partner) Ltd v Powell Williams Partnership (Costs) [2013] EWHC 1859 (TCC) 145, 146
IIG Capital LLC v Van Der Merwe [2008] 1 All ER (Comm) 1173 385
Instance v Denny Bros Printing Ltd [2000] FSR 869 243
International Sea Tankers Inc v Hemisphere Shipping Co Ltd [1982] 1 Lloyd's Rep 128 507
Investec Bank (UK) Ltd v Zulman [2010] EWCA Civ 675 359
Investors Compensation Scheme Ltd v West Bromwich Building Society (No1) [1998] 1 WLR 896 357
Itochu Corp v Johann MK Blumenthal GmbH & Co KG [2013] 1 All ER (Comm) 504 433

Jackson v Tharker [2007] EWHC 271 (TCC) 360
Jameson v Central Electricity Generating Board [2000] 1 AC 455; [1998] QB 323, 357, 517
Jarrom v Sellars [2007] EWHC 1366 (Ch) 128, 131, 141
John Barker Construction Ltd v London Portman Hotel Ltd [1996] 83 BLR 31 387
Jones v Sherwood Computer Services plc [1992] 1 WLR 277 . . . . 384, 385
Joseph Finney plc v Vickers [2001] All ER (D) 235 413

Kagalovsky v Balmore Investment [2014] EWHC 108 (QB) 107
Kastner v Jason [2004] 2 Lloyd's Rep 233 491
Kinstreet Ltd v Balmargo Corporation Ltd [2000] CP Rep 62 112
Kitcat v Sharp [1882] 48 LT 64 88
Kollerich & Cie SA v The State Trading Corporation of India [1980] 2 Lloyd's Rep 32 384

La Société Pour La Recherche, La Production, Le Transport, La Transformation et La Commercialisation des Hydrocarbures SPA v Statoil Natural Gas LLC [2014] EWHC 875 (Comm) 523
Lazari v London and Newcastle (Camden) Ltd [2013] EWHC 97 (TCC) 107
Lazenby (James) & Co v McNicholas Construction Co Ltd [1999] 3 All ER 820 450
Lead Technical Services Ltd v CMS Medical Ltd [2007] BLR 251 522
Leicester Circuits Ltd v Coates Brothers plc [2003] EWCA Civ 333 144
Lesotho Highlands Development Authority v Impregilo SpA [2006] 1 AC 221 . . . . 410, 426, 503, 504, 506
Lilleyman v Lilleyman & Another (No 2) [2012] EWHC 1056 (Ch) 134
Lloyds TSB Bank plc v Crowborough Properties Ltd [2013] EWCA Civ 107 . . . . 295, 371
Lobster Group Ltd v Heidelberg Graphic Equipment Ltd [2008] 2 All ER 1173 . . . . 152, 153
Locabail (UK) Ltd v Bayfield Properties Ltd [2000] QB 451 498
Longstaff International Ltd v Evans [2005] EWHC 4 (Ch) 141

M v M [2014] EWHC 537 (Fam) 119–21
MA Lloyd v PPC [2014] EWHC 41 (QB) 107
McAlpine PPS Pipeline Systems Ltd v Transco plc [2004] BLR 352 . . . . 399, 406
McCook v Lobo [2002] EWCA Civ 1760 . . . . 42, 138
McCosh v Williams [2003] NZCA 192 . . . 250
Macdonald v Livingstone [2012] CSOH 31 385
McE v Prison Service of Northern Ireland [2009] 1 AC 908 480
McGlinn v Waltham Contractors Ltd [2005] 3 All ER 1126 152
McMillan Williams v Range [2004] EWCA Civ 294 144
McTear v Engleheart [2014] EWHC 722 (Ch) 107
Macob Civil Engineering Ltd v Morrison Construction Ltd (1999) 64 Con LR 1 . . . . 393, 405
Magical Marking Ltd v Ware and Kay LLP [2013] EWHC 636 (Ch) 63, 132
Marco v Thompson (No 3) [1997] 2 BCLC 36 385

Margulead Ltd v Exide Technologies [2005] 1 Lloyd's Rep 324 . . . . 421, 503
Mason v Walton-on-Thames Charity [2010] EWHC 1688 (Ch) 243
MD v Secretary of State for the Home Department [2011] EWCA Civ 453 . . . 115
Medway Primary Care Trust v Marcus [2011] EWCA Civ 750 . . . . 131, 132, 135
Mehjoo v Harben Baker [2013] EWHC 1669 (QB) 63
Memory Corporation v Sidhu [2000] 1 WLR 1443 20
Menolly Investments 3 Sarl v Cerep Sarl [2009] EWHC 516 (Ch) 388
Mercury Communications Ltd v Director General of Telecommunications [1996] 1 WLR 48 . . . . 386, 387
Metalfer Corp v Pan Ocean Shipping Co Ltd [1998] 2 Lloyd's Rep 632 430
Metcalfe v Clipston [2004] EWHC 9005 410
Michael v Middleton [2013] EWHC 2881 (Ch) 24
Michael Wilson & Partners Ltd v Emmott [2008] Bus LR 1361 . . . . 440, 441
Midland Linen Services Ltd, Re [2004] EWHC 3380 (Ch) 138
Milsom v Ablyazov [2011] EWHC 955 (Ch) 440
Mitchell v News Group Newspapers Limited [2013] EWHC 2355 (QB) 53, 107, 111
Mobiqa Ltd v Trinity Mobile Ltd [2010] EWHC 253 (Pat) 140
Morris v Davis [2012] EWHC 1981 (Ch). . . 130
MRI Trading AG v Erdenet Mining Corp LLC [2013] 1 Lloyd's Rep 638 359
Muman v Nagasena [2000] 1 WLR 299. . . 112
Murray v Neil Dowlman Architecture Ltd [2013] EWHC 872 (TCC) 53, 111
Myerson v Myerson [2008] EWCA Civ 1376 87

Nagusina Naviera v Allied Maritime Inc [2003] 2 CLC 1 509
National Bank of Jamaica Ltd v Olint [2009] 1 WLR 1405 501
National Grid Co plc v M25 Group Ltd (No 1) [1999] 1 EGLR 65. . . . . 387, 388
National Navigation Co v Endesa Generación SA [2009] 1 Lloyd's Rep 666 473
National Westminster Bank plc v Feeney and Feeney [2006] EWHC 90066 . . . . 59, 151, 153
Neal v Jones Motors [2002] EWCA Civ 1757 143
Nelson's Yard Management Company v Eziefula [2013] EWCA Civ 235 . . . 51, 127
Nema, The [1982] AC 724 507
Newbury v Sun Microsystems [2013] EWHC 2180 (QB) 357
Newfield Construction Ltd v Tomlinson (2004) 97 Con LR 148 504
Newman v Framewood Manor Management Co Ltd [2012] EWCA Civ 1727. . . . . . 55, 130, 135
Nigel Witham Ltd v Smith [2008] EWHC 12 (TCC) 143, 225
Nikko Hotels (UK) Ltd v MEPC plc [1991] 2 EGLR 103 386
Nisshin Shipping Co Ltd v Cleaves and Co Ltd [2004] 1 Lloyd's Rep 38 416
Noble Denton Middle East v Noble Denton International Ltd [2011] 1 Lloyd's Rep 387 497
Nokia Corp v HTC Corp [2012] EWHC 3199 (Pat) 496
Norbrook Laboratories Ltd v Carr [2013] EWHC 476(QB) 51, 142
Nordsee Deutsche Hochseefischerei GmbH v Reederei Mond Hochseefischerei Nordstern AG & Co KG (Case 102/81) [1982] ECR 1095 414
North Oxford Golf Club v A2 Dominion Homes Ltd [2013] EWHC 852 (QB) . . 152
North Shire Ventures Ltd v Anstead Holdings Inc [2011] EWCA Civ 230. 386
Northern Pioneer, The *see* CMA CGM SA v Beteiligungs-KG MS 'Northern Pioneer' Schiffahrtgesellschaft mbH and Co
Nova (Jersey) Knit Ltd v Kammgarn Spinnerei [1977] 1 WLR 713. 472

Oceanbulk Shipping & Trading SA v TMT Asia Ltd [2010] 1 WLR 1803 88
Oceanografia SA de CV v DSND Subsea AS [2007] 1 Lloyd's Rep 37 417
Ofulue v Bossert [2009] 1 AC 990 87
Oliver v Symons [2012] EWCA Civ 267 41
Omnibridge Consulting Ltd v Clearsprings (Management) Ltd [2004] EWHC 2276 (Comm) 503
Ondhia v Ondhia [2011] EWHC 3040 (Ch) 357
Oxford Shipping Co Ltd v Nippon Yusen Kaisha [1984] 3 All ER 835. 440

P4 Ltd v Unite Integrated Solutions plc [2007] BLR 1 . . . . 128, 133
Pacific Maritime (Asia) Ltd v Holystone Overseas Ltd [2008] 1 Lloyd's Rep 371 500

Painting v Oxford University [2005] PIQR Q5 136
Palfrey v Wilson [2007] EWCA Civ 94 . . . 137
Park Promotion Ltd (t/a Pontypool Rugby Football Club) v Welsh Rugby Union Ltd [2012] EWHC 2406 (QB) 137, 143
Patel v Patel [2000] QB 551. 410
Patley Wood Farm LLP v Brake [2013] EWHC 4035 (Ch) 450
PC Harrington Contractors Ltd v Systech International Ltd [2013] Bus LR 970. . . .399
Peacock v Peacock [1991] Fam Law 139 520
Pell Frischmann Consultants Ltd v Prabhu [2013] EWHC 2203 (Ch) 128, 130
Persimmon Homes Ltd v Woodford Land Ltd [2011] EWHC 3109 (Ch) 388
Petroships Pte Ltd v Petec Trading and Investment Corporation [2001] 2 Lloyd's Rep 348. 503
PGF II SA v OMFS Company [2012] EWHC 83 (TCC). 141
PGF II SA v OMFS Company 1 Limited [2014] 1 WLR 1386 . . . . . . .11, 38, 64, 116, 134, 138, 139, 141, 146, 147
PHI Group Ltd v Robert West Consulting Ltd [2012] EWCA Civ 588. 64
Pickersgill v Riley [2004] PNLR 31 20
Pinnel's Case (1602) 5 Co Rep 117a 519
Pitt v PHH Asset Management [1993] 4 All ER 961 . . . . 40, 357
Porter v Magill [2002] 2 AC 357 . . . . 435, 498
Practice Note [1927] WN 290 369
Practice Note (Civil Litigation: Case Management) [1995] 1 All ER 385 . . . . 8, 95
Practice Note (Commercial Court: Alternative Dispute Resolution) [1994] 1 All ER 34 . . . . 8, 95
President of India v La Pintada Cia Navegacion [1984] 2 All ER 773. 360
Project Services v Opek Prime Development Ltd [2000] BLR 402 522

R (Bradley) v Secretary of State for Work & Pensions [2009] QB 114 345
R (Cowl) v Plymouth City Council [2002] 1 WLR 803 . . . . 62, 114, 115
R (on the application of Crookenden) v Institute of Chartered Accountants in England and Wales [2013] All ER (D) 352 (May) 55, 130
R (on the application of Royal London NHS Foundation Trust) v Secretary of State for the Home Department [2013] EWHC 4010 (Admin) 107
R (on the application of S) v Hampshire County Council [2009] EWHC 2537 (Admin) 115
R (Prudential plc) v Special Commissioner of Income Tax [2013] 2 AC 185. 86
Raggett v Governors of Preston Catholic College [2012] EWHC 3641 (QB) 63
Raj v Charity Commission for England and Wales [2013] EWHC 1425 (Ch) 111
Raja v Van Hoogstraten (No 9) [2009] 1 WLR 1143 458
Ranko Group v Antarctic Maritime SA (1998) LMLN 492 490
Rederij Lalemant v Transportes Generales Navigacion SA [1986] 1 Lloyd's Rep 45. 412
Reed Executive plc v Reed Business Information Ltd [2004] 1 WLR 3026 . . . . 88, 143, 147, 243
Reid Minty (a firm) v Taylor [2001] EWCA Civ 1723 145
Reliance Industries Ltd v Enron Oil and Gas India Ltd [2002] 1 All ER (Comm) 59 506
Retla Steamship Co v Gryphon Shipping Co SA [1982] 1 Lloyd's Rep 55 502
Ridehalgh v Horsefield [1994] Ch 205. 19
RJT Consulting Engineers Ltd v DM Engineering (Northern Ireland) Ltd [2002] 1 WLR 2344 392
Rofa Sport Management AG v DHL International (UK) Ltd [1989] 1 WLR 902 521
Rolf v De Guerin [2011] EWCA Civ 78 . . . 141
Rondel v Worsley [1969] 1 AC 191 20
Rose v Rose [2002] 1 FLR 978 305
Roult v North West Strategic Health Authority [2010] 1 WLR 487 369
Roundstone Nurseries Ltd v Stephenson Holdings Ltd [2009] EWHC 1431 (TCC) 144, 146, 152, 153
Rowallan Group Ltd v Edgehill Portfolio No 1 [2007] EWHC 32 (Ch) 145
Royal Bank of Canada v Secretary of State for Defence [2003] EWHC 1841 (Ch). . . . 128
Rush & Tompkins v Greater London Council [1989] AC 1280. . . . . 27, 86–7
Rustal Trading Ltd v Gill and Duffas SA [2000] 1 Lloyd's Rep 14 477

S v Chapman [2008] EWCA Civ 800 143
S v S [2014] Fam Law 448 426
SAB Miller Africa v East African Breweries [2010] EWCA Civ 1564. 501

Savings & Investment Bank Ltd v Fincken [2004] 1 WLR 667. 88
Sayers v Clarke Walker [2002] EWCA Civ 910 88
Scott v Avery (1856) 5 HL Cas 811; (1856) 25 LJ Ex 308 . . . . 39, 418, 419
Seabridge Shipping AB v AC Orssleff's Eft's A/S [1999] 2 Lloyd's Rep 685 410
Secretary of State of the Environment, Transport and the Regions, *ex p* The Channel Group Ltd [2001] EWCA Civ 1185. 418
Seeff v Ho [2011] EWCA Civ 186 142
Shashoua v Sharma [2009] 2 Lloyd's Rep 376. 468, 474
Shell Egypt West Manzala Gmbh v Dana Gas Egypt Ltd [2010] 1 Lloyd's Rep 109 . . . 506
Sheltam Rail Co (Proprietary) Ltd v Mirambo Holdings Ltd [2009] Bus LR 302. 476
Shirayama Shokusan Co Ltd v Danovo Ltd (No 1) [2003] EWHC 3306 (Ch). 112
Siebe Gorman and Co Ltd v Pneupac Ltd [1982] 1 WLR 185. 369
Slick Seatings Systems v Adams [2013] EWHC B8 53
Smith v Shirley and Bayliss (1875) 32 LT 234 517
Smiths Group Ltd v George Weiss (unreported, 22 March 2002) 243
Société Internationale de Télécommunications Aéronautiques SC (SITA) v The Wyatt Co (UK) Ltd [2002] EWHC 2401 (Ch) 137, 148, 153
Sonatrach Petroleum Corp v Ferrell International Ltd [2002] 1 All ER (Comm) 627 473
Soulsbury v Soulsbury [2007] EWCA Civ 969 358
Southwark LBC v IBM UK Ltd[2011] EWHC 653 (TCC). 145
Stax Claimants v Bank of Nova Scotia Channel Islands Ltd [2007] EWHC 1153 (Ch) . . . 87
Stretford v Football Association [2007] Bus LR 1052 426
Strover v Harrison [1988] Ch 390 20
Sucafina SA v Rotenberg [2013] Bus LR 158 487
Sudbrook Trading Estate Ltd v Eggleton [1983] 1 AC 444 382
Sulamerica CIA Nacional de Segueros SA v Enesa Engenharia SA [2013] 1 WLR 102 . . . . 118, 119, 470, 473
Summers v Fairclough Homes [2012] 1 WLR 2004 132
Sumukan Ltd v Commonwealth Secretariat [2007] Bus LR 1075 427
Sunrock Aircraft Corporation Ltd v Scandinavian Airlines System Denmark-Norway-Sweden [2007] 2 Lloyd's Rep 612. 120, 379
Sutcliffe v Thackrah [1974] AC 727. 389
Swain Mason v Mills & Reeve [2012] EWCA Civ 498 . . . . 41, 129, 130
Sycamore Bridco Ltd v Breslin [2013] EWHC 583 (Ch) 134

TAG Wealth Management v West [2008] 2 Lloyd's Rep 699 450
Tapoohi v Lewenberg [2003] VSC 410. . . . 250
Thames Valley Power Ltd v Total Gas & Power Ltd [2006] 1 Lloyd's Rep 441. . . . 380, 383
Thevarajah v Riordan [2014] EWCA Civ 15 107
Thomas and Co Ltd v Portsea SS Co Ltd [1912] AC 1. 416
Thomas-Fredric's (Construction) Ltd v Wilson [2004] BLR 23. 522
Thorne v Courtier [2011] EWCA Civ 460 . . . . 360, 387
Thornhill v Nationwide Metal Recycling Ltd [2011] EWCA Civ 919. . . . . 127, 137
Three Rivers District Council v Bank of England (No 5) [2003] QB 1556 . . . . 86, 246
Thwaite v Thwaite [1982] Fam 1. . . . 369, 520
Thyssen Canada Ltd v Mariana Maritime SA [2005] 1 Lloyd's Rep 640 477
Tilia Sonera Ab v Hilcourt (Docklands) Ltd [2003] EWHC 3540 (Ch) 491
Toepfer International GmbH v Societe Cargill France [1998] 1 Lloyd's Rep 379. 419
Tomlin v Standard Telephones & Cables Ltd [1969] 1 WLR 1378. 88
Tongyuan (USA) International Trading Group v Uni-Clan Ltd (unreported, 19 January 2001). 523
Transport for Greater Manchester v Thales Transport & Security Ltd [2013] EWHC 149 (TCC). 86
Troy Foods v Manton [2013] EWCA Civ 615 . . . . 53, 111
Turville Health Inc v Chartis Insurance UK Ltd [2012] EWHC 3019 (TCC) . . . 380, 409

U & M Mining Zambia Ltd v Konkola Copper Mines plc [2013] 2 Lloyd's Rep 218. . . . 468
UBS AG v HSH Nordbank AG [2009] 2 Lloyd's Rep 272 416
UK Highways A55 Ltd v Hyder Consulting (UK) Ltd [2012] EWHC 3505 (TCC). . . 113
Unilever plc v Procter & Gamble Co [2000] 1 WLR 2436 . . . . 87, 88, 244

Union Discount v Zoller [2002] 1 WLR 1517 . . . . 120, 379
Universal Satspace (North America) LLC v Kenya (QB) (unreported, 20 December 2013). 245, 257
Ursa Major Management Ltd v United Utilities Electricity plc [2002] EWHC 3041 (Ch) 382

Vale of Glamorgan Council v Roberts [2008] EWHC 2911 (Ch) 135–7
Veba Oil Supply and Trading GmbH v Petrotrade Inc [2002] 1 Lloyd's Rep 295. 384, 385
Vedatech Corp v Crystal Decisions (UK) Ltd [2003] EWCA Civ 1066. 296
Venture Investment Placement v Hall [2005] EWHC 1227 (Ch) 243, 247, 257
Vernacare Ltd v Environmental Pulp Products Ltd [2012] EWPCC 49 131
Vertase Fli Ltd v Squibb Group Ltd [2013] BLR 352 406
Vimercati v BV Trustco Ltd [2012] EWHC 1410 (Ch) 382
Virani v Manuel Revert Y CIA SA [2004] Lloyd's Rep 14. 143

Wah v Grant Thornton International Ltd [2012] EWHC 3198 (Ch) 119
Walford v Miles [1992] 2 AC 128 . . . . 40, 118
Walker v Wilsher [1889] 23 QBD 335 . . . . 88, 147
Walker Construction (UK) Ltd v Quayside Homes Ltd [2014] EWCA Civ 93 135
Walton Homes Ltd v Staffordshire CC [2013] EWHC 2554 (Ch) 385
Watson v Sadiq [2013] EWCA Civ 822 . . . 107
Watkins Jones and Sons Ltd v Lidl UK GmbH (2002) 86 Con LR 155 413
Webb Resolutions Ltd v JV Ltd (t/a Shepherd Chartered Surveyors) [2013] EWHC 509 (TCC) 294
Webb Resolutions Ltd v Waller Needham & Green (a Firm) [2012] EWHC 3529 (Ch) 51, 128
Weissfisch v Julius [2006] 1 Lloyd's Rep 716. . . . . 472, 478
Wentworth v Bullen (1840) 9 B & C 840 369
West Tankers Inc v Riunione Adriatica di Sicurtà SpA (Case C-185/07) [2009] 1 AC 1138 478
Westwood Shipping Lines Inc v Universal Schiffartsgesellschaft MBH [2012] EWCA 3837 (Comm) 86, 441
Wethered Estates Ltd v Davis [2006] BLR 86 . . . . 140, 148
Whitworth Street Estates (Manchester) Ltd v James Miller and Partners Ltd [1970] AC 583. 468
Wicketts v Brine Builders [2001] CILL 1805. 450
Widlake v BAA Ltd [2010] PIQR P4 136
Wilky Property Holdings plc v London & Surrey Investments Ltd [2011] EWHC 2888 (Ch) 384
Williams v Hull [2009] EWHC 2844 (Ch). . . . 87
Willis v MJR Rundell & Associates Ltd [2013] EWHC 2923 (TCC) 53, 109
Wilson v Haden (t/a Clyne Farm Centre) [2013] EWHC 1211 (QB) 49, 134, 138, 140
Woodward v Santander UK plc (formerly Abbey National plc) [2010] IRLR 834 89
World Trade Corporation v Czarnikow Sugar Ltd [2005] 1 Lloyd's Rep 422 . . 490
Worldwide Corporation Ltd v Marconi Communications Ltd (2004) *The Times*, 2 March. 20
Wright v Michael Wright Supplies Ltd [2013] EWCA Civ 234. . . . . 12, 42, 123, 219

Yan Seng Pte Ltd v International Trade Corp Ltd [2013] EWHC 111 (QB) 382
Yeates v Line [2013] Ch 363 362
Youell v La Réunion Aérienne [2009] Bus LR 1504 473
Youlton v Charles Russell (a firm) [2010] EWHC 1032 (Ch) 154, 248

Zurich Insurance Co plc v Hayward [2011] EWCA Civ 641 372

TABLE OF STATUTES

UK Statutes

Administration of Justice Act 1920
s 11 . . . 62
Arbitration Act 1697 . . . 7, 31
Arbitration Act 1950 . . . 31, 410
Arbitration Act 1979 . . . 31, 410
Arbitration Act 1996 . . . 19, 31, 386, 389, 408, 410, 411, 413–16, 419, 421–3, 425–9, 431, 438, 440–3, 445–8, 451, 453, 455, 457, 461, 465, 468, 471, 473, 476, 485, 488, 493, 494, 497, 499, 503, 509, 513, 514
Pt I . . . 416
ss 1–84 . . . 473, 477
s 1 . . . 419, 435, 494
s 1(a) . . . 409, 419, 421, 447, 453
s 1(b) . . . 447, 494
s 1(c) . . . 450, 475, 494, 514
s 2(1) . . . 473
s 2(2)(a) . . . 469
s 2(2)(b) . . . 469
s 2(3) . . . 469
s 3 . . . 423, 468, 474
s 4 . . . 423
s 4(2) . . . 443
s 4(3) . . . 423, 443
s 5 . . . 417, 506
s 5(1) . . . 416
s 5(2) . . . 416
s 5(3) . . . 416
s 5(4) . . . 417
s 5(6) . . . 417
s 6 . . . 425
s 6(1) . . . 413, 427
s 7 . . . 411, 423
s 8 . . . 423
ss 9–11 . . . 422
s 9 . . . 411, 414, 469, 476, 495, 496, 514
s 9(1) . . . 495, 496
s 9(3) . . . 495, 496
s 9(4) . . . 496
s 12 . . . 422, 431
s 12(1) . . . 497
s 12(2) . . . 431
s 12(3) . . . 497
s 12(4) . . . 497
s 13 . . . 422
s 13(1) . . . 431
s 14 . . . 423
s 14(1) . . . 431
s 14(3) . . . 431
s 14(4) . . . 431, 432
s 14(5) . . . 431
ss 15–22 . . . 423
s 15(1) . . . 433
s 15(2) . . . 433
s 15(3) . . . 433
s 16 . . . 433
s 16(1) . . . 433
s 16(3) . . . 434
s 16(4) . . . 434
s 16(5) . . . 434
s 16(6) . . . 434
ss 17–19 . . . 434
s 17(1) . . . 497
s 17(3) . . . 497
s 18 . . . 475
s 18(3) . . . 497
s 20(3) . . . 433, 489
s 20(4) . . . 433, 489
s 21(3) . . . 433
s 21(4) . . . 433, 489
s 22 . . . 490
s 23 . . . 423
s 23(1) . . . 436
s 23(3) . . . 436
s 23(4) . . . 436
s 24 . . . 422, 435, 436, 497, 509
s 24(1) . . . 497
s 24(4) . . . 436
s 25(1) . . . 436
s 25(3) . . . 436, 498
s 25(4) . . . 436, 498
s 26(1) . . . 422, 436
s 27(1) . . . 437
s 27(2) . . . 437
s 27(3) . . . 437, 497
s 27(4) . . . 437
s 28 . . . 422, 509
s 28(1) . . . 437
s 28(5) . . . 437
s 29 . . . 422
s 29(1) . . . 437
s 29(3) . . . 437
s 30 . . . 423, 475, 478
s 30(1) . . . 478
s 31 . . . 422, 477

s 31(1) 475, 477
s 31(4) 477
s 31(4)(b) 477
s 32. . . . . 422, 475
s 32(2) 475
s 32(2)(b) 513
s 32(4) 475
s 33. . . . . 422, 435, 460, 502
s 33(1) 421, 457
s 33(1)(b) 435, 447
s 34. 423
s 34(1) 447, 451
s 34(2) 447
s 34(2)(b) 479
s 34(2)(d) 451, 455
s 34(2)(e) 421, 458
s 34(2)(f). 453
s 34(2)(g) 404, 421, 458
s 34(2)(h) 457
s 34(3) 448
s 35. 423
s 36. 423
s 37. . . . . 423, 498
s 37(1) 457
s 37(2) 422
ss 38–41 423
s 38. . . . . 428, 480
s 38(3) 447, 480
s 38(4) 448, 498
s 38(6) 498
s 39. . . . . 428, 447
s 39(2) 447
s 39(3) 447
s 40. 422
s 40(1) 419
s 40(2) 419
s 41(1) 449
s 41(3) 450
s 41(5) 449, 450
s 41(6) 449
s 41(7) 449, 450
s 42. . . . . 403, 420, 450
s 43. . . . . 420, 422, 459, 498, 499
s 44. . . . . 420, 423, 499–501
s 44(2) 500
s 44(2)(b) 500
s 44(2)(c) 448
s 44(2)(e) 500, 501
s 44(3) 500
s 45. . . . . 423, 513
s 45(1) 488, 501, 502
s 45(2) 502
s 45(2)(b) 502, 513
s 45(3) 502
s 45(4) 501
ss 46–58 499
s 46. 423
s 46(1) 461, 470
s 46(1)(b) 471
s 46(2) 470
s 46(3) 470, 471
ss 47–49 423
s 47. 487
s 47(2) 487
s 48. 499
s 48(1) 491
s 48(3) 491
s 48(4) 491
s 48(5) 428, 491
s 48(5)(a) 491, 499
s 48(5)(b) 491
s 48(5)(c) 491
s 49. 491
s 49(3) 491
s 49(4) 491
s 51(1) 487
s 51(2) 487
s 51(3) 487
ss 52–58 423
s 52(1) 487
s 52(3) 487
s 52(4) 488
s 52(5) 488
s 53. . . . . 469, 490
s 54(1) 490
s 54(2) 490
s 55(2) 491
s 55(3) 491
s 56. . . . . 491, 509
s 56(1) 437
s 57. 506
s 58(1) 491
s 60. 422
s 61(1) 492
s 61(2) 492
s 66. . . . . 422, 425, 475, 523, 525
s 66(1) 523
s 66(2) 475
s 66(3) 523
s 66(4) 523
ss 67–69 514
s 67. . . . . 422, 476, 509
s 67(2) 476
s 68. . . . . 412, 422, 477, 490, 502–5, 509
s 68(1) 502
s 68(2) 502, 504
s 68(2)(a) 503
s 68(2)(b) 503
s 68(2)(d) 504
s 68(2)(g) 504

s 68(3) 505
s 68(3)(b) 505
s 68(3)(c) 505
s 68(4) 514
s 69 . . . . . 423, 427, 488, 503, 505–7, 509, 511, 513
s 69(1) 505, 506
s 69(2) 507
s 69(3) 507
s 69(3)(a) 508
s 69(3)(b) 506, 508
s 69(3)(c) 508
s 69(3)(c)(ii) 508, 509
s 69(5) 513
s 69(7) 508
s 70 422
s 70(2) 476, 492, 506, 509
s 70(3) 476, 490, 492, 507, 509, 513, 514
s 70(4) 504, 505
s 71 422
s 72 . . . . . 411, 422, 475, 477
s 72(1) 475, 477
s 73 . . . . . 422, 475–7, 505, 514
s 73(1) 477, 505
s 74 422
s 74(1) 437
s 74(2) 437
s 75 422
ss 76–79 423
s 79 509
s 80(5) 509
s 81(1)(b) 417
s 82 . . . . . 394, 413
s 82(1) 476, 506
ss 85–88 466
ss 89–91 . . . . . 425, 439
s 90 439
s 93(1) 434
s 93(6) 434
ss 94–98 425
s 99 524
s 100(2) 523
s 100(2)(b) 491
s 101 523
s 101(3) 523
s 102(1) 524
s 102(2) 524
s 103 524
s 103(2) 475
s 103(2)(a) 418
s 104 523
s 105(1) 514
Sch 1 421
Sch 2 434

Children and Families Act 2014 . . . . . 100, 307, 308
s 10 100
s 10(3) 100
Companies Act 1985 451
Companies Act 2006
s 31 418
s 996 495
Consumer Credit Act 1974
s 60 360
s 61 360
s 65 360
Contracts (Applicable Law) Act 1990 471
Contracts (Rights of Third Parties) Act 1999
s 1(1) 416
s 1(2) 416
s 8(1) 416
s 8(2) 416
Courts and Legal Services Act 1990 60
s 58 61

Employment Act 2008 338
Employment Rights Act 1996 328
Employment Rights Act 2003
s 203 311
s 203(3) 311
Employment Tribunals Act 1996
s 18(7) 87
Enterprise and Regulatory Reform Act 2013 334
Equal Pay Act 1970 328
Equality Act 2002 328
Equalities Act 2010 336

Family Law Act 1996 307
Financial Services and Markets Act 2000
ss 225–234A 343
s 228(5) 345
s 229(5) 345
Foreign Limitation Periods Act 1984 328

Housing Grants, Construction and Regeneration Act 1996 . . . . . 392–4, 398, 400, 406, 522
Pt II 392, 393, 406
s 104 393
s 104(1) 394
s 104(2) 394
s 104(3) 394
s 104(6)(b) 394
s 105 393
s 105(1) 394
s 105(2) 394
s 105(2)(d) 394

s 106 . . . 393, 406
s 107(1) . . . 395
s 108 . . . 393, 522
s 108(1) . . . 394
s 108(2) . . . 393, 395, 396
s 108(2)(c) . . . 395, 405
s 108(2)(d) . . . 395
s 108(2)(e) . . . 404
s 108(2)(f) . . . 404
s 108(3) . . . 396, 405
s 108(3A) . . . 395, 396
s 108(4) . . . 406
s 108(5) . . . 396
s 108A(2)(a) . . . 405
s 109 . . . 393
s 112 . . . 393
s 113 . . . 393

Insolvency Act 1986 . . . 519

Judgments Act 1838
s 17 . . . 523

Land Registration Act 2002 . . . 328
Law of Property Act 1925
s 136 . . . 360
Law of Property (Miscellaneous Provisions) Act 1989 . . . 360
s 2 . . . 362
Legal Aid, Sentencing and Punishment of Offenders Act 2012 . . . 61, 62
Pt 2 . . . 61
Legal Services Act 2007
s 129 . . . 344
Limitation Act 1980 . . . 11, 328, 330, 431
s 2 . . . 431
s 5 . . . 431
s 14A . . . 431
s 14B . . . 431
s 33A . . . 328, 330
s 33A(2) . . . 328
s 33A(3) . . . 328
s 33A(4) . . . 328
s 33A(6) . . . 328
s 33A(7) . . . 328
Local Democracy, Economic Development and Construction Act 2009
ss 138–145 . . . 392
s 139 . . . 395

Mental Capacity Act 2005 . . . 418

National Insurance Act 1911 . . . 7

Parliamentary Commissioner Act 1967 . . . 7

Prescription Act 1832 . . . 328
Proceeds of Crime Act 2002 . . . 85, 86, 248

Senior Courts Act 1981
s 31 . . . 495
s 33(2) . . . 500
s 34(3) . . . 500
s 37 . . . 475, 501
s 37(1) . . . 478
s 51 . . . 126, 150, 153
s 51(6) . . . 66
Sex Discrimination Act 1975 . . . 328
Statute of Frauds 1677
s 4 . . . 360

Trade Union and Labour Relations (Consolidation) Act 1992 . . . 338
Tribunals, Courts and Enforcement Act 2007 . . . 7
Trusts of Land and Appointment of Trustees Act 1996 . . . 351

Unfair Contract Terms Act 1977 . . . 251, 389

Secondary Legislation

Administration Act 1996 (Commencement No 1) Order 1996 (SI 1996/3146) . . . 466
Arbitration (Foreign Awards) Order 1984 (SI 1984/1168) . . . 524

Civil Procedure (Amendment) Rules 2011 (SI 2011/88) . . . 11, 324
Civil Procedure Rules 1998 (SI 1998/3132) . 3, 4, 6, 8, 21, 22, 37, 63, 65, 95–7, 100, 105, 106, 114, 118, 126, 151, 223, 224, 264, 371, 372, 427, 428, 441, 495
Part 1 . . . 143
r 1.1 . . . 8, 10, 77, 105, 419
r 1.1(2) . . . 105
r 1.3 . . . 77, 106
r 1.4 . . . 77
r 1.4(1) . . . 105
r 1.4(2) . . . 105
r 1.4(2)(e) . . . 8, 114
r 1.4(2)(f) . . . 106
Part 2 . . . 359
Part 3 . . . 10
r 3 . . . 10
r 3.1 . . . 107
r 3.1(2)(f) . . . 113
r 3.1(4) . . . 107
r 3.1(5) . . . 107, 108
r 3.1(8) . . . 106

r 3.4 139
r 3.4(2) 372
r 3.9 10
r 3.12 . . . . 109, 111
r 3.13 111
r 3.14 111
r 3.15 109
r 3.17 111
r 3.18 111
rr 3.19–3.21 111
PD 3A 10
PD 3E 10, 109, 111
PD 3F 111
Part 5
r 5.4C 328
Part 7 . . . . 476, 495
Part 8 . . . . 326, 327, 372, 388, 406, 500, 508, 515, 521, 522
rr 8.3–8.8 326
Part 10
r 10.3(1)(b) 513
Part 16 451
Part 18 . . . . 102, 463
Part 19
r 19.45 327
Part 21 356
r 21.10 . . . . 356, 519
Part 23 . . . . 326, 327, 475, 513
r 23.7(1) 501
PD 23A
para 10 367
Part 25 475
r 25.7 108
r 25.13 480
Part 26
r 26.3(1) 112
r 26.4 . . . . 113, 227
r 26.4(2A) 113
r 26.4(3) 113
r 26.4(4) 113
r 26.4(5) 113
r 26.4A 300
r 26.4A(5) 300
r 26.5 113
r 26.5(2AA) 300
PD 26 . . . . 112, 113
para 3.1 113
para 3.4 113
PD 26B
para 1.1 298
para 2 298
para 5 298
para 6 298
Part 28
r 28.6 112
Part 29
PD 29
para 4.10(9) 108
Part 31 455
r 31.6 . . . . 90, 455
r 31.17 500
r 31.22 456
Part 32
r 32.7 327
Part 33
r 33.4 327
Part 34
r 34.8 327
r 34.10 327
r 34.11(4) 328
r 34.13(1A) 328
Part 35 . . . . 280, 378
r 35.12 244
PD 35 39
para 11 459
Part 36 . . . . 25, 38, 39, 50, 51, 53, 55, 62–4, 67, 99, 106, 107, 125, 126, 132–6, 141, 142, 144, 211, 228, 244, 262, 264
r 36.10 . . . . 63, 132
r 36.10(5) 134
r 36.14 63
r 36.14(2) 107
r 36.14(3) 107
r 36.14(4) 133
Part 38
r 38.6 367
r 38.6(1) 55
r 36.7 367
Part 39
PD 39
para 4.2 373
Part 40
r 40.6 . . . . 359, 367
r 40.6(7)(b) 368
r 40.11 364
PD 40B
para 3.5 370
Parts 43–48
PDs 43–48 . . . . 151, 152
Parts 44–48 151
r 44.2(1) 126
r 44.2(2) 126
r 44.2(2)(a) 149
r 44.2(4) 126
r 44.2(5) 126
r 44.2(6) 126
r 44.3(2) 111, 373
r 44.3(4) 66
r 44.3(5) 111

r 44.4 . . . . . 111, 126
r 44.4(2)(a) 372
rr 44.13–44.17 96
PD 44
para 4.2 150
Part 46
r 46.14 . . . . . 521, 525
r 46.14(3) 521
r 46.14A 372
Part 47 . . . . . 373, 521
PD 47—
para 5.12(8) 151
Part 48
r 48.7 66
Part 51
PD 51G 109
PD 51H 11
PD 51I 300
PD 51L 11
Part 52
r 52.3(6) 514
Part 58 496
PD 58 496
paras 13.1–13.4 496
Part 62 . . . . . 476, 502, 508, 515
r 62.3(1) 508
r 62.3(2) 509
r 62.3(3) 495
r 62.4(2) 513
r 62.5 513
r 62.6 509
r 62.7 513
r 62.8(1) 496
r 62.8(2) 496
r 62.8(3) 496
r 62.9 509
r 62.9(3) 509
r 62.10 513
r 62.18 523
PD 62 . . . . . 476, 500
para 2.3(1) 509
paras 6.1–6.7 513
para 8.1 500
para 9.2 502
para 9.3 502
para 10.1 . . . . . 502, 513
para 10.2 513
para 11.1 509
para 12.2 507
Part 74 330
Part 78 . . . . . 11, 250, 324, 325, 329
Part III 324, 325, 329
r 78.23(2) 327
r 78.24 . . . . . 295, 326
r 78.24(2) 326
r 78.24(3) 326
r 78.24(4) 326
r 78.24(5) 326
r 78.24(6) 326
r 78.24(7) 326
r 78.24(8) 326
r 78.25 326
r 78.26 . . . . . 85, 327, 328
r 78.26(2) 327
r 78.27 . . . . . 327, 328
r 78.28 . . . . . 327, 328
PD 78 326
para 22.1 326
para 22.2 326
para 22.3 328
Civil Proceedings (Fees) Order 2008 (SI 2008/1053) 373, 434
Civil Proceedings Fees (Amendment) Order 2014 (SI 201/874) 96
County Court Rules 1981 (SI 1981/1687) . . 95
Cross-Border Mediation (EU Directive) Regulations 2011 (SI 2011/1133) . . . 324, 325, 327, 328
reg 3 324
reg 4 324
reg 8 327
reg 9 327
reg 10 327

Damages-Based Agreements Regulations 2013 (SI 2013/609) 61

Employment Equality (Religion or Belief) Regulations 2003 (SI 2003/1660) 435
reg 2(3) 435
Employment Tribunals (Early Conciliation: Exemptions and Rules of Procedure) Regulations 2014 (SI 2014/254) 334
reg 3 334

Family Procedure Rules 2010 (SI 2010/2955) 10, 100, 308
Part 3 . . . . . 100, 307
r 3.3(1) 100
r 3.4(1) 100
r 3.8(1), (2) 101
r 3.10 101
PD 3A 100, 307
Part 7
r 7.29 307
Part 9 . . . . . 305, 307
r 9.17(1) 305
PD 9A 101, 305
para 6.1 305
Part 12 307

PD 12B 87, 305, 336
para 8.1 305
para 14.11 305
Family Procedure (Amendment No 3) Rules 2014 (SI 2014/843) 100

Offers to Settle in Civil Proceedings Order 2013 (SI 2013/93) 63

Rules of the Supreme Court (Revision) 1965 (SI 1965/1776) 95

Scheme for Construction Contracts (England and Wales) Regulations 1998 (SI 1998/649) 396

Unfair Terms in Consumer Contracts Regulations 1999 (SI 1999/2083) 440
reg 3(1) 440

EU legislation

Directive 2002/22/EU on the provision of electronic communications networks . . 122
Directive 93/13 on unfair terms in consumer contracts 425
Directive 2000/31 on certain legal aspects of information society services, in particular electronic commerce, in the Internal Market 73
Directive 2008/52 on certain aspects of mediation in civil and commercial matters 11, 121, 238, 249, 250, 319, 322–4, 327, 329, 330
Recital 8 324
Recital 11 324
Recital 23 327
Recital 25 329
Art 1 323
Art 2 . . . . 324, 329
Art 2(a) 325
Art 3(a) 323
Art 4 . . . . 238, 325
Art 4(1) 325
Art 4(2) 325
Art 5 . . . . 121, 122
Art 5(1) 323, 325
Art 5(2) 323, 325
Art 6(1) 325
Art 6(2) 325
Art 7 249
Art 7(1) 327
Art 7(2) 327
Art 8 328
Art 9 329
Art 13 323
Directive 2013/11/EU on consumer ADR . . 74, 322, 323

Regulation 44/2001 on jurisdiction and the recognition and enforcement of judgments in civil and commercial matters 330, 473, 478
Art 1(2)(d) 473
Regulation 2201/2003 concerning jurisdiction and the recognition and enforcement of judgments in matrimonial matters and the matters of parental responsibility 330
Regulation 864/2007 on the law applicable to non-contractual obligations (Rome II) 472
Regulation 593/2008 on the law applicable to contractual obligations (Rome I) 471, 485
Art 3(1) 472
Art 3(2) 472
Arts 4–8 472
Art 4(1)(a) 472
Art 4(1)(b) 472
Art 4(3) 472
Art 5(1) 472
Art 5(3) 472
Regulation 524/2013 on online dispute resolution 74, 323

International law

Brussels Convention on Jurisdiction and the Enforcement of Judgments in Civil and Commercial Matters 1968 (Brussels Convention) 473

Convention on the Law Applicable to Contractual Obligations 1980 (Rome Convention) 471

European Convention on Human Rights 1950 (ECHR)
Art 6 . . . 12, 107, 120–3, 419, 426, 427, 429
Art 6(1) 414, 427
Art 8 114

Geneva Convention on the Execution of Foreign Arbitral Awards 1927 524

ICC Rules of Arbitration 2008 (ICC Rules) . . 19, 467, 468, 479, 480, 485
Art 2(1) 480
Art 3(1) 480
Art 4(1) 480
Art 4(5) 481
Art 5(1) 481

Art 5(4) 481
Art 5(6) 481
Art 11(2) 481
Art 12(1) 481
Art 12(4) 481
Art 18(1) 481
Art 18(2) 482
Art 20. 479
Art 23. . . . . 435, 481
Art 23(2) 481
Art 24. 482
Art 25(1) 482
Art 25(2) 482
Art 25(3) 482
Art 25(4) 482
Art 25(6) 482
Art 26(3) 482
Art 26(4) 482
Art 27. 482
Art 30(1) 482
Art 30(2) 482
Art 31(2) 482
Art 33. 482
Art 34(6) 481, 506
Art 36(1) 481
Art 37(4) 482
International Convention on the Recognition and Enforcement of Arbitration Awards 1958 (New York Convention). 330, 389, 418, 425, 428, 439, 466, 475, 487, 491, 493, 522–5
Art 1. 523
Art 5. 469
UNCITRAL Model Law on International Arbitration 1985. . . 19, 322, 410, 424, 442, 466, 467, 470, 479, 482, 483, 485
Art 1(1) 440
Art 1(3) 467
Art 1(4)(a) 467
Art 1(4)(b) 467
Art 2A(1) 482
Art 10(1) 483
Art 10(2) 483
Art 11(3)(a) 483
Art 11(4) 483
Art 12. 435
Art 12(1) 498
Art 16. 483
Arts 17–17J 483, 499
Art 17. 483
Art 17(1) 483
Art 17(2) 483
Art 17A 483, 499
Art 17B(1) 483
Art 17B(2) 483
Art 17C(4) 483
Art 17E. 483
Art 17F. 483
Art 17G 483
Art 17H 484
Art 17I 484
Art 18. 484
Art 19(1) 484
Art 19(2) 484
Art 21. 483
Art 22(1) 479
Art 22(2) 479
Art 23. 484
Art 23(1) 484
Art 24(1) 484
Art 24(2) 484
Art 24(3) 484
Art 26(1)(a) 484
Art 26(1)(b) 484
Art 26(2) 484
Art 28. 484
Art 28(4) 471
Art 29. 484
Art 31(2) 484
Art 32. 484
UNCITRAL Model Law on International Commercial Conciliation 2002 322
United Nations Convention on Contracts for the International Sale of Goods 1980. 471

US Legislation

Uniform Mediation Act 2001. 19

PART I

HISTORY AND RANGE OF ADR METHODS

1

INTRODUCTION

A BACKGROUND 1.01
B WHAT IS ADR? 1.12
C WHY IS THERE A NEED FOR ADR? 1.17
D THE GROWTH OF ADR OPTIONS 1.21
E COURT RECOGNITION OF ADR 1.23
F ADR AND THE REVIEW OF CIVIL LITIGATION COSTS 1.26
G RECENT DEVELOPMENTS 1.29
H THE INTERNATIONAL CONTEXT 1.31
I SOME ISSUES WITH REGARD TO ADR 1.33
J POTENTIAL ADVANTAGES OF ADR 1.34
K POTENTIAL DISADVANTAGES OF ADR 1.47
L WEIGHING UP DISPUTE RESOLUTION OPTIONS 1.57
M THE PSYCHOLOGY OF DISPUTE ESCALATION 1.59
N ASSESSING THE SUCCESS OF ADR 1.65
O OVERVIEW OF REGULATORY FRAMEWORKS 1.67
P OVERVIEW OF TRAINING AND ACCREDITATION 1.75
Key points summary 1.81

A BACKGROUND

In many jurisdictions a court system is seen as a superior way of settling civil disputes, especially where that system is seen as independent, inspires the respect of society, and has rules for procedure and evidence that have been refined over a long period of time to seek to ensure fairness. **1.01**

The strength of the court system in England and Wales is such that over several centuries it has evolved as the standard method for resolving legal disputes within the jurisdiction. The respect in which this system is held can be seen in the extent to which other jurisdictions have copied aspects of it, the extent to which parties making commercial contracts will often select English law as the law of the contract, and the extent to which litigants in commercial and other civil cases may choose to use the English courts. London is seen as one of the main litigation capitals of the world, with confidence shown in the system and in judicial decision making. **1.02**

The pre-eminence of the court system is such that other forms of dispute resolution are commonly called 'alternative' dispute resolution (or ADR), carrying the implication that litigation is the norm. However, increasingly doubts are expressed as to whether litigation is always the most efficient way of dealing with a dispute. The potential for delay, complexity, and cost was illustrated by the fictional case of *Jarndyce v Jarndyce*, in *Bleak House* by Charles Dickens. Many cases have always settled rather than go to trial, and over the last few decades there has been fast increasing growth in the use and variety of forms of ADR. **1.03**

In 1998 ADR was formally acknowledged by the Civil Procedure Rules (the CPR) as being potentially relevant to all civil actions, to the extent that use of ADR is part of the overriding objective, and is positively encouraged both at a pre-action stage and after litigation has **1.04** commenced, with potential sanctions in appropriate cases where an ADR process is not followed, for which see 1.23–1.25 and Chapters 7, 8 and 9. In the 'Review of Civil Litigation Costs' carried out by Lord Justice Jackson, the Final Report issued in December 2009 went further in embedding the use of ADR, with recommendation 6.3 saying that ADR has a vital role to play, and that there should be a serious campaign to ensure that all litigation lawyers are properly informed of how ADR works and the benefits that it can bring. The Jackson Review also recommended amendments to the CPR to promote the use of ADR, most of which were implemented as a package in April 2013, see 1.26–1.28.

1.05 Government policy has shown increasing support for ADR, expressing a belief that 'access to justice for all parties depends on costs being proportionate and unnecessary cases being deterred'. There is also a concern that 'cases are resolved too late, too expensively, with complex procedures and an adversarial climate imposing costs that sometimes dwarf the value of a contested claim', which led in March 2012 to proposals that all small claims be referred to mediation (though it will not be compulsory that they be resolved in that way)—see 'Solving Disputes in the county courts: creating a simpler, quicker and more proportionate system' at www.justice.gov.uk/downloads/consultations/solving-disputes-county-courts.pdf.

1.06 These developments mean that it is now crucial that all lawyers be aware of:

- the ADR options that may be available for a client;
- how each ADR process operates;
- the potential strengths and weaknesses of each option, as regards other ADR options and litigation;
- the potential impact of ADR options with regard to matters such as costs, disclosure, and enforcement;
- what the role of the lawyer is with regard to each ADR process.

1.07 The reasons why litigation lawyers in particular need such knowledge are:

- the provision of a good service to a client requires the recommendation of an ADR option where that offers potential benefits, eg as regards costs and time;
- lawyers who do not advise sufficiently on appropriate ADR options may leave their clients open to significant penalties in costs, even if a case is won;
- in areas such as commercial law, employment law, and family law ADR solutions are increasingly the norm, and if a lawyer cannot provide a service that includes ADR a client may go elsewhere;
- it is foreseeable that lawyers will be subject to complaints, and possibly even wasted costs orders or actions for negligence, if they proceed with litigation in a case where ADR could have achieved a quicker, cheaper, or otherwise better outcome.

1.08 The purpose of this book is to provide an overview of the ADR options that a lawyer in practice in England and Wales should be aware of. We outline the processes involved, the options that should be put to a client, and the sorts of decision that may need to be taken. In doing this we take a practical approach that should be of value to a lawyer in a case. Due to the relative informality of some ADR processes it is not always possible to provide a systematic guide, but the summaries and checklists should provide a sound foundation.

1.09 We seek to cover the full range of ADR options, with a focus on negotiation, mediation and arbitration, as those are most commonly encountered in practice. Some ADR options are quite specialist, or not commonly used, in which case we provide an overview with references to other books and resources. Some ADR options, such as mediation and arbitration, are quite well supported by not-for-profit or commercial providers, and reference is made to publications and websites that provide useful further information.

It is important to appreciate that ADR does not provide a single 'menu' of alternatives to litigation from which a lawyer and client select a single option when a dispute arises. Many cases will move from one option to another—a case that is eventually decided by a judge may have gone through some negotiation, or a case that has been substantially prepared for litigation may be resolved by mediation. The effective lawyer needs not only to advise on an appropriate dispute resolution option, but to keep options under review, prepared to move from one option to another, and to consider how one dispute resolution process might impact on another. **1.10**

ADR processes are not used only by lawyers. Techniques such as negotiation and mediation are often used in business, and dispute resolution processes are common in relation to employment and sale of goods and services. Many clients will therefore have some experience of such processes. **1.11**

B WHAT IS ADR?

The term 'alternative dispute resolution' or 'ADR' does not have an agreed definition. Some might argue that arbitration is not a form of ADR because it is a regulated adjudicative system, and others might say that negotiation is not technically a form of ADR as it involves lawyers and their clients but no third party. Terminology and methodologies are still evolving. For the purpose of this book we take the phrase to cover the full range of alternatives to litigation that might be available to a lawyer and client to resolve a civil dispute. **1.12**

There are also debates as to whether the term 'alternative dispute resolution' should be used at all. Options are only really 'alternative' if the use of litigation is seen as the norm, but statistics show that most cases settle rather than going to court for decision, so that settlement rather than litigation is actually the norm. Also many cases use a mixture of court procedure and ADR rather than relying solely on one 'alternative'. For such reasons it has been argued that it may be more accurate to talk of 'appropriate dispute resolution'. Rather than be drawn into such debates, we take the pragmatic view that 'ADR' is a term generally accepted as covering alternatives to litigation, defined as follows. **1.13**

'ADR' is taken to cover alternatives to litigation where: **1.14**

- there is a dispute between two (or more) parties;
- that dispute relates to civil legal rights and/or duties;
- the dispute could potentially go to court for resolution;
- the dispute can be resolved through some other process, usually with a more flexible structure;
- the process is essentially confidential;
- the process involves individuals other than the parties in dispute who add some degree of objectivity, be it lawyers, or an independent and normally neutral third party.

Alternatives to litigation potentially include the following factors: **1.15**

- a process that is formal (like arbitration), or informal (like negotiation);
- the involvement of lawyers and clients only (like negotiation) or third parties (like mediation);
- the involvement of specialists or experts;
- a process provided or facilitated by a commercial or not-for-profit organization;
- processes that operate within this jurisdiction, or are available in this jurisdiction but can operate internationally (with national and international systems for arbitration, and few jurisdictional limits for processes such as mediation);
- a process that is based on meetings, or documents, or that is wholly or partly remote (with growth of online dispute resolution or 'ODR').

1.16 There is no single appropriate terminology for those participating in an ADR process. If a dispute is settled before the issue of proceedings there will never be a claimant or a defendant. The general approach in this book is to refer to those involved in a dispute as the 'parties' to the dispute, whether or not they are formally parties to an action. Much of the text is directed to lawyers advising 'parties'.

C WHY IS THERE A NEED FOR ADR?

1.17 A sound and just court system is undoubtedly a primary choice for dispute resolution. Clear and fair procedural rules should ensure that both parties are able to put their case properly. Balanced and transparent rules for evidence should ensure that relevant information is admissible, and that irrelevant or prejudicial information is excluded. A respected judicial system and a process for appeals should ensure justice is done. A state-supported system should ensure reasonable access for potential litigants, and support for the enforcement of judgments.

1.18 That said, no system can be perfect, and there are various ways in which a good court system may nonetheless fail to meet the needs of individual litigants. Any of the following factors might cause a potential litigant to look for alternatives to litigation.

- The strengths of a court system can include potential weaknesses. Rules for civil procedure may need to be complex to be fair, but this complexity may of itself extend the time and costs needed to resolve the dispute.
- Evidence rules for disclosure and inspection may assist justice, but may be burdensome where a wide range of documents are potentially relevant, or where a client is concerned about confidentiality.
- It is a central objective of the court system to provide justice for individual litigants—in terms now enshrined in the overriding objective in the CPR: see Chapter 7. However the court system has other objectives, such as the development of law through the precedent system. Going to the Court of Appeal or the Supreme Court to resolve a point of law may be important for the system but something an individual litigant would prefer to avoid.
- The court process in England and Wales is adversarial. This ensures that the case for each side is fully presented and effectively challenged. However, an adversarial process may not always be appropriate, for example where the parties are likely to have an ongoing relationship (maybe as regards business dealings or the care of a child) that may be threatened rather than assisted by an adversarial approach.
- The stages of the litigation process may not all be appropriate—if a case turns largely on a specialist matter requiring expert evidence it may be more appropriate to focus on determination by an expert rather than follow a full trial procedure.
- The court system is based on the role of the judge, a point reinforced by the growth of judicial case management. While this offers clear benefits for justice and the conduct of cases, it may not suit clients who would prefer more personal control over a dispute resolution process.
- Normally the focus in court is on a past factual scenario, such as how an accident happened. Sometimes a party might prefer a dispute resolution process to cover a wider range of matters, to take into account points that are not necessarily technically relevant, or to look more clearly to the future.
- In court a judge can only make such decisions or orders as he or she has the power to make, with some flexibility as regards what might be put into a schedule to a consent order. A party might prefer a process that could look at decisions and outcomes beyond the technical powers of a judge.

1.19 None of these points means that an ADR process is necessarily better than a court process. Indeed each of these points is open to argument—for example civil litigation procedure rules include significant flexibility for controlling time and cost, and options such as the fast track. The point is rather that these factors may be relevant in considering options for resolving a dispute.

Also these points are not necessarily reasons for rejecting litigation. Many clients will continue to see bringing a legal action as the natural choice when a dispute arises, and if a negotiation or mediation is not successful then litigation remains the fallback. Most ADR processes will take place within the context of what a judge might decide if the case went to court, and an outcome to a mediation or negotiation is only likely to be agreed if it compares adequately to the likely outcome of litigation. The point is rather that a lawyer should not focus exclusively on litigation without considering the possible benefits of alternatives, and should not allow a case to move automatically from one step in litigation to the next without reviewing options. **1.20**

D THE GROWTH OF ADR OPTIONS

There might be a perception that ADR options are a relatively recent development. However it has always been possible to settle a case rather than go to court, and the range of alternatives to litigation has developed over a prolonged period. The following outline of major developments provides a context for the current position. **1.21**

- The first English statute relating to arbitration was the Arbitration Act 1697 (9 & 10 Will III c15), which stopped parties from withdrawing from arbitration right up to the last moment if the case seemed to be going against them. It is clear that arbitration was being used well before that date, with the earliest reported case being *Anon* [1468] YB 8 Edw IV, fo1, p1. The Victorians developed the use of arbitration, with further regulation by statute.
- Tribunals to adjudicate disputes with administrative agencies grew throughout the last century. It is generally thought that the first tribunal was that set up under the National Insurance Act 1911, and there was substantial growth and review throughout the century, leading to the creation of a new unified structure for tribunals under the Tribunals, Courts and Enforcement Act 2007.
- A different option for dealing with disputes relating to administration is the use of an ombudsman. The term 'ombudsman' is derived from old Swedish, and from about 1800 the term has been used to mean an independent official who could review the actions of executive government to address the concerns of individual citizens. In the United Kingdom the term is used for the Parliamentary Commissioner for Administration, whose office was set up under the Parliamentary Commissioner Act 1967. This initiative has been followed by the creation of a range of other 'ombudsmen' whose role is to address complaints by investigation and attempt to resolve matters without litigation: see Chapter 21.
- The area of employment saw substantial growth of the use of ADR processes during the last century. In 1975 the Advisory, Conciliation and Arbitration Service (commonly known as ACAS) was set up. Although funded by the government, this body is independent, and focuses on supporting employment relationships, where it is often more important to seek to resolve a dispute and move forward rather than to take an adversarial approach. For more information see www.acas.org.uk.
- In 1990 the Centre for Effective Dispute Resolution (commonly known as CEDR) was launched with the support of the Confederation of British Industry and some leading law firms. This body is based in London but has a national and international presence with regard to promoting and facilitating ADR, especially with regard to commercial cases. For more information see www.cedr.co.uk.
- Over the last 20 years there has been steady growth in the numbers of commercial and not-for-profit bodies, and the number of solicitors' firms and barristers' chambers, offering mediation and other ADR services.

1.22 There has also been a steady growth in recognition of, and support for, ADR options within the litigation system:

- The use of offers to settle was judicially encouraged in *Calderbank v Calderbank* [1976] Fam 93, which made it clear that a written offer to settle could be brought to the attention of the judge when costs were considered. This was formalized into the system for Part 36 offers, with clear potential costs penalties where a party presses on with litigation but fails to improve upon an offer for settlement, see 4.58–4.63.
- Initial interest in the use of ADR arose in the context of commercial cases. In 1994 the Commercial Court issued the 'Practice Note: Commercial Court; Alternative Dispute Resolution' [1994] 1 All ER 34, requiring lawyers to 'consider with their clients and the other parties concerned the possibility of attempting to resolve the particular dispute or particular issues by mediation, conciliation or otherwise', and to 'ensure that parties are fully informed as to the most cost-effective means of resolving the particular dispute'. This approach produced quite successful take-up rates and improved client satisfaction, and the commercial courts have led developments in the use of orders to support ADR.
- The High Court Practice Note (Civil Litigation: Case Management) [1995] 1 All ER 385 provided for greater judicial control of cases, including questions on whether legal advisers had discussed the possibility of using ADR with their client and the other side, and whether they had considered that some form of ADR might assist in resolving or narrowing issues. This showed recognition of ADR, while not at that stage taking significant steps to support its use.
- In 1996 a pilot scheme in the Central London County Court offered time-limited voluntary mediation in any defended case where the claim was for over £3,000. This led to pilot schemes in other county courts, and evaluation of these schemes provided the foundation for county court mediation, with a nationwide scheme from 2004.
- A mediation scheme attached to the Court of Appeal was established on a voluntary basis in 1997. As leave to appeal is given on the basis that there is a real prospect of success it is logical that the parties should review their positions prior to the appeal hearing. The scheme has a reasonably good success rate. On 30 March 2012 it was announced that as a pilot all appeals would be referred to mediation unless a judge ordered otherwise, and this pilot was extended to April 2014.

E COURT RECOGNITION OF ADR

1.23 Following the general initiatives discussed in 1.22, the past decade has seen moves to embed acknowledgement of the potential benefits of ADR more clearly within the civil litigation system. The current position is considered fully in Chapters 7–9, but key developments are summarized here as they provide an important context for the general development of ADR within this jurisdiction.

- Some encouragement of the use of ADR was part of the Woolf reforms, and the Civil Procedure Rules 1998 that followed. The overriding objective expressly includes saving expense and dealing with case in a proportionate way, CPR r 1.1. Judges are expected to encourage the parties to co-operate, 'encouraging the parties to use an alternative dispute resolution procedure if the court considers that to be appropriate and facilitating the use of such procedure' and 'helping the parties to settle the whole or part of a case', CPR r 1.4.2(e).
- ADR is expressly encouraged prior to litigation see 7.20–7.38. The reasonableness of pre-action conduct can be relevant to a costs order, see 8.42–8.50. Pre-action protocol requirements were amended from 2003 to say that the letter of claim should state if a party wishes to enter into mediation or another form of ADR. In 2006 the approach to ADR in the protocols was standardized to say that the parties should consider whether some form of alternative

dispute resolution would be more suitable than litigation and, if so, that they should endeavour to agree which form to adopt. Parties may be required by the court to provide evidence that ADR was considered, and conduct in this regard can be relevant to costs: see 7.20–7.38.

- ADR is also expressly encouraged during litigation. It was provided that on filing the completed allocation questionnaire after issue a party might make a written request for the proceedings to be stayed while the parties tried to settle the case by ADR, or that the parties could request or the court of its own initiative could consider a stay for a period of one month for ADR to be considered. These provisions have been extended following the Jackson reforms.
- From 2007 the use of ADR has been standardized in county courts, and from 2008 there has been a full-time mediation officer in each area. This provides a common and subsidized mediation procedure which was supported by a National Mediation Helpline, replaced in 2011 by an online scheme with government and Civil Mediation Council support: see 14.80–14.100, and www.civilmediation.justice.gov.uk/.

This development of procedural regulation was accompanied by a development of judicial attitude. This is important because the rules have expressly opened up options for the discretion of a judge, but have stopped short of making any requirement that a party enters ADR. The following key cases are fully discussed in later chapters. **1.24**

- In *Dunnett v Railtrack* [2002] 1 WLR 2434 the courts showed that they were prepared to impose a costs penalty on a party who failed to take part in an ADR process. Although the defendants won their case on appeal they were denied their costs because the court had stated that the parties should attempt mediation but the defendant had refused to consider it. See 8.78.
- In *Halsey v Milton Keynes NHS Trust* [2004] 1 WLR 3002 the court reviewed practice relating to ADR, and accepted the potential benefits of ADR, especially a voluntary process such as mediation. It concluded that a party could not be compelled to use ADR, but that a costs penalty could be imposed on a party who unreasonably refused to consider ADR. See 7.106 and 8.12–8.18.
- In *Burchell v Bullard* [2005] BLR 330 a dispute over building work involved a claim for £18,000 and a counterclaim eventually judged to be worth about £14,000, so that less than £5,000 changed hands following judgment. The costs of the case were over £160,000. The claimant had suggested mediation at an early stage but the defendants refused. Although the judge was not prepared to impose a penalty as the original case was some years old he made it very clear that ADR should have been attempted. See 8.24.

These changes led to a significant growth in the use of ADR in the first decade of this century. Most recently the Jackson reforms have embedded its use within civil litigation, see 1.26–1.28, and judicial support for the reasonable use of ADR has grown even stronger, see 1.29–1.30. That said, there are some significant issues in relation to the use of ADR, see 1.33, and research shows some mixed results in relation to the success of ADR, see 1.65–1.66. **1.25**

F ADR AND THE REVIEW OF CIVIL LITIGATION COSTS

The question of costs is one of the main reasons for choosing ADR, and has been driving most recent developments of policy. The Review of Civil Litigation Costs carried out by Lord Justice Jackson provided a significant step forward in promoting the use of ADR, with a thorough review of many relevant issues. The Final Report concluded that 'ADR (particularly mediation) has a vital role to play in reducing the costs of civil disputes, by fomenting the early settlement of cases'. Lord Justice Jackson also recommended 'a serious campaign to ensure that all litigation lawyers and judges are properly informed of how ADR works, **1.26** and the benefits that it can bring', 'Recommendation 6.3'. A guide to the use of ADR for the use of judges and lawyers has been published as *The Jackson ADR Handbook* (OUP, 2013).

1.27 The 'Review of Civil Litigation Costs: Final Report' was published in January 2010, see www.judiciary.gov.uk/publications-and-reports/review-of-civil-litigation-costs/reports. The Ministry of Justice published a consultation paper relating to the proposals, and on 29 March 2011 the Government published 'Reforming Civil Litigation Funding and Costs in England and Wales—Implementation of Lord Justice Jackson's Recommendations: The Government Response', see www.justice.gov.uk/consultations/566. This indicated that the government would implement the main proposals of the review, and this was done as a package on 1 April 2013.

1.28 The main changes with implications for the use of ADR are in summary as follows:

- A change in the wording of the overriding objective requires that cases be dealt with 'justly and proportionately', CPR r 1.1. This is likely to encourage the use of ADR, especially in cases of modest value, if the costs of litigation could easily become disproportionate to the sum in dispute. It remains to be seen how the court will interpret the word 'proportionately' in this context.
- Active case management is supported by a new directions questionnaire, CPR Part 3. The Directions Questionnaire includes in section A guidance on the need to make every effort to settle a case, with relevant information. For fast-track and multi-track cases, legal representatives have to confirm that the need to try to settle, the options available, and the possibility of costs sanctions for a refusal to try to settle have been explained to the client.
- Case management is also supported by new standard directions, several of which are relevant to the use of ADR. In particular direction A03 ADR provides: 'At all stages the parties must consider settling this litigation by any means of ADR (including mediation); any party not engaging in any such means proposed by another must serve a witness statement giving reasons within 21 days of that proposal; such witness statement must not be shown to the trial judge until questions of costs arise.' (The period of 21 days may be varied.)
- The introduction of costs management and the more focused use of costs budgets is likely to make the potential cost of litigation more transparent, making parties more likely to consider ADR seriously, CPR r 3 and Practice Direction 3E Costs Management. The courts are showing willingness to enforce the use of budgets, see for example *Henry v News Group Newspapers Ltd* [2013] EWCA Civ 19.
- There is a stronger use of sanctions to impose compliance with the CPR, CPR r 3.9. For more detail see Chapter 8. A greater use of sanctions could promote the use of ADR, but it remains to be seen what the revised approach will mean.
- A new test requires that costs should be proportionate as well as reasonably incurred in order to be recoverable. This is likely to encourage the use of ADR as a way to keep costs in line with the amount in dispute. However, the meaning of proportionality is as yet far from clear.
- The use of online portals to support the settlement of some types of lower value case has been extended. See chapter 5.

G RECENT DEVELOPMENTS

1.29 There have been many significant recent developments regarding the fast-growing use of ADR. The most important are as follows, and they are picked up in more detail as relevant in later chapters.

- The Family Procedure Rules 2010 (SI 2010/2955), which came into force on 6 April 2011, brought about substantial changes in the procedure of the family courts. As regards ADR, the most important changes are contained in Part 3, Alternative Dispute Resolution: the court's powers, and Practice Direction 3A, Pre-Application Protocol for Mediation Information and Assessment. The court must consider at every stage in proceedings whether ADR is appropriate and should facilitate its use. It is a requirement that where an application is to be made the parties should normally attend a mediation awareness session with a mediator to learn about mediation. While this approach is in principle to be welcomed, there are concerns about resourcing, and research has shown mixed success. See 18.49–18.64.

- The European Union Directive on mediation in civil and commercial matters (Directive 2008/52/EC) was implemented as required by 20 May 2011, encouraging the use of mediation in cross-border disputes within the EU. The Civil Procedure (Amendment) Rules 2011 made amendments to Part 78 of the Civil Procedure Rules and provide for a mediation agreement to be recorded as a court order, and to support confidentiality. The Limitation Act 1980 and other relevant legislation has been amended to provide that time spent in mediation should be excluded in calculating whether a limitation period has expired in cross-border disputes, see 19.12–19.59.
- On 23 June 2011 the government signed a new Dispute Resolution Commitment, requiring all government departments and agencies to use alternatives such as mediation and arbitration whenever possible before taking a dispute to court. For the full text see www.justice.gov.uk/guidance/mediation/dispute-resolution-commitment.htm.
- The Institute of Family Law Arbitrators launched a new Family Law Arbitration Scheme on 26 March 2012. This is supported by the Chartered Institute of Arbitrators, the Family Law Bar Association and Resolution. It provides a scheme under which family law disputes can be decided through a decision-making process that is within the control of the parties, see www.ifla.org.uk.

More significant developments are planned for the near future. These are covered in outline in this book, and will be covered in more detail in the Online Resource Centre related to this book in due course. **1.30**

- In line with the implementation of the Jackson Reforms, judges are delivering judgments expressing strong support for the use of ADR in appropriate cases, especially where costs appear to be unnecessarily high. They are also expecting parties to show reasonable engagement with ADR, for example saying that a failure to respond to a proposal that ADR be used may be treated as a refusal to engage in ADR, *PGF II SA v OMFS Company 1 Limited* [2014] WLR 1386.
- A compulsory Mediation Information pilot scheme has taken place in the Central London, Birmingham and Manchester County Courts, based on the Mediation Information and Assessment Meetings (MIAMs) used in family cases since 2011, Practice Direction 51H The Mediation Service Pilot Scheme. A separate pilot scheme for the use of mediation in relation to some types of case issued through the County Court Money Claims Centre was extended to 31 March 2014, Practice Direction 51L The Second Mediation Service Pilot Scheme. These pilots are likely to lead to the development of the use of mediation in county courts.
- The government is working to implement EU proposals for substantial extension of the use of ADR in relation to consumer disputes, including online dispute resolution options, see Chapter 5.

H THE INTERNATIONAL CONTEXT

There has been a significant growth in the use of ADR in many other jurisdictions round the world. While the details of these developments are beyond the scope of this book, they provide valuable context, especially with the growth of disputes including international factors. **1.31**

- There is a separate system for international arbitration based on international arbitration institutional rules: see Chapter 29. This should be distinguished from the system for arbitration within the jurisdiction which is based on statute: see Chapter 26.

- Mediation is an informal process based on agreement, and it is therefore not necessarily jurisdiction specific, though its use is regulated in different ways in some jurisdictions, for example within the European Union. For further discussion, see Chapter 19.
- Options developed in different parts of the world in relation to different types of cases can provide useful models for effective dispute management and resolution processes. Some states in the USA have experimented with the use of more compulsion as regards the use of ADR, with for example case settlement conferences and court-directed arbitration or mediation.

1.32 The use of 'collaborative law', developed in North America, is now used in this jurisdiction, especially with regard to family law. It is promoted by the Resolution group, which trains lawyers in collaborative techniques, see www.resolution.org.uk. Essentially each party has a lawyer, and all lawyers and parties meet together to seek to settle matters in dispute. Initially each party gets legal advice from their own lawyer as to legal rights and potential entitlements. The two lawyers then set up a meeting for both parties and both lawyers, and all four sign an agreement making it clear that the intention is to resolve matters without going to court. If the process breaks down and the case goes to court, the parties will each appoint a new lawyer. The first meeting will often include a general review of issues and agreement about exchange of information. Later meetings will focus on specific issues, and may include relevant experts (for example as regards asset valuation). A final meeting will agree outcomes and implementation. This offers the parties a high level of control, and each has the advice of a lawyer throughout. It tends to be successful, but the significant involvement of lawyers means that this process is significantly more expensive than negotiation or mediation.

I SOME ISSUES WITH REGARD TO ADR

1.33 The speed and level of development might make it appear that ADR is now fully formed and accepted, but there is still significant ongoing evolution and some significant issues.

- A key issue is whether a party can be forced to use ADR. It is possible that this might be a breach of Art 6 of the European Convention on Human Rights which provides that 'In the determination of his civil rights and obligations . . . everyone is entitled to a fair and public hearing within a reasonable time by an independent and impartial tribunal established by law'. An order to use ADR that prevented access to a court would potentially breach this right, though the European Court has accepted that a party can waive Art 6 rights in for example agreeing to a binding adjudicative process, so long as there is not undue pressure and the right to trial is retained: *Deweer v Belgium* (1980) 2 EHRR 239. The use of ADR is compulsory in some circumstances in a few EU countries. Within this jurisdiction judges considered the issue of compulsion in *Halsey v Milton Keynes NHS Trust* [2004] 1 WLR 3002, though possible breach of Art 6 was not fully argued and comments by Dyson LJ were *obiter*. The position is that no party can be forced to enter into any form of ADR, or to agree an outcome to a non-adjudicative ADR process. It is acceptable that a party should have to consider ADR, and risk a costs penalty where ADR is unreasonably refused. Obligations on parties to litigation, such as compliance with pre-action protocols, are not seen as breaching Art 6, and the distinction seems to be that sanctions can be used to support compliance with procedural requirements, so long as enforcement is not by penal sanctions such as imprisonment or a fine for contempt, and the party is not deprived of a right to trial. It is interesting to note that the Court of Appeal has commented on whether some compulsion to use ADR should be introduced where litigants in person proceed with litigation in circumstances where this is not the best option for the case, *Wright v Michael Wright Supplies Ltd* [2013] EWCA Civ 234.

- There are significant concerns that a wide use of ADR may undermine the development of legal principle in a common-law jurisdiction where law is based on precedent. Where a case is settled through ADR the outcome is often not reported publicly, and the outcome may not have been based on a strict application of legal principle. See for example Hazel Genn and Linda Mulcahy, 'The collective interest in private dispute resolution', *Oxford Journal of Legal Studies* vol 33, no 1 (2013) 59–80.
- There are some concerns in relation to the professionalization, regulation and oversight of mediators and arbitrators. Various respected bodies have taken a lead, but there is limited standardization, which can cause difficulties for those seeking to offer or use ADR services.
- There are a number of jurisprudential issues to be developed with regard to the inter-relation of litigation and ADR. For example, there are issues with regard to the traditional concepts of privilege and confidentiality and ADR processes. Confidentiality is protected by legal professional privilege, which protects communications between a lawyer and client when preparing a case, and the privilege protecting communications made with a view to settlement. However problems can arise if the ADR process fails or there is any dispute about it, and with regard to issues such as whether a mediator can be called as a witness: see 6.48–6.50.

J POTENTIAL ADVANTAGES OF ADR

There are many potential advantages ADR can offer, though the actual advantages for a specific case will need careful professional consideration. The potential advantages are summarized here, and are developed in Chapter 3 with regard to selecting a specific ADR process. Whether potential advantages are actually achieved will depend on the type of ADR selected and how the case is pursued. **1.34**

Lower cost

Using ADR may be significantly cheaper than going to court, especially if the case is settled at a relatively early stage before costs build up, and if a relatively inexpensive method such as negotiation is used. This potential advantage will decrease if ADR is not attempted until a relatively late stage (as costs will already have accumulated), and/or if a relatively expensive form of ADR such as arbitration is selected. See Chapter 4 for more guidance on costs. **1.35**

Speed of settlement

A case can take months or even years to reach resolution in court, and that time frame may be extended if there is an appeal. Some forms of ADR, such as negotiation or mediation, can be conducted quite quickly and quite soon after the dispute arises. This potential advantage may be less fully enjoyed if ADR is not used until a relatively late stage in the case, or if the ADR process used is itself protracted, as an arbitration might be. Speed of settlement can substantially reduce the stress and distraction that may be caused to the parties in the case. **1.36**

Control of process

Once proceedings have been issued, a court case is essentially under the control of the judge. A lawyer should always act within client instructions, but in practice many clients may feel that litigation is substantially guided by the lawyer because the client is unfamiliar with procedural rules. Many clients may prefer the greater control that can come with an ADR process such as mediation. **1.37**

Choice of forum

1.38 In litigation there are some choices, for example as regards the court in which a claim is commenced. However there are many rules about case management, tracks for different types of cases etc, and the parties will have no choice as to the judge in the case. In a process such as arbitration or mediation the parties are able to agree who should hear the case or provide the mediation process, taking expertise and experience into account.

A wider range of issues may be considered

1.39 Sometimes a client will present a lawyer with issues that are not easy to categorize in legal terms, or where the law is complex or unclear. Such issues may be difficult or expensive to litigate and ADR may provide a more practical alternative. That said, ADR should never be followed simply in an attempt to sidestep a problem—the need for case analysis and legal research are just as high in an ADR process because of the need to convince an opponent or third party.

Wider range of potential outcomes

1.40 A judge in court can only order something that is within the powers of the court, such as damages or an injunction, and the order can only relate to the issues before the judge. If a judge makes a consent order it may be possible to put wider terms into a schedule to an order, but such a schedule may not be appropriate, for example, to govern an ongoing commercial relationship. Negotiation or mediation can result in any terms that suit the parties, and can be particularly useful to regulate a future relationship.

Flexibility of process

1.41 A case that goes to court must follow a set process that generally includes a pre-action protocol, rules for commencing the claim, rules for possible interim applications, rules for trial etc. Some rules are quite detailed and technical. The range of ADR options provides for less formality, and parties can often agree the process to be followed in a mediation or arbitration.

Flexibility with regard to evidence

1.42 The rules for evidence in civil cases have been relaxed in various ways over recent years, but litigation still involves detailed rules for disclosure and inspection and the admissibility of evidence. An ADR process will normally be much more flexible as regards information and evidence—indeed in negotiation and mediation it is essentially for each party to decide what to reveal. This does not mean that the rules of evidence can be ignored—the lawyer will still need to consider what information might be obtained through litigation, and must take some care over what is revealed in ADR in case the process fails and the case goes to trial. Disclosure can be burdensome and expensive and this can be avoided through ADR.

Confidentiality

1.43 Most litigation processes are open, so justice can be seen to be done. There may be reasons why a client would prefer a more private settlement, for example to keep personal or business information or the outcome of the case confidential. This can be achieved through ADR, which is a private process, and confidentiality clauses are a normal part of an agreement for or reached as a result of ADR.

Use of a problem-solving approach

Litigation tends to focus on what happened in the past and on allocating blame. This can be a negative process for both sides, and the adversarial process can lead to parties becoming entrenched. ADR options can be more forward looking and constructive—for example, mediation can help to move parties away from intransigence. **1.44**

Possible reduction of risk

In aiming to find a winner and a loser, litigation can be a relatively blunt instrument. Liability is decided on the balance of probabilities, which could potentially be as close as winning if the judge is 51% convinced of a case, or losing on 49%. The level of risk is heightened by the rule that costs will normally follow the event, so that the loser will potentially bear the costs of both sides. If the chances of winning in litigation are not very clear cut, proceeding to trial can carry significant risks that need to be carefully evaluated. An ADR process may provide better ways of managing risk. **1.45**

Client satisfaction

Even parties who win express some dissatisfaction with the litigation process. This is perhaps inevitable—a client can have unrealistic expectations, or underestimate the strength of the case for the other side. Nonetheless this cannot be ignored by any lawyer concerned to provide a good service for a client. Clients tend to express higher levels of satisfaction with a successful negotiation or mediation process, perhaps because they have been involved in agreeing the outcome, and have felt more in control of the process. **1.46**

K POTENTIAL DISADVANTAGES OF ADR

The potential disadvantages will not apply to every case, and they may be largely avoided with careful choice of an appropriate ADR option, and careful pursuit of the case. The potential disadvantages are also developed in more detail in relation to ADR options in Chapter 3. **1.47**

Increased expense

An ADR process needs to be carefully selected and efficiently handled to be successful. If ADR is used in an inappropriate way or at an inappropriate time, the process may fail. Failed ADR is likely to add expense to resolving the case if the case still has to go to trial. The cost implications of different types of dispute resolution must be kept in mind. A party who wins in court is likely to get an order that his or her reasonable costs will be paid by the loser, whereas a settlement will normally leave the party liable to pay his or her own costs unless some payment of costs is agreed as part of the settlement. This is considered further in Chapter 4. **1.48**

Additional delay

An ADR process that fails may cause delay if the case then has to go to court for resolution. It is important to assess carefully when ADR has a reasonable chance of success. This can be complex where one party is keen to use ADR but the other is obstructive. **1.49**

Possible reduction in outcome compared to a court judgment

A client who feels he or she has a strong case may prefer to go to court to achieve the full potential of the case, including a costs order. ADR may involve some concession or **1.50** compromise. That said, a non-adjudicative ADR process can never force a client to accept anything less than the client thinks is fair, and some reduction may be justified where time and costs have been saved.

1.51 This can be a strategic issue—a party with a relatively weak case may seek ADR in the hope of getting an offer where going to trial might mean losing and having to pay the winner's costs. Litigants with a strong case may understandably be reluctant to enter ADR in such circumstances, and may need persuasion to do so.

Lack of a clear and public finding

1.52 Some clients value a public finding by a judge that they have 'won'. It may vindicate a stand the client has taken, or create a precedent that the client can rely on in relation to other potential claims. However an agreement reached through ADR can always be made public by agreement.

1.53 There is a public interest in having a sufficiently comprehensive range of court judgments for the law in an area to be reasonably clear. An ADR process will usually take place within the context of what would happen if the case went to court, so ADR is to some extent reliant on continuing litigation producing precedents. As ADR reports are not normally published it can be very difficult for anyone other than a practitioner regularly involved in ADR in an area to see how practice in settlements is developing.

Loss of potential strategic use of procedural steps

1.54 The range of pre-action and interim applications that can be made in relation to court proceedings can be strategically very useful. For example it may be relevant to a particular case to seek an interim injunction, or security for costs. Summary judgment can resolve a case quickly. Some such outcomes may be achieved in an ADR process, but arbitrators have much more limited powers, and mediators rarely have such power. It is important to consider what procedural applications might be useful before selecting an ADR process. This may be a reason for starting an action and making constructive use of procedural possibilities before moving to an ADR option.

Loss of potential advantages of evidential rules

1.55 If court action is contemplated, evidential rules provide for disclosure and inspection of relevant documents held by the other side, with a variety of possible applications to court if information and material is not made available. Pre-action protocols provide for early availability of key material. The importance of litigating with 'cards on the table' is now the norm. Adjudicative ADR options may have some requirements as to the material to be made available, though this is usually subject to the agreement of the parties. Mediation and adjudication do not normally have mandatory requirements for the disclosure of evidence, and a party may choose to keep relevant material secret. It is important to consider what information and evidence you may need from the other side, as well as what information and evidence you might disclose voluntarily, before selecting an ADR option. This may be a reason for at least going through the pre-action stages of litigation before moving to ADR.

Confusion of process

1.56 In some cases there is a clear choice—for example to use arbitration instead of litigation. However, the fact that ADR is not always a full alternative to a court process can lead to real difficulties in analysing a case and pursuing it in a comprehensively strategic way. Negotiation and mediation can arise at various stages before and during a court action in a way that can hamper coherent progress of the case. For example a phone call from one solicitor to another or a discussion by barristers prior to an interim application may give rise to suggestions relevant to settlement while a litigation process is in progress. It is important to try to define ADR and settlement possibilities separately from the steps for ongoing litigation.

L WEIGHING UP DISPUTE RESOLUTION OPTIONS

The discussion at 1.34–1.56 shows that there can be quite strong reasons for using, or not using, ADR. They also show that the situation can be complex, with some factors favouring ADR and others not. The factors are considered more fully in Chapter 3 in relation to advising a client in relation to selecting an ADR option in a particular case. It should be noted that courts now normally expect reasonable grounds to be given for refusing to engage in ADR, so factors need to be weighed up carefully. **1.57**

A decision about ADR is rarely taken once only in a case. Relevant factors may change over time, so a decision about ADR may need to be reviewed. A case may move between litigation and ADR options, for example starting under a pre-action protocol, then attempting mediation, but if that fails moving to the issue of proceedings and perhaps some interim applications. A Part 36 offer may lead to negotiation, but then perhaps go to court for a consent order. It may not be so much a question of alternative dispute resolution, but more a question of blended dispute resolution. **1.58**

M THE PSYCHOLOGY OF DISPUTE ESCALATION

Insight into the psychological dynamics of how disputes escalate can be of great assistance. This is a substantial area of academic study, the detail of which lies beyond the scope of this book. For further study see for example Richard Birke and Craig Fox, 'Psychological Principles in Negotiating Civil Settlements', *Harvard Negotiation Law Review* 4, (1999) 1 and Russell Korobkin and Chris Guthrie, 'Psychological Barriers to Litigation Settlement: An Experimental Approach', *Michigan Law Review* 93 (1994) 107. **1.59**

In terms of simple principles, someone who has suffered harm is likely to want to blame a person rather than a pure accident, whereas someone who has caused harm is more likely to look for an explanation than take personal blame. Where harm has happened, people naturally see what they want to see, and start to put together a story that interprets events well for them personally rather than being inclined to objectivity. Individuals tend to assess themselves positively—a high proportion of people see themselves as 'better than average' drivers! In the commercial world many people believe themselves to be rational and hard headed, but they can still bring a surprisingly high level of emotion to a dispute. A breach of contract claim may seem to call personal judgment or integrity into question, so the individual will easily be motivated by self-justification rather than objectivity. A claim easily becomes a personal attack on self-esteem, so the reaction may well be anger, especially if there is a need to retain reputation with colleagues. In 'Pride comes before a Claim—The Psychology of Dispute Resolution' on the Field Fisher Waterhouse website, over two thirds of those surveyed thought that emotion and personal pride adversely affected resolution of a commercial dispute. See www.FFw.com/publications/all/articles/psychology.dispute-resolution.com. **1.60**

1.61 These typical psychological approaches mean that most civil claims will have significant emotional currents just below the surface even where a client appears calm. These are best dealt with not by ignoring them, but by appreciating what effect they may have on what the client says in relation to objectives and evidence. A natural response to the serious challenge of a dispute is to seek vindication, and therefore to 'beat' the person making the challenge. A small initial loss of objectivity can quite quickly become an entrenched position that informs the approach to the dispute—an offer from the other side may be rejected because it comes from the other side rather than because it is a bad offer, and negotiation may be seen as weak. Research has shown that who presents an offer and how it is phrased can have a significant effect on whether it is accepted.

1.62 The adversarial process can be psychologically satisfying in terms of a staged contest to try to prove that one is 'right'. However the adversarial process can be led by, and indeed exacerbate, feelings of self-righteousness that are natural, but which are not objectively justified. The adversarial process can easily increase rather than resolve conflict because it is designed to divide those involved into two parties with most people concerned being 'for' a party, and the focus being on 'issues'. The procedure can easily be one of exchanging blows, rather than trying to focus more positively on interests and the resolution of problems.

1.63 This is not to suggest that litigation is bad—many civil disputes need to be approached in a structured and managed way with a focus on issues and evidence. The point is rather that litigation should not necessarily be seen as an automatic best choice, and that psychological and emotional factors may need to be addressed and taken into account in making a sensible choice. Few clients would invest £20,000 without cold, hard analysis, and £20,000 should not be put into litigation costs without similar consideration.

1.64 Psychological insight into how clients take decisions can also be of great assistance, see for example Randall Kiser, *Beyond Right and Wrong: The Power of Effective Decision Making for Attorneys and Clients* (Springer, 2010). Kiser quotes research showing that in a majority of cases a party at some stage rejects a settlement offer that is better than the final outcome.

N ASSESSING THE SUCCESS OF ADR

1.65 Both lawyers and clients may be interested in information as to how successful an ADR process may be. Substantial research has been carried out in a range of jurisdictions in relation to how successful ADR is, and there is for example a body of research into negotiation and mediation in the USA. In particular the Harvard Negotiation Project has a strong international reputation: see www.pon.harvard.edu/research-home/.

1.66 In England and Wales there has been research in particular into the usefulness of mediation. Some of this research can be accessed online, see for example http://asauk.org.uk/alternative-dispute-resolution/adr-research/. The Ministry of Justice also provides access to relevant research through its website: see www.justice.gov.uk/publications/research-and-analysis/moj. Probably the most important studies are those that have assessed the relative success of court-related mediation, for which see 18.16–18.33. Some of the key studies of ADR are:

- *Twisting Arms: Court referred and court linked mediation under judicial pressure. A review of the Central London County Court Scheme* by Professor Hazel Genn and Professor Paul Fenn (Ministry of Justice, 2007);
- *Small Claims Mediation. A collection of 4 research reports on pilot schemes in County Courts* (Department for Constitutional Affairs, 2006);

- *Picking up the Pieces: Marriage and divorce two years after Information Provision. A study of the pilot scheme for the use of mediation as a part of the divorce process* by Professor Janet Walker (Department for Constitutional Affairs, 2004);
- *Court of Appeal Mediation Scheme. Court-based initiatives for non-family civil disputes* by Professor Hazel Genn (2002).

O OVERVIEW OF REGULATORY FRAMEWORKS

The regulatory framework for arbitration in England and Wales is provided by statute, the current codification being the Arbitration Act 1996: see Chapter 26. There is ultimate oversight by the courts: see Chapter 31. **1.67**

The regulatory framework for international arbitration is provided by international treaties. There are also various agreements that provide a framework for international arbitration including the International Chamber of Commerce Arbitration Rules 1998, and the UNCITRAL Model Law on International Arbitration. Detail is provided in Chapter 29. **1.68**

There is as yet no formal statutory or regulatory framework for mediation in England and Wales, though there is in some other jurisdictions, such as the Uniform Mediation Act in the USA. There are a number of mediation schemes linked to courts (see Chapter 19), but these provide access to a process rather than regulation by the courts. The European Union has drawn up a Directive relating to the general provision of mediation, and a Code of Conduct for Mediators, and this is quite widely adopted (see Chapter 19). **1.69**

Some other ADR processes take place within a statutory or regulatory framework, and where this is the case it is covered in the relevant chapter of this book. **1.70**

There is no regulatory framework for lawyers taking part in a negotiation or mediation, save the need to abide by appropriate rules of professional conduct and ethics (see Chapter 6). If a client is dissatisfied with the standard of work done by a lawyer then a range of options will be available, though how these rules apply with regard to ADR processes is still being developed. **1.71**

- Each firm of solicitors and each set of barristers' chambers is required to have a procedure for dealing with complaints under the requirements of the relevant codes of conduct. A dissatisfied client should normally use this as a first step.
- A complaint may be made to the appropriate professional body.
- A complaint can be raised with the Office for the Legal Services Complaints Commissioner: see www.olscc.gov.uk, and 21.06.
- The concerns may be addressed as part of decisions about costs, so that costs are not granted or are disallowed: see Chapter 9.
- There may be a wasted costs order due to an improper, unreasonable, or negligent act or omission on the part of the lawyer, provided there is a causal link between the poor conduct and the costs wasted: *Ridehalgh v Horsefield* [1994] Ch 205. This could include a failure to secure a reasonable outcome to an ADR process.
- In an extreme case, a claim may be brought for professional negligence. The standard to be expected is that of such care and skill as would be exercised by a reasonably competent practitioner in conducting an ADR process, and it remains to be clarified what standards will be seen as the norm. In making an assessment the court can take into account that the case may settle or proceed to court: *Harrison v Bloom Camillin* (1999) Times, 12 November. It will also be relevant if a client could still litigate even if ADR has failed. The immunity from an action for negligence based on anything done in court defined in

Rondel v Worsley [1969] 1 AC 191 was limited in *Arthur JS Hall & Co (a firm) v Simmons* [2002] 1 AC 615, where the House of Lords held that there should no longer be a general immunity in respect of the conduct of a case in court.

1.72 Examples of claims for professional negligence that have succeeded include:

- The failure of a lawyer to investigate the facts of a case properly so that the client recovered less than he should: *Dickinson v Jones Alexander & Co* [1990] Fam Law 137.
- The failure by lawyers to pass on important information to their clients: *Strover v Harrington* [1988] Ch 390.
- The failure by lawyers who had negotiated a business lease to notify the client of an unusual clause with regard to rent that was used to raise the rent dramatically: *County Personnel v Alan R Pulber* [1987] 1 All ER 289.

1.73 Examples of where a claim for negligence has not succeeded include:

- The mere fact that advice given by a lawyer is not ultimately successful cannot found an action, or no lawyer would risk giving advice where the law was not clear: see *Buckland v Farrar & Moody* [1978] 3 All ER 229.
- A lawyer only has to act within the scope of the instructions. If for example the client is an experienced businessman the lawyer has no obligation to investigate matters outside their instructions, or to provide warnings about the commercial risks of a transaction: *Pickersgill v Riley* [2004] PNLR 31.
- A lawyer is not necessarily in breach of duties of competence and care by pursuing a very weak case, though this will depend on the circumstances: *Harley v McDonald Harley (a firm)* (2001) Times, 15 May.

1.74 Note that a client is bound by a lawyer's assurances to a court even if the lawyer may be subject to a negligence claim: *Worldwide Corporation Ltd v Marconi Communications Ltd* (1999) Times, 7 July. If there is a conflict of duties, the court will look at the background: see *Memory Corporation v Sidhu* [2000] 1 WLR 1443, where on an interim application there were problems with what the lawyers told the court as regards the terms of an order, and as regards the evidence supplied by the client.

P OVERVIEW OF TRAINING AND ACCREDITATION

1.75 There are separate training and accreditation systems for arbitrators and for mediators. Many barristers and solicitors train as arbitrators or mediators in addition to their legal qualification, usually with a view to working in such a role in the area in which they practise. Some firms and chambers offer mediation and/or arbitration services, usually putting summary information on their website.

1.76 While the majority of arbitrators and mediators have a legal background many have other professional backgrounds, as accountants, for example. It has become increasingly common for senior managers in business to have negotiation or mediation training, so it is important to remember that a client may have relevant expertise.

1.77 The professional training and accreditation of barristers is overseen by the Bar Standards Board. From September 2010 training in ADR has become a compulsory part of the Bar Professional Training Course. The professional training and accreditation of solicitors is overseen by the Solicitors' Regulation Authority. Training in ADR is not compulsory for solicitors. Relevant sections of the relevant professional Codes of Conduct are addressed in Chapter 6. Some Bar and Law Society associations support the use of ADR, for example in commercial and family law areas.

Training and accreditation for arbitrators is overseen by the Chartered Institute of Arbitrators: see www.ciarb.org. They provide three levels of membership, associate, member and fellow, based on specific training courses that include arbitration, international arbitration and adjudication. They also provide accreditation for training meeting their standards that is provided by other bodies. A variety of other bodies provide training for international arbitrators. **1.78**

The training and accreditation for mediators is provided by a range of bodies. It is important to note the requirements of training set by the Civil Mediation Council are the widely acknowledged standard, see www.civilmediation.org. Internationally, standards are set by the International Mediation Institute, see www.imimediation.org/. Courses can focus on different specializations such as commercial law or family law, and have different coverage and length. It is important to check the content of training you might undertake, and to get information about those who have undergone the training to evaluate a course. When looking for a mediator, qualifications and experience should be checked with the body providing mediation services, and/or with the individual mediator, which is normally available on the relevant website. The following are examples of mediation training providers: **1.79**

- The Centre for Effective Dispute Resolution: www.cedr.com/training/;
- The ADR Group: www.adrgroup.co.uk;
- National Family Mediation: www.nfm.org.uk.

No formal training is needed to negotiate. However, many training courses are available, for example from CEDR, and many practical and accessible books provide insight, for example *Getting to Yes: Negotiating Agreement Without Giving In* by Roger Fisher and William Ury (Random House Business Books, 2003). Such sources can be important because of the extent to which success can depend on the skill and experience of the negotiator. **1.80**

KEY POINTS SUMMARY

- The use of ADR has grown substantially over the last 20 years, with support now being embedded in the Civil Procedure Rules, and seen frequently in judicial comment. **1.81**
- Government support for ADR is now significant, especially in terms of expecting parties to get information about mediation, and using mediation more frequently in relation to small claims.
- It is now crucial that a lawyer has sufficient knowledge of ADR options to provide a full range of advice for a client.
- There is no agreed definition of ADR, and this book takes a wide approach, looking at all the alternatives to litigation.
- ADR options offer many potential advantages in terms of saving time and costs, providing confidentiality and increasing client control.
- ADR has some potential disadvantages, especially if it is not used appropriately, and some of the strategic opportunities available in litigation may be lost.
- Arbitration is founded on statute law, but most ADR options have a less formal basis.
- Training is available for arbitrators and mediators.

2

OVERVIEW OF ADR OPTIONS

A KEY ELEMENTS OF ADR OPTIONS 2.06
B THE ROLE OF THE LAWYER WITH REGARD TO ADR OPTIONS 2.09
C NON-ADJUDICATIVE ADR OPTIONS......2.12
D ADJUDICATIVE ADR OPTIONS.......................2.42
E OTHER OPTIONS.....................2.60
Key points summary 2.68

2.01 The range of ADR options is wide. At one end of the scale are adjudicative processes such as arbitration that have similarities to litigation in that they involve a set procedure and result in the giving of a decision. At the other end of the scale are processes that are relatively informal, such as a negotiation between lawyers representing the parties. The range continues to extend as online options are developed, see Chapter 5. This chapter provides an overview of the ADR options available to parties to a dispute in England and Wales, and outlines the most commonly used processes. A lawyer should have a working knowledge of the ADR options that may be relevant to the fields in which he or she practises, so as to be able to advise a client on which option(s) might best meet the client's interests. It is important to make reasonable use of ADR options to meet CPR rules and avoid sanctions, and the factors relevant to choice are outlined in Chapter 3.

2.02 There is no overall system for the provision or oversight of ADR. For example, mediation services may be provided by courts, commercial providers, not-for-profit providers, solicitors' firms, or barristers' chambers. However, there is some coherence, for example through the role of the Civil Mediation Council (CMC), see 14.84–14.103. The wide range of types of ADR is inevitable given the need for flexibility and the range of types of case to be resolved. This book seeks to include references to all the main current sources of information, including websites, though the position is constantly developing.

2.03 An ADR option may be selected in advance and built into a contract, especially in a commercial agreement. In some areas, such as construction disputes, a particular form of ADR is commonly used within the industry: see Chapter 25. In some areas a particular type of ADR is seen as normally appropriate for a particular type of dispute, as is for example the case with mediation and conciliation for employment disputes, or ombudsman-type processes for complaints against public bodies. It has also become the norm for certain types of ADR to be used in certain areas of practice—for example mediation is more commonly used in commercial and family disputes.

2.04 If no ADR option has been selected in advance, or if there is no norm for a particular type of dispute, a range of ADR options may need to be considered. Those most commonly used are arbitration, mediation, and negotiation, which are each developed further in later chapters. While only one type of ADR should be used at a time, options are not necessarily exclusive. For example if negotiation between lawyers has led to deadlock, perhaps because of the strict instructions given by clients, a good mediator may still be able to take matters forward.

There is no definitively agreed terminology with regard to ADR options. ADR processes have developed in different ways, in different jurisdictions, and in different areas of law, so words can have slightly different meanings. There is no need for this to lead to confusion—it is rather a question of avoiding assumptions and checking if the meaning of a term is important. **2.05**

A KEY ELEMENTS OF ADR OPTIONS

The main purposes of ADR are as follows, though each occurs to a different extent in different forms of ADR: **2.06**

- The focus is on settlement rather than conflict (though the need for those involved to be able to put their case is important).
- Some level of objectivity is introduced to try to assist the achievement of a settlement through facilitating communication.
- The parties have some level of control over the process and the decision taken.
- There is a level of flexibility in the process.

This does not of course provide a complete contrast between ADR and litigation in that the purpose of a trial is to provide objective determination by an independent judge. The difference is really one of emphasis, in that in litigation the main focus is on the adversarial process right up to the time that the judgment is given. In ADR processes there is more focus on agreement. **2.07**

The main factors that differentiate ADR options are: **2.08**

- whether the process involves an independent third party (as most ADR options do), or only the parties and their representatives (as is the case for negotiation);
- whether a binding decision at the end of the process is made by a third party (adjudicative) or by the parties themselves by agreement (non-adjudicative);
- whether the process may result in a non-binding finding or proposal being made by a third party and, if so, what the role of that finding or proposal is. For example early neutral evaluation normally produces a report for the parties to consider;
- the extent to which there is a set procedure—which is more likely in an adjudicative process so the parties have a fair opportunity to put their case to the third party. There is no set procedure for a negotiation;
- the extent to which a third party controls or facilitates the process. In adjudication the adjudicator normally has a high level of control, whereas the role of a mediator is largely facilitative;
- the extent to which the parties control the process. There is always some control, in that for example the parties will agree on the appointment of an arbitrator, even if the arbitrator then takes over control of the process. In a negotiation the parties keep substantial control through the instructions given to the lawyers;
- the role of lawyers varies in different ADR processes. This is dealt with in 2.11;
- the potential costs of ADR processes vary substantially, depending on the process and the individual case. An arbitration might cost as much as a trial, whereas a negotiation may only cost the fees paid to the lawyers for the time spent negotiating: see Chapter 4. The costs of an ADR process can normally be reasonably predicted and agreed in advance, whereas it can be more difficult to provide a budget for likely litigation costs, despite the move to budgeting for litigation.

B THE ROLE OF THE LAWYER WITH REGARD TO ADR OPTIONS

2.09 A lawyer might conduct an ADR process. A number of lawyers train as arbitrators and mediators, and this is covered in 1.75–1.80. More commonly a lawyer may represent a client with regard to a dispute. In any ADR process the lawyer must of course act within the instructions given by the client, and where the lawyer plays a role in agreeing the final settlement, as in negotiation, the lawyer must act within the authority to settle provided by the client. The role of lawyer in relation to ADR has developed in the light of the Jackson Reforms and recent case law. For example, a lawyer needs to advise that reasonable use be made of ADR so that there is no risk of cost sanctions, and will need to bear in mind the importance of costs being proportionate to the amount in dispute. The tighter approach to case management and tougher enforcement of sanctions means there may be a greater likelihood of actions for professional negligence against lawyers, *Michael v Middleton* [2013] EWHC 2881 (Ch).

2.10 There are various points at which a lawyer may be involved in an ADR process:

- The lawyer should be prepared to advise orally or in writing on what ADR options might be appropriate as an alternative to litigation.
- That advice should include sufficient information on the relative strengths and weaknesses of each ADR option to assist the client in taking an informed decision. Either the lawyer or the client can consult a potential ADR provider if more detail would be useful.
- The lawyer will need to consider how and when ADR might best fit with a litigation process, and advise the client on that.
- The lawyer will need to help to prepare the case for the ADR process appropriately. This will include defining client objectives, preparing information for use, and preparing relevant arguments. Consideration should also be given to how the case should proceed if the ADR fails. For preparing for a negotiation see Chapter 12, and for mediation see Chapter 15.
- If the ADR process produces a potential settlement, or an objective evaluation, the lawyer will need to advise the client on how that relates to what is realistically obtainable if the case is pursued in any other way, eg litigation. In non-adjudicative ADR this might include advising the client on whether to accept a proposed settlement.
- If the ADR process results in agreement, the lawyer is likely to be involved in reviewing the proposed terms and helping to convert them into a final agreement. See Chapters 17 and 23 for the options for recording a settlement.
- The lawyer might be asked to advise on enforcing a settlement: see Chapter 32.

2.11 When an ADR process is undertaken, the role the lawyer varies with the process:

- In an adjudicative process such as arbitration the role of the lawyer may be broadly similar to the role of the lawyer in a trial in presenting the case.
- In early neutral evaluation or expert-assisted determination the process may be largely paper based, and the lawyer may be mainly involved in providing information and assisting in defining issues. If an evaluation is produced the lawyer might advise with regard to its effect.
- In mediation the lawyer will have a more mixed and less formal role, sometimes playing a part in presenting the case, and sometimes advising the client on options. This is developed in Chapters 14–16.
- In a negotiation the lawyers of one party will often deal directly with the lawyers for the other party, a process that gives the lawyer a large role in taking the case forward. This is developed in Chapters 11–13.

C NON-ADJUDICATIVE ADR OPTIONS

In a non-adjudicative process a third party will not take a decision, or impose an outcome upon the parties. The purpose is rather to investigate options for settlement, leaving control of the process and the possible outcome with the parties. **2.12**

Inter-client discussion

A party to a dispute may settle the dispute personally. Even if a party has consulted a lawyer for advice on rights and possibly as regards a letter before claim, the party may then seek to resolve the dispute personally rather than instructing the lawyer to negotiate. For example this may happen with a commercial client who has experience of negotiating and simply wants advice on the legal context. The lawyer might wish to warn the client of any possible admissions etc that might prejudice the position of the client should the case not settle. The lawyer might also usefully advise about how any agreement should be made legally enforceable. **2.13**

Written offers

An offer to settle a dispute can be made in writing, normally in the form of letter. If the offer is accepted then an agreement is reached. While an oral acceptance could be binding, acceptance would normally also be in writing. Enforcement of such an exchange of letters would follow normal contractual principles: see Chapter 23. The importance of making written offers is if anything growing as a way of protecting the position of a party, to facilitate the use of ADR, and to protect the position as regards costs. **2.14**

Many written offers are made under the CPR Part 36. The main advantage of this procedure is that it potentially shifts the burden of costs if the offer made is not exceeded in a later court judgment. This potential advantage is such that a Part 36 offer should normally be made if litigation is likely to be pursued, once the case has been sufficiently explored and evaluated for the appropriate level for a Part 36 offer to be calculated. Case law shows the importance of fulfilling the requirements carefully. See 4.58–4.63 for more detail. **2.15**

A written offer is a simple way to seek to settle a dispute. However, significant analysis and skill may be required to calculate what should be offered and to make the offer in a clear form. This approach is probably most suited to a case with a relatively limited number of issues to avoid complexity and misunderstanding with regard to the terms of the written offer. A written offer normally relates to a figure for damages, but a more complex offer can be made with careful drafting. **2.16**

There are potential problems in making a written offer in a letter. In keeping the terms of an offer clear it is best to leave out much by way of justification or persuasion, which may limit the chance that the other side will accept the offer. Exploration of terms may lead to a further exchange of letters, and confusion as to what is being offered may arise if this is not carefully controlled. A written offer may lead to a negotiation, and this is further explored in 2.18–2.24. **2.17**

Negotiation

A negotiation is a relatively informal process involving the discussion of some or all of the issues in a case with a view to resolving them on agreed terms. The process may be quite simple, or may involve substantial use of strategy and tactics. A negotiation may be carried out in writing (by letter or email) if the issues are relatively few or simple. Alternatively a negotiation may be carried out by telephone or conference call. If the negotiation is carried out face **2.18** to face, this often happens at the office of one of the lawyers, or at some other location that the parties agree as being appropriate and neutral. Negotiation between lawyers can happen at the door of the court when the parties to litigation go to court for an interim hearing or for trial. For the purpose of this book it will be assumed that lawyers are involved when negotiation is used to settle a legal claim. A negotiation between lawyers would typically last up to an hour (though possibly much less outside court before an interim hearing), though a complex negotiation with clients in attendance could last half a day or more.

2.19 There is no set procedure for a negotiation, and the process is within the control of those taking part. This can be challenging for a lawyer more comfortable with a set process, but it also offers opportunities for a lawyer who prepares well to present a case in its best light, and to use strategy and tactics to best effect (see Chapters 11–13). The key elements of a negotiation are as follows:

- The lawyer analyses the factual background, and ascertains the client's objectives. The lawyer advises when the case is in a state where it can appropriately be negotiated. A lawyer should act within the instructions provided by the client, and any terms agreed are normally subject to client approval before becoming fully effective. Detailed preparation is the key to success in a negotiation (see Chapter 12).
- The lawyers agree when and where the negotiation will take place and who will attend.
- The negotiation process normally starts with the agreement of an agenda to decide what issues will be covered in what order (see Chapter 13).
- The negotiation normally goes through a discussion stage where the parties seek and provide information relating to facts, objectives etc.
- Either as part of the discussion stage or immediately afterwards the parties use argument, persuasion, strategy and tactics to seek to secure the agreement of the other side (see Chapters 11 and 13).
- The parties then seek and offer concessions with a view to reaching a settlement.
- The parties make offers for settlement of each issue, or of the case overall, and explore those offers.
- To the extent agreement is reached, the terms need to be clarified and put into an enforceable form (see Chapters 17 and 23). It is very important to agree the essence of the terms in writing before the end of the meeting to avoid any later misunderstanding. Outline terms are normally subject to client approval.

2.20 Attendance at a negotiation is a matter of agreement based on what is appropriate to the case. The following are all possible, though coverage in later chapters is based on the norm that each client instructs a lawyer to negotiate on their behalf.

- It is possible for the parties to negotiate between themselves on the basis of advice given, if for example the issue in the case is one of interpretation, rather than a personal dispute where there is significant acrimony.
- The solicitors in a case might negotiate, if instructed by their clients to do so. Solicitors might negotiate by exchange of letters or telephone.
- The solicitors and clients in a case might negotiate together, especially in a case where litigation is unlikely.
- The barristers in a case might negotiate. This is quite common in a case where litigation has been commenced or is a serious likelihood. While barristers might negotiate by telephone they normally negotiate face to face, in chambers, or at the door of the court if there is a court hearing.
- The barristers, solicitors, and clients in a case might all meet to negotiate. This is a more expensive and complex option, but it might be justified by what is at stake in the case if there is a realistic hope of settlement.

- In complex or commercial negotiation, it may be necessary to take careful decisions as to who should attend. It is important to involve either directly or through availability on the telephone those with relevant information, and those with the ability to take and implement decisions.
- Because the process is informal it is possible to agree that someone else be present at a negotiation, eg an expert.

A negotiation may take place at any stage in a case and may relate to any issues. There may **2.21** well be more than one negotiation in a case. The timing of a negotiation is very important. The case must be properly evaluated and researched before any negotiation takes place so as to enable proper preparations to be made and to enable the negotiator to act effectively. The main stages at which lawyers may be instructed to negotiate a settlement are:

- early in the case, shortly after initial instruction and evaluation, and before proceedings are issued. Negotiation at this stage is supported by pre-action protocols;
- following a written offer to settle the case, where the offer is sufficiently tempting to be explored, but not good enough for immediate acceptance;
- in relation to interim applications. For example an application for an interim injunction may lead to negotiation outside court that may relate to the application itself, and also to the whole case;
- outside court before trial. The attractions of negotiating at this stage are that both sides have fully prepared their case, and a resolution may be reached while the parties still have control of the case saving the expense of the trial. The drawback of leaving negotiation till this stage is that the majority of the costs are likely to have been incurred.

The main potential advantages of negotiation are: **2.22**

- It is very flexible and comparatively low cost, making it the most common form of ADR.
- Clients retain control of the outcome through giving instructions and approval of any agreement reached.
- Many lawyers favour negotiation because of the control over process and outcome that it offers.
- The negotiation process is private, confidential, and 'without prejudice'; *Rush & Tompkins v GLC* [1989] AC 1280. This means that no reference can be made to what happened in the negotiation, save for example as regards the terms of any agreement reached.

The main potential drawbacks of negotiation are: **2.23**

- Success depends to a significant extent on how well the case has been researched and analysed, so that the case on each issue can be put strongly.
- Success can depend on the skill of the negotiator, and the strategy and tactics employed.
- Negotiation can lead to a relatively weak outcome for a client if the strengths of a case are not properly exploited.
- Some clients may be dissatisfied if they not involved in the negotiation and are left feeling that the lawyers have taken over the case.
- The relative informality of negotiation can lead to confusion if a negotiation drags on in a vague way through prolonged correspondence.

A negotiation is most likely to succeed if the lawyers are properly prepared and if the clients **2.24** on both sides are prepared to make sufficient concessions. There are four main reasons why a negotiation might fail:

- Over-optimistic client expectations and instructions can bind a lawyer too tightly. If there is little flexibility then offers and possible concessions may be difficult to address. This is best avoided by the lawyer discussing reasonable expectations sufficiently with the client

before the negotiation, and seeking to ensure that instructions include adequate flexibility. It may mean that mediation might be a better option than negotiation.
- Insufficient preparation may make it difficult to make headway.
- The negotiation process can get bogged down. If issues are quite complex and neither side is open to making concessions it may prove difficult to reach agreement.
- If the lawyers see litigation as the primary process and are not fully committed to achieving settlement negotiation may fail. This is to some extent understandable—a lawyer might feel he or she has more expertise in litigation. While the lawyer may get higher fees if the case continues, it is clearly the lawyer's duty to settle if that is the best option.

Mediation

2.25 Mediation involves a neutral third party who seeks to facilitate the resolution of a dispute. The process is quite flexible, and will normally be agreed in advance in a written agreement. The third party will meet the parties together and/or separately, helping them to find possible terms of settlement. It can be agreed who will attend a mediation session, but later chapters are largely based on both the parties and their lawyers attending.

2.26 Various types of mediation services are available, provided by the courts, or by commercial or not-for-profit organizations or by individuals. Some services provide for specific types of case such as commercial disputes, family disputes, or landlord and tenant disputes. It is not compulsory for a mediator to be trained, but normally parties will want to use someone with appropriate training and experience. Government policy is increasingly encouraging the use of mediation where it is more cost effective than litigation.

2.27 There is no set procedure for a mediation. A mediation service provider may offer a standard process, but details are usually a matter of a written mediation agreement, which will be an enforceable contract between the parties: see 15.01–15.06. The time frame can also be agreed—many mediations take a day, though a court-based programme may be much simpler, offering a limited time frame of one to three hours, and a complex commercial mediation may last a week or more. The normal key elements of a mediation process are as follows (more detail can be found in Chapters 14–16):

- The possibility of using a mediation process is raised at an appropriate point in a case by one of the parties or, possibly, if litigation has been commenced, by the court.
- If both parties are prepared to consider mediation, the parties will agree which mediation process or mediator should be used. The choice of a mediation service and/or individual mediator can be key to the success of the process.
- A mediation agreement will be signed. Some mediation services offer a set service (as tends to be the case with court mediation models), or offer a standard form agreement (as tends to be the case with major mediation service providers). The agreement will usually cover details such as when and where the mediation will take place, the format to be followed, and the fee to be paid: see 15.28–15.32.
- Lawyers usually prepare a mediation file with key documents etc., which is normally shared with all parties or just with the mediator. They also draft a written position statement.
- The mediator may be briefed prior to the mediation.
- A mediation will normally start with a joint meeting of the mediator and the lawyers and clients for both sides. This may be the first time the clients have met face to face so as to put their cases directly to each other. Opening statements may be made by lawyers and/or clients (see 16.13–16.25), followed by questions and discussion. The intention is to clarify objectives, and the strengths and weaknesses of each side's case.

- There may then be separate meetings between the mediator and the lawyers and/or clients for each side to explore their cases. There can also by agreement be meetings with an expert etc. There may be further joint meetings if that might be useful.
- Depending on what has been agreed in the mediation agreement, the mediator may seek to facilitate agreement in a very general way, exploring options with each side, and/or may make non-binding suggestions for settlement.
- If an agreement is reached the mediator will confirm the details of the agreement and ask the parties to sign a written memorandum of agreement.

It is a matter of agreement who should attend a mediation: see 15.36–15.47. The main **2.28** options are:

- The mediator talks to the parties without their lawyers, but the parties act on advice provided in advance by their lawyers. This may be effective if the problem is mainly a personal one, or if the parties do not necessarily need lawyers with them (eg a family case).
- The mediator meets the parties and their lawyers. This is a common format, though the mediator may meet the parties and the lawyers separately if this might help to take the case forward. The relevant lawyers may include in-house lawyers, solicitors, and barristers.
- Exceptionally and by agreement a mediation may be attended by another relevant person such as an expert, or an insurer or a key witness.
- There may be an imbalance if one party is legally represented and the other is not, which can make the role of the mediator rather complex.

The timing of a mediation is important, or the mediation may fail and the fees wasted. **2.29** Mediation should not happen before the case is sufficiently evaluated, but it may be most effective before the parties become too focused on trial.

The lack of a formal process in mediation can be challenging for a lawyer used to litigation, **2.30** especially as mediation tends to focus on clients, and the mediator takes some control from the lawyer. The role of the lawyer may be very different depending on the type of dispute, the client, and the composition of the legal team. The main role of the lawyer is as follows (this is developed at 16.85–16.102):

- advising on when to mediate, and who to use as a mediator;
- advising on the terms of the mediation agreement;
- drafting a written position statement to brief the mediator, and/or making an opening statement. An opening statement can be strong, but needs slightly different presentation skills from trial advocacy to include the client and address the opponent;
- it may be advisable to have a meeting to prepare the client for the mediation, to discuss the strengths and weaknesses of the case and the possible outcomes, and the role of the client in the process. A client has a much more direct involvement in a mediation than in a negotiation;
- advising the client on any offers or options that may emerge;
- looking carefully at the position as regards evidence. While the process is confidential, if there is a risk the process may fail it will be important to keep an eye on what may happen if the process reverts to litigation;
- ensuring any agreement reached is properly recorded and enforceable. It is often a term of the mediation agreement that the parties enter a written agreement at the end of the process, and some standard forms are available.

The key potential advantages of mediation are as follows (and see 14.14): **2.31**

- A neutral third party may be able to help a party to see the strengths and weaknesses of a case more clearly, and/or may help them to see the dispute in a different light.

- A mediator can help parties step outside an adversarial framework and entrenched positions, which can help mediation to work where negotiation has failed.
- A mediator can strip away false optimism and make possible concessions look more acceptable.
- Mediation offers a potentially much larger role for clients than negotiation, and this can assist clients in feeling that they have had their say, and in seeing the case for the other side.
- Because the process is flexible, a client can be allowed to make a statement to give the client the feeling of 'having their day in court'. A mini trial or an examination of a key witness can be included by agreement.

2.32 The potential disadvantages of mediation are:

- The involvement of a third party removes some control from the parties themselves.
- Success depends partly on the abilities of the mediator.
- Lawyers may feel less comfortable with mediation as they have less control than in a negotiation.
- Mediation may make a party feel they are expected to make concessions, though there is no reason why this should be the case.
- Mediation is unlikely to work if the parties are deeply antagonistic.

2.33 A mediation is most likely to succeed if both parties take a realistic view of the strengths and weaknesses of their case, if care is taken to agree a process that is likely to work, and if the mediator is reasonably skilled.

2.34 A mediation is most likely to fail if the parties are unrealistic in their objectives, are falsely optimistic about the strengths of their cases, or are very antagonistic. A mediation can be defeated by one party being unreasonable.

Conciliation

2.35 The term conciliation has no fully agreed meaning, and it is sometimes used interchangeably with mediation. Both processes involve a neutral third party who helps the parties to reach settlement. In conciliation the neutral third party tends to facilitate negotiation between parties rather than to mediate between their positions. There can be other differences between particular types of mediation and conciliation. A number of bodies offer conciliation services, and probably the best known is the Advisory, Conciliation and Arbitration Service (ACAS). There is more detailed consideration of conciliation in Chapter 20.

Early neutral and/or expert evaluation

2.36 An early neutral evaluation is an assessment of some or all of the issues in a case by an independent third party. This may be appropriate where the case wholly or largely turns on limited issues that may require particular expertise or interpretation, and an appropriate agreed expert can provide a view that both parties will respect, which should help them in evaluating their own case and reaching a resolution. The third party may be an expert or an independent person with legal knowledge, and will normally be asked to produce a written report on specified issues. The report can include findings or provisional recommendations as requested by the parties.

2.37 There is no set procedure. The key elements of the process are likely to be:

- A contract specifies that early neutral evaluation should be used in the event of a dispute, or the parties agree that it would be useful once a dispute has arisen.
- The parties agree who to approach for an evaluation, what issues to seek evaluation of, what information should be provided to the evaluator, and what fee should be paid. An

evaluator can be asked to make findings of fact, findings on likely outcome, proposals for appropriate remedies etc.
- Agreed information will be provided to the evaluator. This is normally done in writing, but there can be a meeting for discussion with any agreed relevant people present if this might be useful.
- The evaluator produces a report as requested.
- The parties decide how to take the case forward in the light of the report. The report may be so clear that terms may be agreed by letter, or a negotiation or mediation might take place.

To be most effective it is clearly important that the early neutral evaluation be held as early as is reasonably possible, once the parties have sufficient information to identify the issues to be addressed, and to brief the evaluator. **2.38**

The potential advantages are that an independent report may well facilitate the early settlement of the whole case, or at least some of the issues, especially where the third party has a good professional reputation and is respected. This can avoid or limit litigation and save costs, not least as there is little point in using a full litigation process for limited or technical issues. An agreed evaluation can be less intrusive and expensive than a full mediation. Difficulties in agreeing and getting permission to use expert evidence in a trial can be avoided. **2.39**

Possible drawbacks are that work will be required to agree what materials and issues to put to the evaluator, and success will depend on the quality of the report produced. It is of course possible that an independent report will fail to support a party's case, though it is probably better to see potential weaknesses at an early stage. **2.40**

There are some special forms of early neutral evaluation, for example in the Commercial Court and Technology and Construction Court, where a senior judge or lawyer can evaluate the likely outcome of a case on the basis of a summary brief. For more detail on early neutral or expert evaluation see Chapter 22. **2.41**

D ADJUDICATIVE ADR OPTIONS

Adjudicative ADR involves a decision on the case being made by an impartial third party. The main difference from litigation is that the parties have much more control over the process, and the choice of the arbitrator. **2.42**

Arbitration

An arbitration is a consideration of a case by a specially appointed impartial third party that leads to a decision about the case being taken by that arbitral tribunal. The tribunal and the process to be followed are agreed in advance by the parties. There is a great deal of variation, and an arbitration can be anything from a consideration of written submissions to a process which is broadly similar to that of a trial. **2.43**

Arbitration has developed as an alternative to litigation over many years. Because it can lead to a decision binding the parties, arbitration is formally regulated in many jurisdictions. In England and Wales this is done by the Arbitration Act 1996. Because it can operate outside the courts of individual jurisdictions, arbitration is very popular in commercial cases and in other cases with an international dimension. In a case with international elements it is important to distinguish between a case where the parties have agreed to an arbitration in England under the Arbitration Acts (see Chapter 26), and a case where the parties have **2.44** agreed to an international arbitration under a relevant treaty or agreement (see Chapter 29). Arbitration may also be used where the parties want a binding decision to be reached using a code different to that of the legal jurisdiction, for example applying sharia law.

2.45 The key elements of an arbitration are:

- An agreement to go to arbitration is triggered by a clause in a contract, or by an agreement between the parties once a dispute has arisen: see Chapter 26.
- The parties agree which arbitration service/arbitrator to use. This may be decided by the arbitration clause, or by agreement at the time. For more detail on arbitral tribunals see Chapter 27.
- The parties enter a written agreement setting out how the arbitration will be conducted. This will normally include timescale, how evidence and other submissions will be made, what form the arbitration decision will take, and how costs and fees will be paid. Many arbitration providers or regulators provide model rules.
- The parties take such pre-hearing steps as have been agreed. This may include providing information etc to the arbitrator.
- The arbitration takes place. In a simple case this may just involve the consideration of written submissions and other material by the arbitrator. In a more complex case the procedure can be very similar to a court hearing with lawyers on both sides making oral submissions, calling witnesses etc.
- The arbitration decision is given. This is normally a written award delivered after the arbitration. Depending on what was agreed it may or may not include detailed reasons: see Chapter 30.
- In certain circumstances there may be an appeal to a court from an arbitration award.
- As regards the enforcement of arbitration awards, see Chapter 30.

2.46 An arbitration can be held in any suitable, and usually neutral, place agreed by the parties. It is for the parties to agree who should attend where there is to be a hearing. It would be normal for lawyers to attend and to conduct the case. As it is a decision-making process, an arbitration should not be held until both sides have adequately prepared their case, the timing being a matter of agreement between the parties.

2.47 The main attractions of arbitration are that:

- the process can be closely tailored to the needs of a specific dispute, for example providing for specific evidence to be submitted by both sides, rather than the need to follow generic procedural rules for disclosure;
- the parties can select an arbitrator with appropriate expertise and experience, rather than being allocated any judge from the court where proceedings are issued;
- the process is private, unlike a trial in open court, so privacy can be maintained, save to the extent that the parties agree to make any statement about the case and its outcome;
- the fact that the process can resemble a trial may make it relatively attractive to lawyers.

2.48 The potential drawbacks of arbitration are that:

- the fact that some arbitrations can be similar to a court trial can mean that arbitration is not necessarily a cost-saving option;
- the process results in a decision by the arbitrator, so the parties do not have the control over the outcome that they would have in a non-adjudicatory process;
- an arbitration process cannot deal as easily as a court with a party who fails to co-operate;
- an arbitrator may have relevant knowledge without necessarily having the robustness of a judge with substantial experience of litigation.

Arbitration is most likely to succeed where the parties put sufficient effort into agreeing the arbitration process, are adequately committed to the process, and select the arbitrator with care. 2.49

It is more likely to fail where the arbitrator is not appropriate for the case, or fails to understand the case for a party properly so that the party is dissatisfied with the outcome. 2.50

Adjudication

There is a variety of other processes in which a neutral third party acting under an agreed process can reach a decision on the whole case, or on specified issues. Some operate under regulation, and some by agreement between the parties. An adjudication process is most likely to be appropriate in a specialist commercial field where the parties prefer a system adapted to the needs of their industry or business. The adjudicator used is most likely to be someone with appropriate specialist knowledge. One of the best known adjudication processes is that used for construction disputes: see Chapter 25. 2.51

An adjudication process should be agreed between the parties. The process to be used is normally laid down in advance in terms agreed by the industry, and/or by the body or person who provides the adjudication. The parties normally agree in a commercial contract to be bound by the relevant adjudication process should there be a dispute. 2.52

The key elements of an adjudication process tend to be broadly similar to those of an arbitration, but they are adapted to industry needs and may provide for processes to deal with particular types of dispute quickly. By agreement, the adjudication may lead to a binding decision, or to a decision that will only be binding if the parties agree to it, or if neither party appeals within a set period. 2.53

The potential benefits of adjudication are that: 2.54

- the process can be carefully adjusted to the needs of a particular industry or business;
- the process may be governed entirely by agreement between the parties, and can therefore be more flexible than arbitration or litigation;
- an adjudication can be one of the most cost-effective ways of getting an independent decision in a case.

The possible drawbacks are that: 2.55

- tailored adjudication processes are not available for all types of dispute where they might be useful;
- adjudication may be quite expensive if the adjudicator has to do a lot of work to understand the case;
- if the adjudication agreement does not provide that the adjudicator's decision will be final and binding on both parties, costs may be wasted and litigation still necessary.

Expert determination

The possibility of an expert opinion assisting non-adjudicative dispute resolution was considered at 2.36–2.41. The view of an expert may be equally useful in an adjudicative process. There are various possibilities depending on the needs of the case. 2.56

One option is that the expert may be appointed to decide the case. This may be appropriate where the only or main issues in the case require expert knowledge and a full adjudication procedure is not needed. For more information on expert determination see Chapter 24. 2.57

2.58 Another option is that an adjudication may take place, but the adjudicator may not necessarily have the required specialist knowledge, so it may be appropriate for an expert to assist in the determination of a case. This might for example be on the basis that a neutral expert would report on specified issues to the adjudicator.

2.59 Using an agreed independent expert may well save both time and costs, especially if the alternative would be that the parties would both get reports from separate experts and present them to an arbitrator or adjudicator. However, it is important that the expert be carefully chosen so that the parties will respect the expert's report.

E OTHER OPTIONS

2.60 The options most commonly used for ADR are those set out above. However, this is not a definitive list. People with a dispute can agree to any approach that they think can assist them in reaching a resolution, and any government or private body can offer dispute resolution processes. There is constant development, and some further options that do not fit neatly under the headings of adjudicative or non-adjudicative.

Hybrids

2.61 It is possible to choose an option that combines the advantages and disadvantages of different ADR options. For example a 'med-arb' can be set up with an agreement to mediate, but to allow the mediator to impose an outcome if the parties fail to reach agreement. This means that the dispute will be resolved by agreement if possible, but by a decision from an agreed informed person in default of that: see 16.73–16.76. An alternative is an 'arb-med', where the parties may set up an arbitration, but then the arbitrator may try to mediate an agreed outcome before giving a decision: see 16.77–16.79.

2.62 Such hybrids can present problems, but if the goal is to settle the dispute they may provide the best way forward. All ADR processes in any event have such flexibility that they can be adjusted according to need. For example, an arbitration may be delayed while the parties negotiate, or a mini trial may take place within a mediation.

Processes for dealing with grievances

2.63 There are various processes that provide for a person or body to look at a dispute or complaint. The process may provide for various forms of investigation, suggestions for outcome, or decision making. One example is the use of ombudsman-type processes, for which see Chapter 21. Such processes generally apply to concerns in a particular area. An ombudsman may have a facilitative role, or may be empowered to take a decision.

Specialist systems

2.64 Some industries have developed special procedures to meet specific needs. One example is the removal industry, where many removal contracts require a dispute to be referred to a settlement process. Such processes may be advantageous, or may effectively limit the options for a customer with a concern.

IT-based options

2.65 Over the last few years there has been a substantial increase in the provision of ADR options via the internet. In some cases technology is used to support a specific process such as mediation or arbitration, but increasingly new options for Online Dispute Resolution or 'ODR' are being developed that use technology to create new processes. For more detail see Chapter 5.

Online options can be particularly useful to deal with relatively low-value consumer disputes, especially in relation to e-commerce. However, it should be appreciated that national and international frameworks for the use of ODR are still being developed. This is also discussed further in Chapter 5. **2.66**

Dispute management systems

Some disputes can be very large or complex, and may involve a large number of potential parties. It can be very difficult to find a single appropriate process to manage and resolve such a dispute, but the flexibility of ADR methods can be used very imaginatively to address needs. It may prove possible to adapt and mix ADR approaches to put together a system for moving forward. One example of this is the way in which complex disputes relating to the building of the channel tunnel were addressed: see *Channel Tunnel Group Ltd v Balfour Beatty Ltd* [1993] AC 334. Another example is the way in which concerns relating to the retention of organs from dead children by hospitals were dealt with. Group mediations were used to raise and vocalize the sometimes emotional concerns of parents, and this helped to settle many issues so that only limited parties and issues eventually went to trial. **2.67**

KEY POINTS SUMMARY

- A lawyer should be familiar with the range of ADR options and be able to advise a client on them as appropriate. This includes familiarity with each process, when it should be used, who might attend, and key strengths and weaknesses. **2.68**
- All ADR options focus on settlement and offer process control to the parties. A process may be set in advance or agreed after a dispute arises.
- Mediation and arbitration processes are often based on a written agreement between the parties.
- ADR options can be broadly divided into processes that are adjudicative (where a third party takes a decision) and those which are non-adjudicative (where the parties approve any proposed settlement).
- The main non-adjudicative options are negotiation and mediation. In both cases the outcome is by agreement of the parties. The main difference is that a negotiation is normally conducted by lawyers, whereas a mediation includes a neutral third party.
- The main adjudicative options are arbitration and expert determination. These provide for a third party to take a decision.

3

FACTORS INFLUENCING THE SELECTION OF AN ADR OPTION

A LEGAL ADVICE ON APPROPRIATE DISPUTE RESOLUTION OPTIONS 3.02
B ADVANCE SELECTION OF AN ADR OPTION 3.11
C FACTORS INFLUENCING ADR SELECTION 3.16
D POTENTIAL CONCERNS ABOUT ADR 3.50
E SECURING AGREEMENT TO ADR 3.64
F CONFIDENTIALITY IN RELATION TO ADR PROCESSES 3.71
G TIMING THE USE OF ADR 3.74
Key points summary 3.76

3.01 The range of ADR options and the potential main advantages and drawbacks of each was considered in Chapter 2. Many factors may influence the selection of an appropriate dispute resolution option for an individual case, and it will be necessary to consider carefully which factors are most important. Sometimes the selection of an option may be relatively straightforward, but in a large or complex case it may be necessary to compare different ADR options carefully with litigation. One of the main potential factors is cost, and this is considered more fully in Chapter 4.

A LEGAL ADVICE ON APPROPRIATE DISPUTE RESOLUTION OPTIONS

3.02 If ADR may be appropriate in principle, then the lawyer should consider and advise a client on the most appropriate form of ADR for the case. As with all advice, at the end of the day the decision lies with the client. The role of the lawyer is to provide sufficient advice for the client to take an informed decision, explaining the need to make reasonable use of ADR.

Overcoming possible problems in advising on ADR

3.03 Practical knowledge of ADR within the legal profession is currently somewhat uneven, ranging from lawyers who are themselves qualified as arbitrators or mediators, through lawyers who use at least one form of ADR within their practice on a fairly regular basis, to lawyers who rarely if ever use ADR.

3.04 There are reasons why a lawyer may not find it easy to advise on ADR:

- Litigation lawyers are familiar with the litigation process, and may feel they can do the best job for their client working in the area with which they are familiar.
- Lawyers may think it is difficult to advise on ADR before a certain stage in litigation. It may be difficult to assess a case fully prior to disclosure. Indeed in a complex case the lawyer may fear a complaint or even an allegation of negligence if the case is settled for less than it is worth before full information is available.
- The litigation process has a life of its own and naturally moves from one step to the next following a timetable so that ADR might appear to be an intrusion.

- The position of a lawyer is less clearly defined in ADR processes than it is in litigation, and the lawyer may have concerns about having less control of the process.
- A lawyer will have a natural concern about fee income, and may not find it easy to advise on options that will potentially reduce fees.
- It can be quite challenging to compare the potential advantages and disadvantages of litigation and a form of ADR, because of the number of possibly relevant factors.

The position is changing rapidly, so that lawyers should feel more confident in giving advice: **3.05**

- ADR options are not far outside the experience of most lawyers. The main ADR options are broadly based on negotiation (eg mediation) or a trial-type process (eg arbitration).
- Most ADR processes involve similar elements to litigation. A settlement should always be based on a careful assessment of the best the client can hope to get in legal terms, and what would be the most likely outcome if the case went to court.
- The importance of disclosure has changed with the growth of pre-action protocols. Much of the key information in a case is now potentially available before the issue of proceedings.
- With the growth of judicial case management under the CPR, lawyers have less control over the conduct of litigation. ADR processes are flexible and subject to agreement, so potentially offer more control.
- Clients are likely to be attracted to lawyers who offer a service that includes ADR options for quicker and cheaper settlement given the often high cost of litigation. This is happening with the growth of alternative business structures.
- There has been a massive growth in the availability of information and training with regard to ADR, including internet resources, and ADR providers who offer quite comprehensive packages.

The professional duty to give advice

General legal professional and ethical duties with regard to advising on ADR remain to be more fully developed by the relevant professional bodies. Currently it is the general professional duties with regard to advising a client that apply. As an example, the Code of Conduct for the Bar provides that a barrister must act in the best interests of each client (Core Duty 2) so that the client's best interests are protected and promoted (Outcome 11) fearlessly and by all proper and lawful means without regard to the lawyer's own interests or to any consequences to himself (Conduct Rule RC15). Similarly the SRA Code of Conduct provides in Chapter 1 Outcome 1.12 that a solicitor must ensure that clients are in a position to make informed decisions about the services they need, how their matter will be handled and the options available to them. For possible penalties where proper advice on ADR options is not provided see 1.67–1.74. **3.06**

It is the question of what is in 'the client's best interests' that governs how far it is a duty to offer advice on ADR. It is suggested that it is normally in the client's interests to be made aware of relevant ADR options where they could lead to a more cost-effective or quicker resolution of the client's case, with an outcome that meets the client's objectives to the best reasonable extent. This approach is supported by judicial statements including: **3.07**

- Dyson LJ in *Halsey v Milton Keynes NHS Trust* [2004] 1 WLR 3002: 'All members of the legal profession who conduct litigation should now routinely consider with their clients whether their disputes are suitable for ADR';
- Ward LJ in *Burchell v Bullard* [2005] EWCA 358: 'The court has given its stamp of approval to mediation and it is now the legal profession which must become fully aware of and acknowledge its value'.

3.08 It is clear that a lawyer has a professional duty to discuss ADR with a client to comply with relevant civil litigation rules (and this is considered further in Chapters 7–9):

- in order to comply with a pre-action protocol, or the spirit of a pre-action protocol;
- in order to consider the possibility of a stay for ADR to take place once proceedings have been issued;
- where there is any possibility of a costs sanction if there were any refusal to engage in ADR;
- if the other side proposes an ADR process, where a failure to reply can be treated as a refusal to use ADR, see *PGF II SA v OMFS Company 1 Limited* [2014] WLR 1386;
- in order to ensure that costs remain proportionate to the amount in dispute.

When to give advice on ADR options

3.09 The main opportunities for giving general advice on ADR options are as follows:

- *When giving initial advice*. Relevant ADR options can be broadly outlined, including pros and cons, implications, and potential cost. This could be done generally through a website or brochure.
- *When holding a conference or meeting*. It is natural to review when a Part 36 offer should be made and how much should be offered, see 4.58–4.63. It is equally useful to review when and how negotiation or mediation might assist in taking the case forward, helping to achieve the client's objectives.
- *When writing an opinion*. As part of advising on next steps a barrister might well advise on Part 36 offers and/or ADR options.
- *When reviewing a case prior to issuing proceedings*. ADR should be considered not just in relation to a pre-action protocol, but as part of a comparison of litigation and ADR options.
- *When reviewing a case prior to a court hearing*. Preparation of a case for hearing often leads to a consideration of when and how the case might be settled. This may lead to negotiation or mediation.

3.10 The main stages in litigation where the position relating to ADR might most usefully be reviewed are:

- *When the case first comes to the lawyer.* This is the best opportunity to save costs and time if there is an appropriate ADR option, such as expert determination. However ADR should not be used before it is possible to assess the strengths and weaknesses of a case properly.
- *Before proceedings are issued*. Pre-action protocols require the exchange of information that is normally sufficient to allow an assessment of the strengths and weaknesses of a case, and require the consideration of ADR. There is still an opportunity to save significant costs and time, unless there is a good reason to start litigation, for example to make use of procedural and evidential rules.
- *At the track allocation stage or a case management hearing, to comply with civil litigation rules*. There may be a risk of sanctions for failing to consider or engage in ADR: see Chapters 7–8. The Directions Questionnaire (Fast track and Multi-track) on Form N181 asks in section C whether a pre-action protocol has been fully complied with, and for an explanation of any failure to comply or partial compliance.
- *After disclosure and inspection of evidence/exchange of witness statements*. It is often suggested that this is a good time to review ADR options because this is the stage at which you are likely to know the full case for the other side. However this is not necessarily true—collecting and dealing with all this material can be very time consuming and expensive so it is only important to wait till this stage when you expect something important from it.

- *On consideration of expert evidence.* An application to use expert evidence needs to identify the issues the expert will address as well as an estimate of costs, which may lead to agreement as to what is reasonably required. The concurrent hearing of expert evidence can also be used to reduce issues, CPR Practice Direction 35, paras 11.1–11.4.
- *When a Part 36 offer is made.* The offer is in itself an attempt to settle, but the options are not only to accept or reject it. The making of an offer can be an appropriate time to consider negotiation or mediation if the offer has some possible merit but is not good enough, see 4.58–4.63.
- *Just before trial.* A significant amount of negotiation and some mediation takes place just before trial. This is the time when lawyers and clients will have made a final assessment of the strengths and weaknesses of the case, and it offers a chance to save some of the cost of trial, and to agree an outcome rather than leaving it to a judge whose view may not be easy to predict. On the other hand, if there is no real reason why the case could not have settled much earlier, it is a waste of time and cost to leave settlement to the door of the court.

B ADVANCE SELECTION OF AN ADR OPTION

It is increasingly common for parties entering an agreement, especially a commercial contract, to include a term that in the event of a dispute arising, a form of ADR will be used to settle it. Lawyers advising on the drawing up of an agreement should consider whether such a term should be included, and while a standard term can be used, the clause can be tailored to meet specific requirements. There are many potential advantages in taking decisions about dispute resolution options while a relationship is positive: **3.11**

- It can be useful where informal or private resolution is desirable, for example in a partnership agreement, or where specialist knowledge might be needed.
- The parties can agree on the form of ADR to be used, and can even identify an ADR body or an individual to act if needed.
- The parties can agree the process and the timescale for the ADR, and how costs will be met.
- The parties can effectively draw up their own pre-action protocol for what should happen in the event of a dispute before courts are involved.
- This can help to ensure a constructive approach if there is a dispute, so that parties focus on trying to find resolution rather than escalating the dispute.

In addition to prescribing ADR in an individual agreement, some large bodies and other organizations have made public commitments to use ADR where appropriate. This includes a public pledge made on 23 March 2001 by the government of the United Kingdom to use ADR whenever it was sought by parties with whom the government was in dispute, in appropriate cases. This commitment was reinforced in 2011 and is supported by annual reports on the use of ADR by the government. **3.12**

Any clause agreeing to the use of ADR must be drawn up carefully as it will potentially be enforceable as a term of contract. The terms must be sufficiently clear to be enforced: *in Cable & Wireless v IBM* [2002] EWHC 2059 (Comm) there was comment *obiter* by Colman J that clear procedures, such as those of the Centre for Effective Dispute Resolution (CEDR), should be enforceable. It would seem that an agreement to use a named expert, or a named ADR provider, or a process such as early neutral evaluation would be specific and enforceable. A court can require the fulfilment of certain procedures before the start of arbitration proceedings: *Scott v Avery* (1856) 5 HL Cas 811. However, if the early stages are too vague a court may not be prepared to enforce them, so a stay will not necessarily be ordered to force **3.13** the use of non-determinative ADR: *Halifax Financial Services Ltd v Intuitive Systems Ltd* [1999] 1 All ER 303. For more detail on the enforcement of agreements to go to arbitration see 26.10–26.44.

3.14 However, the form of ADR selected may have implications for whether the agreement can be enforced. Negotiation and mediation are consensual processes and a court cannot force a party to take part in them, and certainly cannot force a party to agree an outcome. In *Walford v Miles* [1992] 2 AC 128 it was said that an agreement to negotiate is not enforceable, though that case related to interpreting a collateral provision rather than the use of ADR. This approach was endorsed in *Pitt v PHH Asset Management* [1993] 4 All ER 961, where Bingham LJ emphasized that the problem was that negotiation was a wide and vague obligation, a party could stop negotiating at any time and the court could not really assess if that was for good reason, or force the party to reach an agreement. Even if a term to negotiate were enforceable, it is difficult to see how damages for breach would be assessed, or whether damages could be more than nominal.

3.15 As both the CPR and the approach taken by judges have moved to support the use of ADR it is to be anticipated that courts will move further to support the enforcement of clearly defined and reasonable ADR agreements. However, it is likely that the focus will remain on supporting clearly defined processes. In practice enforceability is rarely a problem. If the parties have voluntarily agreed to ADR they are likely to comply voluntarily. In any event they should normally follow a pre-action protocol, which will require the consideration of ADR, and the pre-agreed form of ADR may be an appropriate way to do this.

C FACTORS INFLUENCING ADR SELECTION

3.16 In most cases there will be no pre-agreement as to the form of ADR to be used. This means that the following factors will need to be weighed up. In each case consideration will have to be given to which factors apply, and to their relative importance. This may change at different stages in the case. In taking decisions about dispute resolution options it is vital to consider the advantages and disadvantages of each ADR option as against litigation. The details of the litigation process itself are well dealt with in other sources and are referred to rather than dealt with fully here.

Is jurisdiction an issue?

3.17 Jurisdiction may be a crucial issue for litigation. In many cases both parties will be based within a single legal jurisdiction. If they are not then the procedural rules of any potentially relevant jurisdiction will need to be used to determine where litigation should take place. Some forms of ADR are only available in a particular jurisdiction, for example because they have been set up by legislation or by court rules.

3.18 Jurisdiction is not normally an issue for ADR, because it is undertaken by agreement, and indeed ADR can provide a way of overcoming jurisdictional issues. International arbitration may be a solution where for example parties from different jurisdictions do not wish to submit to the courts of a single jurisdiction: see Chapter 29. There is also potential for international mediation: see Chapter 19. By its very nature, negotiation can take place without regard to jurisdiction. Many ADR organizations can provide services both within and outside specific legal jurisdictions. Remember, however, that jurisdiction may be relevant to any appeal, or be crucial to enforcement of an agreement. If this may be an issue, check what appeal or enforcement options will be available before agreeing to a mediation or arbitration that will have potential effect beyond a single legal jurisdiction.

Is ADR inappropriate?

It is sometimes said that some types of case are inherently unsuitable for ADR. It is certainly right that ADR is not the best way forward for some individual cases, but query if any category of cases should never use ADR. Some of the possible problems with ADR generally can be resolved by choosing a specific method of ADR. **3.19**

The main areas where it might be suggested that ADR is not appropriate are where: **3.20**

- *A court judgment is needed as a precedent.* Only a court judgment can provide a precedent to bind other cases. Query, however, whether the parties to an individual case need a legal precedent—they can for example agree that the outcome of one ADR process will bind them for other similar cases. See 3.21–3.23.
- *Where the powers of the court to make interim orders are important.* In particular cases the powers of the court may be needed, for example to grant an interim injunction or provide security for costs. Note, however, that this does not rule out using ADR in a case once appropriate interim orders have been made, see 3.24 and 3.44. It is also possible to agree that arbitrators have power to make interim orders, though an arbitrator will not have the same range of enforcement powers as a judge.
- *If the client has a very strong case.* There may be a fear that agreeing to an ADR process will necessitate the making of concessions, so that ADR should not be used where a case is strong. It may be better to issue proceedings and apply for summary judgment. However, if a case is put strongly in mediation it may force the other side to see that their expectations are unrealistic and save costs on a longer litigation process. There is authority that a party with a strong case may not act unreasonably in refusing ADR, *Swain Mason v Mills & Reeve* [2012] EWCA Civ 498 (per Davis LJ). The belief that a case is strong must be objectively justified, *ADS Aerospace Ltd v EMS Global Tracking Ltd* [2012] EWHC 2904 (TCC).
- *The law is very complex.* An area where the law is complex may be best dealt with by a court, especially if clarity of law in that area is important. However it is not necessarily in the interests of an individual client that his or her case be used to clarify the law, especially if the area of law is not of general importance. ADR may achieve a practical solution without the need for full legal debate. Alternatively, early neutral evaluation may assist in clarifying the legal issues. The courts have said on several occasions that it is not necessary to go to court simply because the law in an area is complex or unclear if that would lead to disproportionate costs, see for example *Faida v Elliott Corporation* [2012] EWCA Civ 287 and *Oliver v Symons* [2012] EWCA Civ 267.
- *The facts are very complex.* Complex facts may be appropriately considered in court, especially if there is a fear that witnesses are not telling the full truth and cross-examination may be important. However, it can be very difficult for a judge to reach a decision on complex facts, which can leave the parties at risk of losing in court. An arbitration or expert-assisted determination may be just as effective in dealing with complex facts in a specialist area. Negotiation or mediation where key facts are discussed but the parties focus on a satisfactory outcome rather than on detailed analysis of past facts may lead to a satisfactory result.
- *There are many parties to the action.* The rules for civil litigation provide a structured way for a number of parties to be engaged in a dispute. However, it is quite possible for an ADR process to be structured to involve a number of parties, with mediation being used where there are a number of potential claimants in a negligence action.
- *There is great animosity between the parties.* A process that has to work by agreement may be doomed to failure if there is great animosity between the parties. However, providing a day in court is not necessarily the best way forward if one party will win and the other

will remain resentful. A good mediator can be very effective in managing emotion at face-to-face meetings, helping the parties to reach a more mutually acceptable outcome. The courts have said that ADR can be appropriate even if trust has broken down: *Wright v Michael Wright (Supplies) Ltd* [2013] EWCA Civ 234.

- *There are quasi-criminal allegations.* Cases involving allegations such as fraud or libel may not be suitable for non-adjudicative ADR, though this will depend on the facts of the case. Cases involving domestic abuse or similar allegations may be unsuitable for non-adjudicative ADR, unless it is possible to facilitate a real change of attitude to protect the abused party.
- *A matter of public policy is involved.* It is said that public matters such as environmental or government regulation issues are not suitable for ADR because the process is essentially private, but ADR has been used successfully in many cases as the government is committed to the use of ADR where appropriate.
- *The claimant wants to make a public point of going to court.* Some claimants see having a day in court, with publicity for their case, as being one of their primary objectives, as may happen for example where a well-known figure brings an action for libel. However it is worth remembering that a court hearing will be public whatever the outcome. While ADR processes are private, a public statement can be one of the agreed outcomes, with the client having more control over the words that reach the press.

Is a court decision creating a precedent important?

3.21 It may be important that a judicial precedent is created, eg interpretation of a clause in a standard form contract (see *McCook v Lobo* [2002] EWCA Civ 1760). An important concern about the growth of ADR is the extent to which the doctrine of precedent may be undermined. The development of the common law depends on courts taking decisions which are reported and used as the basis for later decisions. An ADR process is private, with only such public report as the parties may agree, and a consensual agreement or a decision by an arbitrator or expert cannot have the precedent value of a decision by a judge.

3.22 This is an important concern, not least because ADR is partly dependent on court decisions. In presenting a case in an arbitration, or in deciding what to accept in a negotiation, the lawyer will always take as a benchmark what would be likely to be the outcome if the case went to court. ADR processes would be undermined without the development of the law through reported cases, and there is a risk that the law would ossify, or would develop in a way that lawyers could not easily track due to the lack of reported cases. It is vital that a sufficient number of cases continue to go to court for the law to continue to be publicly developed and clarified.

3.23 That said, for many years only a small percentage of disputes have gone to trial, with an even smaller percentage resulting in reported decisions. Individual parties should not be expected to go to the expense and stress of trial if it is not in their own interests, and the need for precedent should not hold back appropriate development of ADR.

Is a court order necessary?

3.24 Sometimes a court order is the only way of achieving a particular outcome. For example a declaration of legal rights or an injunction can only be ordered by a court. Some technical orders can only be made by a court, for example an amendment of the register of members of a company. Even if an ADR process is followed, a court order may be required to approve it, for example court approval is required for a settlement made on behalf of a minor or a patient.

What is the relative cost of possible options?

The cost of litigation is one of the main concerns of those who have a legal case, and can remain a complaint even of parties who win in court and recover the major part of their costs from the loser. Costs will be an even greater concern for a loser who may have to pay the costs of the winning party as well as his own. The level of concern about costs is such that this is one of the main reasons for choosing an ADR process. While ADR is likely to prove cheaper than taking a case to trial, ADR carries its own costs, and savings will depend on the form of ADR chosen and how early in the case it is used. An arbitration might be as expensive as a trial, and negotiation may not save a lot of money if it takes place just before trial. For more detail see Chapter 4. **3.25**

How important is expert knowledge?

Expert knowledge is relevant to a wide range of cases, and the normal approach is to try to have this admitted through an expert report. If an expert can be agreed and jointly briefed this is a cost-effective approach. However, some cases require general expert knowledge, for example of how a particular industry functions, or very specific expert knowledge on a core part of the case, such as the maintenance of specialist machinery. It may be expensive to litigate such a case because of the amount of evidence that will need to be presented to a judge, and the clients may not have great faith in a judge without specific expertise. An ADR process may be very helpful, and in particular an adjudicative form of ADR would allow the parties to agree on an arbitrator or adjudicator with appropriate expertise, or expert-assisted determination might be appropriate. It is possible for experts to be involved in a negotiation or mediation, but this may be less successful if the issue needing expert input is strongly contested. **3.26**

Is confidentiality important?

A desire for confidentiality is another important reason why a client may choose ADR. Most civil trials are held in public, whereas ADR processes are agreed and carried out privately. A desire to avoid publicity may be a key reason for using ADR, for example to protect information about a business, or to keep personal matters private. **3.27**

That said, the position on publicity is not entirely straightforward. There can be some privacy in a trial process, for example the detailed outcome of a case can be kept confidential through a schedule in a Tomlin order. Equally there are ways in which an ADR process may become at least partly public. It is quite possible to agree that any kind of public statement be made as part of the outcome of ADR if the matter is resolved. Many arbitration findings are made publicly available, or there may be an appeal from an arbitration to a court. There are some problems as regards the application of traditional concepts of privilege and confidentiality to some ADR processes, especially mediation: see 3.71–3.73 and 6.43–6.74. **3.28**

How much control does the client want?

On the face of it an adversarial court process provides a large degree of control for the parties as each side prepares and presents their own case. The degree of control can appear particularly strong for a litigation lawyer who is familiar with the process. However, there are limits to the control that the parties have, especially with the growth of judicial case management and the use of sanctions for non-compliance. Process control is especially limited when the case reaches trial—a judge is allocated to the parties, that judge can only make such orders as he or she has power to make, and the parties are faced with the decision of the judge, the only option if they do not like it being an appeal. **3.29**

3.30 ADR options potentially offer much more control. The parties can agree the process that they wish to follow, making decisions about time frame, presentation of evidence etc. They can also select and agree an arbitrator, mediator or other third party to suit their needs. The control that they have over the decision made in the case depends on the type of ADR selected. An adjudicative form of ADR will normally reach a binding decision, whereas in mediation or negotiation the outcome will remain within the control of the parties and they only need to accept it when they are satisfied.

What are the main objectives of the client?

3.31 Any dispute resolution process should centre on the objectives of the client. The litigation process has many strengths in obtaining objectives for a client—a range of remedies has been developed over many centuries with great sophistication in areas like the assessment of damages. Court orders are authoritative, and they carry with them the enforcement powers of the court. An adjudicative ADR process such as arbitration can lead to a decision, but that will only be binding as regards the parties who have agreed to the arbitration.

3.32 A possible drawback of litigation is that a judge only has the power to make such orders as remedy the cause of action argued by the successful party, though this can be mitigated if a judge makes a consent order in terms agreed by the parties. In contrast an arbitrator or adjudicator can make a decision within whatever parameters have been agreed by the parties, which potentially offers the possibility for innovation, and remedies tailored to meet the case. In mediation or negotiation the parties can focus entirely on their objectives and can agree any outcome that is acceptable to the parties. Mediators will normally focus on the objectives of the parties, and a mediation can be very forward looking, without the need to reach a decision on factual issues from the past that are not of ongoing interest to the parties.

Is a future relationship important?

3.33 Litigation is adversarial—it is based on a contest between the parties. It is also essentially an historic process. It is designed to look at the facts of a contract made in the past or an accident that happened in the past, to try to establish truth and apply existing law to issues. A court only looks forward where there is a specific reason for doing so, to assess damages for future losses, for instance.

3.34 An ADR process can take a similar approach, for example if expert-assisted determination is a useful way to decide why a machine malfunctioned. However, an ADR process can take a rather different approach, because it does not have to take decisions about the past, and does not necessarily have to apply existing law. Mediation in particular can be a creative and forward-looking process, which can focus on future relationships. This is why mediation is already used to a significant extent in commercial cases, where businesses may want an ongoing commercial relationship, and in family cases, where parents may need to deal with contact with children for some years.

What is the relevance of the chances of success?

3.35 Some clients are very competitive and focus primarily on 'winning', and being 'proved right' by the endorsement of a decision by a judge. Such clients tend to see any form of compromise or concession as a weakness. This approach is fostered by the adversarial system, and indeed can be the main objective of litigation. This is the approach of many litigation lawyers. Such an approach is entirely understandable where a client has been injured in an accident, or has a business put at risk by a breach of contract. However 'winning' is essentially an emotional need rather than logically necessary. The process used should depend on a careful assessment of the strengths and weaknesses of the case, and a careful examination of the likely chance of success. A case with at least an 80% chance of success may justify going to trial, but the client should understand clearly the risks where there is only a 60% chance of success.

The point is not that ADR is necessarily more appropriate for weaker cases. The point is rather that a decision on appropriate dispute resolution should not be based on the emotional concept of a 'win' but on a hard-headed analysis of the comparative strength of the case and the most cost-effective way of achieving a good outcome. A case with a good chance of success may achieve just as good an outcome more quickly and cheaply through ADR. A case with weaker chances of success may be resolved with less risk through the use of ADR. **3.36**

Does the client want a 'day in court'?

Some clients are very keen to have a 'day in court'. The client may want to be present at the event of a trial, seeing the process as providing an appropriate end to a very serious experience. The client may want to have the attention of a judge, and to see cross-examination of an opponent. However this experience may only prove satisfactory and provide a vindication if the case has a good chance of success. Also the fact that much evidence is now provided in writing in advance as witness statements can make a day in court a much less cathartic experience. There are ways in which a day in court can actually be quite frustrating for a client, for example because he or she can only sit and watch for most of the time. Some of the aspects of 'a day in court' are available in ADR—for example an arbitrator can reach a decision that endorses a client's position, and clients can find that they can be more involved in putting their case personally in a mediation. Witnesses can be called and questioned as part of many ADR processes. **3.37**

Other clients may see an apology from the other side as being of crucial importance. Mediation is likely to be the best process for a client for whom an explanation and/or apology is an important objective. Mediation may also prove a satisfactory experience for a client who wishes to play a greater role in talking through the experience that is the basis of the action. **3.38**

With competition between legal service providers, levels of client satisfaction cannot be ignored. Research tends to show that clients are often dissatisfied with litigation even when they have won a case—the outcome may not be what they wanted and costs may be resented. Clients tend to be more satisfied with an ADR process, probably because they have had a greater role in agreeing the outcome. **3.39**

Would neutral assistance be valuable?

It is part of the role of a legal representative to provide objectivity in a case, with a dispassionate analysis. In many cases lawyers provide sufficient objectivity to be able to negotiate a settlement to a case. That said, a lawyer is briefed by a client as a representative, and it is the lawyer's task to act within instructions. If the client is too controlling or too optimistic about a case the instructions may not leave a lawyer with scope to negotiate. An experienced mediator may be able to assist as a mediation process can be quite effective in showing a client the weaknesses in a case—the client then has the option of agreeing an outcome rather than going to court with a significant risk of losing. Expert evaluation early in a case can be very useful in ensuring expectations are realistic. **3.40**

What stage has the case reached?

The stages at which a lawyer might be asked to advise on ADR are outlined at 3.10. Some forms of ADR are likely to achieve best results if commenced at an early stage. Adjudicative **3.41**

ADR such as arbitration is effectively a direct alternative to litigation and should therefore normally be selected before steps are taken with regard to litigation. Some non-adjudicative ADR, such as early neutral evaluation, is by its nature effective if it is incorporated into a case reasonably quickly. Any form of ADR is most likely to be most cost effective if it is carried out sooner rather than later—before costs have already accumulated.

3.42 It would be far too simplistic, however, to suggest that ADR should only be considered at an early stage. Deciding on the best time to try ADR is an important professional judgment. ADR should not normally be recommended before sufficient information is available to evaluate the case. Presentation of a case in a negotiation or mediation normally requires just as much analysis as for advocacy in court. The lawyer will need to consider very carefully whether, for example, information provided under a pre-action protocol is sufficient to settle the case without seeing a formal particulars of claim or defence. It may or may not be important to wait for disclosure or exchange of witness statements. Specific information can be sought from the other side if needed. ADR may be best considered when there is realistically little likelihood of further significant information emerging.

3.43 Thus non-adjudicative ADR may be considered at any stage. Indeed most cases that are being litigated will at some point be negotiated, and/or go to mediation. This is most likely to happen when one or both parties feel they are able to evaluate their case sufficiently. It may be triggered by an interim hearing or a Part 36 offer, or the court may order a stay: see Chapters 7–8.

How important might interim orders be?

3.44 Judges have wide powers to make interim orders, including security for costs, interim injunctions, and freezing injunctions. As non-adjudicative ADR is carried out by agreement no such orders are available. The parties can by agreement give an arbitrator or adjudicator some powers in regard to giving directions, but these will never have the potential range and force of court orders. If interim orders are needed it does not mean that ADR is not an option. Proceedings may be commenced to provide a basis for seeking relevant interim orders, but once that is done the case could move to an ADR process.

Might orders relating to evidence be needed?

3.45 The litigation process provides for the systematic disclosure of relevant evidence. This is done in stages with key material normally being exchanged pre-action, but then with disclosure of all relevant documents and later of witness statements. There are also court powers with regard to the production of evidence, search orders etc. In non-adjudicative ADR information will only be disclosed by agreement. In adjudicative ADR the arbitrator or adjudicator may have agreed powers to ask for information, but will not have the powers of a judge to compel the production of material. For clients who are concerned about confidentiality and who do not wish to make full disclosure, for example to protect commercially sensitive information, this may make ADR positively attractive. On the other hand a client whose case depends on getting information that the other side will not easily make available voluntarily may need to start an action to get disclosure.

What is the attitude of the court?

3.46 As there is a right to a court hearing, no party can be compelled to settle a case through an ADR process. At most a party can be asked to consider ADR, and the strongest power available to the court is to stay an action, normally for no more than a month, for ADR options to be considered: see Chapters 7–8. Failure to comply may lead to a sanction. The increased use of sanctions and case management to support the reasonable use of ADR means that parties may engage in tactics in relation to ADR to get the support of the court.

The wording of a stay is quite important, and it will usually require 'best endeavours' or 'good faith' with regard to seeking a solution through ADR. Courts increasingly go so far as to propose a particular form of ADR such as mediation. Courts will make orders to support ADR during the stay, for example by ordering the disclosure of documents of particular relevance. The order can provide a strong form of encouragement provided there is not compulsion. If there is a stay the lawyer would need to consider all the factors relevant to ADR with the client, and in particular the likely chance of success of the case in litigation, and the risk and possible implications of a cost penalty. Serious thought should be given to doing at least enough to comply with the order, such as seriously discussing ADR with the other side, making an offer to settle, or proposing a negotiation, and having evidence of taking these steps to show to the court to avoid a sanction. **3.47**

Might enforcement be an issue?

A potential advantage of ADR is that because the parties agree to the process (in the case of adjudicative ADR), and in many cases also agree to the outcome (in non-adjudicative ADR) there is less likely to be a difficulty with enforcement. Enforcement is a much greater potential problem in litigation where a party who has lost in court may well be unwilling to meet the judgment. **3.48**

In any case where enforcement might be a problem, enforceability options must be considered. A court judgment will carry the advantage of the full enforcement powers of the court. An agreement reached without any court involvement will normally be enforceable as a contract, and a separate action will need to be brought to enforce the agreement, which would be more complex than enforcing an existing judgment: see Chapter 32. Note, however, that ADR can result in a court order where negotiation or mediation takes place after the issue of proceedings and the judge is prepared to make a consent order, or there has been a cross-border mediation within the EU. See Chapter 19. **3.49**

D POTENTIAL CONCERNS ABOUT ADR

Many lawyers and clients see the potential benefits of ADR in appropriate cases. However, it is only realistic to accept that a number of lawyers and clients are resistant to the concept of ADR. Some of the most common concerns, and the potential response, are as follows: **3.50**

ADR can undermine litigation

It is understandable that litigation lawyers, and barristers in particular, might see their expertise in litigation as being of primary importance in taking a case forward. They focus on statements of case to define issues, the use of interim orders etc. The lawyer may want to keep key points to be used in advocacy at trial. An ADR process may be seen as a threat because it may remove attention from preparation for trial, and may make the other side aware of points so that they can prepare better for trial. **3.51**

Query how far such a view is justified with the modern 'cards on the table' approach to litigation, where substantial information is available at an early stage under pre-action protocols, and where it is virtually impossible to keep any significant point secret until trial in a civil case. A case should not be allowed to take on a life of its own so that the next step in litigation is seen as more important than reviewing whether litigation remains in the client's best interests. The Jackson reforms have now placed an emphasis on reasonable use of ADR. **3.52**

Proposing ADR suggests a lack of faith in your case

3.53 In an adversarial system where the lawyer is the representative of a client a competitive approach is inevitable. It is the basis upon which the adversarial system is founded. The client will want to see his or her case in the best light, and it is the lawyer's task to argue the client's case in the best possible way. It might therefore be seen as a sign of weakness to talk of settlement rather than going to court.

3.54 In a world where many commercial organizations choose arbitration or mediation such a view is clearly outdated. The less formal process of a negotiation or mediation can provide a very good platform for presenting a strong case. The 'see you in court' attitude can now only be sustained in limited circumstances where ADR can reasonably be used.

ADR can undermine a lawyer's control of a case

3.55 It is understandable that litigation lawyers feel they have best control of a case within a litigation process. It is not always easy to see where a quick-fire negotiation might go, and an informal mediation process may be controlled as much by the mediator as by the parties and the lawyers.

3.56 While this has some truth, it is only *some* truth. In litigation it is the judge rather than the lawyer who is in charge of the trial, and it can be much easier to deal with an arbitrator or a mediator under an agreement than it can with a judge in court. A lawyer has more direct control in negotiation than in any other process. The lawyer's analysis of the case will remain key in any ADR process, and the client can be briefed in advance about how to approach an ADR process. If the lawyer lacks personal knowledge of an ADR process, that can be remedied quite easily through information from an ADR provider.

ADR does not really save costs

3.57 While saving costs is often an important factor in choosing ADR, it is quite true that ADR will not always save costs. Arbitration can be as expensive as a court hearing, and a settlement negotiated at the door of the court may not save much. A non-adjudicative ADR process that does not resolve the case might be seen as wasted expenditure.

3.58 To achieve the best cost savings it is important to select the most appropriate form of ADR at the earliest reasonable opportunity. It is also important to plan for what may be gained from an ADR process even if the case does not settle. Mediation and negotiation can be used to gather information, and to convince the other side of your case in certain areas, even if immediate concessions are not forthcoming. Even if there is not an overall settlement, most ADR processes help to limit the issues, or lead to a settlement at a later date even if not immediately.

ADR is a way of getting something for a weak case

3.59 There is some concern that an ADR process may be abused by a party with a weak case who would lose if the case went to court, and who tries to use ADR to get an offer 'to go away'. This may cause the party on the other side to resist ADR. Such an attitude may be justified in some cases, but it is not justified as a generic response to ADR. A mediation process where lawyers and clients are all in the room can be very effective in making it clear to a potential litigant how weak their case is (subject to keeping the cost of the mediation itself low).

ADR involves too much pressure to settle

In a non-adjudicative ADR process such as negotiation or mediation a main purpose of the process is to reach a settlement. An effective negotiator or mediator can certainly exert pressure to try to ensure that a settlement is reached, which may put pressure on a party. **3.60**

However, it is equally true that non-adjudicative ADR can only reach settlement by agreement. It is always possible to say no and walk away, and that provides a strong weapon. A claim can be resisted by making the strengths of your own case and your own bottom line very clear, and this resistance can put pressure on the other side. Testing your case can also help you to prepare it more fully if you do go to trial. **3.61**

ADR is used as a delaying tactic

It is sometimes said that an ADR process may be used as a delaying tactic to put off the issue of proceedings or the setting of a trial date. This may have some truth where for example a letter is sent that vaguely suggests a possibility for settlement without engaging in realistic negotiation. That said, ADR cannot easily be used by one party to cause any substantial delay. A party seeking to make progress can call a delaying party's bluff, and more robust case management means that a court will not normally countenance delay. **3.62**

ADR is not a robust process

Lawyers may have some concern that an ADR process may lack robustness. While arbitrators and mediators are trained they may not have the same length of training and experience as a judge, and they may not have the standing or personality to take a robust approach. While this may have some truth in some cases it is again not a generic concern. Arbitrators and mediators may be like judges in being qualified lawyers with many years of experience in practice, and they may also have substantial experience in ADR processes. They may also have other relevant experience. The need for a robust approach is relevant to deciding on an arbitrator or mediator. **3.63**

E SECURING AGREEMENT TO ADR

Litigation may be forced on a defendant by the issue of a claim form, but ADR can only be carried out by agreement. It will be necessary to get the other side to agree to the use of ADR. This may just be a matter of asking, but if the lawyers on the other side have some reservations, or have a different view of the interests of their client, then they may need to be persuaded to agree. It is best to use a positive approach, and the following points provide options. If they do not work more pressure may be required. The other side may be reminded of their obligation to make reasonable use of ADR, and the possibility that you may make an application as to costs if they do not do so. If the other side refuses a request to use ADR the court may order them to file a witness statement indicating why ADR is thought to be inappropriate, and a failure to file such a statement may be penalized in costs: *Wilson v Haden (t/a Clyne Farm Centre)* [2013] EWHC 1211 (QB). **3.64**

Suggest specific benefits that ADR might offer

Potential benefits that you identify for your client may also be potential benefits for the other side. There may be other benefits listed in 1.34–1.46 that might apply to the other side. Try to identify positive suggestions, and possibly ways ahead on some issues. **3.65**

Offer information about ADR options

3.66 While not being patronizing, it may be possible to form some view as to whether the lawyer on the other side has significant knowledge and experience of ADR options. Even with lawyers you do not know it may be possible to get information from the website of the chambers or firm. If the lawyer may not have significant relevant knowledge or experience it may be possible to suggest tactfully how they get information from relevant ADR service providers. Do not rush to suggest a specific mediator as this may make an opponent suspicious, but recommending a provider website or sending a copy of a typical mediation agreement for consideration might be helpful.

Propose a simple ADR option

3.67 It may be possible to tempt a party into ADR. A Part 36 offer may encourage a party to enter a negotiation. A suggestion of a negotiation may succeed as many lawyers feel confident with the control they can have. A well-handled negotiation that fails to resolve all issues may encourage the use of mediation to reach a full agreement.

Address any concerns that you think an opponent might have

3.68 You may form the impression that an opponent has a general concern about ADR, like those raised in 3.50–3.63. If so, try to find out what their concerns are so that you can try to address them. Make it clear that you are open to their arguments about ADR, and perhaps leave it to them to suggest a form of ADR. It may be possible to offer a carrot, such as a willingness to consider a particular concern their client has, so long as ADR is attempted.

Offer to pay reasonable ADR fees

3.69 Any such offer should be clear and not open to any misunderstanding as to what will be covered, but one party might for example offer to bear the whole fee of a mediator to encourage the other to enter mediation.

Seek to persuade a judge to order a stay

3.70 Once proceedings have been started it may be possible to ask a judge to order a stay for ADR: see Chapter 7. This should be a last resort rather than a first step as ADR is most likely to be successful if it is used by agreement rather than being forced. It may be most useful to try at least one of the suggestions above first, and this may assist in preparing an application to the judge.

F CONFIDENTIALITY IN RELATION TO ADR PROCESSES

3.71 Privacy can be one of the main attractions of an ADR process. Whereas litigation normally takes place in open court, ADR processes are private. It is vital to be aware that there is no absolute right of privacy for ADR processes. Privacy depends on three concepts developed in relation to litigation, and it is maintained by:

- any contractual agreement between the parties, a confidentiality clause being normal in mediation and arbitration agreements;
- by legal professional privilege, which protects any communication between a lawyer and client made for the purposes of giving or receiving legal advice;
- by the privilege from disclosure of oral or written 'without prejudice' communications made with the intention of seeking a settlement.

These concepts, especially the third, are very useful, but they do not provide blanket protection. Problems may arise for example if: **3.72**

- the ADR process breaks down and there is any attempt to use something revealed in later litigation. (Note that if a document is disclosable, using it in an ADR process will not give it any privilege);
- there is any dispute about the terms agreed in settlement;
- there is an attempt to call anyone involved in the ADR process as a witness in later proceedings.

The application of the principles developed in relation to litigation are still being developed in relation to ADR processes. For details on the principles of legal professional privilege in relation to ADR see 6.57–6.59. For details on the protection of without prejudice communications in ADR see 6.60–6.68. It is normal for an arbitration or mediation agreement to include a confidentiality clause, and this is also the case for many other ADR processes which are based on agreement. For a discussion of the use of confidentiality clauses in mediation see 6.48–6.50. **3.73**

G TIMING THE USE OF ADR

It is important to use ADR at the right stage in a case. This will be different for each case, depending on the issues, the information available, and the conduct of the case by the other side. Strategically there should be a time when enough is known to evaluate the case, and when appropriate ADR can best save costs. It is best to have an overall strategy as to the coherent use of ADR, as there have been several cases where confused use of negotiation, Part 36 offers and so on has led to a very confused position as regards case resolution and costs. Various points about timing are made above, for example as regards timing advice (3.09–3.10) and the stages of a case (3.41–3.43). **3.74**

Courts are taking an increasingly strict view of failures to comply with pre-action requirements, *Fons HF v Corporal Ltd* [2013] EWHC 1278 (Ch), including the failure to respond to an offer of ADR, *Nelson's Yard Management Company v Eziefula* [2013] EWCA Civ 235, though if both sides act unreasonably at the pre-action stage the court may not impose a costs penalty on either side, *Norbrook Laboratories Ltd v Carr* [2–13] EWHC 476 (QB). A failure to provide information that could facilitate ADR may be penalized in costs, *AP(UK) Ltd v West Midland Fire and Civil Defence Authority* [2013] EWHC 385 (QB) and *Webb Resolutions Ltd v Waller Needham & Green (a firm)* [2012] EWHC 3529 (Ch). **3.75**

KEY POINTS SUMMARY

- A lawyer has a general professional duty to advise on ADR options, and there are identifiable points in a case and in litigation where this is particularly important. **3.76**
- There are many factors that may be relevant to the use of ADR, and to which form of ADR is most appropriate, including cost, the nature of the dispute, and the objectives of the parties. It is important to select the ones relevant to each case.
- No type of dispute is inherently unsuitable for ADR, though an individual case may be.
- Various concerns may be expressed in relation to ADR, but they can be addressed.
- There are ways to encourage a reluctant opponent to use ADR.
- ADR processes are private, but confidentiality depends on contractual provisions, legal professional privilege and privilege for without prejudice communications.

4

FUNDING ADR PROCEDURES

A THE FUNDING CONTEXT 4.01
B GENERAL CONSIDERATIONS 4.06
C ELEMENTS OF EXPENSE 4.17
D WHAT ADR PROCESSES COST 4.23
E EFFECTS OF THE FUNDING BASIS 4.47
F SHIFTING THE LIABILITY FOR COSTS—PART 36 OFFERS 4.58
G CONSIDERATIONS FOR THE PARTIES . . . 4.63
H OVERALL FINANCIAL ANALYSIS AND RISK ASSESSMENT. 4.64
I BASIC EXAMPLE OF ADR FINANCIAL CONSIDERATIONS. 4.72
Key points summary 4.77

A THE FUNDING CONTEXT

4.01 Financial concerns are fundamental to decisions in relation to dispute resolution options. There is widespread concern amongst potential litigants as regards the possibly very high cost of litigation, and the problems of controlling cost. A desire for cost effectiveness may be one of the most important factors in choosing to use an ADR alternative. This concern is also central to current government policy in relation to dispute resolution, and is for example a motivation for the moves to increase the use of mediation in relation to lower value civil cases, see 1.29–1.30.

4.02 There are many reasons why litigation costs are high. The work needed to prepare a case for court in terms of collecting evidence, preparing papers, and research is time-consuming. The costs of lawyers, parties, and witnesses attending court can be high. It is government policy that the civil court system be self-funding, so the level of court fees has risen. It is not surprising that costs can sometimes outstrip the amount in dispute in a case, attracting adverse comment from judges, as in *Finesse Group Ltd v Bryson Products* [2013] EWHC 3273 (TCC), and that even clients who win a case in court may express concern about the costs involved.

4.03 The Final Report of the Review of Civil Litigation Costs carried out by Lord Justice Jackson issued in December 2009 (see www.judiciary.gov.uk/publications-and-reports/review-of-civil-litigation-costs) contained a number of provisions for reducing and controlling costs, including the following general endorsement of the use of ADR:

> Alternative dispute resolution ('ADR') (particularly mediation) has a vital role to play in reducing the costs of civil disputes, by fomenting the early settlement of cases. ADR is however under-used. Its potential benefits are not as widely known as they should be. I therefore recommend that:
>
> - There should be a serious campaign to ensure that all litigation lawyers and judges are properly informed of how ADR works, and the benefits that it can bring.
> - The public and small businesses who become embroiled in disputes are also made aware of the benefits of ADR. An authoritative handbook for ADR should be prepared, explaining what ADR is and how it works, and listing reputable providers of ADR services. This handbook should be used as the standard work for the training of judges and lawyers.

> Nevertheless ADR should not be mandatory for all proceedings. The circumstances in which it should be used (and when it should be used) will vary from case to case, and much will come down to the judgment of experienced practitioners and the court. (Recommendation 6.3)

The Review of Civil Litigation Costs included recommendations for greater attention to be paid to costs management (Recommendations 6.10 and 6.11), and a greater use of costs budgets. The government response made it clear that the government is convinced that access to justice for all parties depends on costs being proportionate, and the primary recommendations of the Jackson Review were introduced in April 2013. In brief, the key changes relevant to the funding of litigation and the use of dispute resolution are: **4.04**

- The overriding objective has been amended to include proportionality as a consideration throughout litigation, and this may increase the extent to which cases are directed into ADR.
- Costs management has been introduced alongside case management, so that judges will take a proactive role in controlling costs.

In many cases, budgets using Form H need to be agreed or approved. The form includes a specific section for the estimated costs of ADR and settlement discussions. The Guidance Notes on Precedent H make it clear that this should cover settlement negotiations, including Part 36 and other offers, and advising the client, as well as drafting a settlement agreement or Tomlin order. The Guidance Notes also make it clear that pre-action costs in the budget should include considering ADR, advising on settlement, and Part 36 offers.

- A new test of proportionality with regard to the recovery of costs has been introduced.
- The encouragement of the use of damages-based agreements, and of third-party funding, have implications for when ADR may be used and settlements agreed.

These provisions provide a substantial change to the context within which the potential cost of litigation and of ADR fall to be considered. The use of budgets in particular provides a much stronger focus on the potential cost of litigation at an early stage, and importance of proportionality makes it important to consider the relative expense of litigation and ADR. Case law is starting to show how these provisions will be interpreted. The courts have endorsed the benefits that budgeting can bring: *Slick Seatings Systems v Adams* [2013] EWHC B8 (Mercantile, making it clear that failure to engage with discussions as to a budget or to file a budget may be met with a sanction); *Mitchell v News Group Newspapers Limited* [2013] EWHC 2355 (QB). Once a budget is approved it is likely to be extremely difficult to persuade a court to allow a revised budget simply because of inadequacies or mistakes: *Murray v Neil Dowlman Architecture Ltd* [2013] EWHC 872 (TCC). Budgets will not be approved where they are disproportionate or unreasonable in relation to the sum that may be recovered: *Willis v MJR Rundell & Associates Ltd* [2013] EWHC 2923 (TCC). Costs will not necessarily be reasonable and proportionate just because they fall within an agreed budget: *Troy Foods v Manton* [2013] EWCA Civ 615. It has become important to consider the potential cost of ADR when drawing up a budget and when considering the costs as related to the potential outcome of a case. **4.05**

B GENERAL CONSIDERATIONS

Although financial considerations are of key importance, the relevant rules are not straightforward. Initial payment or 'funding' needs to be distinguished from possible later orders as to whether one party should pay 'costs' to the other. There are several interrelated factors: **4.06**

- Paying for any dispute resolution process in terms of paying the lawyers, court fees etc is primarily the responsibility of the party to the dispute. The overall expense is therefore of prime importance to a client.
- As this is likely to be expensive, clients with limited resources will look for alternative ways of funding the process, but that funding method may have implications for ADR, see 4.47–4.57.
- Courts have a general power to make orders as regards the costs of litigation, and will generally order that a loser pays the reasonable costs of a winner. An arbitrator may be given a power to make an award of costs, but in non-adjudicative ADR costs will remain with the party incurring them.
- There are various ways in which liability to pay costs may change or shift, but the position is not entirely coherent, see 4.14–4.16. In any case where costs are or may become significant, considering options in relation to costs will need to be done alongside considering options for ADR.

4.07 The full rules for funding systems and potential costs orders are beyond the scope of this book. They are discussed in Sime, *A Practical Approach to Civil Procedure* (17th edn, OUP, 2014). Further detail can be found in *Blackstone's Civil Practice 2014* (OUP). These rules provide the background against which a lawyer and client must consider the relative expense of litigation and ADR processes, and the possibility of recovering at least part of that expense.

4.08 The likely expense of an individual ADR process can be estimated as set out in 4.17–4.46. However, the expense of ADR can only be considered in isolation where it is decided to use ADR at the very start of a case. The position is usually more complex. Some costs may already have been incurred before ADR is considered, and in some cases the proceedings may move from one process to another, for example from litigation to negotiation to litigation to mediation, so the expense of an ADR process will need to be put into a wider context. The main factors to be considered in relation to the financing of a case in the light of 4.06 are as follows.

What are the main elements of expense in the case?

4.09 The inherent likely expense of pursuing the case. This will depend on factors like the complexity of the factual issues, how expensive it may be to collect evidence and carry out research, whether expert evidence will be required etc. The lawyer needs to identify as early as possible in each case what the main expenses are likely to be. Strategic decisions may need to be made as to how much of this potential expense is essential, and how much might be avoided or controlled through the use of ADR. Budgeting now requires that such an exercise be done, at the latest, soon after issue of proceedings.

How much is at stake in the case?

4.10 The realistic sum being claimed and the level of importance of any key non-financial objectives, are central to informed financial decisions. The proportionality of expense in relation to what is sought is important as it is part of the overriding objective under the CPR, and also a test for the recovery of costs. ADR in the form of mediation may well be the most proportionate way of dealing with a relatively small-value dispute.

How is the case being funded?

4.11 The guidance in this book relates primarily to privately funded cases. Some different considerations may apply to ADR options where the case is being funded in some other way, such as a conditional fee agreement, or by third-party funding. See 4.48–4.57.

The extent to which expense has already been incurred

A lawyer will need to carry out some evaluation of a case before advice on how to pursue it can be given. The extent to which expense has already been incurred, and whether that expense might or might not be potentially at least partly recoverable, must be part of considering the overall possible financial attractiveness and timing of an ADR process. **4.12**

The chances of success

The chances of success must also be factored in. Asking a client to pay £10,000 for litigation you have advised is 90% likely to succeed carries limited risk, but if litigation costs are likely to be £10,000 with only a 60% chance of winning the risk is much greater, making an ADR process rather more attractive as a way of lessening risk. See 4.64–4.71 for more detail. **4.13**

The possibility that costs may be recovered or liability for costs may shift

An expense incurred in relation to ADR is the responsibility of the party which incurred it, but this may change in the following circumstances: **4.14**

- by agreement within the ADR process (see 4.36 and 4.41);
- by an award in an adjudicative process (see 30.28–30.30);
- by a court award of costs (see Chapter 9);
- through automatic shifting of costs under Part 36 (see 4.58–4.62);
- if proceedings have been issued and the action is discontinued the claimant will be liable for the defendant's costs, CPR, r 38.6(1). Unless this outcome is intended, if a case is settled it is important that the claimant should not agree to discontinue the action. The court has a power to order some other outcome as to costs, but this power has been interpreted restrictively, *Brookes v HSBC Bank* [2011] EWCA Civ 354.

Potential cost shifting may greatly complicate a decision as to whether an ADR process may be cost effective. Even if the costs of litigation are relatively high, the party incurring those costs may be less concerned if the costs will be substantially recovered if the case is won. This makes it particularly important to assess the chances of success of a case as accurately and realistically as possible. False optimism may lead a client to reject ADR but then go on to lose a case and have to bear the reasonable costs of the other side in addition to his own costs, when ADR could have provided a much better outcome. The relevant arithmetic and the choices that may be available are explored further in 4.72–4.76. **4.15**

It is essential to be clear that if the parties settle a dispute without any agreement as to costs, one party cannot later argue that costs should be awarded on the basis that party had effectively won, *R (on the application of Crookenden) v Institute of Chartered Accountants in England and Wales* [2013] All ER (D) 352 (May). It has been held that it may be reasonable to refuse an offer to settle if it is made on the basis that each side bear their own costs and this could have an unfair effect on the party, *Newman v Framewood Manor Management Co Ltd* [2012] EWCA Civ 1727. **4.16**

C ELEMENTS OF EXPENSE

There are basic elements of cost in any process for dispute resolution. In a privately funded case each party will incur their own costs for having a case investigated and getting advice on it. Each party will be liable to pay these costs, which will normally be incurred on the basis of a retainer agreement between a client and solicitor. Liability to pay these costs will remain **4.17** with the party who incurs them unless there is a court order as to costs (which can only be made as part of a litigation or arbitration process: see Chapter 9), or by agreement (which may be done as part of an ADR process). Someone other than the party may be liable to pay the costs depending on how the case is being funded: see 4.47–4.57.

Solicitor fees

4.18 A solicitor will normally charge an hourly rate, the details of which will be set out in a client care letter soon after the solicitor is first retained. This rate will be charged when the solicitor is working on the case in any capacity, including advice and research as well as engaging in correspondence, drafting, and attending meetings. Different rates may be charged where solicitors with different levels of experience work on a case under the supervision of the solicitor with primary responsibility. The solicitor should provide updates on accumulated fees, and is likely to ask for payments on account to cover fees.

Barrister fees

4.19 A barrister will normally be paid a separate fee for each task for which the barrister is instructed. There will be separate brief fees for providing an opinion, for appearing in court to deal with an application etc. Each fee will cover ancillary work such as research.

Evidence and information

4.20 Normally the solicitor will be responsible for collecting information and evidence. Much of the cost will therefore be paying for the solicitor's time to do this. There will be additional costs where a third party charges for information or for copies of documents—for example an expert will charge a fee for a report, and copies of documents on disclosure must be paid for.

Disbursements

4.21 All cases will have incidental costs such as travel costs, photocopying etc. The solicitor will normally add such disbursements to the bill that is payable by the client.

Process fees

4.22 Fees will be charged for any formal process, eg court fees for issuing proceedings.

D WHAT ADR PROCESSES COST

4.23 Many of the costs for an ADR process will fall under the heads outlined in 4.17–4.22. If lawyers are instructed to negotiate or assist in a mediation they will need to be paid to prepare and attend. There will often be a process fee for the ADR process. This means that ADR is not necessarily cheaper if lawyers are involved and a case is fully prepared for hearing, as in an arbitration. What will often make an ADR process less expensive is that it will take significantly less legal time, and that potentially time-consuming and expensive processes such as disclosure can be avoided.

4.24 Most ADR processes can be carried out at various levels with a range of costs. Just as litigation costs can vary substantially between a small case in the county court and a large case in the

High Court, so mediation may cost very little if the parties attend a free service without lawyers, but can be very expensive if a big case is mediated over several days with lawyers attending. An indication of possible fees is given in the following sections, but actual fees should be checked at the time—many ADR providers include information on fees on their website.

ADR provider's fee

Some ADR provision is free. An ombudsman or complaints process may make no charge. Some mediation processes are offered without charge by a court or by a charitable or not-for-profit organization. As an example, the Law Works organization offers up to three hours of mediation free to a party who is on benefits or has a very low income: see www.lawworks.org.uk. **4.25**

Most ADR service providers will charge a fee. The fee may be charged by an ADR organization that provides a service package for an ADR process. Some of the bigger providers, such as the Centre for Dispute Resolution, offer a range of services related to ADR, and these are outlined on their website: www.cedr.com. This fee may cover the cost of a location for the ADR process, support services, refreshments etc. If it does not, this cost may need to be added. There may be a set fee, or a fee that is negotiable depending on what is included. Most fee structures relate to the time that will be taken and/or the value of the claim. The government has set up a website enabling an enquirer to find a mediator who will act for set fee rates of £50 plus VAT to resolve a dispute worth up to £5,000 in up to an hour, up to £425 plus VAT to solve a dispute worth up to £50,000 in a period of up to 4 hours, see www.civilmediation.justice.gov.uk. **4.26**

Most individuals who provide ADR services will also charge a fee. A mediator or arbitrator may be engaged personally, and may charge a set fee or an hourly rate. If the mediator is paid hourly, he or she will want to be paid for preparation as well as the mediation itself. An arbitrator or mediator might also expect to have travel expenses paid. Some mediators charge a higher fee if they do facilitate a settlement of the case. Many firms and chambers offer ADR services, and details are often available on their websites. **4.27**

The fee for an arbitration may be several thousand pounds for a hearing that may take more than a week. If the case is more straightforward and can be completed in less than a week the fee might be similar to that for a mediation. A paper-based or IT-based arbitration might be based on an hourly fee for the arbitrator and cost only a few hundred pounds. **4.28**

A mediator might typically charge £500 for a case worth less than £10,000 that can be settled within a day. Many mediations are concluded in less than a day. For a case that might take two to three days and be worth over £100,000 the fee would typically be a few thousand pounds. For more detail on mediator fees see 14.37–14.44. **4.29**

There is government interest in ensuring that ADR services are provided in a form that is convenient and reasonably cost effective for potential litigants in lower value cases. To take this forward, the government has set up the site referred to in 4.26 to assist litigants in finding mediators to act for a set fee. In addition the government is planning to substantially extend the use of mediation for lower value cases in county courts. An initial consultation paper in March 2011 was followed by a response, 'Solving disputes in county courts: creating a simpler, quicker and more proportionate system', in February 2012—see www.justice.gov.uk/consultations/consultation-cp6-2011.htm. The following proposals relevant to costs have been taken forward: **4.30**

- Expanding the limit for the small claims track (with a simplified litigation process) to £10,000.

- Providing that small claims will be automatically referred to a small claims mediator. This would not make mediation compulsory for resolving these claims, but would make consideration of ADR the norm. At the time of writing these schemes are being piloted.
- Extending the fixed-cost simplified online claims procedure for road traffic accidents to a wider range of personal injury claims.

Negotiation

4.31 The format for a negotiation will be entirely a matter of agreement between the parties. The very wide variation in potential methods for negotiating, from a brief telephone discussion or exchange of letters to a formal meeting, leads to an equally wide variation in potential cost, from almost negligible to several thousand pounds.

4.32 The main cost of a negotiation will be the fees charged by the lawyers. A negotiation may be carried out by solicitors alone, or barristers may be briefed, in which case they may be accompanied by instructing solicitors. Overall cost will depend on the hours of work for the solicitors, and any brief fee for a barrister. The charge for the lawyers may increase if additional time is needed to draw up a settlement after the negotiation. A telephone conversation might take relatively little time, but preparing for and attending a negotiation meeting would be likely to cost a minimum of several hundred pounds.

4.33 A further significant cost might be the cost of a location for the negotiation, though many negotiations take place at the office of one of the solicitors or at no extra cost. Clients may or may not attend a negotiation, as agreed. If they do attend the clients may themselves incur costs in taking time off work, travelling etc.

4.34 A negotiation in a major case may thus be quite expensive. If for example barristers, solicitors and clients agree to meet on neutral ground for at least a day the costs could easily be several thousand pounds. There are, however, many circumstances in which a negotiation would be much cheaper. Lawyers attending court in relation to an application may, if so instructed, take the opportunity to try to negotiate a settlement and this may be at no greater cost than that incurred to attend the hearing.

4.35 Each party will pay their own costs in a negotiation, unless it is a term of the negotiation that all or part of the costs of one party are paid by the other party. This may be used as a tactic, with one party offering to pay the reasonable costs of the other for the negotiation in order to secure a concession, or an overall agreement. It would be possible for a judge to make an order as to costs if court proceedings have been initiated, though this would normally only be by agreement if there had been a successful negotiation.

4.36 If a negotiation is otherwise successful, it may be relevant to agree what should happen as regards other costs previously incurred in the case. It is important to have a reasonably accurate estimate of costs to date available at the negotiation for this purpose. If, for example, one party has been largely successful that party might ask for reasonable costs spent in pursuing the claim, as might have been ordered had the case gone to court. The parties might agree a global payment to include damages and costs, or a separate additional payment in respect of costs. Other options may be appropriate; for example, if a case is settled after proceedings are issued it may be agreed one party will pay the other party's costs on the standard basis, subject to detailed assessment if not agreed. If nothing is agreed, each party will pay their own costs.

Mediation

4.37 A major potential expense is the fee for the mediation service provider, and/or the mediator, see 4.25–4.30. There may be no expense beyond that if the fee is comprehensive, and fees may be kept down where for example the mediation is conducted by telephone. A possible additional expense is for a location as it is common for a mediation to take place on neutral ground. This may be an office provided by the mediation service, or possibly a conference facility in a hotel. It is important to have sufficient space for joint and separate meetings.

It is a matter for agreement whether lawyers attend a mediation, and if so which lawyers. **4.38**
In a commercial case both parties may bring in-house lawyers, a solicitor, and a barrister to provide ongoing input as to the legal options. In family cases the parties may attend without lawyers, though often on the basis of having consulted a lawyer about their potential rights in advance, and possibly seeking advice about a potential agreement after the mediation. If lawyers attend they will normally charge an hourly rate or brief fee, including time for preparation, which may well involve the preparation of a written and/or oral summary of the case. The extent of lawyer involvement will of course have a major impact on the overall cost of the mediation.

While clients will not always attend a negotiation, they will always be part of a mediation. **4.39**
This may not be very expensive where they attend a local service, but it can be expensive for a big case. In a case involving a business it is important that sufficiently senior people with decision-taking powers attend, and it may also be important to have others with direct knowledge of the matters in dispute. If these people do not attend the mediation itself, it may be desirable to have them available for telephone or conference calls. While it is not common for experts or other witnesses to attend, this can be done by agreement. All these matters will affect expense.

The way in which the costs of a mediation will be met will normally be covered by the written **4.40**
mediation agreement. Many mediation providers offer standard form agreements, though these may be varied with consent. A mediation agreement is a contract, enforceable as such, and a court will not have power to vary it: *National Westminster Bank v Feeney* [2006] EWHC 90066. Normally each side will bear their own costs, and the fees for the mediation will be shared equally whatever the outcome of the mediation. Alternatively it may be agreed that the fees will count as costs in the case if the dispute is not settled and goes to trial. If one party has much greater resources than the other party, or is keen to use mediation, that party might agree to pay the whole fee.

If a mediation is otherwise successful, it may be relevant to agree what should happen as **4.41**
regards other costs previously incurred in the case, on a similar basis to the comments in 4.36 in relation to negotiation.

Arbitration

An arbitration procedure is broadly similar to a trial procedure in that both sides present **4.42**
their case to an arbitrator with a view to the arbitrator reaching a decision. There may be less formality than in a litigation process as regards procedure before the hearing. At the hearing witnesses and experts may be called as agreed. This all has implications for the expense incurred, which can potentially be similar to the cost of a trial. However, if the arbitration is conducted on the basis of papers alone and/or online the likely cost will be significantly lower.

One major potential cost is the fee for the arbitration service provider, or the arbitrator, see **4.43**
4.25–4.30. It is common for an arbitration to take place on neutral ground, and a relatively large room may be required, depending on the number of people attending. The hearing may only take a day, but in a complex case an arbitration may last for several weeks, with

consequently high tribunal and accommodation costs. In an international arbitration, costs of travel and hotels may be substantial.

4.44 It is normal for each party to have legal representation at an arbitration, with possibly a barrister, a solicitor, and an in-house lawyer. The cost of legal representation may be similar to the cost at a trial, with the lawyers charging hourly rates or brief fees. The clients may choose to attend an arbitration as they may attend a trial, with consequent costs to them as regards loss of earnings and travel.

4.45 The payment of the arbitration fee will normally be covered by the arbitration agreement, which will often provide for the fees to be shared equally. The costs incurred by each party before the arbitration and at the arbitration will be borne by the party incurring the cost, although often the arbitrator is given discretion to make orders about the tribunal's fees and the parties' costs.

Other forms of ADR

4.46 It is not feasible to run through the potential costs of every possible form of ADR. Each will be based on the same elements as the main types of ADR. A complaint procedure or an ombudsman system may be free or relatively inexpensive, but an adjudicator or an expert carrying out an early neutral evaluation will require an appropriate fee, which may be substantial if for example site visits or research are involved.

E EFFECTS OF THE FUNDING BASIS

4.47 The actual effect of costs on a party will depend on the way in which the party is being funded. The basis for funding may also be relevant to the relative attractiveness of an ADR process. This area is potentially quite complex and the following points are simply indicative of what may need to be considered in relation to ADR as regards the main alternatives to private funding.

Conditional fee agreement funding

4.48 If a client enters a conditional fee agreement (CFA) there is a shift in some of the dynamics relevant to ADR options. A CFA must comply with the Courts and Legal Services Act 1990, and provides that the client will not pay legal fees if the claim is lost, but if the claim is won the client will pay the lawyer's normal fee plus a success fee, which may be up to a 100% increase on the normal fee. A party using a CFA may also take out after the event (ATE) insurance, to cover the potential liability to pay the costs of the other side if the case is lost. A CFA will usually include terms regarding fees if the case is settled. The settlement of the case will normally mean that the fee and success fee are payable, on the basis that the case has effectively been won. The overall figure that the client will be left with needs to be considered—a negotiation or mediation may provide that the costs and success fee of a winning party are paid by the other side, but this can be a very contentious issue. A lawyer may sometimes reduce a success fee to help to ensure agreement. Note that the success fee does not have to be revealed in advance as part of discussions as this would disclose the lawyer's view of the chance of success, but otherwise there are clear rules relating to notifying the other side where a party has CFA funding.

4.49 The client will be less concerned about expense as the lawyer's fee will only be payable if the case is won, though the client will still be liable to pay disbursements (which will include the costs of expert fees and also possibly the barrister's fee if the barrister does not also act under a CFA in addition to the solicitor). The lawyer may be more concerned to keep expenses down, especially if there is a significant risk that the case may not succeed, as the lawyer might be left out of pocket (though a weak case would not normally be taken on a CFA basis in the first place). A CFA can therefore provide a problem for settlement for the claimant. In the past a CFA could put pressure on a defendant to settle because if the defendant was unsuccessful the success fee and the ATE insurance premium were potentially recoverable by the claimant as part of the costs. This has ceased from 1 April 2013 as the Legal Aid, Sentencing and Punishment of Offenders Act 2012, Part 2 has amended s 58 of the Courts and Legal Services Act 1990 to prevent the recovery of success fees, so that they now come from the claimant's damages rather than being paid by the defendant. It is also no longer possible for the cost of after the event insurance to be recoverable.

Damages-based agreement

For funding arrangements entered into on or after 1 April 2013 it is possible for a lawyer to conduct a case on the basis he or she will be paid by a share of the damages recovered, rather than getting the sum of costs under a CFA. The Damages-Based Agreements Regulations 2013 provide for the information that should be given to a client before such a damages-based agreement (DBA) is entered into. The agreement may include some terms relating to the reaching of a settlement. The use of DBAs has significant implications for the dynamics of settlement. **4.50**

The terms of a DBA may make it more profitable for a lawyer to settle early rather than go to trial. The fact that a lawyer has a direct interest in the sum recovered may have implications for whether an offer is made or accepted. There are potential professional and ethical issues in relation to this. It is possible that the best return for a lawyer might be obtained by entering into a DBA where a lawyer can take 50% of the damages, and then settle the case quickly before costs rise. Such an approach could easily be subject to criticism so the lawyer should take care to ensure terms are fair. A solicitor has a professional duty to enter into a fee agreement that is suitable for the client's needs, and which is in the client's best interests. If in doubt, it may be appropriate to ensure that the client gets independent advice before entering the agreement, or at least ensure that the client has written information about funding options, and why the DBA is considered appropriate. **4.51**

Insurance

A party may have insurance for legal costs, or an insurance company may take over the conduct of the case where for example the party has relevant insurance as a driver or a professional. The insurer may then have a view on whether ADR is appropriate, and on what form of ADR should be used. The insurance may provide a maximum amount for legal costs (and note that the maximum may need to cover all costs if for example the party has to pay any costs for the other side). **4.52**

Third-party funding

There has been significant growth in the number of bodies prepared to fund litigation or some other form of dispute resolution on the basis that the fund is essentially making an investment in the outcome of the case. The terms of that interest depend on the agreement made. A Code of Conduct for Litigation Funders has been drawn up by the **4.53**

Association of Litigation Funders of England and Wales, but its provisions are relatively general. A written Litigation Funding Agreement (LFA) should state whether and how the third party may have input into settlement issues, such as deciding whether to make an offer to settle, or to accept an offer that has been made. There are potential concerns regarding how the interests of a party and of the third party funder may be properly met and balanced in an ADR process. The lawyer should of course act in the best interests of the client.

Legal Aid Agency funding

4.54 From 1 April 2013 the possibility of public funding has been removed from most types of civil case, with the Legal Services Commission being renamed the Legal Aid Agency (LAA), under the Legal Aid, Sentencing and Punishment of Offenders Act 2012. This has removed the availability of legal aid from private family law cases (including divorce and custody matters, but with an exception for cases where there is domestic violence), clinical negligence claims, employment- and education-related cases, immigration cases (save where someone is detained) and some debt housing and benefit matters. The government was concerned that the legal aid scheme was very expensive, and that the availability of legal aid might encourage people to bring a dispute to court where an adversarial approach might not be the best way to find a resolution. A party who does meet the conditions for funding and makes a successful application for funding is in a relatively strong position. As the other side will face paying their own costs even if they win (as a result of the Administration of Justice Act 1920 s 11), they are more likely to make an offer for settlement. LSC/LAA funding will normally cover reasonable costs of negotiation or mediation provided that is the most cost-effective way of proceeding, but this should be checked before undertaking the process in a specific case. The costs of other ADR processes such as early neutral evaluation or expert determination may also be covered as a disbursement.

4.55 Public funding may not cover a trial unless reasonable attempts to settle have been made, and it may be withdrawn if a party unreasonably refused to settle a claim in mediation. The Court of Appeal has said that publicly funded claims should be mediated, if appropriate, in order to save costs: *R (Cowl and other) v Plymouth City Council* [2002] 1 WLR 803. The Funding Code recognizes that mediation costs can be publicly funded in family work and family mediation procedures are funded directly.

4.56 The LSC/LAA must be told of a Part 36 offer, as the chance of success of the case is relevant to funding. If an assisted party fails to beat a Part 36 offer they will have to pay the defendant's costs since the offer could have been accepted, which will eat into the sum recovered. The case may need to be compromised to avoid such an effect.

4.57 The client with LSC/LAA funding is in a weaker position in that the statutory charge may reduce the sum the client actually receives. The change can bite where costs incurred by the LSC/LAA in relation to a party are not fully recovered in an order made against the other side. There is a statutory charge over money or assets recovered or preserved to recover such costs. This needs to be taken into account in the arithmetic in a negotiation or mediation, and steps should be taken to avoid or decrease the effect of the charge. One approach is to keep the issues in the case to a minimum as the charge will only bite on property and money at issue. Another possibility is to keep costs low so that the charge is relatively small. A third possibility is to agree that the other side will pay the costs so that no charge arises. If the case proceeds to litigation and the party with LSC/LAA funding wins, that party would normally get a costs order against the other side, and this point should be pursued in an ADR process.

F SHIFTING THE LIABILITY FOR COSTS—PART 36 OFFERS

Although based in the Civil Procedure Rules rather than being a form of ADR, it is very important to consider the making of a Part 36 offer when reviewing ADR options. It can be said that Part 36 in some ways lies on the interface between litigation and ADR. The details of the operation of Part 36 are beyond the scope of this book and can be researched separately in S. Sime, *A Practical Approach to Civil Procedure* (17th edn, OUP, 2014) or *Blackstone's Civil Practice 2014* (OUP). In brief, a Part 36 offer can be made by a claimant or a defendant, and it can be made at any time from before the issue of proceedings up to and including any appeal. It must be made in writing and state that it is intended to have effect as a Part 36 offer. It must specify a period of at least 21 days within which it can be accepted, and must state whether it applies to the whole claim, or if not which issues. Any acceptance of the offer must also be in writing. The important consequence is that if the offer is accepted within the relevant period the proceedings will be stayed, and the claimant accepting the offer will be entitled to the costs of the proceedings assessed on a standard basis to that date, CPR r 36.10. **4.58**

Part 36 is therefore effectively a way of settling a case by negotiation through a written offer. It has the advantages of being a relatively quick and cheap way to settle. The potential consequences as regards costs mean that pressure is put on the offeree to take the offer seriously, and the intention is that a realistic offer should be accepted. If it is not, the party who fails to accept it is at risk as regards the ongoing costs of litigation. An offer made but not accepted cannot be used during trial, but can be revealed in relation to an application for costs. Essentially a claimant who wins a case but fails to obtain a judgment more advantageous than a Part 36 offer from the defendant will have to pay the defendant's costs from the end of the relevant period in which the offer could be accepted, CPR r 36.14. A claimant who wins a case with a judgment at least as advantageous as a Part 36 offer made by the claimant will have costs awarded on favourable terms. Following a recommendation in the Jackson Review of Costs, the rules were amended from 12 February 2013 to incentivize both claimants and defendants to accept offers, see The Offers to Settle in Civil Proceedings Order 2013, SI 2013/93. **4.59**

The potential for protecting the client's position as regards costs, and for encouraging the parties to consider settlement, is such that a party to a civil dispute should regularly consider making or reviewing a Part 36 offer. It may be difficult to frame a Part 36 offer where a case is complex, includes significant non-financial issues, or where face-to-face engagement with the other side to examine issues is important, see for example *Raggett v Governors of Preston Catholic College* [2012] EWHC 3641 (QB) and *Mehjoo v Harben Baker* [2013] EWHC 1669 (QB). In strategic terms, a Part 36 offer may nonetheless stimulate ADR, or follow an attempt to negotiate or mediate. If a party is not realistically able to make a Part 36 offer (because of the exposure to liability for costs if the offer is accepted), that party should still make an offer that is expressed to be without prejudice save as to costs: *Magical Marking Ltd v Ware and Kay LLP* [2013] EWHC 636 (Ch). **4.60**

Assessing what figure to put into a Part 36 offer is an important professional skill. It requires a full assessment of the strengths and weaknesses of the case, and of the figures involved on the basis of assessing a proper range of information. An offer that is unreasonably low may lead to settlement at too low a figure for a claimant, or a figure that does not really protect the defendant as to costs, as the claimant easily beats it. An offer that is much too high will not lead to settlement for a claimant, and is not in a defendant's interests. The trick is to offer a figure that is at the edge of what is reasonable for settlement, but at the edge that favours your client. **4.61**

4.62 While the use of Part 36 offers is important, the provisions are quite complex and there is a significant amount of recent case law on how Part 36 should be interpreted. An offer must meet the detailed requirements of Part 36 to attract Part 36 consequences, *PHI Group Ltd v Robert West Consulting Ltd* [2012] EWCA Civ 588. An unsuccessful Part 36 offer cannot be treated as if it were successful just because it is very close to the final outcome of the case, *Hammersmatch Properties (Welwyn) Ltd v Saint-Gobain Ceramics and Plastics Ltd* [2013] EWHC 2227 (TCC). For a useful summary of current issues, endorsing the view of Lord Justice Jackson that Part 36 should be re-written in a simpler form see S Sime, 'Offers to settle: incentive, coercion and clarity', *C.J.Q.* (2013), 182. A Part 36 offer will often be part of a range of ADR strategies, see for example *Bellway Homes Ltd v Seymour (Civil Engineering Contractors) Ltd* [2013] EWHC 1890 (TCC). Making a Part 36 offer does not exempt a party from making reasonable use of other forms of ADR such as mediation, *PGF II SA v OMFS Company 1 Limited* [2014] WLR 1386. For an analysis of how making a Part 36 offer may be relevant to a sanction see 8.34–8.41.

G CONSIDERATIONS FOR THE PARTIES

4.63 Pulling together the above elements into key principles:

- The costs of each party will be made up of the elements set out in 4.17–4.22, and each party will normally bear their own expenses, subject to how the case is being funded.
- The costs of ADR processes vary substantially, and this needs careful consideration in relation to the form of ADR to use and when to use it.
- There is no doubt at all that the expense of dispute resolution can be kept down through the use of appropriate ADR, and this has been reinforced by the use of budgeting, costs management, and the added importance of proportionality.
- A lawyer should constantly review the sum potentially recoverable in a dispute, the chances of success, the expense already incurred in relation to the dispute, and the relative expense of different options for resolving the dispute and advise the client accordingly. Even if ADR is not used, consideration should be given to protecting the position of a client through a Part 36 offer.
- When resolution of a dispute is considered, be it through litigation or a form of ADR, consideration should be given to seeking an order or award as to costs (in litigation or arbitration) or reaching an agreement as to costs (in ADR).

H OVERALL FINANCIAL ANALYSIS AND RISK ASSESSMENT

4.64 The above elements and factors outline how complex financial decisions relating to a case can be. The lawyer will need to take a relatively systematic approach to collecting relevant data, the analysis of figures, and considering potential future expenses before advising a client. In addition to detailed arithmetic it is important to take into account cost effectiveness, looking at the relative benefits and possible costs of each option, and also managing risks by looking at the relative chances of success of possible ways forward. For more detail on the importance of managing risk see S. Blake, *A Practical Approach to Effective Litigation* (8th edn, OUP, 2014), ch 6.

4.65 As regards figures, the following is a basic checklist of figures that may be relevant:

- the maximum and minimum sum of damages that is realistically at stake in the case, taking into account all heads of loss and matters such as interest;

- your own side's costs to date;
- your side's likely further costs up to and including trial if the case is litigated;
- the extent to which your side's costs are likely to be recoverable, on assessment if you win at trial, or by negotiation in ADR;
- the likely costs to date of the other side;
- the likely further costs the other side will incur up to and including trial if the case is litigated;
- the costs of the other side you are likely to have to pay, on assessment if you lose at trial, or through negotiation in ADR;
- the potential costs of each potentially appropriate ADR process.

This task is part of professional responsibilities. A solicitor has a duty to keep a client updated as to costs, and the CPR provides for budgets, costs management, and estimates of costs to be made available as a case progresses through litigation, so many relevant figures should be to hand. However, complexity arises because a decision cannot be taken on arithmetic alone. A decision on cost effectiveness will be based primarily on the relative likely costs of litigation and of ADR options, but one must also consider how likely it is that each process will succeed so as to take a realistic decision. **4.66**

Risk assessment will include considering the likelihood that the case will be won if it proceeds to trial. In an extreme case it is possible to win at trial, but to lose overall because of the impact of costs. As an example, say that the damages in a case are likely to be £25,000: **4.67**

- If the likely costs are £10,000 and there is a 90% chance of success then the likely outcome is that the claim will be won, and therefore reasonable costs will be paid on a standard basis. While the standard basis is unlikely to cover all costs, it will normally cover about 80% of them, so £8,000 in costs will be reimbursed leaving the party only £2,000 out of pocket on costs. The claimant will get £25,000 plus £8,000 and be out of pocket by only £2,000.
- If the likely costs are £10,000 and there is only a 60% chance of success there is a 40% chance the claim will be lost. If that happened the claimant would have to bear those costs, and would be likely to be ordered to pay the costs for the other side. If the other side has costs at a similar level, and with a similar assumption as regards the assessment of costs, the party will pay £10,000 plus £8,000 in costs and be £18,000 out of pocket. As the damages of £25,000 are not recovered, the total sum by which the claimant is out of pocket is £43,000.

The first scenario is reasonably attractive, to the level where a client may be attracted to incurring extra costs to try to ensure that the case is won. This has an element of gambling, but it may seem sensible to spend more even if the chance of winning is only increased marginally to get the best chance of a positive outcome. The second scenario is very unattractive, but the contrast between being £33,000 in pocket and £43,000 out of pocket shows how crucial it is that the chances of success in a case are carefully assessed. The chances of success will of course include such matters as how clear the law is, how strong the evidence is, whether cross-examination will succeed, and so on. **4.68**

It is this sort of calculation that can illustrate the potential value of ADR. Rather than go to court and risk the difference between these two scenarios it may be worthwhile spending a few thousand pounds on an ADR process to manage risk. This may require some compromise as regards the first scenario, but it can help to avoid the second scenario. Of course thought must also be given to how likely it is that an ADR process might work, and what expense that might incur. Options might include making a Part 36 offer to encourage **4.69** negotiation. If the other side has not done a realistic risk assessment, this may be something that a mediator may be able to help with as part of encouraging a settlement.

4.70 The calculation may be made more complicated because developing case law gives rise to some uncertainty about likely costs orders. Rather than a simple order for costs based on a winner and loser, an order may be made on the extent to which a case has been won—if there were several issues in the case and some were won and others lost an appropriate proportion of costs may be ordered, or there may be an issues-based assessment under CPR r 44.3.4.

4.71 Despite these complexities, the lawyer should deal with arithmetic and risk assessment objectively and put the options to the client. The lawyer's motivation may be complex if he or she might be paid more if the case went to trial in some months rather than settling soon. Nonetheless the client's best interest must come first. As clients become more aware of ADR there may be a possibility of a complaint if options are not fully considered, or possibly a wasted costs order against the lawyer if litigation is prolonged improperly when a case could be settled: Senior Courts Act 1981 s 51(6) and CPR r 48.7.

I BASIC EXAMPLE OF ADR FINANCIAL CONSIDERATIONS

4.72 The claimant's lawyer in a negligence claim assesses potential damages at £50,000 minimum to £70,000 maximum if the case is won. The chance of winning on the balance of probabilities is assessed at about 70% (because there are some weaknesses in the evidence). The defendant has indicated that he will claim contributory negligence of 25%. Appropriate pre-action steps have been taken, but a claim form has not yet been issued.

4.73 The costs to date of the claimant are £10,000, and it is thought that the defendant's costs are about £8,000. If the case goes to trial the costs might be up to £10,000 more each, largely because of disputes in the evidence about what caused the accident.

4.74 The claimant's calculations might be:

- It is clearly more likely than not that the case will be won. The best case scenario is that the claimant would get damages of £70,000 with no finding of contributory negligence. His costs after trial will be £20,000, and he would be likely to get about £16,000 reimbursed after assessment. Thus the most attractive outcome is getting a payment of £86,000 for damages and costs, which will leave the claimant with £66,000 due to costs not being fully recovered. This may make litigation look attractive, but it is the most favourable rather than the most likely outcome.
- At the other end of the scale, the worst case scenario is that there is a 30% chance that the case will be lost at trial. With weaknesses in the evidence this risk must be taken seriously. If the claimant lost there would be no recovery of damages, and the claimant would bear costs that would by then be £20,000. In addition the claimant would have to pay the defendant's costs, which would by then be £18,000, of which the claimant might have to pay £15,500 after assessment. This would leave the claimant £35,500 out of pocket, and with no damages.
- Depending on the details of the case, a reasonable mid-range outcome might be that the claimant would win, but might get only £60,000 in damages, with a finding of 20% contributory negligence. This would provide a payment of £48,000, plus costs.

4.75 The defendant's calculations might be:

- There is a 30% chance the claimant will not win. If the claimant does lose at trial the defendant will not have to pay damages. The claimant will have to pay his reasonable costs, so he will only be out of pocket to the extent his costs are not reimbursed, so perhaps £2,500 down. This is the defendant's best case scenario on the facts given.

- Even if the claimant wins at trial he may only get damages of £50,000, less 25% for contributory negligence, which is £37,250, though the defendant would have to pay the claimant's costs (say £16,000 on assessment) as well as his own (£18,000), a total of £34,000. He would pay £71,250 overall, nearly half of that being in relation to costs rather than damages.
- The worst case scenario is that the defendant loses at trial and has to pay the claimant £70,000 in damages. With costs this would be a total payment of £104,000.

Possible options as regards dispute resolution and costs are: **4.76**

- Proceedings are issued and the case goes to trial. This holds some attraction for each side because it might achieve their own best case outcome. However there is significant risk that their best case outcome will not be achieved. This option will incur £20,000 extra in costs, and total costs will then be £38,000 against a maximum claim of £70,000. Although the damages claimed are only £70,000, the potential outcomes for each side are more than £100,000 apart.
- Either side might make a Part 36 offer. This will potentially protect their position as regards costs not yet incurred. The offer should be pitched to give away as little as possible, but should be sufficient for the other side to consider it. The defendant might offer £37,250 on this basis. The claimant might not be prepared to accept less than £60,000 on a Part 36 basis.
- The parties might instruct their lawyers to negotiate, exploring the ground between their potential Part 36 positions. This might work, but if one or both parties are still primarily focused on their best case scenario the lawyers may not be given sufficient scope within their instructions to reach a settlement.
- The parties might use mediation. Mediation could probably be completed within at most a day with a total cost of perhaps £2,000 or less. The mediator would objectively help the parties to look at the strengths and weaknesses of their cases, and assess the financial risk. This might lead to settlement, or it might help the parties to refine their Part 36 offer, thus limiting the risk each faces.

KEY POINTS SUMMARY

- Costs are a major motivation for undertaking ADR, but the costs position can be quite complex. **4.77** The separate elements of costs must all be considered.
- The Review of Civil Litigation Costs carried out by Lord Justice Jackson recommended that ADR has a vital role to play in reducing the costs of civil disputes. His main recommendations were implemented as a package in April 2013.
- It is government policy to make the costs of dispute resolution proportionate to the amount at stake, for example through extending the use of mediation in lower value cases.
- Although a process like arbitration can be expensive, most ADR processes are relatively inexpensive, and information on costs is quite easily available from ADR providers.
- The basis on which a party is funded is relevant, and the implications of CFA, third party, and other types of funding must all be taken into account where appropriate in an ADR process.
- It is important for the lawyer to make an overall analysis of the financial position and risks to assist the client in taking an informed decision about litigation and ADR options.
- Costs may be considered as part of a negotiated or mediated settlement.

5

ONLINE ADR OPTIONS AND ODR

A INTRODUCTION 5.01
B BACKGROUND 5.07
C THE MAIN BODIES CONCERNED WITH ODR 5.11
D THE CURRENT ROLE OF ICT IN ADR 5.14
E ODR SOFTWARE OPTIONS 5.21
F DEVELOPMENT OF ADR AND ODR WITHIN THE EU 5.26
G LOOKING FORWARD 5.31
Key points summary 5.33

A INTRODUCTION

5.01 The use of information and communication technology (ICT), in relation to all forms of dispute resolution, has developed massively in recent years, and is a significant area of ongoing development. In terms of saving time and money in resolving disputes, ICT has much to offer, especially in relation to lower value cases, and this has been picked up in the growing use of online portals and software-based support for dispute resolution. Whereas litigation and ADR have traditionally been seen as paper-based processes, with face-to-face meetings very important for trial, negotiation or mediation, it is increasingly important to distinguish what really needs hard copy and physical presence from what can be managed electronically and using processes such as video-conferencing.

5.02 In its widest sense, ICT now plays some role in most dispute resolution processes. Online options are increasingly used for processes such as the service of documents and disclosure. Communication is now frequently by email rather than letter. Laptops are used to access legal authorities and information, and to make use of pro-forma documents to create settlements and orders. All the ADR processes covered in this book are increasingly being supported by ICT, and negotiation, mediation, and arbitration can all now be carried out entirely online where appropriate.

5.03 Initially ICT was used primarily to support existing processes, with documents being exchanged online. However, portals and software are now available to carry out some stages of dispute management processes entirely electronically, particularly in relation to small-scale consumer disputes and lower value personal injury claims. Interactive online documents can be used to capture information, for example through drop-down menus for cause of concern and remedy sought, and then software can process information to automate exchanges between the parties, and sometimes even to propose solutions. Sophisticated software can even mimic some of the functions of a negotiator or mediator, for example processing figures in a case to take into account various heads of loss and chances of success and risk, thus helping to define and narrow the field for potential settlement.

5.04 The stage has now been reached where disputes may be handled and resolved wholly online using new processes which may draw on techniques used in negotiation, mediation, and arbitration, but which do not wholly fall into the definition of any of those processes. This is starting to create distinct forms of ADR in which the whole process is automated, facilitating the resolution of disputes through innovative techniques and online technologies. This

Online Dispute Resolution is now commonly called 'ODR'. ODR options are developing around the world, and some proponents are keen on how valuable online systems can be in dealing with disputes using proportionate resources, and in areas where ODR can offer special benefits, as in dealing with provision after divorce, where software might help to diffuse emotions that may arise in face-to-face meetings or direct exchanges.

The use of ICT/ODR is currently most strongly established in relation to smaller scale commercial transactions, and in particular in relation to e-commerce. Major current initiatives include European Union Directives to bring in by 2015/16 online ADR/ODR options for disputes relating to goods and services, see 5.26–5.30. In addition, at international level, guidelines on the use of online ADR have been developed by UNCITRAL, see 5.11. **5.05**

The current use of online ADR and the developing use of ODR are complex and cannot be dealt with fully in a single section of one book. This chapter provides an overview of the main areas where online options are available or are being developed. Further detail can be found through the websites noted in this chapter. **5.06**

B BACKGROUND

The terminology used in relation to online ADR has evolved slowly and is not yet fully standardized. Terms used include Internet Dispute Resolution (iDR) and Electronic ADR (eADR). However, the most commonly generally used term is 'ODR'. There is no fully common agreement as to what ODR is, but the term is primarily applied to a dispute resolution process that is conducted online (rather than only being supported by ICT), and/or to a process where online software carries out all or a major part of a dispute resolution process. **5.07**

The development of the use of online dispute resolution or ODR was initially piecemeal, but it is now reaching the stage where it has been shown to be reliably successful in a range of areas so that its use is growing. Three factors have driven the development of ODR. The first is the growing need for reasonably quick methods of dispute resolution at proportionate cost. Combining ADR and ICT offers potential solutions where traditional means of dispute resolution are proportionately too expensive or impractical. **5.08**

Secondly, ODR can be particularly useful in resolving small-scale consumer and personal injury disputes, because software can process basic issues and figures. Within England and Wales, online portals have been developed. For road traffic accidents occurring after 30 April 2010, personal injury claims are dealt with through an online process for filing and managing documents, for which see the Pre-action Protocol for Low Value Personal Injury Claims in Road Traffic Accidents and www.claimsportal.org.uk/. The process is designed to facilitate settlement, and lawyers are remunerated through fixed fees. From 31 July 2013 the use of the portal was extended to cover claims with a value up to £25,000. A further portal to deal with Employers' Liability and Public Liability Claims was added on the same date, see the Pre-action Protocol for Low Value Personal Injury (Employers' Liability and Public Liability) Claims. It is logical to use the internet for the resolution of e-commerce disputes, not least as parties to an online transaction are often located some distance from each other. Developments in this area by the EU are outlined at 5.26–5.30. Common terminology in this area is C2C (where the dispute is between consumers) and B2C (where the dispute is between a business and a consumer). **5.09**

Thirdly, ODR can be attractive where the parties are some distance apart, or meetings are inconvenient. This has led to the development of ODR to address international disputes. ODR may also be useful where face-to-face meetings are inappropriate or may be counterproductive, for example in dealing with an acrimonious dispute. **5.10**

C THE MAIN BODIES CONCERNED WITH ODR

5.11 One body that has played a major role in the development of ODR is the United Nations Commission on International Trade Law (UNCITRAL), a body which has also been particularly concerned with the development of arbitration. For more than a decade UNCITRAL has been developing principles for the use of online ADR, and it provides a wide range of relevant documents, reports, and links to a range of national and international schemes and resources, see www.uncitral.org/uncitral/publications/online_resources_ODR.html. UNCITRAL has also set up a Working Group on Online Dispute Resolution, and the papers of this group can be found at www.uncitral.org/uncitral/commission/working_groups/3Online_Dispute_Resolution.html.

5.12 A further body of particular importance is the National Center for Technology and Dispute Resolution. The NCTDR was founded in 1998 at the University of Massachusetts by two Professors, Ethan Katsh and Janet Rifkin. It has a website that provides access to a wide variety of information and resources relating to the international development and use of ODR, see www.odr.info. The Center runs international forums and provides updates on developments. In addition it provides information about online ADR providers. Like UNCITRAL, the Center provides links to standards relevant to ODR. The Center carries out practical work assisting in developing ODR systems and software and it has also worked on projects to model mediation-type processes for use online.

5.13 The European Union is also strongly involved in developing the use of ODR in relation to e-commerce. The above sites give links to this work, and the current position is outlined below, see 5.26–5.30. There are other websites that provide helpful material on the use of ODR and are seeking to build a cross border infrastructure, such as www.odrexchange.com.

D THE CURRENT ROLE OF ICT IN ADR

5.14 Many mediation and arbitration providers make substantial use of the internet to promote and support their services. This includes provision of a substantial amount of information about process, and often about the mediators and arbitrators themselves. The government also makes substantial use of the internet directly and indirectly to provide information about ADR processes and providers.

5.15 The main ADR providers use their internet sites actively to support the setting up of a mediation or arbitration process. It is often possible to apply online through the website to initiate a process or to get more detailed information. Sample mediation or arbitration agreements are available online, and can increasingly be wholly or partly completed online. It is very constructive to start an ADR process online because the parties can work together on drafts of documents, encouraging a co-operative approach.

5.16 A mediation process may be conducted at least partly online. This includes finalizing the initial agreement, exchanging evidence and opening statements, and sometimes drafting a settlement, which may be done by uploading documents to a shared site. Note that an online interface and/or email may involve some different issues of confidentiality from a face-to-face mediation, but this remains to be explored as problems arise. A telephone or conference call mediation may be supported by documents exchanged electronically. There may be virtual meetings via webcam conferencing facilities, including Skype. A number of providers offer online mediation or e-mediation. Providers are best searched online at the time of need, but at the time of writing options include: The Mediation Room (www.themediationroom.com), E-Mediator (www.e-mediator.co.uk), Dispute Doctor (www.dispute-doctor.co.uk),

Resolute Systems (www.settleonline.com), Cybersettle (www.cybersettle.com) and NCTDR (www.odr.info). For an example of phone mediation backed up with online communication, see LawWorks (www.lawworks.org.uk).

In a similar way an arbitration may be carried out wholly or partly online, so long as this is what the parties agree in an arbitration agreement that otherwise meets appropriate requirements, see Part VI. A number of arbitration providers offer a paper-only service where an award is made on the basis of written submissions and evidence only, and this is often done with electronic exchange of documents, thus effectively amounting to online arbitration. As noted in 5.11 above, UNCITRAL is very much involved in the use of online arbitration and their website is a useful source of information. Providers are best searched online at the time of need, but at the time of writing options include many of the main arbitration providers, and also organizations such as www.net-arb.com, www.onlinearbitration.net, and www.oanlive.com. **5.17**

Training and continuing professional development for ADR providers is also offered online. This offers benefits in terms of access to training and staying up to date, though it is important to note that standards set by the Civil Mediation Council include significant live experience of mediation. One example of online ADR training can be found at www.adr-international.com. **5.18**

Potential problems in relation to ODR arise because this area is still developing fully agreed national and international standards. Arbitration and mediation are based on contract law, statute law in relevant jurisdictions, and international agreements as set out in other chapters in this book. An online process that is based on a mediation or arbitration contract but where agreement takes place online will in principle be valid and enforceable in the same ways as any other mediation or arbitration. However, ODR processes are emerging that are carried out by agreement, but do not follow generally accepted routes. These processes can be very useful and effective, but there may be questions about the formal legal validity and enforceability of any agreement reached. Such ODR works because the parties agree to it, or because there is a motive to comply—for example an online international seller or service provider has an online reputation to protect. ODR enforcement can sometimes be facilitated by being built into a transaction, as happens for example in the chargeback process, which reverses a credit or debit card payment in the case of fraud or other breach of contract terms, but there may otherwise be enforcement problems. **5.19**

Some of the problems which may arise in the case of cross-jurisdictional ODR can be seen in relation to the Uniform Domain Name Dispute Resolution Policy (UDRP) developed by the International Corporation for the Assignment of Names and Numbers (ICANN), see www.icann.org/en/help/dndr/udrp. This is a streamlined process intended to deal with disputes about the use of domain names on the internet. This is web based, but it also makes use of a panel to take decisions. It has dealt with many thousands of cases successfully, but there has been some criticism of the fairness of some of the rules in this process, the lack of an appeal process, and problems caused by a range of legal traditions giving different expectations. **5.20**

E ODR SOFTWARE OPTIONS

Software has already been designed and is in use to carry out some parts of an ADR process. **5.21**
Given that many negotiation/mediation processes work through the parties each doing their own calculations, then defining parameters for settlement and moving on to exchanging demands and offers within those parameters, it is quite logical that software could in a

number of cases mimic such calculations. Software can have added benefits in terms of keeping some information private, and carrying out quickly a number of calculations that might be quite complex to speed up the process and open up options.

5.22 Software 'automated negotiation' has been primarily developed and used in the United States, particularly in relation to settling insurance claims. Software for 'blind-bidding' can assist in deciding on a figure for damages after liability is agreed. This works on a sort of auction system where some information about offers and the reason for them is shared by the parties and some is stored within the software and is known only to the party who inputs the data. If there is only one financial issue between two parties 'double blind-bidding' may be used. If the parties agree to do this, parameters are agreed for the process and how a final outcome may be reached (eg that offers be within 10–20% of each other, and each party may make three settlement offers). Each party then makes a settlement offer in secret, and the software calculates whether the offers meet the agreed parameters. If they do, the software will carry out an agreed computation (eg split the difference between the two offers) to produce a settlement figure. If the offers do not meet the parameters, each party can make another secret bid and the software will again see if they meet the parameters. This may seem a little rough and ready, but it may in a number of cases be more cost effective than paying for lawyers to negotiate face to face. As the settlement offers are hidden, if the figures do not meet the agreed parameters the parties will simply know that their figures are too far apart for settlement, without knowing any detail of what figures the other side provided. This may be quite attractive to a lawyer seeking secrecy for information.

5.23 Software for 'visual blind-bidding' may be used where there are more issues and parties. If the parties agree to this, each provides a defined optimistic outcome for each issue. The software makes all of these optimistic outcomes visible, as they define the highest and lowest possible outcome. The software then generates a range of outcomes that all fall within the range of these outcomes. A party may also contribute options that fall within the outcomes, but it will not be clear from the display which options are machine or party generated. The parties may agree on one of the possible outcomes generated, or each may choose a different option from those generated, in which case the software will use an algorithm to combine those options. The algorithm can take into account matters such as which party moves into a potential settlement zone quickest, thus encouraging the making of concessions rather than positional bargaining. Such software lacks the refinement to deal with complex and non-financial issues, but it can provide assistance in dealing with a range of financial issues. It may also assist in avoiding deadlock. Such software is potentially attractive to lawyers as only a best case outcome has to be revealed by each side rather than a bottom line, and, as it is not clear whether a party or a machine has generated a potential outcome, an adequate offer may be accepted without loss of face. Such software can assist wherever there are several financial heads of loss, for example in a personal injury claim.

5.24 One might assume that mediation always requires a neutral third person, but there are ways in which software may provide 'automated mediation', mimicing functions a mediator might perform. This may assist with disputes in areas such as the online sale of goods, where there are a significant number of relatively small-scale disputes relating to matters such as mis-description or non-arrival. For several years software has provided online mediation services to sites such as eBay to assist in resolving disputes between sellers and buyers. The process involves a buyer or a seller completing a web-based claim form that gathers information about the type of dispute and the solution sought. This triggers an email to the other party asking if he/she is prepared to agree to online resolution, and if so to complete an online form. The software is able to detect agreement on the basis of comparing the forms, or to move the parties into an electronic interface that shapes a constructive dialogue through reply options, limited free text boxes and set deadlines. This is, at a very basic level, what a mediator does. If the dispute is not resolved, the parties are given the option of getting the services of a live mediator for a low fee. This type of system has been successful in resolving millions of disputes across many countries in several languages, with high success rates.

Similar but even more sophisticated software could go further in collecting and analysing information from parties in a way that makes only selected information available to another party. The process could analyse information and create options for settlement using algorithms so that use of the software would be in some ways broadly similar to the input a mediator might have in a relatively short mediation session. Such software could be used to define issues or support negotiation, or could be a preliminary stage to narrow a dispute before mediation or arbitration and therefore limit costs. Software of this kind is being developed by a range of academics and lawyers around the world. **5.25**

F DEVELOPMENT OF ADR AND ODR WITHIN THE EU

The European Union has sought to develop a common approach to dealing with disputes relating to goods purchased online, to support the development of a common commercial market across all EU countries. The E-Commerce Directive was adopted in 2000, setting up a framework for electronic commerce, EU Directive 2000/31/EC. The Directive established harmonized rules on matters such as transparency and information requirements for online service providers, electronic contracts, and limitations of liability of intermediary service providers. An Internal Market clause provides that services are in principle subject to the law of the member state in which the service provider is established, but that the member state in which the service is received cannot restrict incoming services. Services covered by the Directive include the online sale of products and services (eg financial services, travel services and goods), online information services (eg online newspapers), and online advertising and entertainment services. Professional services provided for example by lawyers, doctors, accountants, and estate agents are also covered. The development of a common consumer market is constantly being taken forward. For example in 2009 the European Small Claims Procedure (ESCP) was introduced to seek to overcome problems caused by small claims procedures operating only in limited national jurisdictions. This facilitates enforcement in relation to claims for under €2,000 arising in cross-border disputes, and provision was made for the use of new technologies in transferring information and evidence between the courts of the different member states. See europa.eu/legislation_summaries/consumers/protection_of_consumers/l16028_en.htm. **5.26**

To support the e-commerce market, the Commission is concerned that all EU consumers be able to resolve problems without going to court, regardless of the kind of product or service that the contractual dispute is about and regardless of where they bought it within the European Single Market. On 29 November 2011 the European Commission published a Communication on Alternative Dispute Resolution for consumer disputes in the Single Market, with legislative proposals for a draft Directive on ADR, and a draft Regulation on ODR, with a call for the views of EU governments, ending on 31 January 2012. The British Government consulted on these proposals, getting some mixed responses, see www.bis.gov.uk/consultations. The draft proposals were revised and approved, and the government is working towards implementation in 2015. The changes are important as they will potentially affect all consumers and businesses, even if they already operate a system for dealing with complaints, but significant further work is being undertaken prior to implementation, so they are only outlined here. **5.27**

5.28 The proposals fall into two parts. The first part is a Directive on Consumer ADR, published on 18 June 2013, Directive 2013/11/EU, see http://eur-lex.europa.eu/LexUriServ/LexUriServ.do?uri=OJ:L:2013:165:0063:0079:EN:PDF. There is a concern that take-up rates for ADR are relatively low in consumer cases across the EU, not least due to uneven provision of ADR, variable quality of process, and lack of information. This is perceived to discourage cross-border purchases and therefore depress trade. The intention is that all consumers within the EU should have access to ADR options that meet set quality principles, with national networks developing to become international. This will cover a range of relevant ADR options. The changes will apply to disputes in relation to contracts for goods or services. Traders will be required to provide information to consumers about ADR options, and member states will provide some monitoring of standards in ADR entities.

5.29 Secondly there is a Regulation on Online Dispute Resolution published on 21 May 2013, Regulation (EU) No 524/2013, see http://eur-lex.europa.eu/LexUriServ/LexUriServ.do?uri=OJ:L:2013:165:0001:0012:EN:PDF. This will cover consumers making purchases online from a business seller in another EU country. The intention is to set up a single EU-wide online platform to provide information and deal with complaints, linking consumers and traders with ADR-providing entities. Each complaint will be registered online through an interactive multilingual system, and the intention will be to resolve all disputes entirely online within 30 days. Should this not prove possible, use will be made of facilitators.

5.30 As a further initiative, it is a concern that there is currently a very wide range of ADR processes and providers across the EU, and there is a desire to harmonize the position. The intention is to cover a wide range of legal areas, including family law, employment law, and so on. With this in mind a European e-Justice portal has been set up, with the intention that this be developed as a one-stop shop, see https://e-justice.europa.eu/home.do?action=home&plang=en.

G LOOKING FORWARD

5.31 Existing ADR processes such as mediation and arbitration are increasingly being delivered at least partly online. In addition, purely online processes that do not necessarily fit within existing ADR definitions are being developed as ODR. This has increasing support at national and international level, and development is coming quite quickly, with ODR becoming a major way of addressing a range of smaller value disputes. In more complex cases, ODR can increasingly support the role of a third-party mediator or arbitrator. The potential use of ODR is so significant that it is referred to as a 'fourth party' by some authors because ODR processes are seen as being capable of having an independent input to the management of the dispute, in addition to the two parties and an independent third party.

5.32 As technologies continue to develop they are changing the way in which people communicate and interact, which will inevitably have an impact on the ways in which conflicts are managed and resolved. There will of course be scepticism as to how far technology can deal with complex relationships and propose solutions that are likely to be accepted, but already software can mimic some of the processes in a mediation or negotiation, see 5.21–5.25. In addition, a secure website can provide virtual collaborative workspaces or e-rooms in which the parties can exchange messages, share documents, and engage in synchronous or asynchronous negotiations, see for example www.juripax.com. Multi-faceted programs could also integrate information and generate options in a variety of ways, including exploiting the possibility of using virtual reality and avatars to rationalize intensity in some areas where issues are complex and/or strong emotions are involved.

KEY POINTS SUMMARY

- ADR processes such as mediation and arbitration can take place partly or wholly online, and can be facilitated by advancing technology in various ways. 5.33
- In addition, online dispute resolution or ODR is fast developing. This comprises systems designed to work online that do not necessarily fit within existing ADR definitions.
- International and cross-border ODR is being developed, especially to support e-commerce.
- Software is already used successfully to mimic some negotiation and mediation processes, and this is likely to develop.
- Provisions are in place to substantially develop the use of ODR in relation to sales and services in the EU.

6

PROFESSIONAL ETHICS

A INTRODUCTION 6.01
B ADVISING ABOUT ADR OPTIONS 6.05
C LAWYERS PROVIDING AN ADR SERVICE 6.14
D COMPLIANCE WITH CORE PROFESSIONAL DUTIES 6.17
E SPECIFIC DUTIES IN MEDIATION 6.33
F SPECIFIC DUTIES IN NEGOTIATION 6.39
G THE DUTY OF CONFIDENTIALITY 6.43
H LEGAL PROFESSIONAL PRIVILEGE 6.55
I WITHOUT PREJUDICE COMMUNICATIONS 6.57
J PRACTICAL CONSIDERATIONS 6.67
K DISCLOSURE OF INFORMATION IN ADR PROCESSES 6.69
L AUTHORITY TO SETTLE 6.75
M THE RELATIONSHIP BETWEEN BARRISTERS AND THEIR PROFESSIONAL CLIENTS IN ADR 6.77
Key points summary 6.81

A INTRODUCTION

6.01 ADR processes, in particular negotiation and mediation, can give rise to a number of ethical considerations for lawyers that differ from those that arise when conducting litigation. Lawyers acting in an ADR process will owe duties to their professional client, the lay client, the neutral third party (such as the mediator, adjudicator, expert, or arbitrator), and the court (if settlement occurs that is to be embodied in a court order). The growing use of ADR is creating some tensions as regards ADR and ethics, for example because professional codes of conduct tend to focus on duties to the court rather than duties in ADR. Developments in funding are also creating some tensions, for example where a lawyer is acting under a DBA, or the client has third-party funding. The professional codes of conduct for solicitors and for barristers have been substantially revised in recent years. While underlying duties to clients and to the courts remain similar there has been a move to a focus on outcomes and underlying principles with detail moved to guidance notes. While slightly different terminology is used in the different codes, core outcomes and principles will normally apply to ADR as well as to litigation, though it is not always clear how duties to the court might operate in ADR.

6.02 Solicitors and those regulated by the Solicitors Regulation Authority have to comply with the Code of Conduct set out in Version 9 of the Solicitors Regulation Authority Handbook, which came into effect on 1 April 2014. This includes ten mandatory core principles ('SRA Principles'), which regulate all aspects of practice and the mandatory outcomes ('SRA Outcomes'). The SRA recognizes that the SRA Outcomes can be satisfied in a number of ways, so they are supplemented by 'SRA Indicative Behaviours', which give guidance on whether or not the solicitor is likely to have complied with the SRA Outcomes and Principles. For details see www.sra.org.uk/solicitors/handbook/code/content.page

6.03 Barristers and those regulated by the Bar Standards Board (BSB) must comply with the Code of Conduct, which came into effect from 6 January 2014 as part of the new Bar Standards Board Handbook. Those regulated by the BSB must meet ten core duties ('BSB Core Duties')

which regulate all aspects of practice, and are supplemented by mandatory rules ('BSB Rules'), and outcomes to be met ('BSB Outcomes'), with guidance notes to assist ('BSB Guidance'). Many of the duties, rules, and outcomes are broadly relevant to the appropriate use of ADR to resolve a dispute, and only the most directly relevant points are covered here. The Code has been completely restructured from earlier versions but while there are modifications of wording there are no major changes as regards duties relevant to ADR. For details see www.barstandardsboard.org.uk/handbook.

Mediators also have to adhere to ethical standards of behaviour in mediation, see 14.104–14.122. **6.04**

B ADVISING ABOUT ADR OPTIONS

ADR affords clients many advantages over litigation (see Chapter 1). A key advantage is the cost savings that can be achieved by settling a case. If a case settles by ADR, particularly before proceedings have been issued, the lawyers in the case will obviously earn less fee income, but lawyers must not let this fact influence them in any way. Equally a lawyer acting under a DBA might wish to settle quickly for a good sum rather than build up fees, but client interests must prevail. **6.05**

Lawyers have a professional duty to help the court to further the overriding objective (CPR r 1.3). They are therefore under a duty to save expense, ensure that the case is dealt with expeditiously and fairly and in a way that is proportionate to the issues, the importance of the case, the amount of money involved, and the financial position of each party (CPR r 1.1). Helping the court to further the overriding objective will also mean that they must encourage the parties to co-operate with each other and facilitate the use of ADR if that would be appropriate (CPR r 1.4). **6.06**

Legal representatives are under a positive duty to consider routinely with their clients whether the dispute is suitable for ADR. This has been the subject of judicial comment in several cases (see 7.80 and (in relation to mediation in particular) 14.06–14.12). This duty has been made even more important due to the possibility of a costs sanction if reasonable use is not made of ADR, and the need to keep costs proportionate. **6.07**

The duty on the parties to consider ADR should be exercised at all stages of the dispute, not just before proceedings are issued. It should be considered, in particular, before issue, at track allocation stage, after disclosure, and before the costs of a trial have been incurred (see Chapter 7). **6.08**

Solicitors are obliged to act in good faith and in the best interests of each client (SRA Principle 4) and to provide a proper standard of service to clients, which includes exercising competence, skill, and diligence, and taking into account the individual needs and circumstances of each client (SRA Principle 5). Solicitors must also achieve the following outcomes under the Code of Conduct: **6.09**

- treat the client fairly (SRA Outcome 1.1);
- provide services to the client in a manner which protects their interests in the dispute or matter, subject to the proper administration of justice (SRA Outcome 1.2);
- provide a competent service to the client, delivered in a timely manner which takes account of the client's needs and circumstances (SRA Outcome 1.5);
- ensure clients are in a position to make informed decisions about the services they need, how their matter will be handled, and the options available to them (SRA Outcome 1.12);
- ensure clients receive the best possible information, both at the time of engagement and when appropriate as the matter progresses, about the overall cost of the matter (SRA Outcome 1.13). This outcome can be achieved by discussing whether the potential outcomes of a client's matter are likely to justify the expense or risk involved, including any

risk of having to pay someone else's legal fees (SRA Indicative Behaviour 1.3) and clearly explaining the likely fees and warning about other payments for which the client may be responsible (SRA Indicative Behaviours 1.14 and 1.15).

6.10 To comply with these principles and outcomes, it seems likely that the solicitor must discuss whether mediation or some other form of ADR procedure would be more appropriate than litigation. The solicitor should also ensure that the client understands that there may be adverse costs consequences if a party unreasonably refuses ADR. Advice about ADR procedures must be given at any appropriate stage of the proceedings, not just at the outset of the dispute. In assessing whether the matter is suitable for ADR, the solicitor should bear in mind the factors discussed in Chapters 3, 7 and 8.

6.11 Both barristers and solicitors are required to act in the best interests of the lay client without regard to their own interests (SRA Principle 4, BSB Core Duty 2, and BSB Rule C3.R1). This will require them to consider, and discuss with the lay client, the most cost-effective and timely way of resolving the dispute by using the most appropriate ADR method. This professional duty is also reinforced by the key court guides (see the *Chancery Guide* para 17.4; the *Admiralty and Commercial Court Guide* para G1.4 and the *Technology and Construction Court Guide* para 7.1.3).

6.12 Where ADR process is to be used in an effort to resolve the dispute, the extent of each lawyer's involvement in the process should be clearly agreed with the lay client in advance. Appropriate costs advice should also be given to the client in relation to this, and recorded in writing (see SRA Outcome 1.13 and SRA Indicative Behaviours 1.1, 1.3, 1.14, and 1.15). This has become more important with the focus on cost budgeting.

6.13 If a lawyer fails to give appropriate advice about ADR or negligently advises the client to reject an offer from the opposing party to use ADR, the lawyer may expose their client to a costs penalty (see Chapter 8). The lawyer could be personally liable for a wasted costs order and/or a professional negligence action could be brought against him or her.

C LAWYERS PROVIDING AN ADR SERVICE

6.14 A solicitor or a solicitor's firm may offer ADR services to third parties, either as mediator, neutral evaluator, adjudicator, or expert determiner. A solicitor undertaking an ADR service of this kind must be truly neutral. They must ensure there is no prior personal knowledge of or relationship with either of the parties to the dispute. They should also ensure that no one within the firm has acted for any of the parties, even an unrelated matter. This is important to avoid the appearance of bias. If the lawyer, or any member of the firm, has acted or had any connection with any of the parties to the dispute, this must be disclosed to all parties, and the lawyer should not proceed unless all parties consent in writing to the provision of the agreed ADR service. Solicitors must act in the best interests of each client and that includes complying with their obligations with regard to conflict of interests contained in Chapter 3 of the SRA Code of Conduct (see SRA Principle 4). Solicitors must have in place proper systems which enable them to identify and deal with potential conflicts (SRA Outcome 3.1). Solicitors must not act if there is a conflict or a significant risk of conflict between two or more current clients (SRA Outcome 3.5). Some exceptions are provided by SRA Outcomes 3.6 and 3.7, but these are not likely to apply in this context.

6.15 Barristers are also permitted to offer ADR services, and many barristers' chambers now offer a mediation service. Although barristers are not generally permitted to make any payment to any person for the purposes of procuring professional instructions, they are permitted to pay a reasonable fee required by an ADR provider that appoints or recommends them to conduct mediation, arbitration or adjudication services (BSB Guidance C2.G18). They are also permitted to enter into a reasonable fee-sharing arrangement with such an organization on comparable terms to other mediators.

Barristers are required to act with independence and be impartial (BSB Core Duty 4, BSB Rule C1.R1). A barrister is personally responsible for her or his conduct and professional work, should use personal professional judgment, and should be able to justify decisions and actions regardless of the views of a client, solicitor, or other person (BSB Rule C3.R6). **6.16**

D COMPLIANCE WITH CORE PROFESSIONAL DUTIES

Lawyers acting for a client in an ADR process must act in compliance with their core professional duties, which apply in all cases. The precise wording of the core obligations differ in the codes of conduct applicable to each side of the profession, although the fundamental obligations are very similar. Lawyers will be expected to comply with these core duties in all areas of their professional practice, including acting for clients in the full range of ADR processes. Lawyers who are qualified mediators, adjudicators, arbitrators, or neutrals or determiners in any other ADR processes will also be expected to comply with these duties. The core obligations are as follows. **6.17**

To act within the client's instructions

It is vital that a lawyer acts at all times within the client's instructions. The objectives in the case, and the priorities, must come from the client and be confirmed with the client, and should not be assumed. In the relative informality of some ADR processes it may be tempting for a lawyer to aim for an outcome that is broadly 'fair', but it must be remembered that the lawyer is in no way a judge who may impose an outcome. The lawyer should advise the client on the strengths and weaknesses of a case, and what might amount to a realistic outcome, but must leave decisions to the client. This is particularly important as regards authority to settle in a non-adjudicative process, which is dealt with at 6.75 below. **6.18**

To act at all times in the client's best interests

SRA Principle 4 and Outcome 1.2 require a solicitor to act in good faith and in the best interests of the client, subject to the proper administration of justice. The obligation to act in the client's best interests is unlikely to prevail where there is a conflict between this duty and the solicitor's duty to uphold the rule of law and the proper administration of justice (SRA Principle 1), to act with integrity (SRA Principle 2), or not to permit their professional independence to be compromised (SRA Principle 3). **6.19**

The duty owed by barristers is in similar terms. A barrister must act in the best interests of each client (BSB Core Duty 2), which includes promoting fearlessly and by all proper and lawful means the client's best interests, without regard to his own interests or to any consequences to himself or to any other person (including any professional client or other intermediary) (BSB Rule C3.R2). **6.20**

Advising on settlement

In advising on any settlement proposal a lawyer must act clearly within the two duties just outlined. It is important to ensure that the lay client is properly informed about the merits of the case, the prospects of success, any evidential weakness in the case, the likely outcome **6.21** at trial and the costs of proceeding to trial so that the client can make an informed decision. The decision whether to accept an offer (or make an offer) must be that of the lay client. The lawyer must ensure the lay client is fully informed about his or her position to provide a sound basis for a decision. The lawyer can give the lay client the benefit of an opinion, but the ultimate decision is that of the client. Care must be taken not to put improper pressure on a lay client to enter into a settlement if the client is unwilling to do so. If the lay client is publicly funded, the lawyers will have an obligation to report if a reasonable offer to settle is refused (Funding Code Procedures, Part 2, Reporting Obligations C43.2 and C44(i)). The Legal Services Commission may withdraw public funding in that event, and the lay client should be advised about this possibility (Funding Code C13.4(f)). If there is third-party funding there may be a requirement that the funder be made aware of an offer.

6.22 A lawyer acting in the lay client's best interests should seek to ensure that any settlement reached using an ADR process is a reasonable one. It may not be reasonable to advise a client to settle a claim for a sum significantly below that which is likely to be received at trial. A lawyer should also ensure that any settlement agreement is drawn up in a way that best protects the client's interests. This may determine the form the settlement takes. For example, it may be more advantageous to record a settlement in a Tomlin order rather than invite the court to make an order by consent for a specified amount (see Chapter 23).

Conditional fee agreements (CFAs) and damages-based agreements (DBAs)

6.23 The lawyer needs to consider the best interests of the client when acting under a CFA or a DBA (see Chapter 4), as this can potentially give rise to a conflict of interest between the lawyer and the lay client when considering ADR options or potential terms for settlement. This is because the level or amount of the lawyer's fee is likely to be dependent on the fact and terms of settlement. In order to act in the client's best interests, the lawyer may have to advise the client to accept a reasonable offer by the other side even if it provides for payment of a lower success fee than that set out in a CFA. This may also require the lawyer to agree with the client to reduce the success fee in a CFA in accordance with the terms of an offer, although it should be noted that there is no legal obligation to do this. The solicitor must at all times give the client all relevant information relating to the agreement (see SRA Indicative Behaviour 1.17).

6.24 A lawyer acting under a DBA will have appropriate professional and ethical duties, though such duties have not been very clearly defined by professional bodies. Under a DBA a lawyer will have a direct interest in the damages recovered in the case, and therefore how quickly a case is settled, and for what sum. The lawyer's interest is, however, subject to the normal duties to the client in relation to instructions and acting in the client's best interests. It is very important that a lawyer gives objective and transparent advice and acts in a fully professional and ethical way in relation to any offer to settle to avoid any complaints, or a possible action for professional negligence.

To be independent

6.25 SRA Principle 3 provides that a solicitor must not allow his independence to be compromised. A barrister owes an overriding duty to the court to maintain independence (BSB Core Duties 1 and 4 and Rule C1.R1) and not knowingly or recklessly mislead or attempt to mislead the court. The proper administration of justice, access to justice, and the best interests of justice should be served (BSB Outcome C2.O2). A barrister should not let a solicitor or other person limit his or her discretion as to how the interests of a client can best be served (BSB Rule C3.R1).

Solicitors also owe similar duties to the court (see SRA Outcomes 5.1, 5.2, 5.5 and 5.6) when conducting litigation or acting as advocates. In particular they must uphold the rule of law and proper administration of justice (SRA Principle 1) and act with integrity (SRA Principle 2). **6.26**

Duties to act independently and in the interests of justice, together with the following duties in relation to integrity and fairness have implications for what is acceptable in terms of strategy and tactics in an ADR process. **6.27**

To act with integrity

A solicitor must uphold the rule of law and the proper administration of justice and this duty is owed not only to clients but also to the court and third parties (SRA Principle 1). A solicitor must also act with integrity towards clients, the courts, other lawyers, and the public (SRA Principle 2). Solicitors must act in a way that maintains the trust the public places in them and in the provision of legal services (SRA Principle 6). **6.28**

A barrister should: **6.29**

- act with integrity and honesty (BSB Core Duty 3);
- maintain standards of integrity, honesty, and independence, and be seen to be doing so (BSB Outcomes C2.01 and C2.04 and Rule C2.R1), and not behave in a way likely to diminish the trust and confidence which the public place in the barrister or in the legal profession (BSB Core duty 5);
- not behave in a way which involves offensive or discreditable conduct to a third party, or which is an abuse of a professional position (BSB Guidance C2.G12).

Fairness

Lawyers must always act with fairness and must not discriminate directly or indirectly because of race, colour, ethnic or national origin, nationality, citizenship, sex, sexual orientation, gender reassignment, marital status, civil partnership status, pregnancy and maternity, disability, age, religion, or belief (BSB Regulation C2.R5; SRA Principle 9 and Outcomes 2.1 and 2.2). **6.30**

Competence

A solicitor must only act if he is able to provide a proper level of service and this includes exercising competence, skill, and diligence, taking into account the needs and circumstances of the client and delivering the service in a timely manner (SRA Principle 5 and Outcome 1.5). A barrister owes similar duty to provide a competent standard of work and service to each client (BSB Core Duty 7), with an expectation that clients receive a competent standard of work and service (BSB Outcome C3.01). A barrister should not accept instructions he or she is not competent to handle or does not have enough experience to handle (BSB Rule C3.R7). A barrister should ensure that a client knows what to expect and understands the advice given to them (BSB Outcome C3.04). A client should be able to have confidence in those instructed to act for him (BSB Outcome C3.06). A barrister should take reasonable steps to avoid incurring unnecessary expense (BSB Guidance C3.G3). **6.31**

Duties when advancing a client's case and drafting documents

A barrister must not knowingly or recklessly mislead or attempt to mislead anyone (BSB Rule C2.R2). In addition a barrister must not draft any statement of fact or contention **6.32** which is not supported by the lay client or his instructions; any contention which he does not consider to be properly arguable; or any allegation of fraud unless he has clear instructions to make such an allegation and has before him reasonably credible material which as it stands establishes a prima facie case of fraud (BSB Rule C2.R2). Similar duties are imposed on solicitors by SRA Principle 1 and Indicative Behaviour 5.7.

E SPECIFIC DUTIES IN MEDIATION

6.33 When drafting a position statement, case summary, or any other document for use in an ADR process, a barrister should ensure that all allegations and assertions are properly arguable and supported by instructions (BSB Rule C2.R2). This also applies to drafting a confidential document for submission to a mediator.

6.34 A barrister instructed in a mediation must not knowingly or recklessly mislead the mediator or any party or their representative (BSB Rule C2.R2). This obligation is quite wide, and taken with other duties outlined above means effectively that ADR processes should not be conducted in a dishonest way. A lawyer cannot say anything to the mediator, expert or evaluator that he or she knows or suspects is not true (BSB Rule C2.R2) even if the client wishes this to be done in order to have a stronger bargaining position over the opposing party (BSB Rule C3.R6). A solicitor acting in this way is likely to commit a breach of SRA Principles 1, 2, and 6.

6.35 It is likely under these rules that a lawyer cannot withhold information which may be detrimental to a client's case if the failure to disclose it renders false and misleading related information that has been communicated to the mediator and the opposing party and on which they have been asked to rely. It is less clear that there is any duty to correct a misunderstanding an opposing party may have formed, though this may be open to debate in some circumstances.

6.36 If the mediator or other neutral in an ADR process has grounds to believe that a position is being misrepresented or that information given is not accurate, those concerns should be expressed to the party. The mediator is also likely to warn the party and the lawyers of the dangers of misrepresenting the position either positively or by concealing information that renders untrue or misleading a position they adopted in the mediation. If appropriate, a halt will be called to the process. Any lawyer supplying false information may be reported to the appropriate professional body and face disciplinary proceedings.

6.37 A lawyer will not be acting with integrity if he or she knows that the lay client is engaging in a non-adjudicative ADR process with an improper motive (such as to gain information about the other side's case or delay the eventual resolution of the matter by litigation) rather than with the intention of genuinely attempting to reach a settlement.

6.38 The matters discussed in 6.39–6.76 below are also relevant to a lawyer instructed to act for a client in a mediation.

F SPECIFIC DUTIES IN NEGOTIATION

6.39 A lawyer must take care not to mislead the opponent in direct negotiations. A barrister must not engage in conduct that is discreditable, or which would diminish public confidence in the profession (BSB Core Duty 5). Similar duties are imposed on solicitors by SRA Principles 1, 2, and 6.

The different strategies and tactics that may be used in negotiation are dealt with in Chapter 11. A competitive strategy may involve bluff, or sometimes what amounts to threats. There are grey areas about how far it is acceptable to go, but in broad terms in negotiating with the opposing party, a lawyer should not: 6.40

- pretend to have evidence if this is not the case;
- misrepresent the evidence;
- indicate that it is the client's final offer if it is not;
- indicate that he/she has instructions on a matter if this is not the case;
- indicate that he/she has no instructions on a matter if this is not the case;
- conceal information that should properly be disclosed;
- provide information that the lawyer knows or believes to be false or misleading;
- threaten the other side with improper adverse consequences if they do not accept the client's position/offer;
- make a clear threat that is nothing to do with the issues in the case, eg to report the client or the other side to the tax authorities on the basis of accounts produced in a case.

If an opponent in a negotiation appears to be behaving in an unethical way, the behaviour should be challenged. This does not need to be confrontational, but should be done in a way that diffuses any possible benefit from the behaviour. For example: 'What you just said sounded a bit like a threat and I don't think that will help us to move forward. What is your argument on the law on this point?' 6.41

Any allegation or contention that a barrister puts forward in face-to-face negotiations must also be properly arguable. The lawyer should not advance a claim that is so lacking in merit that it is not properly arguable. The lawyer should only assert an allegation of fraud or dishonest conduct if there are clear instructions to do so and reasonably credible evidence that establishes a prima facie case of fraud. 6.42

G THE DUTY OF CONFIDENTIALITY

Introduction

Privacy can be one of the main attractions of an ADR process. Whereas litigation normally takes place in open court, ADR processes are private. There is no absolute right of privacy for ADR processes. Privacy depends on several concepts, some of which have been developed in relation to litigation. Privacy in ADR processes is maintained by the following principles discussed in this chapter: 6.43

- professional duties imposed on lawyers to maintain confidentiality;
- any contractual agreement between the parties;
- by the principle of legal professional privilege;
- by the privilege from disclosure of oral or written communications made with the intention of seeking a settlement (the without prejudice rule). The rule applies to settlement discussions in both non-adjudicative and adjudicative ADR processes.

While these concepts are very useful, they create drawbacks as well as advantages. Problems may arise in particular if: 6.44

- the ADR process breaks down and a party would like to use something revealed in later litigation;
- what happened during the ADR process is open to later dispute eg as regards the terms agreed;

- there is an attempt to call anyone involved in the ADR process as a witness in later proceedings.

6.45 The principles relating to confidentiality are still being developed in relation to ADR. Whilst these developments are mentioned in outline in this chapter, reference should be made to 14.120–14.145 for a more detailed consideration of these topics in the context of mediation.

The extent of the duty

6.46 As explained above, SRA Principle 1 provides that solicitors must act in the client's best interests and this includes observing the duty of confidentiality owed to the client. Chapter 4 of the Code of Conduct states 'Protection of confidential information is a fundamental feature of your relationship with clients. It exists as a concept both as a matter of law [from the concept of legal professional privilege] and as a matter of conduct. This duty continues despite the end of the retainer and even after the death of the client'. The SRA Code provides that solicitors must achieve the following outcomes:

- keep the affairs of the clients confidential unless disclosure is required or permitted by law or the client consents (Outcome 4.1);
- ensure that where the duty of confidentiality to one client comes into conflict with the duty of disclosure to another client, the duty of confidentiality takes precedence (Outcome 4.3);
- there are effective systems and controls in place to enable the solicitor to identify risks to client confidentiality and to mitigate those risks (Outcome 4.5).

6.47 A similar duty of confidentiality is imposed on a barrister. A barrister has a duty to keep the affairs of each client confidential (BSB Core Duty 6), and this is supported by guidance which provides that the duty of confidentiality is central to the administration of justice, such that clients who put their confidence in their legal advisers must be able to do so in the knowledge that the information they give, or which is given on their behalf, will remain confidential (BSB Guidance C3.G7–C3.G10). A barrister must protect the confidentiality of a client's affairs, except where disclosure is required by law, or the client gives informed consent (BSB Rule C3.R1).

Confidentiality in mediation

6.48 The confidentiality of mediation is based on contractual agreement and on the 'without prejudice' principle. Communications that take place between the parties themselves, and between each party and the mediator should not be revealed to the court (if agreement is not reached) or a third party, whether or not settlement is reached in that process.

6.49 A separate duty of confidentiality exists in mediation where communications take place between a party and the mediator in private meetings. These communications are confidential unless the disclosing party agrees otherwise. The mediator owes a separate and enforceable duty of confidentiality to each party in relation to information communicated to him or her during these private meetings, and this is usually reinforced by the terms of the mediation agreement and the Code of Conduct governing the mediator's conduct.

6.50 The confidentiality of communications in mediation is not absolute. Communications taking place in mediation can be disclosed in the following circumstances (discussed in more detail in 14.138–14.148):

- The court may order disclosure where it is in the interests of justice to do so, and may override confidentiality in the following circumstances. The parties may agree, by the terms of the Mediation Agreement, that the mediator is not bound by the obligation of confidentiality in some or all of these circumstances:

- Where one party seeks to set aside a settlement agreement reached in mediation on the grounds of economic duress (see *Farm Assist Ltd (in Liquidation) v Secretary of State for the Environment, Food and Rural Affairs* [2009] BLR 399);
- where a claim is being brought against a mediator for misconduct or negligence in the mediation;
- where there is a risk of harm to any person, including children;
- to determine whether a settlement was reached at mediation (see *Brown v Rice* [2007] EWHC 625);
- to prevent the committing of a criminal act;
- where there is a statutory duty to disclose information, for example under the Proceeds of Crime Act 2002.

• In mediations in cross-border disputes, confidentiality can be overridden in the circumstances set out in CPR r 78.26 (see 19.41–19.49).

• An express confidentiality clause in the mediation agreement binds all parties to the agreement, including the mediator, so the parties cannot waive confidentiality if the mediator wishes to maintain it (see *Farm Assist Ltd (in liquidation) v Secretary of State for the Environment Food and Rural Affairs* [2009] EWHC 1102). However, confidentiality may be waived in the following circumstances:
  - The parties agree it is important that a public rather than a private meeting takes place during the mediation to air issues which affect a number of interested parties (eg where mediation occurs in a planning or environmental dispute).
  - The parties want a provision of their settlement agreement to be made public (eg in regulatory matters, or where the provision of a public apology is part of the agreement made).
  - The parties agree that confidential information given to a mediator during a private meeting can be revealed to the opposing party.

Confidentiality in Early Neutral Evaluation and Expert Determination

Confidential information can be provided to an expert in expert determination or to an evaluator in early neutral evaluation unless the parties agree that this should not be done (see Chapters 22 and 24). However, it is generally unwise for confidential information to be provided by one party to the expert or evaluator where a decision or evaluation has to be issued with reasons. In such cases, the expert (or evaluator by analogy) should summarize the information provided in private so that all parties can ascertain the information relied upon in reaching the decision or evaluation (*Halifax Life Ltd v Equitable Life Assurance Society* [2007] 1 Lloyd's Rep 528) (see Chapter 24). Private communications, whether oral or written, between one party and the evaluator or determiner may give rise to the appearance of impartiality or lack of neutrality. **6.51**

Confidentiality in adjudicative processes such as arbitration and adjudication

Arbitration and adjudication are confidential processes and this is often a reason for choosing these processes rather than litigation, which is carried on publicly. Confidentiality is often reinforced by an express clause to maintain confidentiality in the arbitration agreement or the applicable Arbitration Rules. The Court of Appeal has upheld the confidentiality of arbitration proceedings in *Ali Shipping Corp v Shipyard Trogir* [1999] 1 WLR 314. The duty of confidentiality is likely to extend to all documents produced in or prepared for the arbitration (see *Dolling-Baker v Merrett* [1990] 1 WLR 1205). **6.52**

6.53 However, confidentiality of the process is not absolute. There are exceptions, and these were noted by the Court of Appeal in *Emmott v Michael Wilson & Partners Ltd* 1 Lloyd's Rep 233, and see also *Westwood Shipping Lines Inc v Universal Schiffartsgesellschaft MBH* [2012] EWCA 3837 (Comm). These exceptions permit disclosure of confidential communications made during the process in the following circumstances (although the category of exceptions should not be regarded as closed):

- the parties consent to disclosure;
- the court orders disclosure;
- disclosure is required in the public interest, for example to prevent physical harm to a person, or to prevent the commission of a criminal offence;
- disclosure is necessary to protect the legitimate interests of a party to the arbitration;
- there is a statutory duty to disclose information such as under the Proceeds of Crime Act 2002;
- disclosure is necessary to protect a party's legal rights;
- the parties expressly or impliedly waive confidentiality.

6.54 In adjudicative processes, unlike mediation, it is not generally possible for one party to place confidential information before the tribunal that has not been disclosed to the other side or to have private meetings with the tribunal. To enable private and confidential meetings and communications to take place between a party and the adjudicator would offend the rules of natural justice and due process.

H LEGAL PROFESSIONAL PRIVILEGE

6.55 Legal professional privilege applies to communications between a lawyer and client made for the purposes of giving or receiving legal advice: *Three Rivers District Council v Bank of England (No 5)* [2003] QB 1556. Privilege applies to the giving of advice on what should be done, and should therefore include advice on ADR options, so long as obtaining legal advice is the dominant purpose of the communication. Note that legal advice privilege only extends to communications between lawyers and their clients, and not communications from other professional people, even if their advice relates to legal matters, *R (Prudential plc) v Special Commissioner of Income Tax* [2013] UKSC 1. Where a mass of different reports are prepared which may at least partly have management functions, it may be difficult to show that the reports are privileged, *Transport for Greater Manchester v Thales Transport & Security Ltd* [2013] EWHC 149 (TCC).

6.56 Legal professional privilege can be waived by the parties and it can be lost by inadvertent disclosure (see *Guinness Peat Properties Ltd v Fitzroy Robinson Partnership* [1987] 1 WLR 1027).

I WITHOUT PREJUDICE COMMUNICATIONS

6.57 In litigation, all communications passing between the parties, whether orally or in writing, which are made in an attempt to settle a dispute, are protected from disclosure in both the present and in any subsequent proceedings between the same parties and connected with the same subject matter: *Cutts v Head* [1984] Ch 290. Public policy operates to protect those communications from being disclosed to third parties: *Rush and*

Tompkins Ltd v Greater London Council [1989] AC 1280. The strength of this principle has been reasserted by the courts: *Ofulue v Bossert* [2009] 1 AC 990.

The without prejudice rule will prevent disclosure of communications aimed at settling a dispute, even if litigation has not yet begun, the relevant question being whether both parties contemplated or might reasonably have contemplated litigation if they could not agree: *Barnetson v Framlington Group Ltd* [2007] 1 WLR 2443. Communications are protected from disclosure whether or not the word 'without privilege' is used, provided the communications are genuinely aimed at settlement of a dispute. **6.58**

The rule is founded on the public policy of encouraging litigants to settle their differences rather than litigate. They should not be discouraged by the knowledge that anything said in negotiations may be used to their prejudice in the course of proceedings. They should be able to put their cards on the table, without fear that any statements made in settlement negotiations might be used against them later. The rule therefore enables the parties to conduct negotiations freely, in the knowledge that they can make concessions and offers and change their positions in settlement discussions, without these matters being used against them in the litigation if settlement is not reached. **6.59**

The court will not dissect negotiations in order to isolate statements that will be admissible from those that are not. That would give rise to practical problems and would undermine the whole purpose of without prejudice communications: *Unilever Plc v Procter & Gamble Co* [2000] 1 WLR 2436 and *Williams v Hull* [2009] EWHC 2844 (Ch). **6.60**

The rule has no application to communications sent on an open basis, such as those sent to discuss payment in relation to an admitted claim, rather than to negotiate a compromise in respect of a disputed liability: *Bradford & Bingley Plc v Rashid* [2006] 1 WLR 2066. **6.61**

In the following cases, the without prejudice rule is protected by rules of court or by statute: **6.62**

- Communications between the parties and a conciliation officer in employment cases are protected from disclosure (s 18(7) of the Employment Tribunals Act 1996).
- Private law family cases concerning children, in court conciliation led by the judge in collaboration with the Cafcass officer and any mediator will be protected from disclosure in any subsequent hearing before another judge (see *Myerson v Myerson* [2008] EWCA Civ 1376 and FPR 2010, PD 12B). The same approach will apply to settlement discussions that are explored with a judge in financial remedies cases.

The without prejudice rule gives rise to the widest potential protection for communications in an ADR process. The principles have been developed to apply to settlement attempts during litigation, but they clearly apply to mediation (see 14.123–14.135 for more detail in relation to mediation). It is likely that the principles also apply where the parties attempt to reach a negotiated settlement during an adjudicative ADR process. It has been held that a meeting between lawyers on opposing sides to discuss 'battle tactics' will not be protected, *Stax Claimants v Bank of Nova Scotia Channel Islands Ltd* [2007] EWHC 1153 (Ch). **6.63**

It should be noted that the privilege belongs to the parties only, so if the parties wish to waive it, the mediator or evaluator or expert determiner or the adjudicator or arbitrator cannot rely on it to protect communications aimed at settlement. However, third parties may be able to rely on the separate concept of confidentiality discussed in 6.43–6.54 above to prevent disclosure. **6.64**

Exceptions to the without prejudice communications rule

6.65 The rule is not an absolute one and there are a limited number of situations when without prejudice communications can be disclosed to the court in the interests of justice. The main exceptions are as follows:

- to determine whether a settlement was reached, or to prove the terms of the settlement: *Walker v Wilsher* [1889] 23 QBD 335 and *Tomlin v Standard Telephones and Cables Ltd* [1969] 1 WLR 1378;
- to assist in the proper interpretation or construction of the terms of an agreement or to ascertain the objective meaning of the parties' intentions (*Oceanbulk Shipping and Trading SA v TMT Asia Ltd* [2010] 1 WLR 1803);
- if rectification of the agreement is required: *Oceanbulk Shipping and Trading SA v TMT Asia Ltd* [2010] 1 WLR 1803;
- to determine whether any settlement agreement apparently reached during the negotiations should be set aside on the grounds of misrepresentation, fraud, or undue influence (see *Unilever Plc v Procter & Gamble* [2000] 1 WLR 2436);
- even if there is no concluded settlement agreement, communications may be admissible to show that a statement was made by one party in negotiations with the intention that the other side should rely on it, and on which they acted, thus giving rise to an estoppel: *Hodgkinson & Corby Ltd v Wards Mobility Services Ltd* [1997] FSR 178 and *Unilever plc v Procter & Gamble Co* [2000] 1 WLR 2436 per Walker LJ at 2443;
- where the rule is being abused eg by threats, dishonest, oppressive or disreputable conduct: *Kitcat v Sharp* [1882] 48 LT 64; *Best Buy Co Inc v Worldwide Sales Corpn Espana SL* [2011] EWCA Civ 618;
- where the rule is being used as a cloak for perjury, blackmail or other 'unambiguous impropriety' (*Unilever plc v Procter & Gamble Co* [2000] 1 WLR 2436). However the privileged nature of the communications will not be lightly lost; an inconsistency between a pleaded case and the stance taken in negotiations will not result in the privilege being revoked, nor will putting forward an implausible case; nothing less than unambiguous impropriety will suffice: *Savings and Investment Bank Ltd v Fincken* [2004] 1 WLR 667; *Berry Trade Ltd v Moussavi (No 3)* [2003] EWCA Civ 715; *Aird & Aird v Prime Meridian* (2006) BLR 105 and see also *AAG Investments Ltd v BAA Airports Ltd* [2010] EWHC 2844 (Comm);
- where there is a risk of serious harm to a child: *Re D (Minors)* [1993] 2 All ER 693.
- in some interim applications to explain delay in commencing or prosecuting litigation, or to obtain relief from sanctions: *Berg v IML London Ltd* [2002] 1 WLR 3271.
- where both parties to the dispute consent to the privilege being waived so that documents can be put before the court, although no inferences should be drawn from a refusal to waive privilege: *Sayers v Clarke Walker* [2002] EWCA Civ 910; *Reed Executive plc v Reed Business Information Ltd* [2004] 1 WLR 3026.
- if the parties have made it clear that the communications can be looked at on the question of costs (for example, by marking the documents 'without prejudice save as to costs'), the court can look at the communications after judgment has been given on liability and before it determines the question of costs: *Cutts v Head* [1984] Ch 290. However the court has no power to look at without prejudice communications on the question of costs unless the parties have negotiated on the basis that they reserve the right to bring the communications to the court on the question of costs, or all parties subsequently agree to waive the privilege: *Reed Executive plc v Reed Business Information Ltd* [2004] 1 WLR 3026.

The categories of exceptions to the without prejudice rule are not closed, but new exceptions have to be consistent with the overall policy that parties should not be discouraged from settling their disputes (see *Woodward v Santander UK plc (formerly Abbey National Plc)* [2010] IRLR 834). **6.66**

J PRACTICAL CONSIDERATIONS

In practical terms, professional duties of confidentiality, contractual provisions for confidentiality in ADR processes, and the without prejudice rule mean that a lawyer should take the utmost care not to: **6.67**

- inadvertently or deliberately reveal private and confidential information relating to their client. This may be a particular risk when negotiating face to face with the other side in the absence of the lay client, when discussions can be fast paced and informal. Lawyers must always guard against revealing something that would be damaging to the client's case during these discussions that ought not to be revealed. If information is revealed by the other side during these negotiations which would assist the lay client's case then this information should be brought to the lay client's attention.
- disclose any information gained during the ADR process or reveal details of what took place during that process to any third party, or to the court (if settlement is not reached);
- reveal information that the client wishes to be kept confidential to the lawyers acting for the opposing parties in any joint meetings that take place during mediation or in direct negotiations. A lawyer should obtain permission from a client in advance to reveal anything protected by legal professional privilege.

Before acting for a client in negotiations and mediation and at all times during those processes, the lawyer must take care to obtain clear instructions from the client about: **6.68**

- the information that the client wishes to withhold from the other side (and, if applicable, from the mediator);
- the information that can be disclosed to the mediator on the basis that the mediator treats the information as confidential;
- any open offers that the client wishes to make to settle the dispute (these will not be protected by the 'without prejudice' rule and will not be treated as confidential information);
- any admission that the lay client is willing to make. An admission is not protected by the 'without prejudice' rule and thus can be disclosed by the other side. It is also important to make sure that the client appreciates the difference between a clear admission and a concession. An admission is an unqualified acceptance of a fact (eg I accept my client must pay for the radios in the sum of £600 as there is no defence to that aspect of the claim). A concession on the other hand is an offer to concede a fact or position in order to reach an overall settlement and without any admission of liability (eg I will agree to pay for the radios if you will waive your claim for the iPods), and is protected by the 'without prejudice' rule.

K DISCLOSURE OF INFORMATION IN ADR PROCESSES

Non-adjudicatory ADR and expert determination

In most non-adjudicatory ADR processes and also expert determination, the parties usually retain control of how much information to put before the mediator, facilitator, neutral **6.69** evaluator, or expert, as formal rules of evidence and procedure do not apply. As a general rule, the parties will disclose information and evidence that is relevant to the dispute and helpful to the case of the disclosing party.

6.70 The difficulty lies in deciding whether information should be disclosed that is adverse to the client's case. In litigation, the parties are required to give appropriate disclosure, the normal standard being disclosure of the documents on which they rely, as well as those that adversely affect their own case, adversely affect another side's case or support another party's case (CPR r 31.6). However, there is no obligation to disclose such documents in advance of the disclosure stage in litigation (unless the documents are required to be disclosed by a pre-action protocol). The party may therefore have a choice whether to make such disclosure in the ADR process.

6.71 The lawyer acting in such cases may be asked to give advice on whether disclosure should be made. The guiding principles are as follows:

- Adverse information may need to be disclosed if failure to do so renders false or misleading some fact or information that has already been disclosed by that party, unless the misleading fact or information can be withdrawn or corrected in some other way.
- Otherwise, however potentially helpful to the opposing party, information will not usually have to be disclosed. The lawyer would not have to disclose, for example, the fact that the lay client is terrified about giving evidence in court and is likely to be a nervous and unimpressive witness (but equally, you could not positively mislead the other side by saying the client is looking forward to the trial and will be a confident witness).

6.72 In order to ensure that a lawyer acts with integrity, and does not knowingly or recklessly mislead anyone, great care will need to be taken in relation to information that is communicated to the mediator and the other side. See in particular 6.33–6.38.

6.73 An ADR process will have most value if the other side can rely on information and representations made to them during the course of the process. Lawyers and parties should be aware of the fact that although any settlement agreement reached during a non-adjudicative ADR process cannot be the subject of appeal, it can be set aside if one or both parties entered into it under a mistake or misrepresentation or because of duress or undue influence.

Adjudication and arbitration

6.74 These processes are more akin to litigation. The parties will usually agree the ambit of disclosure and, in the absence of agreement, the court will determine the scope of disclosure. See Chapters 25–32 for those processes. In practice, the ambit of disclosure tends to be more akin to litigation.

L AUTHORITY TO SETTLE

6.75 Lawyers acting in non-adjudicatory ADR processes must ensure that they:

- have clarified any limitations on their authority to effect a binding settlement agreement with the client in advance. If in doubt, always make it clear to the opposing party that any negotiations are on the basis that no binding agreement can be reached until the lay client's express approval or authorization has been obtained;
- do not exceed the authority given by the client. By virtue of the ostensible authority that a lawyer has as the client's agent, the lawyer can bind the client to an agreement without

actual authority to do so. Doing this would be likely to result in the lawyer being sued for negligence and breach of contract. If a solicitor proceeds with a case in the hope of securing some outcome despite the expressed view of the client that he did not wish to proceed, the solicitor may be liable to pay costs, see *Flatman v Germany* [2013] EWCA Civ 278.

- do not mislead the opposing party or a mediator as to the authority given, for example by representing that he or she has authority to settle the dispute up to the maximum value of the claim (say £1,000,000), when in fact the authority is limited to £500,000.
- understand the 'bottom line' figure below which the client is not prepared to settle the dispute, and the range within which the lay client would be prepared to settle the claim.
- make and keep an accurate note of offers, counter-offers and concessions that may be made during negotiations. Some barristers will ask the lay client to sign a note of an offer before it is made or rejected. This can be a good idea to ensure that there can be no misunderstanding between lawyer and client.

When conducting direct negotiations or acting in mediation, it is preferable to have the client available so that instructions can be obtained in relation to the settlement proposal. It is particularly important to ensure that the lay client or person who has authority to settle the dispute (for example a representative of an insurer) is present at a mediation. The mediation agreement will typically provide that the person signing the agreement on behalf of a party warrants that they have authority to bind that party to the terms of any settlement. **6.76**

M THE RELATIONSHIP BETWEEN BARRISTERS AND THEIR PROFESSIONAL CLIENTS IN ADR

A barrister may be instructed to attend an ADR process such as mediation instead of the instructing solicitor. If this is the case, the barrister must ensure that an accurate record of what occurs during the process is made and kept. The barrister may be asked to make a copy of this attendance note for his instructing solicitors. At the very least, he or she will have to inform the instructing solicitors of the important events that occurred during the process. **6.77**

If a barrister is instructed to attend an ADR process with a solicitor, it will need to be made clear where the division of roles lies between them. For example in a mediation the barrister may be briefed to attend a mediation, to advise on the merits of offers, carry out a re-assessment of the case in the light of information revealed during the process and to draft the settlement agreement, but the solicitor may wish to take the lead in the negotiations. It may be that the solicitor will wish the barrister to assume a lead role in the mediation (which is more usual where counsel is instructed). It is important that all parties are clear about this. In any event, a barrister should always treat the instructing solicitor with courtesy, and listen to their views and opinion with respect. A solicitor should act likewise. **6.78**

A barrister must bear in mind that the primary duty is owed to the lay client rather than the professional client (the instructing solicitor) and must not permit the instructing solicitor to limit the barrister's discretion as to how the interests of the lay client can best be served (BSB Rule C3.R1 and Rule C3.R6). **6.79**

If a barrister forms the view that there is a conflict of interest between the lay client and the instructing solicitor (for example because the barrister considers the instructing solicitor has been negligent), then he or she must consider whether it would be in the lay client's best interests to instruct another professional adviser. If the barrister considers that it would be, **6.80** then the instructing solicitor must be advised about this and take steps to ensure that this advice is brought to the attention of the lay client, if necessary by sending a copy directly to the client as well as to the instructing solicitor (BSB Rule C3.R3 and BSB Guidance C3.G16).

KEY POINTS SUMMARY

6.81
- Lawyers must advise their clients about ADR options, at all stages of the dispute.
- Lawyers can provide an ADR service for clients, provided there is no conflict of interest.
- In ADR processes, lawyers must observe the rules of the Bar Code of Conduct or the SRA Principles and Code of Conduct.
- If the lawyer is acting under a CFA, a DBA, or in a case with third-party funding, care must be taken to ensure that the settlement is in the client's best interests.
- When acting in mediation or negotiation, a lawyer must act within the client's instructions and take care not to:
  - mislead the other side;
  - disclose confidential information to the other side (or the mediator) unless the client consents;
  - reveal the details of the negotiation or what took place in mediation to third parties or to the court;
  - exceed the limits of his authority.
- Mediators are also required to act in accordance with ethical standards, explained at 14.104–14.122.

PART II

THE INTERPLAY BETWEEN ADR, CPR, AND LITIGATION

7

THE APPROACH OF THE COURTS TO ADR

A INTRODUCTION 7.01
B PRE-ACTION PROTOCOLS 7.12
C THE COURT GUIDES 7.32
D THE OVERRIDING OBJECTIVE AND ADR 7.48
E ACTIVE CASE MANAGEMENT AND ADR 7.50
F COSTS MANAGEMENT AND ADR 7.64
G DIRECTION QUESTIONNAIRES AND ADR . . . 7.69
H GRANTING STAYS FOR ADR 7.75
I JUDICIAL ENCOURAGEMENT OF ADR 7.80
J THE APPROACH OF THE COURTS TO CONTRACTUAL ADR CLAUSES 7.83
K CAN THE COURT COMPEL THE PARTIES TO USE ADR? 7.94
Key points summary 7.109

A INTRODUCTION

ADR has grown at a rapid rate in the last 20 years, initially mainly in America and Australia, but then also in the UK and throughout Europe as a direct response to the cost and delay that were the main criticisms of litigation systems. Several comprehensive empirical studies carried out in the USA showed that those who used ADR processes enjoyed substantial savings in costs in comparison to those incurred in litigation, a speedier resolution of the dispute and a more satisfactory outcome for the parties. The historical background to ADR is set out in more detail in Chapter 1. **7.01**

In the UK, although the Supreme Court Rules and the County Court Rules (the predecessors to the Civil Procedure Rules (CPR)) did not promote ADR, the courts started to do so from about the mid-1990s onwards. The Commercial Court and the High Court required lawyers to consider with their clients the possibility of resolving the dispute by mediation, conciliation, or otherwise and to ensure that parties were fully informed about the most cost-effective means of resolving their dispute (*Practice Note: Commercial Court: Alternative Dispute Resolution* [1994] 1 All ER 34; *Practice Note (Civil Litigation): Case Management* [1995] 1 All ER 385). **7.02**

However, the main growth in ADR in recent years has occurred as a direct result of the Woolf Reforms and the introduction of the CPR on 26 April 1999. **7.03**

In the final Access to Justice Report of 1996, Lord Woolf regarded delay and expense as the twin scourges of the civil justice system. One of his aims was to encourage a less adversarial approach to litigation by encouraging co-operation between the parties and the ethos that litigation should be seen as the last and not the first resort in the attempt to settle a dispute. Parties should settle their dispute before resorting to the courts wherever possible. Where litigation could not be avoided, then the parties should attempt to settle their dispute at the earliest possible stage in the litigation. **7.04**

The Woolf reforms placed ADR at the centre of the civil justice system and the spirit of the CPR is that ADR should be the primary method for resolving a dispute, with litigation the **7.05** last resort. It is therefore not surprising that since the CPR came into force in April 1999 there has been a marked increase in the use of ADR processes, particularly mediation, both before and after the issue of proceedings. There has been a corresponding increase in the number of ADR service providers and the number of lawyers being trained as mediators.

7.06 This trend is set to continue following the implementation of the Jackson Review of Civil Litigation Costs, Final Report, which came into effect on 1 April 2013. In the Final Report, Lord Justice Jackson reported that 'ADR, particularly mediation, has a vital role to play in reducing the costs of civil disputes by fomenting the early settlement of cases. The aim is that no case should come to trial without the parties having undertaken some form of ADR in an attempt to settle the case. Parties should be encouraged to settle their case before proceedings are issued and, if that is not possible, they should attempt settlement at the earliest possible stage in the litigation.'

7.07 On 1 April 2013, a major package of reforms came into effect in civil litigation. Two of these reforms, in particular, have major implications for ADR: firstly the changes made to the legal aid scheme, which substantially reduced the availability of legal aid for civil and family litigation; and secondly the amendments to the CPR to implement the Costs Review Final Report.

7.08 In relation to the costs reforms, the limitations on the availability of legal aid (and consequential increase in Litigants in Person), as well as the fact that since 1 April 2013, Success Fees and After the Event (ATE) insurance premiums are no longer recoverable from the losing party in most cases, and instead must be paid by the winning party out of any damages they recover in the action (see Chapter 4), are likely to result in the robust encouragement of ADR by the courts. Although contingency fees are now lawful in the form of DBAs, so far these have proved to be unpopular. Claimants in personal injury cases are now protected by Qualified One Way Costs Shifting (QOCS) which, in most cases, will mean that orders for costs against such a claimant can be enforced without the permission of the court only to the extent that the costs do not exceed the damages and interest recovered. If such claimants recover no damages at all, unless certain limited exceptions apply, no costs order can be enforced against them (see CPR rr 44.13 to 44.17). Therefore, if such claimants lose their cases, they will not have to contribute towards defendants' costs. In addition, following consultation by the Ministry of Justice, a sweeping reform of civil court fees has been implemented with effect from 22 April 2014 (see Civil Proceedings Fees (Amendment) Order 2014 (SI 201/874)). These reforms to court fees were introduced because the Government considered it was untenable for the taxpayer to continue to subsidize deficits in court income. These changes have resulted in issue fees for claims between £3,000 and £50,000 almost doubling in cost, and with significant increases in fees for most other cases and applications. The government also proposes to remove hearing fee refunds (although it is also planned to make hearing fees payable closer to the hearing date). These reforms will put an even greater onus on parties to resolve their disputes out of court and as early as possible.

7.09 Furthermore, since 1 April 2013, judges have been given more rigorous powers to enable them to actively manage cases and the new concept of judicial costs management was introduced in multi-track cases (and any other proceedings where the court so orders). These provisions require the court to actively engage in both case management and costs management at all stages of the action so as to further the overriding objective. All of these changes make it more important than ever before to use ADR to resolve disputes.

7.10 The encouragement to parties to use ADR to resolve their dispute comes from a variety of means set out below, all of which are considered in this chapter

- pre-action protocols;
- court guides;

- the court's inquiry at track allocation stage whether ADR could be employed;
- case management ADR orders;
- the court's willingness to grant a stay for ADR to be considered and used;
- judicial encouragement for ADR as developed in case law;
- the willingness of the courts to uphold and enforce ADR clauses in a contract.

In addition, the courts and the government have encouraged the use of ADR in other ways, which are discussed in other chapters of this book. In particular: **7.11**

- the government's pledge to use ADR to resolve disputes involving government departments or agencies where it is appropriate to do so (see 1.29);
- the government's continuing policy initiatives to promote alternative methods of dispute resolution so that the courts are the last resort for those involved in civil or family disputes (considered in Chapters 1 and 4);
- the court's willingness to make adverse costs orders or other sanctions against a party who unreasonably refuses to consider ADR (considered in Chapter 8);
- proposals to develop and regulate ODR for consumers (see Chapter 5);
- the promotion of ADR, in particular mediation, by the European Union and the issue of a Directive regulating the use of mediation in cross-border cases and the implementation of these provisions by the government (see Chapter 19);
- the establishment and promotion of court mediation schemes (see Chapter 18) and judicial evaluation schemes (see Chapter 22) and the development of the Civil Mediation Online Directory, which replaced the National Mediation Helpline with effect from 1 October 2011 (see 18.31–18.33).
- the promotion of the use of ADR by parties using Tribunals by HM Courts and Tribunals Service. The use of ADR is now widely promoted to parties using the Upper Tribunal (Lands Chamber) and the Employment Tribunal.

B PRE-ACTION PROTOCOLS

Under the CPR, protocols were introduced to set out the steps that the parties should follow before issuing proceedings, as part of reasonable pre-action conduct. These marked a very significant change in the culture that had prevailed in litigation prior to the CPR. **7.12**

There are currently 14 specific protocols relating to personal injury claims, low value personal injury claims in road traffic accidents, low value personal injury (employers' liability and public liability) claims, disease and illness claims, clinical disputes, obtaining hospital medical records, housing disrepair, defamation, judicial review, professional negligence, construction and engineering disputes, possession claims based on rent arrears, possession claims in respect of mortgage or home purchase plan arrears in residential property, and the Pre-Action Protocol for Claims for Damages in Relation to the Physical State of Commercial Property at Termination of a Tenancy (the 'Dilapidations Protocol'). There is also an overarching Practice Direction – Pre-Action Conduct that applies in all cases, including those that have no specific protocol. **7.13**

Practice Direction – Pre-Action Conduct

The aims of the Practice Direction (PD) – Pre-Action Conduct are to enable parties to settle disputes without the need to start proceedings, and to enable proceedings to be efficiently managed by the court and the parties if litigation cannot be avoided. These aims are achieved by encouraging the parties to exchange information and consider using ADR (see paras 1.1 and 1.2). **7.14**

In cases not subject to a particular protocol

7.15 Proceedings should only be started as a matter of last resort, and they should not be commenced if a settlement is still being actively explored. Although ADR is not compulsory, the parties should consider whether some form of ADR process should be used before starting proceedings, and the court may require evidence that the parties considered ADR (PD – Pre-Action Conduct, para 8.1). ADR procedures can include negotiation and discussion, mediation, early neutral evaluation, or arbitration. The parties should also explore settlement at all times, even after proceedings have been issued, and up to and during any trial or final hearing (see para 8.4).

7.16 Unless the circumstances make it inappropriate (eg because the limitation period is about to expire), the parties should exchange sufficient information about the matters in dispute to enable them to understand each other's position and make informed decisions about settlement and how to proceed. They should also make appropriate attempts to resolve the matter without commencing proceedings, and in particular consider the use of an appropriate ADR process in order to do so (see para 6.1). The parties should act in a reasonable and proportionate manner in all dealings with one another. In particular, the costs incurred in complying should be proportionate to the complexity of the matter and any money at stake (para 6.2).

7.17 Before starting proceedings, the claimant should send the defendant a detailed letter before claim and the defendant should send the claimant a detailed response (paras 7.1 and 7.2). The letter before claim and the defendant's response should contain the information set out in Annex A in respect of the substantive issues in the claim, and should set out the form of ADR that the claimant considers suitable and invite the defendant to agree to this (Annex A, para 2.2(2)). As well as dealing with the substantive claim, the defendant's response should indicate whether the defendant agrees to the claimant's proposals for ADR and, if not, it should state why not, and suggest an alternative form of ADR or give reasons why ADR is not appropriate (Annex A, para 4.2(4)).

7.18 The court will expect the parties to comply with the Practice Direction and any applicable protocol, and may ask them to explain what steps have been taken prior to the start of the claim. Where a party has failed to comply, the court may ask that party for an explanation (see para 4.2).

In all cases

7.19 If expert evidence is required, the parties should consider how best to minimize expense (see para 9.4 and Annex C). The claimant is required to state in the claim form or the particulars of claim whether he has complied with the requirements of the PD – Pre-Action Conduct and any relevant protocol (see para 9.7). The defendant will have to admit or deny this statement in the defence (he cannot require the claimant to prove it because it will be within the defendant's knowledge whether there was compliance or not). This therefore makes the reasonableness of the pre-action conduct one of the issues in the case that the court will consider in making case management directions, orders about costs, and other sanctions for non-compliance (see Chapter 8).

The pre-action protocols

The general position

7.20 All of the protocols have the same common purpose, which is to:

- encourage pre-action conduct between the parties;
- encourage the early exchange of information about the issues in dispute;

- encourage the parties to use ADR processes to settle the dispute before proceedings are issued; and
- enable proceedings to run to the court's timetable and efficiently if litigation cannot be avoided.

Although the precise detail varies a little from protocol to protocol, all of them have the same general requirements in relation to the substantive dispute. The relevant protocol should be consulted for details of precise requirements in each case. In general terms: **7.21**

- The claimant should give early notification of the claim to the defendant.
- The claimant should send the defendant a detailed letter before claim before issuing proceedings, which gives sufficient information about the claim and the remedies sought.
- The defendant should be given a reasonable time to investigate the claim and respond (this can range from seven days to three months or perhaps more in complex claims).
- The defendant should send a detailed letter of response, indicating whether the claim (including the remedies sought) is disputed in whole or in part.
- The parties should give early disclosure of relevant documents.
- They should co-operate by jointly selecting (or jointly instructing) experts.

All of the protocols encourage the use of ADR, and cover whether to make an offer to settle, including a Part 36 offer (see 4.58–4.62). All of them require the parties to consider whether some form of ADR would be more suitable than litigation and, if so, endeavour to agree which form to adopt. The parties may be required to provide evidence that ADR was considered, and if the terms of the relevant protocol are not followed, the court must have regard to such conduct when making case management orders and determining sanctions and costs. However, all of the protocols recognize that no party can be forced to mediate or enter into any form of ADR. **7.22**

The Pre-action Protocol for Possession Claims based on Mortgage or Home Purchase Plan Arrears in Respect of Residential Property

This protocol was amended with effect from 6 April 2011 to provide that starting a possession claim should normally be seen as a last resort, and such a claim must not normally be started unless all other reasonable attempts to resolve the matter have failed. The protocol sets out a number of actions that the parties should consider taking to resolve the matter, including extending the term of the mortgage, changing the type of mortgage, deferring payment of the interest or capitalizing the arrears, voluntary sale by the mortgagor, or applying for support for mortgage interest to the Department of Work and Pensions. The parties must be able to explain to the court the actions that they have taken to comply with the Protocol (see paras 7.1–9.1 of the protocol). **7.23**

The Pre-action Protocol for Construction and Engineering Disputes

This protocol applies to all professional negligence disputes against building professionals. Although this protocol has the same general aims of all of the others, it is unique in requiring the parties to have a pre-action meeting within 28 days of receipt of the defendant's letter of response (or, where there is a counterclaim, within 28 days of the claimant's response to the counterclaim) (see para 5.1). The aim of the meeting is for the parties to agree the main issues in the case, to identify the cause of disagreement in respect of each issue, to consider how the issues might be resolved without litigation and, if litigation is unavoidable, how it can be conducted in accordance with the overriding objective (see 7.48 for the meaning of the overriding objective). In such cases there may be a need for more than one meeting. **7.24**

7.25 The court will normally expect the meeting to be attended by the parties, representatives who have authority to settle the dispute, legal representatives, a representative of insurers and a representative of any relevant third parties (such as sub-contractors) (see para 5.3 of the protocol). Any party who attended a pre-action meeting is at liberty to disclose to the court:

- the fact that the meeting took place;
- when and who attended the meeting;
- the identity of anyone who refused to attend and the grounds for the refusal;
- reasons why the meeting did not take place (if that was the case);
- any agreement reached between the parties; and
- whether any form of ADR was considered or agreed.

7.26 Otherwise the pre-action meeting is to be regarded as 'without prejudice' (see paras 5.6 and 5.7) and the detail of any discussions at the meeting or any note of the meeting cannot be referred to the court unless all parties agree.

Family proceedings

7.27 The Family Procedure Rules 2010 ('FPR') and supporting Practice Directions came into force on 6 April 2011. They are very closely modelled on the CPR and set out a comprehensive and unified set of rules for all family proceedings in the High Court and the Family Court. The FPR, by Part 3 and PD 3A, were instrumental in providing that a Mediation Information and Assessment Meeting (MIAM) should take place, except in very limited circumstances, before making any application to the court in any private law proceedings relating to children and in proceedings for a financial remedy. The MIAM is a meeting between the parties and a mediator to consider whether the dispute can be resolved by mediation and/or other forms of dispute resolution instead of litigation.

7.28 By s 10 of the Children and Families Act 2014, which came into force on 22 April 2014, the requirement to attend a MIAM has been put on a statutory footing. Section 10 provides that before making a relevant family application to the Family Court (that being defined, by s.10(3), as an application in or to initiate family proceedings), a person must attend a MIAM. By s 10(3) of the 2014 Act, a MIAM is defined as a meeting held for the purposes of enabling information to be provided about mediation, the way in which family disputes can be resolved otherwise than by the court, and the suitability of mediation or any other such way of resolving disputes. The FPR 2010, in particular Part 3, have been revised and replaced, from 22 April 2014, to give effect to these provisions by the Family Procedure (Amendment No 3) Rules 2014.

7.29 Part 3 of the FPR 2010, as amended, sets out the court's powers to encourage the parties to use ADR (now known as non-court dispute resolution in the Family Court) and to facilitate its use. This is supplemented by PD 3A, The Pre-Application Protocol for Mediation Information and Assessment. The court must consider, at every stage of the proceedings, whether non-court dispute resolution is appropriate (FPR r 3.3(1)). In considering whether a non-court dispute resolution is appropriate, the court must take into account whether a MIAM took place, whether a valid MIAM exception was claimed or mediator's exemption was confirmed, and whether the parties attempted mediation or another form of non-court dispute resolution and the outcome of that process. If the court considers that non-court dispute resolution is appropriate, it can adjourn the proceedings for such time as it thinks appropriate to enable the parties to obtain information and advice about non-court dispute resolution or to enable it to take place (FPR r 3.4(1)).

7.30 The requirement to hold a MIAM applies to any application to initiate private law proceedings relating to children, or proceedings for a financial remedy which are specified in FPR, PD 3A. There are a limited number of circumstances in which a MIAM need not be held, such as cases of domestic violence, child protection cases, urgency where there is a risk to life, liberty, or safety of the applicant or a child or a member of the family, or a MIAM has been held within the previous four months in relation to the issues in dispute (see FPR r 3.8(1)). An authorized mediator can also grant an exemption by confirming that mediation is not suitable either at all or because the respondents are unwilling or have failed to attend a MIAM (FPR r 3.8(2)). An application to initiate any proceedings must contain a confirmation from an authorized family mediator that the prospective applicant has attended a MIAM, or that one of the exemptions applies or that a mediator's exemption applies. The court has power to enquire into whether an exemption has been validly claimed, and if it finds that an exemption does not apply, it can direct the parties to attend a MIAM and adjourn the proceedings until that takes place (FPR r 3.10). Further detail about mediation in family cases can be found in Chapter 18.

There is also a Pre-Action Protocol for financial remedies cases (FPR, PD 9A). This protocol is similar to the protocols introduced under the CPR in its general objectives and aims of requiring an early exchange of information between the parties and early consideration of ADR. **7.31**

C THE COURT GUIDES

There are a number of specialist court guides, each of which contains guidance relating to the use of ADR. The main guides are as follows: **7.32**

- *The Admiralty and Commercial Courts Guide* (9th edn, 2011, as updated in October 2011, March 2012, March 2013, and April 2014);
- *The Chancery Guide* (7th edn, October 2013, amended December 2013 and February 2014);
- *The Queen's Bench Division Guide* (2007);
- *The Technology and Construction Court Guide* (2nd edn, revised October 2010).

The Admiralty and Commercial Courts Guide

Section G of the guide encourages the parties to consider the use of ADR to resolve their dispute or issues within it. It requires legal representatives to consider with their clients and the other parties involved whether their dispute, or particular issues in it, could be resolved through ADR (para G1.4). Parties who consider that ADR is appropriate can apply to the court for directions at any stage, including before service of the defence and before the case management conference (para G1.5). **7.33**

All parties attending a case management conference must complete and file a detailed case management information sheet which is set out in Appendix 6 of the guide. This requires the parties to answer the following specific questions about ADR (see paras 18 and 19 of the Case Management Information Sheet): **7.34**

(a) Might some form of Alternative Dispute Resolution procedure assist to resolve or narrow the dispute or particular issues in it?
(b) Has the question at (a) been considered between the client and legal representatives (including the advocate(s) retained)?
(c) Has the question at (a) been explored with the other parties in the case?
(d) Do you request that the case is adjourned while the parties try to settle the case by Alternative Dispute Resolution or other means?
(e) Would an ADR order in the form of Appendix 7 to the Commercial Court Guide be appropriate?
(f) Are there any other special directions needed to allow for Alternative Dispute Resolution?

7.35 If the parties ask the court to hold the case management conference on paper (which rarely is appropriate in the Commercial and Admiralty Courts), then the documentation to be lodged with the court must include a statement signed by each advocate which sets out information about any steps that had been taken to resolve the dispute by ADR, any future plans for ADR or an explanation why ADR would not be appropriate (see para D8.3(e)).

7.36 At any case management conference, the judge can invite the parties to use ADR, and he may adjourn the case for a specified period of time to encourage and enable the parties to use ADR and, in doing so, he may extend the time for the parties to comply with any requirement under the CPR, the guide, or any order of the court. If the court makes an order providing for ADR, it will also consider at which point in the timetable there should be compliance with it. For that purpose it will take into account the likely costs of litigation and ADR and whether the ADR process is likely to be more successful if there has been completion of statements of case, disclosure of documents, the provision of further information under CPR, Part 18 or the exchange of witness statements and expert evidence (paras G1.6 and G1.7). The courts are increasingly prepared to make an order directing a party to disclose documentation or provide further information about their case to assist resolution of the dispute using an ADR process.

7.37 At a case management conference the court may consider that an order directed to encouraging bilateral negotiations between the parties' respective legal representatives is likely to be a more cost-effective and productive route to settlement than that afforded by a formal ADR or early neutral evaluation (ENE) order (see Chapter 22 for ENE). If so, the court will set a date by which there is to be a meeting between the respective solicitors and their respective clients' officials responsible for decision making in relation to the case (see para G1.12).

7.38 An example of an ADR order made in the Commercial Court is set out in Appendix 7 of the Guide (see Figure 7.1). This order has also been followed in other courts.

The Chancery Guide

7.39 The Chancery Division of the High Court similarly encourages the parties to use ADR to resolve their dispute and if they consider ADR to be appropriate, they can apply for directions at any stage (see *The Chancery Guide*, Chapter 17). The court will, in an appropriate case, invite the parties to consider whether their dispute, or particular issues in it, could be resolved through ADR. A judge or master at any case management conference will usually inquire about steps that can usefully be taken to resolve the dispute by settlement negotiations, ADR, or other means. The parties should be in a position to tell the court what steps have been taken or are proposed to be taken (para 17.3). Like the Commercial Court, the Chancery Court will extend the time for compliance with the CPR or court orders to enable ADR to be attempted. In particular, the court will readily grant a short stay at allocation or at any other stage to accommodate mediation or any other form of settlement negotiations. However, the court will not normally grant an open-ended stay for such purposes and if a lengthy stay is granted, it will be on terms that the parties report to the court on a regular basis in respect of their negotiations (see para 3.3 of the guide). Appendix 3 of the guide contains draft case management directions, and the parties are required to make use of these when drafting proposed directions for submission to the court.

7.40 Figure 7.2 shows a typical ADR order that may be made in the Chancery Division.

7.41 In the Chancery Modernisation Review: Final Report, December 2013, Sir Michael Briggs concluded that there were compelling reasons why the court should take a more active role in the encouragement, facilitation, and management of dispute resolution. Firstly, it would encourage

Figure 7.1 An example of an ADR order in the Commercial Court

IN THE HIGH COURT OF JUSTICE 2014 Folio 276
COMMERCIAL COURT

BETWEEN

BEELER ENGINEERING PAGE PLC

Claimant

and

GREEN AND MORROW LIMITED

Defendant

IT IS ORDERED THAT:

1. On or before 6th October 2014, the parties shall exchange lists of 3 neutrals or individuals who are available to conduct ADR procedures before 24th November 2014.
2. On or before 13th October 2014 the parties shall in good faith endeavour to agree a neutral individual or panel from the lists so exchanged and provided.
3. Failing such agreement by 4pm on 20th October 2014 the Case Management Conference will be restored to enable the Court to facilitate agreement on a neutral individual or panel.
4. The parties shall take such serious steps as they may be advised to resolve their disputes by ADR procedures before the neutral individual or panel so chosen by no later than 4 pm on 24th November 2014.
5. If the case is not settled by 24th November 2014, the parties shall inform the court by letter by 1st December 2014 what steps towards ADR have been taken and (without prejudice to matters of privilege) why such steps have failed. If the parties have failed to initiate ADR procedures the Case Management Conference is to be restored for further consideration of the case.
6. Costs in the case.

Dated 22nd September 2014.

a more widespread appreciation that ADR must be treated as an integral part of the process, rather than an optional extra. Secondly, it would enable the court and the parties to build ADR into the process both by identifying the most appropriate time for it to be undertaken and by ensuring that, at that time, the parties are not so heavily engaged in compliance with directions for trial preparation that ADR has to be left on one side. Thirdly, the court could adapt its case management directions in ways that would maximize the likelihood of a successful outcome of ADR, for example by ensuring that parties have the requisite information for effective ADR. A more hands-on approach is also likely to lead to a greater development of experience of the appropriate choice and timing of ADR, which the court could use to assist litigates lacking that experience. The report makes the following recommendations in relation to ADR:

- The parties should focus in more detail, and inform the court of their views, on the suitability, type, and timing of ADR before the first case management conference (see para 5.17).
- Thorough review of ADR options should be a normal feature of every case management conference (paras 5.18 and 5.19).
- A Financial Dispute Resolution hearing should take place in individual property litigation cases, such as Inheritance Act or Probate Claims. (see paras 5.20 to 5.22 and Chapter 14 of the report).
- Judicial ENE should be available in a range of chancery cases (paras 5.23 to 5.35).

Figure 7.2 A typical ADR order that may be made in the Chancery Division

IN THE HIGH COURT OF JUSTICE 2014 HC 1276
CHANCERY DIVISION

BETWEEN

TIMOTHY SMALL

Claimant

and

PRICE WATCH PROPERTIES LIMITED

Defendant

IT IS ORDERED THAT:

(1) This claim be stayed for a period of one month until 8th December 2014 for the parties to try to settle the dispute by alternative dispute resolution or other means.
(2) The parties shall notify the Court in writing at the end of that period whether settlement has been reached. The parties shall at the same time lodge either:
   (a) (if settlement has been reached) a draft Consent Order signed by all the parties; or
   (b) (if no settlement has been reached):
      (i) a statement of agreed directions signed by all the parties or (in the absence of agreed directions) statements of the parties' respective proposed directions;
      (ii) the parties' Disclosure Reports; and
      (iii) the parties' Costs Budgets.

Dated 3rd November 2014

The Queen's Bench Guide

7.42 This is in much the same terms as *The Chancery Guide* (see para 6.6 of the guide).

The Technology and Construction Court Guide

7.43 *The Technology and Construction Court Guide* also encourages the parties to use ADR. The court will, wherever appropriate, facilitate the use of ADR. Legal representatives must ensure that clients are fully aware of the benefits of ADR and that the use of ADR has been carefully considered prior to the first case management conference (para 7.1.3). ADR may be appropriate before proceedings are issued or at any subsequent stage (para 7.2.1). The Technology and Construction Court Pre-action Protocol (see 7.24–7.26) itself provides for a form of ADR because it requires there to be at least one face-to-face meeting between the parties before the commencement of proceedings. There should be sufficient time at this meeting to discuss and resolve the dispute. As a result of this procedure having taken place, the court will not necessarily grant a stay of proceedings upon demand and it will always need to be satisfied that an adjournment is necessary for ADR to take place (para 7.2.2).

7.44 At the first case management conference, the court will want to be addressed on the likely efficacy of ADR, the timing of it, and whether a short stay of proceedings should take place. Having considered the representations of the parties, the court may order a short stay to facilitate ADR at that stage. Alternatively, the court may simply encourage the parties to use ADR without imposing a stay of proceedings (para 7.2.3). At any stage after the first case management conference and prior to the commencement of the trial, the court will, either on its own initiative, or if requested to do so by one or both of the parties, consider afresh the likely efficacy of ADR and whether or not a short stay of the proceedings should be granted to facilitate ADR (para 7.2.4). The court may make an ADR order at any stage of the proceedings in the terms of Appendix E. If such an order is made at the first case management conference the court may go on to give directions for the conduct of the claim up to trial (in the event that ADR fails). Such directions may include provision for a further case management conference to take place (para 7.3.2).

The usual ADR order will provide for the parties to agree on the identity of the mediator or other neutral person. If they do not, the court will usually select such a person from the lists provided by the parties. To facilitate this process, the court would also need to be provided with the CVs of each of the individuals on the lists. **7.45**

If an ADR order has been made, the court will expect each party to co-operate fully with each other in making arrangements for the process, otherwise cost orders or other sanctions may be ordered against the party in default (para 7.4.2). **7.46**

The guide also sets out two ADR processes that can be carried out by the court if the parties agree, namely the Court Settlement Process (a form of judicial mediation—see para 7.6 of the guide and also Chapter 18) and Judicial Early Neutral Evaluation (see para 7.5 of the guide and also Chapter 22). **7.47**

D THE OVERRIDING OBJECTIVE AND ADR

The fundamental overriding objective of the CPR is set out in CPR r 1.1, which provides that the CPR are a new procedural code with the overriding objective of dealing with cases justly and at proportionate expense. CPR r 1.1(2) provides: **7.48**

> Dealing with a case justly and at proportionate expense includes, so far as practicable:
>
> (a) ensuring that the parties are on an equal footing;
> (b) saving expense;
> (c) dealing with cases in ways which are proportionate to the amount of money involved, the importance of the case, the complexity of the issues and to the financial position of each party;
> (d) ensuring that it is dealt with expeditiously and fairly;
> (e) allotting to it an appropriate share of the court's resources, while taking into account the need to allot resources to other cases; and
> (f) enforcing compliance with rules, practice directions and orders.

The phrase 'and at proportionate cost' was added to CPR r 1.1 as part of the Jackson reforms, with effect from 1 April 2013. **7.49**

E ACTIVE CASE MANAGEMENT AND ADR

The court is required to further the overriding objective by actively managing cases (CPR r 1.4(1)). This, in effect, moved control of the pace and form of litigation from the parties to the court. In furthering the overriding objective, the court can and will encourage the parties to use ADR methods to resolve the dispute. Active case management includes (CPR r 1.4(2)): **7.50**

(a) encouraging the parties to co-operate with each other in the conduct of the proceedings;
(b) identifying the issues at an early stage;

(c) deciding promptly which issues need full investigation and trial and accordingly disposing summarily of others;
(d) deciding the order in which issues are resolved;
(e) encouraging parties to use an ADR procedure if the court considers that appropriate and facilitating the use of such procedure;
(f) helping the parties to settle the whole or part of a case;
(g) fixing timetables or otherwise controlling the progress of the case;
(h) considering whether the likely benefits of taking a particular step will justify the cost of taking it;
(i) dealing with as many aspects of the case as it can on the same occasion;
(j) dealing with the case without the parties needing to attend court;
(k) making appropriate use of technology; and
(l) giving directions to ensure that the trial of a case proceeds quickly and efficiently.

7.51 The parties and their lawyers are under a duty to assist the court to further the overriding objective (CPR r 1.3). The court can contact the parties from time to time to monitor compliance with directions and the parties are required to respond promptly to any such enquiries from the court (CPR r 3.1(8)).

7.52 Active case management includes encouraging the parties to co-operate with each other, and Lord Justice Jackson in the Final Report on Costs emphasized that the court should use its powers in relation to costs to discourage unreasonable conduct by the parties, both before and after the issue of proceedings. See Chapter 8 for more detail on the sanctions that can be awarded by the court for unreasonable conduct in respect of ADR.

7.53 Active case management also includes helping the parties to settle the whole or part of a claim (CPR r 1.4(2)(f)). Lord Justice Jackson in the Final Report emphasized that the court must do more to encourage the resolution of disputes before proceedings are issued and to encourage the settlement of proceedings commenced in court.

Part 36 offers to settle

7.54 Amendments were made to CPR Part 36, which deal with offers to settle (see 4.58–4.62) in an effort to encourage the parties to settle a dispute before or during the course of proceedings.

7.55 In particular, if a claimant makes an offer to settle and obtains at trial a judgment against the defendant which is at least as advantageous as the claimant's Part 36 offer, then the court can order, unless it is unjust to do so, that the claimant is entitled to:

- interest on the whole or any part of any sum awarded at a rate not exceeding 10% above base rate for some or all of the period starting when the relevant period expired (the relevant period being, in most cases, the period of 21 days from the date of the offer);
- costs on an indemnity basis from the end of the relevant period;
- interest on those costs at a rate not exceeding 10% above base rate;
- an additional amount, not exceeding £75,000, of 10% of any damages awarded up to the value of £500,000, and an additional 5% on any damages awarded between £500,000 and £1,000,000. If the claimant recovers no damages because it is a non-monetary claim, the additional amount can be applied to the sums awarded in respect of costs.

7.56 The additional amount, which was added to the CPR with effect from 1 April 2013 as part of the Jackson reforms, puts an incentive on a defendant to accept a reasonable offer made by the claimant, otherwise they will have to pay an enhanced sum in respect of damages, as well as perhaps additional interest and indemnity costs. Defendants need to give careful consideration to these provisions before ignoring or rejecting a claimant's Part 36 offer. See CPR r 36.14(3).

In respect of a defendant's Part 36 offer, if the claimant fails to beat it, the claimant will be liable to pay the defendant's costs from the end of the relevant period to the date of judgment (even though they have won the action by obtaining a judgment in their favour (albeit a judgment sum that is less than the Defendant's Part 36 offer). See CPR r 36.14(2). **7.57**

A more robust approach since 1 April 2013

The general case management powers of the court are set out in CPR r 3.1. They include powers to extend or shorten the time for compliance with any rule, practice direction or court order, adjourn hearings, and stay the whole or part of proceedings. These powers can be exercised to encourage the parties to use ADR. Where the court gives directions, it will take into account whether or not a party has complied with the Practice Direction – Pre-Action Conduct and any relevant Pre-Action Protocol (see CPR r 3.1(4). The court may also order a party to pay money into court if that party has, without good reason, failed to comply with a rule, practice direction, or relevant pre-action protocol (CPR r 3.1(5)). **7.58**

It is clear that since 1 April 2013 when the Jackson reforms were implemented, the courts are less tolerant of delay and non-compliance with court orders, rules and practice directions and more robust in encouraging the parties to use ADR. Non-compliance is only likely to be excused if the failure to comply is trivial or there is a good reason for it; overlooking a deadline or an obligation, however innocent, is unlikely to be regarded as a good reason for granting relief (see, for example *Mitchell v News Group Newspapers Ltd* [2013] EWCA Civ 1537). Even where non-compliance, taken by itself, might be characterized as trivial, for example where a party narrowly missed a deadline, it might be more significant when viewed against the whole circumstances of the case (see *Durrant v Chief Constable of Avon & Somerset Constabulary* [2013] EWCA Civ 1624). The new, stricter approach to compliance with Rules, Orders, and Practice Directions, and the unwillingness of the court to grant relief from sanctions imposed for non-compliance, has been demonstrated in numerous cases reported since 1 April 2013 (see, for example, *Thevarajah v Riordan* [2014] EWCA Civ 15; *Chartwell Estate Agents Ltd v Fergies Properties SA* [2014] EWCA Civ 506), and *McTear v Engleheart* [2014] EWHC 722 (Ch)). The fact that the application for an extension of time for compliance is made before the deadline and that non-compliance caused no prejudice to the opposing party is not, in itself, a ground for excusing non-compliance or granting relief (see *R (on the application of Royal London NHS Foundation Trust) v Secretary of State for the Home Department* [2013] EWHC 4010 (Admin) and *Kagalovsky v Balmore Investment* [2014] EWHC 108 (QB)). Even if the parties agree that the time for compliance with a Rule, Order, or Practice Direction should be extended, they should not assume that the court will rubber stamp their agreement (see *MA Lloyd v PPC* [2014] EWHC 41 (QB)). The Court of Appeal has also made it clear that it will support robust and fair case management decisions at first instance and it will not lightly interfere with them. A judge who repeatedly encouraged the parties to settle and who adjourned a trial on multiple occasions to enable settlement negotiations to take place did not breach common law notions of fairness or Article 6 of the European Convention on Human Rights. It was also not appropriate to set aside the consent order made between the parties on the grounds that it was vitiated by duress or improper pressure by the judge to settle the case (*Watson v Sadiq* [2013] EWCA Civ 822). In *Lazari v London and Newcastle (Camden) Ltd* [2013] EWHC 97 (TCC), Aikenhead J (at 26–36) noted that CPR r 3.1 gave the court **7.59** very wide powers of case management. The court ordered the defendant to pay the sum of £30,000 into court under CPR r 3.1(5) (and under r 25.7 as those provisions were also satisfied on the facts) because the defendant had failed to comply with the rules of court and the overriding objective. The court noted that the case ought to be resolved by mediation or some other settlement process, and the relatively small payment into court would concentrate the minds of the parties in that respect. Such a payment would not stifle the defendant's defence to the proceedings as there was no suggestion that it would give rise to any financial embarrassment or default.

Case management orders and ADR

7.60 The court can also direct the parties to consider ADR at a case management conference or pre-trial review. The Court of Appeal approved the use of such an order in *Halsey v Milton Keynes General NHS Trust* [2004] 1 WLR 3002 at para 32, describing the Commercial Court order (see Figure 7.1) as the strongest form of encouragement, but falling short of compulsion.

7.61 An order (referred to as the Ungley Order, after Master Ungley) may also be made in the form set out in Figure 7.3 (see PD 29 para 4.10(9)).

7.62 New model standard directions have been devised which contain a standard form of ADR order. Although these standard directions were designed for multi-track cases, they are also being used in fast-track cases. The standard form of ADR order is shown in Figure 7.4.

7.63 The model directions can be found on www.justice.gov.uk/courts/procedure-rules/civil.

Figure 7.3 The Ungley Order

IN THE HIGH COURT OF JUSTICE 2014 HC 1276
CHANCERY DIVISION

BETWEEN

JOHN SMITH

Claimant

and

LEAKE CONSTRUCTION LIMITED

Defendant

IT IS ORDERED THAT:

1. The parties shall by 22nd December 2014, consider whether the case is capable of resolution by ADR.
2. If any party considers that the case is unsuitable for ADR, that party shall be prepared to justify that decision at the conclusion of the trial, should the trial judge consider that such means of resolution were appropriate, when he is considering the appropriate costs order to make.
3. The party considering the case unsuitable for ADR shall, not less than 28 days before the commencement of trial, file with the court a witness statement, without prejudice save as to costs, giving the reasons upon which they rely for saying that the case was unsuitable.

Dated 8th December 2014

Figure 7.4 Multi-track Standard Directions: ADR Order

ORDER Case number: A00 BR 3455
In the County Court at Bristol
District Judge Steel

Parties BLACK ASSOCIATES LIMITED

Claimant

and

JOHN BLOGGS

Defendant

Warning: you must comply with the terms imposed upon you by this order otherwise your case is liable to be struck out or some other sanction imposed. If you cannot comply you are expected to make formal application to the court before any deadline imposed upon you expires.

On 25th April 2014
District Judge Steel sitting at the County Court at Bristol, considered the papers in the case and

ordered that:

1) The Claim is allocated to the Multi-Track and is assigned to District Judge Steel for case management.
2) At all stages the parties must consider settling this litigation by any means of Alternative Dispute Resolution (including Mediation); any party not engaging in any such means proposed by another must serve a witness statement giving reasons within 21 days of that proposal; such witness statement must not be shown to the trial judge until questions of costs arise.

Dated 25th April 2014

F COSTS MANAGEMENT AND ADR

From 1 April 2013, the new concept of judicial costs management will apply in most multi-track cases (and any other proceedings where the court so orders), other than multi-track cases commenced after 22 April 2014 that have a value of £10 million or more. The purpose of costs management is that the court should manage both the steps to be taken and the costs to be incurred by the parties to any proceedings so as to further the overriding objective (see CPR r 3.12). Each party must file and exchange a costs budget in the form of Precedent H, annexed to PD 3E. This requires the parties to set a budget for each stage of the litigation, including both pre-action costs and for ADR/settlement discussions. An extract from Precedent H in relation to settlement/ADR is set out in Figure 7. 5. **7.64**

Unless budgets are agreed, the court can make a costs management order, and that can include revising the parties' budgets (see CPR r 3.15). The court can refuse to approve the budgets if the figures claimed are disproportionate and unreasonable (see *Willis v MRJ Rundell & Associates Limited* [2013] EWHC 2923 (TCC)). Parties are expected to review budgets and either agree or apply to vary them as appropriate. An application to amend or revise a costs management order pursuant to CPR PD 51G Para 6, should be made as soon as it becomes apparent that the original costs budget for any stage in **7.65**

Figure 7.5 Extract from a costs budget in relation to settlement/ADR (from Precedent H, PD 3E)

In the: [to be completed]
Parties: [to be completed]

Claim number: [to be completed]

		RATE (per hour)	SETTLEMENT / ADR				CONTINGENT COST A: [EXPLAIN]				CONTINGENT COST B: [EXPLAIN]			
			Incurred costs	Estimated costs		TOTAL	Incurred costs	Estimated costs		TOTAL	Incurred costs	Estimated costs		TOTAL
			£	Hours	£		£	Hours	£		£	Hours	£	
	Fee earners' time costs (fee earner description)													
1		£0.00			£0.00	£0.00			£0.00	£0.00			£0.00	£0.00
2		£0.00			£0.00	£0.00			£0.00	£0.00			£0.00	£0.00
3		£0.00			£0.00	£0.00			£0.00	£0.00			£0.00	£0.00
4		£0.00			£0.00	£0.00			£0.00	£0.00			£0.00	£0.00
5	**Total Profit Costs (1 to 4)**		**£0.00**		**£0.00**	**£0.00**	**£0.00**		**£0.00**	**£0.00**	**£0.00**		**£0.00**	**£0.00**
	Expert's costs													
6	Fees	£0.00				£0.00				£0.00				£0.00
7	Disbursements					£0.00				£0.00				£0.00
	Counsel's fees [indicate seniority]													
8	Leading counsel					£0.00				£0.00				£0.00
9	Junior counsel					£0.00				£0.00				£0.00
10	**Court fees**					£0.00				£0.00				£0.00
11	**Other Disbursements**					£0.00				£0.00				£0.00
12	Explanation of disbursements [details to be completed]													
13	**Total Disbursements (6 to 11)**		£0.00		£0.00	£0.00	£0.00		£0.00	£0.00	£0.00		£0.00	£0.00
14	**Total (5 + 13)**		0			**£0.00**	0			**£0.00**	0			**£0.00**

the litigation, including ADR, has been exceeded by more than a minimal amount, and such an application must be made before the trial. The court will not approve a variation unless the applicant has shown a good reason to depart from the approved budget (see *Elvanite Full Circle Ltd v Amec Earth and Environmental (UK) Ltd* [2013] EWHC 1643 (TCC) and *Henry v News Group Newspapers Ltd* [2013] EWCA Civ 19). The court is unlikely to allow a party to revise a budget where a careless mistake occurred during the preparation of the original budget (see *Murray v Dowlman Architecture Ltd* [2013] EWHC 872 (TCC)).

When making case management directions, the court is required to take into account the available budget and the costs of each procedural step (see CPR r 3.17). A party will not be permitted to recover more than the costs set out in the budget for each phase of the litigation unless there is good reason to do so, and that will include the costs budgeted for ADR (see CPR r 3.18 and PD 3E). If any party fails to file a budget despite being required to do so, unless the court otherwise orders, they will be treated as having filed a budget comprising only the applicable court fees (CPR r 3.14). This is a very draconian rule because the effect of it is that the party will not be able to recover the vast majority of their legal costs, even if they win the action. Furthermore, in *Mitchell v News Group Newspapers Ltd* [2013] EWCA Civ 1537, the Court of Appeal held that r 3.14 applies not only to parties who fail to file a budget, but also to parties who fail to file a budget within the period prescribed by CPR r 3.13. In that case the court declined to grant any relief to the defaulting party, and indicated that relief would only be granted if the breach is trivial or there is good reason for it, neither of which applied on those facts. **7.66**

The court also has power to make a costs capping order limiting the amount of future costs (including disbursements) that a party may recover in relation to the whole litigation or one or more of the issues (CPR rr 3.19 to 3.21 and PD 3F). Costs can only be incurred or recovered to the extent that they are proportionate (see CPR rr 44.3(2), 44.3(5), and 44.4). Moreover, the court's approval of a budget does not mean, without further consideration, that the costs incurred were reasonable and proportionate simply because they were within the approved budget (see *Troy Foods v Manton* [2013] EWCA Civ 615). On an assessment of costs at the conclusion of the case, the costs judge on a detailed assessment will still consider whether the budgeted costs were reasonable and proportionate. **7.67**

All of these changes make it more important than ever before to use ADR to resolve disputes. The courts are unlikely to find that it is reasonable and proportionate to litigate the claim to trial if the costs of doing so are weighed against the complexity of the issues and the sums in dispute. The filing and exchanging of costs budgets also means that each party's costs are transparent to the other party, and that may also be a factor which motivates the parties to use ADR, and to do so at the earliest opportunity. Parties are required to include ADR costs in their costs budgets. The courts will be able to reduce the amount set out in the budgets for specific items, including the costs estimated for ADR (see *CRM Trading Ltd v Chubb Electronic Security Ltd* [2013] EWHC 3482 (QB), where the court held that as the prospect of formal alternative dispute resolution was minimal, the amount for that in the budget should be reduced from £10,830 to £4,000). Likewise the court may wish the parties to revise the budget in respect of ADR costs if it is apparent that the parties have not given enough consideration to ADR. The court has power to make a costs management order even if proceedings were commenced before 1 April 2013. In *Raj v Charity Commission for England and Wales* [2013] EWHC 1425 (Ch), following an unsuccessful mediation, the court ordered that a case management conference be held so that a costs management regime under CPR r 3.12 could be imposed because of concerns that the costs of the litigation would become disproportionate to the issues at stake. **7.68**

G DIRECTIONS QUESTIONNAIRES AND ADR

7.69 Cases proceeding in the courts will be allocated to one of three tracks: the small claims track, the fast track or the multi-track, depending on the value of the claim or any counterclaim or additional claim, the nature of the remedy sought, the complexity of the issues in dispute, the number of parties, the importance of the case, and the circumstances of the parties (see CPR r 28.6).

7.70 On receipt of a defence, unless a court officer considers that the case should be referred to the judge for directions, the court will provisionally decide the track which appears to be most suitable for the claim and serve on each party a notice of proposed allocation (see CPR r 26.3(1)).

7.71 The notice of proposed allocation requires the parties to file a completed Directions Questionnaire and to serve copies on all other parties. The notice of proposed allocation will be in Directions Form N149A, N149B, or N149C, depending on whether the claim is to be allocated to the small claims track, the fast track, or the multi-track. The Directions Questionnaire must be in Form N180 or Form N181 (see CPR, Practice Direction 26).

7.72 In the Directions Questionnaire, the parties can make a request for the litigation to be stayed whilst they attempt to settle the case. If they decline, they must explain why it is not appropriate to settle the case at this stage. Legal representatives are required to confirm that they have explained to the client the need to try to settle, the options available, and the possibility of costs sanctions (see Chapter 8) if they refuse to try to settle.

Parties are also asked to confirm whether they have complied with the relevant pre-action protocol and if not, to explain why there has been non-compliance.

7.73 The court does not have to accept the reasons put forward by any of the parties for refusing to try to settle the action or consider ADR at this stage. If the court considers those reasons to be weak or inadequate, it will direct the parties to attend an allocation hearing or case management conference, to consider whether ADR should be attempted. In *Kinstreet Ltd v Balmargo Corporation Ltd* [2000] CP Rep 62, the court directed the parties to attempt ADR, even though one party objected to this, because the costs of going to trial would exceed the amount claimed. In *Shirayama Shokusan Co Ltd v Danovo Ltd (No 1)* [2003] EWHC 3306 (Ch) the defendant sought an order for mediation in the terms of the Commercial Court ADR order (see Figure 7.1). The claimant resisted the application on the grounds that the court did not have jurisdiction to order mediation where one party was unwilling to mediate and, in any event, since the defendant had made allegations that the claimant was dishonest, mediation stood little chance of success. Blackburne J held, granting the application, that the court did have jurisdiction to order mediation irrespective of one party being unwilling to mediate and that a mediation order was in accordance with the overriding objective. He relied on the fact that the court had ordered that the parties attempt mediation, even in the face of objections from one party, in *Guinle v Kirreh* [2000] CP Rep 62 and *Muman v Nagasena* [2000] 1 WLR 299. *Shirayama* was cited in the skeleton arguments in *Halsey v Milton Keynes General NHS Trust* [2004] 1 WLR 3002 and, although it was not considered in the judgments of the court in *Halsey*, it is still good law, as the order was made in the form set out in Figure 7.1 and this form of order was approved in *Halsey*.

7.74 The court can therefore critically review the reasons put forward by the party for their contention that ADR was not appropriate or a stay should not be granted to attempt it. If those reasons are plainly inadequate or ill-founded, the court may direct the parties to consider ADR, and grant a stay of its own motion, at the track allocation stage or at any other time, for ADR to be considered, but it will stop short of actually compelling them to undertake ADR (see 7.94–7.108).

H GRANTING STAYS FOR ADR

The court's general powers of management include the power to make orders staying the whole or part of any proceedings until a specified date or event (CPR r 3.1(2)(f)). Any such stay will usually be for a period of one month although the court has power to extend this period. If the court has stayed proceedings at track allocation stage, then the case will not be allocated to the appropriate track until the end of that period (CPR r 26.4 and 26.5). Even if the parties do not request a stay, if the court considers that a stay is appropriate, it can stay the proceedings, in whole or in part, for one month or such period as it considers appropriate (see new CPR r 26.4 (2A)). The court can also extend a stay for such specified period as it considers appropriate (CPR r 26.4(3)). If the parties apply to extend the stay, the court will usually treat a letter from any party or their solicitor as an application, and the letter should confirm that the application is made with the agreement of the parties and explain the steps being taken and identify any mediator or expert assisting with the process. Any extension granted will usually be for no more than four weeks unless clear reasons are given to justify a longer time (see CPR, PD 26 para 3.1). An application for a consent order to give effect to any settlement reached is treated as an application for the stay to be lifted (see PD 26, para 3.4). **7.75**

A stay operates to suspend the directions that the court has made or the steps that the parties would be required to take in relation to the proceedings so that the parties are spared the expense of complying with the procedural timetable and case management orders (such as disclosure of documents and exchange of witness statements). A stay therefore enables an ADR process to be explored while the litigation is suspended avoiding a party having to prepare for the ADR process and the various stages of the litigation process at the same time. In *UK Highways A55 Ltd v Hyder Consulting (UK) Ltd* [2012] EWHC 3505 (TCC) the court held that the effect of a stay was to suspend proceedings until the stay was lifted or until it expired by effluxion of time. When the stay no longer applied, the proceedings resumed automatically from where they had left off when the stay was imposed. Any outstanding time limits by which future steps in the action had to be taken would not be abrogated, but would simply be pushed back by an amount of time equivalent to the length of the stay. **7.76**

A stay can be ordered at track allocation stage (see 7.69) or at any stage of the proceedings, and on application by one or both parties, or by the court of its own motion. The courts have also been willing to grant a stay to enforce an ADR clause in the underlying contract between the parties (see 7.83–7.93). **7.77**

If a stay is granted for ADR to be attempted, the parties must keep the court informed about the outcome of the ADR process. If it results in settlement, the parties will probably wish to lodge a settlement order with the court (see Chapter 23). In any event, the claimant must tell the court if settlement is reached (CPR r 26.4 (4)). If no settlement is reached during the ADR process, then the claimant will need to apply to the court to get the stay lifted (if it has not expired) and for any further relevant directions so that the litigation can proceed. If the claimant does not tell the court by the end of the period of the stay that a settlement has been reached, the court will give such directions as to the management of the case as it thinks appropriate (CPR r 26.4(5)). **7.78**

An example of an order granting a stay is set out in Figure 7.6. **7.79**

Figure 7.6 An example of an order granting a stay

IN THE HIGH COURT OF JUSTICE 2014 HC 2745
QUEEN'S BENCH DIVISION

BETWEEN

JOHN BULL LIMITED

Claimant

and

PALM OIL PRODUCTS LIMITED

Defendant

IT IS ORDERED THAT:

1. These proceedings be stayed until Friday 24th October 2014 to enable the parties to continue to complete the requirements of the pre-action protocol, and thereafter to consider and adopt any appropriate course of alternative dispute resolution to include but not necessarily limited to mediation.
2. Either party shall have permission to apply for the stay to be lifted and request the court to fix the case management conference on the first available date with a time estimate of 30 minutes.
3. The parties to notify the court in writing by 31st October 2014 whether the action has settled.
4. If the action has not settled by 31st October 2014 then the Case Management Conference be restored for hearing at 2 pm on 10th November 2014.
5. Costs in the case.

Dated 29th September 2014

I JUDICIAL ENCOURAGEMENT OF ADR

7.80 The courts have repeatedly encouraged the parties to use ADR. Judicial encouragement to use mediation in particular is dealt with at 14.06–14.12.

- In *Dyson v Leeds City Council* [2000] CP Rep 42, in a claim brought by executors against an employer for causing death from mesothelioma due to exposure to asbestos, Lord Woolf stated [at 16]: '. . . this is pre-eminently the category of case in which, consistent with the overriding objective of the Civil Procedure Rules and the court's duty to manage cases as set out in r 1.4(2)(e), we should encourage the parties to use an alternative dispute resolution procedure to bring this unhappy matter to the conclusion it now deserves sooner than later'.
- In *R (Cowl) v Plymouth City Council* [2002] 1 WLR 803, an appeal was brought by the claimant against the refusal of his application for judicial review of the council's decision to close the residential home in which he was a resident. The council was willing to deal with the matter by a statutory complaints procedure. The claimant contended that this was an inadequate alternative to judicial review. In dismissing the appeal, the court held that it was of paramount importance that litigation should be avoided in disputes between public authorities and members of the public wherever possible. The courts should use their powers under the CPR to ensure that such disputes were resolved with the minimum of judicial intervention. To this end, an inter-partes hearing might be required to establish

whether a complaints procedure or other form of ADR could be used. Judges could question the parties as to the steps taken to avoid litigation, including requiring them to justify their decision not to embark on ADR. The court should not permit, except for good reason, proceedings for judicial review to continue if a significant number of the issues between the parties could be resolved outside the litigation process. Lord Woolf gave strong encouragement to parties to use ADR to resolve disputes between public authorities and members of the public (at [1] and [25]):

The importance of this appeal is that it illustrates that, even in disputes between public authorities and the members of the public for whom they are responsible, insufficient attention is paid to the paramount importance of avoiding litigation whenever this is possible. Particularly in the case of these disputes both sides must by now be acutely conscious of the contribution alternative dispute resolution can make to resolving disputes in a manner which both meets the needs of the parties and the public and saves time, expense, and stress.

Today, sufficient should be known about alternative dispute resolution to make the failure to adopt it, in particular when public money is involved, indefensible.

- In *MD v Secretary of State for the Home Department* [2011] EWCA Civ 453, the claimants commenced proceedings for a declaration that the defendant's delay in issuing their refugee status papers violated their Art 8 right to respect for private and family life and also compensation. The Court of Appeal, applying *R (Cowl) v Plymouth City Council* [2002] 1 WLR 803 upheld the first instance decision of Mr Justice Tracey, who decided that the continuation of the proceedings would be pointless and disproportionately expensive. The Secretary of State had made an open admission and apology, implemented a complaints procedure, and steps had been taken to avoid such delays in the future. This provided as much as the applicants could hope to achieve by court proceedings. Extra-judicial acknowledgement was sufficient vindication of a person's human rights, even without an award of compensation.
- An application for permission to bring judicial review was also refused in *R (on the application of S) v Hampshire County Council* [2009] EWHC 2537 (Admin) where the applicant had an alternative remedy, namely the local authority's complaints procedure and had failed to comply with the pre-action protocol nor made any attempt to avoid litigation, both of which also warranted peremptory refusal of permission.
- In *Brookfield Construction (UK) Limited v Mott Macdonald Limited* [2010] EWHC 659 (TCC), a number of claims were brought arising out of the late completion of Wembley Stadium. Coulson J set out recommendations for the future progress of the claim. In particular, at paras 52–55 he urged the parties to co-operate and use ADR and emphasized that a party's unwillingness to do so would be taken into account by the court when assessing costs.

> I have been concerned about what I perceive to be a lack of co-operation between the parties. . . . As the parties prepare for the sub-trial, I would urge solicitors and counsel to meet on a regular basis, and to endeavour to iron out the minor differences between them, leaving only the significant disputes between them (if any) to be dealt with by the court.
>
> I am required to provide the parties with robust encouragement to explore all ways of resolving their differences without a trial. It seems to me that the size of this case (both financially and in terms of documents) makes it ideally suitable to all the many forms of ADR. In particular, I would have thought that a mediation, conducted by one of the many experienced construction practitioners who offer a mediation service, would be a sensible next step, to be taken sooner rather than later . . . In the present case, there is a clear and obvious alternative: ADR. In my view, the parties need to explore that option as soon as possible . . . . I should make it clear that at the end of the sub-trial, I will make detailed costs orders and that, on the

basis of the documents, my perception of one side's willingness (or otherwise) to participate in ADR will be an important element of my deliberations on costs.

- In *PGF II SA v OMFS Company 1 Limited* [2014] WLR 1386 [at para 27] it was observed that:

> The constraints which now affect the provision of state resources for the conduct of civil litigation (and which appear likely to do so for the forseeable future) call for an ever-increasing focus upon the means of ensuring that court time, both for trial and case management, is proportionately thrown upon the parties to civil litigation to engage in ADR, wherever that offers a reasonable prospect of producing a just settlement at proportionate cost. Just as it risks a waste of the court's resources to have to try a case which could have been justly settled, earlier and at a fraction of the cost by ADR, so it is a waste of its resources to have to manage the parties towards ADR by robust encouragement, where they could and should have engaged with each other in considering its suitability, without the need for the court's active intervention.

7.81 Lord Neuberger, Master of the Rolls, giving The Fourth Keating Lecture at Lincoln's Inn on 19 May 2010 entitled '*Equity, ADR, Arbitration and the Law: Different Dimensions of Justice*' described ADR as 'litigation's invaluable twin' but that care should be taken to ensure it does not become its identical twin. He remarked, at para 44:

> The ... post-Woolf commitment to proportionality weaves ADR more tightly into the fabric of civil justice, to borrow Sir Jack Jacob's phrase, than ever before: it gives it a crucial role to play in dispute resolution. It does so not because it requires courts to divert cases from their formal adjudicative processes to ADR as part of a downgrading and downsizing of the civil justice system. It does so because it is an expression of our commitment to civil justice for the public good. Proportionality and the overriding objective increase ADR's importance, but it will never render it a substitution for adjudication in every case. Promoting and facilitating the use of ADR for those cases where it will be of genuine advantage to the parties, because of, for instance, its informality, the flexibility of its processes and the availability of remedies not available to the litigation process—is of benefit not only to those litigants but also to the justice system. It is of benefit because it ensures that only those cases which truly call for, truly require, formal adjudication utilise the limited resources available to the justice system.

The lecture can be viewed at www.judiciary.gov.uk/NR/rdonlyres/CBC3DC2C-DE43–43EC-8A02–3D3CADCB0442/0/mrkeatinglecture19052010.pdf.

7.82 The typical stages of a claim at which ADR may be attempted are shown in Figure 7.7.

J THE APPROACH OF THE COURTS TO CONTRACTUAL ADR CLAUSES

7.83 The court will give effect to ADR by upholding and enforcing ADR clauses. An ADR clause is a clause in a contract by which the parties agree to resolve their dispute primarily by ADR. The clause may define a particular ADR method which should be used, such as mediation, or it may specify a number of methods that need to be exhausted in turn before litigation can be commenced or continued. If an adjudicative form of ADR procedure is specified by the clause (such as expert determination, adjudication, or arbitration), the clause may also specify that the parties are to be bound by the decision. Such clauses are becoming increasingly common, particularly in contracts for services, insurance contracts, and construction contracts. Some examples of ADR clauses are set out below:

> Any dispute, question or difference of any nature arising under or contained in or arising out of or in connection with this contract, or as to the rights, duties or liabilities under it of the parties shall, in the first instance, be submitted to adjudication in accordance with the Association of Independent Construction Adjudicators (AICA) adjudication rules and thereafter to the exclusive jurisdiction of the English Courts. If the parties fail to agree on the identity of the adjudicator

Figure 7.7 The typical stages of a claim at which ADR may be attempted

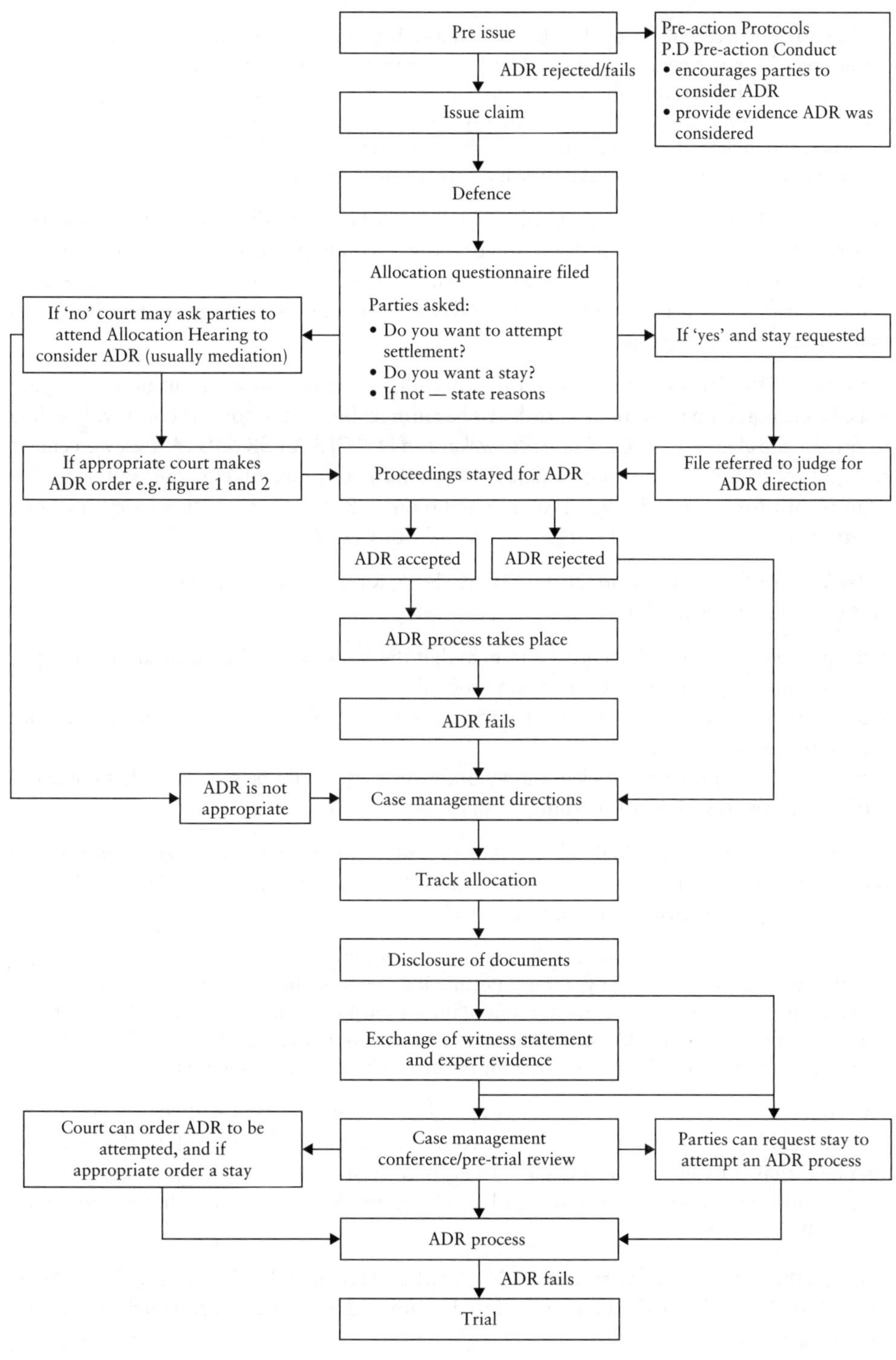

within five days of the dispute, question or difference arising, the adjudicator shall be appointed by the AICA.

The parties shall attempt in good faith to resolve any dispute or claim arising out of or in connection with this Agreement through negotiations between the Managing Directors of each Party. If any dispute is not settled through negotiation, then the Parties shall attempt in good faith to resolve the dispute or claim by an Alternative Dispute Resolution procedure agreed by both parties, and in default of agreement as recommended to the parties by the Centre for Effective Dispute Resolution, before court proceedings are issued to resolve the dispute.

7.84 If the parties have agreed on a particular method by which their disputes are to be resolved, then the court has an inherent discretionary power to stay proceedings brought in breach of that agreement and require the parties to pursue the dispute resolution process that they agreed to use. The court will give effect to ADR clauses regardless of the type of ADR process that the parties have agreed to use.

7.85 However, ADR clauses need to be drafted carefully. The procedure set out in the contract must be clear and unambiguous in order to be enforceable. If it is not, the court will decline to enforce the clause (*Cott UK Ltd v FE Barber Ltd* [1997] 3 All ER 540). A mere agreement to negotiate in good faith is not sufficiently certain to be enforceable by the courts (see for example *Walford v Miles* [1992] 2 AC 128 and *Balfour Beatty Construction Northern Ltd v Modus Corovest (Blackpool) Ltd* [2008] EWHC 3029 (TCC)).

7.86 In *Holloway v Chancery Mead* [2007] EWHC 2495, Ramsey J set out three requirements for an ADR clause to be binding:

- the process has to be sufficiently certain, in that there should not be the need for an agreement at any stage before matters could proceed;
- the administrative processes for selecting a party to resolve the dispute and to pay that person had to be defined;
- the process or at least a sufficient model of the process should be set out so that the detail of the process is sufficiently certain.

7.87 The court has upheld an ADR clause that provided for no particular agreed method to resolve the dispute. In *Cable and Wireless plc v IBM United Kingdom Ltd* [2002] EWHC 2059 (Comm), the clause in the contract provided that:

The parties shall attempt in good faith to resolve any dispute or claim arising out of or relating to this Agreement ... promptly through negotiations between the respective senior executives of the parties ... If the matter is not resolved through negotiation, the parties shall attempt in good faith to resolve the dispute or claim through an Alternative Dispute Resolution (ADR) procedure as recommended to the parties by the Centre for Dispute Resolution.

The court held that the procedure envisaged by the contract was sufficiently certain to be enforceable, and granted a stay of proceedings commenced in breach of the clause. It also held that for the courts to decline to enforce contractual references to ADR on the grounds of intrinsic uncertainty would be to fly in the face of public policy as expressed in the CPR.

7.88 On the other hand in *Sulamerica CIA Nacional de Seguros SA v Enesa Engelharia SA—Enesa* [2013] 1 WLR 102, the court refused to uphold an ADR clause which was in the following terms:

If any dispute or difference of whatsoever nature arising out of or in connection with this Policy including any question regarding its existence, validity or termination, hereafter termed the Dispute, the parties undertake that, prior to a reference to arbitration, they will seek to have the Dispute resolved amicably by mediation .... If the Dispute has not been resolved to the

> satisfaction of either party within 90 days of service of the notice initiating mediation, or if either party fails or refuses to participate in the mediation, or if either party serves written notice terminating the mediation under this clause, then either party may refer the Dispute to arbitration. . . .

The court applied *Holloway v Chancery Mead* and *Cable and Wireless plc v IBM United Kingdom Ltd* and held that this clause provided no unequivocal commitment to engage in mediation, there was no agreement to enter into any clear mediation process whether based on a model provided by a particular ADR provider or otherwise, and no provision was made for the selection of a mediator. There were therefore stages in the process where the parties would need to agree on a course of action before a mediation could proceed. In those circumstances, the clause did not give rise to a binding obligation to mediate which the court could enforce.

In *Wah v Grant Thornton International Ltd* [2012] EWHC 3198 (Ch) the court considered *Cable & Wireless plc* and *Sulamerica Cia Nacional de Seguros SA* and other authorities, and reiterated the general principle that agreements to agree and agreements to negotiate in good faith would generally be unenforceable, because good faith was too open-ended a concept to provide clarity for the purposes of legal obligations. However, the court will try to find an interpretation to give effect to a dispute resolution clause, particularly if the clause is contained in a legally enforceable contract between the parties. It might do this by implying criteria to enable it to determine what process to follow, and when and how that process might be considered successful, exhausted, or properly terminated. The court should consider each case on its own terms, rather than tick off minimum requirements for validity. The court considered (at para 60) there needed to be: **7.89**

(a) a sufficiently certain and unequivocal commitment to commence a process;
(b) a means of discerning the steps each party was required to take to put the process in place;
(c) a process which was sufficiently clearly defined to enable the court to make an objective determination of the minimum each party must do to participate in it and an indication of how the process would be exhausted or properly terminable without breach.

In *M v M* [2014] EWHC 537 (Fam), the court, applying *Wah v Grant Thornton International* held that an agreement to mediate was enforceable because the subject matter of the mediation and what the parties must do was clear. The court held that the fact that the clause did not say how the parties can end the ADR process is of no consequence as the intrinsic nature of mediation is that either party can abruptly bring it to an end, and the reason for doing so would be cloaked with privilege (for privilege, see Chapter 6). **7.90**

Provided the clause is sufficiently clear, in exercising its discretion to enforce such clauses by staying or adjourning proceedings commenced in breach of the clause, the court may consider the following factors (*DGT Steel & Cladding Ltd v Cubitt Building & Interiors Ltd* [2007] BLR 371): **7.91**

- the extent to which the parties had complied with the requirements in any pre-action protocol;
- whether the dispute is suitable for determination by the agreed ADR process;
- the costs of that ADR process compared to the costs of litigation;
- whether a stay would accord with the overriding objective.

The courts have enforced ADR clauses and stayed litigation commenced before the agreed ADR process had been utilized in *Channel Tunnel Group Ltd v Balfour Beatty Construction Ltd* [1993] AC 334 (where the ADR process agreed upon was expert determination); *Cape Durasteel Ltd v Rosser & Russell Building Services Ltd* [1995] 46 Con LR 75; *Herschel* **7.92**

Engineering Ltd v Breen Property Ltd [2000] 70 Con LR 1; and *DGT Steel & Cladding Ltd v Cubitt Building & Interiors Ltd* [2007] BLR 371 (adjudication).

7.93 The courts may also be willing to award damages for breach of an ADR clause. Those damages could consist of the costs reasonably incurred by a party in relation to proceedings brought in breach of an ADR clause which could not be recovered in those proceedings (*Union Discount v Zoller* [2002] 1 WLR 1517). However, it is important to note that costs cannot be recovered as damages if the party seeking to recover those costs could have sought an order for their payment in the proceedings brought in breach of the contract between the parties (see *Carroll v Kynaston* [2010] EWCA Civ 1404). Damages for breach of an ADR clause could also be assessed on the basis of the amount that a party could have obtained had the contractually agreed dispute resolution procedure been followed (*Sunrock Aircraft Corp Ltd v Scandinavian Airlines System Denmark-Norway-Sweden* [2007] 2 Lloyd's Rep 612).

K CAN THE COURT COMPEL THE PARTIES TO USE ADR?

7.94 Most ADR processes are entered into by the parties on a voluntary basis in order to reach a faster, more cost-effective, or creative settlement of the matters in dispute. The court can encourage the parties to attempt ADR by the various means described in this chapter.

7.95 Although the court can direct that the parties should attempt to resolve the dispute by ADR, it cannot make them use ADR and, if they do so, it cannot make them reach a settlement in the selected ADR process. This was recognized in *Halsey v Milton Keynes General NHS Trust* [2004] 1 WLR 3002 and more recently restated in *M v M* [2014] EWHC 537. In *Halsey*, the court accepted that to require unwilling parties to mediate would infringe Art 6 of the European Convention on Human Rights by which everyone is entitled to a fair and public hearing within a reasonable time by an independent and impartial tribunal established by law. The Court of Appeal also accepted that mediation is a process that is most effective if undertaken on a voluntary basis. A court can encourage the parties to engage with ADR, rather than compel them to do so. The Commercial Court order was seen as the strongest form of encouragement. If such an ADR order is ignored, then the court could penalize the defaulting party by making an adverse costs order against them. Dyson LJ stated at paras [9] and [10]:

> We have heard argument on the question whether the court has power to order parties to submit their disputes to mediation against their will. It is one thing to encourage the parties to agree to mediation, even to encourage them in the strongest terms. It is another to order them to do so. It seems to us that to oblige truly unwilling parties to refer their disputes to mediation would be to impose an unacceptable obstruction on their right of access to the court. The court in Strasbourg has said in relation to Article 6 . . . that the right of access to a court can be waived, for example by means of an arbitration agreement, but such waiver should be subjected to 'particularly careful review' to ensure that the claimant is not subject to 'constraint': see *Deweer v Belgium* [1980] 2 EHRR 239 at para 49. If that is the approach of the European Court of Human Rights to an agreement to arbitrate it seems to us that compulsion of ADR would be regarded as an unacceptable constraint on the right of access to the court and, therefore, a violation of Article 6. Even if (contrary to our view) the court does have jurisdiction to order unwilling parties to refer their disputes to mediation, we find it difficult to conceive of circumstances in which it would be appropriate to exercise it.
>
> If the court were to compel parties to enter into a mediation to which they objected, that would achieve nothing except to add to the costs to be borne by the parties, possibly postpone the time when the court determines the dispute and damage the perceived effectiveness of the ADR process. If a judge takes the view that the case is suitable for ADR, then he or she is not, of course, obliged to

> take at face value the expressed opposition of the parties, In such a case, the judge should explore the reasons for any resistance to ADR. But if the parties (or at least one of them) remain intransigently opposed to ADR, then it would be wrong for the court to compel them to embrace it.

Dyson LJ went on to add that the form of encouragement can be robust, and an order set out in the terms of the ADR order made in the Commercial Court in the form set out in Appendix 7 of the *Admiralty and Commercial Courts Guide* (see Figure 7.1) is the strongest form of encouragement. He noted that this form of order stops short of actually compelling the parties to undertake ADR. He also added: 'Nevertheless, a party who, despite such an order, simply refuses to embark on the ADR process at all would run the risk that for that reason alone his refusal to agree to ADR would be held to be unreasonable, and that he should therefore be penalised in costs.' **7.96**

In *M v M* [2014] EWHC 537 (Fam), the divorcing parties reached an agreement which provided that the husband would make interim financial payments to the wife and they would attempt to compromise all existing legal disputes including the determination of the balance payable and to that end they would participate in mediation by an agreed date. The mediation did not take place and instead the wife issued an application for enforcement of her husband's financial obligations under the agreement. The husband claimed that the wife was debarred from proceeding to enforce because by the agreement, they agreed to refer all outstanding disputes to mediation. The court, applying *Halsey*, held that it was clear that the agreement could not be given effect so as to prevent one party from applying to the court for enforcement unless and until mediation had taken place. A bar of that nature would operate as a restriction on the right to apply to the court. The most that could be done in balancing the obligation to mediate and the right of access to the court was to adjourn the proceedings for a specified period to give the parties a final opportunity to engage in ADR. The parties could not be compelled to engage in the mediation, but the court could robustly encourage engagement by means of an Ungley Order (see Figure 7.3) in terms that failure to justify a decision not to engage in mediation could result in sanctions. **7.97**

There are many commentators who consider that *Halsey* is wrong in holding that the court could not compel the parties to engage with an ADR process on the basis that it would infringe their Art 6 rights. For example Lightman J in a speech entitled 'Mediation: Approximation to Justice' (28 June 2007) criticized the decision on the ground that the court failed to differentiate between different ADR processes such as arbitration (which does impose a permanent stay on proceedings) and mediation or negotiation (which do not prevent the parties resolving their dispute by trial). Even if a stay is granted, that simply delays the trial process for a short time. He also points out that a number of other nations, who are signatories to the European Convention on Human Rights, such as Belgium, Greece, and Germany, have compulsory mediation processes. **7.98**

Support for the view that compulsory ADR orders for mediation would not infringe the Art 6 rights of the parties can also be derived from the EU Mediation Directive 2008/52/EC. This recommends that courts in member states should encourage parties to mediate. Art 5 provides that: **7.99**

> (1) A court before which an action is brought may, when appropriate and having regard to all the circumstances of the case, invite the parties to use mediation in order to settle the dispute. The court may also invite the parties to attend an information session on the use of mediation if such sessions are held and are easily available.
> (2) This Directive is without prejudice to national legislation making use of mediation compulsory or subject to incentives or sanctions, whether before or after judicial proceedings have started, provided that such legislation does not prevent the parties from exercising their right of access to the judicial system.

7.100 In other jurisdictions, for example, Italy, Belgium, Greece, Canada, and the USA, parties are ordered to proceed to mediation, even if this is against their wishes.

7.101 In *Alassini v Telecom Italia SpA* (Joined Cases C-317–320/08 [2010] 3 CMLR 17 ECJ), the European Court, on a preliminary reference from Italy, ruled that even if domestic law made commencement of legal proceedings conditional on attempting settlement at a mediation, this would not infringe Art 6. In that case customers brought proceedings against a telephone company claiming damages for breach of mobile telephone contracts under the EU Directive on the Provision of Electronic Communications Networks. Italian law provided that if the parties did not attempt ADR first, then they would forfeit their right to bring legal proceedings in court. The ECJ held that this did not contravene Art 6. It was appropriate to have rules and procedures which governed admissibility to the court. However, any rules which restricted access to the court had to be proportionate and in the general interest by resolving disputes with more speed and less expense. It was proportionate and in the general interest as an optional out-of-court settlement procedure would not have achieved those objectives as efficiently. The court also found that the law did not make it impossible or excessively difficult to bring court proceedings, as although the parties were forced to mediate before issuing proceedings, they were not forced to settle and if they failed to achieve settlement in the mediation, they could then commence proceedings. The ECJ also found that the delay caused by the mandatory mediation law was minimal, because the time limit for completion of the mediation process was 30 days and during this period the limitation period was suspended and the mediation process was free to the parties.

7.102 Lord Dyson (who gave the judgment of the court in *Halsey*), in a talk given at the CIArb Third Mediation Symposium in October 2010 (reported in *Arbitration* 77(3), 2011, 375–381) accepted, in light of the *Alassini* case and Art 5 of the Directive, that a form of compulsory mediation, which requires parties to mediate, but does not penalize them if they fail to do so (so that at most trial is delayed) involves no breach of Art 6. In that talk, he also pointed out the disadvantages of compulsory mediation:

> I remain of the view I advanced in *Halsey*, that if the court were to compel parties to enter into mediation to which they objected, that would achieve nothing except to add to the cost to be borne by the parties. It would possibly postpone the time when the court determined the dispute and damage the perceived effectiveness of the ADR process.

7.103 The Jackson Review on costs also endorsed the view that '... mediation should never be compulsory, although courts should in appropriate cases encourage mediation by pointing out its benefits, by directing parties to meet and discuss mediation and by using the Master Ungley form of order in the field of clinical negligence.' (See Figure 7.3 for the Ungley Order).

7.104 It would therefore seem to be the case that ordering the parties to take part in a non-adjudicative ADR process, such as mediation, is not a breach of Art 6 provided the parties can still issue (or continue) with court proceedings if they failed to reach a settlement. A compulsory order to attempt ADR might not even result in a delay in the trial process because the litigation timetable does not need to be stayed or extended in most cases to accommodate ADR although it may be practical to do so. In light of the *Alassini* case, requiring mediation to be undertaken as a pre-condition to issuing proceedings on the basis that the right to issue proceedings would be forfeited if mediation was not attempted is also not likely to be a breach of Art 6 (although it may well be a breach if the parties had to pay for the mediation and the claim became statute-barred by the operation of a limitation period whilst the mandatory mediation was attempted).

In light of the *Alassini* case, it is also doubtful whether a breach of Art 6 would occur if a court made a mandatory mediation or other non-adjudicative ADR order on the condition that the proceedings would be struck out if the parties failed to take part in the process, although this matter has yet to be resolved. It is clear that a breach of Art 6 would occur if a party was prevented from instituting or continuing proceedings because they failed to reach a settlement in a non-adjudicative ADR process. **7.105**

In *Wright v Michael Wright (Supplies) Ltd* [2013] EWCA Civ 234 Sir Alan Ward expressed concern that the case demonstrated that despite robust encouragement from the court, it was not possible 'to shift intransigent parties off the trial track and onto the parallel track of mediation' and noted (at [3]) that it might be time to review the rule in *Halsey v Milton Keynes General NHS Trust* [2004] EWCA Civ 576, where at [9] Dyson LJ said **7.106**

> It seems to us that to oblige truly unwilling parties to refer their dispute to mediation would be to impose an unacceptable obstruction on their right of access to the court.

He also remarked that the costs consequences spelt out in *Halsey* should be rigorously applied, and expressed the wish that the court should review *Halsey* in light of the past 10 years' development in the field of ADR.

In some courts, cases are referred for compulsory consideration of mediation (see the Small Claims Track Mediation Service and the Court of Appeal Mediation Service and Chapter 18) and also the requirement to attend a MIAM in family cases (see 7.29–7.30 and 18.53–18.55). However, automatic referral for consideration of mediation in such cases is simply a mandatory requirement to engage with a mediator to obtain information on mediation and then undertake mediation if it is appropriate. It is not to be confused with mandatory mediation in the sense that mediation is made compulsory. **7.107**

In summary, the present position in the courts of England and Wales is that the court will, if appropriate, encourage a party to attempt to resolve their dispute by ADR, and the strongest form of encouragement lies in the form of order made by the Commercial Court (see Figure 7.1). The courts are not prepared to compel parties to engage in an ADR process if they are unwilling to do so. It can, however, penalize a party in costs if they unreasonably refuse to attempt ADR, particularly if they are ordered by the court to do so (see Chapter 8). In some cases there is a requirement of mandatory *consideration* of mediation (eg the mandatory MIAMs in family cases—see Chapter 18) and automatic referral to mediation is proposed for small claims cases. However, this is not the same as compulsory mediation. At present, it does not appear that the government intends to introduce any form of compulsory mediation in the sense of compelling and/or enforcing (for example by dismissing or striking out an action) a party to undertake mediation if they are unwilling to do so. It should also be noted that Art 6 is not, in principle, infringed if a party waives their right to a trial process, for example by contractually agreeing to resolve a dispute by an adjudicative ADR process such as Expert Determination or Arbitration (see *Deweer v Belgium A/35* [1980] 2 EHRR 239). **7.108**

KEY POINTS SUMMARY

- Parties are required to consider ADR before proceedings are issued by the protocols and PD – Pre-action Conduct. **7.109**
- The courts will actively encourage the parties to attempt to resolve their dispute by an ADR process after proceedings have been issued.
- The parties may request or the court may order a stay for ADR to be attempted at the track allocation stage or at any other time.

- If ADR is not undertaken before issue, then it should be considered at the track allocation stage (when all the statements of case have been filed), and again after exchange of documents, and also when witness statements and expert evidence have been exchanged.
- The court will actively consider whether attempts have been made to settle the dispute by ADR at any case management conference, and may direct the parties to attempt ADR.
- If the parties reject ADR, before issue or at any stage of the litigation, they should have reasonable and cogent reasons for doing so and may be required to explain these reasons to the court.
- The courts will seek to uphold and enforce ADR clauses in contracts.

8

THE SANCTIONS FOR REFUSING TO ENGAGE IN ADR PROCESSES

A INTRODUCTION 8.01
B THE COURT'S GENERAL POWERS TO MAKE COSTS ORDERS. 8.04
C ADVERSE COSTS ORDERS AGAINST A PARTY WHO FAILS TO COMPLY WITH THE PRE-ACTION PROTOCOLS 8.09
D ADVERSE COSTS ORDERS AGAINST A PARTY WHO UNREASONABLY REFUSES TO CONSIDER ADR 8.12
E OTHER FACTORS 8.60
F REJECTING ADR AFTER JUDGMENT AND BEFORE THE HEARING OF AN APPEAL 8.77
G DELAY IN CONSENTING TO MEDIATION (OR ANOTHER ADR PROCESS) 8.82
H BACKING OUT OF AN AGREED ADR PROCESS 8.84
I UNREASONABLE CONDUCT IN THE MEDIATION 8.88
J IMPOSING A COSTS CAP ON SOLICITOR-CLIENT COSTS FOR FAILING TO PURSUE ADR 8.90
K INDEMNITY COSTS ORDERS FOR FAILING TO CONSIDER ADR 8.92
L WHAT PRACTICAL STEPS SHOULD BE TAKEN BY A PARTY TO AVOID SANCTIONS 8.97
M HOW DOES THE COURT TREAT PRIVILEGED MATERIAL WHEN SEEKING TO IMPOSE SANCTIONS? 8.99
Key points summary 8.104

A INTRODUCTION

The court can penalize a party who unreasonably refuses to: **8.01**

- comply with an order made by the court directing the parties to attempt to resolve the dispute by ADR;
- accept an offer made by the other side to attempt to settle the dispute using an ADR process before the issue of proceedings;
- accept an invitation by the other side to use an ADR process during the course of litigation, or even after judgment and prior to the hearing of an appeal;
- accept a reasonable offer to settle the case, including a Part 36 offer;
- make a reasonable Part 36 offer, or other offer, to settle the dispute.

The orders that the court can make include: **8.02**

- depriving the party of costs even if they are successful in the litigation;
- ordering them to pay some or all of the other side's costs even if they are successful in the litigation;
- ordering them to pay costs on an indemnity basis;

- ordering a higher rate of interest to be paid on damages awarded; or
- depriving a party of interest on damages awarded by the court.

8.03 The most common sanction that is imposed for unreasonably failing to consider or use an ADR process to resolve the dispute is to make an adverse order for costs. Since the Jackson reforms were implemented in April 2013, it is anticipated that the courts will be more robust in penalizing parties who fail to take reasonable and proportionate steps to settle their dispute where it is appropriate to do so. This will be particularly the case where a case management order has been made directing the parties to seek to resolve their dispute using an ADR process. It is likely that any case management order made by the court, including those encouraging the use of ADR, in particular mediation, will be enforced more rigorously than has previously been the case. A stricter, more robust approach has already been demonstrated in case management decisions made since the Jackson reforms were implemented in the Civil Procedure Rules on 1 April 2013 (see the decisions mentioned in para 7.59).

B THE COURT'S GENERAL POWERS TO MAKE COSTS ORDERS

8.04 Costs payable by one party to another are in the discretion of the court (Senior Courts Act 1981 s 51). The court has a wide discretion in relation to costs, both in respect of costs orders made on interim applications and costs orders following trial. The court has discretion whether costs are payable by one party to the other, the amount of those costs, and when they are to be paid (CPR r 44.2(1)). The usual order is that costs will follow the event (ie the overall loser will pay the overall winner's costs), but the court can make a different order (CPR r 44.2(2)).

8.05 In deciding what order to make about costs, the court will have regard to all the circumstances, including the specific factors set out in CPR r 44.2(4), namely:

- the conduct of the parties;
- whether a party has succeeded in part of his case, even if he has not been wholly successful; and
- any admissible offer to settle made by a party that is drawn to the court's attention (which is not an offer to which the costs consequences in Part 36 apply).

8.06 In looking at the conduct of the parties, the court will look at the circumstances, including the matters set out in CPR r 44.2(5):

- conduct before, as well as during, the proceedings, and in particular the extent to which the parties followed Practice Direction – Pre-action Conduct and any relevant pre-action protocol;
- whether it was reasonable for a party to raise, pursue, or contest a particular allegation or issue;
- the manner in which a party has pursued or defended his case or a particular allegation or issue; and
- whether a claimant who has succeeded in his claim, in whole or in part, exaggerated his claim.

8.07 Costs must also be reasonably incurred and proportionate to the subject-matter of the claim and the amount in dispute (see CPR r 44.4).

8.08 The orders that a court may make include an order that a party must pay (CPR r 44.2(6)):

- a proportion of another party's costs;
- a stated amount in respect of another party's costs;

- costs from or until a certain date;
- costs incurred before proceedings have begun;
- costs relating to a particular step in the proceedings;
- costs relating to a distinct part of the proceedings; and
- interest on costs from or until a certain date, including a date before judgment.

C ADVERSE COSTS ORDERS AGAINST A PARTY WHO FAILS TO COMPLY WITH THE PRE-ACTION PROTOCOLS

The court can take into account the extent of the parties' compliance with the pre-action protocols when making case management and costs orders (PD – Pre-Action Conduct, paras 4.1 and 4.2). Non-compliance can include an unreasonable refusal to consider ADR (PD – Pre-Action Conduct, para 4.4(3)). The court can ask the parties to explain what steps they took in relation to ADR and for evidence that they considered the use of ADR (PD – Pre-Action Conduct, paras 4.2 and 8.1). The court can impose sanctions for non-compliance with the protocols (see PD – Pre-Action Conduct, paras 4.5 and 4.6). In addition to the orders set out above, these sanctions can include: **8.09**

- staying the proceedings until the steps which ought to have been taken have been taken;
- an order that the party at fault pays the costs, or part of the costs of the other party;
- an order that those costs are paid on an indemnity basis;
- if the party at fault is the claimant, an order that the claimant is deprived of interest on all or part of any damages or sums awarded by the court, or interest is awarded at a lower rate;
- if the party at fault is the defendant, an order that the defendant pays interest on all or any part of a sum awarded to the claimant at a higher rate, not exceeding 10% above base rate, than would otherwise have been awarded.

A number of cases demonstrate that the courts are prepared to penalize a party for not complying with the protocols: **8.10**

- In *Daejan Investments Ltd v Park West Club Ltd* [2003] EWHC 2178 (TCC), the court stayed proceedings as the claimant had not complied with the Pre-action Protocol for Construction and Engineering Disputes, and there was a real possibility of settlement had the parties complied with the protocol.
- In *Thornhill v Nationwide Metal Recycling Ltd* [2011] EWCA Civ 919 the Court of Appeal, upholding the decision of the trial judge, held that the claimants failed to comply with the requirements of the PD – Pre-Action Conduct in a number of respects and the fact that they were seeking urgent injunctive relief did not provide them with any excuse on the facts of the case. However, the claimants were penalized in costs by the costs order that was made on the interim injunction when they were ordered to pay 80% of the defendant's costs of that application. By the time that application was heard, the shortcomings of the claimants' pre-action conduct had been put right, so the defendants were not entitled to any further relief at trial for the claimants' pre-action conduct.
- In *Nelson's Yard Management Co v Eziefula* [2013] EWCA Civ 235 the court, in making a costs order, took into account the defendant's unreasonable pre-action behaviour in failing to respond to pre-action correspondence and his unwillingness to set out his position, narrow the issues, or discuss mediation or settlement (see paras 30–32, 37, 40, 42–44, and 46 of the judgment).
- In *AP (UK) Ltd v West Midland Fire and Civil Defence Authority* [2013] EWHC 385 (QB) the successful party only received 50% of their costs as they had failed to implement the

provisions in the PD – Pre-action Conduct to engage in pre-action exchange of information and to seek a stay pending the implementation of those steps, or attempt ADR.

- In *Webb Resolutions Ltd v Waller Needham & Green (a firm)* [2012] EWHC 3529 (Ch) the claimant was ordered to pay the defendant's costs after a particular date because it had failed to disclose relevant documents pre-action under the Professional Negligence Protocol.
- In *Chemistree Homecare Ltd v Abbvie Ltd* [2013] EWHC 264 (Ch) the claimant was ordered to pay the defendant's costs, on an indemnity basis, up to the date of issue because of unreasonable pre-action conduct in making complaints pre-issue that were not included in the proceedings as issued. Costs were also awarded on an indemnity basis in *Forstater v Python (Monty) Pictures Ltd* [2013] EWHC 3759 (Ch), as the claim had been started without any real warning, and without compliance with PD – Pre-action Conduct, the court holding that this alone was not enough to justify indemnity costs, but indemnity costs were justified because the claim was also brought by the wrong claimant, for a modest amount, and in the face of a sensible offer of settlement by the opposing party.
- The court has been prepared to penalize successful parties for failing to accept the claimant's offers to use ADR and in particular mediation, before issue of proceedings, in *Burchell v Bollard* [2005] BLR 330; *Jarrom v Sellers* [2007] EWHC 1366, and *P4 Ltd v Unite Integrated Solutions plc* [2007] BLR 1.

8.11 The court refused to strike out a claim for non-compliance with the pre action protocols in *Pell Frischmann Consultants Ltd v Prabhu* [2013] EWHC 2203 (Ch). The court found that although the claimant was aware that a dispute resolution procedure was in progress when they issued proceedings, to do so without any further reference to the defendant was not within the spirit of the protocol. However, by the time the proceedings were commenced, each party knew what the issues were between them, and a breach of the protocol did not justify striking out the claim.

D ADVERSE COSTS ORDERS AGAINST A PARTY WHO UNREASONABLY REFUSES TO CONSIDER ADR

8.12 The leading case is *Halsey v Milton Keynes General NHS Trust* [2004] 1 WLR 3002. Although there were many cases that dealt with this issue before *Halsey*, this case is a convenient starting point from which to analyse the cases on this subject.

8.13 In *Halsey* (which concerned two conjoined appeals), the defendants succeeded at first instance and were awarded the costs of the proceedings. The claimant in each case appealed against the costs order on the basis that the defendant should be deprived of costs for unreasonably refusing mediation. The Court of Appeal dismissed the appeals and held that the general rule that costs follow the event should not be departed from unless it is shown that the successful party acted unreasonably in refusing to agree to ADR. The unsuccessful party bears the burden of proving this. The court also found that the Lord Chancellor's ADR pledge in March 2001 (revised in 2011, see 1.29) was simply an undertaking to use ADR in all suitable cases. The court should not discriminate against successful public bodies when deciding whether a refusal to agree to ADR should result in a costs penalty. The court found that the judge in *Royal Bank of Canada v Secretary of State for Defence* [2003] EWHC 1841 (Ch) was wrong to attach great weight to the ADR pledge in making no order for costs in favour of the successful defendant.

8.14 In the first appeal, the defendant refused to mediate on the grounds that it had a strong defence, the claimant's offers to mediate were tactical, and the costs of mediation would be disproportionately high compared to the value of the claim. There had been no ADR order and, in the circumstances, the court accepted that the defendant had not acted unreasonably in refusing to mediate for these reasons. It also found that the claimant had not discharged the burden of proving that the mediation would have had a reasonable prospect of success.

In the second appeal, the defendant refused mediation because the issue concerned a point of law that required a decision of the court. Again, in the absence of any court encouragement for ADR to be used, the court held that the defendant was not unreasonable in refusing to mediate for this reason. **8.15**

In deciding whether the refusal to consider ADR was unreasonable, the court should consider all the circumstances of the case, including the following matters, which are discussed in more detail in 8.17–8.59: **8.16**

- the nature of the dispute;
- the merits of the case;
- the extent to which other settlement methods have been attempted;
- whether the costs of the ADR process would be disproportionately high;
- whether any delay in setting up and attending the process would have been prejudicial;
- whether the ADR process has a reasonable prospect of success.

The nature of the dispute

Most cases are not, by their very nature, unsuitable for ADR. However, there may be some cases in which ADR may not be suitable because: the court is required to determine issues of law or construction; a legal precedent is necessary; issues involving allegations of fraud or other commercially disreputable conduct may be raised that require resolution at trial; injunctive relief, a search order, or a freezing order may be required; a point of law may need to be resolved; or the case may be a test case. In such cases, a party will not be acting unreasonably in refusing to use an ADR process. **8.17**

The merits of the case

The fact that a party reasonably believes he has a strong case is relevant to the question of whether a refusal of ADR is reasonable, otherwise a claimant could use the threat of a costs sanction to force a settlement in respect of a case lacking merit. The courts will be astute to prevent a party using an offer of mediation as a tactical ploy to obtain a nuisance-value offer from a defendant. If a party reasonably believes he has a very strong case, that may well be a sufficient reason for refusing to mediate (or negotiate), particularly if this is borne out at trial. Dyson LJ in *Halsey v Milton Keynes General NHS Trust* [2004] 1 WLR 3002 rejected the view to the contrary expressed by Lightman J in *Hurst v Leeming* [2003] 1 Lloyd's Rep 379. However, if the case is a borderline one, then it is likely to be suitable for ADR, and thus a party is likely to be held to be unreasonable in refusing ADR, unless there are factors that tip the scales the other way. A party may reasonably believe that they have a strong case even if they did not succeed in some issues at trial. (*Swain Mason v Mills & Reeve* [2012] EWCA Civ 498). **8.18**

In *Daniels v Commissioner of Police for the Metropolis* [2005] EWCA Civ 1312, the Court of Appeal held that if defendants, who routinely face what they consider to be unfounded claims, wish to take a stand and contest them rather than make payments (even nuisance-value payments) to buy them off, the court should be slow to characterize such conduct as unreasonable so as to deprive defendants of their costs, if they are ultimately successful. **8.19**

In *Hickman v Blake Lapthorn* [2006] EWHC 12 (QB), it was held that the second defendant (a barrister) was not unreasonable for refusing to mediate on the grounds that he believed **8.20** that he had a strong case. He also refused to participate in any settlement that provided for the claimant to receive the sum of £150,000 against both defendants plus costs. This was an offer the claimant put forward, and amounted to a significant reduction in the total value of the claim. At trial, the claimant recovered £130,000 (which was split 33:66 against the first and second defendant respectively). Despite finding that (i) the settlement could have been achieved at or close to the £130,000 that the claimant was eventually awarded, (ii) settlement had not occurred due to the second defendant's failure to negotiate or mediate and (iii) the total costs spent by the parties since the refusal of the claimant's offer was £205,000, the court decided that the second defendant had not acted unreasonably in failing to mediate or negotiate. The second defendant's estimation of the strength of the claimant's case was optimistic but not unreasonable, and it was not unreasonable in light of that estimation to refuse mediation. On the facts, this seems a very surprising decision, and one that it is difficult to justify given the outcome at trial (which was very close to the sum that the claimant indicated he would accept), and the costs that had been expended (£435,000 in total).

8.21 The key consideration is whether the party's assessment of the merits of the case was reasonable. The court did not accept, on the facts, that the successful party was guilty of general unreasonable conduct by failing to respond to offers to undertake mediation, or negotiate, or engage in proposals for compromise in a reasonable way in *Newman v Framewood Manor Management Co Ltd* [2012] EWCA Civ 1727. A successful party will not be deprived of some or all of their costs for rejecting mediation if the claim did not warrant any issues of sufficient substance to justify mediation. See *Morris v Davis* [2012] EWHC 1981 (Ch) per Robert Ham QC at [11] to [17] and [21] and also *ADS Aerospace Ltd v EMS Global Tracking Ltd* [2012] EWHC 2904 (TCC). A defendant who rejected mediation where there was no merit in the claim, but who indicated on a 'without prejudice save as to costs' basis that it was prepared to forgo its costs if the claim was dismissed, is unlikely to be found to be acting unreasonably (*Euroption Stragetic Fund Ltd v Skandinaviska Enskilda Banken AB* [2012] EWHC 749 (Comm); *Swain Mason & Others v Mills & Reeve (A firm)* [2012] EWCA Civ 498 at [18] to [23]). However, a party rejecting an offer of ADR on the basis of their assessment of the merits of the dispute should bear in mind the positive effect that ADR, particularly mediation can have in breaking deadlock, or in resolving disputes which have no merit.

8.22 The court is also not likely to penalize a party from commencing or continuing with court proceedings where there is a genuine right to be vindicated and there remains a dispute for the court to decide (*Pell Frischmann Consultants Ltd v Prabhu* [2013] EWHC 2203 (Ch)). See also *R (on the application of Crookenden) v Institute of Chartered Accountants* [2013] EWHC 1909 (Admin).

The extent to which other settlement methods have been attempted

8.23 The court will expect the parties to have complied with the PD – Pre-action Conduct or any relevant pre-action protocol, and sanctions can be imposed for failing to comply with the provisions of the protocols in respect of ADR (see 8.09–8.11).

8.24 The nature of any sanctions that should be imposed on a party for rejecting ADR before issue of proceedings was reviewed by the court in *Burchell v Bollard* [2005] BLR 330. The Court of Appeal stated that a party should not ignore a reasonable request to negotiate or mediate before proceedings are started. It found that the defendant was unreasonable in refusing an offer to mediate before proceedings were issued, as a small building dispute is, par excellence, the kind of dispute that lends itself to ADR and the merits favoured mediation. The defendant's reason for rejecting mediation because the case was too complex was 'plain nonsense', and any belief that the defendant had in the strength of its own case was unreasonable.

The claimant established that mediation would have had a reasonable prospect of success. Despite this, the court declined to make an adverse order for costs because the defendants rejected mediation before the law was clearly developed by cases like *Dunnett v Railtrack* [2002] 1 WLR 2434 (see 8.78) and *Halsey v Milton Keynes General NHS Trust* [2004] 1 WLR 3002. However a party was penalized for rejecting ADR before issue of proceedings in *Jarrom v Sellers* [2007] EWHC 1366 (Ch) (see 8.69).

The court will also take into account the fact that settlement offers have already been made, but rejected. However, this is unlikely to be a decisive factor in deciding whether a party should be penalized for refusing ADR. Much will depend on the facts of the case. In *Vernacare Ltd v Environmental Pulp Products Ltd* [2012] EWPCC 49 the successful party's costs were reduced by 5% for its failure to engage more constructively with the defendant's attempts to negotiate. **8.25**

On the other hand, if reasonable offers have been made by the successful party and rejected by the unsuccessful party, then this may show that the unsuccessful party had an unreasonable view of the merits of their case and that mediation may serve no purpose and therefore the successful party may not have been unreasonable in refusing to agree to it. Likewise, it may not be unreasonable for a successful party with a strong case to refuse to engage in mediation where they had indicated at all times that they were prepared to engage in without prejudice discussions and there was no good reason why that approach should not be tried, particularly where those negotiations would be quicker and would cost substantially less than mediation. (See *ADS Aerospace Ltd v EMS Global Tracking Ltd* [2012] EWHC 2904 (TCC)). **8.26**

In making a decision, the court will also bear in mind that ADR processes such as mediation may succeed where direct settlement discussions between the parties have failed. (*Halsey v Milton Keynes General NHS Trust* [2004] 1 WLR 3002, per Dyson LJ at [20]).

A defendant's failure to make a timely offer

Recent cases have demonstrated that the courts will not only take into account an unreasonable refusal to consider ADR in making adverse costs orders, but they are also prepared to penalize a defendant in costs if they fail to make any offer at all to settle the claim. **8.27**

In *Fitzroy Robinson Ltd v Mentmore Towers Ltd* [2010] EWHC 98 (TCC), in making an order in relation to the costs of the proceedings, the court took into account the defendant's conduct after the trial of liability. The defendant knew at the conclusion of that trial that they were liable to pay substantial damages to the claimant. Despite that, they took no reasonable steps to protect their position in advance of the quantum trial, and instead attempted to put off the quantification of the claim as long as possible and refused offers to mediate. The defendant only made an offer in respect of damages after their attempt to adjourn the pre-trial review was unsuccessful, and they should have been aware that their liability would be much more than that offered. The court therefore ordered the defendant to pay the claimant's costs on an indemnity basis from the date of the pre-trial review. **8.28**

In *Fox v Foundation Piling Ltd* [2011] 6 Costs LR 961 (see 8.47), the Court of Appeal in deciding the issue of costs took into account the fact that the defendant failed to make a realistic offer to settle the case until late in the day. **8.29**

The Court also penalized the defendant in costs in *Medway Primary Care Trust v Marcus* [2011] EWCA Civ 750. In this case, the claimant only recovered £2,000 (about 0.25% of the sum claimed) in respect of a personal injury claim for which damages were agreed in the sum of £525,000, subject to liability. Despite this, the judge at first instance awarded the claimant 50% of his costs of the action (those total costs being in the region of £480,000). On appeal by the defendants against the costs order, the Court of Appeal held that the successful parties **8.30** in the action were really the defendants but the issue was whether there should be a reduction in their costs to reflect the facts that the claimant had succeeded to a small extent, the defendants did not concede liability until a late stage, and they had failed to make an offer to settle the claim. In relation to the failure to make any offer of settlement, Sir Anthony May (President QB) with whom Tomlinson LJ agreed (Jackson LJ dissenting) found that there should be no reduction in costs for the defendants' failure to make a Part 36 offer on the basis that had a Part 36 offer been made at an early stage of the proceedings it would have entitled the claimant to costs in the region of £100,000, which would have been unjust and disproportionate. However, the court did take into account the fact that the defendants could have written a Calderbank letter offering £3,000 and costs proportionate to that sum. Accordingly, the Court of Appeal reversed the order and held that the defendants should only be entitled to recover 75% of their costs from the claimant. Jackson LJ (dissenting) took a more robust approach and would have dismissed the appeal on the grounds that, as the defendants made no offer to settle the claim, they should accept the consequences (namely not recover any of their own costs and pay 50% of the claimant's costs as ordered by the judge at first instance).

8.31 In *Summers v Fairclough Homes* [2012] 1 WLR 2004 the claimant's claim, which he put at more than £800,000, was dishonest and exaggerated, but nevertheless, at trial, he was awarded damages in the sum of £88,716. The defendant was aware of the claimant's dishonesty because it obtained video surveillance evidence. The Supreme Court, approving *Fox v Foundation Piling Ltd* [2011] EWCA Civ 790, noted that defendants in such cases, who wished to protect their position on costs, could not make a Part 36 offer because of the automatic costs consequences in CPR r 36.10 that would flow from that if the offer was accepted. However, defendants faced with a dishonest or exaggerated claim could make a Calderbank offer to settle the genuine parts of the claim, and the costs of that part, but on the basis that the claimant would pay the defendant's costs in respect of the fraudulent parts of the claim on an indemnity basis.

8.32 It is clear that there is an obligation on both parties to proactively look for ways to settle a case, particularly where the costs far exceed the value of the claim and any counterclaim. In *Bellway Homes Ltd v Seymour (Civil Engineering Contactors Ltd* [2013] EWHC 1890 (TCC), the parties eventually settled the dispute between them, but referred the issue of costs to the court. The court penalized the claimant for exaggerating its claim by ordering that it should recover only 50% of its costs for a certain period. For the remainder of the period, the court ordered that there should be no order for costs. In making this order, Akenhead J noted that the order reflected the 'almost complete pointlessless of the litigation proceeding' and that both parties should have been proactively looking for ways to settle the case sooner rather than later.

8.33 In *Magical Marking Ltd v Ware and Kay LLP* [2013] EWHC 636 (Ch) the claimant sued a firm of solicitors for professional negligence but only recovered £28,000 at trial, this being less than 1% of the sum claimed. Briggs J, in applying *Medway Primary Care Trust v Marcus* (see 8.30), held that the defendants were in substance to be regarded as the successful party and so the claimant should pay their costs of the proceedings. However, although the defendants could not be criticized for failing to make a Part 36 offer because that would have exposed them to an unreasonable costs liability had it been accepted, the defendants should have conceded the limited negligence that the court found proved, and so the court ordered a 15% reduction in the costs found payable because of their failure to do so.

The impact of Part 36 offers on a refusal to use ADR

8.34 Some recent robust decisions have shown that a successful party may be penalized in costs for rejecting mediation, even if they have made an effective Part 36 offer or unreasonably refused an offer to settle made outside the regime in CPR Part 36.

In *Corenso (UK) Ltd v Burnden Group plc* [2003] EWHC 1805 (QB), a defendant made two Part 36 offers, the last of which was made (and accepted by the claimant) less than 21 days before trial. In the usual course of events, the claimant would have been entitled to costs up to the date of acceptance, but the defendant argued that the claimant should pay some or all of the defendant's costs because of its failure to respond to its offers to mediate the dispute. The court rejected this submission holding that a party could properly discharge its obligations to consider ADR and to attempt to engage in it, without necessarily being prepared to enter into mediation, if it took the view that there were other forms of ADR that were more appropriate or more likely to produce a result. Provided the parties showed a genuine and constructive willingness to resolve the issues between them, a party could not be automatically penalized because they did not agree to a form of ADR proposed by the other side. The court could only speculate on whether or not a mediator would have achieved any better or quicker result or could have persuaded the defendant to make the eventual offer at an earlier stage. **8.35**

However, a very robust order was made in *P4 Ltd v Unite Integrated Solutions plc* [2007] BLR 1. The claimant's claim was for £70,000. A number of Part 36 offers were made by the defendant, the last one being for £6,000. The claimant recovered £387 at trial. The defendant sought indemnity costs for the whole period; the claimant submitted there should be no order for costs because the defendant had refused an offer to mediate the dispute before proceedings were issued. The defendant rejected the offers of mediation on the following grounds: **8.36**

- It believed the claim was fundamentally flawed on an issue of law.
- It had made other settlement attempts that had been rejected, including a Part 36 offer of £10,000 within a few days of proceedings being issued. Instead the claimant offered to accept £42,000, then increased its proposal to £50,000, showing that the parties were moving further apart.
- It also considered that mediation would be an expensive exercise bearing in mind the sums at stake.
- Mediation did not have a reasonable prospect of success because neither party was willing to concede ground on the issue of law.

The judge (Ramsey J) did not find these to be cogent reasons for failing to engage in mediation. He did not consider that offers of settlement 'can be a proper substitute for the process of ADR which involves clients engaging with each other and a third party, such as a mediator, to resolve a dispute. In such circumstances, the aspirations of each party are soon brought within realistic bounds and a situation in which one party makes increasingly unrealistic offers is avoided. There was no central engagement in the correspondence on the central issues and concerns which are usually the focus of ADR, through such things as position papers in mediation.' He took the view that mediation would have had a good prospect of success, particularly if, at an early stage, the defendant had provided the claimant with information about a particular payment to a sub-contractor. He held that ordinarily, in light of the small amount recovered by the claimant and its failure on the main issues and the early offers made by the defendant, it would have been a case where the defendant would have been awarded the costs of the claim. However, up to the date of its Part 36 offer, the defendant's conduct in failing to mediate and provide information deprived the parties of being able to resolve the case at minimal cost. The defendant was therefore ordered to pay the claimant's costs up to the latest date for acceptance of the Part 36 offer and the claimant was to pay the defendant's costs after that point. **8.37**

Pursuing litigation in a 'no holds barred' manner and failing to make reasonable early concessions so as to reduce the scope and costs of the trial are factors that the court can take into account as part of 'all of the circumstances of the case' under CPR r 36.14(4), in deciding **8.38** whether it would be unjust to order that a defendant, who had made an effective Part 36 offer, which the claimant failed to beat at trial, should recover some or all of its costs from the claimant from the expiry of the relevant period for accepting the Part 36 offer. See *Lilleyman v Lilleyman & Another* (No 2) [2012] EWHC 1056 (Ch), where Briggs J ordered that a defendant, who made an effective Part 36 offer that the claimant failed to beat at trial, should nevertheless only recover 80% of its costs incurred after the time for acceptance of the offer, the 20% disallowance being an appropriate reflection of the defendant's unreasonable conduct in failing to make sensible early concessions and for the no holds barred approach to the litigation.

8.39 An even more robust approach was taken by the court in *PGF II SA v OMFS Co* [2014] WLR 1386. This was a case brought by a landlord against a tenant for breaches of repairing and reinstatement covenants. The defendant tenant made a Part 36 offer to settle the proceedings, but the claimant did not accept this offer within the relevant period of 21 days following the offer. The claimant then made a number of offers to mediate, but the defendant did not respond to these offers. Eventually, on the day before trial, the claimant accepted the defendant's Part 36 offer, leaving the issue of costs to be determined by the court. The claimant argued that, contrary to the usual costs order made under CPR r 36.10(5) (namely, where the claimant accepts an offer outside the 21-day period for acceptance, it should pay the defendant's costs from the expiry of the relevant period until the date of acceptance), the defendant should pay the claimant's costs because it refused the claimant's offers to mediate. The claimant also relied on other grounds but these were summarily rejected by the court. The Court of Appeal, upholding the decision of the judge at first instance, held that it was unreasonable for the defendant (who in this context was regarded as the successful party) not to respond to the offers of mediation. The defendant's silence in the face of two requests to mediate was itself unreasonable conduct sufficient to warrant a costs sanction. The court applied the *Halsey* principles and found that there was a reasonable prospect that the mediation would be successful. The dispute was well suited to mediation and there was no unbridgeable gulf between the claimant's and the defendant's offers that could not have been overcome in mediation. There was nothing to indicate that the defendant thought its case was so strong that it was reasonable to refuse mediation. There was no suggestion that either party had taken an unrealistic view of the merits of the case and in any event a mediator's skill lies in drawing out seemingly intractable positions. The court also considered that the costs of mediation would not have been disproportionately high nor would it have caused delay and that well-advised commercial parties would have been able to reach a settlement in the mediation. Accordingly, the Court of Appeal, upholding the earlier decision of the court, deprived the defendant of their costs from the expiry of the relevant period for accepting the offer until the date of actual acceptance, but it did not order the defendant to pay the claimant's costs.

8.40 In *Sycamore Bridco Ltd v Breslin* [2013] EWHC 583 (Ch), the court considered *Lilleyman*, and although it found that the claimant had not pursued the litigation in a 'no holds barred' manner, and it had beaten a Part 36 order made by the defendants, it should nevertheless only recover 60% of its costs to reflect the issues that it had fought and lost at trial. The court found that there were no grounds for disapplying the normal consequences of failing to beat a Part 36 offer.

8.41 A claimant, who made a successful claimant's Part 36 offer, which was not accepted by the defendant, nevertheless only recovered 95% of its costs, despite having gained a more advantageous outcome at trial. The 5% deduction was appropriate to reflect the fact that the claimant did not succeed in one issue relating to causation (see *Wilson v Haden (t/a Clyne Farm Centre* [2013] EWHC 1211 (QB)).

By contrast, in *Hammersmatch Properties (Welwyn) Ltd v Saint-Gobain Ceramics & Plastics Ltd* [2013] EWHC 2227 (TCC), the court held that where a party makes a Part 36 offer which is *ineffective* because the party to whom it is made recovers more than the sum offered at trial, the court should not impose costs penalties on the 'near miss' grounds that the offer was almost appropriate and the successful party should have negotiated, particularly where the court did not have full information about negotiations which may have taken place and the parties sought costs protection by making Part 36 offers.

Unreasonable refusal of other offers

A successful party may also be deprived of some or all of their costs if they act unreasonably in failing to accept a Calderbank offer made by a defendant to settle the case, and they fail to recover more than that offer at trial. (*Brit Inns Ltd (in Liquidation) v BDW Trading Ltd* (Costs) [2012] EWHC 2489 (TCC)). However, an offer which is not made under Part 36 should not be treated as directly analogous to a Part 36 offer when considering what costs orders to make under CPR Part 44 (see *F & C Alternative Investments (Holdings) Ltd v Barthelemy* (Costs) [2012] EWCA Civ 843). **8.42**

In *Walker Construction (UK) Ltd v Quayside Homes Ltd* [2014] EWCA Civ 93, the Court of Appeal held that a costs order requiring a claimant to pay the defendant's costs of over £345,000, where the defendant had recovered only 12% of its amended counterclaim and only 6% of its original counterclaim (a total net sum of £10,885) was disproportionate, and the judge at first instance had failed to give appropriate weight to a Calderbank offer made by the claimant at an early stage in the proceedings in the total sum of £30,000, which included a figure of £19,000 in respect of the defendant's costs. The Court of Appeal, applying *Medway Primary Care Trust v Marcus* [2011] EWCA Civ 750 and *Fairclough Homes Ltd v Summers* [2012] 1 WLR 2004 – see also 8.31) found that the judge at first instance had failed to give appropriate weight to the fact that the claimant could not have made a Part 36 offer because acceptance of that would have entitled the defendant to all of their costs. The court also found that the claimant's Calderbank offer of £30,000 was reasonable and proportionate and the defendant was unreasonable in not accepting it when it was made. The allowance in that offer of £19,000 for costs, given the defendant's ultimate recovery of approximately £11,000, represented a reasonable offer on costs. The judge was entitled to look at the matter with the benefit of hindsight and in the knowledge that the defendant had made a very small recovery in its counterclaim. Accordingly, the costs order was reversed and the claimant was ordered to pay 50% of the defendant's costs up to the date of the Calderbank offer, and the defendant was ordered to pay the claimant's costs from the date of the Calderbank offer until the date of judgment. **8.43**

However, in *Newman v Framewood Manor Management Co Ltd* [2012] EWCA Civ 1727, a successful claimant was not held to be unreasonable in refusing the defendant's without prejudice offers to settle which were made on the basis that each party pay their own costs. Acceptance of these offers would have deprived her of the right to recover costs as the successful party.

The claimant's failure to initiate ADR

The court makes a distinction between cases where the successful party *rejects* an offer of ADR made by the other side and those cases where there has been a failure by the successful party to *initiate* ADR proceedings. **8.44**

In *Vale of Glamorgan Council v Roberts* [2008] EWHC 2911 (Ch), proceedings were commenced by the local authority in relation to a boundary dispute. It succeeded in the litigation. The defendant argued that it should not have to pay all of the council's costs because it failed **8.45** or refused to accept or engage in serious settlement negotiations or mediation. The court found that none of the defendant's offers positively suggested mediation, so the local authority did not positively refuse to mediate. The court distinguished *Halsey* on the basis that those guidelines did not apply to a case where the successful party did not initiate ADR, and held that it would be going too far to disallow costs incurred by a successful party simply because that party did not initiate suggestions for mediation (or, by analogy, any ADR process).

8.46 However, the court in *Vale of Glamorgan Council v Roberts* did not consider the case of *Painting v Oxford University* [2005] PIQR Q5. This was a personal injury case in which the claimant was claiming £400,000. Initially the defendant paid £184,442 into court. Surveillance evidence showed the claimant's injuries were less severe than she alleged, so the defendant withdrew the payment in and substituted a Part 36 payment of £10,000. At trial, the claimant recovered the sum of £23,331. The defendant argued that it should not have to pay the claimant's costs on the grounds that she had exaggerated her claim and, had it not been for the exaggeration, the matter would have been settled early with minimal costs. They also criticized the claimant for failing to take any steps to negotiate, make counter-offers or accept the offers that had been made. The Court of Appeal held that the judge had failed to give proper weight to the fact that the claimant had exaggerated her claim, and had also failed to take into account the fact that, but for the exaggerated claim, the matter would probably have been settled at an early stage. The court also noted that the claimant had not made an offer or a counter-offer and that the court could take a failure to negotiate into account when determining costs. The Court of Appeal therefore ordered that the defendant should pay the claimant's costs up to the date of the payment into court and the claimant should pay the defendant's costs from that date.

8.47 In *Widlake v BAA Ltd* [2010] PIQR P4, the court applied *Painting v Oxford University* and the successful party was deprived of costs because of exaggeration of the claim, the deliberate concealment of facts relevant to her condition, and the fact that she failed to negotiate. The court ordered that there should be no order for costs. By contrast, in *Fox v Foundation Piling Ltd* [2011] 6 Costs LR 961, the Court of Appeal refused to penalize a claimant in costs who had exaggerated his claim (but where there had been no finding of dishonesty or misrepresentation against him) and where he realistically and promptly accepted the defendant's offer to settle which was made after they had disclosed surveillance evidence. The court was also influenced by the fact that the defendants had obtained the video surveillance evidence in September 2004 but they did not disclose it in the proceedings until March 2009 and they failed to make a realistic offer reflecting the true value of the claim until November 2009, which the claimant then promptly accepted. Jackson LJ stated at para 63:

> In the context of personal injury litigation where the claimant has a strong case on liability but quantum is inflated, the defendant's remedy is to make a modest CPR Part 36 offer. If the defendant fails to make a sufficient CPR Part 36 offer at the first opportunity, it cannot expect to secure costs protection. Different considerations may arise where the claimant is proved to have been dishonest but (on the judge's findings) that is not this case.

8.48 It is not possible to determine how seriously the court viewed the claimant's mere failure to take part in negotiations in any of these cases. In *Painting v Oxford University* and in *Widlake v BAA Ltd* there was a combination of exaggeration and a failure to negotiate and in *Fox v Foundation Piling Ltd* there was exaggeration of the claim by the claimant but prompt acceptance of a realistic offer and culpable conduct on the part of the defendant by delaying in disclosing video surveillance evidence and making a realistic offer in light of that late in the proceedings. In the absence of any exaggeration, *Vale of Glamorgan v Roberts* establishes that an adverse costs order should not be made against the successful party for failing to initiate ADR or mediation in situations where there is no offer to engage in ADR processes by the unsuccessful defendant. It would be unfair to justify giving a costs advantage to the losing party if they too have ignored the need to consider ADR.

In *Vale of Glamorgan v Roberts*, there was no suggestion that the claimant failed to comply with the terms of the relevant pre-action protocol or PD – Pre-Action Conduct. It is clear in light of *Thornhill v Nationwide Metal Recycling Ltd* [2011] EWCA Civ 919 (see 8.10) that a party who fails to comply with the requirements of the Pre-Action Protocols and PD – Pre-action Conduct to a significant extent is likely to find his failure to do so penalized in costs. **8.49**

Whether the costs of ADR would be disproportionately high

This is a factor that will also be taken into account and may be of particular importance if the sums at stake are relatively small. This is because ADR processes, such as mediation, in such cases may cost as much as a day in court. However this is unlikely to be a significant factor in the vast majority of cases, and certainly not in low value cases in the small claims track, where the court operates a free mediation scheme, nor may it be a relevant factor in many fast-track cases where fixed-fee mediations can be arranged through the Civil Mediation Online Directory. **8.50**

Whether any delay in setting up and attending ADR would be prejudicial

If an ADR process is proposed at a late stage of the litigation and is likely to result in the trial being delayed, this may be a reason to refuse to agree to it. An example is *Palfrey v Wilson* [2007] EWCA Civ 94, where no adverse costs order was made for refusing mediation that was proposed only two months before trial. **8.51**

In *Société Internationale de Télécommunications Aéronautiques SC (SITA) v The Wyatt Co (UK) Ltd* [2002] EWHC 2401 (Ch), the defendant settled the claimant's claim at mediation and failed to recover anything against the third party at trial. The claimant contended the third party should be deprived of its costs as it had refused the defendant's offer, made on three separate occasions, to take part in mediation. The court accepted that the third party was not unreasonable in refusing the defendant's first two offers to take part in mediation for the following reasons: **8.52**

- The mediation concerned the claim between the claimant and the defendant.
- The third party had insufficient time to prepare for the first mediation round as it had only recently been brought into the claim as a third party.
- The defendant's reasons for suggesting mediation were not to settle the third-party claim, but rather to persuade the third party to contribute something to the settlement of the claimant's case.
- The offers to mediate were disagreeable in tone and designed to bully and browbeat the third party into mediation.
- The third party was not likely to be liable (an event which was borne out by the trial).

The third offer to mediate related only to the third-party claim, and the court also found that the third party acted reasonably in refusing this offer because it was made too close to the trial (which was due to take place three weeks later). The court therefore declined to make any reduction in the third party's costs. **8.53**

Successful parties were judged not to be unreasonable in refusing mediation where it was proposed only 20 days before trial (see *ADS Aerospace Ltd v EMS Global Tracking Ltd* [2012] EWHC 2904 (TCC), or 13 days before trial (see *Park Promotion Ltd (t/a Pontypool Rugby Football Club) v Welsh Rugby Union Ltd* [2012] EWHC 2406 (QB). **8.54**

Whether ADR had a reasonable prospect of success

8.55 In *Halsey v Milton Keynes General NHS Trust* [2004] 1 WLR 3002, Dyson LJ stated that if mediation (or another ADR process) has been refused on the basis that it would have no reasonable prospect of success, then the burden is on the unsuccessful party seeking to avoid paying costs to show that the successful party unreasonably refused mediation and that it would have had a reasonable prospect of success. Dyson LJ remarked that this should not be an unduly onerous burden to discharge, because the unsuccessful party does not have to show that mediation would have succeeded. Mediators and commentators have questioned what is meant by 'success' in mediation. They argue that mediation may be successful even if it does not result in a settlement because it assists with narrowing and clarifying issues, which can save time at trial and even lead to a settlement at a later date. That may be so; however it is clear that the court in *Halsey* was equating success with settlement.

8.56 The courts have refused to penalize a party for refusing to agree to ADR in the following circumstances:

- where the relationship between the parties was so bad that mediation did not have a realistic prospect of success (*Re Midland Linen Services Ltd* [2005] EWHC 3380 (Ch));
- where the defendant had 'a resounding success' before the trial judge and before the Court of Appeal, and that there was 'insufficient room for manoeuvre to make mediation a venture which might have real prospects of success in achieving compromise' (*McCook v Lobo* [2002] EWCA Civ 1760), where the defendant refused mediation in view of the claimant's attitude, character, and the fact that the claimant was incapable of a balanced evaluation of the facts and therefore mediation had no real prospect of success (*Hurst v Leeming* [2003] 1 Lloyd's Rep 378). Lightman J, however, pointed out that to refuse mediation on the grounds that it has no reasonable prospect of success, although justified on the exceptional facts of this case, was a 'high risk course to take' because it relies on the court agreeing that there is no real prospect of ADR being successful;
- where a party had a strong case and the conduct of the other party indicated that they were not willing to accept a nuisance payment and there was no evidence that they would have settled the claim at that level, even through the good offices of a mediator (*ADS Aerospace Ltd v EMS Global Tracking Ltd* [2012] EWHC 2904 (TCC)).

8.57 However, an adverse costs order is likely to be made if there is no objective reason for concluding that ADR has no reasonable prospect of success. In *Gaston, Boughton v Courtney* [2004] EWHC 600 (Ch), the court ordered the defendant to pay the claimant's costs of the action for refusing to participate in mediation, despite the fact that the court had ordered, on two separate occasions, a 28-day stay to enable the parties to consider in good faith whether they could settle the dispute by ADR and despite a number of offers being made by the claimant to engage in mediation. The defendant refused to do so on the grounds that there was no foreseeable or realistic prospect of success. The court found that there was no objective reason to conclude that mediation had no reasonable prospect of success and that the repeated attempts of the claimant to persuade the defendant to participate in it and to explain its basis and rationale gave positive grounds to encourage hope of success. A defendant was also penalized in the overall costs order made for failing to respond to the claimant's suggestions to use ADR and for ignoring correspondence. The court noted that ADR might not have been successful, but the defendant failed to consider how it might assist (see *Wilson v Haden (t/a Clyde Farm Centre* [2013] EWHC 1211 (QB). See also *PGF II SA v OMFS Company* [2014] WLR 1386 (discussed at 8.59).

Extension of the Halsey *guidelines to a failure to use compulsory ADR schemes*

8.58 The *Halsey* factors also apply where a claimant pursues proceedings rather than considering ADR through a compulsory scheme established by the Financial Services Authority (see *Andrew v Barclays Bank Plc* [2012] CTLC 115)).

The courts will refuse to allow a claim to proceed if the action is brought only to recover costs in circumstances where full compensation, but not costs, could be obtained under an ADR scheme, and such a claim could be struck out under CPR r 3.4 (*Binns v Firstplus Financial Group plc* [2013] EWHC 2436 (QB)).

Silence in the face of an ADR invitation

8.59 In *PGF II SA v OMFS Co 1 Ltd* [2014] WLR 1386, the Court of Appeal, endorsing advice given in The Jackson ADR Handbook, extended the *Halsey* guidelines, and held that as a general rule, silence in the face of an invitation to participate in ADR was itself unreasonable, regardless of whether there was a good reason for the refusal to engage in ADR. It was possible that there might be rare cases where ADR was so obviously inappropriate that to characterize silence as unreasonable would be pure formalism, or where the failure to respond was as a result of a mistake, in which case the onus would be on the respondent to the invitation to prove that explanation. The court held that there were sound practical and policy reasons for such a modest extension to the *Halsey* guidelines, firstly because an investigation of the reasons for refusing to use ADR, advanced for the first time at a costs hearing perhaps months or years later, posed forensic difficulties for the court deciding whether those reasons were genuine. Secondly, a failure to provide reasons was contrary to the objective of requiring parties to consider and discuss ADR. Any difficulties or reasonable objection to a particular ADR proposal should be discussed, so that the parties could narrow their differences. The court noted that that happened routinely in cases involving the use of expert evidence, and there was no reason why the same approach should not be used in relation to ADR. The court found that this would also serve the policy of proportionality.

E OTHER FACTORS

8.60 The court in *Halsey* made it clear that the six factors described in 8.16 to 8.57 above were not exhaustive. The court, in deciding whether a failure or refusal to consider ADR was unreasonable would also consider all the circumstances of the case. These include matters such as:

- whether an ADR order was made by the court;
- the extent to which further information or evidence was required before ADR was attempted;
- the extent to which both parties were at fault.

Whether an ADR order was made by the court

8.61 Where a successful party refuses to agree to ADR despite court encouragement, the court will take this into account in deciding whether the refusal was unreasonable. In *Halsey* Dyson LJ pointed out at [29]: 'The court's encouragement may take different forms. The stronger the encouragement, the easier it will be for the unsuccessful party to discharge the burden of showing that the successful party's refusal was unreasonable.' If a party refused to engage in ADR, despite the fact that an order was made in the form in Appendix 7 of the *Admiralty and Commercial Court Guide* (see Figure 7.1), then 'he runs the risk that for that reason alone his refusal to agree to ADR would be held to have been unreasonable, and that he should therefore be penalised in costs'.

8.62 In *Dyson v Leeds City Council* [2000] CP Rep 42, Lord Woolf [at 18] stated:

> I would also add the reminder that the court has powers to take a strong view about the rejection of encouraging noises we are making [about ADR] if necessary by imposing eventual orders for indemnity costs or indeed ordering that a higher rate of interest be paid on any damages that might at the end of the day be recoverable.

8.63 The successful party was penalized in costs for ignoring two ADR orders made by the court in *Gaston, Boughton v Courtney* [2004] EWHC 600 (Ch) (see 8.57). In *Wilson v Haden (t/a Clyne Farm Centre)* [2013] EWHC 1211 (QB), the court, in awarding costs, took into account the fact that the defendant did not attempt ADR despite the court ordering that the parties should do so, it ignored correspondence from the claimant suggesting the use of ADR, and, even more importantly, it did not file a witness statement indicating why it considered ADR to be inappropriate in accordance with the ADR order made by the court. The court held that it was unacceptable for a party to flout a court order in that way and that there was no real consideration on the defendant's part as to how ADR might assist. The court took all of these matters into account and awarded the claimant 95% of the costs of the action. See also *Ali Ghaith v Indesit Company UK Limited* [2012] EWCA Civ 642 where the Court of Appeal criticized the parties for failing to use mediation when the court granting permission to appeal had recommended they should do so (per Longmore LJ at [26] and Ward LJ at [29].

Requesting further information or evidence before using ADR

8.64 The court in *Halsey v Milton Keynes General NHS Trust* [2004] 1 WLR 3002 made it clear that the factors listed above were not exhaustive. In deciding whether a party was unreasonable in refusing ADR all the facts and circumstances of the case must be considered.

8.65 These include whether a party was unreasonable for refusing ADR where it considered further information or clarification of the opposing side's case had to be provided, or expert evidence had to be obtained and/or disclosed before it was willing to do so.

8.66 In *Wethered Estates Ltd v Davis* [2006] BLR 86, the defendant had made a number of requests for mediation, both before and after issue. The claimant expressed willingness to engage with mediation but felt that it was important that each party's case was set out in court statements of case before doing so. After issue of court proceedings, the defendant again asked the claimant to agree to mediation on several occasions. The claimant indicated that it was willing to do so, but it first needed to understand the defendant's case (although it had, by then, the defendant's defence and witness statements) and that mediation would be best undertaken when the evidence was final. The claimant only agreed to participate in mediation 15 months after it was first proposed by the defendant. The court held that the claimant had not acted unreasonably by refusing to mediate until the issues in the case were clarified, as the nature of the dispute was difficult to fathom.

8.67 In *Corby Group Litigation v Corby DC* [2009] EWHC 2109 (TCC), the court found that the unsuccessful defendant had not acted unreasonably in refusing to mediate in group litigation brought by the claimants until expert evidence had been obtained. Once that evidence had been obtained, the defendant again rejected mediation on the basis that it was unlikely to reach a conclusion of the matter because the defendant's expert evidence supported its stance on each issue and the claimants were adopting a 'scatter-gun' approach. Although with hindsight the defendant was wrong in their assessment of the litigation, their decision to refuse ADR had to be judged at the time the decision was made, and no adverse costs order was made against them.

8.68 The court also considered no adverse costs order should be made against a defendant in *Mobiqa Ltd v Trinity Mobile Ltd* [2010] EWHC 253 (Pat) in circumstances where the defendant (who was treated effectively as the successful party as the claimant discontinued the claim) refused the claimant's offers of settlement and mediation on the grounds that it would prefer to embark on mediation once expert evidence had been exchanged. The court held it was reasonable for the defendant to wait until expert evidence had been exchanged before embarking on mediation so that it could be seen whether the claimant had a case.

A different view was taken by the court in *Jarrom v Sellars* [2007] EWHC 1366 (Ch). In this case, the court deprived the claimants of costs in a probate claim for refusing the defendant's offer of a settlement meeting before the proceedings were issued. The claimants refused to attend such a meeting until the defendant had provided an agenda, witness statements, and detailed proposals. The court found that these reasons were not sufficient to justify the claimants refusing a meeting, as such a meeting would have given them the chance to find out what the defendant wanted, what she proposed, and may have enabled the parties to explore how to take the matter forward without the necessity for litigation. The court therefore made no order for costs. **8.69**

In *PGF II SA v OMFS Co* [2013] EWCA Civ 1288, at first instance (see [2012] EWHC 83 (TCC)) the defendant's failure to respond to the claimant's suggestions to use ADR was not held to be a refusal, and in any event, if it was a refusal, that refusal was justified on the following grounds. **8.70**

- Firstly, it was not unreasonable for the defendant to refuse mediation given what had occurred between the parties at a previous mediation in relation to a different dispute. The court rejected this argument on the basis that the previous mediation proceedings were covered by without prejudice privilege which was not waived by the claimant (see Chapter 6) and also because this was not something that the defendant had raised in answer to the invitation to mediate.
- Secondly, a successful mediation could only take place later in the year when expert reports on diminution in value were available. The court rejected this argument also as it was open to the defendant to ask for the claimant's report and to obtain their own report in reply prior to a mediation taking place. Any such inhibitions to mediation could have been overcome had they been raised by the defendant at the time. The first instance decision was upheld by the Court of Appeal.

Both parties at fault

Where both parties are at fault in failing to consider ADR, the court may penalize both of them by refusing to make any costs order at all, whatever the outcome of the case (*Longstaff International Ltd v Evans* [2005] EWHC 4 (Ch)). **8.71**

The court penalized both parties by making no order for costs in *Rolf v De Guerin* [2011] EWCA Civ 78. The claimant issued a claim against a builder claiming £50,000 for breach of a small building contract for renovation works to a garage and a loft extension. After proceedings were issued, the claimant, in writing, on two separate occasions, indicated that she was willing to consider settlement negotiations, but these were ignored by the defendant. The claimant then made a claimant's CPR Part 36 offer to settle in the sum of £14,000 plus costs and again sent several letters indicating that she would be willing to have a settlement meeting or mediation. These letters were ignored by the defendant until approximately one week before trial when he made his own Part 36 offer and indicated that he would agree to mediation or a settlement meeting. The claimant succeeded at trial, but only recovered damages of £2,500 in respect of one defect (all other aspects of the claim being dismissed). The trial judge considered that the defendant was right to reject the claimant's offer and made no order for costs up to the expiry of the period for acceptance of the offer and that **8.72** the claimant should pay the defendant's costs after that period, including the costs of trial. The claimant appealed.

8.73 The Court of Appeal reviewed the key authorities, including *Halsey*, reversed the costs order, and ruled that the appropriate order was to make no order for costs as this did substantial justice between the parties. In making this order, the Court of Appeal was influenced by the fact that the claimant was the winner, but only just (she had failed in most of her claim) and the defendant was unreasonable in rejecting the claimant's offers to attempt to settle by negotiation or mediation. The court found that this unreasonable refusal should be taken into account when the court exercised its discretion as to costs, particularly as a trial should be regarded as the last resort in a small building case and that mediation was particularly appropriate for cases of this type.

8.74 The defendant put forward three reasons for refusing to agree to mediation or a settlement meeting until the eve of the trial, all of which were rejected by the Court of Appeal:

- the behaviour of the claimant's husband and the fact that, at mediation, the defendant would have been unable to persuade the mediator what he was like;
- he would have had to accept 'his guilt' at mediation;
- he wanted his day in court and he was proved correct.

8.75 A similar result was reached in *Seeff v Ho* [2011] EWCA Civ 186. The claimant brought proceedings against the defendant for carrying out conversion work to his garage which trespassed onto his property. Before the issue of proceedings the defendant failed to respond to the claimant's suggestion that they mediate the dispute. The Court of Appeal, in reversing the order made below, decided that there should be no order as to costs. In doing so, the court took into account all of the circumstances of the case, including the fact that the claimant did not succeed in a substantial part of the claim, and that the defendant failed to take part in mediation when suggested by the claimant.

8.76 In *Abbott v Long* [2011] EWCA Civ 874, the Court of Appeal dismissed an appeal by the claimant against a decision of the first instance judge to make no order for costs on the grounds that the claimant had exaggerated his claim and recovered £8,600, which was about one-sixth of the amount claimed, and the defendant had made no offer to settle the claim. In Norbrook Laboratories Ltd v Carr & others [2013] EWHC 476 (QB), the court made no order for costs where both parties had acted unreasonably before proceedings were issued, and during the litigation.

F REJECTING ADR AFTER JUDGMENT AND BEFORE THE HEARING OF AN APPEAL

8.77 The court has on several occasions penalized a successful party for refusing ADR after trial and pending an appeal. Sanctions are more likely to be imposed if a successful party ignores the Court of Appeal's encouragement to attempt ADR, or a recommendation that the parties should attempt mediation using the Court of Appeal Mediation Service (see 18.24–18.26).

8.78 In *Dunnett v Railtrack plc* [2002] 1 WLR 2434, the single judge, Schiemann LJ, granting leave to appeal, recommended that the parties should try to mediate the dispute using the Court of Appeal Mediation Scheme (which was free to the users at that time). The defendant refused to engage in mediation on the grounds that it was confident it would succeed at trial. Despite the fact that the defendant won the appeal, and the claimant failed to beat a modest Part 36 offer of £2,500 that the defendant had made after leave to appeal had been granted, the Court of Appeal refused to award the defendant the costs of the appeal. The court held that if a party rejected ADR out of hand when it had been suggested by the court, they would suffer the consequences when costs came to be decided. As the defendant had refused to contemplate ADR at a stage prior to the costs of the appeal beginning to flow, it was not appropriate to take into account the fact that offers had been made to compromise the appeal. Brooke LJ stated (at [15]):

> It is to be hoped that any publicity given to this part of the judgment of the court will draw the attention of lawyers to their duties to further the overriding objective in the way that is set out in CPR Part 1 and to the possibility that, if they turn down out of hand the chance of alternative dispute resolution when suggested by the court, as happened on this occasion, they may have to face uncomfortable costs consequences.

In *Neal v Jones Motors* [2002] EWCA Civ 1731, the winning party to an appeal had its costs reduced by £5,000 because it failed to heed advice given by the court to attempt mediation. **8.79**

In *Virani v Manuel Revert Y CIA SA* [2004] 2 Lloyd's Rep 14, on granting leave to appeal, the single judge suggested to the appellant that they could use the Court of Appeal mediation service. They declined to do so and lost the appeal. The respondent was awarded costs to be assessed on the indemnity basis because of the appellant's refusal to mediate. **8.80**

However, a different view was taken by the court in *Reed Executive plc v Reed Business Information Ltd* [2004] 1 WLR 3026. Here, the Court of Appeal refused to penalize the successful appellants/defendants for refusing an offer by the claimant to mediate that was made late in the day after the claimant had obtained judgment in its favour, when the defendants would have been negotiating from a position of weakness and on the grounds that it had a reasonable and justifiable belief in its prospects of success in the appeal. This decision is more likely to be in line with the factors that the court considered in *Halsey v Milton Keynes General NHS Trust* [2004] 1 WLR 3002. See also *Ali Ghaith v Indesit Company UK Ltd* [2012] EWCA Civ 642, where the Court of Appeal criticized the parties for failing to use mediation, despite the court recommending that they should do so. **8.81**

G DELAY IN CONSENTING TO MEDIATION (OR ANOTHER ADR PROCESS)

In *Nigel Witham Ltd v Smith* [2008] EWHC 12 (TCC), the court considered whether a party could be penalized for agreeing to mediation late in the day when the majority of costs had been incurred, although they did in fact mediate the dispute. The court held that where the successful party has unreasonably delayed in consenting to mediation, this may lead to an adverse costs order, but no order should be made on the facts. The court found that it was not unreasonable for the defendant to refuse to mediate before the proceedings were issued as it was entitled to see how the claimant set out its claim and the claimant's uncompromising attitude meant that an earlier mediation would have had no reasonable prospect of success. The defendant had not unreasonably delayed in consenting to a judicial settlement conference. **8.82**

A party did not act unreasonably in refusing to consider mediation until its application to strike out the other side's case had been disposed of by the court (*S v Chapman* [2008] EWCA Civ 800). Successful parties were judged not to be unreasonable in refusing mediation where it was proposed only 20 days before trial (see *ADS Aerospace Ltd v EMS Global Tracking Ltd* [2012] EWHC 2904 (TCC), or 13 days before trial (see *Park Promotion Ltd (t/a Pontypool Rugby Football Club) v Welsh Rugby Union Ltd* [2012] EWHC 2406 (QB). **8.83**

H BACKING OUT OF AN AGREED ADR PROCESS

8.84 The court has considered whether a successful party should be penalized for agreeing to explore settlement in an ADR process, and then backing out of it at the last moment.

8.85 In *Leicester Circuits Ltd v Coates Brothers plc* [2003] EWCA Civ 333, the parties agreed to mediate and even got as far as appointing a mediator and arranging the date of the mediation meeting. However, the defendants withdrew from the mediation the day before it was due to take place on instructions from their insurers. They lost at first instance but won on appeal. Although the defendants were granted the costs of the appeal, the Court of Appeal was not prepared to allow them to recover costs that were incurred from a date nine days before the date they withdrew from the mediation on the basis that there was at least a prospect that the mediation process would have succeeded if it had been allowed to proceed. Per Longmore LJ:

> The whole point of having mediation, and once you have agreed to it, proceeding with it, is that the most difficult of problems can sometimes, indeed often are, resolved . . . . Having agreed to mediation, it hardly lies in the mouths of those who agreed to it to assert that there was no realistic prospect of success.

8.86 In *McMillan Williams v Range* [2004] EWCA Civ 294, the parties agreed, after encouragement from the court, to attempt to resolve their dispute by mediation. Two days before the date fixed for the mediation, the appellant decided not to proceed with it, on the grounds that it was not likely to be successful as neither side was willing to change their positions. Despite winning the appeal, the Court of Appeal refused to award the appellant the costs of the appeal. As Ward LJ put it: 'this is a case where we should condemn the posturing and jockeying for position taken by each side in this dispute and thus direct that each side pay its own costs of their frolic in the Court of Appeal'.

8.87 In *Roundstone Nurseries Ltd v Stephenson Holdings Ltd* [2009] EWHC 1431 (TCC), the defendant withdrew from a mediation meeting days before it was due to take place. The court ordered the defendant to pay the claimant's costs thrown away by the late cancellation of the mediation process.

I UNREASONABLE CONDUCT IN THE MEDIATION

8.88 The principles in *Halsey v Milton Keynes General NHS Trust* [2004] 1 WLR 3002 were extended in *Carleton (Earl of Malmesbury) v Strutt and Parker* [2008] EWHC 424 (QB), to unreasonable conduct in the mediation. The court held a party who agreed to mediation and then took an unreasonable stance in that mediation was in the same position as a party who refused to mediate and that *Halsey* applied to this situation. The parties agreed that privilege should be waived in all 'without prejudice' matters. The court found that the failure to mediate before the trial was due to the attitude taken by both parties, and it was not therefore open to one party to claim that the failure of the other should be taken into account on the question of costs. In relation to the mediation that took place following judgment on liability, the judge found that the claimant's position at the mediation was plainly unreasonable and unrealistic and that if they had made an offer that reflected their true position the mediation might have succeeded. He found that the defendants could have protected themselves by making a Part 36 offer, but that justice would be done by awarding the claimant only a portion of their costs to reflect the unreasonable stance they took in the mediation.

8.89 It is likely that the court can only enquire into conduct that took place in the mediation if all parties to the mediation consent to waive privilege and confidentiality (see 14.120–14.145). As this is not likely to happen often, an order of this type is likely to be very rare.

J IMPOSING A COSTS CAP ON SOLICITOR-CLIENT COSTS FOR FAILING TO PURSUE ADR

8.90 In *Brownlee v Brownlee*, a decision of the South Gauteng High Court of South Africa, 2008/25274, the parties unreasonably failed to mediate in a family dispute. The judge made an order imposing a cap on the solicitor–client costs that could be recovered because he was '. . . persuaded that the failure of the attorneys to send this matter to mediation at an early stage should be visited by the court's displeasure'.

8.91 It is quite possible that the courts in England and Wales could be persuaded to make a similar order if the circumstances of the case merited it. The court could also exercise its powers to make a wasted costs order against a legal adviser who failed to give his client proper practical and commercial advice about the benefits of ADR.

K INDEMNITY COSTS ORDERS FOR FAILING TO CONSIDER ADR

8.92 Although the courts have warned that they have powers to take a strong view about the rejection of ADR, if necessary by imposing indemnity costs orders, or ordering that a higher rate of interest should be paid on any damages that might be recoverable (see the comments of Ward LJ in *Dyson v Leeds City Council* [2000] CP Rep 42 at [18]), until recently there were few reported cases in which orders of this kind have been made. Before indemnity costs are imposed, the case in question must fall outside the norm and there must be unreasonable conduct to a high degree (see *Reid Minty (a firm) v Taylor* [2001] EWCA Civ 1723). The principles relating to indemnity costs orders have been recently restated in *Euroption Strategic Fund Ltd v Skandinaviska Enskilda Banken AB* [2012] EWHC 749 (Comm). If the claims advanced are unreasonable, speculative, and opportunistic, and the manner in which they are litigated is disproportionate, an order for indemnity costs is likely to be appropriate (see *Excalibur Ventures LLC v Texas Keystone Inc (Costs)* [2013] EWHC 4278 (Comm).

8.93 An indemnity costs order was made in *Rowallan Group Ltd v Edgehill Portfolio No 1* [2007] EWHC 32 (Ch) where the claimant issued proceedings during the course of a mediation hearing, with no prior letter before claim.

8.94 In *Southwark LBC v IBM UK Ltd* [2011] EWHC 653 (TCC) and *Barr v Biffa Waste Services Ltd (Costs)* [2011] EWHC 1107 (TCC), indemnity costs were awarded from a certain date in circumstances where there was a failure to accept a reasonable offer which ought to have been accepted. These cases were considered in *Epsom College v Pierse Constructing Southern Ltd (in Liquidation) (Costs)* [2011] EWCA Civ 1449, where the court upheld the indemnity costs order made by the judge at first instance but on different grounds. Lord Justice Rix (at para 71) stated that the requirements for making an indemnity costs order could be met where there has been an unreasonable failure to accept offers of settlement, or a party has resisted a sensible approach to finding a solution to the proceedings.

8.95 A defendant was awarded indemnity costs where enormous amounts of time, costs, and court resources had been wasted as a result of the claimant's unwillingness to accept an offer of settlement from the defendant that they had indicated they were prepared to settle for only a few days earlier, and there was no justification for the claimant's change of position (*Igloo Regeneration*

(General Partner) Ltd v Powell Williams Partnership (Costs) [2013] EWHC 1859 (TCC)). The court also accepted that there was unreasonable conduct to a high degree on the part of a party that justified an award of indemnity costs in *A & E Television Networks LLC v Discovery Communications Europe Ltd* [2013] EWHC 276 (Pat). In this case, the claim and counterclaim were dismissed at trial after costs had been incurred by the parties in the total sum of £3 million. The defendant applied for indemnity costs. The court made an order that the claimant should pay the defendant's costs on the standard basis up until the date on which the period for accepting the defendant's early 'drop hands' offer expired, and on the indemnity basis after that date, on the grounds that the claimant's case had been wholly without merit, and that the claimant unreasonably failed to accept the early 'drop hands' offer from the defendant.

8.96 On the other hand, the court refused to award costs on an indemnity basis against a party who unreasonably withdrew from mediation in *Roundstone Nurseries Ltd v Stephenson Holdings Ltd* [2009] EWHC 1431 (TCC). The court accepted that the defendant's conduct justified them paying the claimant's costs thrown away, but it did not merit assessment of those costs on an indemnity basis. An award of indemnity costs is also not appropriate where the claimant's claim was dismissed at trial, but the issues it raised were plainly arguable, the claim was not pursued in a disproportionate or unreasonable way, and where it was not unreasonable to reject the defendant's low offer to settle inclusive of costs, which would have rendered the claimant out of pocket had it been accepted, even though the claimant would have been better off accepting the offer than pursuing the claim to trial (*Elvanite Full Circle Limited v AMEC Earth & Environmental (UK) Limited* [2013] EWHC 1643 (TCC)).

The court has sounded a warning note to parties who seek indemnity costs after settlement. Such parties must behave in a proportionate way, and where an indemnity costs application depended on evidence which was likely to involve material conflicts of evidence, the applicant needed 'to think long and hard about whether it was appropriate to pursue the application' because there could be few, if any, cases in which there should, in effect, be a trial of issues settled by acceptance of an offer or by settlement reached in some other ADR process (see *Courtwell Properties Ltd v Glencore PF (UK) Ltd* [2014] EWHC 184 (TCC)). Furthermore, in *Forstater v Python (Monty) Pictures Ltd* [2013] EWHC 3759 (Ch), the court noted that the policy of encouraging the abandonment of unsustainable claims should not be undermined by awarding indemnity costs, unless there was a really strong case for doing so.

L WHAT PRACTICAL STEPS SHOULD BE TAKEN BY A PARTY TO AVOID SANCTIONS?

8.97 Recent cases have demonstrated that the court is more likely to be sceptical about arguments raised retrospectively to justify a refusal to engage in ADR. Any objection to ADR must be raised at the time the invitation is made. In *PGF II SA v OMFS Co* [2014] WLR 1386, the court held that silence in the face of an invitation to participate in ADR is, as a general rule, of itself unreasonable, regardless of whether an outright refusal, or a refusal to engage in the type of ADR requested, or to do so at the time requested, might have been justified by the identification of reasonable grounds. The court noted that there were sound practical and policy reasons for this decision, including the fact that reasons advanced for the first time at a costs hearing, where none were given at the time of the invitation, pose forensic difficulties for the court and the inviting party, including, in particular, the question of whether the advanced reasons are genuine at all. The court also noted that a failure to provide reasons for the refusal is destructive of the real objective of encouraging parties to consider and discuss ADR, in short to engage with the ADR process. If an objection is raised at the time, it may be capable of being addressed, for example, where cost of ADR is an issue, by agreeing on a cheaper ADR process or by the proposing party offering to bear the whole of the ADR fees, or asking the court to provide ADR by judicial neutral evaluation or financial dispute resolution. If a lack of information is advanced as an objection to ADR, it may be possible to address that difficulty by limited voluntary disclosure or by ADR taking place at a later date than that proposed. It is essential that parties discuss these difficulties and seek to narrow their differences. The court also noted that a positive engagement with an invitation to participate in ADR may lead to a number of alternative directions, such as settlement, a narrowing of the issues, or an appreciation of the need for an early trial on a point of law only, each of which would save the parties court time and resources.

It is therefore essential that a party who is faced with a request to engage in ADR, but who believes that they have reasonable grounds for refusing to participate in an ADR process at that stage of the proceedings should consider the following practical steps: **8.98**

- Do not ignore an offer to engage in ADR. Failure to respond is very likely to be treated as an outright refusal (see *PGF II SA v OMFS Company 1 Limited* [2014] WLR 1386).
- Respond promptly, in writing, giving clear and full reasons why ADR is not appropriate at this stage of the dispute or proceedings. The reasons given, where possible, should be justified in light of the relevant principles derived from *Halsey* and subsequent cases, which are explained in this chapter. The response should be contained in an open letter or in a letter marked 'without prejudice except as to costs'.
- If lack of evidence or information is an obstacle to a successful ADR process being undertaken at that time, this must be canvassed with the other party to the dispute in the correspondence, and consideration should be given to whether that evidence or information can be obtained during the ADR process or in advance of the process. If court proceedings have already commenced, a judge may be prepared to make an order against a recalcitrant party directing further information or evidence to be disclosed prior to using ADR.
- Letters replying to requests to engage in ADR should be written with care. A party may have good reason to refuse ADR at that time, but the correspondence should not be written in such a way that closes off exploration of ADR processes at a later date. An outright refusal to use ADR at any time is more likely to be construed as unreasonable.

M HOW DOES THE COURT TREAT PRIVILEGED MATERIAL WHEN SEEKING TO IMPOSE SANCTIONS?

Any communications passing between the parties that are aimed at settlement are privileged from disclosure by operation of the without prejudice rule (see Chapter 6). In *Halsey v Milton Keynes General NHS Trust* [2004] 1 WLR 3002, the court accepted that if the integrity and confidentiality of the mediation process is to be preserved, the court should not know, and therefore should not investigate, why the process failed to result in an agreement. **8.99**

In *Reed Executive plc v Reed Business Information Ltd* [2004] 1 WLR 3026, the Court of Appeal applied *Walker v Wilsher* [1889] LR 23 QBD 335 and held that the court has no jurisdiction to order disclosure of oral or written communications that were expressed to be 'without prejudice' (whether in party-to-party negotiations or third-party assisted negotiations) for the purpose of deciding the question of costs and whether a party acted unreasonably in refusing ADR. It found that the decision in *Halsey* did not change that general rule. Even if there were such a jurisdiction, disclosure should be refused as a matter of discretion. It is open to a party to avoid the rule by providing that the communications are taking place expressly on the basis that they are 'without prejudice save as to costs'. The court can then look at those communications after issues of liability and remedies have been determined, in order to decide the question **8.100** of costs. The court recognized that the fact that it cannot look at 'without prejudice' material means that in many situations it may not be able to determine whether the winning party has acted unreasonably in refusing an offer to attempt to resolve the matter by an ADR method.

8.101 In *The Wethered Estate Ltd v Davis* [2006] BLR 86, the defendant submitted that the mediation failed because no agreement could be reached about costs and that this was due to the claimant not agreeing to mediation at an earlier stage of the dispute when the costs were significantly lower. The court was not prepared to enquire into the reasons why the mediation failed as it was important that the without prejudice nature of the mediation process was maintained unless the parties themselves waived it by clear and unequivocal consent.

8.102 There clearly have been cases where the court has been referred to without prejudice material in order to decide the question of costs, and in particular whether an adverse costs order should be made against a party for refusing to participate in ADR. This was the case, for example, in *Société Internationale de Télécommunications Aéronautiques SC (SITA) v The Wyatt Company (UK) Limited* [2002] EWHC 2401 (Ch). Here it was apparent that without prejudice material was shown to the judge after judgment on liability had been delivered and before argument took place about costs. The material provided to the judge included letters written in an attempt to persuade the third party to take part in mediation, including attendance notes of without prejudice meetings of the lawyers, which also recorded events that took place at the mediation meeting and remarks alleged to have been made by the mediator. It is not clear whether all of the communications that were referred to the judge were marked 'without prejudice save as to costs'. To the extent that they were not, the parties waived privilege. Such cases are likely to be rare.

8.103 It is clear from these cases that if a party makes an offer to explore settlement using some form of ADR process, they should make sure that correspondence is marked 'without prejudice except as to costs' if they want to refer it to the court on the question of costs if the other side unreasonably refuses to consider the ADR process. Otherwise a party will not be able to refer to the without prejudice material in making submissions about costs, unless all parties to the dispute waive privilege.

KEY POINTS SUMMARY

8.104

- The court will look at whether a party complied with the requirements of PD – Pre-Action Conduct and the Pre-Action protocols in making decisions about costs.
- If a party unreasonably refuses to consider ADR, before issue, after issue, or after judgment and pending appeal, they can be penalized in costs.
- In considering whether a party has unreasonably refused to consider ADR, the court will look at all the circumstances in the case, including the factors identified in *Halsey v Milton Keynes General NHS Trust* [2004] 1 WLR 3002.
- If a successful party unreasonably refuses ADR, they may be deprived of some or all of their costs or ordered to pay some or all of the losing party's costs, including costs on an indemnity basis.
- Pulling out of an ADR process at the eleventh hour is likely to be judged unreasonable conduct and may result in an adverse costs order.
- The court will not consider 'without prejudice' material in considering costs, unless privilege is waived by all the parties to the dispute, or the correspondence is explicitly written on the basis that it is 'without prejudice except as to costs'.

9

RECOVERY OF ADR COSTS IN LITIGATION

A INTRODUCTION 9.01
B COSTS OF INTERIM APPLICATIONS RELATING TO ADR .9.05
C RECOVERY OF THE COSTS OF UNSUCCESSFUL ADR PROCESSES. 9.09
D RECOVERING THE COSTS OF AN ADR PROCESS AS DAMAGES 9.28
Key points summary 9.30

A INTRODUCTION

The costs of using an ADR process can be significant. If the ADR process results in settlement of the dispute, that may represent a significant saving over the costs of proceeding to trial in litigation. The settlement agreement is also likely to make provision for the costs of both the litigation (if any) and the ADR process. **9.01**

The ADR costs will include the costs of lawyers preparing documents for and attending the ADR process, as well as any fees paid to a neutral party such as the mediator's fees or an evaluator's or determiner's fees and other costs such as venue fees (see Chapter 4 for more detail). If the ADR process is unsuccessful, the costs of that process will have increased the overall costs of the parties in resolving the dispute. **9.02**

This chapter considers the extent to which the court can make orders about costs if: **9.03**

- an interim application takes place in relation to ADR;
- ADR is attempted, but fails to result in any resolution of the dispute due to no fault of either party (unreasonable conduct by a party could result in an adverse costs order as explained in Chapter 8); and
- the main issues are resolved by an ADR process, leaving costs to be determined by the court.

As mentioned above, if the ADR process is successful, the settlement should deal with costs, which is why costs in cases that are settled are not discussed in this chapter, unless there is no agreement between the parties about costs. **9.04**

B COSTS OF INTERIM APPLICATIONS RELATING TO ADR

As stated in Chapter 8, the court has a wide discretion in making orders about costs in legal proceedings. The usual order is that the unsuccessful party will pay the costs of the successful party (see CPR r 44.2(2)(a)). **9.05**

Occasionally an application or a hearing will take place in relation to an ADR process. This can happen if: **9.06**

- the court orders that an allocation hearing or a case management conference should take place to determine whether an ADR order should be made directing the parties to attempt to resolve their dispute by a particular ADR process;

- the court has made an ADR order, perhaps in a form similar to that set out in Figure 7.1, but the parties have not been able to agree on the selection of a suitable neutral person for the ADR process, and a further case management conference is required for the court to facilitate the selection of the neutral person;
- an application is made by one or all parties for a stay to enable ADR to be attempted;
- an application is made to deal with an issue arising during an ADR process.

9.07 The costs of interim applications made in connection with an ADR process will usually be 'costs in the case'. This means that the costs of the interim application or hearing forms part of the costs of the court proceedings, so the party who is awarded costs at the end of the trial process will recover the costs of the interim application (see PD 44, para 4.2). Such an order is made because generally there is no overall winner in case management conferences or hearings at which the court gives directions, because such directions (for example ordering a stay) tend to be for the benefit of all the parties.

9.08 However, if a hearing has taken place due to one party's unreasonable refusal to engage with or act reasonably in an ADR process (for example an unreasonable refusal to consider ADR or to co-operate in the selection of a mediator), and the court decides their conduct was unreasonable or unmeritorious, then, as discussed in Chapter 8, there is no reason why that conduct should not be penalized in costs. The court could order the party acting unreasonably to pay the other side's costs of and occasioned by the application or hearing.

C RECOVERY OF THE COSTS OF UNSUCCESSFUL ADR PROCESSES

ADR processes that deal with costs

9.09 Applications in court proceedings for the costs of unsuccessful ADR processes are only likely to arise where the process selected does not include a power to award costs in the event that the process is unsuccessful. ADR processes therefore fall into two groups, as set out in Table 9.1.

Table 9.1 ADR processes: power to award costs if the process is unsuccessful

ADR process with no power to award costs if the process is unsuccessful	ADR process with power to award costs if the process is unsuccessful
negotiation	adjudication
mediation	arbitration
conciliation	expert determination with power to award costs
evaluation	
expert determination with no power to award costs	

Costs of failed ADR as part of the costs of litigation

9.10 Whether the costs of a failed attempt at ADR are recoverable in court proceedings depends in part on whether the costs are 'incidental' to the proceedings for the purposes of the Senior Courts Act 1981 s 51, and in part on the agreement of the parties. Costs cannot be incidental to proceedings if no proceedings are issued in relation to a substantive dispute (see *Citation Plc v Ellis Whittam Ltd* [2012] EWHC 764 (QB). If proceedings are issued in relation to the dispute, in general terms, the costs of negotiations are regarded as part of the overall costs of the proceedings (see PD 47, para 5.12(8), which provides that the bill of costs can include work done in connection with negotiations with a view to settlement). Otherwise, the costs of work done in relation to other ADR processes are not specifically mentioned in CPR, Parts 44–48 or PD 43–48, which are the provisions dealing with costs.

Despite this omission in the CPR, there is no reason in principle why the costs of the unsuccessful ADR process should not be regarded as part of the costs of the litigation. The court guides published for the specialist courts recognize this. An example is the *Admiralty and Commercial Court Guide* (9th edn, 2011), which states at para G1.10: **9.11**

> At a case management conference or at any other hearing in the course of which the judge makes an order providing for ADR he may make such order as to the costs that the parties may incur by reason of their using or attempting to use ADR as may in all the circumstances be appropriate. The orders for costs are normally costs in the case, meaning that if the claim is not settled, the costs of the ADR procedures will follow the ultimate event [so the unsuccessful party will be ordered to pay the successful party's costs incurred in connection with the ADR process], or that each side will bear their own costs of those procedures if the case is not settled.

In *Halsey v Milton Keynes General NHS Trust* [2004] 1 WLR 3002, the court accepted that the costs of an unsuccessful mediation can be the subject of a costs order by the court after the trial. **9.12**

However, whether or not the court can treat the costs of an unsuccessful ADR process as part of the costs of litigation, and order the unsuccessful party to pay the costs that the successful party has incurred in connection with the ADR process, will depend on whether the parties have made any contrary agreement in relation to the costs of the ADR process. **9.13**

The agreement between the parties determines liability in respect of ADR costs

If the parties have agreed, for example in a mediation agreement, that they will each bear their own costs of the ADR process, then the court will not look behind this agreement and make a different costs order in the event that the ADR process is unsuccessful. **9.14**

Typically, the parties will enter into an agreement in respect of an ADR process, for example a neutral evaluation agreement, or a mediation agreement, which provides that the expenses of that process will be borne equally by the parties and that each party will be responsible for their own costs, whether or not settlement is reached during the process. Such an agreement will bind the parties, and the court will not be able to go behind it to apportion responsibility for costs in any other way. This is so even if the settlement agreement that is reached in the mediation provides for one party's costs to be assessed on the standard basis if not agreed and this is reflected in a Tomlin order (see Chapter 23) signed by the parties, but the settlement agreement does not explicitly deal with the costs of the ADR process (which are covered by the ADR agreement). In such a case the Tomlin Order covers the costs of the parties other than the costs of the ADR process, with the costs of the ADR process being borne equally by the parties in accordance with the ADR agreement. **9.15**

This was the case in *National Westminster Bank plc v Feeney and Feeney* [2006] EWHC 90066 (costs). The mediation agreement provided that the mediator's fee would be borne equally by the parties and that each party would bear their own costs. Guidance notes to the agreement indicated that if the parties wished the costs of the mediation to be taken into account in any court orders if settlement was not reached, then the standard terms should be amended accordingly. No such amendment was made. The Tomlin order that was made at the mediation provided for the claimant to pay the defendant's costs of the counterclaim, **9.16** to be assessed, but did not mention the costs of the mediation process. The defendant then sought to obtain the costs of the mediation in the assessment of costs undertaken by the court. It was held that, as a matter of general principle, the costs incurred in a mediation could form part of the costs of the claim just as the reasonable costs of negotiation could be recovered as costs of the proceedings (see PD 43–48, para 4.8(6)). However the mediation agreement showed that the parties' intention was that those costs should not be recovered as part of the costs of the litigation, and it could not be said that the Tomlin order varied or discharged or took precedence over the terms of the ADR agreement. The Tomlin order also did not include the costs of mediation by necessary implication. The defendant was therefore not entitled to recover its costs of and in connection with the mediation from the claimant. The decision was upheld on appeal (unrep. 14 May 2007).

9.17 In *Lobster Group Limited v Heidelberg Graphic Equipment Limited* [2008] 2 All ER 1173 it was held that if the parties agree to bear their own costs of a pre-action mediation, regardless of the outcome, they cannot subsequently seek to recover these costs from the other party to the proceedings.

9.18 It is likely that if the parties had explicitly stated in the settlement agreement that one party should indemnify the other party in respect of their mediation costs and expenses, or if they had agreed to vary the mediation agreement to provide that one party should bear the costs and expenses of mediation, the decisions in these cases would have been different. Parties should therefore give careful thought to the costs position in drawing up the terms of any settlement agreement.

The parties make no agreement about the costs of the ADR process

9.19 In *Roundstone Nurseries Ltd v Stephenson Holdings Ltd* [2009] EWHC 1431 (TCC) the claimant applied for an order that the defendant should pay the costs thrown away as a result of the defendant's withdrawal from the mediation process. Unlike the cases in the previous section of this chapter, the parties had made no agreement about the costs of the mediation. The court held that the costs of separate stand-alone ADR processes, particularly where they took place before proceedings were commenced, did not usually form part of the costs of or incidental to the proceedings. However, applying *McGlinn v Waltham Contractors Ltd* [2005] 3 All ER 1126, it was clear that costs incurred during the pre-action protocol process could be recovered as costs incidental to the litigation. The court found that the mediation had been arranged so that the parties could comply with the Construction and Engineering Disputes Pre-action Protocol, which required the parties to have a without prejudice meeting. It was common for this to take place under the umbrella of mediation. In the absence of any agreement between the parties about the costs of that process, the parties could ask the court to determine who should bear the costs of the mediation proceedings. The court held that the defendant was wrong to cancel the mediation days before it was due to take place and, that being so, the defendant should pay the claimant's costs thrown away by late cancellation of the mediation as costs 'incidental to the litigation'.

9.20 Even if the mediation had taken place after litigation commenced rather than pursuant to a pre-action protocol, in the absence of any specific agreement between the parties as to who should bear the costs of the process it is likely that the court has jurisdiction to determine the costs of the process, particularly bearing in mind the court's encouragement of ADR (see Chapter 7). The issue of whether mediation costs could be recovered as part of the costs of the proceedings arose for consideration in *North Oxford Golf Club v A2 Dominion Homes Ltd* [2013] EWHC 852 (QB). There the parties attempted mediation after proceedings had been issued, but it failed to result in settlement. The agreement to mediate contained usual terms that the mediator's fees and the costs of the mediation venue and any costs attributable to the mediator such as refreshments or printing should be shared equally between the parties. The case eventually settled on the second day of the trial, with the defendant agreeing to pay the claimant's reasonable costs. The claimant claimed the costs of the mediation as part of the inter partes costs, but the defendant argued that mediation was separate from the action and it was not liable to pay those costs.

At first instance, the master concluded that there was a distinction between the participation costs such as the mediator's fees and the costs of the venue on the one hand and the costs of the preparation for and presentation at the mediation on the other hand. The former were not recoverable, but the latter could be recovered as part of the costs of the action.

On an appeal by the defendant, the court reviewed the cases of *National Westminster Bank plc v Feeney* [2006] EWHC 90066, *Lobster Group Limited v Heidelberg Graphic Equipment Limited* [2008] 2 ALL ER 1173, and *Roundstone Nurseries Ltd v Stephenson Holdings Ltd* [2009] EWHC 1431 (TCC). The court (Royce J) concluded that none of these authorities provided a clear answer to the question of whether a party's preparation and participation costs in respect of mediation that occurred after issue of proceedings could be recovered as part of the costs of the action. He concluded [at 20] that 'This is an area where there is room for argument. However, we consider that the master was probably entitled to reach the conclusion he did.' Further, as the costs of the mediation were very small in the context of the overall costs claimed, it was not consistent with the overriding objective to grant permission to appeal on that ground alone.

Agreement between the parties for the costs of the ADR process to be costs in the case

The court will have power to determine the costs of an ADR process if the parties agree that the costs of the ADR process are to be regarded as costs in the case in the event that settlement is not reached in the ADR process. The same result will apply if settlement is reached on the substantive issues, but not on costs. In these cases the court can regard the costs of the ADR process as part of the overall costs of the litigation. **9.21**

In *Chantrey Vellacott v The Convergence Group plc* [2007] EWHC 1774 (Ch) and *Société Internationale de Télécommunications Aéronautiques SC (SITA) v The Wyatt Company (UK) Ltd* [2002] EWHC 2401 (Ch), the courts were prepared to treat mediation costs as costs of and incidental to the proceedings, which meant the court had a discretion to determine who should pay those costs pursuant to the Senior Courts Act 1981 s 51. However neither the parties nor the court considered the effect that the mediation agreement had on recovery of these costs. **9.22**

To get round the decision in *National Westminster Bank v Feeney* [2006] EWHC 90066, many ADR providers provide in the ADR agreement that the fees and the party's legal costs and expenses incurred in preparing for and attending the ADR process may be treated as costs in the case in any litigation where the court has power to order or assess costs, even where the agreement also provides that the expenses of the process (such as the mediator's or evaluator's fees) are to be borne equally by the parties. For example, clause 9 of CEDR Model Mediation Agreement (13th edn) provides: **9.23**

- Unless otherwise agreed by the Parties and CEDR Solve in writing, each party agrees to share the Mediation Fees equally and also to bear its own legal and other costs and expenses of preparing for and attending the Mediation ("each Party's Legal Costs") prior to the Mediation. However, each party further agrees that any court or tribunal may treat both the Mediation Fees and each Party's Legal Costs as costs in the case in relation to any litigation or arbitration where that court or tribunal has power to assess or make orders as to costs, whether or not the Mediation results in settlement of the dispute. (see Appendix 2)

Settlement or determination on all issues apart from costs

9.24 A separate issue in respect of costs can arise where the parties resolve the main dispute between them by an ADR process (such as mediation or expert determination), but they cannot reach an agreement on the costs of the process or the proceedings, or where an expert determiner has no power under the contract appointing him to award costs between the parties. In that situation, in the absence of agreement about costs, the parties are likely to refer the question of liability for costs to the court.

9.25 This happened in *Dearling v Foregate Developments (Chester) Limited* [2003] EWCA Civ 913. The parties settled the claim and counterclaim at the trial (after pressure from the judge) but referred the issue of costs to the court. Dyson LJ noted that the principles that were to be applied when a claim is settled without the parties reaching agreement on costs derived from *Brawley v Marczynski (Nos 1 and 2)* [2003] 1 WLR 813. These principles are:

- the court has power to make a costs order when the substantive proceedings have been resolved without a trial but the parties have not agreed costs;
- it will ordinarily be irrelevant that the claimant is legally aided;
- the overriding objective is to do justice between the parties without incurring unnecessary court time and consequently additional cost;
- at each end of the spectrum there will be cases where it is obvious which side would have won had the substantive issues been fought to a conclusion. In between, the position will, in differing degrees, be less clear. How far the court will be prepared to look into the previously unresolved substantive issues will depend on the circumstances of the particular case, not least the amount of costs at stake and the conduct of the parties; and
- in the absence of a good reason to make any other order, the fallback position is to make no order for costs.

9.26 As mentioned by Dyson LJ, it is difficult, if not impossible to reach a conclusion on the merits without hearing evidence and submissions. The trial judge also accepted that he could form no view on whether the claimant would have recovered more than the settlement figure had the case been fought. In those circumstances, in the absence of a good reason to make any other order, the fallback position of no order for costs was inevitable. However, where it is possible to determine which party was successful, the court can make a costs order to do justice between the parties (see *Hirani v Hirani* [2012] EWHC 1645 (Ch)).

9.27 If the court is able to work out, without conducting a detailed investigation into the issues, which party is clearly the overall successful party, then a different costs order may be made.

D RECOVERING THE COSTS OF AN ADR PROCESS AS DAMAGES

9.28 It is clear that a party's costs of an ADR process such as mediation can, in certain circumstances, be recovered as damages in subsequent litigation against a third party.

9.29 In *Youlton v Charles Russell (a firm)* [2010] EWHC 1032 (Ch), the defendants were retained to give advice to trustees of a pension scheme. A dispute arose between the trustees and a company to whom the trustees rented a property as to whether an Apportionment Agreement and a Side Letter were enforceable. The Side Letter and Apportionment Agreement had been drafted by the defendants who were the trustees' solicitors. The claim between the trustees and the company was settled at mediation and the trustees then sued the defendants for professional negligence in relation to the drafting and execution of the Side Letter and the

Apportionment Agreement. In the professional negligence action, Mr Justice Warren found that the solicitors were negligent in relation to the drafting and execution of these documents and, but for that negligence, the claimants might have achieved a different outcome than that achieved in the mediation. Damages were assessed on the basis of the lost chance of settling the original action had those documents been valid. The court was prepared to award as damages some of the claimant's costs of and associated with the mediation, including counsel's fees in attending the mediation as well as half of the mediator's fees. The court held that counsel's attendance at the mediation would not have been required had the documents been valid and enforceable, and although there may have been a mediation, it would not have been as long or as costly as the mediation which took place.

KEY POINTS SUMMARY

- The court does have power to make an order that the costs of interim applications in connection with ADR should be borne by one party if that party has acted unreasonably, otherwise the usual order will be 'costs in the case'. **9.30**
- If the parties embark on an ADR process and make a clear agreement as to their respective liabilities for the costs of that process, the court will not look behind it.
- If the parties make no agreement about the costs of an ADR process, the court can determine liability for the costs of the ADR process.
- If the parties agree that the court can treat the costs of the ADR process as costs in the case, irrespective of who pays the costs, and irrespective of whether settlement is reached in that process, then the court can determine liability for the costs of the process.
- If the parties reach agreement on the main issues by an ADR process and agree that ADR costs should be determined by the court, the court is likely to make no order for costs (meaning each party will bear their own costs) unless it can determine, without trying the case, who would have won at trial.

PART III

NEGOTIATION AND MEDIATION

10

OVERVIEW OF NEGOTIATION AND MEDIATION

The processes of negotiation and mediation are dealt with in the same part of this book because the basic underlying principles are very similar. This brief overview is provided to assist understanding of Chapters 11–19, as a number of matters are looked at from the point of view of negotiation and then mediation, covering a number of similarities and differences. Duplication is avoided as far as possible by cross-referencing. **10.01**

Both processes can take place at any stage in a case, whether or not proceedings have been issued. Neither has formal procedural rules save for those agreed by the parties. Both will only result in a settlement with the agreement of the client. In very broad terms it might be said that mediation is a facilitated and more structured form of negotiation. **10.02**

One area of similarity is preparation in terms of case analysis and research, which is dealt with in Chapter 12 (Preparing for negotiation) and Chapter 15 (Preparation for the mediation). However, preparation for mediation will involve more stages in terms of selecting a mediator, preparing an opening statement, and so on. There may also be some similarity in terms of the strategies and tactics that may be used (see Chapter 11), though these may be more overt in negotiation than where there is a mediator to manage the process. **10.03**

There is also some similarity in terms of process, in that both negotiation and mediation will tend to move from exchange of information to the making of offers and bargaining, see Chapter 13 (The negotiation process) and Chapter 16 (The mediation process). However, the process is likely to have a more clearly staged structure where this is facilitated by a mediator. **10.04**

Whether negotiation or mediation is used, there will be a similar need to ensure that all matters in dispute are addressed, and that details are fully agreed and properly recorded (see Chapter 17 in relation to both processes). In a mediation, the mediator will seek to ensure that this happens. **10.05**

Despite the broad similarities, the role of a lawyer in these two processes can be very different. Negotiation is normally carried out by the lawyers acting for each party, often without clients being present. This gives the lawyers substantial control, but the fluid process can be more challenging to manage, and much depends on the preparation and skill of the lawyer. In mediation the mediator may deal only with the parties, especially in a small case, or both parties and lawyers may attend with the lawyer providing advice to the client at all stages. While this may give the lawyer a less obviously prominent role, the role is in essence very similar to that in a negotiation, and greater structure and facilitation may be more likely to lead to settlement. **10.06**

It is quite possible that both negotiation and mediation may be used in relation to the same case. If an attempt to negotiate becomes deadlocked the parties may agree to try mediation. A mediation may fail in the early stages of a case, but a negotiated settlement may still be reached before the case comes to trial. It is important to use judgment as to which process is best used when, and guidance on this is given in Chapters 2 and 14. **10.07**

11

STYLES, STRATEGIES, AND TACTICS IN NEGOTIATION

A THE IMPORTANCE OF STYLE, STRATEGY, AND TACTICS 11.01
B STYLES 11.06
C STRATEGIES 11.12
D TACTICS 11.36
Key points summary 11.73

A THE IMPORTANCE OF STYLE, STRATEGY, AND TACTICS

11.01 In a courtroom, rules of evidence and procedure, and the oversight of the judge, provide structure and relative certainty. In a negotiation there is no set structure (save for whatever is agreed by the parties), and no rules (save for those that come from the context of possible litigation and as matters of professional conduct). This leaves substantial scope for the use of strategy and tactics, to the extent that these can have a significant effect on the outcome of the process and how much a lawyer can achieve for a client.

11.02 It is therefore vital to have a practical understanding of what strategy and tactics may be used, and what they may achieve. Even if you do not use them yourself they may be used by an opponent, and you will need sufficient insight to identify what is happening and to address it effectively. A confrontational opponent may appear intimidating, and you need to be able to ensure that this does not undermine what you achieve for your client.

11.03 It may be tempting to think that decisions on strategy can be left until one meets an opponent, and that good tactics will occur to you on the spur of the moment, but this risks losing many of the benefits that strategy and tactics can achieve. The negotiation process offers substantial control to a lawyer, and the opportunities are best exploited with planning. Strategy and tactics may need to be adapted as a negotiation develops, but options should be planned in advance so they can be properly set up and quickly deployed.

11.04 This chapter provides an overview of the general styles, strategies, and tactics that may be employed in negotiating. There is no clear agreement on the meaning of these terms, but broadly:

- a *style* is the manner of delivery, a negotiator's attitude and demeanour;
- a *strategy* is the overall approach taken to achieve a good settlement;
- a *tactic* is a specific action used to try to achieve a particular end.

11.05 In developing skills, psychological and sociological insights can be helpful. For example some research studies show that those who aim high tend to do better. Research and books on communication skills, emotional intelligence, and working with difficult people can all assist.

B STYLES

Everyone has a personal style. This may be a natural part of their personality, or a matter of how they wish to be seen professionally. A person's style includes factors such as use of language, tone and volume of voice, and physical presence (eg the way someone sits or stands). It includes such things as being relatively talkative, or relatively reserved, and can include matters such as use of humour. Two main styles can be identified. **11.06**

Co-operative

A co-operative style is normally seen as being friendly, courteous, and conciliatory, seeking to gain trust. This style is often characterized as being relatively open, providing information, and seeking to co-operate with an opponent in trying to reach an agreement. Some lawyers will go so far as to try to charm an opponent as they might seek to charm a judge. **11.07**

Such a style can be very productive if the opponent also seeks to be co-operative, but it is important not to be naive and assume that an opponent will be co-operative simply because a settlement is in the interests of both parties. A co-operative style can easily be exploited by a competitive opponent. Also be careful of someone who apparently has a co-operative style but who is using it to mask a competitive strategy. **11.08**

Competitive/confrontational

A competitive style is usually based on making demands, and it is often argumentative. Emphatic language and a strong tone of voice may be used to make the opponent feel uncomfortable and intimidated. It tends to put pressure on an opponent to agree, or may seek to wear down an opponent. In an extreme form this style could be seen as bullying. **11.09**

Such a style can be quite effective, especially if an opponent dislikes confrontation or is poorly prepared. However this style can be risky, especially if it is sustained throughout a negotiation, as it can easily alienate an opponent, who may refuse to make concessions, so that no progress is made. It is not uncommon for a lawyer to start a negotiation with a competitive style, but to do so with an underlying collaborative strategy that may emerge later in the negotiation once the case has been put in strong terms. **11.10**

Choice of style

It is sometimes suggested that one style is inherently more likely to be successful than another, but this is not the case. You should consider what style is most effective for you. Some individuals are naturally more inclined to be co-operative or competitive, but choice of style should also depend on the type of case, and what you know of the negotiator for the other side. If you have a strong case a competitive style may well be justified even if your natural style is co-operative. It is also important to distinguish style from strategy—the use of a competitive style does not necessarily mean that the underlying strategy is competitive. **11.11**

C STRATEGIES

Your strategy is your overall plan for getting the best possible outcome in a negotiation. Style is essentially a matter of presentation and may be relatively superficial, but underlying strategy is key to success. Strategy and style may coincide so that one reinforces the other, or **11.12** style may be used to mask strategy. A strategy may be selected for a whole case, or for part of a case.

Co-operative

11.13 A co-operative strategy focuses on reaching an agreement that is adequately fair and acceptable to both sides. Concessions are expected on both sides, and information is shared. The negotiator tries to be reasonable and open, and to engender trust.

11.14 The characteristic approach is to:

- open by stressing the importance of settlement, and trying to build openness and trust with the opponent;
- offer information to try to promote understanding;
- move relatively quickly to make and seek concessions at a reasonable level;
- explain the basis for offers to show that they are fair;
- use a conciliatory approach to try to secure agreement;
- use tactics constructively to foster agreement.

11.15 The main strengths of a co-operative strategy are:

- Provided an opponent responds by being co-operative, this strategy has a good likelihood of reaching agreement.
- Appropriate concessions are seen as principled and not a weakness.
- It can support a continuing relationship between the parties.
- There are fewer risks that the negotiation will break down, and it may result in agreement being reached relatively quickly.

11.16 The main weaknesses of co-operative strategy are:

- This strategy can be undermined by a competitive opponent, who may treat co-operation as a weakness.
- It can be too easy to see settlement as the main goal, rather than ensuring that the client's objectives are met as fully as possible.
- Without detailed planning, this strategy can lead to unnecessary concessions and a weaker outcome for the client.
- A co-operative negotiator may be tempted to make unilateral concessions or early concessions to encourage co-operation. This may leave limited room for manoeuvre later.
- A co-operative negotiator may volunteer information while getting little or nothing in return.
- A co-operative negotiator may try to avoid confrontation, ignoring rather than seeking to challenge competitive techniques.
- A co-operative negotiator may fail to press the strengths of a case fully.

Competitive or positional

11.17 A competitive strategy seeks to win, getting the best possible outcome for the client, especially as regards financial issues. The negotiator takes a strong stance on each issue, focusing on demands rather than concessions, and is generally slow to yield. The negotiator will show little if any interest in the concerns and objectives of the opponent. Settlement is not seen as a goal in itself, and the negotiator will walk away rather than accept terms seen as unsatisfactory. A positional strategy is very similar, with the focus being on the position of the client. This strategy is basically adversarial and may therefore come most easily to a litigation lawyer. It is also commonly perceived as an appropriate strategy for success in business. A competitive strategy is not necessarily presented with a confrontational style.

The characteristic approach is to: 11.18

- open by making strong statements about the client's position, with little or no attempt to engage constructively with the opponent;
- make high opening demands (often unrealistically high), and maintain high demands for as long as possible;
- demand large concessions from the opponent;
- make few and small concessions, save on things that do not matter to the client;
- provide limited argument to support demands, but demand full justification for the opponent's position;
- give limited information, but often seek detailed information from the opponent;
- seek success on every issue, including interest and costs;
- use tactics such as threats or bluffs.

The main strengths are: 11.19

- This strategy can be very successful in achieving a good outcome, especially against a weak or poorly prepared opponent.
- Research has shown that a high starting position tends to lead to a better settlement.
- It is likely to be most successful where there are few issues, and where the issues are money based.
- It can also be particularly successful for the party with the stronger case.
- There is little chance of exploitation by the opponent because few concessions are made.
- The strategy is relatively easy to understand and use because it involves simple statements and blocking rather than engaging with the complexity of issues.

The main weaknesses are: 11.20

- Many lawyers are not susceptible to the aggressive and manipulative behaviour of a competitive negotiator, so this strategy can make it difficult to reach an agreement.
- This strategy can be damaging in a case where there will be an ongoing relationship between the parties as it can lead to bad feelings.
- The tendency to focus on 'winning' or 'losing' may ignore some of the potential advantages of collaborative negotiation (see 11.24).
- The use of pressure increases tension and stress levels, which may make settlement less likely.
- This strategy can be undermined by a well-prepared opponent who is confident in making good arguments and pointing out weaknesses so that the 'bluster' that is inherent in a competitive strategy is exposed.
- A competitive strategy is not the most effective to deal with complex issues. The hard stance limits the possibility of exchanging information or discussion, and it is difficult to explore options.
- A competitive strategy is unlikely to work well if you hope to get a significant amount of information from your opponent, who will be unlikely to be disposed to answer questions.
- A competitive strategy tends to emphasize differences, and can increase misunderstanding.
- The negotiation can too easily become a battle between the lawyers who jockey for position over issues—losing sight of the client's interests.

Collaborative—principled or problem solving

A collaborative strategy assumes that the parties can work together to reach an agreement that meets the needs of both and is objectively fair. The process includes the parties exploring their underlying interests, sharing information, and being creative in the options considered. 11.21

The agreement will not necessarily focus solely on the original issues between the parties but will try to identify options for mutual gain. This strategy involves more than co-operation—it is based on mutual effort and requires advance analysis and planning. Collaborative strategies may be used to reach settlement in difficult political situations, and may be particularly useful where the parties will have an ongoing relationship.

11.22 Within the term 'collaborative' different strands may be identified:

- A 'principled' strategy tries to achieve an outcome that is objectively fair against some external authoritative norm, for example based on the view of an agreed expert. The principled approach was developed by Roger Fisher and William Ury of the Harvard Negotiation Project. It is well explained in *Getting to Yes: Negotiating Agreement Without Giving In* by Roger Fisher and William Ury (Random House Business, 2012). This strategy is developed further at 11.26.
- A 'problem-solving' strategy focuses on both parties' real needs and interests, and tries to get a practical solution without building costs. The 'problem-solving' approach was set out by Carrie Menkel-Meadow in her paper 'Toward another View of Legal Negotiation: The Structure of Problem Solving' (1984) 31(4) *UCLA Law Review* 754–842.

11.23 The characteristic approach of collaboration is:

- Working together is stressed at the start of the negotiation, and this approach is sustained throughout.
- Each issue is approached constructively, focusing on the best possible outcome for both parties.
- Issues are likely to be approached from the point of view of needs, interests, and options rather than fault and blame.
- Both sides work to maintain an open and reasonable atmosphere.
- The negotiators are likely to emphasize objectivity, and a potential settlement is often judged against agreed criteria to test fairness.

11.24 The main strengths are:

- A collaborative strategy is capable of achieving very good outcomes because it opens the process to anything of potential benefit to the clients, such as creating new shared marketing opportunities.
- This strategy has a good chance of success because it focuses on the interests of the parties going forward, rather than the issues of the past (though those issues must be resolved as part of the agreement).
- Even if there is no agreement, the areas of conflict are usually decreased.
- Techniques to expand resources rather than simply divide them can be beneficial, especially in a case relating to business interests.
- The rational and reasoned approach is reasonably easy to manage, provided both sides follow this strategy.
- A well-prepared collaborative strategy can be successful against a competitive opponent, so long as you are able to demonstrate the potential advantage for their client.

11.25 The main weaknesses are:

- A collaborative strategy can only fully succeed where both parties are prepared to collaborate (though an initial stage of the strategy may be to persuade an opponent to collaborate).
- Effective collaboration may require substantial preparation of options.
- Attempts to collaborate may be defeated, or even exploited, by a competitive opponent, if attempts to collaborate lead to unnecessary concessions.

- This strategy may be difficult to use in court-door negotiations because of time pressure, and limited opportunities to look at options fully.
- A collaborative approach may be exploited by a competitive negotiator, who pretends to be collaborative, but who actually seeks to get concessions while offering little.
- A collaborative strategy may have little to offer in a case where options cannot be developed.

The concept of 'principled' negotiation as developed in books such as *Getting to Yes* includes elements that may be useful whether or not used as part of a collaborative strategy. **11.26**

- *Separate the people from the problem.* This involves defining the difficulty to be addressed objectively, rather than seeking to attach blame to people. It is sometimes expressed as being hard on the problem but soft on the people. This helps to avoid emotion, and can help people to save face. It can help the parties to understand different perceptions of the problem, and thus make agreement more likely.
- *Focus on interests rather than positions.* A negotiation can too easily focus on who is right or wrong. Issues, positions, interests, and needs should be carefully distinguished. To get progress it is more constructive to look at what underlies an issue or a position and see whether a need can be met in a different way (eg through a structured settlement rather than a single financial award). If one person wants a window opened and one wants it closed, it may be more productive to focus on other ways to provide fresh air or to avoid a draught than to argue only about whether to open or close the window.
- *Look for options that may benefit both sides.* This is sometimes called win–win, or increasing the pie, contrasted to any view that one party will 'win' and the other 'lose' as regards an issue. For example if a business contract has been breached, an advantageous deal for future trading may more than wipe out the losses incurred as a result of the breach. An illustration sometimes used is of two sisters arguing over an orange. Just before they cut it in half their mother asks why they want it—and finds out that one sister wants to eat the inside but the other wants the peel to go into a cake she is making. Both can have what they want—a better result than half each.
- *Use objective standards to justify offers and concessions.* Because a negotiation does not involve a judge, this is an effective way to show that a proposal is principled and justified. This can be done by use of an independent expert, an independent standard, setting objective criteria, or following a precedent.
- *Develop a best alternative to a negotiated agreement (BATNA).* This provides a practical framework against which to judge any possible settlement. For guidance on developing a BATNA see 12.58–12.63.

Pragmatic

A pragmatic strategy involves adapting strategy to meet the needs of the particular negotiation. **11.27**
There is a sharp distinction to be made here. Planned pragmatism, especially in the hands of an experienced negotiator, can be very effective. It involves careful forethought about potentially effective strategy for each separate issue, with provisional decisions about an appropriate strategy for each, leaving options open for final decisions during the negotiation. Such a strategy may be most effective where you have limited information and need to get more facts in the negotiation before finally deciding how to proceed, and it may be appropriate where you do not know your opponent and cannot predict what strategy he or she might adopt.

In contrast, unplanned pragmatism that amounts to little more than 'making it up as you go **11.28**
along' carries a high risk of failure, especially in the hands of an inexperienced negotiator, or against an opponent who has a well-prepared strategy. A negotiation can move very quickly, and as you need to take complex decisions about facts, figures, and options, it is very difficult to take and implement the best decisions about strategy at the same time.

Choice of strategy

11.29 Many lawyers have a personal preference for the type of strategy they find it most natural to pursue. However, the strengths and weaknesses of different strategies should be taken into account in making the best choice for each case. Whereas consistent use of a single strategy can help to build expertise, it can also leave you more vulnerable to an opponent—someone who knows you will use a particular strategy to undermine you. For a comparison of strategies see Table 11.1.

11.30 As part of planning for each case, the planning of strategy should include:

- a preferred overall strategy for the case, especially where the strategy needs to be followed clearly and consistently, as with a collaborative strategy;
- how you will open the negotiation to provide a firm foundation for your strategy. This needs care—your opponent may be co-operative and let you follow your strategy, but a

Table 11.1 Basic comparison of the main negotiation strategies

	Co-operative	Competitive	Collaborative
Objective	To get a settlement acceptable to both parties	To win best outcome on every issue	To achieve the best outcome for both parties
Manner	Reasonable and seeks to build trust	Tends to ignore needs or interests of others	Open and constructive Focus on working together
Opening	Stress the desire to be co-operative	Strong statement on client's position and demands	Set out the benefits of collaboration
Information	Tries to build openness by sharing information	Demands information be given Slow to provide information	Shares information and tries to open out options
Argument	Explains basis for proposals	Strong stance on every issue Does not justify position, but demands other side justifies position	Justifies proposals in terms of both clients' best interests Looks at needs and interests rather than fault
Tactics	Used constructively to support settlement	Used wherever an advantage may be secured eg threats and bluffs	Used constructively to open discussion and promote settlement
Concessions	Relatively quick to make and expect concessions	Focuses on demands. Slow to make concessions and few concessions	Focus on best outcome and objective criteria
Key strengths	Good chance of success Supports ongoing relationship	Can secure a good outcome for client Limited chance of exploitation Tends to get good outcome on financial issues	Can secure a good outcome for both clients Good chance of success Good for continuing relationships
Key weaknesses	Can be exploited by opponent Tends to focus on settlement rather than getting best for client Tends to concede too easily May fail to press strengths of case	Significant risk negotiation will fail Not good for ongoing relationship Can be challenged by well-prepared opponent Not good for exploring complex issues Fosters stress	Can be difficult to implement unless both negotiators are prepared to collaborate Requires significant preparation Can be difficult to use in limited time May be exploited

competitive opponent may ignore your strategy, and a very competitive opponent may try to force you to change strategy to undermine your confidence;

- a fallback option for overall strategy should it prove difficult to implement your first choice, for example because of the strategy used by your opponent, or because unexpected information emerges;
- any appropriate change of strategy. You might for example choose to be competitive in going through issues to test your opponent, but then be co-operative in reaching an agreement;
- if appropriate, separate strategies for separate key issues—for example you might chose to be competitive on financial issues, but then collaborative in for example negotiating the terms of an injunction.

There is much discussion and disagreement about whether one strategy is inherently more effective than another. Perhaps the best overall conclusion is that no strategy is inherently better, but that different options are better for different types of case, depending on the strengths and weaknesses of each strategy as outlined above. There is some research into the effect of strategy, and also gender and culture on negotiations (in particular by the Harvard Negotiation Project). The outcomes of research cannot easily be summarized, but it may be a useful area of study if you would like to become a really effective negotiator. **11.31**

Interaction of strategies

It is not just the strategy you choose that matters, but rather the choice of strategy of each negotiator. Some strategies work very well together but others do not. It is important to be aware of the potential interaction of strategies—one does not necessarily trump another. **11.32**

Clearly two collaborative negotiators should be able to make effective progress. Two co-operative negotiators are likely to be able to agree, but they may not get the best agreement for their clients if there is too much focus on agreeing rather than on analysing the case fully and securing the best possible outcome for each client. **11.33**

Two competitive negotiators may reach deadlock. This has been confirmed by an American study *Legal Negotiation and Settlement* by G Williams (West Publishing, 1983). However, it is possible that two competitive negotiators can cover issues in a way that makes compromise appear unlikely, but then trade offers quite quickly at the end of the negotiation when all issues have been tested. **11.34**

Where two negotiators are using different strategies, knowledge of the strengths and weaknesses of each strategy as outlined above is important in dealing with the opponent effectively. It is not essential to change your own strategy to meet an opponent using a different strategy—you can use the strengths of your own choice, and use the weaknesses in their own strategy against them. To give just one example, a collaborative negotiator can succeed against a competitive negotiator by pointing out potential mutual benefits. You should not go too far in exploiting the weaknesses in an opponent's strategy—if a competitive negotiator secures too good an outcome against a co-operative negotiator then the latter's client may simply refuse to accept the provisional agreement. You should of course take care not to let the potential weaknesses of your own strategy be used against you. **11.35**

D TACTICS

A 'tactic' is a type of behaviour or a specific action used in a negotiation to try to achieve a particular end. The term 'tactic' is sometimes seen as negative—associated with manipulating or even tricking an opponent to get an unfair advantage. This is not the case—a tactic can be just as useful for a principled negotiator dealing with a confrontational opponent, and a **11.36** proper use of tactics is part of getting the best possible outcome for a client. Understanding the different tactics that can be used in a negotiation enables you to decide whether and how to use them. Tactics should not be used by a lawyer in an unethical or unprofessional way, and you should neither do this nor accept such behaviour from an opponent. Having a good knowledge of tactics will help you to recognize when an opponent is using a tactic, and to know how to deal with it so that it does not undermine your case.

11.37 Some tactics are associated with a particular style or strategy. For example a positional or confrontational approach is most likely to involve bluffs or threats. However, versions of many tactics can be used in relation to most strategies and styles. Tactics need to be planned in advance because they may need to be set up as part of agreeing an agenda for negotiation, or as part of dealing with a specific issue. It is not necessary to plan tactics for every part of a negotiation—focus on tactics for key issues, and the issues that might be most difficult to address.

Tactics relating to information

11.38 Information may be central to a negotiation. You need to gather information to assess the case for each side, to use information as part of persuading your opponent, and to decide what you will and will not reveal.

Questioning

11.39 Questioning is very important in any negotiation. Questions might relate to the facts, evidence, or objectives as seen by your opponent, and can be used to probe the strengths and weaknesses of their case. Put questions in a way appropriate for the strategy you are using—questioning can have a negative effect. Questions can be used tactically to put pressure on an opponent: for example 'What is your bottom line on this?', or 'What are your instructions on this?' Even if the process fails you can use questions to find out more about your opponent's case.

Statements

11.40 It is important to make tactical statements about your case. A positional negotiator will make substantial use of statements, for example as regards what their client expects to achieve. A collaborative negotiator might make a statement about what collaboration might achieve. To be most effective a statement should be relatively short and clear, with words carefully chosen. Think about the effect you want the statement to have on your opponent.

Revealing information

11.41 Treat information as a resource and reveal it for a purpose. It can of course be very helpful to reveal information that shows the strength of your case. However it is important to take tactical decisions about how far to reveal matters such as your client's objectives. To do so may strengthen your case in terms of showing high expectations, but it can be a hostage to fortune if an opponent takes a realistic objective to be merely a starting point to be argued down. Even a co-operative strategy should be conducted tactically—consider not giving information unless you get information in return

Concealing information

11.42 There is no obligation to provide information, so it is quite proper to keep information confidential, or to refuse to answer a question, especially if the information may weaken your case. However, remember that concealing information can have negative effects, for example building up costs if settlement of the dispute is delayed. Remember the duty of client confidentiality—something you are told by a client should only be revealed with the client's consent.

Reframing

This can be a useful tactic to redress how a difficult opponent is presenting their case. A competitive negotiator might summarize the facts of an accident in an exaggerated, antagonistic, or emotive way. Rather than getting irritated you can politely use more objective words to say the same thing, and this can show that you are in control and not prepared to be manipulated. A collaborative negotiator may try to develop a proposal you are not happy with—trying to reframe it at an early stage is better than letting something you are likely to reject develop too far. **11.43**

Tactics relating to offers and demands

Achieving an outcome in a negotiation is done through making and accepting offers, and in some strategies through demands. Within any strategy offers need to be dealt with tactically to ensure the best possible outcome—timing and phrasing can be very important. **11.44**

Pre-conditions and setting parameters

It is possible to have some control over potential offers by setting a pre-condition, for example 'I could not make any offer on this issue unless your client agrees to apologize to mine', or a parameter, for example 'I have instructions to settle for no more than £2,000 on this point'. This sort of approach is most often associated with a competitive strategy, but it can be used appropriately in connection with any strategy. **11.45**

Objective standards

A principled or collaborative negotiator may make frequent reference to objective standards, but any negotiator may refer to an objective standard as a tactic. An objective standard can be any sort of business practice, trade standard etc. The standard may be referred to in order to justify the fairness of an offer or point you make, or to point out the unfairness of an offer or other point made by the other side. **11.46**

Authority to settle

The importance of settling within the authority provided by the client is dealt with in 12.66–12.69. A negotiator may make clear any limit on their authority, but a comment about a possible limit on authority may also be made tactically, for example 'I do not have authority to deal with that issue'. If an opponent suggests that they do not have authority, you may wish to investigate what is being said; for example 'Are you saying your client has specifically told you she will not accept less than £2,000?' Alternatively you can sidestep the problem, as in 'Your client will not have been able to give you instructions on the full offer I have made, and I would like you to put it to your client'. **11.47**

Ultimatums

An ultimatum may be used to try to force a settlement; for example 'Unless you accept £5,000 to settle this issue I will have to withdraw that offer, and I will make no other offer'. An ultimatum might relate to withdrawing from the process, or a step the party will take if agreement is not reached. An ultimatum is most associated with a competitive strategy, but may be used as a tactic within any strategy to try to move to a settlement when a negotiation risks getting bogged down. An ultimatum should be distinguished from a threat—an ultimatum should be justifiable. **11.48**

Proposing additional outcomes

11.49 If it is important to you that a particular offer be accepted, you might choose to tie in some further outcome to make it sufficiently attractive; for example 'If you accept the £10,000, I will propose to my client that he should pay the costs to date'.

Tactics relating to structure

11.50 A normal structure for a negotiation is outlined in Chapter 13, but variations on structure can be used tactically.

Imposing structure

11.51 Structure is normally agreed through negotiating an agenda at the start of a negotiation. One negotiator may seek to impose their agenda, seeing an advantage in choosing the order in which topics are addressed. It may be tactically useful for example to start with an area where one has strength.

Ignoring structure

11.52 One negotiator may choose for tactical reasons to depart from an agreed agenda. This might for example be part of a competitive strategy, to try to control the process. It may also be used to try to confuse or surprise an opponent.

Parking issues

11.53 Once you have dealt with information, strengths, and weaknesses as regards an issue it is normal to move to possible concessions. If this does not lead to agreement you should park the issue. There is little to be gained from repeating what you have said. If an issue needs to be parked it is tactically important to take charge of the parking by briefly summarizing in your words what you want, and why your case merits it. It is useful to note the basis on which an issue is parked.

Moving on

11.54 Part of the purpose of parking an issue is to be able to move on. There may be other tactical reasons for proposing moving on, for example to take charge of the agenda, to avoid discussing a weakness in your case, or to give yourself time to think if you are suddenly confronted with new information.

Reopening issues

11.55 An issue that has been parked should be reopened at a strategic point. It is often best to reopen a parked issue at a time when it may be tied to a concession on another issue so as to reach an agreement on both. It is not good practice to reopen an issue that has already been agreed as this can undermine trust and lead the negotiation to fail. Nonetheless a confrontational or competitive negotiator may seek to reopen a provisionally decided issue as a way to try to make progress on another issue.

'Just one more thing'

11.56 Normally the issues to be discussed are agreed at the start of a negotiation. This is tactically quite important because you are likely to try to balance a concession on one issue against a concession by the other side on another issue, and this can be undermined if you find at a late stage there are more issues than you were aware of. Tactically a negotiator may choose to introduce a new demand near the end of the negotiation, hoping that it will be accepted rather than lose what has been agreed. This is a risky tactic to use as it is likely to irritate an opponent. If it is used against you it is probably best to make it clear that this is an unfair addition and to refuse to accept it.

Avoiding deadlock

Tactics for avoiding deadlock are dealt with in 13.111–13.112. **11.57**

Tactics relating to presentation

Presentation is as important in negotiation as it is in advocacy. It is normal to present each point clearly, pointing out the strengths of your case and the outcome that you hope to achieve and why. Different approaches to presentation may be used tactically. **11.58**

Abruptness

A competitive negotiator may address an issue very briefly, perhaps doing little more than making a demand and/or stating a key strength. This can be frustrating for an opponent, who may have little choice but try to pull out more detail, or to state that detail will be needed for progress. **11.59**

Evasion

Evasion is another tactic most often used by a competitive negotiator. An incomplete or evasive response may be given to avoid providing facts, evidence or arguments in relation to an issue. Again an opponent will need to press for detail, making it clear why it is important. Evasion can be a risky tactic—it may lead an opponent to conclude that a case is weak on a point even if it is not. **11.60**

Silence

Silence can be used to put pressure on an opponent, or to try to ensure that your opponent goes on to provide more information, or to make a concession. It is important to make it clear that you expect your opponent to say something, for example by looking at them expectantly. **11.61**

Time to think

Many negotiations proceed at a fast pace with relatively few pauses. It may be tactically important to have time to review information and/or options. If you need time, ask for a minute to review the figures, or for a five-minute break to talk to the client. Make it clear that this is a positive decision—just flicking through your papers can appear weak. An advantage of mediation can be that time to reflect is built into the process. **11.62**

Prepare a draft

A tactical way to ensure a focus on your view of the issues is to prepare a draft for use in the negotiation. This might relate to a particular aspect of the negotiation, for example presenting the arithmetic on the damages from your point of view. An alternative is to bring a draft agreement and suggest going through the draft, for example if the negotiation relates to an interim injunction. This can help you control the agenda, and can put an opponent on the back foot in terms of trying to introduce and justify their own points. If your opponent uses this tactic, decide carefully whether you are prepared to use their draft—you might look at it quickly to see what it reveals about their case and then say 'That was very helpful, but perhaps we could discuss the matter first and maybe go back to your draft later'. **11.63**

Bluffing

It may be tempting to bluff with regard to the strength of a case, especially if using a competitive style. This can work against a relatively weak opponent, but a well-prepared opponent **11.64** is likely to challenge such a bluff, seeking detail on the strengths of the claim. A claim that is shown to be a bluff tends to undermine belief in other claims made, so a bluff can be a risky tactic. A bluff should not amount to actively misleading an opponent with regard to facts or evidence, which is likely to amount to unprofessional conduct, see Chapter 6.

Aggression

11.65 Lawyers normally behave in a controlled and objective way. However in negotiation a competitive negotiator might use aggressive tactics to try to put pressure on an opponent and undermine their confidence. There may not be overt aggression, but sarcasm, ridicule, or expressions of exasperation. If such approaches are used against you, do not react. Ignore it or respond in a rational way, or label the behaviour to defuse it, for example 'Sarcasm is not going to persuade me!'

Threats

11.66 A competitive negotiator may be tempted to make threats, and even a collaborative negotiator might consider some form of threat to try to reach an agreement they think is fair. A client may propose the making of threats in a difficult case where much is at stake. There are grey areas with regards to threats, and careful distinctions may need to be drawn.

11.67 A pure and unjustifiable threat would normally be unethical and might well amount to unprofessional conduct: see Chapter 6. However a statement of fact in relation to something your client has told you, pointing out potential consequences of a course of action, or setting out a step you feel may be justified if an agreement is not reached, could be seen as a statement, even though it might be perceived as a form of threat by the opponent. Saying 'If we cannot agree on this issue I will have to pursue an application for an interim injunction' is a statement, so long as it is reasonably justified. Saying 'My client has told me that he is thinking of reporting your client for tax evasion on the profit from this deal if we don't reach an agreement today' is on the face of it a statement, but is probably an unjustified threat in a case that relates to contract law and has nothing directly to do with tax. Much may depend on exactly what is said and how it is said. For the sake of professional probity it is best to err on the side of caution.

11.68 There are a variety of ways of responding to a threat. You could ignore it, you could state openly that you refuse to deal on the basis of threats, or you could push it aside with words such as 'If making a threat is your best line of argument...'. In appropriate circumstances you could challenge whether the threat would really be carried out. Making a counter-threat is rarely helpful as it escalates hostility.

Tactics relating to law

11.69 Although legal analysis is vital in preparation, use of detailed law has a limited role in the negotiation itself. As lawyer–negotiators have legal knowledge there is no need for law to be explained in detail. A collaborative negotiator may not see it as productive to carry out a detailed legal analysis of past events. That said, law provides a vital context for the negotiation, and law can and should be used tactically.

Using legal terminology and tests

11.70 A point about the legal strength of a case can be made in a shorthand way; for example 'My client properly mitigated his loss and I am not going any lower', or 'If we go to court I will succeed on the balance of convenience test'.

11.71 Equally, a weakness in an opponent's case can be pointed out briefly, as in 'You may say that, but you would not be able to prove it on the balance of probabilities', or 'Your client may want £500 on that, but there is no causation'. This can be successful against a poorly prepared opponent, who may make a concession rather than get into debate about a point of law they have not prepared.

Using research

Mentioning a recent or obscure case as an authority can be an effective tactic in getting a concession from an opponent. It is important to do sufficient legal research in relation to key issues to be able to do this. If this tactic is used against you, take care not to reveal that you have not heard of the case and are a bit shaken. Say something like 'Interesting point, but have you got a copy of the case with you so I can deal with the detail?' **11.72**

KEY POINTS SUMMARY

- A proper understanding and use of style, strategy, and tactics is a very important part of securing the best possible outcome for a client. **11.73**
- Style should be distinguished from strategy as an apparent style can mask a different strategy.
- Specific strategy and tactics should be planned in advance for each case so that they can be implemented to best effect.
- The main strategies are: co-operative, competitive, collaborative, and pragmatic. Each has strengths and weaknesses.
- A wide range of tactics can be used, relating to information, offers, demands, structure, and presentation. Tactics can and should be used to support any strategy.
- In addition to using strategy and tactics effectively yourself, you should use your understanding to identify and address the strategy and tactics used by your opponent.

12

PREPARING FOR NEGOTIATION

A THE IMPORTANCE OF PREPARATION. . . .12.01
B IDENTIFYING THE OBJECTIVES 12.04
C THE IMPORTANCE OF THE PROCEDURAL STAGE THE CASE HAS REACHED 12.07
D IDENTIFYING THE ISSUES. 12.15
E THE RELEVANCE OF THE LEGAL CONTEXT 12.18
F PREPARING TO DEAL WITH FACTS AND EVIDENCE. 12.21
G PREPARING TO DEAL WITH FIGURES . . .12.31
H IDENTIFYING PERSUASIVE ARGUMENTS. 12.33
I PLANNING POTENTIAL DEMANDS, OFFERS, AND CONCESSIONS. 12.48
J LINKING CONCESSIONS. 12.57
K IDENTIFYING THE BATNA. 12.58
L IDENTIFYING THE WATNA 12.64
M CLARIFYING YOUR INSTRUCTIONS AND AUTHORITY .12.66
Key points summary 12.70

A THE IMPORTANCE OF PREPARATION

12.01 A negotiation offers great potential to a lawyer. There is a level of control that is not available in a relatively formal trial process. The flexibility of the process provides possibilities for the use of strategies and tactics, and the availability of outcomes, that may not be possible in a court. However, comprehensive preparation is essential to make the best use of the available opportunities so as to secure the best possible outcome for the client.

12.02 To mould a negotiation to suit your purpose you need a clear list of what you want, and clear plans for how you might get it. While a negotiation normally follows a staged process (see Chapter 13), it often moves very quickly, and is likely to bring surprises and challenges, especially if your opponent is experienced and/or determined. With preparation you can move forward confidently, make the most of a possible advantage and take the unexpected in your stride.

12.03 Because negotiation is a relatively informal process, it might be tempting to just see how it goes. For a lawyer such a view is unprofessional and potentially disastrous. Without full familiarity with the strengths and weaknesses on each issue it can be very difficult to put the case coherently and effectively to an opponent, and without a sufficiently detailed analysis of possible concessions it can be very difficult to take justifiable decisions on what to offer or accept. Strategy and tactics also require planning for best effect (see Chapter 11). A flexible pro-forma for a negotiation plan is provided at Figure 12.1.

B IDENTIFYING THE OBJECTIVES

12.04 The starting point is to be clear on exactly what the client hopes to achieve. Ask the client to provide clear objectives, and check that the list you have is complete. Get a full list and then review what is realistically achievable. Ask the client to identify priorities—do not make assumptions.

- *Money claims*
  - List every potential head of loss, for example in a road accident claim the client may be seeking damages to cover loss of wages, other benefits lost from being laid off at work as a result of the accident, medical expenses, the cost of repairing the car, etc.
  - Consider future loss as well as past loss, such as ongoing loss of wages. Consider whether there are any problems with regard to recoverability of each head, such as foreseeability, mitigation etc.
  - Reach a figure or a range of figures for each head of loss. If it is difficult to calculate a loss eg loss of profit, you will have to propose a method for assessment, as you would have to do if the case went to court.
  - Consider associated matters: when should the sum be paid? Should it be paid as a lump sum or in instalments? Is there a claim for interest? If so, what is the rate of interest and over what period has it been calculated? Are there any VAT or other tax implications for the sum?
- *Other legal rights.* If there is a possible claim for a non-financial remedy such as a declaration or an injunction relating to legal rights, consider whether this can be addressed without going to court, eg through a written agreement. Consider the wording that will best meet the client's objectives.
- *Future relationship.* If there will be a future relationship, for example because the dispute relates to arrangements for care of a child, because there is a commercial relationship, or because the parties are neighbours, establish what your client's objectives for the future are. Are there existing terms for the relationship, such as a contract? If so, will those terms be varied or will there be a new agreement?
- *Personal objectives.* The client may wish to achieve something in addition to enforcing legal rights, for example an apology.
- *Costs of the litigation.* Check the costs of the case to date, and the costs of the negotiation itself. Get a breakdown rather than just global figures, and identify any arguments as to which party should pay each element of the costs.

It is also important to try to anticipate your opponent's objectives as far as you can—what they are likely to want from any settlement, and their probable priorities. Consider what might motivate them to settle. If you are not clear about their objectives you might wish to ask in the negotiation. This will be important to your whole approach if you are likely to use a collaborative strategy. It will in any event be relevant to planning possible concessions. **12.05**

Once you have identified and attempted to prioritize the objectives of both sides, you should consider whether there are any that are shared (ie that both parties want), compatible (ie where the parties value things differently), or where there is conflict. This will help you to formulate possible offers. **12.06**

C THE IMPORTANCE OF THE PROCEDURAL STAGE THE CASE HAS REACHED

The stage that the case has reached provides a crucial context for the preparation that needs to be done. It also gives rise to different procedural possibilities and points that may be made during the negotiation. The main options are as follows. **12.07**

The case is at a very early stage

Considering a negotiation shortly after the client has approached a lawyer may be good in terms of keeping costs to a minimum. If you have a relatively strong case there may be benefits in trying to settle before the other side has time to marshal arguments. A solicitor may **12.08** send a letter proposing a negotiation, on the basis that if agreement can be reached the case will proceed no further.

12.09 However a very early settlement carries risk, unless the case has only one or two issues, such as a claim for money owed. At this stage the lawyer will often have little more than the client's informal statement and any documents the client may have to hand on which to assess the case and the appropriate remedies. Equally the other side may well only have an informal statement from their client. Sufficient information exchange and discussion to gain a clearer picture may be necessary before trying to settle. You are likely to be taken by surprise by some of the points raised by the other side, as each client is likely to have described events from a very different point of view.

The case is at a pre-action protocol stage

12.10 Solicitors will often attempt to negotiate a settlement before a claim form is issued in an attempt to avoid going to court. Consideration of settlement is required under pre-action protocols, and indeed an unreasonable failure to engage in ADR at this stage may be penalized in costs. As the pre-action protocols require the exchange of quite a lot of relevant information, and a correspondence file is likely to have built up, it should be easier to assess the strengths and weaknesses of the case.

12.11 As neither side is yet committed to a statement of case there will be no formal definition of issues. This can be an advantage in terms of flexibility in the negotiation, though it may be a disadvantage in terms of there being less information about your opponent's case. The possibility of issuing proceedings can be used as a tactic in a negotiation.

After the issue of proceedings

12.12 Once all statements of case have been served, both sides will have a much clearer picture of the issues and the allegations of fact made. It will also be clear what will go to court if the case is not settled. Further information becomes available step by step as directions are given with regard to disclosure and inspection of evidence, and then the exchange of witness statements. This gives you the advantage of a clearer picture of your opponent's case, the disadvantage being that your opponent will also know more about your case. Appropriate procedural steps, for example with regard to getting further evidence, can be taken before a negotiation, or raised tactically during a negotiation.

12.13 At this stage you may be negotiating at the court door prior to an interim application, for example an application to obtain summary judgment, or an interim injunction. This can be a challenging type of negotiation because there may be very limited time outside court, and there are several factors to consider.

- Be clear whether you have authority to negotiate the outcome of the whole case as well as the interim application. Ensure you have a full list of issues if you can deal with both, eg costs of the case and of the application.
- If you have authority to settle, remember that you will still need to go into court to address the judge as regards the interim application, so you need to decide whether that goes ahead, is abandoned etc.
- Be aware of the possible effect of the application on the whole case.
- As regards negotiating the outcome of the interim application, bear in mind the test that the court will apply, for example in a claim for an interim injunction, whether there is a serious issue to be tried, whether damages would be an adequate remedy and where the balance of convenience lies. The chances of winning in court are the basis for negotiating.

The case is being prepared for trial

A negotiation at the door of the court just before trial has particular characteristics. This is the last stage at which the parties have control of the outcome rather than leaving it to the judge. The imminence of trial may focus the minds of the parties on trying to avoid the risk, stress, and costs of a full trial. At the door of the court there will be particular considerations, such as trying to avoid keeping the judge waiting for too long, and recording any agreement reached in a consent order. Although the costs may be greater, there may be merit in having a separate meeting before the trial date. **12.14**

D IDENTIFYING THE ISSUES

Identify clearly what parts of the case and what issues you are instructed to negotiate. **12.15**

- You may be instructed to negotiate the whole case, or the outcome of a specific application, see 12.12–12.13.
- You may be instructed to deal with certain issues. Some issues may have been settled already, for example through correspondence. It may be agreed you negotiate a specific part of the case, leaving other matters for a later date. For example there may be a negotiation about liability for an accident, leaving damages till later. You might be instructed to negotiate a claim but not the counterclaim.

If litigation has been commenced the issues should be largely defined in the statements of case. If litigation has not been commenced the issues will need to be identified from client statements and correspondence with the other side. **12.16**

- Identify the alleged or potential causes of action.
- For each cause of action, identify the elements that would need to be proved if each went to court, for example the making of a contract, relevant express or implied terms and breaches.
- Identify which elements are actually in dispute. For example there may be no dispute about the making of the contract or its express terms, but there may be a dispute about implied terms, or there may be an argument that a term was in fact varied.
- Identify on whom the burden of proof lies with regard to each issue.
- Identify alleged or potential defences, eg limitation or contributory negligence.
- Identify the remedies that are or might be sought.
- Identify any legal issues with regard to each remedy; for example if damages are claimed there may be issues of causation, remoteness, foreseeability, or mitigation.
- Is there a counterclaim?

The flexibility of the negotiation process allows you to deal with additional or non-legal issues, especially if your strategy will be collaborative. The above list will need to be adapted as appropriate if you are acting for the defendant rather than the claimant. In any event you should go through the list from the point of view of your opponent to get insight into the lines he or she is likely to pursue in negotiation. **12.17**

E THE RELEVANCE OF THE LEGAL CONTEXT

Legal principles are central to a trial. The issues in the case are defined by law, the lawyers on each side focus their arguments on how the law supports their case, and the judge makes a decision based on and often setting out the application of the law to the case. For a negotiation the legal context is different, but potentially equally important. **12.18**

- The potential outcome if the case were to go to court is a key standard against which the parties should measure proposals for settlement.
- Where your case has legal strength you should use this in argument in the negotiation, albeit with reference to relevant legal principles rather than a long argument based on law.
- Where your case has legal strength you should not make significant concessions.
- You can use points of law, such as a recent case, tactically.

12.19 Many negotiations turn on arguments on fact and evidence rather than on law, though there are still likely to be legal issues such as the wording of an implied term, or whether a particular head of loss was foreseeable. Ensure you identify and are familiar with relevant legal principles as your opponent may take a more legalistic view of the case than you. Also ensure that your knowledge of the law is up to date so that you cannot be taken by surprise.

12.20 If there is a more complex issue of law in the case you need to research it as thoroughly as you might in preparing the case for court. Consider taking copies of key cases or relevant practitioner texts with you to the negotiation to show your opponent. If case law is relevant, decide which cases support your position, and consider the level of the court involved, and whether the case has been subsequently considered by the courts, including whether it was approved, distinguished, or overruled. Consider how you will argue in what way the case supports your client. Also consider how your opponent is likely to argue the point, and which cases they might use. Summarize research that you have done in a way that can be referred to easily in your preparation and in the negotiation itself.

F PREPARING TO DEAL WITH FACTS AND EVIDENCE

12.21 Most legal negotiations turn wholly or partly on disputes of fact. Indeed it may be problems of potential cost with regard to clarifying facts and collecting evidence that lead to a decision that negotiation should be attempted. It is a vital part of preparation to decide how you will deal practically and persuasively with each issue of fact and evidence, especially where there are gaps in information.

12.22 Dealing with fact and evidence can be one of the most difficult parts of a negotiation. Unless you are negotiating after the action has been started and after disclosure and inspection and exchange of witness statements have taken place, you will have less information than would be available at trial. This makes it particularly important to be methodical and strategic in dealing with the information you have, and with the information you do not have.

The client's view of the facts and evidence

12.23 You need a full version of your client's view of the facts. Later in the case this will take the form of a sworn statement, but at a relatively early stage in the case there will be an informal summary of what the client says. While you must accept what your client tells you, be wary of assuming that your client has told you the whole truth, or has given an objective summary. The two parties are likely to view the events leading to potential litigation very differently, and are likely to have developed a mental picture to support what they wish to see as an outcome. If you have only an unsworn statement that is likely to be incomplete and over optimistic, you may wish to test what the client says in a meeting or conference to avoid being taken by surprise by your opponent in the negotiation.

12.24 Consider next what information and evidence currently available supports your client's view of the case as regards each issue likely to be in dispute. While it is not formally necessary to prove an allegation of fact to an opponent in a negotiation, proof or potential proof will be important tactically in convincing an opponent. Where you do not have evidence, identify what is likely to be easily available, so that you can say at the negotiation that you will seek to get that evidence if the case goes to trial. The relevance, admissibility, and weight of existing and potential evidence is important as part of the strength of your case. You can show an opponent evidence that is not technically admissible, but they are likely to be quick to point out that inadmissibility in court is a weakness. Remember that an item shown in a negotiation is privileged and the process confidential and cannot be used at trial unless it is otherwise admissible, but the opponent will be aware of it once shown. Remember that information that has not been disclosed has lawyer–client privilege, and you should have the approval of your client to use it.

The opponent's view of the facts and evidence

To determine what an opponent might accept, look at the facts from their point of view. **12.25**
Close to trial you will have sworn statements from the other side to support their case, but at an earlier stage you may have very limited information about how the other side's version of the facts differs from your own. To avoid being taken by surprise at the negotiation, draw everything you can from what your client says and from what documentation is available to try to predict how the other side sees the case. If there is a key issue on which you would like to know their view prior to negotiation it may be possible to ask with a letter or a phone call.

Early in a case you will know little or nothing about the evidence the other side may have. **12.26**
Make best use of the pre-action protocols to request relevant evidence in the possession of the other side. If you would like to see evidence that is not strictly available under a pre-action protocol you can ask—they can only say no. Bear in mind that when a negotiation precedes formal exchange of evidence, an opponent may produce evidence in support of their case at a negotiation as a tactic to try to surprise you.

Dealing with gaps and ambiguities

Having followed all the above steps, there will be gaps and ambiguities in the information **12.27**
you have, especially early in a case. A successful negotiator is often someone who is able to deal effectively with such gaps. You do not need to know everything about a case to be able to negotiate effectively. Even if a case goes to trial you will not find out exactly what happened—the judge will decide on the balance of probabilities. Do not get distracted by or feel insecure about the various things you do not know—focus on what you really need to know to deal effectively with those issues that are in dispute. Focus on information that is most relevant to winning on the main issues, and to getting the results the client hopes for. This will help you to see which gaps in information are important.

When a gap in information is important it may be dealt with as suggested above—by asking **12.28**
the client, or by a request to the other side prior to the negotiation. You may collect extra evidence before the negotiation, but only seek evidence that is key, and can be found at reasonable cost.

Where gaps remain you will need to present arguments to convince your opponent. Develop **12.29**
arguments on key gaps in the case in advance—good arguments will rarely occur to you on the spur of the moment, and arguments need to be integrated with your strategy and tactics. The following might provide a line of argument:

- Given the disparity between the two versions of events, which seems more plausible? Why?
- How can the facts that are known be most convincingly put together?

- What further evidence might each party gain if they needed to?
- Which side would be most likely to persuade a judge if the case went to trial?
- Which side would have the burden of proof on the disputed issue? Will that party be able to meet the standard of proof of the balance of probabilities?
- Will their evidence be admissible and their witnesses credible?

Preparing to deal with facts and information in negotiation

12.30 Going through the above stages should prepare you to deal efficiently and confidently with the facts in a case. There are just a few more things to do to ensure that you can deal with factual information quickly and fluently. Having to check facts in your papers during a negotiation wastes time and provides your opponent with an opportunity to take control of the process. If you make a mistake about facts it may impact on how the negotiation proceeds, and misleading your opponent about facts can be an issue of professional conduct.

- Ensure that you are fully familiar with the facts so you can deal with them accurately. You also need to be able to absorb new information quickly to adjust your view of the case during the negotiation.
- Be ready to put the facts on each key issue in dispute clearly and confidently from your client's point of view.
- Be ready to use evidence that you have or could easily obtain to best effect to support your client's view of the case.
- Think about which facts are known to both sides and which are not. You may be able to make tactical use of information known only to you.
- Prepare a list of questions to put to your opponent to get information to support you client's version of the case and to undermine your opponent's version.
- Have arguments ready to deal with gaps in your case that cannot be addressed in any other way.
- Consider where there may be gaps in the information your opponent has.
- Decide whether there is any information about your case that you might wish to keep secret in case the negotiation fails.

G PREPARING TO DEAL WITH FIGURES

12.31 Virtually every negotiation includes at least some issues relating to figures. Some negotiations turn almost entirely on figures, for example where a commercial contract has been breached, or where liability has been admitted, so that only a figure for damages remains to be negotiated. It is vitally important to be prepared to deal with figures in detail to ensure you get the best outcome for your client.

- You cannot afford to get confused or make errors about figures in the heat of a negotiation. If you do you will undermine your confidence and lose the initiative.
- Presenting figures to an opponent who is almost certainly going to argue is more difficult than presenting figures to an objective judge.
- If you are not prepared to deal with detailed figures you may easily make concessions unnecessarily and end up with a deal that is unfavourable to your client.
- The process of dealing with offers and concessions means that you need to be able to amend your figures quickly and accurately.
- Many negotiators will choose a competitive strategy with regard to money, whatever strategy they might use on other issues.

Steps to take with regard to preparing figures are: 12.32

- Identify all issues to which figures are relevant, including each head of loss.
- Collect the figures you need to address each issue, or decide how you will deal with a figure that is not to hand. You might for example propose accepting a figure for damage assessed by an agreed independent expert.
- Ensure that you can justify the case for the figure you say is payable—that the loss is foreseeable, is caused by the breach, etc, as relevant.
- Check whether there is any basis on which the figure should be reduced—mitigation, contributory negligence, etc, as relevant.
- Consider any issues relating to calculation, eg how loss of profit should be calculated.
- Consider whether any figure should be adjusted, for example to take VAT into account.
- Consider which figures should have interest added and, if so, the rate and period.
- Consider any issues about when and how money should be paid.
- Ensure you have figures for costs to date, and for the costs of the negotiation.
- Consider how your opponent will see each of the above issues.
- Prepare a summary of your figures to include all the above elements as any of them might be argued in the negotiation. Prepare the summary in a flexible way so that you can quickly adjust figures and recalculate in the negotiation if necessary.

H IDENTIFYING PERSUASIVE ARGUMENTS

The real challenge in any negotiation is getting your opponent to concede what you want for 12.33 your client. A good negotiator is properly prepared, as outlined in this chapter, and makes effective use of strategy and tactics as outlined in Chapter 11. A good negotiator is also able to persuade their opponent to make concessions. Persuasive arguments need to be prepared in advance for negotiation just as much as they do for advocacy. It could be said that preparation of argument is even more important in negotiation because it can be more difficult to persuade an opponent than an objective judge.

The first step is to identify where you will need persuasive arguments. This should emerge 12.34 from putting together your analysis of your client's objectives (see 12.04–12.06), of the issues in the case that are in dispute (see 12.15–12.17) and of how far facts and evidence support your case (see 12.21–12.30). You will need the most persuasive arguments where issues are most in dispute, and where those issues are most important to your client's objectives. The importance of developing arguments where there are gaps in the facts was dealt with in 12.27–12.29. Here we look at the wider need to develop arguments to support the case overall.

Use of argument in negotiation is in some ways similar to use of argument in advocacy. In 12.35 both you seek to persuade another to meet the claims of a client through promoting the strengths of a case and minimizing the weaknesses. Both may depend to some extent on developing a coherent theory of the case, or at least a coherent approach to key issues.

A major difference from advocacy is the way in which you put your case. A case is put in 12.36 a structured way in court, with a set role for an opening and/or closing speech. In negotiation the process is more fragmented, and tends to focus on what is really is dispute. Use of argument in negotiation can be more challenging because the process moves much more quickly than a trial, your opponent may well interrupt, you are more likely to have to deal with new information and points, and the opponent is not an independent arbitrator but a person with a different viewpoint. These differences can make it difficult to present a full and detailed case. If time is limited you may need to focus on identifying about three of the best arguments on each issue and present those arguments in the most persuasive way. Note other arguments, but they can be kept in reserve.

12.37 Be aware of the arguments that are most likely to be used to test you or to justify your opponent's proposals so you can be ready to respond. This will help you to be proactive rather than merely reactive; for example you may be able to reduce the impact of any argument that may be raised by your opponent before they use it.

Arguments based on the application of the law

12.38 If there is a significant argument on what the relevant law is, it is more likely that the case will go to court, especially if either party wishes to create a precedent. An argument may arise because a legal principle is not well established, or if it is argued that it should be reinterpreted or applied in a different way. Reference to the law may be needed where there is dispute about the interpretation of the law as regards a statute, regulation, or case law. The lawyers cannot establish what the law is in the way a judge can, but the lawyers can try to reach agreement on what the law will be seen as being for the purposes of settling the case if the parties wish to avoid the cost of going to court.

12.39 Argument is more commonly about how the law applies to facts, for example what the standard of care is in a case where negligence is alleged, or whether representations induced a contract. In a negotiation between lawyers there is no need for law to be stated at length—more commonly there is a brief reference to principle and then a statement as to how it is seen to apply. For example 'We will of course need to satisfy the balance of convenience test and we do that because…' When arguing about law, lawyers typically use shorthand references to principles; for example 'We will not pay £1,000 because you have a forseeability problem in employing a chef for a day'.

Arguments based on facts

12.40 Commonly, at least some of the arguments in a negotiation relate to what the facts are. In a contract case there may be a dispute about whether there was an oral variation of contract, which essentially sets one person's word against another's. In a negligence case there may well be a dispute about exactly how an accident happened. How to deal with argument where there is a gap in the information available is dealt with in 12.27–12.29.

Merit-based or moral argument

12.41 A merit-based argument is one that seeks to show an objective reason why a specific approach should be adopted, for example by relating an issue to a set standard. An argument on law will be merit based where you are seeking to argue that a specific outcome is justified by legal principle. An argument on evidence will be merit based where you have clear admissible evidence on a point. A merit-based argument should have a sound base, not relying on an assumption or partisan view, to be successful.

12.42 A moral argument might relate to the beliefs or circumstances of the parties to a case. A specific outcome might be seen as 'right' for those involved, perhaps for cultural or personal reasons. In negotiating a separation between a couple it might be right to take such factors into account.

12.43 More frequently an argument about what is 'fair' might be used. A negotiator might say 'it would be fairer to…', but this is a very vague term. You need to be able to justify on what basis a particular approach is 'fairer'. Is it more equal? Is it more justified because of the way someone has behaved?

Practical or personal arguments

Practical arguments might relate to a party's circumstances, or to the practicalities of achieving a possible compromise. Practical arguments might be very relevant in a case relating to a sale between two businesses, or as regards the terms of a proposed interim injunction. A practical argument might also relate to the terms of a settlement, for example terms for payment. **12.44**

An argument in a negotiation might relate to the particular people involved, especially where a collaborative strategy is employed. In a neighbour dispute an elderly person might primarily want to secure a peaceful and quiet life. In a business dispute a hairdresser might want to get the right ambience for a new salon. Personal arguments can be powerful if used carefully and at the right time, but they can show weakness if used wrongly, especially if used against a competitive opponent. **12.45**

Mixed arguments

An issue might be addressed using several types of argument. A single issue might be addressed with an argument about the application of the law, and an argument about personal needs. Alternatively an issue might involve an argument about facts, then an argument about the application of the law, then a moral argument about what is fair. The force of some key arguments can be lost if too many arguments are put together. **12.46**

First identify the main types of argument that might be used on an issue. Then think carefully about which arguments are strongest, and whether you might use only key arguments, keeping others in reserve. If you might need to use more than one form of argument, for example about facts and about application of the law, then plan the use of each argument as regards the order in which they are best presented, and how they are best linked. **12.47**

I PLANNING POTENTIAL DEMANDS, OFFERS, AND CONCESSIONS

A negotiation is a process for moving towards agreement. It may start from positions that are quite far apart, especially where two competitive negotiators are involved. From there a process of demands and proposals will potentially lead to offers and concessions, and hopefully to a point where the parties can agree. In order to ensure you get the best possible outcome for your client it is important to plan in advance when you would envisage these steps taking place. Without planning it can be very difficult to know what to offer when, and it is all too easy to ask for too little or concede too much. **12.48**

Overall you need to work within a clear understanding of the client's priorities, the most the client might possibly achieve, and the least that the client might accept: see 12.04–12.06 and 12.66–12.69. There should rarely if ever be a concession on something that is important to your client and where the case is strong. Any concession should be justifiable by a proper evaluation of the case. It is your professional duty to seek the best available outcome for your client, and your plan should be reasonably optimistic. It is not your role just to aim vaguely for a position some way between yourself and your opponent, or to try to impose something you see as roughly 'fair', and such an approach could be exploited by a competitive opponent. **12.49**

Plan what you will seek from the other side

12.50 Planning involves systematic consideration of the client's objectives, the client's priorities, and the strengths and weaknesses of the case. It is psychologically helpful to start by identifying where you will seek concessions from the other side.

- What are your client's main objectives? Work from a detailed and prioritized list. Concessions may come from the lower part of the list, but should be limited in the upper part.
- Which issues relate to your client's main objectives? Plan primarily with regard to those issues.
- How exactly is your case strong in relation to key issues? Is it a matter of law, fact, and/or evidence? What sort of legal or evidential issue is it? How good are the arguments you can develop?
- Is your strength on the issue clear (for example because of evidence you hold), or might you need to investigate the issue with them before seeking a concession (eg to ask what evidence they have)?
- What exactly are the weaknesses of the case for the other side in relation to the key issues? Are the weaknesses legal, factual, or evidential? How can you point out those weaknesses most clearly?
- What are the relative strengths or weaknesses? Can you argue the other side should acknowledge you should win (eg because you have a letter proving a variation of contract, or you will argue a head of loss was unforeseeable)? Can you argue the other side should make a significant concession (eg because you think you can prove 30% contributory negligence)? Can you only argue they should make a small concession (for example because of a limited failure to mitigate loss)?
- Based on the previous point, identify as accurately as possible the largest concession on the issue you can expect the other side to make.
- Identify fallback positions as accurately as possible. For example if they will not concede 30% contributory negligence, might you argue for 20%? Why?

Plan how and when you will ask

12.51 Gaining a significant concession from an opponent in a negotiation will not be easy. If you just ask an opponent to concede 30% contributory negligence you are likely to be met with a refusal. You need to lay foundations for when and how you will seek a concession to maximize your chances of success.

- Decide whether you will make a demand or ask for a concession, or use other terminology, depending on how this fits with your strategy.
- It is usually best to seek a concession specifically, clearly, and once. This is most likely to stick in your opponent's mind and to have some effect.
- Support this with a clear summary of reasons. For example 'I think you need to drop your claim for £2,000 for the loss of the wife's earnings. That head of loss was not foreseeable to my client and he had no notice of it. In any event I would argue it did not flow from the breach.'
- Relate concession planning to structure planning and time your approach for best effect. A competitive negotiator might well demand early in a negotiation that an opponent makes a number of concessions. This can be effective as it will often lead to the other side making concessions on at least some of those points. However early demands that are unrealistic and unjustified are likely to fail as they can be challenged relatively easily by the opponent. More commonly a concession would be requested after the relevant issue has been discussed and the case made, so you might want to cover areas where your case is strong early so that you can get justified requests for concessions on the table.

You may obtain a concession quite quickly if your case is strong (though if you obtain a concession too easily it might mean that you have asked for too little). However you will rarely get a full concession immediately. Once you have made your opponent aware of what you are seeking you may need to move to another issue. You might well be able to get the concession in return for something else later. Repetition is more likely to weaken your position rather than help because your opponent may well repeat a refusal. Do not rush to reduce the concession you are seeking unless there is a good reason—this can look weak. **12.52**

Plan what you will offer

You also need to plan carefully what concessions you might make to the other side. You will rarely if ever be able to reach a settlement without making some concessions. Your client will want to achieve their objectives as far as possible, so success depends on making as few concessions as are necessary, with each concession being as small as possible. A co-operative strategy should not lead to unnecessary concessions any more than a competitive strategy. **12.53**

The process for identifying possible concessions is similar to that for identifying demands: **12.54**

- How exactly is your case weak or their case strong? Is it a matter of law, fact, and/or evidence? What sort of legal or evidential issue is it?
- Should you investigate the issue with them before offering any concession (eg ask what evidence they have)?
- What is the relative weakness in your case? Are you clearly going to lose on the issue (eg because your client admits to you that a key term was not part of an oral contract)? Might you have to make a significant concession (for example because the burden of proof on an issue is on you and you think it unlikely you will be able to get enough evidence)? Are you thinking of a small concession (eg that you will not force the other side to get formal evidence on a particular point)?
- Based on the type and size of the weakness, should you really make any concession at all? Is the weakness something you might address by getting further evidence if the case went to trial? What is the smallest concession on the issue you can expect the other side to consider?
- Is there any more you might concede in any circumstances? If you make any concession an opponent might press for more—your concession should not be more than the relative weakness of your case justifies. Be slow to concede more on an issue of real importance to the client.
- Ensure you are clear what concession you might make—for what reason, how much, and in what circumstances.
- Prioritize potential concessions in order of importance to the client, and try only to make ones that are of least importance to the client. The fact that you could make a concession does not mean that you should!

Plan how and when you will make offers

Plan carefully when and how to offer a concession to ensure that you make as few concessions as are really necessary. This might well be a part of planning the structure of a negotiation. You might want to make any concession that you offer 'provisional', that is that the concession would only become operative as part of an overall deal with concessions from both sides, and is not a concession that would stand alone. **12.55**

There may be a tactical reason for making a provisional concession at an early stage; for example 'I am prepared to say immediately that we will not be pressing ahead with our **12.56** application for an interim injunction so long as all the issues relating to the agreement between the parties can be settled today.' This can help to lay a foundation for a collaborative strategy.

- You might start with an area where you can make a few unimportant concessions so that you can appear generous. If these are provisional concessions you can use that to put pressure on your opponent to make concessions later.
- You might start with an area where you do not feel you need to make any concessions, to lay a foundation for a competitive strategy.
- It is risky to start with an area where you think you may need to make significant concessions as this can make you look weak, unless perhaps you are sure that both negotiators are committed to a collaborative approach.
- If you need more information to be sure whether a concession is justified, make sure that you ask relevant questions before raising any possible concession.
- Plan to stage concessions. Make small fallback steps between your opening offer and the least you can accept. Avoid big or rapid increases in concessions or your opponent will realize that more may be gained by pushing you.

J LINKING CONCESSIONS

12.57 In seeking to do the best for the client, a concession should rarely be made without getting something in return. In addition to having a good reason for making a concession on a particular point, you should try to make sure that the concession takes the case forward. This is most likely to happen if your concession is linked to a concession by your opponent on another point. Make this clear by saying when you offer a concession that it is provisional on getting something in return. Make sure that you try to link getting a concession on something important to your client to making a concession on something of limited importance. Avoid vaguely trading one concession for another if you are giving away much more than you get.

K IDENTIFYING THE BATNA

12.58 In addition to planning potential demands and concessions in relation to individual issues, it is vital to be able to put any potential settlement into an overall context, so that you will be in a position to judge whether a particular overall set of terms should or should not be accepted. This requires comparing whatever potential overall deal you are able to achieve in a negotiation with the best realistic alternative there would be if no settlement were reached. This involves identifying the BATNA (best alternative to a negotiated agreement). If the deal you have negotiated is at least as good as the BATNA then it should potentially be accepted. If it is worse, then you should probably walk away. The BATNA is not something to aim for—if you are negotiating effectively you should get much more—but it is effectively a bottom line. It is rarely in your interests to reveal a BATNA as a competitive opponent will try to force you down to that figure.

12.59 BATNA is not a concept of law, but a practical tool for risk management. A lawyer will not necessarily use the term 'BATNA' (which was developed by academics with expertise in negotiation), but will fully appreciate the need to have a defined plan B. For a legal negotiation the alternative to settlement will be going to court, so the BATNA is what the client is realistically likely to get if he or she were to go to court. A BATNA can be used in advising a client whether to accept an offer. Assessing the likely BATNA of your opponent can help you to assess offers.

There is no single way to identify a BATNA with accuracy, and these paragraphs provide a guide to key factors rather than a definitive approach. The following stages are most important: **12.60**

1. Calculate the figure that is realistically achieveable in damages if the case goes to trial.
   Calculate the most realistic figure recoverable for each head of loss. Rule out optimistic hopes, and take proper account of rules for the calculation of damages such as causation and mitigation. Add figures for interest to date where relevant. Add together the figures for all heads to identify an overall figure.

2. Take into account how likely the case is to succeed at trial.
   It would be quite unrealistic to have the same bottom line if you have a strong case that is 90% likely to succeed as you would if there were weaknesses in your case such that it is only 60% likely to succeed. Chances of success are assessed by thorough examination of the factual, legal and evidential strengths and weaknesses in a case. If the law is clear, there are no gaps in the facts, and all relevant matters in issue can be proved in the client's favour, then the chances of success are likely to be close to 100%. If the law is not entirely clear, if some facts are disputed, and if the evidence available is open to challenge then the chances of success will be much lower. It is not easy to assess chances of success and skill in this only really develops with experience. However, this is a key skill for a lawyer. A lawyer in practice needs to be able to calculate chances of success for a variety of purposes (for example in relation to a CFA agreement or in an opinion relating to possible legal aid funding), and clients are often keen to have chances of success expressed in percentage terms rather than in vague words such as 'good'. The chance of success is taken into account in a broad-brush way by multiplying the likely damages by the chances of winning those damages. (This is not a matter of legal principle but just taking the risk of not getting the damages into account.) If a negotiation takes place at a very early stage in a case when facts and evidence are not fully known it can be quite difficult to make an accurate calculation of chances of success. If in real doubt the options are to collect more information relevant to chances of success, or to assume that the chance of success is 100% until risks are known.

3. Take into account the further costs likely to be incurred to obtain the damages if the case were to go to trial.
   If the case does not settle, further costs will be incurred going to court. To the extent your client may end up bearing these they must be taken into account in assessing what to accept. Even if the case is won and the other side is ordered to pay the claimant's reasonable costs, some part of what the claimant has actually paid in costs may not be recoverable. As a rough rule of thumb, about 20% of costs in a civil case may prove irrecoverable on taxation. Deduct from the likely damages the costs that would be likely to be incurred to secure the damages, but would then be likely to be irrecoverable.

To give a very simple example, you may assess realistic total potential damages if the case went to trial as £40,000. However due to doubts as to whether a legal argument will succeed, or as to whether a key witness will come up to proof, you might assess the chances of success at trial as being 75%. To reflect the level of risk the damages should be discounted by the risk: £40,000 × 75% = £30,000. If going to court would be likely to incur further costs of £5,000, of which you think that £1,000 might not be recoverable even if the client won the case and was awarded standard costs, then the figure should be further reduced by the potentially unrecoverable costs: £30,000 – £1,000 = £29,000. **12.61**

On these figures the BATNA would therefore be £29,000. In a negotiation you would still seek damages of £40,000 for the client and argue hard to get as close to that figure as **12.62** possible. However, if the negotiation does not go well you need to bear in mind that there is a risk that the case will not be won in court, and that even if the client were to win it might cost more to go to court. The BATNA takes these things into account. The client should seriously consider accepting an offer of £29,000 or above if that is the best you can achieve as that is the figure at which in broad terms it is more risky to go on than to accept the offer.

12.63 It can be difficult to assess a BATNA very accurately if there are several financial issues in a case with different chances of success. In such circumstances it is probably best to calculate the BATNA only on the basis of the main issues that are worth most money. There can also be problems if the client's objectives are not all financial. You should still calculate a BATNA for the financial issues, but discuss priorities with the client in advance of the negotiation, so that you have a clear view on what the client might be prepared to concede in financial terms to obtain a non-financial objective. You should still not settle financial issues below the BATNA unless you have achieved a substantial non-financial goal.

L IDENTIFYING THE WATNA

12.64 Identification of the worst alternative to a negotiated agreement (WATNA) is less important, and it can be rather depressing, but it can also provide useful contextual information when assessing offers. The point here is to assess the worst that could happen if there were no negotiated agreement, so that you do at least consider an offer if there is a risk that the outcome could be even worse than the terms offered. A WATNA can also be used tactically, by pointing out to an opponent what his or her WATNA might be if your offer is not accepted, especially if their chance of success might be relatively low. It may not be easy to assess the worst that could happen, partly because a doomsday scenario may not be very likely, and also because it may be difficult to engage a client in considering a very poor outcome when you are trying to show that you are acting in his or her best interests.

12.65 In the scenario dealt with above in calculating the BATNA, if the chance of success in the case was 60% rather than 75%, there would be a 40% risk that the client would lose at trial, therefore getting nothing. If the client lost he or she would have to bear his or her own costs, which might be say £5,000. In addition he or she might be ordered to pay the opponent's costs, which might be a figure of say £10,000. The WATNA would be that the client would end up £15,000 out of pocket. This is not the likely outcome and should not of itself lead to unnecessary concessions, but the possibility should not be ignored. While at one end of the scale the client is likely to get £40,000 and his reasonable costs paid, the fact that it is possible that at the other end of the scale the client will be £15,000 out of pocket cannot be ignored.

M CLARIFYING YOUR INSTRUCTIONS AND AUTHORITY

12.66 In professional terms it is vital to be absolutely clear what you are instructed by the client to do, and what authority you have from the client to settle. If you have any doubts you should check, and if the client is indecisive or vague it may be best to record the instructions and authority in writing. If any doubts arise you may also wish to check during a negotiation that your opponent is acting with instructions and within the authority given.

12.67 Your instructions relate to whether you can negotiate at all and what you can negotiate on. Do you have a clear instruction to negotiate? Does it apply to all issues? If not, which issues are you instructed to deal with? Any doubts must be resolved with the client as it is a matter of professional conduct to act within your instructions. If any proposals for settlement are made by the other side get instructions with regard to those proposals.

Your authority to settle is a different matter. 'Authority' relates to what you are authorized to accept on your client's behalf. A lawyer normally has apparent authority to settle on behalf of a client, and if you do not act within actual authority you may put yourself in the very difficult position of having made an agreement with the other side that your client is not prepared to honour. A client will often give general authority to negotiate, but on the basis that any agreement you reach with the other side will only be provisional and subject to client approval. This is a helpful basis for you as it gives you flexibility but enables you to make it clear to your opponent that only a provisional agreement can be reached and it will be subject to client approval. You may need to raise any limit on authority in the negotiation: see 13.49–13.52. **12.68**

A client may give guidelines as to what sort of figures are acceptable on specific issues, often based on the advice the lawyer has given to the client on what can realistically be gained. Sometimes a client will insist on being unrealistically optimistic so that the lawyer only has authority to settle for a high figure. This may make it unlikely the negotiation will be successful. **12.69**

KEY POINTS SUMMARY

- The negotiation process is very flexible, which offers a lot of opportunities to a lawyer who is properly prepared to get the most out of the process. **12.70**
- The purpose of a negotiation is to get the best possible outcome for the client, so planning should be based on a careful identification and prioritization of the client's objectives.
- Context is very important—consider carefully the implications of the stage the case has reached.
- Identify the issues that need to be negotiated, and analyse the facts, evidence, and law to put together persuasive arguments on each issue.
- Be ready to deal with figures fully and in detail so that you can deal with them fluently in the negotiation.
- Evaluate your case carefully to plan potential concessions, demands, and offers, so that you are clear what you want to get on each issue, and what the possible fallback positions are.
- Have planned positions so that you can avoid 'splitting the difference'—this may appear to be fair but is often not justified by relative strengths and weaknesses.
- Plan a BATNA and WATNA to provide a context for assessing offers and the possible overall outcome of the negotiation.

Figure 12.1 Pro-forma negotiation plan

PRO-FORMA NEGOTIATION PLAN

This is a flexible basic pro-forma for planning a negotiation.

NEGOTIATION PLAN

A. CONTEXT

- What stage has the case reached?
- If litigation has not been commenced, are there any issues relating to compliance with pre-action protocols?

B. ISSUES IN THE CASE

(*List clearly and objectively all the issues that are in dispute in the case. Include financial and non-financial issues.*)

1. …
2. … *(etc)*

C. OBJECTIVES OF CLIENT

(*Prioritize the issues from your client's point of view. Assess what your client wants to achieve in relation to each issue as specifically as possible.*)

1. …
2. … *(etc)*

D. LIKELY OBJECTIVES OF THE OTHER SIDE

(*Being as clear as possible as to what your opponent is likely to be seeking will help you to prepare strategy and tactics.*)

1. …
2. … *(etc)*

E. LEGAL CONTEXT

- What is the legal basis for the claim?
- Does the claim have particular legal strengths?
- Is there a legal defence to the claim?
- Are there legal principles relevant to the quantification of damages, such as causation or remoteness?

F. INFORMATION AND EVIDENCE SUPPORTING YOUR CASE

- How can you best use the facts and evidence you have to support your client's case on each issue?
- Is there specific information or evidence you might offer to get as part of the negotiation?

Figure 12.1 Pro-forma negotiation plan (*Continued*)

G. INFORMATION AND EVIDENCE YOU MAY SEEK FROM THE OTHER SIDE

- What information do you need to assess what demands or offers you might make?
- What information do you need to assess the strengths and weaknesses of your opponent's case?

H. INFORMATION AND EVIDENCE THAT MAY BE SOUGHT FROM YOU

- What questions is your opponent most likely to ask on key issues? How far should you provide answers?

I. STRENGTHS AND WEAKNESSES OF YOUR CASE
As regards each main issue:

- What are the key legal strengths?
- What are the key factual and evidential strengths?
- What are the key weaknesses in your case, and how can you best address each?

J. WEAKNESSES AND STRENGTHS OF THE CASE FOR THE OTHER SIDE

- What are the key legal, factual, and evidential strengths your opponent's case is likely to have as regards each main issue, and how will you address them?

K. CALCULATIONS

(*For any financial objective you need to carry out detailed calculations in advance. This is an essential basis for framing offers and concessions. Include interest etc.*)

L. STRATEGY AND TACTICS

- What is the best overall strategy and style for use in this case?
- What specific tactics might be used on specific issues?
- How would you plan to open the negotiation?
- In what order would you prefer to deal with topics?

M. POTENTIAL DEMANDS, OFFERS, AND CONCESSIONS, AND THE BATNA

(*It is vital to have a clear BATNA before starting any negotiation. Potential demands and concessions should also be planned in advance.*)

N. OPTIONS FOR RECORDING THE SETTLEMENT

- In what form can the outcome of this negotiation be recorded? If there are options, which is best for the client?
- Are there existing proceedings or applications to be brought to a close? If so, how is that best done?
- Are there any particular terms to include, eg to protect confidentiality?

13

THE NEGOTIATION PROCESS

A WHEN, HOW, AND WHERE 13.04
B WHO 13.08
C COMMUNICATING EFFECTIVELY 13.11
D STRUCTURE AND AGENDA SETTING 13.26
E OPENING. 13.32
F SEEKING INFORMATION 13.57
G MAKING YOUR CASE ON THE ISSUES . . .13.63
H PLANNING AND TIMING CONCESSIONS, OFFERS, AND DEMANDS 13.77
I MAKING PROGRESS 13.107
J DEALING WITH DIFFICULTIES 13.109
K REACHING A CLOSE—SETTLEMENT OR BREAKDOWN. 13.122
Key points summary 13.127

13.01 There is no defined negotiation process, but almost all negotiations include similar identifiable stages. Understanding those stages will help you to control the process and work with confidence, so that you can get the best achievable outcome. Many negotiators prefer the relative security of a conventional structure based on an agenda, though it is inevitable that discussion will sometimes move away from what was planned, and some negotiators will fail to follow a set structure as a matter of tactics.

13.02 The main stages that can be identified are as follows. They normally come broadly in the order listed, though stages 2–3 are often followed through separately in relation to each issue. The stages are illustrated in Figure 13.1.

1. Agenda setting/opening (see 13.26 and 13.56).
2. Seeking information (see 13.57–13.62).
3. Discussion of the merits on the issues (see 13.63–13.76).

13.03 That said, each negotiation is unique. Each case will have different issues and clients with different objectives. There will be different legal and evidential strengths and weaknesses, and the negotiation may take place at a different stage in the case. The negotiators will use different strategies and tactics that affect how the process unfolds. Analysis and preparation, as outlined in Chapter 12, will help to ensure that you can predict and control these differences rather than be confused or tripped up by them.

A WHEN, HOW, AND WHERE

13.04 The first decision to make is that negotiation is an appropriate process for settlement of a case, and that a good point in the case has been reached to try negotiation. The parties need adequate information to be able to analyse the case sufficiently as outlined in Chapter 12.

13.05 The next question is what form of negotiation to use. A negotiation may be conducted wholly or partly face-to-face, by telephone, or in writing. Exchange of letters or emails may be appropriate if there are limited issues in the case and proposals can be put quite briefly without the need for much explanation or discussion—this book does not deal further with

Figure 13.1 Overview of the negotiation process

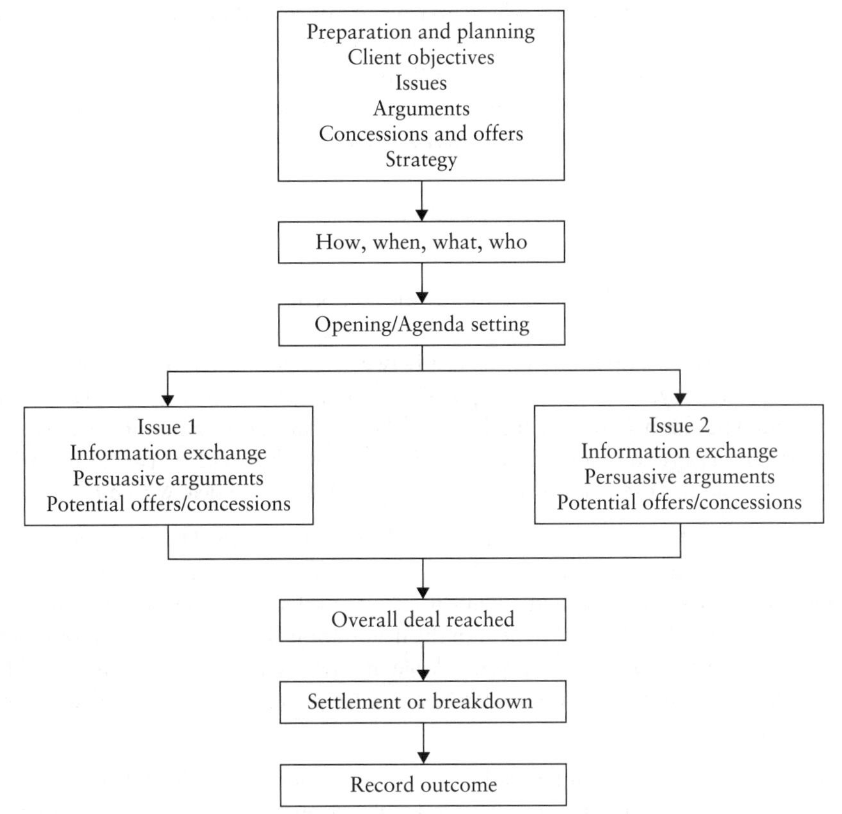

making written offers. Negotiating by telephone might be appropriate where the barristers or solicitors on each side are instructed to investigate settlement and it is thought that the process will not take too long. A number of the points made in this chapter could apply, but this chapter deals primarily with face-to-face negotiation involving lawyers.

An appropriate location for the negotiation must be agreed, depending on who will attend: see 13.08–13.10. Solicitors will often negotiate in the office of one of the solicitors, and barristers may negotiate in the chambers of one of the barristers. A sufficiently large space will be needed for the number of people involved, and a space appropriate for the length of time the negotiation might last. There may be advantages in holding the negotiation in a space you have control of so that you can arrange seating, offer refreshments, and so on. Alternatively you may prefer to visit a space where you have no responsibilities, and where you can threaten to leave if you are not happy with progress. A negotiation can be facilitated or frustrated by simple things like comfortable chairs and adequate table space for papers. Space can support your strategy and tactics. Do you want to show a competitive start by taking all the space available for your papers, or do you want to make a facilitative start by arranging chairs comfortably round the table? Making a point about the arrangements at the start of a negotiation may be done as a tactic. **13.06**

You may have little choice over location if the negotiation takes place outside court. This will happen quite often for a barrister early in practice, when appearing on an interim application may provide an opportunity to negotiate. It may also happen when lawyers meet **13.07** outside court before a case management conference or trial. Many courts have small interview rooms that may be available, but there is often no choice but to use the corridor outside court, which may be noisy or busy. There may be no tables, and possibly no seats, so that it may be difficult to manage or refer to papers. There can also be stress if a case will be called into court at a particular time. You should still do what you can to control the space. Court door negotiations are often carried out between counsel, and it may be important to find space where the solicitor and client can wait away from counsel.

B WHO

13.08 Decide who needs to attend the negotiation. Relevant people need to be included, but additional people will increase cost, may slow the process down, and may make it more difficult to control. The negotiation may be just between solicitors, just between barristers, or between teams of lawyers on both sides, possibly including in-house lawyers. The number of lawyers should be justified by the complexity of the case and/or the amount at stake. If there is more than one lawyer on each side the role of each should be decided in advance—will one take the main role and the others provide information? Will each deal with different issues?

13.09 The clients may wish to be present. This can make it easier for the lawyers to take instructions and review the acceptability of options. However, it may be undesirable because clients may undermine the strategy or tactics being used with oral interjections or body language. If the client is present, the role of the client in the negotiation should be clearly agreed beforehand. It may be better for clients to be available in separate rooms nearby or available for consultation by telephone so that they can be asked for instructions or be briefed on what is happening as and when appropriate.

13.10 Others might usefully attend, or be available for consultation, especially if there are complex issues. An accountant might be present for at least part of the negotiation to assist with figures, or an expert might be asked to attend to help to deal with a specific issue. Such individuals may be available to telephone rather than attend the venue.

C COMMUNICATING EFFECTIVELY

13.11 Effective communication is central to effective negotiation. The main purpose of the process is for sufficient communication about the case for each side to take place so that agreement can be reached. Unfortunately the lack of a clear process, different strategies and tactics, and factors such as stress can make communication difficult. This might prevent agreement being reached if you avoid or do not address problems.

13.12 Psychological factors and non-verbal communication should not be ignored. Sitting back, smiling, and making open and relaxed body movements can suggest confidence and might encourage negotiation. Nodding normally indicates support. Crossed arms and looking away can show hostility. Failing to meet someone's eyes might indicate that what is being said is misleading. Hunching over a desk or sitting uncomfortably can indicate lack of confidence.

13.13 Make sure that you control your own body language—sitting and moving in a confident way can help to convey your message. Sitting forward with interest when your opponent outlines a point of importance to them can help progress a collaborative approach. Body language can provide clues that you can follow up, for example saying 'You do not look comfortable—you don't seem to think your case on this point is strong'.

Reciprocal or 'mirroring' behaviour

When two people are involved in a discussion, they often unconsciously 'mirror' each other's behaviour. If one starts to express annoyance, the other may take a similar course. You can sometimes take advantage of this to help you to progress a negotiation. If you want to take a collaborative or co-operative approach it can be very helpful to model it by smiling, listening carefully, and expressing what you say supportively. Unless your opponent has a clear plan for another strategy, he or she is likely to be prepared to follow your lead. Do not go too far—do not make too large a concession just to try to encourage an opponent to do likewise. **13.14**

Two competitive negotiators can make effective progress, but mirroring can be a problem if one negotiator is confrontational or aggressive and the other is pulled in to behaving in a similar way. This serves little purpose, and deadlock is likely to result. If your opponent's conduct is unhelpful try to remain calm and constructive. Do not feel compelled to make concessions to appease them—this may be what the tactic is trying to achieve. **13.15**

Effective presentation

The way you present your case is likely to have a major impact on the outcome. A mediocre case will often get a better outcome if it is presented confidently and coherently. Being well prepared is half the battle—if you know how you want to argue each issue and what concessions you will seek you can concentrate on what you say and how you say it. A strong case can be completely undermined by mediocre presentation. **13.16**

- The way you speak can be important—choose your language and tone of voice carefully.
- Keep up a good pace, but do not rush so that points get lost.
- Focus on your opponent as your audience—the point is to ensure that your opponent understands your case and is persuaded by it.
- Make each point as clearly and concisely as you can. Say what you want and why. Focus on your strongest points on each issue.
- Construct arguments carefully, making all your points on an issue together so they build on each other.
- Use appropriate legal terminology, not setting out law at length, but using the right legal words, for example 'Your client is clearly in breach of an implied term' or 'I can't see that there is any problem with foreseeability here'.
- Objective language is often most persuasive, 'My client has good evidence on this issue' is stronger than 'I think my client has a good point here'.
- Reference to the client is generally better than making things personal; for example 'My client would not accept that', rather than 'I won't accept that'.

Presentation can be undermined in various ways. **13.17**

- Speaking at too great a length—if you ramble, or recite information your opponent is already aware of at length, your opponent will cease to listen and is likely to interrupt you.
- Presenting too many arguments together in a way that is difficult to follow, so good arguments get lost among weaker ones.
- Repeating points at length—this is more likely to bore your opponent than lead to concessions.
- Failing to notice how your opponent is taking your presentation. If your opponent misunderstands or is bored you need to deal with that.

Presentation should of course be varied to fit with strategies or tactics. A competitive or confrontational negotiator is likely to present with extreme self-confidence, whether or not **13.18** this is justified, and may make sarcastic or condescending remarks about an opponent. Such a negotiator may be argumentative to try to wear an opponent down.

Responding effectively

13.19 Responding can be challenging, as you may have to take into account new information that alters your assessment of the case. It is easy to focus so much on presenting your own case that you fail to respond properly—both are equally important.

- You need to understand facts presented by an opponent. Follow up detail if you need to. Check key allegations and figures.
- You may need to understand the arguments made by your opponent, but take care how you ask for clarification. Do not help an opponent to develop an argument, or allow a weak argument to appear important.
- Test and challenge what your opponent says—if a statement is not properly justified ask for reasons, or for evidence.
- Try to respond as clearly and accurately as you can. Your response should try to move your case forward, keeping a focus on your client's objectives and your view of the strengths and weaknesses of the case. If you disagree with what the other side has said about law, fact or evidence, then make that clear and say why.
- Avoid responding with surprise, or an indication that anything said undermines the strength of your case. If you are aware of a weakness you may have a prepared response; for example 'I accept we do not have evidence on that, but we could seek it if the case were to go to trial'. If you need time to think before you respond, make time by talking about details, or move on to another point and then come back.
- It is normally best not to interrupt an opponent—you may miss something important. If their presentation is long try to make the point by saying something like 'Sorry to interrupt but I think your key point here is that you are denying contributory negligence—can you give me your two main reasons for this'.

13.20 Responding should also fit with strategy and tactics. A competitive negotiator may fail to respond at all to a point made to imply that the point is irrelevant.

Questioning effectively

13.21 Lawyers are used to the need for questioning skills in conferences with clients and in dealing with witnesses in court. Similar skills may be needed to get information from an opponent in a negotiation, be it factual information or reasons for their view of the case. While only a very competitive negotiator would cross-examine an opponent, questions are crucial for testing your opponent in an appropriate way.

13.22 Questions can also be used constructively—a collaborative negotiator will ask questions about what the opponent's client most wants to get from the negotiation. Most questions can be asked in a positive or confrontational way. Saying 'Please could you tell me why your client feels his claim on this issue is strong' is much less confrontational than 'I really can't see why you think you have a leg to stand on. On what possible basis do you make that claim?'

Listening effectively

13.23 A lawyer in a negotiation is often so focused on putting the client's case and on responding robustly that too little attention is given to listening. Indeed there may be a fear that listening is not a good use of time when you could be presenting. Unless you stay quiet for a long time this is not the case—pick up every clue from what an opponent says, what they do not say, and any subtext. A throw-away remark may reveal information you need to follow up, or you may be able to spot a gap in their case from the way an argument is being made.

Concentration is important, and negotiation can be tiring. Make sure you do not miss anything important because you are thinking about something else. Listening can be part of your strategy—listening with interest supports a co-operative strategy, but appearing bored may support a competitive strategy. **13.24**

What is not said can be important. Something an opponent is trying not to talk about could be an area of weakness. Ask about gaps, and do not feel you need to tiptoe round an issue. Your opponent has a professional duty not to mislead you—if careful but vague wording is being used it may well be because care is being taken not to mislead. Remember there may be a gap between what your opponent has told the client and what they are telling you. The client may have been told the case on a point is not strong, while their lawyer tries to present it to you in a good light—you may be able to pick up your opponent's underlying view if you listen carefully. **13.25**

D STRUCTURE AND AGENDA SETTING

The lack of a set format for a negotiation process means that structure and agenda setting are important. An experienced negotiator will want to use a structure that supports plans for strategy and tactics. An inexperienced negotiator is likely to feel more secure working within an agreed structure. In a big case the coverage and order for a negotiation may well be agreed in advance. In a smaller negotiation the agenda is usually set in the first few minutes of the negotiation. **13.26**

The potential benefits of a clear structure and agenda are that they should help to ensure that: **13.27**

- time is used efficiently, especially if limited time is available;
- you are able to cover all the things you need to;
- you can work coherently to achieve your client's objectives;
- you can implement your chosen strategy and tactics;
- you can deal with topics in a sensible order;
- you have a plan to fall back on if something unexpected comes up.

Choices for structure will normally be based on: **13.28**

- what you judge to be the best opening: see 13.32–13.56;
- what you judge to be the most productive order for dealing with topics;
- the need to resolve some issues before others, eg liability before damages;
- the need to gather information and clarify issues before any discussion of concessions;
- whether a few items will dominate the discussion, or whether there are a lot of items.

Various problems may arise in implementing a chosen structure: **13.29**

- An opponent may make a very different choice about structure, such that it is impossible to implement both.
- Your opponent may interrupt you, either with questions and proposals, or as a tactic to undermine your plans.
- Unexpected information from your opponent may make it difficult to pursue your structure as planned.
- It may prove more difficult than you expect to deal with a particular issue, so that some parts of the structure overlap or get repeated.
- The negotiation may take an unpredictable turn because of an offer made.

13.30 If a difficulty arises try to modify rather than abandon your structure. Abandoning a planned structure might undermine your strategy, or mean that you forget to deal with some important issues. Prepare flexibly, and be prepared to adapt your structure if necessary.

13.31 Sometimes structure is vital to a whole strategy. A problem-solving approach might require the investigation of interests and needs, followed by option-creation, rather than moving straight to issues. A principled strategy might include the consideration of objective criteria for what is fair or just. If you want to follow this kind of strategy there is merit in trying to agree this in advance with your opponent.

E OPENING

13.32 The way in which you open can set the tone for a whole negotiation. One negotiator may be able to take control of the process, to impose decisions as to structure or strategy in a way that may put the other at a disadvantage. How you deal with opening can give messages about what your client wants, what your strategy will be, how good you are at presenting your case, how well prepared you are, and whether you will make efficient progress in dealing with issues. Choose the messages you want to give and make them clear. You will have most energy and focus at the start of a negotiation and should use this to best effect.

13.33 Possible choices for opening are as follows. Some can be combined by starting with one and then moving quickly to another. Some openings are only appropriate in some circumstances—for example a long statement proposing a collaborative approach is unlikely to prove effective if there is limited time to reach an agreement outside court.

Open by agreeing an agenda

13.34 This is the normal way to open when no agenda has been agreed in advance. It has advantages in allowing both negotiators to influence structure, and it provides a relatively objective start in which each negotiator can form an impression of the views and strategy of the opponent.

13.35 An agenda is often proposed by one negotiator. You could start by listing the matters that you consider need to be discussed, and the order in which you would like to consider them. If there is limited time, take this into account to ensure you cover key matters. Your opponent may draw conclusions as to your interests and strategy from what you propose.

13.36 An agenda may be evolved collaboratively. You could open by saying: 'I thought it would be a good idea to agree an order in which to discuss the matters. The order I think would be best is ... What do you think?' You can still keep relative control if you set up and manage this approach.

13.37 Alternatively one party may try to take control of the process by imposing an agenda—the other negotiator might choose to go along with this but then start to impose their own agenda at a later stage. Alternatively an objection can be raised—challenge if you are prepared to be competitive, or point out the benefits of a different agenda.

Open with a statement or a proposal

13.38 You can start by outlining your view of the case, and of the negotiation. A general outline of the merits of the case may be useful if you have a strong case overall that is weak on some minor issues. If for example there is a single breach of contract where your case is relatively clear, but then several heads of loss of mixed strength, it could be helpful to present your overall view of the contract at an early stage. It can also be helpful if you want to stress some particular aspects of the case, or state views about the potential outcome, especially if this includes some things your opponent may not be aware of. A statement can also be useful if you want to set up a particular strategy, for example to explain how a collaborative approach might help.

It might be tempting to provide an overview of your case, but this can be risky where there are several issues of equal importance and you have a good case on some but not others. You will simply make it clear from the start that your case has a mixed chance of success, and give your opponent advance notice so he or she will be better prepared to respond. If you over-emphasize a readiness to settle, a competitive opponent might see this as a weakness. Keep any statement you make relatively short and clear or there is a risk your opponent will start to argue with you before you can finish it. **13.39**

It can be tempting to start a negotiation by setting out the strengths of your client's case and, possibly, the weaknesses of your opponent's case. You might include what your client is expecting to achieve, and you might include strong confidence in achieving much of what your client seeks. This sort of opening will appeal particularly to a competitive negotiator, who might use an extreme form, such as 'Well, I am here to get the £15,000 my client demands, and I expect interest on it and costs. I can't see that your client has a leg to stand on, so I hope this won't take long.' **13.40**

It is not very common to start with a proposal related to settlement, but it can be helpful to set up a co-operative strategy, or as a tactic to take forward a specific element of your case. For example, if a negotiation takes place just before an application for an interim injunction you might propose at the start that you will not pursue the application provided concessions are made on specific issues. **13.41**

Start by asking some key questions

It is not common to open a negotiation by asking questions, but there are some circumstances in which it may be useful, or even tactical. If there is a key piece of information that you need to be able to assess your case or to frame an offer then you could start by saying 'It would be really helpful if you could let me know the dates when you are saying there was too much noise.' **13.42**

Alternatively you might ask a question about your opponent's objectives, such as 'Could you just tell me how much you are claiming for the damage to the car?' Asking questions constructively can lay a foundation for a collaborative approach, though intrusive questions may alienate the opponent. **13.43**

Invite your opponent to open

It can be a useful tactic to invite your opponent to open, especially if you have limited information about a case, or you are not sure what view of the case your opponent might take. It may help you to evaluate your opponent's likely negotiating strategy, and what they hope to achieve. It may assist you to gauge whether your strategy will work effectively or should be adjusted. With any luck your opponent might reveal information you are not aware of, or possibly even a weakness in their case. In any event you can ask questions or probe issues when your opponent finishes. **13.44**

This way of starting has potential advantages, but you cannot guarantee that they will be achieved. Your opponent might refuse to start, or do little more than make a general comment. This type of opening is also risky, as you are effectively giving the initiative to your **13.45** opponent, who may not cover what you invite them to cover. A competitive negotiator might well see this as an invitation to take control.

Start with items that can be agreed easily

13.46 There may be some issues that can be easily agreed, perhaps because both parties want the same thing, or because the issue is important to one party but of limited interest to the other. This can be especially useful in setting the tone for a co-operative or collaborative strategy. Such an opening must be used with care—if you start offering concessions your position may be exploited by your opponent.

Start with items where your case is strong

13.47 You may wish to start with items where your case is strong, either setting an agenda briefly and then moving straight to this, or by jumping straight in with words like 'I would like to get the issue of whether there was actually a breach of contract sorted out first'. The potential advantages are clearly that you can put your case best while you are freshest, that this can help give a general impression that your case is strong, and that you may get some quick concessions. The possible drawbacks are that your opponent may not be prepared to discuss your strongest issue first, and that if you fail to get a concession on your strongest issue it might undermine your case.

13.48 There are advantages in pitching your case at its best and in 'opening high' in terms of what you expect to achieve. Research has shown that higher opening demands tend to lead to higher outcomes. However, it is important to pitch an opening demand carefully. If the demand is unrealistically high only a weak or poorly prepared opponent will take it seriously. If the demand has no real justification, the opponent may form the view that the negotiator making the demand is not credible. The only way to move from a high demand to compromise is to make concessions, and if the demand is very high the concessions may have to be big. The general risk of starting by focusing on the strengths of your case is that you may set a competitive tone for the whole negotiation, or at least antagonize your opponent.

Make limits on authority clear

13.49 A limit on your authority to settle should be made clear to your opponent, and this is often done with a statement at the start of a negotiation. This is important as an error could lead to the negotiation breaking down, to a breach of professional conduct, and/or to a complaint or legal action by your client.

13.50 In the negotiation you are acting as the agent of the client, and with apparent authority to bind the client to what you agree with your opponent. Any terms you agree will therefore bind the client, unless you have already made a limit on your authority clear. If you bind your client to anything beyond your instructions from your client, you will be in breach of your duty to your client. If you do that, or mislead your opponent about your level of authority, there may be a breach of professional conduct. If you appear to agree something in a negotiation but later try to say it was not agreed due to a limit on your authority your credibility will be undermined and your opponent will probably refuse to negotiate further.

13.51 A common limitation on authority is that an agreement reached will only be provisional and will be subject to your client's approval. This is good for the client as they will have final approval, and it provides protection for the lawyer if the negotiation moves outside areas where instructions are clear.

If your authority to settle is subject to final approval by the client then say so early in the negotiation. Another possible limit on authority is if you negotiate outside court prior to an interim application. If you only have authority to negotiate as regards the interim application but not the main action you should make this clear. **13.52**

Refer to privilege for discussion

Discussions with a view to settlement are generally 'without prejudice'. This means that what is said is privileged and cannot be revealed in court, so that offers or possible concessions will remain private and cannot be referred to if agreement is not reached. It also means that any information provided cannot be used as evidence, though it may be that admissible evidence can be found in another form. There are only a few limited exceptions. It is normal briefly to confirm at the start of a negotiation that the discussion will be 'without prejudice'. (See Chapter 6.) **13.53**

Note that the privilege applies to not referring to the matters discussed in court. It is not a general provision that nothing said in the negotiation can be passed on. If for example one lawyer reveals to the other a detail that benefits the case of the latter's client, the lawyer can tell the client what was revealed. Bar Council guidance makes this clear as regards barristers in its guidance on counsel-to-counsel confidentiality. **13.54**

Dealing with problems in opening

However you plan to open, it may not go as you hope. You should always be ready to modify what you planned, or move to an alternative because you need to start as well as possible to lay a sound foundation for the negotiation. Many negotiators will be prepared to discuss an agenda, but you will need to take on board quite quickly the style and strategy of your opponent, and what opening they have planned. **13.55**

In some cases there will be a real problem and you may need to negotiate how to start. You may plan to be collaborative but be met by an opponent making a very competitive statement to which you may feel you need to respond, or you might plan a competitive start to be met by an equally competitive opponent so that deadlock is reached within minutes. You may need to modify strategy so as to make some progress, hoping to return to the original strategy later. Alternatively you can name the problem and propose a next step; for example: 'Our clients have asked us to try to settle and we have both set out strong positions. Let's see if we can try to agree an agenda as a way forward.' **13.56**

F SEEKING INFORMATION

Knowledge can provide power. The negotiator who knows most about a case is likely to be in a strong position. You will have analysed the information you have as outlined in Chapter 12, but this is likely to leave gaps in your knowledge of facts, and you may well want to know more about matters such as your opponent's objectives. Limited information gathering may be needed in a negotiation just before trial, but if a negotiation takes place early in a case, a substantial part of the negotiation may relate to gathering information. Logically you need to gather information before discussing the merits of the case in detail, either through dealing with information generally early in a negotiation, or through dealing with information at the start of dealing with each separate issue. **13.57**

Information gathering will be affected by the strategy and tactics being used by each negotiator. If both are taking a collaborative or co-operative approach then the exchange of **13.58** information is likely to be relatively free and straightforward. A negotiator following a competitive strategy will use information much more tactically, possibly asking quite intrusive questions, but generally refusing to provide many answers.

13.59 Bear in mind what information is shared. If the case is close to trial then statements of case, formal witness statements, and evidence that have been subject to disclosure and inspection will all be shared. There may be relatively few further questions, and no need to discuss this information save as regards how it shows strengths and weaknesses in the case. Early in a case there may be little information that is shared.

13.60 Word questions with care because the other side does not have to provide answers. Try to show how the information will help to progress the negotiation. The types of information you might wish to seek include the following:

- basic factual information relating to an issue, for example 'Your client says there was a lot of noise and disturbance on the Sunday—it would be useful if I could have more detail';
- a general explanation of how they see an element of the case; for example 'Can you explain how you think my client's children caused the death of the fish?';
- basic factual information relating to a remedy claimed; for example 'Could you outline how that loss of profit is calculated?';
- information about what evidence the other side has to support their allegations; such as 'Do you have evidence from anyone who overheard what your client said?';
- information about the other side's objectives, which might help you in framing offers, as in: 'How important is it to your client to keep running the machine until 6 pm?';
- checking if the other side has information you have (but only if this has a purpose—do not check if you want to use the information strategically later). For example 'There is a letter relating to the cost of repairing the car—do you have that?';
- information that may be useful to you in progressing the case if the negotiation fails (though your opponent may not be prepared to answer such questions).

13.61 You may need to judge carefully how to respond to a request for information. Even if you are trying to be collaborative it is probably not in your client's best interests to give away information without getting enough information in return, especially if it is information that shows any weakness. If your strategy is competitive you may refuse to answer questions, but take care not to force the negotiation to break down. Possible responses include the following.

- You can refuse to reply, especially if the reply might undermine your case. (However be aware that your opponent might interpret a refusal to reply as an acceptance that your case is weak.)
- You might say that you will deal with the matter later. This might be necessary because of strategic plans. It can also be a tactic to deflect a question that you would prefer not to answer (though your opponent might call your bluff and ask the question again later).
- Give a partial answer, or avoid answering the question directly, to avoid revealing a weakness (though an opponent might press you for a fuller answer).
- Give an answer that reinforces a strength in your client's case (especially if you can add detail or evidence that the other side might not yet be aware of).
- Your duty to protect client confidentiality means that you should not reveal anything subject to client confidentiality without the agreement of the client.

13.62 Quite often you will get information that comes as a surprise. Your client may not have been entirely truthful in revealing possible weaknesses in the case, and your opponent may well wish to surprise you as a tactic. It is very important not to react with surprise or your opponent will realize you have seen a possible weakness in your case. Try to give yourself time to absorb the information and to think of a constructive way to respond. If you are not sure how to respond it is probably best to move on to another issue.

G MAKING YOUR CASE ON THE ISSUES

Making your case on the issues is a major element of any negotiation. You may choose to make a general statement about how you see the strengths of the case, but normally the negotiators will go through each issue. The order in which you choose to go through the issues should be dictated by your strategy and planning, and will normally be agreed as part of setting the agenda at the start of the negotiation. **13.63**

Normally the negotiators go through the issues one at a time. On each issue they will deal with information, then discuss strengths and weaknesses, and normally deal with possible concessions before moving to the next issue. This stage of a negotiation can get a little confused if problems are encountered or discussion jumps from one issue to another. Such problems are dealt with below, but it is usually constructive to deal with each issue systematically. **13.64**

Keep a tight focus on the outcome you want to achieve on each issue, and why you should get it. Do not digress into general discussion, unless you do this for tactical reasons to distract your opponent. It is very important to deal with strengths and weaknesses effectively and persuasively to get concessions from your opponent. **13.65**

Remember that the point is to air the merits of the case and get concessions. You do not need to agree on an interpretation of the law, to agree exactly what the evidence proves, or to agree exactly what happened, so do not get distracted. You are trying to see what is reasonably justified as a basis for settlement. As you discuss the merits you will need to monitor how well your arguments are succeeding. Where does your opponent accept a point you make, and where are you impressed by a point your opponent makes? Who would be most likely to win on a balance of probabilities if the case went to court? What remedies would a judge be most likely to award? This will inform what concessions should be demanded or made. **13.66**

Presenting the merits of your case

The importance of preparing persuasive arguments was covered at 12.33–12.47, and of clear presentation at 13.16–13.18. If you are properly prepared it should not be too difficult to present the merits of your case on each issue reasonably briefly and clearly. Avoid reciting facts at length—focus on the key strengths of your case to persuade your opponent. Put your main arguments clearly and concisely. If you get distracted or side-tracked make sure you go back to cover or summarize the merits of your case. **13.67**

Addressing weaknesses in your case

You should choose strategically and tactically how to deal with weaknesses in your case, especially if they are significant weaknesses, related to a key client objective. **13.68**

One possibility is to bring up the weakness yourself, together with an argument to limit the effect of the weakness, as in: 'It could be said that my client might have mitigated his loss by cancelling the holiday, but I would say that would not be reasonable as this was a special holiday for his son's 18th birthday that could never be replaced.' The benefit of this approach is that it can take the wind out of your opponent's sails by undermining an argument they might have made. The possible problem is that you might bring up a weakness that your opponent had not even thought of. **13.69**

13.70 A second possibility is to have a response to each possible weakness ready for use should your opponent raise the weakness. This can be effective as you will see what case your opponent makes and fit your response to that, but the drawback is that it lets your opponent have the first word on the issue, and if they make a point of the weakness it may be difficult to recover.

13.71 A third option is to simply ignore or downplay the weakness. A competitive negotiator might well take this approach. This can be effective against a weak opponent, but is likely to be ineffective against a strong opponent. If you refuse to make a case about a possible weakness your opponent will probably insist on taking the weakness fully into account in making offers.

Bringing out weaknesses in your opponent's case

13.72 It is important to point out the weaknesses in your opponent's case, whether they are in law, fact, or evidence. Any defence to a potential cause of action should be aired, as should any argument against the availability of a head of loss, or the amount of damages. If you are not sure whether there is a weakness, probe your opponent's case to find out. This is all part of doing your job for the client, and getting the concessions you should get.

13.73 A competitive negotiator is likely to be keen to voice and over-emphasize every weakness. A collaborative negotiator might well voice a point more constructively, as in: 'The facts do show 30% contributory negligence, and it is only fair to my client that that be reflected in what you pay'. If you feel that your opponent is being too optimistic about the chances of success, point this out.

Proposing an outcome

13.74 You will normally wish to explore an issue fully before proposing an outcome. Indeed you may choose not to propose an outcome until you get on to the offer and concession stage covered in 13.77–13.106. However it is important that in discussing each issue you raise the arguments that are relevant to how much or little should be offered, and what concessions should be made. This lays a clear foundation so that when you move on to dealing with offers and concessions you have reasons for what you offer or seek. A competitive negotiator might deal with each issue in less detail, but would still be likely to stress the strengths of their case and the weakness of the opponent's case.

13.75 Alternatively, you can state the outcome you seek as part of dealing with an issue, and then deal with strengths and weaknesses as part of justifying that outcome. This can help you to persuade your opponent as regards what you want and why, but there can be some risk in revealing the outcome you seek before your opponent sets out their case.

Additions to oral argument

13.76 The argument in a negotiation is primarily oral. However, there is nothing to stop you using other things to support your argument. Tactically it can be very helpful to support your case with other resources, as this can help you to 'anchor' the discussion on your viewpoint. To give some examples:

- *Evidence*. If you have a letter, report etc that supports your case you might choose to provide a photocopy to your opponent, especially if you think they may not be aware of it. You might want to show this quickly without providing a copy if part of the document does not support your case.

- *Figures*. It can be difficult to discuss figures, and it can be helpful to prepare a schedule from your point of view for discussion and show it to your opponent. This can help you to control discussion, and to get concessions. But make sure your arithmetic is accurate!
- *Law*. If there is a legal issue it can help to bring a copy of a statute, regulation, or case. A lawyer cannot easily refuse to argue a legal point, but may not be able to reply quickly to a point you have prepared.
- *Photos*. Where damages, injuries etc are in issue a photograph can make an impression on an opponent as it can on a judge or jury.
- *Plans*. If any kind of plan can help to understand an accident etc it is a good idea to produce one as it can help you to get control of the discussion.

H PLANNING AND TIMING CONCESSIONS, OFFERS, AND DEMANDS

Dealing with concessions, offers, and demands is central to a negotiation. The point of a negotiation is not to determine whether the claimant or the defendant should win, what would be the outcome in court, or whose version of the facts is 'true'. The purpose is for each negotiator to secure the best possible outcome for their client, which is achieved through getting concessions, while not making too many concessions. **13.77**

Dealing with concessions is inevitably challenging. A competitive negotiator may find it relatively easy to make high demands, but it can be difficult to move from that to realistic settlement proposals. Co-operative negotiators can find it difficult to secure a deal that really meets the client's interests. The following are important to feeling confident about this stage of a negotiation: **13.78**

- Have a clear and full list of the issues in the case, and the client's objectives and priorities, see 12.04–12.06.
- Prepare plans for what concessions you should ask the other side to make, and what concessions you should be prepared to make if necessary, including potential staging of concessions, see 12.48–12.57.
- Have standards against which to compare overall offers, with a calculation of what you might get if you went to court, and a consideration of the BATNA and WATNA, see 12.58–12.65.
- Have sufficient familiarity with the figures to be able to add VAT, take away a month of wages etc without a major delay, see 12.31–12.32.
- Get sufficient further information in the negotiation to refine possible offers and concessions, see 13.57–13.62.
- Explore the strengths and weaknesses of the case sufficiently to have reasonable confidence in demands or offers.

Implementing concession plan

Implementing your plans will rarely be easy, but the earlier stages of the negotiation process should help you to get a feel for the strategy your opponent is following, and where they might be most open to settlement. **13.79**

As regards timing, it is best to try to deal with offers and concessions in a reasonably structured way. There are the following options: **13.80**

- Start with issues where you have a strong case so that you can seek concessions supported by good reasons relatively early on.

- A competitive negotiator might make early demands, though there is normally some discussion of the case before concessions are considered.
- Try to avoid making early concessions unless they are small, part of your strategy, or provisional on you getting something in return.
- Discuss possible offers and concessions at the end of dealing with each issue, once you are able to assess what is reasonable. Either open the discussion yourself with a clear statement of what you want and why, so that you get control of the process, or get your opponent to say what they want and why.
- If nothing can be agreed move on, but take the lead in suggesting an overall deal once other issues have been aired.

13.81 As regards the size of concessions, it should always be your rule to get as much as you can for your client and give away as little as possible. Your planning and further questions during the negotiation should tell you what the range of possible figures is. Start reasonably high, and move down in small, planned, and justifiable stages.

13.82 As regards terminology, you can talk of offers, demands, or concessions. The same potential deal can be phrased in many ways, so you should consider what fits with your strategy and is most likely to get what you want from your opponent. A competitive negotiator might say: 'My client will not accept a penny less than £10,000!', where a collaborative negotiator might say: 'It would be fair for my client to get £10,000 on this issue, but perhaps that would be acceptable if your client got the £3,000 he sought on the item we just discussed'.

Gaining concessions

13.83 Gaining a significant concession from an opponent will require skill. Your opponent will not want to give anything away, and is likely to challenge your points and may even interrupt or distract you. Keep a tight focus on what is most important to your client and the main concessions you need to get.

- Identify clearly the largest concession on each issue you can realistically get. Aim steadily for that, moving to a fallback position only for good reason and if there is no option.
- Identify the legal, evidential, factual, and other arguments that support your claim on each issue. Identify the three strongest arguments in support of the concession you seek and ensure you make those points in the negotiation as clearly and well as you can. Adding weaker arguments can confuse or undermine your case.
- State clearly what concession you are seeking and why.
- Do not be put off. You will rarely get the full concession you want immediately—if you do it may mean that you have asked for too little. Once you have made your case on each issue restate what you want.
- Take time to respond if a concession is made. Accept it if the offer is good, but pause to consider whether you could get a little more. If an offer seems very generous, consider if your opponent is aware of a weakness in their case that you do not know about.
- If there is any ambiguity in a concession then clarify it. If you would like a modification then say so. If it is not good enough ask your opponent to justify it.
- Do not get distracted by small concessions. Check your client is getting a good deal, and ask for more where justified.

Making demands

13.84 While no absolute distinction can be made, concessions generally arise from a discussion of strengths and weaknesses, and tend to come with some justification. A demand tends to be made unilaterally, with little or no discussion, with limited justification and often on the basis the point is non-negotiable.

A competitive negotiator may talk in terms of demands, setting out what their client wants in this form. All negotiators may need to make demands if the client wants something that may be difficult to justify. **13.85**

If an opponent makes a demand you can ask them to justify it. Alternatively you can make it clear that you would only consider it as part of an overall settlement, treating the demand as a potential concession. **13.86**

Making concessions

You will rarely be able to negotiate a settlement without making some concessions. Success normally depends on making as few concessions as are necessary for a settlement, with each concession being only as big as is necessary. It is the duty of a lawyer to get the best possible outcome for a client, and even a co-operative approach should not lead to unnecessary concessions. **13.87**

Before making any concession, check the following: **13.88**

- Has the opponent given a clear legal, evidential, or factual reason why you should make this concession? Be slow to volunteer a concession if your opponent has not asked for it and justified it.
- What is the lowest concession you can make?
- What might you get in return for the concession? Can you link it to the opponent conceding something that is worth as much or more to you?
- Will the client accept the concession as part of the settlement? If not, what do you need to get so the client will accept it?

Making a concession can be seen as winning or losing on an issue. Refusing to make concessions might be seen as a sign of strength, and being slow to make concessions of any size may improve the deal you get. However, unreasonable refusal to make concessions can lead a negotiation to fail, which may not be in the client's interests. If you do make a concession, make it in a clear and confident way with a reason, and make it clear if it is conditional. If you look weak or unsure your opponent may seek a greater concession. Do not leave room for confusion. Do not offer a range or your opponent will press for the best possible figure. Either propose to tie the concession to something you want, or make it clear that the concession will only stand if it is tied in with a concession from your opponent. **13.89**

If your offer is not accepted then make it clear if it is your final offer on that issue, and whether it stays on the table to be possibly tied in with a concession from your opponent later. Do not offer a bigger concession unless you have planned to and/or it is justified. Move by as small an amount as you can. If your opponent sees it is possible to get you to increase concessions they are likely to try to exploit that. **13.90**

Linking concessions

A concession should rarely be made without getting something in return. Even if there is good reason for making a concession on a particular point, there is likely to be a reason why your opponent should make a concession on another point. This can be done most easily where the parties put different values on different items, which can often emerge as the issues and the objectives of each party are discussed. **13.91**

13.92 Trying to tie concessions together to make an overall acceptable settlement can be done by making it clear from the start that all proposals should be treated as conditional until an acceptable overall package emerges. This gives you flexibility to look at different options, or to withdraw a possible concession if your opponent proves difficult.

13.93 Be very wary of linking concessions that should not be linked because they are not equal. The fact that two issues have a similar face value does not mean they should be set against each other if one side has a much stronger case. Do not be fooled by a comment about the number of concession each side has made—it is the trading of equal amounts that are equally justified that matters.

Making offers

13.94 Quite separately from dealing with concessions, you might want to offer something that could assist in the reaching of a settlement. This is particularly likely where a collaborative negotiator wishes to get the best possible outcome, and might for example offer a new business opportunity so long as an agreement can be reached. An offer would rarely be one sided—you would hope to get something in return, linking your offer to a concession by the other side.

Reaching a deal

13.95 An overall settlement is usually based on a proposal for how all the possible concessions, offers, and demands fit together. This may emerge naturally if each issue is provisionally agreed as it is discussed, and/or as possible concessions are traded against each other. If it does not, then it is likely that one of the negotiators will propose an overall settlement for discussion.

13.96 It is useful to propose an overall deal yourself so that you can pitch it as closely as possible to what your client hopes to achieve, and you leave your opponent the burden of arguing why it is wrong. Before proposing an overall deal, make sure that you have a complete list of the issues that are to be covered, or your opponent may try to add extra items. A possible disadvantage is that it shows your opponent what you hope to get, and they might seek further concessions.

13.97 Think carefully about the way in which potential concessions are joined together. Base your proposal on what you have argued for, but building in just enough of the concessions your opponent has sought. At this stage in a negotiation the negotiators tend to be tired and can get confused. Make sure you do not make more/larger concessions than your opponent overall, and check the deal against your client's objectives and your BATNA.

13.98 Different strategies tend to move to an overall settlement in different ways:

- A competitive negotiator will open 'high', setting out the highest sustainable goals. They will demand concessions, and are likely to focus discussion on what concessions the other side should make. They will be slow to concede, and will make only small concessions. The negotiator is likely to attempt to impose a settlement that makes the fewest possible concessions and to try to control the terms and content of the overall settlement.
- A co-operative negotiator will tend to see concessions as important, and is likely to encourage and note potential concessions by each side as each issue is discussed. The overall deal is likely to pull together those potential concessions, with the negotiators looking at options for the overall deal.
- A collaborative negotiator will focus on exploring interests and options, and will tend to think in terms of offers. Concessions have less importance as the focus is on an outcome that is 'fair'. A settlement is likely to emerge from discussion over time.

Bargaining tactics

Pre-conditions

A negotiator might make a demand expressed as a pre-condition—stating for example that the other negotiator must accept a particular point before a topic is discussed. This may be used to try to force a concession from the other side, or at least put them at a disadvantage. If the pre-condition has no justification it is probably best to refuse to be 'bullied'. **13.99**

Extreme demands

An inflated opening demand can influence how the parties see the 'bargaining range' and produce a higher outcome. However, if the demand is not credible it can be easily attacked as being unrealistic. Other ways to deal with an extreme demand are to discuss the issues, or to ignore the demand. Responding with a high demand can make settlement very difficult. **13.100**

False issues

A negotiator may suggest that something is an issue when it is not, making an apparent concession on the issue in an attempt to get a real concession from the other side. If something is unexpected, ask questions to check it is a real issue. **13.101**

Escalating demands

A very competitive negotiator may increase the size of their demands. This is done to try to test how much they can get the other negotiator to concede, and to increase pressure and stress. This is a risky strategy that can lead to a breakdown. If it is used against you ignore it or insist on discussing the merits. **13.102**

'Take it or leave it'

A negotiator may make a single offer and refuse to debate it. A competitive negotiator may do this, or a collaborative negotiator may do this on the basis that what they propose is 'fair'. It may also be done if the negotiation is dragging on. The other negotiator is apparently deprived of the chance of discussing the offer. Asking for the reasons behind the offer may help to open discussion. **13.103**

Multiple concessions

A negotiator may try to deal with several issues together, focusing on the number of concessions they have made to argue a position is fair, whereas in fact the overall amount conceded is lower. Check the arithmetic and do not get confused. **13.104**

Inducing stress

A competitive negotiator may purposefully induce stress, especially if the opponent seems at all uncomfortable with confrontation, trying to force concessions. Try to make steady progress rather than show stress, or make a comment like: 'I prefer to deal with the issues objectively rather than get into pressure and emotion.' Do not make an unnecessary concession. **13.105**

'Splitting the difference'

An inexperienced negotiator might feel that there is some fairness in 'splitting the difference'—that is just taking a figure halfway between what is sought and what is offered. If there is no other way forward you might split the difference, but on many issues it is not at all fair and is a sign of failing to prepare properly or to negotiate effectively. To 'split the difference' is to say that each side has an equal case on the issue, which is rarely true. If your client has a 70% chance of winning a head of damage in court then you are not doing a good job for your client in accepting 50%. Remember that in a civil case the standard of proof is **13.106** the balance of probabilities—if you have a better than 50% case then you should win and not split the difference.

I MAKING PROGRESS

13.107 Making progress means moving through the issues towards a settlement with reasonable efficiency. This is best achieved in a relatively systematic way, reviewing the strengths and weaknesses of each issue, and potential concessions on both sides. This should happen at a good pace, with an appropriate time spent on each issue. If there is limited time outside court it may be particularly important to make key points and move on.

13.108 You should keep progress under review:

- If discussion is spending too long on an issue of limited importance, point this out and suggest moving on.
- If discussion moves away from an agreed agenda, decide what to do. It is not necessarily a problem if something unexpected has come up, and/or if you are still making reasonable progress. If the departure is not justified, suggest returning to the agenda.
- Jumping around from issue to issue almost always causes problems because the case for both sides is not properly explored so it is difficult to move to settlement. If this happens, try to return to a clearer agenda.
- If a problem arises in dealing with an issue, try to identify and deal with it. Is there a problem with information, or a failure to look at possible concessions? Failing to tackle the problem and moving on will often mean you just have to come back to the problem later.
- Sometimes the parties get tired or frustrated and points get repeated. This serves no purpose. If you are properly prepared make your points and move on. If your opponent starts repeating a point, ask them to move on.
- If at the end of discussing an issue you manage to reach a provisional agreement, make a note of it. This helps to ensure the matter is not forgotten or reopened, and that there is no misunderstanding as to what was agreed. If you make an offer that is not accepted but that you want to leave on the table then make a note of that.
- If you cannot reach any agreement on an issue, note the point you have reached; for example: 'I propose your client pays 70% of my client's losses, but you are proposing only 40%.' It is easy to assume you will remember this, but you may not. It may be easier to address the point once other issues are sorted out.
- Try to think of creative options. Structured settlements were invented by lawyers looking at how to meet the needs of claimants and defendants in personal injury cases, see PD 40C Structured settlements.

J DEALING WITH DIFFICULTIES

13.109 Negotiation is a complex and challenging process. Awareness of the sorts of problems that can arise, and potential solutions, can help you to move forward and avoid a breakdown of the negotiation.

Gaps in information

13.110 It may be difficult to reach an agreement because of a lack of a key piece of information. If there is no easy way to check the point, get as close as you can to an agreement, possibly using a formula rather than an immediate solution. For example if you do not know the value of an item you can agree that a party will pay a fair price as assessed by an independent third party. Agree sufficient detail, such as how the valuer will be selected. Be realistic and try to avoid the expense of a further meeting.

Getting bogged down, or reaching deadlock

Even with good preparation, and reasonably effective progress, a negotiation can get bogged down. An item may be particularly difficult, there may be new information the negotiators need to consider, or the negotiators may be tired. Rather than repeating yourself or getting frustrated, try to identify what the problem is, so that you can address it. **13.111**

- In a long negotiation it may best to have a short break.
- It is usually constructive to summarize progress so far and what remains to be done, agreeing an agenda for those items. You may find that one issue has not been fully discussed, or that a new suggestion comes up.
- If it is important to both parties to settle, it may help to focus on the advantages of settlement for both sides. There may be shared interests or a small area of agreement to build on.
- If the problem relates to concessions, you could propose a conditional or hypothetical concession to get things moving.
- If there is no more constructive option, state that progress does not seem to be possible and why you think this is, seeing if either negotiator can propose a solution.
- Propose an alternative way forward if you can. Mediation with the clients can sometimes help.

In an extreme case the negotiation may appear to reach a deadlock, where agreement appears impossible. This may happen if, for example, one side makes a 'final offer' which is refused, if one negotiator is unreasonable or unrealistic in terms of demands, or if one client is over-optimistic about chances of success and has not given realistic instructions about an acceptable agreement. One of the approaches above may help, but if deadlock is inevitable the best tactic is probably to summarize your best reasonable offer, perhaps backing that up with a Part 36 offer later (see 4.58–4.62). **13.112**

Dealing with a poorly prepared opponent

Sometimes a lawyer is not properly prepared, due to lack of time, underestimating the complexity of the case, or over confidence. On the face of it this should not be a problem—the better prepared lawyer should have little difficulty in getting a good outcome—but the lack of preparation can lead to problems. **13.113**

Your job is to get the best realistic outcome for your client, not to make up for the weaknesses of another lawyer. Sometimes an underprepared opponent will fall back into being competitive or positional, and your best course is to proceed to make your prepared case. Sometimes the lack of preparation stops you doing your job, because your opponent is not able to answer questions or deal with possible concessions properly. In such a case you should make progress by taking charge with regard to putting your arguments, proposing concessions etc. However you should not go so far as to propose settlement terms that will not be acceptable to your opponent's client. Get the best deal you can for your client that is likely to be acceptable to the opponent's client. It can be difficult to assess this if your opponent is not very forthcoming, but try to ask your opponent about their client's objectives to check. **13.114**

Dealing with a very competitive opponent

13.115 A competitive opponent can put you under pressure with regard to your case, but at the end of the day a good competitive negotiator knows that an agreement should be reached if possible, and that it needs to be acceptable to both clients. Problems are most likely to arise with a negotiator who chooses a competitive strategy but is not sufficiently skilled, so that the result is inflexibility, failure to discuss, attempts at manipulation, and bad feeling.

13.116 One reaction to a competitive opponent is to be competitive yourself, running a risk of deadlock. Another approach is to be relentlessly reasonable and proactive. Refuse to be manipulated, remain objective, and stay cool. If your opponent's approach interferes with process you may need to point that out and explain why that it is a problem for their client as well as for yours. Continue to make objective and justified proposals, and to ask your opponent for objective justifications.

Frustration and emotion

13.117 A negotiation between lawyers should be objective and detached, removing the emotion between the parties. However, even with appropriate professionalism, there may be clashes of personality, style, or strategy, and there may be frustration where agreement proves elusive. Rather than giving way to feelings, pretending there is no problem, or letting the negotiation break down, there are some steps that may help. At the very least, keep calm and persevere.

13.118 Some useful ways of dealing with a difficult opponent are proposed in *Getting Past No: Negotiating Your Way from Confrontation to Cooperation*, by William Ury (Bantam, 1999). In summary, this book proposes strategies for breaking through five potential barriers to co-operation:

- Your reactions may be a problem, if for example your opponent has irritated you. Deal with this by not reacting. Pause, do not give an off-the-cuff response, and mentally return to a point where you were in control. Keep focused on your objectives. 'Don't get mad, don't get even, get what you want!'
- Your opponent's emotions may have a negative effect, if for example they are nervous or defensive. Deal with this by trying to defuse the emotion. Be conciliatory, encourage them to explain their problem, and try to check you understand. Agree with the problem as far as you can, and put your own point of view objectively, trying to rebuild a working relationship.
- Your opponent may be too embedded in a positional approach. If so, try to reframe the process and alter their perception. Do not get sucked in to win or lose, but try to ask problem-solving questions to get information or reasons. Label their behaviour as argumentative etc and ask how it is helping to try to get them to shift ground.
- Your opponent may have doubts about the agreement and whether it is best for their client. They may wish to focus on their proposals rather than look at something which is your idea. Try to build a bridge by involving your opponent in the proposal, ensuring all interests have been explored, and helping your opponent to save face.
- An opponent may perceive negotiation as a power game. Try to show your opponent that negotiation is not win–lose but win–win. Try to keep a focus on reality, and what will happen if agreement is not reached, and give your opponent space to agree.

Concern about possible inexperience

13.119 In practice, particularly in your early years as a lawyer, you will negotiate with more experienced practitioners. Concerns about a disparity of experience could influence how you negotiate. You might assume that your opponent is more skilled or knowledgeable, and be inclined to accept their suggestions about process. You might find it difficult to argue about their views of the law, or proposals as regards outcome. You must ensure that this does not undermine the outcome for your client. Focus on your preparation and your decisions about the case, and do not accept anything you would not accept in another negotiation.

In any negotiation you may have sudden feelings of weakness or indecision. You may have **13.120** to deal with new information, complex calculations, and difficult decisions very quickly. A proposal from your opponent may surprise you when you are getting tired, or temporarily lose concentration, or it may prove very difficult to achieve something you know is important. Feelings like this are inevitable from time to time, and you should not allow them to prejudice the outcome for a client. If you need a short break ask for it, even if it is just a couple of minutes to check your papers. Alternatively you could move discussion to a more straightforward topic for a few minutes. If the problem is severe, review your analysis of your client's objectives and the merits of the case to check whether there is any alternative.

Once in a while an opponent will make a point that completely undermines your view of the **13.121** case and the chances of your client achieving their objectives. If it is early in the case this may be something you had no chance of finding out, or your client may have significantly misled you. Do not show any sign of surprise. Review whether there is any chance your opponent is bluffing or exaggerating. Go on to complete as much as you can of the negotiation, but it may be that you will only be able to make provisional agreement on a few issues and will need to consult your client about the new information.

K REACHING A CLOSE—SETTLEMENT OR BREAKDOWN

Reaching an agreement in a negotiation is an oral contract, but it is no more than an oral **13.122** contract. When you agree there may well be a sense of relief, and a desire to get on to the next thing you need to do. It is, however, absolutely vital to check that you have tied up all the ends before you leave, or the terms you have agreed may fall apart when it comes to implementation, so that all your effort will be wasted.

Making an oral contract

When you think you have reached a provisional agreement on all issues you should check all **13.123** the terms carefully, see 17.05. Do not shirk from taking the time you need and checking detail pedantically—the terms of the agreement are the whole point of the negotiation. Never leave a negotiation until all the terms are clear and finalized. Make sure the terms are recorded, and you have agreed what will happen as regards a formal record of the settlement.

It is quite common for problems to arise at this final stage, either as final details are ham- **13.124** mered out, or because a negotiator continues to employ tactics. In relation to the problems that may arise and how to address them (see 17.06).

Recording the outcome

An oral agreement is potentially enforceable, and it will be enforceable immediately if it is **13.125** not subject to some condition. Most negotiated agreements are subject to client approval, so will be binding once approved. As regards how to proceed to recording the outcome, see 17.07–17.10. As regards options for how the settlement can be recorded, see 17.11.

No agreement is reached

13.126 If no full agreement is reached, there may still be positive benefits to take away from the negotiation. Think carefully about this before leaving the negotiation. For the things that you might consider even if a negotiation fails see 17.12.

KEY POINTS SUMMARY

13.127
- Good communication skills are very important for effective negotiation.
- Although negotiation is an informal process, it has identifiable stages.
- Using the stages reasonably systematically will assist the negotiator in making best use of the process.
- Each negotiator should make clear any limits on authority, and whether any settlement will be subject to client approval.
- Agenda setting and opening are important in gaining control of a negotiation.
- It is normal to move through each issue reasonably systematically, making best use of information, analysis, and presentation.
- It is important to deal with concessions, offers, and demands effectively to get the best outcome for the client.
- The negotiator should be able to identify the problems that can arise in a negotiation process and the techniques that may be used to overcome them.
- If a negotiation is successful an oral contract is reached. The terms should be clarified and recorded.
- Even if the negotiation is not successful, progress may be made with regard to the case.

14

MEDIATION: GENERAL PRINCIPLES

A WHAT IS MEDIATION? 14.01
B WHY IS MEDIATION AN EFFECTIVE ADR PROCESS? 14.04
C JUDICIAL ENDORSEMENT OF MEDIATION 14.06
D DISPUTES SUITABLE FOR MEDIATION 14.13
E THE ADVANTAGES OF MEDIATION 14.14
F DOES MEDIATION WORK? 14.15
G WHY DO THE PARTIES USE MEDIATION? 14.20
H WHAT CAN BE DONE TO MAKE A RELUCTANT PARTY ENGAGE IN MEDIATION? 14.21
I THE TIMING OF MEDIATION 14.24
J THE COSTS OF MEDIATION 14.37
K THE FUNDING OF MEDIATION COSTS, FEES, AND EXPENSES 14.45
L STYLES OF MEDIATION 14.50
M THE ROLE OF THE MEDIATOR 14.67
N ACCREDITATION AND REGULATION OF MEDIATION 14.75
O THE CIVIL MEDIATION COUNCIL 14.80
P ETHICAL CONSIDERATIONS AFFECTING MEDIATORS 14.101
Q THE WITHOUT PREJUDICE RULE IN MEDIATION 14.120
R LEGAL ADVICE PRIVILEGE IN MEDIATION 14.134
S CONFIDENTIALITY IN MEDIATION 14.135
T THE MEDIATOR AS WITNESS 14.146
U CAN A MEDIATOR BE SUED? 14.153
Key points summary 14.157

A WHAT IS MEDIATION?

14.01 The Centre for Effective Dispute Resolution (CEDR), one of the leading ADR service providers, has defined mediation as '… a flexible process conducted confidentially in which a neutral person actively assists parties in working towards a negotiated agreement of a dispute or difference, with the parties in ultimate control of the decision to settle and the terms of resolution'. The Ministry of Justice has defined mediation in a slightly different way as 'a flexible, speedy and cost effective way to resolve disputes. It is a confidential process that enables both parties to explain and then discuss what their needs and concerns are to each other in the presence of an independent third party—the mediator—so that they reach an agreement between themselves. The individuals concerned have greater control and responsibility in resolving disagreements rather than lawyers or the courts. In this way, mediation empowers parties to control the length of the process, the issues they would like to discuss, and the outcome.'

14.02 Instead of conducting a negotiation face to face with the other side, the parties do so through a neutral third party whom they select by mutual agreement. Mediation is therefore a form of neutrally assisted negotiation (see *Aird & Aird v Prime Meridian Ltd* [2006] BLR 105 at [5] per May LJ). The negotiations will take place with the help of a neutral third party, within a structured process, in a formal setting, during a defined period of time, all of which will help to create an impetus for settlement. The mediator will work to facilitate a settlement between the parties, but will not himself impose one, or decide the outcome of the dispute. There is no determination of liability in mediation, and any settlement that is reached is not necessarily based on the underlying legal rights or obligations of the parties. Instead, the parties, with the assistance of the mediator, can reach a solution which is tailored to their real needs and interests.

14.03 Mediation is a voluntary process. The court can offer strong encouragement to the parties to mediate their dispute, but it cannot compel them to do so (see 7.94–7.108). Despite the fact that there is some support among commentators and ADR providers for compulsory mediation (as opposed to compulsory consideration of whether to use mediation) to be introduced, it looks as though this is unlikely to happen. Lord Justice Jackson, in his Final Report on the Review of Costs in Civil Cases, reported at Chapter 36, para 3.4: 'In spite of the considerable benefits which mediation brings in appropriate cases, I do not believe that parties should ever be compelled to mediate.' Even if the parties do mediate their dispute, they have the right to go to court to resolve the dispute if mediation does not result in settlement. Mediation can take place before litigation is commenced or it can be a parallel process to it.

B WHY IS MEDIATION AN EFFECTIVE ADR PROCESS?

14.04 Mediation can be effective if direct negotiations between the parties have failed. There are many similarities between negotiation and mediation in terms of cost effectiveness, and, keeping control of the outcome and negotiation, of course, plays a central part in mediation. However, the presence of a mediator can assist the negotiation process (described in Chapter 13) in the following ways:

- The presence of the mediator adds a new dynamic to the bilateral relationship which exists in negotiations between the parties themselves or their lawyers.
- The mediator, as a neutral third party, can help the parties to present their own case more effectively to the other side.
- The mediator can create a balance between the different negotiating styles and personalities of the parties and minimize the pressure that one party can feel when the other side employs a positional, confrontational negotiating style.
- Mediators have a good understanding of the various styles, strategies, and tactics that can be employed in negotiation. A mediator will have a sound understanding of the rules of principled negotiation advocated by Roger Fisher and William Ury in their book *Getting to Yes*. Mediators can help the parties (and their lawyers) to work through the deadlock that can be created by purely positional or competitive negotiation by helping the parties to devise strategies that are more likely to lead to settlement.
- Proposals offered through a mediator can be perceived as being more attractive than an offer made by the party directly, and a concession conveyed by the mediator may be seen to be more valuable than if it were made by the other side directly. In simple terms, this is because arguments put forward by one side are automatically psychologically devalued by the other side (a process known as 'reactive devaluation').
- The appointment of a mediator introduces an element of detachment into the negotiation process and mediation avoids the need for direct confrontation and an immediate response that occurs in face-to-face negotiation between the parties.
- The mediator can be skilled at calming and diffusing strong feelings such as anger or pride that may lead the parties to adopt entrenched positions in, or even walk away from, direct negotiation.

- Mediators will bring their own personal attributes to the table, such as patience, empathy, ability to listen, good judgment, good communication skills, creativity, the ability to think 'outside the box', impartiality, authority, and the ability to command respect, all of which can help the parties to review and re-evaluate their case.
- The mediator can help the parties to communicate constructively and effectively with each other.
- The mediator will also encourage a more accurate and honest assessment by each party of the strengths and weaknesses of their own case.
- Mediation can avoid over-ready concessions between the parties as the mediator will advise on the timing of offers and concessions.
- Mediators tend to be highly skilled at getting to grips with the needs, interests, and positions of the parties and at guiding them towards a settlement that they can live with.

Table 14.1 The differences between negotiation and mediation

Characteristic	Negotiation	Mediation
A voluntary process?	Yes.	Yes—although the court may order the parties to attempt mediation, it cannot compel them to do so. The court can impose sanctions, such as an adverse costs order, if the parties unreasonably refuse to engage with the process.
A structured process?	Not usually.	Yes.
It takes place through a neutral third party who assists in formulating proposals and testing claims?	No.	Yes (a mediator)—although he will not usually evaluate claims or advise on the likely outcome unless the parties ask him to perform this role.
The parties themselves will have the chance to be heard and will be active participants in the process?	Not usually, if they have instructed lawyers to act for them.	Yes—even if lawyers are instructed and attend the mediation on behalf of the lay clients, the mediator will ensure that the parties themselves directly participate in the process.
Witnesses of fact or expert witnesses may be directly involved in the process?	Not usually.	Although this is unusual, they can be asked to attend the mediation and give a summary of their evidence and, in some cases, can be questioned on their evidence by the parties or the mediator.
The parties choose: (i) the date; (ii) the venue; (iii) the issues to be negotiated; (iv) who should take part?	Yes—although usually negotiations will be conducted between lawyers for the parties rather than the parties themselves.	Yes—although (i) will be subject to the mediator's availability and the mediator may give guidance on (iii) and (iv) and may provide (ii).
The process is likely to result in settlement if the parties have reached deadlock?	No.	Yes—the mediator can help the parties work through the deadlock.

14.05 Mediation is also perceived to be effective for other reasons:

- Negotiations take place in a structured process (see Chapter 16) within a defined time frame.
- The parties are likely to be paying for the mediation, both in relation to their own legal costs and their contribution towards the expenses of the mediation (such as the venue) and the mediator's fee as well as any indirect costs such as their time, lost wages or holiday entitlement caused by their attendance at the mediation. This generates an impetus to settle, so that the costs and time spent in relation to the mediation should not be in vain.
- The court may direct the parties to attempt mediation, thus imposing a requirement on the parties to engage with the process seriously and with the intention of settling the case.
- Mediation puts control into the hands of the parties themselves. It allows the parties 'to have their day in court'. It empowers them to resolve the dispute themselves rather than relying on others. It gives them a forum where they can air their grievance in a confidential process, without the risks inherent in litigation and this can make them more amenable to settlement.
- The parties can explore options for settlement that could not be ordered by a court and can thus reach more creative settlements that reflect their underlying needs and concerns.

C JUDICIAL ENDORSEMENT OF MEDIATION

14.06 The courts have readily endorsed and encouraged the use of ADR in general (see 7.80–7.81). However, in many cases, the courts have stressed the importance of mediation in particular, and the flexibility this process provides for resolving disputes.

14.07 In *Dunnett v Railtrack plc* [2002] 1 WLR 2434 per Brooke LJ at [14]:

> Skilled mediators are now able to achieve results satisfactory to both parties in many cases which are quite beyond the power of lawyers and courts to achieve. This court has knowledge of cases where intense feelings have arisen, for instance in relation to clinical negligence claims. But when the parties are brought together on neutral soil with a skilled mediator to help them resolve their differences, it may very well be that the mediator is able to achieve a result by which the parties shake hands at the end and feel that they have gone away having settled the dispute on terms with which they are happy to live. A mediator may be able to provide solutions which are beyond the power of the court to provide. Occasions are known to the court in claims against the police, which can give rise to as much passion as a claim of this kind where a claimant's precious horses are killed on a railway line, by which an apology from a very senior officer is all that the claimant is really seeking and the money side of the matter falls away.

14.08 In *Halsey v Milton Keynes General NHS Trust* [2004] EWCA Civ 576 Dyson LJ at [15] said:

> We recognise that mediation has a number of advantages over the court process. It is usually less expensive than litigation which goes all the way to judgment.... Mediation provides litigants with a wider range of solutions than those which are available in litigation: for example, an apology; an explanation; the continuation of an existing professional or business relationship perhaps on new terms; and an agreement by one party to do something without any existing legal obligation to do so.

14.09 In *Burchell v Bullard* [2005] EWCA Civ 358 Ward LJ (at para 43) endorsed mediation in these terms:

> *Halsey* has made plain not only the high rate of a successful outcome being achieved by mediation but also its established importance as a track to a just result running parallel with that of the court system. Both have a proper part to play in the administration of justice. The court has given its stamp of approval to mediation and it is now the legal profession which must become fully aware of and acknowledge its value. The profession can no longer with impunity shrug aside reasonable

requests to mediate. The parties cannot ignore a proper request to mediate simply because it was made before the claim was issued. With court fees escalating it may be folly to do so.

In *Egan v Motor Services (Bath) Ltd* [2008] 1 WLR 1589 Ward LJ stated: **14.10**

> Mediation can do more for the parties than negotiation. In this case the sheer commercial folly could have been amply demonstrated to both parties sitting at the same table but hearing it from somebody who is independent. The cost of such mediation would be paltry compared with the costs that would mount from the moment of the issue of the claim. In so many cases, and this is just another example of one, the best time to mediate is before the litigation begins. It is not a sign of weakness to suggest it. It is the hallmark of commonsense. Mediation is a perfectly proper adjunct to litigation. The skills are now well developed. The results are astonishingly good.

More recently, in *Faida v Elliot Corporation* [2012] EWCA Civ 287, the Court of Appeal has expressed dismay that the parties in a neighbour dispute did not use mediation. Lord Justice Jackson remarked at paras 35 and 36: **14.11**

> Of course there are many cases where a strict determination of rights and liabilities is what the parties require. The courts stand ready to deliver such a service to litigants and must do so as expeditiously and economically as possible. But before embarking upon full-blooded adversarial litigation, parties should first explore the possibility of settlement. In neighbour disputes of the kind now before the court (and of which I have seen many similar examples) if negotiation fails, mediation is the obvious and constructive way forward..... I have little doubt that such a mediation would have been successful. The points of law upon which the litigation has turned are not easy ones and at the time of the hypothetical mediation neither party could have been confident of victory.

Comments to the same effect were made by Lord Justice Elias. He agreed that the case was 'crying out for mediation' and stated:

> It depresses me that solicitors cannot at the very first interview persuade their clients to put their faith in the hands of an experienced mediator, a dispassionate third party, to guide them to a fair and sensible compromise of an unseemly battle which will otherwise blight their lives for months and months to come.

In *Wright v Michael Wright Supplies Ltd* [2013] EWCA Civ 234, Ward LJ stated:

> The parties would be most ill-advised not to seek mediation of not only this dispute but the chancery action which is due to be heard in October...Mediation is the obvious way in which to explore these matters and allow the parties to move on before they cripple themselves with more debt.

Members of the judiciary have also encouraged the use of mediation in numerous speeches and articles. It has been stated on many occasions that ADR in general, and mediation in particular, must become an intrinsic part of the litigation process with lawyers giving it the same automatic attention as routine matters such as disclosure or expert evidence. A direction that the parties consider mediation is now part of the standard case management directions in most cases (see Chapter 7). **14.12**

D DISPUTES SUITABLE FOR MEDIATION

Mediation is suitable for almost all disputes, whatever the subject-matter of the underlying cause of action. It is carried out in all kinds of contract disputes, consumer claims, neighbourhood disputes, housing disputes, tortious claims, regulatory and public sector disputes, and family disputes. Lawyers instructed to advise a client whether to use mediation should bear in mind the factors outlined in Chapter 3, where there is also guidance on the types of case where mediation may or may not be suitable. Chapter 8 also sets out the sanctions that can be imposed for failing to engage in an ADR process such as mediation and the case law described in that chapter also gives guidance on the court's approach to reasons that **14.13** are commonly put forward for rejecting mediation. Those chapters should be consulted when advising a client whether a particular dispute is suitable for mediation either at all, or at a particular point in time, and when advising whether a client's refusal or reluctance to mediate for a particular reason is likely to be accepted by the court as reasonable. Lawyers instructed to advise whether mediation should be attempted should also bear in mind the factors discussed in paras 14.14–14.20.

E THE ADVANTAGES OF MEDIATION

14.14 Many of the advantages of ADR in general that are described in Chapter 1 also apply to mediation. The key advantages of mediation are as follows:

- It is a flexible process and can be tailored to meet the needs of the case.
- It results in a quicker resolution of the dispute than litigation. Although many cases settle during the litigation process, this may be at a later stage than settlement reached by mediation.
- It is cost effective. It tends to be a cheaper method of resolving disputes than the trial process. It can result in a significant saving compared to the costs of litigation. This is particularly important where litigation is being funded by public money, as in the case of publicly funded private parties or public sector disputes involving government departments and agencies and in complex cases.
- It can be arranged relatively quickly. Most mediations (apart from mediations in very complex or multi-party cases) can be arranged within a matter of days or weeks from the date the decision is made to mediate. The mediation will typically last for one day only.
- Negotiations can take place with the assistance of a neutral third party, within a structured process.
- It is a confidential and private process. This is particularly useful if the publicity generated by a trial could damage the reputation or have an adverse effect on the commercial relationships of one or both parties, or would result in disclosure of a trade secret or confidential information. Generally, all communications passing between the parties during the mediation (oral and written) cannot be disclosed to the court or third parties.
- It avoids an adverse precedent being set by the court.
- It avoids the stress and the trauma that some individuals may feel about giving evidence in court.
- A settlement that is reached by mutual agreement is more likely to preserve relationships than a court-imposed solution. This can be important in public sector disputes, involving bodies such as a health or local authority and in continuing employment and commercial relationships.
- Mediation enables the parties to be more creative when reaching a settlement. The terms of settlement may provide for matters that could not be achieved within the constraints of the litigation process. The solutions that are agreed in mediation can include matters such as an apology, an explanation, the continuation of a commercial relationship (perhaps on different terms), replacement of goods or services, an agreement by one party to do something that he has no legal obligation to do so (such as the transfer of land to a neighbour for a sum in excess of its market value as a solution to a nuisance/easement/boundary dispute claim or the renegotiation of the terms of a commercial contract), or a change in policy or procedure to avoid such a complaint/dispute arising in the future.
- Even if settlement is not reached at the mediation, going through the mediation process may help the parties to understand each other's case, narrow the issues and, in some cases, settlement may be more easily achieved after the mediation.

F DOES MEDIATION WORK?

14.15 Research carried out into court-mediation schemes has indicated that mediation is an effective ADR process for timely resolution of many different kinds of dispute: see for example, Professor Hazel Genn's reports into mediation schemes at Central London County Court between 1996 and 1998, 'The Central London County Court Pilot Mediation Scheme: Evaluation Report' (DCA Research Paper 5/98), the report by Professor Hazel Genn and others, 'Twisting Arms: Court referred and court linked mediation under judicial pressure' (Ministry of Justice Research series 1/07), and also Professor Genn's report 'Court-Based ADR Initiatives for Non-Family Civil Disputes: The Commercial Court and the Court of Appeal' (2002). Reference can also be made to the evaluation of Sue Prince and Sophie Belcher 'An Evaluation of the Effectiveness of Court-based Mediation Processes in Non-Family Civil Proceedings at Exeter and Guildford County Courts'.

14.16 Evidence from ADR providers also show that there is increasing use being made of mediation as an ADR method, and that it is very successful at resolving disputes. By way of example, CEDR reports on its website (www.cedr.com) that over 70% of cases referred for mediation do settle at mediation. CEDR has also carried out a number of mediation audits. In 2007, CEDR's third mediation audit showed that the market had grown by 33% in two years, and that mediation saved UK businesses around £1 billion annually and that a quarter of all mediation referrals came through mediation schemes such as the Court of Appeal Mediation Scheme and the National Mediation Helpline (now replaced by the Civil Mediation Online Directory) as well as sector specific schemes (see Chapter 18 for details of these schemes). The average fees of a less experienced mediator for a one-day mediation remained at around £1,200, but those for more experienced mediators had risen by 42% over a two-year period to around £3,100 per day. The audit also showed that mediators reported that around 75% of their cases settled on the day, with another 13% settling shortly thereafter, giving an aggregate settlement figure of 88%. In 2010, CEDR's fourth Mediation Audit (published 11 May 2010) records that there is a continued rise in clients making direct referrals to mediators (nearly 65% in 2009, compared to 60% in 2007, 55% in 2005 and 45% in 2003). In 2010, around 6,000 civil and commercial cases were referred to mediation (over a 40% increase in activity since the 2007 Audit), with the vast majority of the growth being attributed to schemes (see Chapter 18). CEDR's 2012 Mediation Audit showed that the mediation market continued to grow with around 8,000 cases per annum (representing a 15% increase year-on-year since the 2010 audit), with a success rate of 70% on the day, and with an additional 20% settling shortly thereafter. Average fees for the less experienced mediator for a one day mediation increased from around £1,390 in 2010 to £1,517 in 2012 and average daily fees for more experienced mediators rose from £3,450 in 2010 to £4,279 in 2012, an increase of around 24%.

14.17 Some evidence about the success and use of mediation can also be obtained from statistics released by the Ministry of Justice. On 23 March 2001, with the aim of ensuring that the government led by example, the government pledged to use ADR to resolve any suitable dispute involving government departments and agencies if the other side agreed. This pledge was renewed and the government's commitment to ADR strengthened in 2012. Since then and until recently, the Ministry of Justice (and previously, the Department for Constitutional Affairs) published an Annual Pledge Report which monitors the effectiveness of this pledge. The annual reports can be viewed on www.justice.gov.uk. They record the number of cases referred to ADR each year in which the government is involved and the outcome of those cases. Although no breakdown is given in the annual reports between the various types of ADR processes, the illustrative cases used in the reports involve mediation. The following figures are taken from the annual pledge reports from 2001–02 to 2008–09.

Table 14.2 Success rates of ADR in disputes involving government departments

Year	Number of cases referred to ADR	% settled by ADR	Estimated saving made by using ADR
2001–02	49	—	£2.5m
2002–03	163	83%	£6.4m
2003–04	229	79%	£14.6m
2004–05	167	75%	£28.8m
2005–06	336	72%	£120.7m
2006–07	331	68%	£73.08m
2007–08	374	72%	£26.3m
2008–09	314	82%	£90.2m

14.18 While some ADR organizations and the government publish figures on the number of cases referred to ADR processes, a substantial number of mediations take place by mediators in private practice, and it is more difficult to obtain statistics in relation to these.

14.19 Some statistics can also be gleaned from submissions made by interested parties for the Review of Costs in Civil Cases by Lord Justice Jackson (see the Jackson Report 2010 at www.justice.gov.uk). The Civil Mediation Council's submission of 21 July 2009 recorded that its members reported around 6,473 mediations so far in 2009, which was an increase of 171% over the 2007 baseline. Its members conducted 6,473 mediations in 2008, and although that dropped slightly in 2009 to 6,251 mediations, it rose in 2010 to 7,628 mediations, a 22% increase over the previous year. When one takes into account the providers who responded in both 2009 and 2010 (for consistency), the increase in mediation use was more dramatic, with 2010 seeing an increase of 49.8% over 2009. The mediation count carried out by the CMC in 2011 showed that a total of 6,203 mediations were undertaken and this rose to 7,026 in 2012 (an increase of 13.3%). See 14.80–14.100 for more information about the Civil Mediation Council.

G WHY DO THE PARTIES USE MEDIATION?

14.20 There are a number of reasons why the parties choose mediation as an ADR option.

- The parties may have contractually bound themselves by a dispute resolution clause to attempt to resolve any dispute arising out of or in connection with the contract by mediation before embarking on litigation (or arbitration). See for example *Cable & Wireless plc v IBM United Kingdom Ltd* [2002] EWHC 2059 (Comm) (see 7.83–7.93).
- The court may have encouraged or directed the parties to attempt to settle the dispute by mediation, and the parties may fear adverse costs orders or other sanctions if they unreasonably refuse to mediate (see Chapter 8).
- The parties may have voluntarily chosen to mediate their dispute because of its perceived success rate and advantages as an ADR method (see 14.14–14.19).
- The parties may be referred to mediation by an applicable disputes resolution scheme.
- Practical considerations may lead the parties to choose mediation, such as a desire to settle a multiplicity of claims between the parties involving a number of different but related issues, with perhaps each claim proceeding in a different court and perhaps even in different jurisdictions. Mediation can also be an effective process for settling claims with a multitude of parties eg a number of defendants and additional parties. In these types of

cases, all of the parties and claims can be brought into the mediation process and a settlement can be reached that resolves them all.

- The parties may have tactical reasons for choosing mediation. For example, they may wish to seek clarification of one or more of the issues, or assess the strength (or weakness) of the other side's case. None of these reasons are improper provided they are coupled with a genuine intention to explore settlement. Sometimes parties will enter the mediation process in bad faith, for an ulterior motive, for example to engage in a fishing expedition, with no intention of trying to settle the dispute. The mediator will detect this within a very short time, and he or she is likely to terminate the mediation if this occurs.

H WHAT CAN BE DONE TO MAKE A RELUCTANT PARTY ENGAGE IN MEDIATION?

It is not uncommon for one party to want to use mediation but the opposing party is reluctant to agree to mediate. There are a number of reasons why a party may be unwilling to try mediation, either because they perceive it to be inappropriate or disadvantageous (see 1.47–1.56 and Chapter 3). **14.21**

If one party wishes to try mediation, and the other side does not, a number of steps can be explored to bring the reluctant party to the mediation table. **14.22**

- A party may be reluctant to agree to mediation because they feel that agreeing to mediate displays a lack of confidence in their case and gives an impression of eagerness to settle. A letter should be written to the other side, pointing out that the pre-action protocols, the Practice Direction – Pre-action Conduct and the CPR all require the parties to consider using an ADR procedure to resolve the dispute both before issue and at the allocation and case management stages of the case (see Chapter 7). The letter should also put the reluctant party on notice that if they unreasonably refuse to engage in mediation (or another suitable ADR process), then an order for costs, including indemnity costs, will be sought against them at trial (see Chapter 8). Far from demonstrating a lack of confidence in the case, taking the initiative in exploring ADR options shows that the party has confidence in their case, it is in good order, they are complying with the CPR, and are acting in their client's best interests in trying to resolve the dispute by the most cost-effective means.
- A party can suggest that the parties seek help from an ADR provider to give neutral and independent advice on the benefits of mediation, whether it would be appropriate given the facts and circumstances of a particular dispute and, if so, how the process could be tailored so as to best meet the needs of the particular case. Information about mediators and bodies offering a mediation service is widely available on the internet and a search of the Civil Mediation Online Directory (www.civilmediation.justice.gov.uk) will also return details of a number of organizations in the area searched. If only one party approaches the ADR provider, that party will be solely responsible for any fees charged for acting as broker. The person acting as broker will not be involved in the mediation itself. If an individual mediator (as opposed to an ADR provider organization) is approached by one party to act as a broker, he or she may decline to do so on the grounds that it would compromise the other side's perception of the broker as a neutral. The person acting as broker will usually be scrupulous about disclosing his or her dealings and communications with all parties. For that reason, the initiating party should be careful about revealing confidential information to the broker at this stage. If the dispute is suitable for mediation, the broker will liaise with the reluctant party and will seek to persuade that party to engage in the process.
- A party may invite the court to stay proceedings (assuming that proceedings have been issued) and direct the parties to attempt to resolve the dispute by ADR (see 7.75–7.79). The

party reluctant to mediate may do so in the face of robust encouragement from the court. The court can also assist mediation by making appropriate orders for advance disclosure of information or documents on the application of one or both of the parties.

- A party may be unwilling to agree to mediation on the grounds that it would delay the trial or the litigation process. However, lawyers acting for the party wishing to mediate can point out that if mediation results in settlement, a significant saving in the time taken to resolve the dispute is likely to be achieved together with a consequential saving in costs. Even if the mediation takes place after the litigation has commenced, it need not lengthen the litigation process. Mediation can be attempted without the litigation being stayed. Even if a stay is granted, it tends to be for a short period, usually 28 days. The matter would be different if a trial date or window had been arranged, and mediation would result in the trial being vacated. Furthermore, even a mediation which does not result in settlement can narrow the issues and help the parties to prepare effectively for the trial process.
- A party may fear revealing their case. Some parties may view mediation with suspicion because they do not want to reveal the strength of their own case, or fear that the other side is suggesting it to assess the strength of their case. The CPR favour a 'cards on the table' approach to litigation, so this is not likely to be a valid reason for refusing to mediate. If the case has merit, it will be resolved in that party's favour by settlement and/or judgment, so parties with a strong case have nothing to fear. Anything relevant to the litigation will have to be disclosed in any event during the usual process of disclosure. It may cause more concern to parties with a weaker case, because if the weaknesses in the case are exposed, then offers to settle may not be forthcoming at all. However, the parties themselves control the amount of information that they give to the mediator and which they authorize him to disclose to the other side, so parties should not refuse to agree to mediation on that basis. Indeed some parties embrace mediation because it gives them a forum to assess the strengths and weaknesses of their own case and the other side's case which can assist in the preparation for trial if a settlement cannot be reached at the mediation.
- A party may fear that information disclosed in the mediation will be used against them in subsequent litigation. However mediation is a confidential, without prejudice process, and that is only overridden in the most exceptional circumstances (see Chapter 6 , 14.120–14.133, and 14.142–14.145).
- If both parties consent, judicial mediation can be undertaken. At present, this tends to be confined to cases in the Technology and Construction Court under the Court Settlement Process (see 18.37–18.39), some family cases (see 18.40–18.42), and under the Judicial Mediation Scheme in the Employment Tribunal (see 18.43–18.45).

Mediation Information Assessment Meetings

14.23 The government and the judiciary are putting greater emphasis on Mediation Information Assessment Meetings (MIAMs). These are mandatory meetings which the parties must attend with a mediator with a view to obtaining information about mediation, assessing the suitability of the case (and the parties) for mediation and, if appropriate, securing the agreement of all parties to commit to the process. They currently take place in family cases (see 7.27–7.31 and 18.53–18.55 and in relation to some cases in the Court of Appeal (see 18.30). Mandatory referral for consideration of mediation also takes place in the small-claims track in the county court (see 18.19–18.23), and it has also recently been introduced in the Employment Tribunals by the mandatory Early Conciliation scheme (see Chapter 20). The government has consulted on requiring a MIAM to take place in civil cases with a value up to £100,000, but has decided against implementing that proposal for the moment. It is anticipated that the use of MIAMs in these cases will result in more parties becoming aware of the benefits of mediation and that a mediator will be able to persuade unwilling parties to agree to use the process. MIAMs should be regarded as compulsory *consideration* of mediation, rather than mandatory mediation. The parties are compelled to consider mediation, but they are not compelled to mediate if they do not wish to do so.

I THE TIMING OF MEDIATION

Before the parties embark on mediation they should first attempt to settle the dispute by direct negotiation between themselves (see Chapters 11, 12, and 13) as this will normally be less expensive and may narrow issues. If negotiations are unsuccessful and the dispute is suitable for mediation, the lawyers will have to consider the timing of the mediation. Mediation can theoretically take place at any stage of a dispute. It can take place before issue, after issue, or at any time up to trial and even pending an appeal as is aptly demonstrated by the Court of Appeal Mediation Scheme (see 18.24–18.25). It can be an alternative process to litigation or arbitration or it can be used in conjunction with those processes. General points about the timing of ADR are covered in Chapters 2, 3, and 7. Specific points about mediation are as follows: **14.24**

There are two important questions that any lawyer advising a client in relation to mediation must ask: **14.25**

- Should mediation take place before proceedings are issued?
- If mediation is to take place after issue, at which point in the litigation process should it be employed?

Before litigation begins

The court has recognized the success of mediation at an early stage of the dispute, before proceedings begin. See for example *Egan v Motor Services (Bath) Ltd* [2008] 1 WLR 1589, per Ward LJ (see para 14.10). **14.26**

The judge (HHJ Coulson QC, as he then was), had this to say about the timing of mediation in *Nigel Witham Ltd v Smith* [2008] EWHC 12 (TCC) at [32]: **14.27**

> It is a common difficulty in cases of this sort, trying to work out when the best time might be to attempt ADR or mediation. Mediation is often suggested by the claiming party at an early stage. But the responding party, who is likely to be the party writing the cheque, will often want proper information relating to the claim in order to be able to assess the commercial risk that the claim represents before embarking on a sensible mediation. A premature mediation simply wastes time and can sometimes lead to a hardening of the positions on both sides which make any subsequent attempt at settlement doomed to fail. Conversely, a delay in any mediation until after full particulars and documents have been exchanged can mean that the costs which have been incurred to get to that point themselves become the principal obstacle to a successful mediation. The trick in many cases is to identify the happy medium: the point when the detail of the claim and the response are known to both sides, but before the costs that have been incurred in reaching that stage are so great that a settlement is no longer possible.

Some cases may lend themselves more to mediation before issue than others and this should also be borne in mind. In *Bradford v James* [2008] EWCA Civ 837, Mummery LJ remarked: **14.28**

> There are too many calamitous neighbour disputes in the courts. Greater use should be made of the services of local mediators, who have specialist legal and surveying skills and are experienced in alternative dispute resolution. An attempt at mediation should be made right at the beginning of the dispute and certainly well before things turn nasty and become expensive. By the time neighbours get to court it is often too late for court-based ADR and mediation schemes to have much impact. Litigation hardens attitudes. Costs become an additional aggravating

issue. Almost by its own momentum the case that cries out for compromise moves onwards and upwards towards a conclusion that is disastrous for one of the parties, and possibly for both.

14.29 In deciding on the most appropriate time to mediate, a lawyer acting for a party should consider the following matters:

- Are the issues fully defined?
- Is the client's own case in relation to the issues clear?
- Has all the key information been obtained?
- Have the main witnesses been interviewed and statements taken from them?
- Is the other party's case clearly developed?
- Have key documents that are material to the dispute been exchanged? If not, can an order from the court be obtained for limited disclosure to take place for the purpose of a mediation or can the parties agree on a process of disclosure and information exchange as part of the mediation process?
- In a technical case that is likely to turn on expert evidence, is it necessary to obtain an expert's report before attempting to resolve the dispute? It may be that the parties can agree to jointly select the expert, or even jointly instruct the expert for the purposes of the mediation.
- Is this a case where it would be more advantageous to the client to attempt to secure an early resolution of the matter before issuing proceedings, despite the fact that all available evidence has not yet been obtained or disclosed by the parties?

14.30 The advantages and disadvantages of mediating before issue of proceedings are set out in Table 14.3.

Table 14.3 The advantages and disadvantages of mediation before issue

Advantages	Disadvantages
It is likely to achieve the largest saving on costs.	The issues between the parties may not be clearly defined.
It is likely to result in the largest saving on time.	The parties may not have reached an accurate assessment of their own case. Counsel's advice, or an expert's opinion may be needed, or their advice may only be provisional on further information being obtained.
The parties are less likely to have adopted entrenched positions.	It is more difficult to distinguish between a genuine sustainable position and pure posturing.
The parties have greater incentive to settle the dispute so to avoid the stress and costs and time occasioned by litigation.	There may not be full disclosure of all relevant documents and information, including witness statements and expert evidence.
Relationships are more likely to be preserved.	It may not be possible to evaluate strengths and weaknesses of each party's case with the same degree of accuracy.
Total confidentiality is more likely to be achieved.	It may be more difficult to evaluate arguments made by the opposing party in the mediation and to counter them effectively.
	It may not be possible fully to quantify the claim or counterclaim.

14.31 If the parties have fully defined the issues, disclosed key information, and quantified the claim and any counterclaim, then the most advantageous time to embark on mediation will be before proceedings are issued. However, if the issues between the parties are not yet clearly defined, or the information-gathering process is so incomplete that an evaluation of the strengths and weaknesses of each party's position cannot reasonably be ascertained until litigation commences, then early mediation is not likely to result in settlement, and, to save costs, it may be best to postpone the timing of it. If a party decides that it would not be sensible to embark on mediation before issue, then that party must be prepared to explain and justify this to the court. The decision should be objectively reasonable on the facts of the particular case. If it is not, then an adverse costs order may be made against that party (see Chapter 8).

Sometimes the parties may embark on an early mediation, and it becomes apparent that the issues are not clearly defined or that further information needs to be obtained before settlement can be reached. If this happens, the parties, with the assistance of the mediator, may agree a timetable for further information to be obtained and disclosed, and the mediation can be adjourned to another date for that to be done. This will add to the costs of the mediation process. **14.32**

After litigation begins

The later the mediation takes place in the litigation process, the more clearly the issues will be defined between the parties, and the outcome of the dispute can be assessed with more accuracy. This is particularly so if mediation is undertaken after disclosure of documents and exchange of witness statements and experts' reports. However, the costs savings that can result from a mediated settlement decrease the closer mediation is undertaken to the date set for trial. **14.33**

Parties who wish to attempt mediation after issue should consider applying for a stay of the proceedings and a suspension of the timetable set by the court in order to save costs (see 7.75–7.79). **14.34**

The court may take the selection of the timing of the mediation out of the hands of the parties. It can grant a stay to enable the parties to attempt to resolve their dispute by mediation at the track allocation stage (CPR r 26.4) or indeed at any stage of the litigation. **14.35**

If mediation cannot reasonably be undertaken before issue, the best time to attempt it may be after exchange of statements of case or after disclosure of documents. Research carried out by Nicholas Gould, Claire King, and Philip Britton 'Mediating Construction Disputes: An Evaluation of Existing Practice, 2010' (see www.fenwickelliott.com/mediating-construction-disputes-download) found that the largest number of successful mediations took place in the early stages of litigation (specifically during exchange of statements of case or during or as a result of disclosure). A smaller cluster of cases undertook successful mediations shortly before trial after exchange of witness statements and (if applicable) expert's reports. **14.36**

J THE COSTS OF MEDIATION

The general aspects of the costs of ADR processes are dealt with in Chapter 4. The costs of mediation will include the party's own costs, the mediator's fees, and other expenses. **14.37**

The party's own costs of preparing for the mediation

This will include the costs perhaps of lawyers preparing position statements, case summaries, and other documents for use in the mediation and solicitor's and perhaps also counsel's fees of preparing for and attending the mediation. If experts are to attend the mediation, it will also include their costs. **14.38**

The mediator's fee

14.39 The mediator's fee will usually be calculated on an hourly or daily basis or it may be a combination of both. The hourly rates will usually include preparation time. Daily rates may be advantageous because that is the rate that will be paid irrespective of how long the mediation lasts, so if it goes on into the late evening no additional fees will have to be paid by the parties. However, some fees will be set at a certain level for the day (based on an eight or ten-hour day) with additional fees being calculated on an hourly rate for every hour after a certain time, for example, 6 pm. Hourly rates vary greatly between individual mediators, and will depend on the nature and value of the case being mediated, and the experience of the mediator. The hourly rate can range between £200 and £500 plus VAT, and can be more in very high value cases. Daily rates can vary from around £700 to £1,000 per party (for a fast-track case up to £50,000 in value mediated by a mediator with little experience) to £2,500 per party or more in high-value cases with a highly experienced mediator. Mediators' fees may be less if a court or fixed-fee mediation scheme is used (see for example, Chapter 18 for mediations taking place through the Civil Mediation Online Directory, the County Court Small Claims Scheme, and the Court of Appeal Mediation Scheme).

14.40 If the parties use an ADR provider, then it is likely that they will charge a fixed fee that will include all associated expenses as well as the fees of the mediator. The fixed fee will be payable irrespective of the length of time the mediation takes or the amount of preparation that is undertaken by the mediator. It is likely to be higher than the fees that would be payable should a mediator be appointed directly by the parties because the ADR provider has to cover their administrative costs in selecting and referring the case to a mediator on their panel and administering the process. A discount on the usual fee may be offered if the ADR provider operates, and the parties select, an express mediation service by which the parties use the ADR provider to select the mediator, but carry out most of the other administrative work themselves, such as booking the venue and the date.

14.41 Fees payable to a mediator or an ADR provider are usually payable in advance of the mediation (usually around seven days in advance) and if they are not paid the mediation may be cancelled and the parties are likely to have to pay some or all of the cancellation charges. Any additional charges (caused by the mediation taking longer than expected for example) will be billed after the mediation.

Expenses of the mediation

14.42 These will include other associated costs of the mediation such as the venue and the provision of refreshments.

14.43 The mediation agreement will usually provide that the mediation fees and expenses will be borne equally by the parties, and that each side will bear their own costs (ie the mediation party costs). However there is no reason why the parties cannot agree something different if that would be more appropriate on the facts of the case. For example:

- One party could agree to pay all of the fees and expenses associated with mediation.
- One party could agree to pay the other side's mediation party costs.
- The parties may agree that all of costs arising out of the mediation are to be regarded as costs in the case, so the overall winner (whether by settlement at the mediation, acceptance of a Part 36 offer made since the mediation, or by trial) will pay the overall loser's mediation party costs and the fees and expenses of the mediation.

14.44 In some circumstances, a party may be able to recover their mediation party costs and their share of the mediation fees and expenses from the other side in the litigation (see Chapter 9).

Alternatively a party may be able to recover some or all of their mediation party costs and their share of the fees and expenses of mediation by the settlement agreement that is reached in the mediation (see Chapters 17 and 23).

K THE FUNDING OF MEDIATION COSTS, FEES, AND EXPENSES

The different ways of funding ADR costs, fees, and expenses are dealt with in Chapter 4. **14.45**
Specific points in relation to mediation are mentioned in the following paragraphs.

Public funding

The Legal Aid Agency (LAA) is prepared to fund a party's mediation costs, fees, and expenses **14.46**
in appropriate cases. Counsel and solicitors acting in publicly funded cases should ensure that the LAA will fund the costs of mediation before embarking on this process. The Funding Code recognizes that mediation costs can be publicly funded in family work and family mediation procedures are funded directly by the LAA, although other forms of ADR, including non-family mediation, can be funded as a disbursement in suitable cases (see *The Funding Code: Decision Making Guidance 3C-090 – 3C-105*). For more information consult www.justice.gov.uk/legal-aid.

Parties in receipt of public funding can be required by the LAA to attempt mediation before **14.47**
other steps are taken in the litigation, unless the dispute is not suitable for mediation or the other side refuses. However, public funding will only be available for mediation if it appears to be the most cost-effective way of proceeding and the fees of the mediator are reasonable in all the circumstances. When the LAA funds mediation, the funding will include all the reasonable legal costs of and related to the mediation, including payment of the mediator's fees. Public funding may be withdrawn if a party unreasonably refuses to settle a claim at mediation. The LAA provides mediation through LAA-contracted providers under fixed fee arrangements and under the terms of the *LAA Mediation Quality Mark Standard (MQMS)* (July 2012) with which mediators must comply.

Funding under a CFA

Conditional fee agreements (CFAs) are explained in Chapter 4 at 4.48. Where a party is **14.48**
funded by a CFA entered into before 1 April 2013, useful guidance for lawyers and mediators can be found in a paper published by the Civil Mediation Council (CMC) entitled 'Mediation, CFAs and conflicts of interest' which can be downloaded from the CMC's website at www.civilmediation.org/downloads-get?id=373.

Mediators can also be instructed on the grounds that their fee is dependent on the outcome **14.49**
of the mediation. If the case settles they will be paid a success fee, ie an enhancement of the fee that they would otherwise have been paid, but if the mediation is not successful, then the mediator obtains no fees. Many mediators will refuse to accept instructions on this basis as there is a perception that such a fee arrangement compromises the neutrality of a mediator.

L STYLES OF MEDIATION

Mediation tends to follow two main forms: facilitative mediation and evaluative mediation **14.50**
(sometimes called directive mediation). Facilitative mediation is the norm. However one party or both parties may invite the mediator to undertake a wider role by asking for an

evaluation of an issue, the overall case, or the likely outcome of the claim. The mediation will then move from being a purely facilitative mediation to an evaluative one. However this will only happen at the request of both parties. If the mediator does agree to perform an evaluative as well as a facilitative role, this should be recorded in writing in the mediation agreement at the outset, or added to it by way of an addendum if the request is made during the course of the mediation (see Chapter 16).

14.51 The main differences between facilitative and evaluative mediation are explained in the following paragraphs and set out in Table 14.4.

Table 14.4 A comparison of facilitative and evaluative mediation

Characteristic	Facilitative mediation	Evaluative mediation
The mediator will make an assessment of the claims for the parties and may even suggest a range for settlement.	No.	Yes—but usually only if he is specifically asked to do so by the parties and he agrees to do so.
The mediator will be interventionist in challenging the parties to re-assess their claim, and will exert more control over the form of the parties negotiations.	Yes—but to a lesser extent.	Yes—to a greater extent.
The evaluation or determination of the mediator will be binding on the parties.	Not applicable.	No—the parties do not have to accept any evaluation by the mediator.

Facilitative mediation

14.52 The mediator, as a neutral or impartial third party, helps the parties to solve their own problems by negotiations that he facilitates. A facilitative mediator will focus primarily on the real interests and concerns of the parties that underpin the dispute rather than the strict legal merits of the dispute.

14.53 Although the mediator is there as a facilitator, the mediator's role is not a passive one. The mediator will:

- ask questions that test the strength and weaknesses of each side's case;
- explore each party's situation and help them to identify what they really need or want to achieve from the dispute;
- encourage the parties to think about the likely outcome of litigation and the costs of obtaining that outcome;
- focus each party's attention on their underlying objectives and needs, rather than on a strict analysis and evaluation of the merits of their case; and
- help them to work out a creative solution that is in their best interests.

14.54 The facilitative mediator will also help the parties to negotiate more effectively, formulate offers in a way that will be attractive to the other side, and give guidance about the timing and staging of offers and concessions.

14.55 A mediator using a purely facilitative mediation model will not give his own opinions on the strengths and merits of each party's case or evaluate the likely outcome of a dispute or put forward proposals for settlement himself. A facilitative mediator is also likely to exert less control over the process than an evaluative mediator and will generally be less interventionist and challenging in the questions asked of the parties about the way in which they have assessed the merits of the case.

Facilitative mediation is the primary or true form of mediation. Whether any particular mediator favours a facilitative or an evaluative style is something that the parties should take into account when selecting a mediator, or in agreeing the scope of the mediator's role in the mediation. 14.56

Most mediators will use elements of both evaluative and facilitative styles during the mediation, but evaluative mediation in the narrow sense means a mediation in which the mediator will evaluate the dispute and express a non-binding opinion on the likely outcome of it, or about the range within which the parties should settle. 14.57

Evaluative mediation

The evaluative mediator will generally facilitate settlement by using a facilitative style. However, such a mediator will go further and, if asked, will actually evaluate the claim or issue and the strengths and weaknesses of a party's case. The evaluative mediator will evaluate the dispute, exert more control over the process, challenge the parties to re-evaluate their assessment of the case, and give an opinion on the likely outcome. The evaluation will be carried out in a legalistic way, with emphasis on the legal and factual issues and an evaluation of the evidence in relation to the issues. Lawyers or professionals who have expertise in the subject-matter of the dispute have a natural tendency to be evaluative mediators. 14.58

An evaluative mediator will be more challenging in relation to the questions he or she asks the parties about the way in which they have assessed the merits of the issues and the likely outcome at trial. 14.59

The evaluative mediator may also be asked to recommend a form of settlement, or a range of options for settlement. He will usually communicate his opinion to each party in a private meeting, although the evaluation can also take place in a joint meeting. If he is asked to do so, he will set out his opinion in writing. His evaluation is not binding on the parties. 14.60

The parties will determine whether the mediator's role moves from the normal facilitative role to an evaluative one in the narrow sense described in 14.58. Both parties may jointly ask the mediator to evaluate the claim, or one or more discrete issues in the claim, or recommend a suitable range for settlement or one party may do so privately in relation to their own position. The mediator will not usually evaluate a claim or issue unless he is specifically invited to do so because doing so may lead to the appearance that he is not maintaining neutrality (on the basis that his assessment of the merits is likely to be more closely allied to that of one party). It is for this reason that some commentators suggest that if evaluation is to be undertaken, it should be done openly, or at least the same advice should be given to both parties in identical terms. An opinion given jointly to the parties is less likely to give rise to undue pressure or coercion than an opinion given to one party alone. 14.61

Some ADR providers do not permit their mediators to express an opinion on the merits of the dispute or give an indication of the likely outcome or analyse a party's legal position. There is a perception that evaluative mediators can coerce the parties into settlement, and by expressing an opinion on the likely outcome they can compromise their neutrality. The mediator will also seldom be provided with all of the documentation in a case. Any evaluation that he provides may not be based on complete information and may therefore be misleading. Providing an evaluation may also expose the mediator to a potential claim in negligence (see 14.153–14.155). For these reasons, evaluative mediation is more likely to be the exception rather than the norm. However, some commentators and clients favour it; it can speed up the settlement negotiations, and provide the reality check that is needed to enable the parties to move towards settlement. The Law Society's Code of Practice for Civil 14.62

and Commercial Mediation (see paras 3, 4, and 5 and commentary, last updated November 2011) provides that:

> While impartiality is fundamental to the role of the mediator, this does not mean that a mediator may never express a comment or view that one party may find more acceptable than another. However the mediator must not allow his or her personal view of the fairness or otherwise of the substance of the negotiations between the parties to damage or impair his or her impartiality. The mediator must appreciate that his or her involvement in the process is inevitably likely to affect the course of the negotiations between the parties .... This would be the case whether the mediator intervenes directly or whether he or she deals with issues indirectly, for example, through questions. Consequently, all mediator intervention needs to be conducted with sensitivity and care in order to maintain impartiality.
>
> The mediator and the parties should agree, as far as practicable, at the outset whether the mediator's role will be purely facilitative, or whether the mediator may at his or her discretion, provide an evaluative element based on his or her knowledge of the subject matter or legal issues involved. This is rarely used and then, usually, only at the end of the mediation. This would not be precluded by paragraph 5.5 of the Code,which provides that the mediator should not impose his or her preferred outcome on the parties. The mediator may suggest possible solutions and help the parties to explore these where he or she thinks that this would be helpful to them.

14.63 If evaluative mediation is sought from a mediator, this should be specified in advance (as some mediators may be unwilling to do this) and if it is to be undertaken by the mediator, this will usually be agreed at the outset and recorded in the mediation agreement, or added to it by way of addendum if the evaluation is sought during the course of the mediation (see Chapter 15).

14.64 Evaluative mediation is very similar to judicial conciliation (see Chapter 20) and some commentators refer to it as conciliation. However, in this book, where the evaluation and/or recommendation as to the form of settlement take place in the context of mediation, it is referred to as evaluative mediation rather than conciliation. It is also a form of early neutral evaluation (see Chapter 22) in that the outcome is similar, although the process may differ. Where the evaluation takes place in the context of mediation, it is referred to in this book as evaluative mediation, rather than early neutral evaluation.

Transformative mediation

14.65 Some commentators also make reference to a third style of mediation, namely that of 'transformative mediation'.

14.66 Transformative mediation tends to focus on improving the relationship and communication between the parties rather than having the settlement of the dispute as its primary focus. Transformative mediators aim to help the parties to improve their communication so that they can resolve their own dispute. The parties themselves will control the nature of the discussions, with the mediator primarily providing a reflective role. Whilst some mediators will display some aspects of a transformative mediation style during the course of mediation, most will also use elements of a facilitative or an evaluative approach. For further information on transformative mediation see Robert A Baruch Bush and JP Folger, *The Promise of Mediation, The Transformative Approach to Conflict* (Jossey-Bass, 2005) and www.transformativemediation.org.

M THE ROLE OF THE MEDIATOR

14.67 The mediator's role can be said to fall into three discrete areas:

- organizing the mediation process;
- acting as facilitator during the process;
- acting as intermediary between the parties.

Organizing the mediation process

Before the mediation

When appointed, the mediator will usually contact the parties (or their lawyers) and will explain, in a pre-mediation meeting, or by telephone, the nature of the mediation process, how they should prepare for it, the mediator's function, the role that the parties will play in the process, and the costs of the process. He or she will discuss with each party who should attend the mediation and will check that the attendees for each party have authority to settle the case. The mediator will endeavour to find out if there are any limits on their authority and, if so, advise on what needs to be done to ensure that settlement is not thwarted because one party lacks authority at the mediation. The mediator will also set the timetable for events that need to happen prior to the mediation, such as the date by which the mediation agreement should be signed and returned and the date by which position statements and documents should be provided and exchanged (see Chapter 15 for more detail about these matters). If the parties have used an ADR service provider to provide a mediator, then it is likely that the service provider rather than the mediator will make the practical arrangements for the mediation. **14.68**

At the mediation

The mediator will also perform an organizational role at the mediation. In particular, the mediator will: **14.69**

- Chair the meetings and manage the process.
- Set the agenda for the mediation by suggesting the order in which issues should be negotiated, and amend it if necessary as the mediation progresses.
- Control the form that the mediation follows on the day (and discuss with the parties and/or decide whether any modifications should be made to the process to meet the needs of the case or the parties).
- Decide when discussions should take place in joint or private meetings.
- Impose or suggest a time limit for delivery of opening statements in the initial joint meeting.
- Decide whether further joint meetings should take place during the negotiation phase in addition to the opening joint meeting.
- Prevent interventions by the other side during the opening statement of the opposing party.
- Ensure parity, as far as possible, in the amount of time the mediator spends in private sessions with each party.
- Control the form of questions that one party may put to the opposing party in the opening joint session.

All of these matters are dealt with, in detail, in Chapter 16.

Acting as a facilitator

The mediator will assist the parties to negotiate with one another in a more effective manner than they would be able to achieve on their own. The mediator will do this in the following ways: **14.70**

- Gather information from the parties both at the pre-mediation stage (see Chapter 15) and during the mediation (see Chapter 16) about the issues in dispute and their needs and interests.
- Help the parties to identify the legal and factual issues, and their underlying needs and objectives.
- Encourage the parties to treat the mediation as their 'day in court' and to air their feelings and emotions, particularly in private meetings, so that the matter can move forward.

- Help the parties to listen to each other and communicate more effectively with each other.
- Discourage or defuse confrontational or aggressive communications between the parties that will hinder negotiations, and reframe them if necessary.
- Encourage the parties to analyse the strength and weakness of their own case and the case presented by the other side.
- Perform the role of 'reality-checker', perhaps by assuming the role of 'devil's advocate', if the parties are unrealistic in their assessment.
- Encourage the parties to think about the BATNA (best alternative to a negotiated agreement) and the WATNA (worst alternative to a negotiated agreement), and ensure that they have carried out a full risk assessment, including the costs (and irrecoverable costs) of proceeding to trial.
- Review the negotiations that have already taken place between the parties, and encourage each party to reflect on why they failed and how they can change their position to move the matter forward.
- Encourage brainstorming and the generation of options for settlement, including the identification of common ground between the parties.
- Create and use strategies and options to end deadlock between the parties.

14.71 All of these matters are discussed in detail in Chapter 16.

Acting as intermediary

14.72 The mediator will act as the 'go-between' or 'shuttle-diplomat' during private meetings of the parties. He will convey offers, concessions and information, rejections, and counter-offers from one party to another. He will enable the parties to negotiate through him as intermediary, rather than with each other face to face. This can be very effective in achieving progress to an overall settlement. He will keep a record of any agreement reached on individual issues as the negotiation progresses, as this will help with drawing up any final overall settlement agreement.

14.73 In order for the mediator to carry out these functions, it is vital that each party trusts and has confidence in him. To build up that trust, the mediator must ensure that he is even-handed in his dealings with the parties and that he does not do or say anything that may lead one party to think that he is biased in any way. That is not to say that a mediator should not be rigorous and testing in the way he encourages each side to analyse their case. He may play the 'devil's advocate'. But he should not do or say anything that gives the impression he is not impartial, and he should not force a solution on the parties.

Post-mediation role

14.74 Even if the mediation does not result in settlement, it is not uncommon for the parties to engage the mediator to broker settlement negotiations at a future date particularly if both parties trust and respect him.

N ACCREDITATION AND REGULATION OF MEDIATION

Introduction

14.75 The number of ADR professionals is growing year on year and they come from a wide range of professional backgrounds. While some are lawyers, many are not. Mediators may be drawn from other areas of professional practice, such as accountants, engineers and other construction professionals, and from the field of psychology. The ADR profession needs regulation. The market is not served by the fact that:

- there is a variation in the nature of the training courses offered by different ADR providers;
- mediators in private practice do not have to undergo any form of training or accreditation at all. However, as mediation becomes more commonly used and widely publicized, it is unlikely that a member of the public will choose a mediator who has not undergone some form of training accreditation (see 14.78–14.79);
- there is a multiplicity of codes of conduct among providers (see 14.101–14.104).

There is an urgent need for: **14.76**

- uniformity in the professional training and accreditation requirements for *all* mediators leading to a formal qualification;
- a common code of conduct which sets uniform standards, which *all* mediators must adhere to;
- an independent regulatory body to oversee the work of *all* ADR professionals, including setting minimum professional standards in the way mediators carry out their business, monitoring those standards and implementing and operating a standard complaints procedure.

The Civil Mediation Council (CMC) has taken steps in this direction by creating the CMC Provider Accreditation Scheme for organizations who wish to be registered as mediation provider members of the CMC (which is regarded as a kite mark of quality and is relied upon as a requirement for inclusion in the Ministry of Justice's 'Find a Civil Mediation Provider' database—see 18.31–18.33 for more detail about the Civil Mediation Online Directory). However, these measures fall short of what is required; not all ADR provider organizations will choose to become members of the CMC, and individuals, whilst they can become members of the CMC, are not currently accredited by the CMC (see 14.92–14.93). **14.77**

Training and accreditation requirements

In order to become accredited, a mediator must satisfy requirements for training and continuous professional development. Although these vary between providers and organizations, they typically involve attending a training course, which can range between four and eight days in duration. The course will include training in ethics, mediation theory and practice, negotiation, and role-play exercises. Most of the training providers will comply with the minimum requirements of training that are laid down by the CMC for the Provider Accreditation Scheme 2014 (see 14.88–14.91), and in some cases will exceed those requirements. The training requirements differ depending on the date of the training, and are more onerous for those undertaking training from 1 April 2011. For those undertaking training up to 31 March 2011, the training had to include not less than 24 hours of tuition and role play, and this has been increased to 40 hours from 1 April 2011. **14.78**

Accreditation of mediators takes place at present in the following ways: **14.79**

- Many ADR organizations have their own systems in place for training and accrediting member mediators.
- Family mediators are accredited by the Family Mediation Council (FMC). The FMC has recently approved a new 'Assessment of Professional Competence' Scheme which sets out steps that mediators must take to demonstrate their competence in order to apply for Assessed Professionally Competent Mediator (APCM) status before they are competent to practise by the FMC and recognized by the LAA to undertake publicly funded mediation work. Further detail on the scheme can be obtained from www.familymediationcouncil.org.uk.

- The Law Society has prescribed training standards and has a system of accreditation for solicitor mediators on its Family and Civil and Commercial Mediation Accreditation Schemes who comply with those standards. Further detail on each of these schemes can be found at www.lawsociety.org.uk. Law Society accredited practitioner panel civil and commercial members must also have some practical experience consisting of at least 90 hours of mediation experience over the preceding two years including at least four civil and commercial mediations comprising a minimum total of 30 hours. The Law Society maintains a list of approved accredited training providers and members.
- The Bar Council also maintains a Mediation Directory and the barristers who appear in the Mediation Directory have all completed training with an approved training provider. Currently, the course must be at least 40 hours in length and include role playing and teaching in mediation procedure and ethics.
- The CMC provides accreditation to ADR civil and commercial mediation organizations but not individual mediators, although individuals can become members of the CMC (see 14.80–14.100).

O THE CIVIL MEDIATION COUNCIL

14.80 The CMC was constituted in 2003 to represent the interests of mediation providers and mediators, promote civil and commercial mediation and other dispute resolution options, and create a culture of best practice in the field. Family mediation is not currently regulated or represented by the CMC (see 14.79 for the regulation of family mediation). It has currently about 400 individual members and about 90 member organizations across the UK.

14.81 The CMC's mission is 'to inspire all sectors of society to use mediation when managing and resolving disputes' and it has the following key aims (see www.civilmediation.org):

- Promote the highest standards of skill, conduct, and integrity in mediation.
- Enable access to high quality mediation services.
- Lead the development and stimulate the growth of mediation.
- Act as a link between all who are interested in mediation.

14.82 The CMC currently operates three membership schemes and more information on each of these schemes is set out in this chapter:

- The Provider Accreditation Scheme
- The Individual Membership Registration Scheme
- The Workplace Mediation Provider Registration Scheme.

14.83 It is important to note that although both individuals and mediation providers are entitled to become members of the CMC, only mediation providers (defined as organizations, bodies, groups, societies, centres, and the like) can become *accredited* members, assuming they comply with the requirements of the Provider Accrediation Scheme. Individuals, although eligible to apply for membership, are not accredited by the CMC.

14.84 Any mediations that take place through the Civil Mediation Online Directory (see 18.31–18.33) will only be handled by organizations accredited by the Civil Mediation Council under its Provider Accreditation Scheme. A list of accredited mediation providers can be found by searching the Civil Mediation Online Directory's website at www.civilmediation.justice.gov.uk.

14.85 The CMC is currently working with mediation training organizations with a view to establishing and agreeing minimum standards for commercial and civil mediation training courses. Most reputable training courses now comply with the minimum requirements specified by the CMC in respect of the Provider Accreditation Scheme (see 14.88–14.91).

Many ADR providers who are accredited by the CMC will also monitor performance of their mediators through client feedback and peer review, and they may make this available to the parties to assist in the selection of a suitable mediator. **14.86**

The CMC operates an internal Members' Complaints Resolution Service. This enables members (or clients of members) who have a complaint which has not been resolved through the member's own complaints scheme to refer the complaint to the CMC for resolution (if possible) by a fixed-fee, time-limited mediation. **14.87**

The CMC Provider Accreditation Scheme

This scheme was revised by the CMC on 6 November 2013. It only applies to organizations, bodies, groups, societies, centres, and the like. Under this scheme, the provider becomes accredited by the CMC. This means that the provider has demonstrated that it meets minimum requirements set by the CMC, so in that respect accreditation can be regarded as a kite mark of quality. Individual mediators who are employed by or who have work referred to them by that provider are not individually accredited. It continues to be up to the providers to ensure that individual mediators are properly trained and accredited, insured and supervised, and that they fulfil their CPD and practice requirements. **14.88**

The CMC will accredit mediation providers if they satisfy the Board of the CMC that they have reached the standards set by the Board for the provision of mediation services and they have paid the annual membership fee. This scheme is open to providers of civil and commercial mediation. Accreditation is carried out annually. Providers apply for accreditation by completing and submitting the application form which can be found on the CMC's website together with the appropriate fee for accreditation (currently £300 for new accreditations, or £75 for annual re-accreditations). Their application will then be considered by the Accreditation Committee of the CMC. If the application for accreditation is refused, reasons will be provided. When an application for accreditation has been approved, the provider can advertise this fact in its literature or advertising material. **14.89**

In order to be accredited, the provider must meet the following minimum requirements: **14.90**

- It must have at least six trained civil or commercial mediators on its panel.
- Its mediators must have successfully completed an assessed training course, which complies with the requirements set by the CMC at the relevant time. Currently the requirements consist of training in ethics, mediation theory, mediation practice, negotiation, and role play exercises. If the mediator is not a lawyer, s/he must also demonstrate an understanding of basic contract law if s/he is to undertake civil or commercial mediations. From 1 April 2011, the training course must include not less than 40 hours of face-to-face tuition and role play followed by formal assessment. The assessment must comply with the detailed assessment criteria and specifications.
- In addition, all of the provider's mediators must have the prescribed minimum level of practical experience in the 12 months prior to accreditation, the provider must adopt the EU Model Code of Conduct for Mediations (or a similar code), operate a published complaints procedure, capture feedback about its mediators from the parties in mediation, operate a CPD policy for its mediators and have adequate insurance in place (which must be not less than £1,000,000 for each mediator). Full details of the scheme can be found on the Online Resource Centre and at www.cuilmediation.org.

A senior official of the provider is required to sign and date a Statement of Truth personally certifying that the contents of the application form are true and accurate, and the CMC can rely on this in granting accreditation. The CMC can request evidence of the matters stated **14.91** in the form. The names and addresses of Accredited Providers can be found on the CMC's website. See www.civilmediation.org.

The CMC Individual Membership Scheme

14.92 Under this scheme, individual mediators who conduct a professional mediation practice and who certify that they are 'qualified in accordance with such standards as to training, accreditation or otherwise as the Board may publish from time to time' can apply to become members on payment of a fee (currently £75). An individual will comply with this requirement if he or she has been accredited by and currently holds accreditation from an Accredited Mediation Provider member of the CMC, or they completed and passed a mediation training course that complied with the CMC's requirements for accredited mediation providers at the relevant time.

14.93 It should be noted, however, that membership does not amount to accreditation by the CMC, and individual membership is not to be regarded as a mark of quality or accreditation by the CMC. A list of individual members is published on the CMC's website. However, anyone who wants to make a search of the list must tick a box expressly agreeing that the CMC is not making any representation or assuming any responsibility for the accuracy of the information provided or the suitability or competence of any mediator listed, and that the person searching must make their own checks if they wish to instruct a mediator. The individual member is also not permitted to suggest that their inclusion in the list implies any form of accreditation, qualification, or competence as a mediator.

The CMC Registered Workplace Mediation Organisation Scheme

14.94 This was set up in 2009 for mediation organizations who provide mediation services in the workplace in relation to employment related disputes to become registered members of the CMC on payment of an initial fee (currently £300) and then an annual renewal fee (currently £75). Workplace mediation providers who register under the scheme are eligible to use or display any CMC logo. Organizations wishing to register under this scheme must meet the registration requirements, which include a minimum number of two workplace mediators, professional indemnity insurance cover for the organization and each individual mediator, compliance with the European Code of Conduct for Mediators, or an equivalent code, and each mediator must comply with the CMC's minimum training and CPD requirements. As with the provider accreditation scheme, the CMC does not undertake any independent verification that these requirements are met, but rather relies on a self-certifying statement of truth from the applicant that the registration information it has given is correct.

Is further regulation required?

14.95 In March 2011, the government published a consultation paper, CP6/2011 entitled 'Solving Disputes in the county courts: creating a simpler, quicker and more proportionate system'. This can be viewed at http://consult.justice.gov.uk/digital-communications/county_court_disputes. The consultation period ended on 30 June 2011 and the government's response was published in February 2012.

14.96 In the consultation paper, the government noted that although the accreditation scheme operated by the CMC in respect of civil and commercial mediation providers was a mark of quality assurance which was 'very much in line' with the requirements of Article 4 of the EU Mediation Directive (see Chapter 19), it currently has no accreditation scheme for individual mediators who practise on their own account or through a mediation provider which is not accredited by the CMC. In the government response, it was noted that 57% of those who responded to the consultation considered the CMC's provider accreditation scheme was sufficient, although 43% considered it was not adequate.

14.97 The response to the government's consultation is broadly in line with evaluations carried out by both the CMC and CEDR. In the CMC's response to the Ministry of Justice's Consultation on the Civil Court Reforms, only 58.9% of those surveyed by the CMC stated that they felt that the CMC's accreditation scheme for mediation providers was sufficient for the purpose of quality assurance, with 37.8% reporting that it was not sufficient. The Third Mediation Audit report by CEDR (November 2007) also indicated the need for reform, with 52.3% of mediators who responded welcoming the idea of a single standard of basic professional training of commercial mediators and 58.5% agreeing that there should be a single regulatory body for setting and monitoring professional standards of practice by commercial mediators and dealing with public complaints against mediators. These figures were broadly unchanged in the fourth Mediation Audit (2010), being 52.8% and 54.9% respectively. In the fifth mediation audit in 2012, the figures were 52.1% and 61.7% respectively, demonstrating that the clear majority favours a single regulatory body for setting and monitoring professional standards. The CMC retained its position as the most popular body amongst candidates to fulfil each of these roles, although there was also strong interest in a new body taking on these roles.

14.98 Some suggestions which have been proposed for change are as follows:

- Some form of compulsory accreditation for all individual mediators and providers is necessary.
- A regulatory framework is required to set clear standards for training, accreditation, and all aspects of service delivery.
- There should be a disciplinary body which oversees professional standards and operates and implements a complaints service.
- The CMC's accreditation system for providers needs to be more robust—it is essentially a self-certifying process.
- CPD requirements should be in place for all mediators in line with other professionals.

14.99 The CMC published a consultation document, 'The CMC and Accreditation' on 25 March 2013, with a view to ascertaining whether it should extend accreditation to individual mediators, accredit all mediation training courses (and if so, how and in what terms these might be achieved), and finally whether there was a case for the creation of a Mediation Standards Board, which would maintain some autonomy from the CMC, to monitor accreditation standards and deal with complaints. Following that consultation, in December 2013 the CMC has decided to proceed with a registration scheme for individual mediators and a registration scheme for mediation training courses. The CMC intends to remove the word 'accreditation' from all schemes, and instead both individuals and provider organizations will simply become registered members. The requirements for registration of individuals are likely to be based on the present requirements for accredited providers, although the full requirements have not yet been defined.

14.100 The CMC arranged to hold a meeting in May 2014 to seek the authorization of members to establish a company limited by guarantee to take over the affairs of the CMC and then, following incorporation, to apply for charitable status. The proposed name of the company will be the Civil Mediation Council Limited. It is also proposed that the CMC's membership should be widened and opened to other interested parties in mediation, including academics and students. Consult the Online Resource Centre for future developments.

P ETHICAL CONSIDERATIONS AFFECTING MEDIATORS

14.101 Mediators are in a position of considerable power. They have the ability to influence whether or not a settlement takes place between disputing parties and the terms of that settlement. Mediation is conducted on the basis that the parties are encouraged to speak freely and confidentially to the mediator in private meetings about their interests and concerns and their assessment of the merits of their case and the extent of offers or concessions they are prepared to make or accept. It follows from this that mediators are likely to be the recipients of highly confidential and sensitive information from each party to the dispute. It is therefore of crucial importance that mediators act in a professional and ethical way.

14.102 Most mediators do operate under a code of conduct. This may be the Code of Conduct operated by the ADR provider of whom the mediator is a member and by whom the mediator is accredited, or mediators in private practice may devise and operate under their own Code of Conduct. Members of the CMC, whether accredited provider members or individual members, are expected to comply with the European Code of Conduct for Mediators (see the Online Resource Centre). This code is entirely voluntary and mediators or ADR organizations do not have to adopt it or operate under it, but most mediators and ADR organizations offering a mediation service do operate under a code which contains the same or similar provisions to the EU Code.

14.103 Mediators who are professionally qualified in another field of expertise will also be expected to comply with the code of conduct prescribed by their governing or regulatory body. For example, solicitor mediators also operate under the SRA Principles and Code of Conduct and barristers acting as mediators will remain subject to the obligations in the Bar Code of Conduct (see Chapter 6).

14.104 Any mediator who accepts instructions to mediate in a dispute between two or more parties should comply with the ethical standards discussed in the following paragraphs.

Competence

14.105 Mediators must be competent and knowledgeable in the process of mediation. This should include proper training in mediation skills and in the process of mediation, and a system for Continuing Professional Development (CPD) to refresh and update their skills. The mediator should be competent to conduct the mediation, bearing in mind the nature and complexity of the dispute and the needs and objectives of the parties. Mediators should also provide information to interested parties relating to their background and experience so that they can make an informed choice (see European Code of Conduct for Mediators, paras 1.1 and 1.2).

Independence and neutrality

14.106 A mediator must ensure there is no conflict of interest with any of the parties directly or indirectly affected by the dispute. If circumstances exist which do or may give rise to a conflict of interest or affect his neutrality (such as previously acting for or advising one of the parties in an unrelated matter or having a personal or social relationship with one party), these should be disclosed immediately to the parties. The mediator should only consent to act in such circumstances if the parties expressly authorize this (in writing)—see European Code of Conduct for Mediators, para 2. Brown and Marriott in *ADR Principles and Practice* (3rd edn, Sweet & Maxwell, 2011) suggest that there are some situations in which a mediator must refuse to mediate even if there has been full disclosure to and consent from the parties. These situations are as follows:

- The mediator or persons associated with the mediator have a personal or financial interest in the outcome of the mediation.
- The mediator or persons associated with him has acted for any of the parties at any time in relation to the issues that may need to be considered in the mediation.
- A therapist/client or counsellor/client relationship has existed at any time, in relation to any matter, between one of the parties and the mediator.
- The mediator or a member of his organization has previously acted for a third party whose interests may conflict with those of either party in the mediation (eg previously acting for trustees where one of the parties is a beneficiary under the trust).
- The mediator is aware of circumstances or personal or other reasons which make it impossible or difficult for the mediator to act impartially.

Impartiality

The mediator should at all times act, and endeavour to be seen to act, with impartiality towards the parties (see European Code of Conduct for Mediators, para 2.2). Mediators must not do anything which demonstrates actual or perceived bias. Whilst it is perfectly possible for a mediator to carry out an objective assessment of the merits of an issue in order to give a non-binding evaluation or opinion on that issue to one or more of the parties, some commentators and ADR organizations feel that this puts the mediator's impartiality at risk because the assessment in most cases will favour one side's case over another. It is for that reason that purists would argue that mediators should not perform an evaluative role. **14.107**

The mediation procedure

The mediator should ensure the parties understand the nature and purpose of the mediation process, the terms of the mediation agreement, the fees payable, and the obligations of confidentiality imposed on the parties and the mediator. The mediator should also explain the procedure to be followed in the mediation, which can be modified or agreed following discussions between the mediator and the parties (see European Code of Conduct for Mediators, paras 3.1 and 3.4). **14.108**

Fairness

The mediator should act fairly between the parties, ensuring that all parties have adequate opportunities to be involved in the process and that the process is conducted in a manner which is fair to both parties. This may involve the mediator managing dominating parties so that each side can be properly heard. The concept of fairness also means that mediators must take care to avoid any party being forced into mediation or a mediation settlement agreement as a result of abuse or threats or other unconscionable conduct. However, because the essence of mediation is that the parties make their own decisions about how to resolve their dispute, the notion of fairness would not extend to the mediator ensuring that the terms of any proposed settlement are fair to each of the parties, although this is subject to the need to have overall fairness in the process so that each party is in a position to freely make their own decisions about the dispute. **14.109**

The mediator should also be careful not to put undue pressure on a party to settle the dispute. If this happened, the agreement could be set aside for undue influence or duress. The mediator must not press a party into settlement in order to maintain a high personal settlement rate. **14.110**

Confidentiality

14.111 Paragraph 4 of the European Code of Conduct for Mediators provides that:

> The mediator shall keep confidential all information arising out of or in connection with the mediation, including the fact that the mediation is to take place or has taken place, unless compelled by law or public policy grounds. Any information disclosed in confidence to mediators by one of the parties shall not be disclosed to the other parties without permission or unless compelled by law.

14.112 The duty of confidentiality is discussed in general terms in Chapter 6 and specifically in relation to mediation at 14.135–14.145. The mediation agreement will usually spell out exceptions to the general rule in which the mediator can reveal confidential information.

Termination of the mediation

14.113 The mediator should terminate the mediation and inform the parties (if appropriate) if they believe a settlement to be unenforceable or illegal, or that continuing the mediation is unlikely to result in settlement (see European Code of Conduct for Mediators, para 3.2).

14.114 The mediator should also explain that the parties have the right to withdraw from the mediation at any time, and without giving any reason for doing so (see European Code of Conduct for Mediators, para 3.3).

14.115 If agreement is reached at the mediation, the mediator should ensure that all parties understand the terms of the agreement, and that they consent to it. The mediator may, if requested by the parties and competent to do so, give advice on how the agreement can be formalized and made enforceable (see European Code of Conduct for Mediators, para 3.3).

14.116 The mediator should also ensure that any files or documents, including personal notes that are retained following the mediation, should be securely and confidentially stored.

Repeat instructions

14.117 In the Third Mediation Report carried out by CEDR (November 2007), concern was expressed by both mediators and lawyers that a mediator's over-dependence on repeat referrals from a particular firm could also prejudice their neutrality. However, this would not be an issue if disclosure was made of all prior contacts with referring parties, as well as the parties directly involved in the dispute.

Practice administration

14.118 The Civil Mediation Council Code of Good Practice for Mediators also requires mediators to:

- have an efficient system of personal practice administration (para 11);
- have access to a complaints resolution system (para 12);
- make effective arrangements for obtaining peer review and feedback and an effective system for obtaining and reviewing feedback (para 13);
- be insured to cover errors, omissions, and negligence: the CMC recommends a minimum of £1,000,000 of such insurance or a higher level if appropriate (para 14);
- be sensitive to diversity, equality, and anti-discrimination issues (para 15).

14.119 The Agreement to Mediate (see 15.28–15.32) is also likely to contain provisions which set out the ethical conduct to be expected of mediators. Mediators who are drawn from professions such as solicitors, barristers, engineers, architects, or accountants will also operate under Professional Conduct Rules specified by any professional bodies to which they belong (see Chapter 6 for more detail on the ethical considerations affecting lawyers).

Q THE WITHOUT PREJUDICE RULE IN MEDIATION

The without prejudice rule and exceptions to it (see 6.57–6.66) apply to communications passing between the parties made in the context of a mediation, so these cannot be relied on or referred to in subsequent court proceedings if the mediation is unsuccessful (*Aird & Aird v Prime Meridian Ltd* [2006] BLR 105). **14.120**

In *Halsey v Milton Keynes General NHS Trust* [2004] 1 WLR 3002, the court accepted that 'if the integrity and confidentiality of the [mediation] process is to be respected, the court should not know, and should not investigate, why the process did not result in agreement'. The without prejudice rule will clearly apply to communications aimed at settlement that take place between the parties before the mediation agreement is signed, or before the mediation commences, as well as communications that take place during the course of the mediation. **14.121**

The without prejudice rule is often specifically stated in the mediation agreement between the parties and is further strengthened by a confidentiality clause. The court will uphold these clauses and grant an injunction to restrain a party from referring to any part of the discussions that took place during the mediation (*Venture Investment Placement Ltd v Hall* [2005] EWHC 1227 (Ch)). In *Mason v Walton-on-Thames Charity & others* [2010] EWHC 1688 (Ch), the claimant sought permission, in advance of the hearing of a preliminary issue, to rely on without prejudice communications that had been produced in the course of mediation in order to oppose the position one of the defendants adopted in the litigation. The court refused permission as no exceptions to the exclusionary without prejudice rule applied and secondly the claimant contractually agreed, by a clause in the mediation agreement which she had signed, to abide by the without prejudice confidential nature of the process. **14.122**

In mediation, the following communications will be protected from disclosure by operation of the without prejudice rule: **14.123**

- any oral or written communications made specifically for the purposes of settlement, such as position statements, correspondence about the mediation, offers or concessions whether made before, during or after the mediation (see *Reed Executive plc v Reed Business Information Ltd* [2004] 1 WLR 3026; *Brown v Rice* [2007] EWHC 625 (Ch));
- any communications passing between the parties and the mediator before, during or after the mediation with a view to exploring settlement;
- communications created for the purpose of trying to persuade the parties to mediate: *Instance v Denny Bros Printing Ltd* [2000] FSR 869.

The rule will protect communications aimed at settlement which pass between the parties themselves or between their respective lawyers and it is also likely to protect communications passing between the parties and the mediator (*Brown v Rice* [2007] EWHC 625 (Ch)). **14.124**

It will also operate to protect investigations carried out as part of the mediation process. In *Smiths Group plc v George Weiss* (unreported, 22 March 2002), the agreed mediation procedure provided for each party's expert to meet with employees and former employees with a view to establishing work done by them during a particular year. The mediation was adjourned to enable this to be done. The persons interviewed were told informally before each interview that the interview was without prejudice and that the material would not be used in evidence. The mediation failed to result in settlement and the issue before the court **14.125** was whether the claimant's expert should be required to expunge accounts of his interviews with the employees from his report. Despite finding that the interviews were part of the fact-finding process and in no sense related to any attempt to settle the proceedings, Mr Roger Kaye QC (sitting as a Deputy High Court Judge) accepted that these interviews were protected by the without prejudice rule, and that the defendant's conduct was not such that they should be estopped from asserting the privilege.

Communications that are not protected by the without prejudice rule in mediation

14.126 Although there are few reported decisions in the context of mediation, in view of the fact that there is no particular special category of 'mediation privilege', it is likely that the exceptions to the without prejudice rule in general litigation (see 6.65–6.66 will also apply in the context of mediation).

14.127 In mediation, the following communications will not be protected by the without prejudice rule:

- open offers;
- offers that can be communicated to the court on the question of costs, after issues of liability and remedies have been determined. If a party wishes to rely on a document in relation to costs, then they should either mark the document 'without prejudice except as to costs' or make a formal offer under Part 36 of the CPR. If the offer is not accepted by the other party, and they fail to beat it at trial, then it can be drawn to the attention of the court in order to persuade the court to make an adverse costs order against that party;
- communications that are not aimed at settlement of a dispute. Not all documents produced at or prepared for a mediation will be protected by the without prejudice rule. The rule will not protect documents that were not created for the purposes of exploring settlement, such as statements of case or contractual documents, documents relating to loss, accident report forms, maintenance records, or any other documents of this nature that would have to be disclosed during the course of litigation. It will also not apply to a joint statement made following a meeting of the experts instructed by each party that was created for use in the mediation, as such a statement is one that the experts must produce if the court directs it under CCR 35.12 (*Aird & Aird v Prime Meridian Ltd* [2006] BLR 105).

14.128 If the without prejudice rule is abused, eg by a party making a threat about the action they will take if an offer is not accepted during a mediation, then the court will not allow a party to shield behind the rule and will order disclosure (*Unilever plc v Procter & Gamble* [2000] 1 WLR 1436; *Aird & Aird v Prime Meridian Ltd* [2006] BLR 105).

14.129 The court can look at communications that took place in a mediation to decide if the mediation resulted in a concluded settlement. In *Brown v Rice* [2007] EWHC 625 (Ch), an issue arose between the parties as to whether a settlement had been reached at mediation, even though the terms had not been recorded by an agreement in writing and signed by the parties. The ADR Group was given permission to intervene in the proceedings. They submitted that nothing said or done in preparation for or at mediation could be disclosed in the absence of impropriety by a party at the mediation. They also submitted that the clause in a mediation agreement providing that there was no agreement unless it was in writing and signed by the parties prevented the court from looking at the events in the mediation to see if there was a concluded settlement because this clause effectively removed that exception to the without prejudice rule. The court rejected these submissions and held that the fact that communications took place in the context of mediation did not provide the communications with a special status. Mediation was simply a form of assisted negotiation and so the usual exceptions to the without prejudice rule applied in the context of mediation. The court could therefore look at the events in the mediation to decide if there was a concluded agreement as an exception to the without prejudice rule. Although the court accepted that an offer had been made, and accepted by the deadline on the day following the mediation, the absence of any provision as to the manner of disposal of the litigation meant that the offer was incomplete. The court also held that the clause in the mediation agreement requiring there to be a written settlement, meant that any agreement reached between the parties could not be completed until reduced to writing, unless that clause was varied or waived or one party was not able to rely on it. The court therefore found that no binding settlement had been reached.

As mediation increases, so too is there likely to be an increase in litigation arising out of the mediation. There have been a number of recent cases in which the courts have considered what took place in mediation in an effort to determine whether mediation resulted in a binding settlement. **14.130**

- In *AB v CD Ltd* [2013] EWHC 1376 (TCC), the mediator was required to give evidence, and to disclose notes he had made and communications received from the parties from the conclusion of the mediation meeting until settlement was reached by the parties some two weeks later, in order to assist the court to determine whether the dispute had settled by agreement following the conclusion of the mediation meeting. The court considered *Brown v Rice* [2007] EWHC 625 (Ch), but distinguished it on its facts, and held that the mediation ended when the defendant rejected the claimant's offer, which had been left open after the conclusion of the mediation meeting. As the further negotiations after that date were not covered by the clause in the mediation agreement, there was no need for the parties to enter into a written settlement agreement signed by them before the settlement could be legally enforceable.
- The court also admitted evidence of what took place at a mediation in order to determine whether a settlement agreement was binding on the parties in *Universal Satspace (North America) LLC v Kenya* (QB), 20 December 2013 (unrep). The parties reached a settlement at mediation, but the defendant requested a 21-day delay in signing the settlement agreement. The parties therefore made an oral arrangement that they would sign the settlement agreement within that period, Although the claimant signed it, the defendant did not do so. The claimant then made an application to court to strike out the defence and counterclaim, relying on the oral agreement to execute the settlement agreement in the form that had been agreed at the mediation. Teare J held that the oral agreement to sign the settlement agreement within a certain time period was a collateral contract that could be enforced by the court. The provision in the mediation agreement which provided that no settlement reached in mediation would be binding unless and until it was reduced to writing and signed by all parties did not apply, because it was concerned with settlement of the underlying dispute, not a collateral agreement.
- In *Barden v Commodities Research Unit (Holdings) Ltd* [2013] EWHC 1633 (Ch), the parties reached an agreement in mediation, and an issue arose whether that agreement was inclusive or exclusive of tax. The claimant applied to the court for payment of the balance of £673,000 which he claimed was due under the settlement agreement, which the defendant, his employer, had deducted and paid to HM Revenue and Customs. The court had to construe the agreement to determine whether the settlement figure was inclusive or exclusive of tax. The court ordered disclosure of the notes of the mediation. The parties and their lawyers made witness statements describing the course of negotiations in the mediation. The court considered the extent to which the communications between the parties during the mediation were admissible as an aid to construction of the settlement agreement. The court held that much of the parties' evidence surrounding their negotiations and mediation

was not admissible in considering the true construction of the settlement agreement. All that was admissible was the factual matrix, which did not include the parties' negotiations or subjective intent. Taking that into account, the construction of the agreement was clear and the payment was to be made net of tax.

14.131 The mediation agreement itself is not protected by the without prejudice rule and it can be produced to prove its terms (*Brown v Rice* [2007] EWHC 625 (Ch)).

14.132 If *all* parties to the mediation waive privilege, the communications can be placed before the court. In *Cumbria Waste Management Ltd v Baines Wilson* [2008] BLR 330, a mediation took place between the claimant and DEFRA, which resulted in settlement. The claimant then sued its former solicitors, Baines Wilson, for the difference between its original claim and the settlement amount. The shortfall was alleged to be due to their negligence in drafting the underlying substantive contract. The solicitors (who did not act for the claimant in the mediation) sought disclosure of communications in the mediation and argued that, by bringing the action against them, the claimant had waived privilege and they needed to know what happened during the mediation to assess the reasonableness of the settlement. The court held that the court should support the mediation process by refusing, in normal circumstances, to order disclosure of documents and communications that took place within mediation. Mediators should be able to conduct mediations confident that, in normal circumstances, their papers would not be seen by the parties or others. The privilege belonged not only to the claimant but also DEFRA. In the absence of waiver of the privilege by DEFRA, the court could not order disclosure of the communications within the mediation.

Can the mediator rely on the without prejudice rule?

14.133 The without prejudice rule exists for the benefit of the parties and it can be waived by them. It is not a privilege of the mediator, so if the parties waive it, the mediator cannot rely on it to prevent non-disclosure of communications arising out of the mediation process or to justify a refusal to give evidence about such communications. This is so even if the mediation agreement contains an express provision as to the without prejudice nature of the mediation process (*Farm Assist Ltd (in liquidation) v The Secretary of State for the Environment, Food and Rural Affairs (No 2)* [2009] BLR 399).

R LEGAL ADVICE PRIVILEGE IN MEDIATION

14.134 Communications passing between a client and their lawyers made for the purposes of giving or receiving legal advice are protected by legal professional privilege (*Three Rivers District Council v Bank of England (No 5)* [2003] QB 1556). Legal advice privilege will also be upheld in mediation. In *Farm Assist Ltd (in liquidation) v Secretary of State for Environment, Food and Rural Affairs* [2008] EWHC 3079, the claimant and the defendant settled the claim at mediation. The claimant then brought separate proceedings against the Secretary of State seeking an order that the settlement reached at mediation should be set aside on the grounds of economic duress. The Secretary of State sought disclosure of documents covered by legal advice privilege both before and during the mediation, consisting of advice about the merits of the claim, the offers to be made during the mediation, and the response to offers made by DEFRA. It was argued that privilege had been impliedly waived by impeaching the settlement on the grounds of economic duress. The court held that waiver of legal advice privilege could only occur in proceedings between the client and the solicitor, and that legal advice privilege was not waived by suing a third party (DEFRA) in these circumstances.

S CONFIDENTIALITY IN MEDIATION

14.135 The mediation agreement will usually stipulate that neither party can reveal any detail of the mediation process or any information obtained during the mediation without the express consent of the other party. A confidentiality clause in the mediation agreement amounts to a contractual promise on the part of all parties to the contract, including the mediator, not to reveal communications made during the mediation. An injunction can be obtained, in certain circumstances, to restrain breach of this obligation (see *Venture Investment Placement Ltd v Hall* [2005] EWHC 1227 (Ch)). Damages could also be claimed for any breach. Even in the absence of an express confidentially clause, one is likely to be implied, because it would destroy the basis of mediation if either party could publicize the matters that took place between them and the mediator. The mediator also owes a duty of confidentiality to the parties. A confidentiality clause adds weight to the without prejudice rule and it may be wider than it.

14.136 In *Aird & Aird v Prime Meridian* [2006] BLR 105, the court accepted that a confidentiality clause reinforces the without prejudice rule. However May LJ went on to state:

> This cannot of course be taken literally, since it would obviously not apply to documents produced for other purposes which were needed for and produced at the mediation, for example their building contract or the antecedent pleadings in the proceedings . . . . but the general intent of the provision is clear, and it accords with the generally understood 'without prejudice' nature of mediation.

14.137 Unless the mediation agreement provides to the contrary, the mere fact that the parties have agreed to try and resolve the dispute by mediation or have had a mediation hearing is not confidential; the confidentiality therefore attaches to the events during the mediation process, rather than the bare fact that the parties are about to or have embarked on mediation.

Example of a confidentiality clause

14.138 Any information, whether written or oral, which is disclosed to a mediator in private will be treated as confidential by the mediator and will not be disclosed to any other party to the dispute or any person whatsoever or to any judge, court, or tribunal unless:

(a) the party making the disclosure agrees that it should be disclosed;
(b) the law requires the mediator to disclose the confidential information;
(c) the mediator believes there is a serious risk to the life or safety of any person if disclosure is not made.

The parties and the mediator also agree that they will not disclose any information arising out of or in connection with mediation, including the facts and terms of settlement, unless they are compelled by law to do so or except insofar as it is necessary to enforce any settlement agreement.

Information given to the mediator

14.139 Any information given to the mediator during the process and in particular anything revealed to him during the private meetings of the parties is protected by the confidentiality obligation. The mediator cannot reveal this information to the other side or any other party unless the party providing the information expressly consents. The duty of confidentiality will apply even after the mediation process has been completed or terminated.

Can the mediator enforce the confidentiality clause?

14.140 The without prejudice rule exists for the benefit of the parties and it can be waived by them. It is not a privilege of the mediator, and cannot be relied on by him. However the express or implied term of confidentiality is different. The court in *Farm Assist Ltd (in liquidation) v The Secretary of State for the Environment, Food and Rural Affairs (No 2)* [2009] BLR 399 accepted that the express (or implied) obligation of confidentiality exists not just between the parties themselves, but also between the parties and the mediator, and so it could only be waived by them all.

14.141 In *Farm Assist*, the claimant sought to set aside an agreement reached with the defendant at the mediation on the basis of economic duress. Both parties waived the without prejudice privilege and confidentiality in the mediation. A witness summons was issued against the mediator, requiring her to attend court to give evidence about the entire events of the mediation, including private conversations she had with each party. The mediator applied to set the summons aside, relying on the confidentiality provision in the mediation agreement. The mediation agreement also provided that the parties would not call the mediator as a witness in any litigation. The court held that confidentiality can be waived but only by the consent of *all* parties. The claimant and the defendant could not waive confidentiality so as to deprive the mediator of her right to have the confidentiality of the mediation preserved. The court accepted that the mediator has an express enforceable right to keep matters confidential under the terms of the mediation agreement. However, it went on to hold that the obligation of confidentiality is not absolute, and the court has power to permit evidence of confidential communications to be given or produced if it is in the *interests of justice* to do so.

When will the court override the confidentiality provisions in the interests of justice?

14.142 It seems likely that the court will override the confidentiality provisions in the absence of agreement by all parties only in exceptional cases.

- In *Farm Assist*, the court did override confidentiality because it was necessary for the court to ascertain what was said and done at the mediation in order to determine whether the agreement reached at the mediation should be set aside for economic duress.
- The interests of justice are also likely to require confidentiality to be overridden by the court if one party is seeking to vitiate an agreement reached at the mediation on the grounds of undue influence or misrepresentation.
- The court is unlikely to allow a mediator to rely on a confidentiality clause so as to prevent the parties from revealing advice given by him during the mediation in respect of any action against him for breach of contract or negligence.
- The court is also likely to override the confidentiality and without prejudice nature of mediation in order to determine a professional negligence claim against solicitors arising out of their conduct of a claim which was settled at mediation or arising out of their conduct at the mediation—see *Youlton v Charles Russell* [2010] EWHC 1032 (Ch).

14.143 To permit confidentiality to be overridden in anything other than in very exceptional and limited circumstances will seriously undermine the mediation process. In view of the strong promotion of mediation by the judiciary, this is unlikely to happen.

Other exceptions to confidentiality

14.144 Confidential information may have to be disclosed by the mediator in some circumstances. These exceptions may also be spelt out in the mediation agreement:

- where disclosure is required by law, for example where disclosure is required under the Proceeds of Crime Act 2002, or the HM Revenue and Customs exercises its statutory powers to compel disclosure. The CMC has prepared a guidance note on the obligations of mediators under the Proceeds of Crime Act 2002, which can be downloaded from www.civilmediation.org;

- to prevent risk of harm to the public at large;
- if the mediator believes there is a risk of significant harm to the health, life, or well-being of a person or a threat to their safety if confidential information is not disclosed. This can arise particularly in a family mediation concerning children; and
- if disclosure is necessary to prevent criminal activity, or prevent the mediator being charged with colluding in the commission of an offence or if a failure to disclose the confidential information may amount in itself to a criminal offence on the part of the mediator.

Following *Farm Assist (No 2)*, the Civil Mediation Council issued Guidance Note No 1 'Mediation Confidentiality', which can be downloaded from its website at www.civilmediation.org. **14.145**

T THE MEDIATOR AS WITNESS

The EU Mediation Directive, Art 7, provides that member states should ensure that mediators should not be compelled to give evidence regarding information arising out of mediation. It does, however, provide for exceptions where all the parties agree or there are public policy considerations that require the mediator to give evidence. The Directive had to be implemented in member states by May 2011 (see Chapter 19). **14.146**

The mediation agreement will also usually contain a clause by which the parties agree not to call the mediator or any of his employees or agents as a witness or expert or consultant in any proceedings. Such a clause was considered in *Farm Assist Ltd (in liquidation) v The Secretary of State for the Environment, Food and Rural Affairs (No 2)* [2009] EWHC 1102 (TCC). However, the clause in that case prevented the parties from calling the mediator as a witness 'in relation to the dispute', meaning the underlying dispute between the parties that gave rise to the mediation. The court (Ramsey J) found that this was different to the dispute that the court was concerned with, namely whether the mediation agreement should be set aside for economic duress. However, the court went on to find that even if the clause did apply to the current dispute '... I do not consider that it would in itself lead to the witness summons being set aside. Rather, it would be a factor for the court to take into account in deciding whether, in the interests of justice, a mediator should be called as a witness.' The court found that it was in the interests of justice that the mediator should give evidence as to what was said and done in the mediation and it therefore dismissed the mediator's application to have the witness summons set aside. **14.147**

The court was unsympathetic to the mediator's submission that she had little recollection of the mediation as it occurred many years ago and she had conducted up to 50 mediations per year in the intervening period. Ramsey J said this (para 53): **14.148**

> Whilst the mediator has clearly said that she has no recollection of the mediation, I accept that this does not prevent her from giving evidence. Frequently memories are jogged and recollections come to mind when documents are shown to witnesses and they have the opportunity to focus, in context, on events some years earlier .... This is a case where, as an exception, the interests of justice lie strongly in favour of evidence being given of what was said and done.

The court will therefore override the mediation agreement, and require a mediator to give evidence, if it is in the interests of justice to do so. In *AB v CD Ltd* [2013] EWHC 1376 (TCC), at the judge's direction, and in order to assist the court to determine whether a binding settlement agreement had been reached between the parties, the mediator was ordered to give evidence as to the events that took place between the parties at the end of the mediation meeting and during the period following the mediation when they tried to reach settlement through the services of the mediator, on what the judge found was an 'ad hoc' basis, following the conclusion of the mediation meeting. **14.149**

Should the law be reformed?

14.150 The EU Directive on Cross-Border Mediation (see Chapter 19) contains a number of provisions on confidentiality of mediation which protect mediators from being required to give evidence in subsequent proceedings. This Directive has been implemented in the United Kingdom and Part 78 of the Civil Procedure Rules has been amended to give effect to the provisions of the Directive (see Chapter 19). However, these provisions currently only apply to mediations in cross-border disputes. The government consulted on implementing these provisions to domestic mediations but it has decided to review how they operate in cross-border cases before doing so.

14.151 There has been some debate amongst those involved in mediation as to whether a mediator would be entitled to refuse to give evidence about private discussions he had with either party during mediation, even if he is ordered to attend court as a witness to give evidence about events that occurred within the mediation. As yet, there is no reported decision on this point. Mr Justice Briggs, as he then was, in two papers published in the *New Law Journal*, suggested that public policy may require a new 'mediation privilege' which is limited to confidential information given to a mediator by one party and which could operate in a similar way to Legal Professional Privilege. This would encourage parties to be as frank with the mediator as they are with their lawyers (see 159 NLJ 506 and 159 NLJ 550).

14.152 Other commentators go further and suggest that there should be a statutory privilege protecting the confidentiality of communications made by the mediator and the parties in the context of mediation. Such statutory protection exists in the United States and more recently, the Law Reform Commission of the Republic of Ireland in its *Report on Alternative Dispute Resolution: Mediation and Conciliation, 2010*, has recommended that communications made in the context of mediation and conciliation should be the subject of a distinct form of privilege which is protected by legislation.

U CAN A MEDIATOR BE SUED?

Legal proceedings

14.153 A mediator acts under a contract made with the parties. It is probably an implied term of the contract that he should perform his services with reasonable care and skill. Theoretically, it is possible that a claim could be brought against a mediator for breach of contract, or in negligence if he acted in a way that was not consistent with his duty of care and skill. This may be the case for example if he gave the parties legal advice in the mediation that was incorrect, or negligently evaluated their claim, or brought undue pressure or misrepresented anything to them in order to persuade them to settle the case. If a mediator took it upon himself to draft the settlement agreement (few mediators will do this), a claim could also be brought against him for negligence in this respect. Such claims are likely to be difficult to prove, and will raise difficult issues of causation (particularly where the parties are independently advised by lawyers who are present at the mediation) and loss.

14.154 If a settlement was reached as a result of undue pressure exerted on that party by a mediator, then this may provide grounds for overturning the settlement agreement. In *Tapoohi v Lewenberg* [2003] VSC 410 an action to overturn a settlement agreement that one party alleged they had entered into as a result of pressure by the mediator was allowed to proceed. The mediator could also be liable if he personally recommends a settlement at a certain level to the parties, if the settlement was unreasonable on the facts of the case (see *McCosh v Williams* [2003] NZCA 192). There have been no cases, as yet, in this jurisdiction in which a mediator has been sued on this basis.

Some mediation agreements will contain an exclusion clause that purports to exclude the mediator from liability for negligence or breach of contact. This may be unenforceable in law or unfair under the Unfair Contract Terms Act 1977. **14.155**

Disciplinary proceedings

It is possible that disciplinary proceedings could be brought against a mediator who acts improperly or not in accordance with the code of conduct adopted by the ADR service provider by whom he was accredited and appointed or by his professional organization. **14.156**

KEY POINTS SUMMARY

- Mediation is a flexible, voluntary, and confidential process. **14.157**
- The parties retain control of the outcome.
- Almost all disputes are suitable for mediation.
- The assistance of a neutral (the mediator) can result in mediation succeeding where direct negotiations have failed.
- Mediation should only be conducted when the issues are clearly defined and the merits and quantum can be evaluated.
- The earlier mediation can be undertaken the greater the saving in costs.
- Mediation is 'without prejudice', although there are exceptions to the rule.
- Mediation is a confidential process but confidentiality can be overridden by the courts in the interests of justice.
- The mediator may be called to give evidence about the mediation if this is in the interests of justice.
- Mediators must act in accordance with ethical standards.
- The European Code of Conduct for Mediators (which has been adopted by the CMC) provides a useful benchmark for determining the minimum rules of professional conduct that should be expected from a mediator. More needs to be done to ensure all mediators are properly accredited and regulated.

15

PREPARATION FOR THE MEDIATION

A INTRODUCTION 15.01
B SELECTING A MEDIATOR 15.03
C THE DURATION OF MEDIATION 15.20
D SELECTING A VENUE 15.22
E THE AGREEMENT TO MEDIATE 15.28
F PRE-MEDIATION MEETING/CONTACT . . . 15.33
G THE ATTENDEES 15.36
H THE POSITION STATEMENTS 15.48
I THE KEY SUPPORTING DOCUMENTS 15.60
J DISCLOSURE OF POSITION STATEMENTS AND DOCUMENTS 15.70
K OTHER DOCUMENTS THAT THE PARTIES MAY WISH TO BRING TO THE MEDIATION 15.71
L OTHER INFORMATION THAT THE MEDIATOR MAY SEEK FROM THE PARTIES BEFORE THE MEDIATION 15.72
M OTHER STEPS THAT NEED TO BE TAKEN TO PREPARE FOR THE MEDIATION 15.73
N CONCLUSION 15.76
Key points summary 15.77

A INTRODUCTION

15.01 Once the parties have decided to use mediation to resolve the dispute, they need to plan for the process. If the parties to the dispute have appointed lawyers, then the lawyers will undertake most of the preparatory work that is required for a mediation. A lawyer will often be required to describe what happens in the mediation process, select and agree the appointment of a suitable mediator, agree the terms of the mediation agreement, locate and book (if necessary) the venue for the mediation, sort out preliminary ground rules for the mediation with the mediator and the other parties such as the documents that need to be prepared and (if necessary) exchanged, whether expert evidence should be sought on any issue in advance of the mediation, and who should attend the mediation on behalf of each party. All of these matters are covered in this chapter, together with practical considerations that lawyers should bear in mind in order to effectively advise on and prepare a client for the mediation process.

15.02 The lawyer who is instructed to attend the mediation will also need to prepare thoroughly for it and this will include consideration of the negotiating strategy and tactics they will employ during the mediation. Chapter 12 describes the preparation a lawyer needs to undertake for a negotiation and that chapter applies with equal force to the preparation a lawyer should undertake when instructed to represent a client in a mediation.

B SELECTING A MEDIATOR

15.03 The parties can approach a mediator directly; alternatively they can engage the services of one of the ADR providers, who will then recommend one or more accredited mediators on their panel, often leaving the final choice to the parties themselves.

If the parties decide to use a mediation provider, then the shortlist of mediators who have the relevant expertise to mediate the dispute will be drawn from its panel. The ADR provider will also administer the mediation process. It is likely to: **15.04**

- arrange the date of the mediation;
- book the venue;
- provide the parties with the mediation agreement;
- ensure that the mediator has no conflict of interest;
- advise on the documents and statements that each party should provide for the mediation; and
- deal with any concerns or queries that the parties may have about the process.

Some ADR providers may offer a fast-track mediation service for parties who book their own date and venue, and only require a mediator, and a discounted rate will usually operate for this more limited service. **15.05**

In large and complex disputes, the parties may need to appoint more than one mediator. If so, then there may be scope for choosing mediators with different styles and areas of expertise, so that a complementary mediation team is selected to mediate the dispute. **15.06**

The qualities required in an effective mediator

A good mediator is someone who will have some or all of the following qualities: good listening and communication skills, strong observation skills for detecting non-verbal behaviour, persistence, determination, diplomacy, incisiveness, empathy and sensitivity, patience, firmness, good attention to detail, the ability to think creatively when resolving a dispute, flexibility, the ability to inspire trust and respect, good analytical skills, skilled questioning techniques, good judgment, relevant mediation experience, excellent negotiation skills and techniques, and a commitment to reaching settlement. A mediator will also, of course, be neutral, impartial, ethical, and have a balanced and even-handed approach to the dispute and the parties. Depending on the nature of the dispute and the needs of the parties, it may also be important for the mediator to have sound knowledge of the legal, technical, or factual issues in dispute. **15.07**

Factors influencing the selection of a mediator

There are a number of other factors that will determine the selection of the mediator. These include the following matters: **15.08**

Personal recommendation

Lawyers for the parties may be able to recommend a particular mediator based on personal experience or based on the recommendation of others in their firm or chambers. ADR organizations will usually also be able to make available feedback from clients on particular mediators that they recommend. **15.09**

Personality

It is important that the parties have trust and confidence in the mediator and that they feel that they can have an open and effective working relationship. The mediator's personality should work with those of the parties. For example, if one of the participants in the process has a robust personality, it may need a mediator with a strong and authoritative personality to enable the mediation to work effectively. **15.10**

Expertise in the subject-matter of the dispute

The parties may want to select a mediator who is familiar with the subject-matter of the dispute. This is also likely to be helpful if expert evidence is to be employed in the mediation. **15.11**

The parties may not want a mediator who has a specialist family law practice to mediate a technical commercial supply contract or a construction dispute. A mediator who has no underlying expertise at all in the subject-matter of the dispute, whether as a lawyer or an expert in the relevant field, is less likely to focus on the relative merits of each case and the likely outcome if the matter went to trial, and will be more interested in devising a creative solution to the problem. Such a mediator is also more likely to adopt a purely facilitative rather than an evaluative approach to mediation (see 14.58–14.64) and may lack sufficient knowledge about the issues to act as an effective 'reality-tester'.

Expertise gained as a lawyer

15.12 In some cases, expertise acquired as a lawyer may well be very desirable. Such a mediator will appreciate the procedural background and practicalities of litigation, the commercial realities of the matter, and the underlying technical issues or the complexities of the legal or factual position of each party. He will also be trained to look at a matter more widely and creatively when facilitating a settlement. Such expertise is also likely to be essential if evaluative mediation is required. In cases involving difficult legal issues a lawyer mediator may be preferred, particularly one who has special expertise in the subject-matter of the dispute.

Expertise gained as a professional in other fields

15.13 A non-lawyer mediator who has expertise in the underlying nature of the dispute, such as an accountant or an engineer may be essential if the underlying issues are so technical that expertise is required to understand them in order to facilitate meaningful negotiations between the parties, or if evaluative mediation is sought. However the mediator's expertise in the subject-matter of the dispute may make it more difficult for him to remain or appear neutral and to keep the parties (and their experts perhaps) focused on reaching settlement rather than debating the merits of complex technical or legal positions.

Preferred style of mediation

15.14 The choice of mediator may also depend on the style of mediation that the parties prefer. Some mediators work in a more facilitative style, preferring to avoid expressing an opinion on the merits of the case. Others will adopt a more evaluative approach. If the parties do wish the mediator to express a view on the merits of their respective cases, or the likely outcome or offer a range for settlement, it will be particularly important to select a mediator who has expertise in the subject-matter of the dispute. See 14.50–14.66 for details on mediation styles.

Practical experience as a mediator

15.15 Care also needs to be taken to select a mediator with relevant practical experience. The parties will want to ensure that the person selected is a trained and accredited mediator, with a proven track record in relation to the mediations they have undertaken. The parties should not be afraid to ask the mediator to provide a detailed curriculum vitae, information about the number and type of mediations he or she has undertaken, the outcome of those mediations, and the names and addresses of referees.

Accreditation

15.16 The mediator selected should also be properly trained and accredited and operate under an appropriate Code of Conduct (see 14.75–14.79).

Interview

15.17 Bearing in mind the points set out above, the parties may wish to draw up a shortlist of suitable prospective mediators and interview them before selecting and engaging the mediator of their choice. At the interview, the parties will be able to explore some of the points made above which are of particular importance to them.

Language and cultural considerations

The parties should consider whether it is necessary to have a mediator who can mediate in the first language of the parties. This is particularly important in a cross-border or international dispute. The mediator should also share or be familiar with the cultural background of the parties, and should be sensitive to cultural diversity. See the guide to choosing the right mediator produced by the International Mediation Institute (IMI) at www.imimediation.org. In cases with an international or European flavour, the IMI also maintains a directory of accredited mediators, which can be found on its website. **15.18**

A team of mediators

Some very complex or multi-party disputes or international disputes may require more than one mediator to be appointed. In such cases, care needs to be taken to ensure the team of mediators contains the right blend of expertise, language skills, age, gender, professional experience and background as well as compatible personalities and mediation styles. The co-mediators need to ensure that they work as a team in all respects. For a useful perspective on co-mediation, see David Richbell, *Mediators on Mediation* (Tottel Publishing), ch 17 and Lawrence Boulle and Miryana Nesic, *Mediator Skills and Techniques: Triangle of Influence* (Bloomsbury Professional, 2010), ch 9. **15.19**

C THE DURATION OF MEDIATION

A typical mediation will last a day, with negotiations not really commencing until some way into the day. However in a case involving few issues or straightforward issues, it may only take half a day. In time-limited, fixed-fee mediations, the mediation will usually last three hours (and the free mediations offered in the Small Claims Court will only last one hour or less). In more complex, multi-party, or high-value cases, it is not uncommon for mediations to last anything between two and five days. Some mediations can also take place on a number of separate occasions arranged over a number of months. This is particularly the case in complex or multi-party disputes or international disputes. A number of meetings also tend to be held in family disputes, particularly in cases involving children. **15.20**

If in doubt about how long the mediation is likely to last, it may be best to book the mediation for one day, but with all parties prepared to adjourn to another day if further time is needed. **15.21**

D SELECTING A VENUE

If the parties are using an ADR provider then they may select and book a suitable venue for the mediation on behalf of the parties and may even have suitable rooms at their own premises. A mediator in private practice may also conduct the mediation in his or her own premises. Otherwise the parties themselves will have to choose the date and select an appropriate venue for the mediation. A number of practical factors will govern the choice of venue, and these include the costs of the venue, the size of the premises required, and the equipment and facilities needed. **15.22**

A neutral venue is likely to be best, such as a hotel, or a designated conference centre because all participants are away from their familiar environment and so are likely to focus more intensely on the issues. **15.23**

The mediation can sometimes be held at the offices of the solicitor for one of the parties, or even in the chambers of counsel for one of the parties or at the premises of one of the parties. **15.24**

These options may make the other side feel at a disadvantage, although they may result in a cost saving.

15.25 Normally at least three rooms will be required, one for the joint meeting, and two separate rooms, one for each of the parties. Ideally a fourth room is desirable for the private use of the mediator, or for joint meetings (if convened) of lawyers or even experts of the parties during the negotiating phase of the mediation. If there are more than two parties, sufficient rooms should be made available to ensure that each of the parties have their own room. In large multi-party disputes it may be possible for parties of a certain class or those united by a common issue to share a room. It is worthwhile checking that the rooms are sound-proofed if they are next door to one another; if they are not, the parties will not feel comfortable having a frank discussion in private meetings.

15.26 The mediation meeting will frequently last all day, and often run into the evening, so this should be borne in mind when selecting a venue. It would be very inconvenient if the venue had to be vacated at 4.30 pm, just when a crucial stage was reached in the negotiations. It is important that suitable refreshment facilities are readily available in or close to the venue. The venue also should be comfortable, conducive to settlement discussions, and equipped with all of the usual facilities such as flip charts (a necessity in all rooms), telephone, facsimile machine, computer and internet points, and photocopying facilities.

15.27 The layout of the main meeting room that will be used for the joint sessions is particularly important. It should not be laid out in an adversarial style resembling that of a courtroom. A room containing a single table large enough to accommodate all of the parties will be more conducive to a successful mediation.

E THE AGREEMENT TO MEDIATE

15.28 In the United Kingdom, with the exception of mediations arranged in employment cases through ACAS, mediation has no form of statutory framework. In most cases, the regulatory framework for mediation derives from the contract between the parties and the mediator, comprised in the agreement to mediate.

15.29 The parties to mediation will be required by the mediator to sign an agreement to mediate before the mediation meeting takes place. The mediator or the ADR service provider that the parties are using will usually send their standard form agreement to the parties in advance of the mediation (see, for example, CEDR's Model Mediation Agreement, 13th edn, in Appendix 1). These standard form agreements are amended from time to time, so check the website for the latest edition at www.cedr.com. The parties will usually be asked to sign a single copy of the agreement at the start of the mediation because psychologically this can help to reinforce their commitment to the process.

15.30 The agreement to mediate represents the contract between the mediator and the parties appointing him. It sets out the terms on which the mediator is appointed and the scope of the mediation.

15.31 Although the detail of the agreement to mediate will differ from mediator to mediator, most agreements contain the following key clauses. The parties may wish to vary the standard form agreements so that they are more specifically tailored to the circumstances of the particular case.

- The scope of the mediation: reference should be made to the dispute that is being referred to mediation. If only some of the issues are being referred to mediation, the agreement should make this clear.

- Practicalities, such as the names of the parties, the identity of those attending the mediation, the date and time and place of the mediation, and confirmation that the parties attending the mediation have authority to settle the case.
- The process is confidential and that the parties will keep confidential all information arising out of or incidental to the mediation (see 14.135–14.145). If the parties are particularly concerned about confidentiality, they may want to tailor this clause to suit their own circumstances.
- Communications passing between the parties and/or the mediator during the mediation process will be protected from disclosure by the 'without prejudice' rule and should not be disclosed to any third party or used in litigation unless it is disclosable by law (see 14.120–14.133).
- The mediator is neutral and impartial and will not reveal confidential information entrusted to him without the consent of the person who provided it, unless he is required to make disclosure as a matter of law (see 14.126–14.133).
- The parties will not call the mediator as a witness in later legal proceedings in connection with the dispute or in relation to any matter arising out of the mediation, or require him to disclose any notes he made during or in relation to the mediation, and they will indemnify him for the costs of resisting or responding to any application that he should do so (see 14.146–14.149).
- The mediation will be conducted under the Code of Practice of the mediator/organization concerned.
- Any settlement reached at the mediation will not be binding on the parties until it is recorded in writing and signed by the parties. This is a common clause that is found in agreements to mediate. The court has considered the nature and effect of this clause in a number of cases. In *Brown v Rice* [2007] EWHC (Ch) 625, the court held that a clause in this form in an agreement to mediate meant that any settlement agreement reached between the parties was not complete or legally enforceable until it was reduced into writing unless that clause was waived or varied or the parties were otherwise not able to rely on it (see 14.129–14.131 for more detail on *Brown v Rice*). More recently, the courts have upheld a settlement agreement which did not fully conform to this clause by finding that an oral agreement to sign an agreed settlement agreement reached at mediation was a collateral agreement, not caught by the clause in the agreement to mediate (see *Universal Satspace (North America) LLC v Kenya* (QB), 20 December 2013 (unrep). In *AB v CD Ltd* [2013] EWHC 1376 (TCC), the court held that the clause did not apply, because the mediation had ended on the defendant rejecting an offer that the claimant agreed could remain open following the conclusion of the mediation meeting, and the counter-offer and continued negotiations between the parties which took place in the following days were not made in the course of the mediation and therefore a legally enforceable settlement agreement came into being on the claimant's solicitors accepting the defendant's latest offer, even though, by that stage, the settlement agreement had not been recorded in writing and signed by the parties, and even though several matters remained to be resolved during the detailed drafting of the Tomlin Order.
- The agreement will also set out the costs of the mediation and who is responsible for paying them.

The courts have recognized that mediation agreements are valid and that they contain enforceable terms (see eg *Brown v Rice* [2007] EWHC (Ch) 625). The courts have also granted an injunction to restrain breach of a confidentiality clause in such an agreement (*Venture Investment Placement v Hall* [2005] EWHC 1227). **15.32**

F PRE-MEDIATION MEETING/CONTACT

15.33 A pre-mediation meeting may have already taken place in order to give the parties information about mediation and to attempt to persuade them to agree to the process (see 14.21–14.23). Once the parties do commit to the process and a mediator has been appointed, it may be necessary to have some form of pre-mediation contact between the mediator and the lawyers for each party (or perhaps even with the parties) to enable the mediator to get a better understanding of the issues in dispute, and to determine whether the typical mediation process (see Chapter 16) needs to be personalized to meet the needs of the parties and the case. If the parties are referred to or seek the assistance of a mediator or broker to help them decide whether to use mediation, or a MIAM takes place, for example in family cases or under one of the court schemes (see Chapter 18), and the parties decide during the mediation information meeting to use mediation, it may be the case that all of these matters can be dealt with at that meeting. However, the mediator will usually get the parties to sign the Agreement to Mediate before discussing the process further.

15.34 If the mediator has had no prior contact with the parties in order to help them decide whether to use mediation, then he or she will usually contact them (or, more usually, their lawyers) by telephone, video or telephoning conferencing technology or by email before the mediation in order to:

- check that the parties understand the process;
- obtain information on any particular needs and objectives that each party may have;
- discuss practical matters such as the venue, the date and time of the mediation, the duration of the mediation, and any special arrangements that need to be made for any of the parties;
- identify the parties who should attend the mediation, advise on the documents to be provided and the preparation that each of the parties should do for the mediation;
- set the timetable for the mediation and the dates by which steps should be taken by each party in order to prepare for the mediation. This is usually also set out in a letter to the parties;
- explore who is intending to take a lead in the negotiations and in the opening plenary session, and the role that the lay clients will have;
- explore with the lawyers, particularly where the lay client is a public body, a company, partnership, or backed by an insurer, that the representative attending the mediation has full authority to settle the dispute whatever emerges during the negotiation process. If he or she has not, the mediator will try to persuade the lawyer to ensure that someone more senior, who has the appropriate authority, attends the mediation;
- form a view of the personalities of the parties involved and the way they interact with the other parties and the strength of feeling they have in respect of the issues;
- discuss how to approach and structure the mediation.

15.35 All of these matters are discussed in detail in the remainder of this chapter.

G THE ATTENDEES

15.36 It is very important to identify all of the relevant individuals who should attend the mediation. Factors influencing the selection of the participants include the following:

- Who has direct knowledge of the key factual issues in the case?
- Who is most closely and personally affected by the dispute or the resolution of it?
- If relevant, who has the appropriate technical expertise?

- Does resolution of any particular issue require expert evidence and the attendance of an expert at the mediation?
- Who has authority to settle the dispute?
- What message will the identity and status of the participants send to the other side?

The key attendees will include the following individuals. 15.37

Representatives of the parties

Each of the parties will have to determine who should attend the mediation. If the parties are individuals, then it is likely that they themselves will almost invariably attend as they will have direct knowledge of the facts and issues in dispute. If the parties are public bodies, companies, or unincorporated associations or a partnership, then the representative will most likely be the person who has the most direct personal knowledge of the issues in the case. The parties will also be permitted to bring any friend or relative with them for support, although these individuals may not be able to enter the mediation rooms due to shortage of space. If they are permitted to enter they may be asked to sign a confidentiality agreement. 15.38

Person with authority to settle

If one of the parties is a firm, company, public body or an unincorporated body, it is important that someone attends who has authority to settle the action up to the maximum value of the claim. A failure to do so may render the mediation ineffective. It will usually be an express term of the agreement to mediate that each party will ensure that the mediation will be attended by someone who has authority to settle the dispute (in so far as this is possible). If it is genuinely impossible for the party who has authority to settle the dispute to attend the mediation, then they should be available throughout the day to be contacted by email and/or by telephone. It is not uncommon to find that the person attending the mediation only has authority (eg from their board, or claims manager) to settle the dispute up to a prescribed limit. If the proposed settlement exceeds that limit, authorization will have to be obtained from another person, and it may not even be possible to obtain it that day. In such cases, the parties may have to conclude the mediation by signing a 'heads of agreement' document that sets out the agreed terms, subject to formal authorization being obtained by one or both parties. This can be risky because there may be no binding settlement until authorization is obtained and the settlement signed, so the parties can resile from their position. An alternative would be to adjourn the mediation until authority has been obtained, or so that the person who has the relevant authority up to the maximum value of the claim can attend the mediation. 15.39

Lawyers

If the parties have instructed lawyers in relation to the dispute, then the lawyers will usually attend the mediation. Usually solicitors acting for the parties will attend the mediation. Counsel may also be instructed to attend instead of or in addition to the instructing solicitor. It is important to have a lawyer present at the mediation to advise the client on offers, concessions, and any overall settlement proposals. If a party is unrepresented, then a pro bono organization such as the Bar Pro Bono Unit, or LawWorks, can be approached to see if free representation can be arranged. The mediator cannot advise any party on the merits of the proposed settlement or about their legal position, so legal representation for each party at the mediation is essential in complex claims, although it can and often will be dispensed with in small claims mediations. 15.40

Insurers

15.41 Thought needs to be given to the position of insurers. If any party is going to be indemnified under a policy of insurance, then a representative of the insurer, who has the requisite authority to settle the claim, may need to attend the mediation, or at least be available on the day so as to approve any settlement.

Interest groups

15.42 Some mediations may involve other parties, such as representatives of the community.

15.43 Once each party has identified the members of the team who will attend the mediation, the other side and the mediator will need to be notified of the names and position of each of the attendees. The identity and position held by the attendees may send a clear message to the other side about the value that a party places on mediation and the commitment they are making to the process.

Experts

15.44 Sometimes (although this is relatively rare) an expert may need to be consulted during the course of the mediation. This may be the case if there are technical issues that an expert may be able to resolve. Sometimes a mediator may need to obtain assistance from an expert to gain a better understanding of the issues in the case. The expert may be one who has already been instructed for the purposes of actual or proposed litigation. He may have been jointly instructed or jointly selected by the parties, following the steps in a pre-action protocol. Each party may have obtained their own expert evidence, in which case the mediator may ask both experts to be present at the mediation. The experts may be able to meet in a 'without prejudice' meeting during the mediation to see if they can narrow the issues and identify areas of agreement or dispute between them, which may make it easier to resolve the dispute.

15.45 It may also be the case that the parties have not yet obtained expert evidence, but they and/or the mediator consider that it would be beneficial for an expert to be instructed for the purposes of the mediation. Any instruction for these purposes will usually be made on a joint basis.

15.46 An expert attending the mediation may make a statement in a joint session (often the opening joint session), and be questioned by the mediator or by the parties on it. If an expert is required to give oral evidence at a joint meeting then this should be agreed with the mediator in advance so that consideration can be given to the extent of the expert's involvement and, in particular, whether the expert should simply be present and available in private meetings to assist the mediator and the parties with technical issues that arise, or whether the expert should give evidence at a joint meeting. For the difference between joint and private meetings, see 16.10 and 16.32–16.37.

Witnesses of fact

15.47 It is very rare for witnesses of fact to be involved in a mediation. However, occasionally, especially where the dispute revolves around the evidence of conflicting factual witnesses, it may be useful for those witnesses to attend the mediation so that the mediator can clarify their accounts, if necessary, either in private meetings or at the opening joint meeting. Even if the witness does not give evidence in the opening joint session, the parties or their lawyers may wish to have key witnesses attend the mediation so that they can answer any issues that arise, or give assistance to the mediator if required.

H THE POSITION STATEMENTS

The mediator may ask each party to provide him or her with a statement setting out their case. This is sometimes referred to as a position statement (which is the term that is used in this text), a case summary, a statement of case, written submission, party statement, or even an issue statement. However, this is only likely to be required in more complex cases. The parties will rarely be asked to prepare a position statement for mediation in small claims. A position statement is not always required for modest value fast-track county court cases referred to a mediator for a fixed-fee mediation through the Civil Mediation Online Directory (see 18.31–18.33). It will usually always be prepared and provided in multi-track cases. However, lawyers acting for parties in mediation may consider that it is useful to prepare one even if it is not formally requested by the mediator. **15.48**

Where a position statement is required by the mediator, he or she will usually stipulate the time limit within which the position statements (and supporting documents) should be provided. This will usually be around 7–14 days in advance of the mediation. **15.49**

On occasions, particularly if the mediation is taking place before proceedings have been issued, the lawyers should consider and canvass with the mediator whether there should be sequential exchange of position statements, with the claimant having the right to reply to the position statement of the defendant. If an ADR order is made by the court, then this may also direct the parties to exchange case summaries and supporting bundles of documents for use in the ADR process (see the example of the Commercial Court's ADR Order in Figure 7.1). **15.50**

The position statement is not intended to be a formal document like a statement of case used in litigation. The document is primarily intended to ensure that the mediator is fully briefed on each side's case. The statements are also usually disclosed to the other party, so they form an important tactical function of giving the opposing party an insight into the strengths of the other side's case, and what they hope to achieve from the mediation. **15.51**

The aims in drafting the position statement

There are no set rules for drafting the opening statement or case summary. However it should not read like a statement of case. It should be written in plain English. The aim in drafting it, as with so many other legal documents, is that it should be concise and precise. **15.52**

The lawyer or party drafting the statement should bear in mind the following matters: **15.53**

- It should be clearly laid out, easy to navigate, with appropriate use being made of headings and subheadings where necessary.
- It should be logically ordered.
- It must be precise.
- It must be concise. Whilst there is no set page length (unless the mediator imposes one), on average it should be between five to ten pages long, and may be shorter than five pages if the case is relatively straightforward. In any case, it should seldom exceed 20 pages.
- It needs to be persuasive. It should set out the key issues in a focused, concise way, rather than being a detailed discursive document that will lack impact due to over-lengthy explanation.

The content of the position statement

It is suggested that the position statement should set out the following requirements as *essential* matters: **15.54**

- *Heading*. It should be headed up with the names and description of the parties (as in a statement of case) and marked 'Without Prejudice and for use in the Mediation only'.

It should clearly identify the party on whose behalf the statement is made (eg 'Position Statement on behalf of the Claimant, Jane Beggs').

- *Formalities*. It should also include the date and time of the mediation, the name of the mediator, the party on whose behalf the statement is made, a list of the individuals attending the mediation on behalf of that party and their connection with the dispute.
- *Facts*. It should briefly outline the key facts of the case and the nature of the matters in complaint.
- *Issues*. It should identify the issues in the case, both legal and factual. The statement should also identify the key issues that are of vital importance to the parties at the date of the mediation. This may be different from the list of all of the factual and legal issues that arise in the case as it involves focusing on the matters that are of primary concern to the party. If these issues are resolved, all else tends to follow or fall away, so the mediation will primarily focus on these issues.
- *Outline of the party's case on the issues*. The statement needs to clearly set out the party's position in relation to each of the issues, and explain why the issues should be resolved in their favour. The statement should make reference to statements of case, key documents or evidence and matters of law that support the party's position. It is important that this document persuades both the mediator and the other side of the merits of the case, and therefore the strength of the party's negotiating position in relation to the disputed issues of fact or law. However, it should be written in a non-confrontational style.
- *The party's interests and objectives*. The key objectives that the party wants to achieve at the mediation should be identified. This section can draw attention to the costs of proceeding to trial, the element of irrecoverable costs, the desire to preserve relationships, the time it will take to resolve the depute if mediation is unsuccessful or any other factors that influenced the party to mediate rather than litigate the dispute. It should also make clear the party's intention to resolve the dispute, if possible, at the mediation, but also that they are prepared to proceed to trial if no reasonable offers are made by the other side.
- *Further information required*. The statement may identify any further information that needs to be obtained before the matter can be resolved.
- *Negotiations*. Any offers, including offers made under Part 36 of the CPR, or concessions that have already been made, should be explained. It should explain why offers have been rejected. If any issues in the case have already been resolved by negotiation, this should also be noted.

15.55 There should be no objection at all to a statement in this form being provided to the other side. However if the case summary is not disclosed to the other side and it is intended to be a confidential document for the mediator's eyes only, this should be clearly stated on the face of the document.

15.56 The parties may also wish to set out an opening offer, or a road map for settlement (for example, if agreement can be reached in relation to the boundary wall, the claimant will abandon its claim on the driveway).

15.57 If proceedings have been issued and the parties have already prepared an agreed case summary and a list of issues, for example for a case management conference in a multi-track case, then these matters do not need to be set out again in the position statement. Reference can simply be made to that document, and a copy can be annexed to the position statement. If the mediation is taking place before proceedings have been issued, it would be helpful if the position statements set out each party's case as fully and clearly as possible, to enable the mediator and the other side to understand the issues in the case and each side's position in respect of them.

15.58 The position statement should always be accompanied by two separate documents, unless the nature of the dispute renders these unnecessary. These two documents should be agreed with the other side and then all parties can refer to them at the mediation:

- *Chronology*: This should include the chronological dates relevant to the complaint, as well as the chronological negotiation history, and a chronological history of the proceedings (if proceedings have been issued).
- *Dramatis personae*: This document is really for the benefit of the mediator. It should identify the parties, their legal advisers, the experts, the witnesses for each side, the insurers (if relevant), and the name of the person or persons for each party who has authority to settle the dispute.

Joint position statement

The parties can also agree to prepare a joint statement that they can both use at the mediation, although such a statement is likely to be limited to the facts, the issues, and an explanation of each party's case in relation to the issues. 15.59

I THE KEY SUPPORTING DOCUMENTS

Each of the parties will have to select and prepare a bundle of key documents for the mediator. These documents will usually support or even prove the assertions and arguments made in the position statement. 15.60

Some parties will wish to send almost all of the documents that they have to the mediator. In a complex commercial dispute, this can run to many boxes of material. If the mediator is charging an hourly rate for preparation and he is required to read several boxes of documents, then the preparation fee alone is going to be substantial. It is usually not helpful to prepare voluminous bundles of documents for use in the mediation. Each party should endeavour to select the key documents only that will help the mediator to identify the issues in the case, support and strengthen their own position in relation to the liability or quantum issues in dispute, or undermine the case of their opponent. The parties should exercise restraint and ensure that they supply the mediator with key documents only. 15.61

Some mediators may stipulate the maximum length of the bundle of documents that should be provided by each party. This should be adhered to unless there are exceptional reasons why a greater volume of documents should be provided. 15.62

When compiling the documents, the lawyers should bear in mind that the documents are necessary to: 15.63

- inform the mediator of the issues in the dispute, the strength of the party's case in relation to those issues or that undermine the position of the other side;
- enable the mediator to adequately test the other side's case;
- support the negotiating stance taken by the party and the objectives it wishes to achieve at the mediation.

If expert evidence is required to resolve the dispute (eg in the case of a share or asset valuation) but it has not yet been obtained, then the parties may need to agree jointly to commission an expert's report prior to the mediation. If this is a relevant matter, it should be raised with the mediator in advance of the mediation. 15.64

Agreed bundle

The parties should co-operate with one another in relation to the documents that are provided to the mediator and produce agreed bundles where possible. This will be particularly important if the mediator has imposed a maximum page number in relation to the supporting documents that should be provided to him. 15.65

15.66 The agreed bundle should consist of:

- statements of case if proceedings have been issued and detailed letters of claim if they have not;
- witness statements that have been disclosed by the parties;
- any expert reports that have been disclosed, or the key sections of those reports (there is usually no need to include appendices), so that the mediator can fully understand the technical issues in the case;
- any case management orders that have been made (so that the mediator understands the procedural timetable governing the dispute), including costs management orders and approved costs budgets.
- Part 36 offers or other offers;
- any key documents that relate to the issues in dispute. It is helpful if these can be grouped together in relation to the issues to which they relate (eg the contract, documents relevant to breach or causation, or documents that have been disclosed relating to quantum, such as medical reports, schedules of loss, loss of earnings documentation, share valuation documents, or computation of loss of profit;
- any other relevant correspondence between the parties.

Confidential bundles

15.67 If a joint bundle of core documents has been agreed, then each party can produce for the mediator, if required, a small bundle of additional documents that they do not wish him to reveal to the other side. The confidential documents could consist of documents setting out the party's view of the case, issues that they may be willing to compromise on, a draft expert's report or witness statement that has not yet been disclosed to the other side or perhaps counsel's opinion on liability or quantum. Care should be taken to mark this bundle as 'strictly confidential' and to explicitly state that the mediator should not disclose them to the other side.

15.68 Sometimes parties will not want to disclose documents in the mediation because they feel that it will adversely affect the chances of settlement being reached. This may be so if proceedings have not yet been issued or disclosure has not yet taken place. The parties do not have to disclose anything if they do not wish to do so. However in choosing not to disclose documents they should bear in mind the provisions of the CPR and the protocols that encourage a 'cards on the table' approach to litigation. If the document would have to be disclosed in the litigation, it may be best to disclose in the mediation. Failure to disclose crucial documents that have a major effect on the case can give rise to a risk of any settlement being overturned on the grounds of misrepresentation or (less likely, as the parties are not in a fiduciary relationship to one another) material non-disclosure.

15.69 If documents are disclosed to the mediator in confidence he will not reveal the existence or content of these documents to the other side. However, from an ethical point of view, the mediator is likely to refuse to communicate any offer or other information to the other side which is directly contradicted by the existence of a confidential document of which he is aware.

J DISCLOSURE OF POSITION STATEMENTS AND DOCUMENTS

15.70 Lawyers acting for the parties should explore with the mediator whether there should be simultaneous or sequential disclosure of position statements and supporting documents. Any documents or position statements that are provided by one party to the mediator will not be disclosed to the other side by the mediator unless the party providing those documents agrees that the mediator has authority to disclose them to the other side. If there is no objection to disclosure, each party may wish to arrange for copies of these documents to be sent directly to the other party or provide additional copies to the mediator or ADR provider with a request that they be sent to the other side.

K OTHER DOCUMENTS THAT THE PARTIES MAY WISH TO BRING TO THE MEDIATION

Although the documents to be provided to the mediator are likely to be limited in scope, it is often useful to ensure that the complete set of papers relating to the dispute is available at the mediation in case reference needs to be made to them to resolve a matter that arises during the process. **15.71**

L OTHER INFORMATION THAT THE MEDIATOR MAY SEEK FROM THE PARTIES BEFORE THE MEDIATION

The mediator may contact one or more of the parties, by telephone or in writing, before the mediation to seek further information. In particular, the mediator may wish to know about the following matters: **15.72**

- clarification or further information about an issue in the case;
- further information about offers or negotiations that have taken place between the parties and why these have been rejected;
- the key objectives of the party and an indication of concessions or offers that they would be willing to make;
- the method of funding for the case. The mediator will want to know whether the claim is funded by a CFA and ATE insurance (particularly for cases with funding arrangements made before 1 April 2013), or publicly funded by the LAA, or whether the client is funded by a DBA as this is likely to have a bearing on any settlement reached (see Chapter 14);
- the nature of any costs orders that may already have been made in the case. These may need to be considered as part of the overall settlement;
- the costs incurred by the parties to date, and the further costs that they are likely to incur if settlement cannot be agreed at the mediation.

M OTHER STEPS THAT NEED TO BE TAKEN TO PREPARE FOR THE MEDIATION

The lawyers acting for each party should ensure that a full risk assessment is carried out in relation to the client's case before the mediation. In particular, they should identify the client's objectives and plan a route map for how these can be achieved in the mediation. This is likely to involve a detailed analysis of the legal and factual merits of the case, the evidence that is available to support the case and the further evidence that could be obtained, consideration of how the client's case on each issue could best be argued and what arguments can be put forward to refute the claims made by the opposing party. This will also include selection of the appropriate negotiation styles and strategies that could usefully be employed during the mediation, planning offers and concessions to be given or demanded, and the calculation of each party's BATNA and WATNA against which the merits of any offer can be assessed. All of these matters are discussed in Chapters 11 and 12 to which reference should be made when preparing for mediation. **15.73**

15.74 It is also important to ensure that a full costs review is carried out before the mediation and the relevant figures are brought to the mediation. A breakdown should be available of the costs and expenses that have been incurred up to the date of the mediation, and the further costs that are likely to be incurred to take the matter to trial, including the likely amount of irrecoverable costs. These figures will be necessary if an overall settlement is reached because the settlement agreement is likely to make provision for costs.

15.75 The key stages that need to be undertaken in preparation for mediation are shown in Figure 15.1.

Figure 15.1 The key stages in preparation for mediation

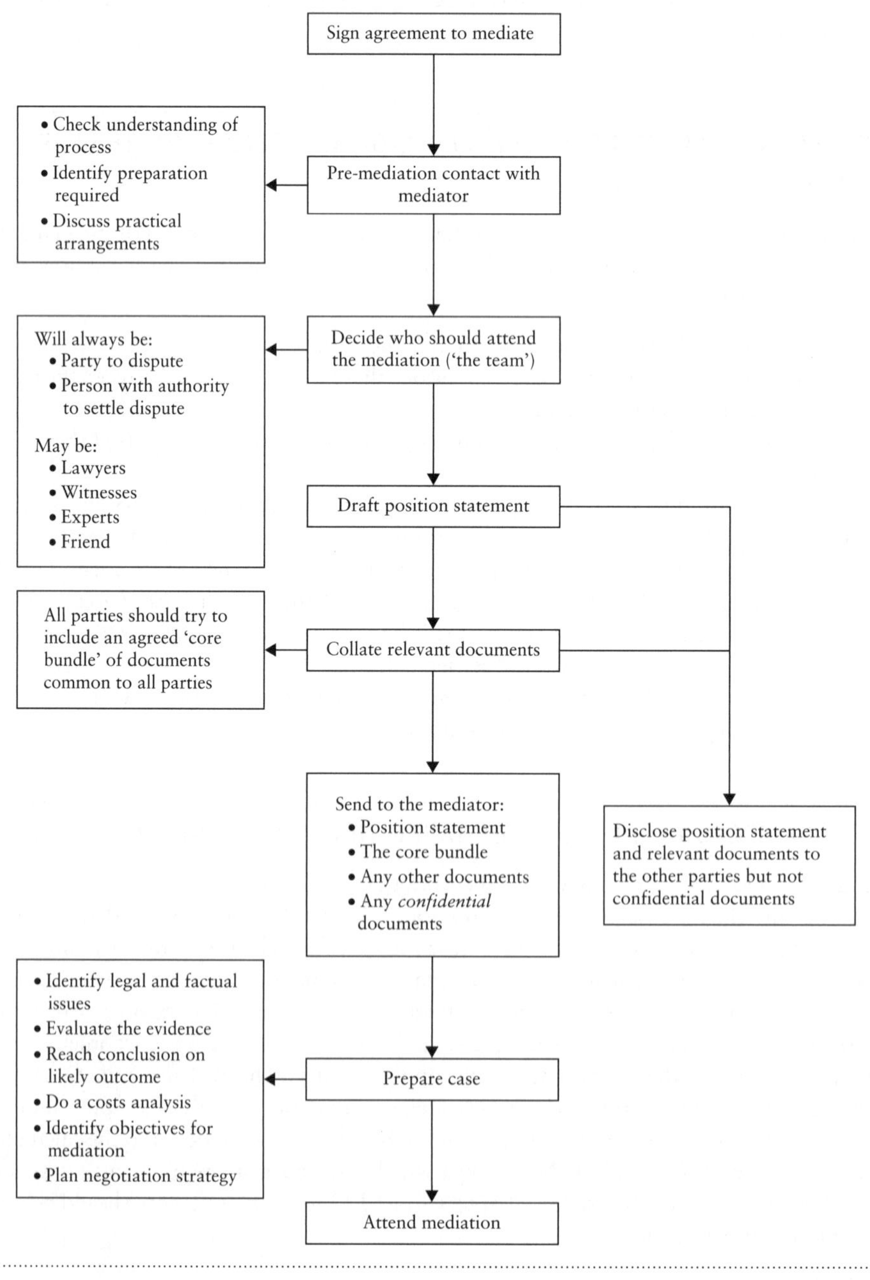

N CONCLUSION

The value of effective preparation for the mediation cannot be underestimated. Effective drafting of position statements and careful compilation of documents will enable a party to influence the mediator so that he is able to be more effective in devising creative solutions and carrying out a 'reality check' with the other side. They will also show the other side the strength of the case. The mediation itself will proceed more effectively and efficiently if each party's position is made clear in advance. In high value cases, the costs of preparation are likely to be very small compared to the sums at stake and the sums that would be spent in litigation or arbitration. However in low value or medium value cases (particularly small claims and fast-track cases) the parties will need to take care to ensure that the costs of preparation remain proportionate to the sums sought to be recovered in the claim. **15.76**

KEY POINTS SUMMARY

- A wide range of factors can influence the choice of mediator. **15.77**
- A suitable venue needs to be chosen for the mediation.
- The parties should agree and sign a Mediation Agreement in advance of the mediation.
- All relevant parties should attend the mediation including someone who has authority to settle the dispute up to the maximum value of the claim.
- Mediation requires thorough preparation. In many cases, this will include the drafting of a Position Statement.
- The lawyer should carry out a legal, factual, evidential, and costs analysis of the case and plan an effective negotiation strategy before attending the mediation.
- The parties should co-operate to produce an agreed bundle of key documents for use in the mediation.

16

THE MEDIATION PROCESS

A WHEN DOES THE MEDIATION START? . . .16.01
B THE STAGES IN MEDIATION 16.06
C THE OPENING STAGE 16.09
D THE EXPLORATION/INFORMATION STAGE 16.38
E THE NEGOTIATING/BARGAINING STAGE 16.42
F JOINT OPEN MEETINGS IN THE EXPLORATION OR BARGAINING STAGE 16.49
G THE SETTLEMENT/CLOSING STAGE 16.52
H THE CLOSING JOINT MEETING 16.58
I TERMINATION AND ADJOURNMENT OF THE MEDIATION 16.59
J THE MEDIATOR'S ROLE FOLLOWING THE CONCLUSION OF THE MEDIATION 16.60
K THE MAIN VARIATIONS IN THE PROCESS 16.65
L THE ROLE OF THE ADVOCATE IN MEDIATION 16.85
Key points summary 16.103

A WHEN DOES THE MEDIATION START?

16.01 It has become increasingly important to know when a mediation starts and ends for a number of reasons:

- In mediations taking place in cross-border disputes, the statutory limitation period is suspended during mediation (see 19. 50–19.55).
- An ADR clause in a contract may require parties to commence or finish mediation by a particular time.
- It may be important to know whether an offer was made during or after the end of the mediation process. This can be illustrated by an issue which arose in *Brown v Rice & Patel* [2007] EWHC 625 (Ch). In that case the mediation agreement contained a fairly typical term to the effect that a settlement reached in the mediation would not be binding until it was reduced to writing and signed by the parties. An issue arose as to whether an oral offer and acceptance was made in the mediation or after the mediation had ended for the purposes of ascertaining whether a legally binding agreement had been made.
- It may be necessary to know if a mediation had commenced or ended for the purposes of ascertaining whether the parties were bound by a particular provision in the mediation agreement at a particular point in time.

16.02 In many cases, it is difficult to pinpoint the moment mediation begins with any accuracy. Does mediation begin when:

- The mediator is appointed?
- The parties pay the mediator's fee in advance?
- The pre-mediation meeting/contact takes place as described in Chapter 15?

- The mediation agreement is signed by each party, or where the parties sign the agreement on different days, at the time on which the last party signed it?
- The substantive mediation meeting takes place?

When the mediation begins and ends can often only be ascertained by examining the intention of the parties from the facts and circumstances of the case. The outcome may not be easy to predict. In *Brown v Rice* [2007] EWHC 625 (Ch), the judge stated [at para 63] that: **16.03**

> Offers made during a mediation are commonly left on the table after the conclusion of the formal mediation hearing itself, in order to enable the parties to reflect and if necessary for the mediator to continue discussions with the parties individually. In my judgment, an acceptance, made after the conclusion of the mediation hearing, of such an offer is just as much made in the mediation as if it was made at the hearing itself.

By contrast, in *AB v CD Ltd* [2013] EWHC 1376, Edwards-Stuart J held that the agreement of the claimants to leave their offer made during the mediation hearing open until after the conclusion of the hearing and the defendant's agreement to consider it did amount to an agreement by the parties to continue the mediation until the defendant either accepted or rejected the offer or it was withdrawn. Once the defendant rejected it, the mediation ended. The continued negotiations between the parties, assisted by the mediator on an ad hoc basis, did not take place in the context of mediation, and so the provisions in the agreement to mediate no longer applied. **16.04**

In the interests of certainty, it would be prudent to give some consideration to the events that will constitute the commencement and termination of the mediation in advance and ensure that this is recorded in the mediation agreement or in correspondence between the parties. If without prejudice negotiations are to continue after the mediation meeting, the parties (and the mediator) should give careful consideration to whether they wish the provisions of the mediation agreement to continue to apply and, if so, they should state this explicitly in writing. **16.05**

B THE STAGES IN MEDIATION

The typical mediation will go through four key stages, which are discussed in detail in this chapter: **16.06**

(1) *The opening stage.* This will consist of introductions and each party setting out their formal position in relation to the issues in the case. It will usually take place in the opening joint session (sometimes called a plenary session, which simply means any session which is attended by representatives of both parties).
(2) *The exploration (or information) stage.* This can take place partly in open joint meetings and partly in closed private meetings, or exclusively in an open joint meeting or alternatively a closed private meeting, depending on the preferences of the parties, the issues in the case and the view of the mediator.
(3) *The negotiation (or bargaining) stage.* This will almost invariably take place in closed private meetings (sometimes referred to as 'caucuses' or 'closed sessions') with the mediator acting as broker between the parties.
(4) *The settlement (or closing) stage.* This will usually take place in joint meetings between all of the parties and/or between the lawyers of the parties who will have the task of drawing up the agreement.

The key stages in the mediation process are shown in Figure 16.1. Although most mediations will go through the stages outlined above, mediation is a flexible process and it is **16.07**

Figure 16.1 The typical mediation process

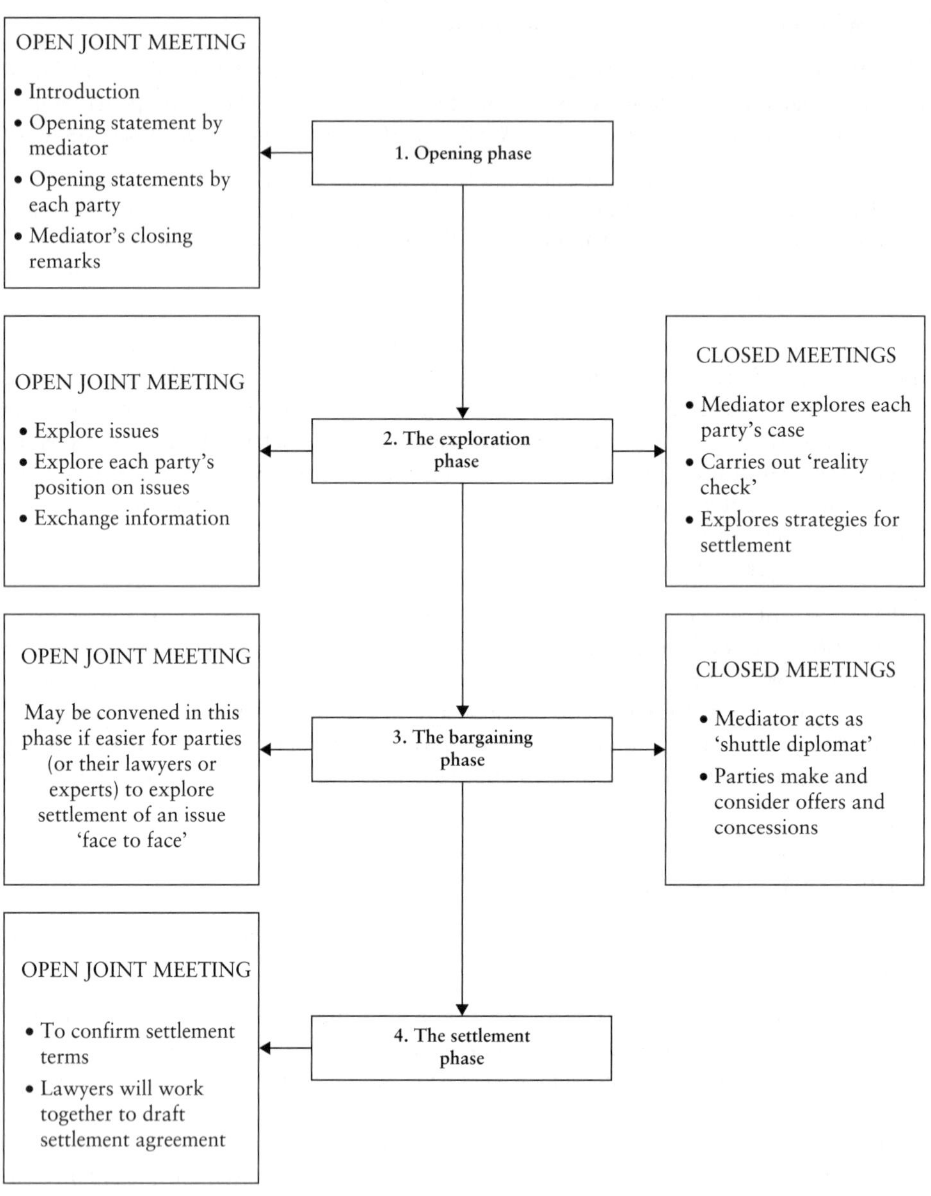

possible to devise a bespoke process to meet the needs of a particular case. In complex cases with multiple issues, the mediation can take place over a number of sessions on different days, with each separate session perhaps focusing on a particular issue. In some cases involving the breakdown of a personal or business relationship such as a partnership, where emotions may run high, it may be beneficial to dispense with all or some part of the opening joint session to lessen the amount of time that the parties spend together. It may be beneficial to have the assistance of expert evidence in some mediations, and that may work best if the expert evidence is received in a meeting other than the main mediation meeting so that the parties have time to consider it. Some mediations may work best if the parties are left to meet together, with or without their lawyers. The mediation process is flexible enough for the parties to personalize it to best fit the facts of the case.

The stages of mediation may not always take place in the strict sequential order described above and not all of the stages will be present in every case. In some mediations, the stages can take place at the same time in relation to different issues. It is quite possible for the parties to be in the bargaining stage in relation to issue one, at the information stage in relation to issue two and even at the settlement phase in relation to issue three all at the same time. 16.08

C THE OPENING STAGE

Introductions

On the day of the mediation, the mediator will usually arrive at the venue early so that he or she can greet the parties as they arrive and show them to their private rooms. Generally, the parties should arrive at the venue in good time for them to be able to have a final conference before the day begins. The mediator is likely to visit the parties in their private rooms before the start of the mediation in order to meet the members of the team in an informal way and to answer any queries about the process or the timetable for the day. The mediator may ask the parties to clarify who will be making the opening statement at the joint meeting and may even briefly discuss the content of the opening statement. The mediator may check how the parties prefer to be addressed, and whether they are comfortable with first names. When everyone has arrived, the mediator will call the parties together for the opening joint meeting. 16.09

The opening joint meeting (plenary session)

The mediator's opening statement

The mediator will direct everyone to their seats and then ask everyone present to introduce themselves. The parties, rather than their lawyers, will usually be seated closest to the mediator. The mediator will take a central position at the table (usually at the end of the table), with the parties on either side of him, usually approximately facing each other unless their relationship is so acrimonious that this would cause tension. The lawyers are likely to sit on the other side of the parties (again usually opposite each other). Any other witnesses, then experts, are likely to be seated on the other side of the lawyers. A diagram showing the typical seating arrangements for joint sessions is set out in Figure 16.2. However the mediator will arrange the parties as he sees fit bearing in mind the relationship between them and the nature of the issues in dispute. 16.10

The mediator will start by asking the parties to introduce themselves (if necessary). The mediator may also ask the parties to sign a copy of the agreement to mediate (even if they have each previously signed a copy provided to them in advance) as doing so can help to reinforce their commitment to the process. The mediator will then open the mediation by making a formal opening statement. The form of the opening will obviously vary from mediator to mediator and will also need to be tailored to the subject-matter of the dispute and the issues that have to be resolved at the mediation. The value of the opening statement cannot be underestimated; it sets the tone for the day and can influence the parties' expectations of and attitude towards the day and encourage them to commit to the process. 16.11

Figure 16.2 A typical seating plan for joint meetings

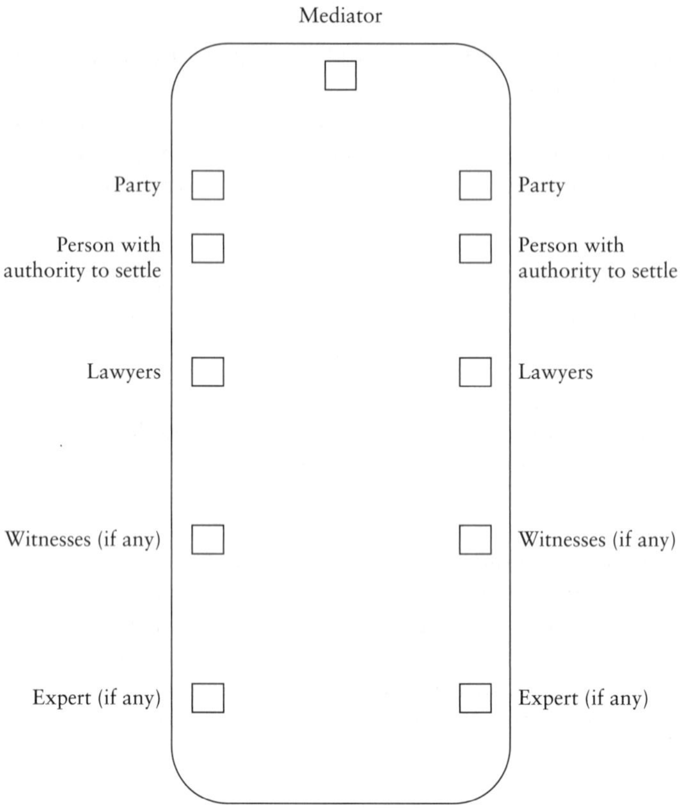

16.12 In the opening statement, the mediator will usually:

- introduce himself or herself and give an outline of his or her qualifications and experience and professional history. This may help the parties to gain confidence in the mediator;
- explain what mediation is about, and perhaps give some general indication of its success rate as a method of dispute resolution. The mediator will explain the course of the mediation, the likely time that each stage of the process will take and the role that each of the parties present will play in it;
- confirm that he or she is neutral and impartial. If he or she has any interest or connection with the parties or the dispute, this will be disclosed;
- explain that the mediator is not there to decide the case, but merely to help the parties reach settlement, that the process is flexible and can be adapted to meet the needs of the parties;
- explain the confidential nature of the mediation process and that anything said during private meetings with the mediator will not be revealed to the other side without the prior express consent of the party making the disclosure;
- explain that anything that occurs during the process cannot be used in subsequent litigation because the mediation process is 'without prejudice'. The mediator is likely to highlight the confidentiality provisions in the mediation agreement that deal with these matters;
- explain the voluntary, non-binding nature of the process and the fact that any or each of the parties can abandon it at any time prior to settlement being reached;

- check that the parties present have authority to settle or, if not, that the person who has ultimate authority is easily contactable by telephone (or email) and will remain so throughout the day;
- explain the procedure in the event that settlement is reached and the need to have a settlement agreement drawn up and signed by the parties before the close of the mediation (unless ratification is required by a board or committee after the mediation).

Opening statements by the parties

The mediator will usually ask each of the parties to outline their case and what they hope to achieve at the conclusion of the dispute. They may do this by reference to the position statement or case summary that they prepared, although they may of course depart from this if they wish. The mediator will ask the other side not to interrupt the party delivering the statement. **16.13**

It is becoming increasingly common for the opening statement to be made by counsel or the solicitor instructed by the party, but it can be delivered by the parties themselves. It should be concise. The mediator may impose a time limit on each party. Generally, each party should aim to make their opening statement in less than 20 minutes, and typically around ten minutes is usual. However the length of the opening will depend on the complexity and number of issues in the case. **16.14**

The rationale for the opening statement is to: **16.15**

- let the parties air their views about the matters in dispute;
- enable the parties to persuade the other side of the strength of their case;
- inform the mediator about the nature of each party's case, so that he or she is in the most informed position from which to facilitate settlement or undertake an evaluative role (if requested) in the mediation;
- point out weaknesses in the other side's case. In effect, the aim is to persuade the other party to take stock of their own case and evaluate it afresh;
- enable the parties to set out the remedy/outcome that they wish to achieve;
- give each party their day in court. Even if the lawyers have delivered the statement, the mediator will almost invariably ask the parties if they wish to add anything and will actively encourage them to do so;
- give the other side (and the mediator) the opportunity to assess the personalities involved in the opposing team and the quality of their arguments and their credibility.

The mediator will fix the order in which the parties are asked to make these statements. The usual order is that the claimant in the dispute will be asked to begin first. **16.16**

Bearing in mind that the purpose of the opening statement is to persuade the other side of the weaknesses of their own case compared to the strengths of the case against them, it should be addressed to the other side, as well as the mediator. In order to persuade the other party and build up a dialogue for negotiation and settlement, good eye contact should be maintained with the other party during the delivery of it. The individuals concerned in the dispute should be referred to courteously by name and title. Some mediators prefer to get the parties at the mediation on first name terms unless they are uncomfortable with this, but sometimes a more formal address such as 'Mr Jones' is to be preferred. However because the opening is delivered directly to the other side, they would not be referred to by description, for example 'the claimant' or 'the claimant's solicitors'. **16.17**

It should be concise yet persuasive. It should aim to cover all of the issues and the strength of the lay client's case in relation to those issues in a focused way that will make a real impact. It should also address the other side's case in relation to those issues, and deal with any arguments that they **16.18** have raised in defence of their position. In doing this, the advocate may wish *briefly* to remind all parties present of key paragraphs in the statements of case, documents, or witness statements that support the lay client's case and that show that the other side's position in relation to the case or issue is much weaker than perhaps they believed it to be. It may also be necessary to explain why the other side's position is wrong or weak as a matter of law. When doing this, it is important to pitch the statement at the right level so that it persuades the parties. It should not be pitched at the level of a judge. It should explain and justify why the party is not prepared to settle at a figure proposed by the other side in any negotiations that took place before the mediation.

16.19 The statement should be delivered with confidence and conviction. Thorough preparation and being totally on top of the issues, law, facts, and evidence will help in presenting the lay client's case in the strongest terms. The advocate should be sensitive and courteous to the other side when delivering the statement. He or she should adopt a reasonable tone that seeks to win over rather than alienate the other side. The advocate may be able to empathize with the other side (for example by expressing regret about an injury) or even explain what happened or what went wrong, whilst still maintaining a strong stance on liability or quantum (or both) on behalf of the lay client.

16.20 If the mediation is to be effective the advocate should ensure that the lay client's willingness to settle the dispute is emphasized. He or she may even offer suggestions for how a settlement could be achieved.

16.21 If the lawyer makes the opening statement on behalf of the client, the client should always be invited to speak at the end of it. The lay client may wish to explain the importance of the case to him or her and state his or her grievances or concerns. The client should be guided to vent grievances in a factual measured way. The aim of the joint meeting is not to escalate or inflame the dispute, but rather to lay the groundwork to enable settlement to be achieved. The lawyers acting for the parties should take great care to explain this to the client. It is often better to ensure that the client vents emotions in the private meetings rather than in the joint meeting.

16.22 The team for each party may divide up the delivery of the opening statement between them, with the lawyer (usually counsel if counsel is present, or the solicitor if not) setting the scene and dealing with the legal merits of each side's case, followed by the lay client who may say a few words about any aspect which is of particular concern to him or her, followed (in some cases, although this is not that common) by an expert if the case raises complex technical issues that call for an expert to be present at the mediation.

16.23 After each party has delivered their opening statement, the mediator will usually ask any other member of the team if they wish to add anything to the opening statement. At the conclusion of each party's opening statement, the mediator may ask questions to clarify anything that is unclear. The mediator will try to frame such questions in an open and neutral way because a closed question (for example, 'You did not heed the large yellow warning notice positioned in the courtyard, did you?') could give the impression that he had formed a view of the merits of the case. The mediator may also give the other side the opportunity to ask questions to clarify any matter that they did not understand. However, such questions should be framed to elicit further information or clarification of an issue. The mediator will not permit the other side to conduct a cross-examination about the submissions made in the opening statements.

16.24 The second party to deliver the opening statement does not have to respond to the first party's statement. Each side should concentrate on their own position, rather than on answering the position of the other side. However if there are points that can be refuted clearly and succinctly, this can be done. The mediator may occasionally allow the first party to reply to something mentioned in the second party's statement, but this is not usual.

Further information about the purpose, content, and delivery of opening statements can be found in Boulle and Nesic, *Mediator Skills and Techniques: Triangle of Influence* (Bloomsbury Professional, 2009), ch 5; and Goodman, *Mediation Advocacy* (2nd edn, Nova), ch 5. **16.25**

Witnesses and experts

Lay witnesses

Sometimes (although this very rarely happens), it is desirable for live evidence to be given at the mediation. This may be necessary if an issue of fact dividing the parties depends on the evidence of a particular witness and an assessment of their credibility by all of the parties. If a party wishes to call any witnesses at the mediation, then this will usually happen after that party has made their opening statement. **16.26**

If a witness is called at the mediation, their evidence will not usually take the form of examination in chief and cross-examination; rather the mediator will ask the witness to give a brief summary of their evidence. The mediator rather than the party calling the witness will usually ask the witness additional questions arising out of his or her evidence. However the mediator may allow each side to ask additional questions of the witness. **16.27**

Expert evidence

The lay witnesses (if any) may be followed by expert evidence (although again, this is rarely necessary). Where there is a dispute between the experts in relation to an important issue in the case, it may be necessary for the parties to reach a view on which expert's opinion is more likely to be accepted by the court before an overall settlement can be reached. The experts can give their evidence at a joint session, or simply be available in private sessions to answer any queries that the parties may have. If the experts do give evidence in a joint session some thought will need to be given as to the form of that evidence. There are two options which may be employed: **16.28**

- The lawyers for the parties can question the experts within a pre-determined time limit.
- The mediator can question the expert, but in doing so he should not cross-examine or challenge the expert because this may cast doubt on his neutrality. The mediator can ask questions that are designed to get at the truth of the matter and enable all present to assess the underlying factual assumptions and the cogency of the reasoning of the expert on a particular point.

Closing the opening joint meeting

When the opening statements have been made, and any relevant witnesses have been heard, the mediator will draw the opening session to a close. The mediator will usually summarize the concerns of the parties and any areas of agreement between them, and the areas they need to resolve in the mediation. He or she will explain that the mediation will now move into the next phase, and that this will take place primarily in private meetings of the parties. The mediator will explain how the private meetings will be conducted and the role that he or she will play in these meetings. The mediator may explain the confidential nature of the private meetings and that he or she will not reveal any information that he obtains during these sessions to the other side without consent. **16.29**

The mediator should set some sort of timetable for these private sessions, and indicate which party he or she will see first and the initial time that is likely to be spent with each party. The mediator should ensure that the parties are given broadly equal amounts of his time during the initial private meetings. After the first private meeting with each party, it is likely that the pace of negotiations will increase and the mediator will be moving from one party to **16.30** another with offers and counter-offers on a very frequent basis and in a way which it would be impossible to timetable.

Extension of the plenary session

16.31 Some mediators may extend the joint opening session in an attempt to get the parties to co-operate with one another or to commence and perhaps even complete the exploratory stage of the mediation in the joint meeting. Such a tactic will not work in all cases, but the process is flexible and can be tailored so that it best meets the needs of the particular case. If the parties are reasonably co-operative and civil towards one another, some mediators have reported that they like to extend the plenary session to do some or all of the following:

- get the parties to agree the key issues that need to be discussed, and to agree the order in which they will deal with these issues (alternatively the mediator will identify the issues and the order of priority and then secure the parties' agreement to the agenda);
- get the parties to work together to explain a particular issue for the benefit of the mediator;
- enable the parties to plug any relevant gaps in the information;
- discuss the figures that comprise the claim and the counterclaim (if any), the costs that each party has incurred to date and the future costs that will be incurred by each party if the dispute is not settled at the mediation. This can be effective in focusing minds on overall figures and settlement, rather than on positional issue-driven bargaining.

The separate private meetings (or closed meetings)

16.32 Almost all mediations will involve the parties spending time in closed meetings. These meetings are sometimes called 'separate private meetings', 'caucuses', or 'closed meetings' to distinguish them from the open joint meetings of the parties. In these meetings the parties will meet privately, without the other side being present, to explore the issues and discuss settlement. This tends to be the key stage in the mediation process. The mediator will attend the private meetings of each party. The key characteristic of these meetings is that any discussion that takes place within them in the presence of the mediator is confidential. To give weight to this confidentiality process, many mediators will not write down any information that they gain during private meetings with the parties unless they are clearly told that the information can be communicated to the other side.

16.33 The key purpose of private meetings is to:

- give the parties privacy to discuss the issues in the case and their own negotiating strategy and proposals for settlement;
- enable the mediator to meet with the parties privately to discuss the dispute and strategies for settlement and to test the reality of their assessment of the case;
- enable the parties to consider proposals from the other side and make a considered response to those proposals. This may be more advantageous than in face-to-face direct negotiations where an instant response of some kind may be required or spontaneously given in the heat of the moment;
- enable the mediator to frame and communicate offers and counter-offers in a constructive way.

16.34 In the closed private meetings, two stages of the mediation usually take place.

- the exploration/information stage (although in some cases, this can take place in a joint session as described above). Some commentators refer to this as the 'problem-solving' stage;
- the negotiating/bargaining stage.

Although these stages usually take place in private meetings, there is nothing to stop the parties and the mediator carrying out these stages of the mediation in an open joint meeting if this would be useful in all the circumstances of the case. Mediation is a very flexible process and the mediator will make use of open and closed meetings in a way that best meets the needs of the parties. **16.35**

Where both the information and bargaining stages take place in closed private meetings, they can happen at the same time, particularly if offers are made early in the process. It may be impossible to draw a clear distinction between the two stages. In other mediations, negotiations will not commence for some time into the process until after the parties have exchanged information and explored positions on the issues in the dispute. However, both stages will feature in almost all mediations to some extent. In some cases, the mediation will be conducted entirely in a joint session (for example, this is usually the norm in family cases, although some mediators are departing from this to some extent nowadays). **16.36**

It is impossible to state with any accuracy the percentage of time spent in the joint or open meetings because the balance between the two will depend on the type of mediation, the subject-matter of the dispute, and the relationship between the parties. To a very large extent, the mediator will go with his or her instinct on the day having observed the parties and the way they are reacting to one another. **16.37**

D THE EXPLORATION/INFORMATION STAGE

In the closed private meetings, in the presence of the mediator, the parties can embark on a rigorous assessment of their case without the other side being present, and without losing face if they revise their positions several times on any issue or in relation to the overall settlement that they hope to achieve. The mediator performs a number of important roles during the closed private meetings and these roles are discussed below. **16.38**

Carrying out a 'reality test'

The neutrality and the 'reality test' that the mediator can provide is an extremely valuable part of the mediation process. The mediator will try to do this as neutrally as possible ('Why', 'What if...?') so as to avoid the perception that he or she is expressing any personal views on the merits of the case. The mediator will carry out a reality check by: **16.39**

- assisting the parties to review and accurately evaluate the strengths and weaknesses of their own case and that of the other side and challenging their factual and legal perceptions about the case;
- focusing each party's attention on gaps in the evidence, facts which they may have difficulty proving at trial, and anything which may affect the court's assessment of the credibility of a particular witness or expert;
- helping the parties to work out what their best, worst, and most realistic case outcomes are if the matter proceeds to trial, together with the costs of legal proceedings, including the element of irrecoverable costs that would be payable even if one party succeeds and gets a judgment and costs order in their favour.

Probing the underlying issues

The mediator will try to work out what concerns and issues underlie the dispute. Many mediators report that the formally presented factual and legal issues in the case are usually only 'the tip of the iceberg'. There are many underlying matters underpinning any dispute, **16.40** such as anger, anxiety, lack of trust, resentment, or competition and economic factors. The mediator will often need to explore these with the parties to assist them to reach a settlement. The mediator may encourage the parties to give vent to their private feelings and concerns (mediators report that if all issues are not brought out in the mediation, the parties have less chance of reaching a settlement they can live with), and absorb these. This fulfils an important role of allowing the parties to 'have their day in court'. This is also cathartic, and the parties are sometimes only able to move forward to resolve the dispute once they have done this.

Devising options for settlement

16.41 The mediator may explore with the parties some or all of the following matters to try to help them to generate options for settlement:

- ask them to consider any wider factors that impact on settlement, such as adverse publicity, the need to maintain a relationship with the other side, damage to reputation, and the effect that a failure to achieve settlement may have on third parties;
- ask them to consider the consequences of a settlement not being reached;
- encourage them to focus on what they could achieve if they were not expending time, money, and energy on the dispute;
- seek to persuade them to evaluate the case in the same way, so that the gap between them is narrowed so that negotiations have a better chance of success;
- require them to focus on their interests (that is commercial and personal needs) rather than their strict legal positions;
- seek to persuade one party to agree to disclose additional documents to the other side, which might encourage some movement in their position;
- encourage them to explore the likely outcome if the litigation proceeds to trial, including the element of irrecoverable costs;
- encourage them to be more creative in looking at options for settlement, particularly options that may not readily be available in court proceedings, but which may nevertheless be of real value to the parties. This can involve consideration of matters that are outside the scope of the dispute and which a court would have no power to order. For example:
  - in a boundary dispute, agreeing to 'sell' a piece of land to the other side for a sum above its true market value that reflects the importance of that small piece of land to the other side;
  - in a commercial case involving the supply of goods, agreeing to supply goods for a prescribed period of time to the other side for an agreed price that is perhaps lower than the usual market price for goods of that type;
  - in a libel case providing a public apology by an agreed method;
  - agreeing to accept damages by way of periodic payments;
  - devising new systems that will prevent a recurrence of the complaint in the future.

E THE NEGOTIATING/BARGAINING STAGE

16.42 At some point during the private meetings, the parties will start to think about putting forward proposals for settlement. They may ask the mediator for guidance on how a proposal or offer should be presented to the other side, and about the value and content of the opening offer and the strategy that they should employ in order to move towards settlement. The mediator will draw on his or her own negotiating experience so as to assist the parties with their negotiations and the mediator will usually do this by helping the parties to move from a positional to a principled negotiating strategy (see Chapter 11) so that a constructive dialogue can take place. The parties may commence with less controversial issues on which agreement can be more readily achieved, before moving to the main contentious issues that need to be resolved. In the later stages of the bargaining phase, small issues may divide the parties and prevent them from reaching overall settlement. Mediation can be more effective than direct negotiation at closing the final gap between the parties and the mediator will employ every skill and technique at his disposal to ensure that the parties make the final push towards settlement. In this stage, the mediator has two main roles and these are described below.

Acting as a shuttle-diplomat

Before the mediator leaves a private meeting with a party, he or she will sum up the discussion that has taken place and any offers or concessions or information that he or she is authorized to communicate to the other side. **16.43**

The mediator will then 'shuttle' between the parties, putting forward offers, concessions, information, and responses to offers for their consideration and generally acting as the intermediary between the parties. This is sometimes referred to as 'shuttle mediation'. The mediator will usually be the judge of when to time offers or concessions and the order in which they should be made during the process, in order to maximize the chances of settlement. **16.44**

There are advantages in the mediator acting as a shuttle diplomat or honest broker in this way: **16.45**

- Offers and concessions made by a mediator will be perceived as having more value than if they had been made by the other side directly.
- It is effective if the parties have a limited range of negotiating skills or the relationship between the parties has broken down.

There are also disadvantages: **16.46**

- The parties are not working together to the same degree.
- Confidential information may be inadvertently leaked by the mediator to the other side.
- The process may take longer.
- It gives the mediator a great deal of control and power.

For these reasons, sometimes rather than engage in 'shuttle mediation', the mediator will convene a joint meeting, so that the parties can negotiate directly between themselves. **16.47**

Devising strategies to help the parties work through deadlock

To move the settlement process forward, some new offer, concession, or information will sometimes have to be placed on the table by the parties, particularly if stalemate has been reached. It is one of the most important parts of the mediator's role to help the parties to explore other remedies and solutions that will enable them to move the settlement discussions forward. The mediator may employ a number of tactics and strategies to move through deadlock, including those set out in 16.38–16.41. **16.48**

- A rigorous reality testing can be undertaken with the parties to get them to reassess their position on the merits.
- The parties can be directed into re-assessing their risk (see Chapter 12).
- One issue can be divided into many, so as to create greater opportunities for settlement. For example if the sticking point is the amount of damages for a breach of contract, that could be divided into several issues consisting of the amount of damages, the amount of

credit that should be given by the claimant, the timing of the payment, how payment will be made, and what interest is payable.

- If one party needs time to absorb and reflect on offers that are made, the mediator may adjourn the mediation to another day, rather than allow the settlement opportunity to be lost altogether.
- If one or more members of a team are effectively frustrating the attempts of the others to settle, the mediator may meet with them individually and encourage them to look at the situation objectively and realistically.
- The mediator may also be able to help the parties to save face in relation to a changing position in a way that cannot be easily achieved in direct negotiations. He may do this, for example, by encouraging the parties to blame him for a proposal, or by reframing the offer to make it seem more attractive, or even by giving a party a 'cop out' for changing position by trying to pin the change of position on matters that emerged during the mediation even if they were obvious and present throughout the process.
- The mediator may suggest that different members of each team should get together to brainstorm settlement options in relation to an issue in the hope that they will introduce new energy into the process;
- If a deadlocked issue could be resolved by obtaining a determination from a third party such as an expert, the mediation could be adjourned for a short time to enable a determination or a non-binding evaluation to be obtained on that issue (see Chapters 24 and 22 respectively). Where an expert is instructed pursuant to a mediation settlement agreement, the appointment of the expert is under the agreement, rather than by a court order, even where the court orders the expert to be appointed pursuant to the agreement that the parties have made, and accordingly, Part 35 of the CPR does not apply to the expert's determination (see *Beauty Star Ltd v Janmohamed* [2014] EWCA Civ 451).
- To bridge the gap in the monetary offers made by the parties, the mediator may suggest, for example, that the claimant accepts less if payment is made immediately, or that the defendant should increase its offer if given a longer period of time in which to pay the agreed sum to the claimant.
- In cases where both teams' lawyers are giving bullish legal advice on an issue, the mediator will work with the parties and their lawyers to help them to appreciate the risks of proceeding to trial.
- The mediator may suggest other options for closing the final gap between the parties such as splitting the difference, tossing a coin to see who wins or loses the final sticking point, one party making a charitable donation instead of a payment to the other side, implementing the agreement in relation to all other matters that have been agreed leaving the remaining issues to go to trial or to be resolved by some other ADR process.
- If the parties agree, the mediator may hold a joint meeting of the parties or the lawyers for the parties or both and suggest terms which he thinks may be mutually acceptable. This is not an evaluation of the merits and neither should it be regarded as the mediator offering his own opinion of the likely outcome. The terms are suggested as a practical and pragmatic solution to the dispute for the consideration of the parties. The parties will then give their response (which can include a revised offer or concession) to these proposals to the mediator in a private meeting.
- If quantum remains the sticking point, the mediator may suggest agreement on liability leaving quantum to be determined by another ADR method at a later date.
- Finally, the mediator may actually advise the parties, by evaluating the dispute and giving them his professional opinion on the likely outcome of it or in respect of an issue raised in it. A mediator who provides an opinion is said to be an evaluative mediator (see 14.58–14.64). Any opinion or advice given by the mediator is not binding on the parties.

F JOINT OPEN MEETINGS IN THE EXPLORATION OR BARGAINING STAGE

Joint meetings of representatives of the parties

The mediator may call the parties together for one or more joint meetings as the day progresses if he or she feels it would help the parties to reach agreement on one issue or an overall settlement. These joint meetings may be attended by the lawyers acting for each party, or by all of the parties and their representatives. Some mediators favour bringing the representatives of the parties together for offers to be made unless the relationship between the parties would make this counter-productive. The mediator is likely to convene a joint meeting during the negotiation phase if it is likely to be more effective for the representatives of the parties to make or explore proposals face to face, rather than through the mediator. **16.49**

Joint meetings between the lay clients

In some mediations, it may be beneficial for the parties to negotiate some or all of the issues directly with one another. This is only likely to be the case if the parties have a reasonable working relationship with one another. Even if the mediator conducts 'shuttle mediation' for most of the bargaining phase, when the negotiations are almost completed, the mediator may often bring the lay clients together to agree the remaining outstanding issues, particularly if the overall settlement is likely to involve a future relationship between the parties. The mediator may also convene a meeting between the lay clients if no movement at all has been made towards settlement in order to explain the benefit of the process and encourage the parties to commit to it. **16.50**

Joint meetings of the experts

If experts are present for each party then joint meetings may be convened between the experts, usually without the representatives of the parties or the parties themselves being present, to see if some agreement can be reached on technical issues or on issues of quantum. **16.51**

G THE SETTLEMENT/CLOSING STAGE

If settlement is reached

If a settlement is reached, the mediator will confirm the terms agreed and ask the lawyers for the parties (if they are present) to draw up the settlement agreement. Whatever form the document takes, the mediator will usually ensure that the parties do not leave the mediation until the agreement is signed by the parties and the mediator as their input is frequently required as the fine points of detail are hammered out between the lawyers. The mediation agreement will usually provide that no settlement is binding on the parties unless it is recorded by the parties and signed by them (see 15.31). Unless this takes place at the mediation, there is always the possibility that the parties may resile from the settlement before the binding agreement has been drawn up. **16.52**

If the parties are represented by lawyers, they will have the task of drawing up the settlement agreement. This will usually be a joint effort of all the lawyers involved. The mediator will, however, oversee the process and will mediate any disagreement that takes place between the parties, or their lawyers, in relation to the detailed terms of the settlement. The lawyers should try to ensure that a laptop computer is brought to the mediation for that purpose, together with some sample precedents. **16.53**

16.54 A number of recent cases have demonstrated how careful lawyers and mediators need to be when drawing up the settlement terms. In *AB v CD Ltd* [2013] EWHC 1376 (TCC), the parties reached agreement shortly after the conclusion of mediation. The defendant alleged that no binding agreement had in fact been reached because the claimant's acceptance of the defendant's offer introduced two new terms: firstly, that the action would be disposed of by a Tomlin order; and secondly, that the payment that the defendant agreed to make to the claimant would be payable within 14 days. The court dismissed both of these points on the basis that professional negligence actions (which this was) are invariably disposed of by Tomlin orders (see 23.46–23.53), and this was envisaged by the negotiations that had taken place between the parties. In relation to time for payment, the court, in effect, implied a term into the agreement and held that parties who are negotiating the settlement of an action by the payment of money must be taken to assume that the period for payment will be 14 days from the date of their agreement unless they have agreed otherwise. The claimant's acceptance therefore did not contain new terms which would have resulted in no binding agreement being created. In *Barden v Commodities Research Unit International (Holdings) Ltd* [2013] EWHC 1633 (Ch), the court had to construe a mediation settlement agreement in order to determine whether a payment was to be made net of tax.

16.55 If the parties are acting in person, the mediator may draw up a heads of agreement or a memorandum of agreed terms and ask the parties to sign it, with the intention of setting out the terms in writing so that the legal representatives of each party can then draw up the formal settlement agreement (perhaps in the form of a Tomlin order) after the mediation. No binding settlement will be achieved, however, until this has been done, so there always remains the possibility that one or more of the parties will have second thoughts about the settlement and try to renege from it. In very simple cases, the mediator may draft a settlement agreement. In order to ensure that a party acting in person fully understands the terms of the settlement and that the settlement is in his best interests, the agreement may provide that it will only be binding if legal advice is obtained within a certain time. The mediator will then maintain contact with the party acting in person after the mediation and oversee the implementation of the agreement.

16.56 Once the final terms of the settlement agreement have been drafted, the mediator will usually convene a final joint meeting of all the parties and will read through the agreement. Once the mediator is satisfied that the agreement fully reflects all of the parties' objectives the parties will be asked to sign it.

If no settlement is reached

16.57 If no settlement is reached, the mediator will record this, and may also set out the reasons why the mediation did not result in settlement. In any event, he is likely to summarize the closing positions of the parties, which may form the baseline for further settlement discussions outside the mediation. In suitable cases, he may invite the parties simply to adjourn the mediation for further information to be obtained, or for the parties to consider their positions. If the parties do not wish to adjourn the mediation, the mediator will remind the parties of the advantages of settlement over litigation and will encourage them to try and close their differences by continuing discussions and negotiations or perhaps by employing some other form of ADR process. He may invite the parties to let their closing offers remain open for acceptance for a limited period of time after the mediation so that the parties can consider them in the meantime. It is important to discuss and agree whether the mediation is to be regarded as continuing during this period for the reasons outlined at 16.03–16.05 and 16.61. If an offer made in the mediation is accepted outside the mediation meeting it may be regarded as a settlement reached in the mediation, so must be recorded in writing to be binding on the parties (*Brown v Rice* [2007] EWHC 625). In fact, many unsuccessful mediations do result in settlement some time after the mediation took place.

H THE CLOSING JOINT MEETING

The mediator will convene the closing meeting if: **16.58**

- a settlement has been reached on all of the issues or on some of the issues, leaving the remainder to be determined by litigation or some other means;
- settlement is not likely to be achieved;
- one of the parties wishes to terminate the mediation;
- the mediation needs to be adjourned eg for an expert to carry out a neutral evaluation of particular issues, for further information to be obtained, or if the day has ended without reaching a settlement but the parties feel that settlement could be achieved if the mediation is adjourned to the next available date.

I TERMINATION AND ADJOURNMENT OF THE MEDIATION

The parties may request an adjournment at any time, to consider proposals, to obtain advice or for any other reason they see fit. The mediation can also be terminated at any time by any of the parties or by the mediator. **16.59**

J THE MEDIATOR'S ROLE FOLLOWING THE CONCLUSION OF THE MEDIATION

In most cases, if mediation does not result in settlement, the mediator will have no further involvement with the case unless, at some future date, the parties refer the dispute back to him for further mediation, or seek his assistance in private negotiations between the parties. The mediator may help to facilitate settlement by conference telephone calls or by correspondence if the parties wish him to do so. **16.60**

In cases where the parties are likely to continue to explore settlement themselves after the mediation, the mediator and the parties should agree whether the mediation has merely been adjourned (so that any further settlement discussions between the parties take place under the terms of the mediation agreement) or whether the mediation has ended, so that any further settlement discussions take place outside of it. This can be important in relation to costs, particularly if the mediation agreement sets out the manner in which the parties will bear the costs of the mediation. It can also be important for determining the form of settlement and for the other reasons mentioned in 16.03–16.05. **16.61**

If the mediation does not result in settlement, the parties may ask the mediator to provide a written opinion on the likely outcome of the dispute or a written settlement recommendation (and thus become an evaluative mediator). A separate fee would be payable for this. **16.62**

If it is clear that the mediator's involvement with the case has come to an end, he or she may return the papers he was given to the parties. However, some mediators will retain their file of papers in case their assistance is required in relation to any matter arising out of the mediation in the future. Some mediators may destroy confidential information that they were given by the parties during the mediation. **16.63**

If settlement is reached at the mediation, the terms of the settlement may state that any dispute about implementation of the settlement must be referred back to the mediator. This is **16.64** not uncommon in complex settlement agreements that require a number of things to be done by the parties to implement the settlement.

K THE MAIN VARIATIONS IN THE PROCESS

16.65 Mediation is designed to be a flexible process. As is mentioned briefly at para 16.06–16.08, the typical stages of the process as described in this chapter can be varied to suit the subject-matter of the dispute and the needs of the parties. For example, in family proceedings, it is rare for the mediator to convene separate meetings with the parties to avoid any impression that he is not completely neutral. In cases that raise public policy or environmental issues the mediation may take place in public before interested parties rather than in private. If the relationship between the parties has broken down completely the mediation can take place in private closed meetings only.

16.66 Full details of the main variations in the process can be found in Laurence Boulle and Miryana Nesic *Mediator Skills and Techniques: Triangle of Influence* (Bloomsbury Professional, 2009), ch 9. The key variants in the process are outlined in the following paragraphs. Reference should also be made to the various mediation schemes described in Chapter 18.

Evaluative mediation

16.67 The parties may, either in advance of the mediation or during the course of the mediation, ask the mediator to give one or both parties a non-binding neutral evaluation of the likely outcome should the case go to trial or an evaluation of the merits of one or more of the issues in the case. The characteristics of an evaluative mediation style are described in more detail at 14.58–14.64.

16.68 An evaluation given in the context of mediation is designed to help the parties themselves to facilitate a settlement of the dispute. However, any such evaluation is likely to favour one side's case over the other and this can lead to:

- a perception that the mediator is not neutral and unbiased and this may destroy the effectiveness of the process.
- a hardening of position on the part of the party whose case is more likely to succeed so unless the other party is prepared to move significantly and offer something close to the evaluation, then the parties will become more entrenched in their positions.

Evaluation of the merits of the case requested by both parties

16.69 An evaluation of the overall merits of the case should only be given if *all* of the parties agree and request this and the mediator is willing and happy to do so. If a mediator is to have this role, this should be agreed at the outset and recorded in the mediation agreement. He is only likely to give an evaluation on the merits of the overall dispute if he has some expertise in the underlying subject-matter of the dispute, and is provided with all relevant documents and information to enable him to properly evaluate the case. He may also be unwilling to do this if each of the parties have lawyers acting for them, as they can properly advise their clients on the likely outcome at trial should settlement not be reached. The evaluation will be given openly and in identical terms to both parties. Evaluation in these terms is rarely undertaken in the UK.

16.70 If a formal non-binding evaluation is sought from the mediator by both parties, it may be advantageous for the evaluation to take place early in the mediation so that the parties can bear it in mind when putting forward proposals for settlement. However, sometimes the mediator may leave the evaluation until near the end of the bargaining phase and then provide his non-binding opinion in a final last-minute effort to help the parties to resolve the differences between them. In giving an evaluation of the likely outcome of the case, or when suggesting a settlement proposal for the consideration of the parties, the mediator must take care not to reveal private and confidential information provided to him by the parties that had a bearing on his evaluation.

Evaluation of one or more issues requested by one party only

A more limited form of evaluation may occur in the exploration or bargaining phase, during private meetings with the parties. One or more of the parties may ask a mediator who is skilled in the particular field, to give his or her opinion about the merits of one or more of the issues in dispute or the range for settlement. Some mediators may be unwilling to do this, but if the mediator does agree, the evaluation is usually requested by and given to one party on a confidential basis. In giving such an evaluation, the mediator is likely to indicate that it is a general 'broad brush' view, given without consideration of all of the evidence and so on. **16.71**

Some commentators and mediators believe that rigorous reality testing is also evaluative, but it is only likely to be so if the mediator strays from playing 'devil's advocate' and inadvertently reveals his own evaluation of the case in the formulation of the questions. **16.72**

MED-ARB

This is a hybrid process which provides that if no settlement can be agreed at the mediation, the parties may invite the mediator to act as arbitrator to determine the dispute and make an award that will be binding or non-binding as agreed by the parties. **16.73**

The main advantage of the process is that the parties have certainty that the dispute will be resolved by one method or the other. The main criticisms of the process revolve around the fact that the same neutral person is both mediator and arbitrator. He or she will therefore be in possession of confidential information provided by the parties, or the parties will be inhibited in providing confidential information to him or her for fear that it could prejudice them in any resulting arbitration. Such a challenge was successfully made on this basis in proceedings to enforce an adjudication award where the adjudicator had previously acted as mediator in *Glencot Development and Design Co Ltd v Ben Barrett & Son (Contractors) Ltd* (unreported, 13 February 2002). This can be overcome by having a different individual to act as mediator and arbitrator, although this is likely to be more costly. **16.74**

The Centre for Effective Dispute Resolution has published a report 'The CEDR Commission on Settlement in International Arbitration' (see www.cedr.com/arbitration) recommending that an arbitration tribunal should facilitate a negotiated settlement unless the parties otherwise agree. It has also published 'CEDR Rules for the Facilitation of Settlement in International Arbitration', which provide for a mediation window to be inserted into the arbitral proceedings at the request of the parties, and when awarding costs the tribunal can take into account any unreasonable refusal by a party to make use of a mediation window. **16.75**

If settlement is agreed at the mediation, the parties may appoint the mediator as arbitrator and ask him or her to draw up the settlement agreement as an arbitration consent award, which would then become enforceable at law. If the parties wish to do this, they should commence the process by an arbitration agreement otherwise, if the dispute is settled by mediation, there will be no 'dispute' within which an arbitral award can be made by consent. **16.76**

ARB-MED

This reverses the process. A simplified form of arbitration takes place first, followed by mediation. The neutral person will make an arbitration award which is sealed and not revealed to **16.77** the parties unless they are unable to reach settlement at the mediation that will follow the arbitration. The same neutral person will change his or her role from arbitrator to mediator. The uncertainty generated by the unknown award often forces the parties to reach a settlement at the mediation. If mediation produces settlement, the arbitral award will not be opened.

16.78 The main criticism of this process is that if mediation results in settlement, the time and money taken to arbitrate the dispute first will have been wasted. There is also the risk that the parties may perceive the mediator as giving some indication of the arbitration award if he or she makes any evaluative comments in relation to the dispute.

16.79 For more detail on med-arb and arb-med, see the paper by Alan L Limbury, 'Hybrid Dispute Resolution Processes—Getting the Best while Avoiding the Worst of Both Worlds?' (January 2010) (published on www.cedr.com).

Telephone mediations

16.80 In some situations, mediation may need to be conducted by telephone rather than in face-to-face meetings. This may happen in:

- the Small Claims Court Mediation Scheme (see Chapter 18);
- if the parties have been restrained by a court order from meeting each other;
- if the parties live a long geographical distance from one another.

16.81 Telephone mediations lack the impact of a meeting and some parties find it very difficult to communicate via a telephone conference call.

16.82 The stages in the telephone mediation process are as follows:

- The mediator will hold pre-mediation discussions with the parties as in the main process. This will take place exclusively by telephone.
- The mediation will take place by a telephone conference, with all the parties being telephoned at the same time by the mediator, so that they can hear what is said, and participate, as if they were present at a joint meeting.
- If separate discussions are needed with the parties (to mimic a separate private meeting), then the telephone conference will be terminated and the mediator will then ring each party on their private telephone line and discuss the case with them in much the same way as he or she would if a private meeting was convened with the parties attending in person.
- The negotiating phase can take place by the mediator acting as shuttle diplomat in separate telephone conversations with the parties, or by the parties making offers and concessions during a joint telephone conference, or a mixture of the two.
- In any event, the mediator should confirm the agreement reached and ensure each party assents by arranging a final joint telephone conference call.
- The mediator may record the terms of the draft agreement in writing and email or fax it to the parties before the end of the joint telephone conference for it to be fully drawn up by their lawyers and signed by the parties.

16.83 There are a number of ADR providers who offer a telephone mediation service.

Mediations conducted online

16.84 Mediation can also take place on the internet (also known as e-Mediation or online mediation). This can be useful if the parties reside in different countries. A number of internet organizations now offer online ADR services (see Chapter 5). Any mediations taking place over the internet will be fully documented by the email and text messaging exchanges that may take place between the various parties, and there may be issues about confidentiality.

It may be possible to arrange virtual meetings via webcam conferencing facilities. It is likely that this will further develop in the future.

L THE ROLE OF THE ADVOCATE IN MEDIATION

Lawyers, whether they are a solicitor or a barrister, will carry out a specific role at a mediation that will involve the exercise of the four main skills in their toolbox. These are: **16.85**

- preparation and case analysis;
- mediation advocacy skills;
- advisory skills;
- drafting skills.

In many cases, the solicitor acting for the party will attend the mediation without instructing counsel. In some cases, however, counsel will be instructed to attend the mediation without a solicitor in attendance. In complex or high value claims, counsel is likely to be instructed to attend the hearing as well as the instructing solicitors. Counsel is also likely to be instructed to attend a mediation on behalf of a child or other person who lacks capacity to conduct legal proceedings on their own behalf. Any settlement reached at the mediation in such cases will only become binding when the approval of the court has been obtained, and counsel's opinion on the merits and quantum of the claim and whether the settlement is reasonable is usually required before the court will approve it. **16.86**

Preparation and case analysis

Preparing effectively for a mediation is just as important as preparing for trial. An advocate who turns up to the mediation without having undertaken a careful analysis of the client's case is not going to be able to persuade the other side of the legal or factual strengths of the case in a joint session or demonstrate to the other side and the mediator that the client's case is likely to succeed at trial. A lawyer who is not properly prepared for mediation will not be in a position to accurately advise the client on offers made by the other side or the extent to which the client should be making reasonable offers and concessions. He or she will not be able to properly guide and advise the client through the mediation process. **16.87**

The advocate instructed to represent a client at a mediation hearing must undertake a great deal of preparation. A thorough analysis of the strengths and weaknesses of the legal, factual, and evidential issues in the case must be carried out and the prospects of success should be evaluated. A thorough analysis of the costs to date, future costs, and the likely element of irrecoverable costs should be carried out. The lawyer should consider the dispute and the position of the client in the broadest possible context, including looking at the practical, commercial, and personal considerations that might influence settlement. Finally, a strategy for the mediation should be devised. All of these matters are dealt with in Chapters 11 and 12 and also see 15.73–15.75. **16.88**

Mediation advocacy

The Standing Council of Mediation Advocates (SCMA) has defined mediation advocacy in the following way (see www.mediationadvocates.org.uk): **16.89**

> Mediation Advocacy is the technique of presenting and arguing a client's position, needs and interests in a non-adversarial way. It recognises the following:-
>
> - The negotiated outcome to a dispute is usually more satisfying, more effective, more workable, more flexible and more durable than an order imposed by a court or other tribunal.
> - The parties to a dispute should control its process and its outcome.

- The parties to a dispute should be assisted by their professional representatives or advisers in coming to a settlement that both deals with all matters in issue and also meets their true needs and wider interests.
- The parties to a dispute should have regard to helping the opposite party secure its needs while at the same time preserving their own.

16.90 SCMA is a multi-disciplinary, cross-professional association established to promote and deliver best practice and professional excellence in mediation advocacy. Its members include barristers' chambers, solicitors' firms, and individual legal, surveyor, and construction professionals who represent parties in civil and commercial mediations in the UK. A useful description of the role of advocates in mediation can be obtained from *Mediation Advocacy* by Andrew Goodman (2nd edn, Nova, 2010).

16.91 There are a number of key differences between mediation and court proceedings, which advocates (and barristers in particular) should bear in mind.

- Mediation is an informal, non-adversarial process.
- There is no opportunity for forensic witness handling skills that are employed in the adversarial process that occurs in the courtroom.
- The aim of the game is not to win, but to ensure that a settlement is reached.
- The focus is on the parties and not the lawyers. The mediator will speak directly to the parties rather than communicating with them through the lawyers. In mediation, the lawyer will have to expect to take a 'back seat' in private meetings with the mediator. The lawyer is a valuable part of the team, but not the leading player in it.
- The mediator will not (usually) be making any determination on the issues on the case, so he does not need to be 'won over' or persuaded of the strength of the lay client's case in the same way as a judge. In saying that it is important that the mediator has a clear appreciation of the merits of the case so that he can effectively counter arguments made by the other side during private meetings with them.
- The mediator is primarily there to facilitate settlement between the parties, not to decide or direct what the outcome should be, and not to give advice on whether any proposed settlement is a reasonable one.

Advisory skills in mediation

16.92 The advocate, whether solicitor or barrister, will have an advisory role in mediation. The advice that the advocate may need to give to his client at mediation covers a wide range of issues:

- The advocate may need to advise the client about whether mediation is suitable, the sanctions that may be imposed if the client unreasonably refuses to mediate, when it should be used, the nature of the process, the role of the mediator, and the roles that each party will play in the process. The lawyer will also give advice on the preparation that needs to be carried out in advance of the main mediation meeting, including the drafting of the position statement. All of these matters are covered in Chapters 8 and 15.
- If the lay client is to deliver part of the opening statement at the opening joint session, the advocate should prepare the lay client to do this.
- The advocate will need to advise the client at mediation about the strengths and weaknesses of their legal position, so that they can evaluate any settlement proposals made by the other side and so that they can make informed offers and concessions themselves as the day progresses.
- The advocate will also be required to give legal advice about issues raised by the other side, the effect of offers and concessions made by the other side and guide the lay client in responding to these.

- The advocate will need to advise the client about offers and concessions that the client may wish to make, or should be advised to make.
- The advocate may need to discuss and agree tactics and a negotiating strategy during the mediation. He may need to 'rein in' a client who wishes to make his best offer first if that would be tactically unwise in the circumstances of the case.
- The advocate will also want to advise the client on any settlement reached during the mediation, and ensure that the agreement is a reasonable one bearing in mind the lay client's underlying interests as well as the merits of his legal position.
- The advocate will also advise the mediator about the issues in the dispute, and the legal and factual strengths of the client's case. This can assist the mediator if he needs to conduct a 'reality test' with the opposing party.

Delivery of the opening statement at the opening joint meeting

It is usual for the advocate to deliver the opening statement in the opening plenary session. **16.93** As is noted above, the purpose of this statement is to persuade the mediator and the other side of the merits of the lay client's case. The advocate should make the statement to the other side, and maintain good eye contact with the other party and their lawyers during the delivery of it. The advocate should seek to persuade the other side of the strength of the case against them. He or she should also acknowledge their concerns and position and try to deal with these. Care must be taken not to construct a wall between the parties, or make it higher than it is already. Instead the opening statement should persuade the other side of the need to dismantle the wall, and show them the route that could be taken or explored during the mediation in order to reach that goal. In delivering the opening statement, it is important to select language that is non-judgmental, non-confrontational, and readily understandable to a lay person. If possible, it can be helpful to explain why differences could have arisen between the parties (eg errors in communication, differences of opinion, mistaken assumptions, etc) whilst still presenting a strong case on behalf of the lay client.

The advocate's role during private closed meetings

During the private meetings, the advocate will seek to persuade the mediator of the merits of **16.94** his client's case and the weaknesses in the other side's case. He may also raise questions that he wishes the mediator to convey to the other side in an effort to obtain further information about their stance on a particular issue, or give the mediator information to pass to the other party. He will discuss the case with the mediator and, if necessary, re-assess the merits of the case and offers and concessions in light of that discussion or following information disclosed during the mediation.

The lawyer will also discuss and explore settlement options in private with the lay client and **16.95** other relevant members of his team, including the timing of offers and concessions and the negotiation strategy to be adopted.

The lawyer also needs to work with the mediator during the closed sessions and embrace **16.96** the skills that the mediator has by virtue of his role and expertise to help further his client's goals. The lawyer can brainstorm ideas and options for settlement with the mediator, and work with the mediator to agree how offers and concessions should be framed or structured so as to be more attractive to the other side. During the private meetings, the mediator may want to know about the client's concerns and the offers or concessions the client is prepared to make. The mediator may ask for an indication of the upper and lower figures that the client is prepared to make or accept so as to establish the parameters for the negotiations. The lawyer will have to decide whether the client's upper and lower limits for negotiations should be revealed at the outset or whether it would be more prudent to reveal the client's position more slowly as the negotiations unfold.

16.97 The lawyer can derive assistance from the mediator when advising a client who has a misguided or unreasonably optimistic assessment of his or her case or position. The lawyer and the mediator can work together to help the lay client come to a more realistic assessment of his or her position and help the client to reach an outcome he or she is happy to live with during the mediation.

16.98 The lawyer should also appreciate that the mediator will wish to talk directly to the lay client during private meetings. The lawyer must be sensitive of the need not to 'take over' the private meetings. The mediator's focus in the private meetings will be on exploring ways to move the settlement process forward with the lay client and the lawyer should respect this and work with the mediator to help the client to achieve a satisfactory outcome.

16.99 During this stage of the mediation, the advocate may propose or be asked by the mediator to meet with the lawyer for the other party in a joint meeting to explore settlement of a particular issue rather than communicate second-hand through the mediator. A joint meeting of lawyers may also be held to enable them to explain their case on a difficult issue to each other in the hope that this will cause some movement in their positions.

Settlement

16.100 If a binding agreement is reached during the mediation process, then the mediation agreement will usually provide for the settlement to be drawn up in writing and signed by the parties before it is regarded as a legally binding contract between the parties. The lawyers' role will be to draft this legal settlement agreement before the close of the mediation. There is always a time pressure in drafting the agreement. The deal is usually struck at the end of the day, but usually no members of the team can be released until the agreement is signed as the drafting of the terms of settlement often throws up points of detail that may need to be further negotiated and agreed between the parties. Reference should be made to Chapter 17 for matters to consider on reaching a negotiated settlement in negotiation or mediation, to Chapter 23 for the options available for recording settlement and to Chapter 32 for consideration of the methods by which settlement agreements can be enforced.

16.101 A number of recent cases have shown that the utmost care needs to be taken when drawing up the settlement agreement and advising the client on its effect. In *Frost v Wake Smith & Tofields Solicitors* [2013] EWCA Civ 772, the parties undertook mediation, but the agreement reached in that mediation was unenforceable. A second mediation therefore took place at which a detailed and legally binding agreement was drawn up. The claimants then sued their lawyers in negligence for failing to ensure that the first mediation ended in a legally binding agreement. The Court of Appeal held that a lawyer owes no duty to the client to ensure that mediation ends in a legally binding agreement. Such an obligation would have been impossible to perform on the facts. It would also be impossible at the outset because a lawyer could not know how a mediation could progress and it was impossible at the conclusion of the mediation because matters had not developed to the point where the parties could reach a final agreement and it was not in the lawyer's powers to fill in the gaps. Tomlinson LJ noted that a more plausible complaint could have been made, but it was not pleaded or pursued at trial, namely that the lawyers were negligent in failing to advise the client that the outcome of the first mediation was not a final and binding agreement from which the other side could not resile. Such a failure to warn or advise could, at best, only lead to the recovery of the wasted expenditure in attempting to enforce the first agreement. In some cases, an immediate and legally binding agreement is possible at mediation, and if that is not achieved as a result of poor drafting on the part of the lawyer, then the client may have a claim in negligence, but that was not the position in this case. See also *Barden v Commodities Research Unit (Holdings) Ltd* [2013] EWHC 1633 (Ch), where the court had to determine the meaning of a settlement agreement reached at mediation.

If it is clear that if an overall settlement cannot be achieved at the mediation, the advocate should ensure that the parties record in writing those issues on which agreement was reached, so as to achieve a narrowing of the issues to be determined at trial. **16.102**

KEY POINTS SUMMARY

- The mediation process is flexible and can be tailored to the needs of the parties. **16.103**
- A typical mediation will go through four stages: opening, exploratory, bargaining, and settlement.
- The mediation will take place in a mixture of joint open meetings and private separate meetings of the parties.
- The opening statement by the parties should be addressed to the other side.
- The mediator will help the parties to work through deadlock in the bargaining phase.
- The advocate in mediation should harness the mediator's skills and work with the mediator to further his client's interests.

17

REACHING A SETTLEMENT

A REACHING AN ORAL AGREEMENT 17.01
B THE ROLE OF THE LAWYER 17.03
C CHECKING COVERAGE AND DETAIL 17.05
D RECORDING THE OUTCOME 17.07
E OPTIONS FOR RECORDING THE SETTLEMENT 17.11
F IF NO AGREEMENT IS REACHED 17.12
G CONTRACTUAL PRINCIPLES 17.13
H ENFORCEMENT OF SETTLEMENT AGREEMENTS 17.14
Key points summary 17.15

A REACHING AN ORAL AGREEMENT

17.01 The reaching of an agreement through a negotiation or mediation will initially constitute an oral contract. In principle an oral agreement is immediately binding, provided it complies with contractual principles. If it is intended that the oral agreement will be subject to some condition such as client approval, or not being binding until it is reduced to writing and signed, this needs to be agreed in advance, as commonly happens in a mediation agreement.

17.02 Reaching an apparent agreement can give a sense of relief, but it is absolutely vital to check that all ends have been tied up and terms are clear. If anything is assumed or left vague, an apparent agreement may fall apart when it comes to making a full record or implementation. The principles that follow apply to both negotiation and mediation, but as regards the process at the end of a mediation and the assistance that a mediator will provide in drawing up terms of settlement see 16.52–16.56. As regards the details of formally recording a settlement and drafting orders see Chapter 23.

B THE ROLE OF THE LAWYER

17.03 In either negotiation or mediation, it is the agreement of the parties that is paramount. A lawyer should only act within instructions, and final approval of terms is a matter for the client. In both processes the role of the lawyer may vary—the lawyer may attend the process with the client, may advise a client before and/or after the process, or in the case of negotiation lawyers may take a primary role in carrying out the settlement process.

17.04 In any event the role of the lawyer is likely to involve:

- advising the client in advance of a settlement process as to what terms of settlement may be appropriate (see Chapters 12 and 15);
- advising the client what terms of settlement to offer, and whether to accept an offer made (see Chapters 12 and 15);
- drafting and/or advising on approving detailed terms of settlement once an agreement is reached.

C CHECKING COVERAGE AND DETAIL

When provisional terms of agreement are reached, whether through negotiation or mediation, the lawyer should do the following: **17.05**

- Double check his or her list of issues to ensure every item is resolved.
- Go through the agreement on each issue to ensure both sides agree exactly what has been agreed. It is not uncommon to find there is a difference of understanding on at least one issue that must be resolved.
- Check that details such as dates for actions to be completed are included.
- If there are still actions to be taken to complete the agreement, e.g. an item to be valued, agree how and when that will happen.
- Ensure you have included all the details relating to figures, such as inclusion of any interest payable (taking into account rate of interest and when it runs from and to), date of payment, any interest or other penalty for late payment etc. If instalment payments have been agreed, there should be absolute certainty as to the time, date, and method for each payment.
- The settlement agreement should also deal with any payment in relation to costs or the parties will pay their own. This may include the costs to date of either party, the costs of litigation to date if proceedings have been issued, and the costs of the negotiation or mediation process itself. A mediation agreement will often provide that the fees and expenses of the mediation should be borne jointly by the parties and that each party is responsible for their own legal costs, but this may be negotiated in the mediation as part of the overall settlement (see Chapters 14 and 16).
- If one party is acting under a CFA or DBA agreement, or has third-party finance then this may be relevant to the terms and implications of a settlement agreement (see Chapter 4).
- Double check all arithmetic. Be clear about what your client gets overall as well as under each head. If both sides are making payments to each other try to combine the figures into one payment—and make sure that figure is right!
- If an apology is to be provided, then the wording of this should be agreed and, if the apology is to be made public, the agreement should set out when and by what means that should happen.
- If one of the settlement terms is that the parties will enter into a new contract, for example because there is an ongoing commercial relationship, the form and terms of that contract should be agreed.
- Check each term is practical and realistic, especially if you are drafting terms that restrict the activities of a party. Attention to the detailed wording of a settlement agreement can be very important as regards sums payable: *Barden v Commodities Research Unit International (Holdings) Limited* [2013] EWHC 1633 (Ch).
- Give thought to methods of enforcement should there be a breach of the terms of the settlement by any party. Penalties may be built into the agreement to ensure compliance.
- Provision may be made for how any disputes arising out of the terms of the settlement be dealt with, e.g. be referred to mediation in the first instance.
- If litigation has already commenced, the settlement agreement should provide for the means by which the litigation will come to an end. This is usually done either by lodging a consent order, staying the action on the terms of the settlement (a Tomlin order), by the claimant applying for the dismissal of the proceedings, or by a consent order made in the proceedings that sets out the terms agreed (for further guidance and sample orders see Chapter 23).
- Check that the agreement on crucial issues, and overall, is within your instructions and reasonably meets your client's objectives. The test is not whether you think it is roughly

fair, but whether the deal is as close to your client's instructions and objectives as is realistically possible.

- Check your client understands the agreement and accepts it. This may be done immediately if the client is present. If not, remind your opponent that the agreement is provisional and subject to client approval.

17.06 This checking process needs to be done carefully. It is not uncommon for a potential agreement to fall apart at this stage. Beware of tactics that may be used by a competitive opponent to try to get more just before final agreement. Note that if a lawyer acts unreasonably in refusing to agree the terms of an order being drawn up following directions from a judge, the lawyer may be liable for costs incurred: *Webb Resolutions Ltd v JV Ltd (t/a Shepherd Chartered Surveyors)* [2013] EWHC 509 (TCC). In a mediation, the mediator should assist in ensuring a provisional agreement is not undermined by unreasonable tactics.

- *Renegotiation of an issue.* One side may claim that the agreement on an issue is not as good as it might be, and will try to renegotiate. Insist that the terms are an oral agreement and cannot now be varied.
- *Adding an issue.* One side may want to add an issue at the last moment, perhaps pretending it was forgotten. Even if it seems a small point, be careful—this may be a tactic to get more and may change the balance of the whole deal.
- *Filling a gap.* One side may suggest there is a small gap in the terms that needs to be filled. Take care that something that may be introduced as minor does not turn out to be a renegotiation or an additional issue.
- *Points of detail.* Getting detail right is important, but can be used tactically as a mask for renegotiation. Try to agree sufficient detail on issues as you go along to avoid this being a potential problem at the end.
- *Confusion.* It may emerge that the parties did not in fact agree a point that they thought had been agreed. This may happen if a party did not express a proposal clearly, or interpreted vague wording in a way favourable to his or her case. Again this is best avoided by clarifying and noting detail as you go along.

D RECORDING THE OUTCOME

17.07 Even if it has taken some time to reach an agreement and those involved are tired, it is vital to record the terms agreed in writing at the end of the negotiation or mediation. Even where the terms are relatively straightforward and the parties trust each other, it is very risky to leave the outcome as an oral contract. It is all too likely that memories of what was agreed will differ, or that one party may on reflection seek to change a detail and the agreement will be lost.

17.08 Very simple terms may be recorded on paper, but it is increasingly common for those acting for the parties to bring a laptop computer to a mediation or negotiation. This can be pre-loaded with possible draft settlement terms and precedents for settlement agreements and orders. This can assist in getting a good settlement as key terms can be thought out in advance and then amended in the light of what has been agreed.

17.09 In a negotiation, it is normal for one or both lawyers to make a note of terms agreed as the negotiation progresses. At the end of the negotiation it is vital to agree the wording of the terms. This should be done accurately as a fresh document. Any crossing out or scribbled notes can cause confusion. It should be agreed what should happen to that note of terms. The note might for example be given to an instructing solicitor to be used as the basis for an exchange of letters, or it may be the basis for reporting to a judge the terms agreed where a negotiation has taken place outside court. A separate copy may be needed for a judge if the terms of agreement are to be taken immediately into court for endorsement in an order.

In a mediation, the mediator will normally lead the process of recording the terms agreed, and insist that the parties sign the terms before they leave. This is likely to be based on notes that the mediator has taken. Some mediation service providers use a pro forma for recording terms of settlement. If the parties are represented by lawyers, they are likely to be asked to draft the settlement. If lawyers are not present, heads of agreement may be signed, and then referred to lawyers for the drafting of a formal settlement or court order. Alternatively the mediator may draft an agreement, but tell the parties the terms will only be binding once the parties have sought legal advice, giving a set period for this to be done. For details see 16.52–16.56. **17.10**

E OPTIONS FOR RECORDING THE SETTLEMENT

The options for recording the terms of a settlement are covered in Chapter 23. An appropriate choice must be made for each case. Note that sometimes more than one option may be needed, for example an interim order may be needed because an injunction has been applied for, with other terms being recorded in an exchange of letters. **17.11**

- *A contract or deed.* The terms of agreement may be drawn up as a contract to be signed by the parties. This is the usual way to record the outcome of a mediation.
- *Exchange of letters.* One solicitor may write out the terms in a letter, with the other side replying to agree those terms. This may be done after a negotiation if it is not thought necessary to record the terms in a separate contract.
- *An interim order.* If the negotiation relates to the terms of an interim application, the terms may be recorded as an interim order to be taken to a judge for approval.
- *A consent order.* The terms may be recorded in a court order by a judge. Note that for a negotiation or mediation this can only be done once proceedings have been issued so a judge has jurisdiction over the case. There is an exception in the case of a cross-border mediation within the EU, in which case there is a procedure for the agreement to be recorded as a consent order under CPR r 78.24, see 19.31–19.40. It can be very difficult to rectify the terms of an order once they have been negotiated and agreed: *Lloyds TSB Bank plc v Crowborough Properties Ltd* [2013] EWCA Civ 107, but there are exceptions. However the court may vary an order if this becomes necessary. See *Community Care North East v Durham County Council* [2012] 1 WLR 338.
- *Endorsement on briefs.* If barristers negotiate and reach a relatively simple agreement the terms may be written onto the backsheet of the brief and signed.

F IF NO AGREEMENT IS REACHED

If no full agreement is reached, there may still be some progress made in mediation or a negotiation. **17.12**

- It may be appropriate to adjourn the attempt to settle rather than abandoning it. If so, the basis on which the process should be resumed should be agreed.
- There may be provisional agreement on some issues. If so, it should be clearly noted which issues have been agreed and on what basis. Is the agreement final so that the point is no longer in issue? If not, on what basis is it provisional? It may be appropriate to confirm this by an exchange of letters or e-mails. This may help to limit the issues to be determined.

- If there has been movement on some issues without agreement being reached, make a note. Extra information may have emerged regarding facts, evidence, or objectives, but remember that the negotiation or mediation process is normally confidential. What has been learned could not normally be used at trial, but may be a basis for reviewing how to progress the case.
- A negotiation or mediation will often provide information on the basis of which a Part 36 offer may be made or updated, see Chapter 4.
- A mediator will often offer to provide the parties with further support in reaching a settlement should they wish it, see Chapter 16.
- Some other form of dispute resolution may still be appropriate. For example if a negotiation does not succeed, a mediation with the clients present might make more progress.

G CONTRACTUAL PRINCIPLES

17.13 A settlement agreement is essentially a contract, and will be bound by contractual principles. The implications of this are, for example:

- The agreement will need to comply with normal contractual principles to be enforceable.
- A party may be able to issue proceedings to set aside a settlement agreement, or defend enforcement proceedings brought in respect of such an agreement, if the contract is vitiated by fraud or misrepresentation, see *Vedatech Corp v Crystal Decisions (UK) Ltd* [2003] EWCA Civ 1066.
- If one of the parties lacks capacity, for example because he or she is a child, then any settlement reached will need the approval of the court and will therefore be conditional on court approval being obtained.
- If one of the parties to the settlement is a public body or a company, the settlement may need to be approved by a committee before it becomes binding. The agreement will therefore again be provisional until it is approved.

H ENFORCEMENT OF SETTLEMENT AGREEMENTS

17.14 A detailed discussion of the methods by which settlement agreements can be enforced can be found in Chapter 32.

KEY POINTS SUMMARY

17.15
- It is very important to check the coverage and detail of a potential settlement fully.
- A potential agreement may be undermined by a failure to agree detail as the settlement process goes forward, or due to tactics in the final stages. Such problems should be avoided as far as possible.
- It is very important to finalize the terms of an agreement at the end of the settlement process.
- There are various ways to record the terms of an agreement and an appropriate method should be identified (see Chapter 23).
- An agreement reached through mediation or negotiation is essentially a contract, so contractual principles will apply.

18

COURT MEDIATION SCHEMES AND OTHER SCHEMES

A INTRODUCTION 18.01
B HISTORIC SCHEMES 18.04
C CURRENT COURT MEDIATION SCHEMES 18.16
D CURRENT MEDIATION INFORMATION PILOT COURT SCHEMES 18.28
E THE CIVIL MEDIATION ONLINE DIRECTORY 18.31
F JUDICIAL MEDIATION SCHEMES 18.34
G MEDIATION IN SPECIFIC CASES 18.46
H MEDIATING MULTI-PARTY DISPUTES 18.76
I OTHER SPECIALIST MEDIATION SCHEMES 18.83
J OTHER MEDIATION PROCESSES 18.84
K RESTORATIVE JUSTICE 18.94
L COMMUNITY MEDIATION 18.97
M PRO BONO MEDIATION AND LAWWORKS 18.101
Key points summary 18.103

A INTRODUCTION

18.01 A number of court and other mediation schemes have developed over recent years. Some of these provide low-cost, time-limited mediations such as the Court of Appeal Mediation Scheme, the Mayor's and City of London County Court Scheme, the Small Claims Court Scheme, and mediation referrals that take place through the Civil Mediation Online Directory, which is maintained by the Ministry of Justice. Some courts also operate judicial mediation schemes (the Family Courts, the Technology and Construction Court, and the Employment Tribunal). More recently, following the introduction of mandatory Mediation Information Assessment Meetings (MIAMs) in family cases, a number of pilot schemes have been set up in some county courts and in the Court of Appeal to see if mandatory referral for consideration of mediation has benefits in other areas.

18.02 There are a growing number of specialist mediation schemes such as the INTA scheme for intellectual property disputes, healthcare sector schemes, and numerous trade association schemes. A small selection of these are mentioned in this chapter. Other, more specialist mediation processes are used in very high-value, high-profile, highly complex claims such as multi-party disputes, deal mediation, consensus building in cases involving public policy issues, project mediation, and the executive tribunal process.

18.03 Whilst community mediation has been used successfully for some time to resolve community disputes, the concept has recently been extended to achieve restorative justice in some criminal cases. These developments are all discussed in this chapter but the topic is so wide that this chapter can only begin to scratch the surface of a rapidly expanding area of work.

B HISTORIC SCHEMES

18.04 A number of mediation pilot schemes took place in the county court, paving the way for the creation of the National Mediation Helpline (which was disbanded with effect from 1 October 2011 and replaced with the Civil Mediation Online Directory (see 18.31–18.33). These schemes were all the subject of research which has done a great deal to influence the development of mediation in the United Kingdom. This section therefore sets out brief details of some of these schemes.

The Central London County Court Voluntary Mediation Pilot Scheme

18.05 In 1996, a pilot scheme was set up in the Central London County Court which offered voluntary mediation in any defended case with a claim above £3,000.

18.06 Under the scheme, parties were offered a voluntary mediation at the court, which was limited to a three-hour slot that took place between 4.30 pm and 7.30 pm. Parties initially paid a fee of £25 each (raised to £100 in 1998) to cover administration costs. Although the scheme was under-used, it was favourably reviewed by those who did use it. The operation of the pilot was reviewed in 1998 by Professor Hazel Genn (see DCA Research Paper 5/98).

18.07 The scheme was rolled out at the Central London County Court between 1998 and 2007.

The Central London County Court Compulsory Mediation Pilot Scheme

18.08 This was set up in 2004 and ran from 1 April 2004 to 31 March 2005. It provided for cases to be automatically and therefore compulsorily referred to mediation unless one or both of the parties gave reasons for objecting to do so. After the decision in *Halsey v Milton Keynes General NHS Trust* [2004] 1 WLR 3002, the judge could not override a party's objections and compel mediation if one party was unwilling to agree to it. If the reference to mediation went ahead, then the proceedings were stayed for an initial period of two months to enable the mediation to proceed (CPR, PD 26B paras 1.1 and 5).

18.09 All cases were automatically referred to the scheme except (see CPR, PD 26B para 2):

- cases on the small claims track;
- cases where one of the parties was a child or a protected person or a person exempt from paying court fees;
- cases in which the court had granted an interim injunction.

18.10 Parties were required to pay for the mediation and the amount of the charge was notified by the court to each party, and was payable within 14 days (CPR, PD 26B para 6). The fee was set at £100 per party.

18.11 The operation of both the voluntary and the compulsory scheme was reviewed by Professors Hazel Genn and Paul Fenn and others in the 2007 report 'Twisting Arms: Court referred and court linked mediation under judicial pressure' (Ministry of Justice Research Series 1/07). This research report showed the following:

- In the compulsory scheme, in 81% of all cases referred in which the court received a reply, one or both parties had objected to the referral. Case management conferences dealing with objections did not generally result in mediation bookings and tended to delay the progress of the case. There was a higher rate of objection in personal injury cases (and this was also the case in the voluntary scheme). Over the year of the pilot, cases in which both parties had initially objected to mediation had a lower settlement rate (48%) than cases where neither party objected (55%). Where mediation had taken place that did not result in settlement, it was felt to have increased overall costs by around £1,000–£2,000.

- In the voluntary scheme, there was a significant increase in the number of mediations following *Dunnett v Railtrack Plc* in 2002. However the settlement rate had declined from 62% in 1998 to below 40% in 2003, and the settlement rate had not exceeded 50% since 1998.
- From both schemes, it was apparent that the motivation and willingness of parties to negotiate and compromise was critical to the success of mediation. Facilitation and encouragement, with appropriate pressure, was felt to be more effective than coercing the parties to mediate. Judicial pressure and fear of costs penalties had resulted in more cases being mediated, but had perhaps brought unwilling parties into the mediation process, which may have accounted for the declining settlement rates since 1999.

The National Mediation Helpline

The National Mediation Helpline (NMH) provided low-cost, fixed-fee, time-limited mediations for disputes in civil and commercial cases. This scheme was administered by the Ministry of Justice (MOJ) in conjunction with the Civil Mediation Council (CMC), but ceased to operate with effect from 1 October 2011. Before it was disbanded, most county court mediation referrals tended to take place using the NMH, with the exception of the Mayor's and City of London County Court Scheme and the Small Claims County Court Scheme (see 18.17–18.18 and 18.19–18.23). The parties in small claims cases could use the NMH, although the service was not free, unlike the Small Claims Mediation Scheme, so there was no incentive for them to use it. Any type of case, proceeding in any track or in any court, could be referred to mediation using the NMH. In practice however, it seemed to be most used for mediating fast-track cases proceeding in the county court. **18.12**

A referral to the NMH could be made by the court or by the parties. If the court made the referral with the consent of the parties, the judge usually stayed the proceedings for 28 days to enable the mediation to take place. **18.13**

The ADR providers who assisted the scheme had to comply with a standard procedure which provided for the ADR provider to take steps within set time frames, and any complaints had to be handled in accordance with the NMH Complaints Procedure. **18.14**

The NMH Scheme was successful, although it did not grow at the same rate as the Small Claims Mediation Scheme. Some commentators suggested that the reason for this may be that solicitors preferred to deal directly with an ADR provider who was known to them rather than use the scheme, which gave them little choice over the selection of the mediator. Around 66% of the cases referred through the NMH resulted in settlement. **18.15**

C CURRENT COURT MEDIATION SCHEMES

Some county courts have their own mediation scheme, as does the Court of Appeal. Some schemes are linked to external ADR providers who supply the mediators, but some may have a mediator attached to the court. **18.16**

The Mayor's and City of London County Court Mediation Scheme

The Mayor's and City of London County Court Scheme was launched in May 2006. It is a fixed-cost, time-limited scheme administered by the City Disputes Panel with the assistance of a number of ADR providers. Mediations take place at the International Dispute **18.17**

Resolution Centre in Fleet Street, London. The cost to each party is £275 plus VAT for a three-hour mediation for claims up to £15,000 and £425 plus VAT for a four-hour mediation. For claims greater than £50,000 a four-hour mediation will cost £550 plus VAT per party. If the mediation extends beyond the fixed time limit any additional fees must be agreed with the mediation administrator.

18.18 In February 2012, Professor Simon Roberts carried out a review into the operation of the first five years of the scheme to 31 May 2011. During that period 106 cases were referred to mediation by the court where both parties agreed (usually this direction was made at the track allocation stage) and the settlement rate achieved over that period was 66%. (The report can be viewed at www.citydisputespanel.org.)

The HMCTS Small Claims Mediation Scheme

18.19 Schemes for mediating small claims track cases (currently, cases up to a value of £10,000) were first piloted in the Exeter and Manchester County Courts. In the Exeter model, the district judge referred suitable cases to solicitor mediators who gave the parties a 30-minute mediation appointment to explore settlement. The Manchester pilot used an in-house court mediator and operated on the basis of one-hour mediation appointments, which initially involved face-to-face meetings and then latterly telephone mediations. It is this model that is primarily followed in the nationwide Small Claims Mediation Service that has been rolled out in the county courts. A further pilot operated in Reading, but this was primarily limited to providing parties with information about mediation.

18.20 The Small Claims Mediation Service was established by Her Majesty's Courts Service (HMCS), now known as the Courts and Tribunals Services (HMCTS) in 2007–08 following the success of the in-house small claims mediation pilot in Manchester County Court. It is a free service for defended small claims cases and it now operates in the county court sitting in all court centres, with the mediators in the employ of HMCTS rather than being paid by the parties. The court will refer the parties to the scheme where the conditions in CPR r 26.4A are satisfied. Rule 26.4A of the CPR came into force on 1 April 2014, and the Small Claims Mediation Pilot Scheme set out in PD 51I was revoked from that date. Small claims cases, with the exception of road traffic accident, personal injury, or housing disrepair claims, or any claim in which a party does not agree to referral, will be automatically referred to the Small Claims Mediation Service if the parties indicate that they agree to mediation. There is nothing to stop the parties agreeing that any case proceeding in the small claims track should be referred for mediation to the Small Claims Mediation Service, even one to which CPR r 26.4A does not apply. If the parties agree to mediate their dispute (and as the service is free, there is little reason for them not to do so), then a court mediator (who is not a member of the judiciary) will contact them usually by telephone. If this is not possible, a meeting can be arranged. The telephone mediations are generally conducted by private discussions with each party rather than in a joint telephone conference call. The mediation, whether conducted by telephone or by a meeting, will typically last about one hour. If the mediation is unsuccessful, then a hearing date is arranged before a district judge. If the court is not notified that a settlement has been agreed, then the claim will be allocated to a track no later than four weeks from the date of the last directions questionnaire (see CPR r 26.5(2AA). It is anticipated that mediation will take place within this four-week period. If the claim is settled by mediation, then the proceedings will automatically be stayed, with permission to apply for judgment for the unpaid balance of the outstanding sum due under the settlement agreement or for the claim to be restored for hearing of the full amount claimed, unless the parties have agreed that the claim is to be discontinued or dismissed (see CPR r 26.4A(5)).

The small claims court scheme has been very successful. It won the 2008 European Crystal Scales of Justice Award given by the European Commission and the Council of Europe for innovative court practice. It also won CEDR's Sector award and was runner up in the Innovation category of The Guardian Public Service Awards. 18.21

The government, in its annual pledge reports, has been monitoring the success of the scheme. The Annual Pledge Report for 2007–08 reported that 3,745 cases had been referred to mediation, with 2,527 of those cases settling at mediation (a success rate of 67.5%). The Report for 2008–09 showed that 9,240 cases had been referred to mediation, with 6,675 settling at that stage (a settlement rate of 72%). At a speech given at the Civil Mediation Council Conference in May 2011, the Justice Minister Jonathan Djanogly stated that as at May 2011, around 10,000 mediations had been conducted under the scheme in each of the previous two years, and the service had a 90% satisfaction rate. The Annual Pledge Reports can be found at www.justice.gov.uk. 18.22

As part of the Reform of Civil Cases (see Chapter 1) the small claims track limit was increased from £5,000 to £10,000 with effect from 1 April 2013. This has resulted in a much greater number of cases being referred for consideration of mediation and many of these will be resolved by mediation under the Small Claims Mediation Service. 18.23

The Court of Appeal Mediation Scheme

The Court of Appeal Mediation Scheme (CAMS) was first set up on a voluntary basis in 1997, although it had a low take-up and a less than 50% success rate. A revised scheme was launched in 2003. With the exception of family cases, the revised scheme is currently administered by CEDR Solve. In family cases, the Court of Appeal will select the mediator from the Law Society's Family Mediation Panel, the UK College of Mediators or the Solicitors' Family Law Association. 18.24

The key features of the scheme are as follows: 18.25

- The court when granting permission to appeal, or when first granting directions in an appeal, will consider whether the appeal should be mediated through CAMS, and the Civil Appeals Office will then notify the parties and CEDR of the court's recommendation. CEDR will then contact the parties and invite them to participate in mediation. There is nothing to stop the parties seeking referral for mediation using CAMS on a voluntary basis, even if the court does not direct them to do so.
- If both parties agree to mediation, CEDR will appoint a mediator from the CAMS panel, which is regulated by the Court of Appeal.
- The parties will usually find and pay for the venue.
- Once the mediator has been appointed, CEDR will agree a date for the mediation with the parties and the mediator and render a fee note in accordance with the fee schedule currently in force for CAMS. The fees are payable no later than seven days before the mediation. The parties will also be sent a draft agreement to mediate, which they must sign by the start of the mediation.
- The preparation for the mediation and the mediation meeting will follow the same steps as those described in Chapters 15 and 16, although no witness of fact or expert witnesses are formally called in appeal mediations, although they can attend and give assistance if required.
- The scheme is entirely voluntary and the parties are free to terminate the mediation at any time and without giving a reason.
- The mediator's role is to facilitate a settlement of the matter.
- The parties can ask the mediator to offer his opinion on issues that arise in the case, although he may not be willing to do so.

- As a condition of entering into the scheme, the parties have to agree not to make any claim in relation to the mediation against the mediator, the court or its officials or CEDR Solve, the administrators of the scheme.
- All discussions in and documents created for the mediation are confidential and 'without prejudice'. The Court of Appeal will receive no report from either the mediator or CEDR as to what happened during a mediation and will make no enquiry about such matters, except to be given confirmation that the mediation did or did not take place, and that settlement was or was not reached so as to end the appeal.
- The mediation is usually completed within three months of referral to CEDR, so there is usually no need to stay the appeal.
- If settlement is reached, the agreement would normally be placed on the court record, although the parties can keep the terms of settlement confidential if they wish.
- The fixed fee for each party is currently set at £850 plus VAT. The fixed fee includes both the fee of the mediator and also CEDR's costs of setting up and administering the mediation. CAMS mediations are expected to take a maximum of five hours. If all parties agree extra hours can be agreed, usually at a cost of £125 per hour plus VAT per party. For very complex cases, or claims with a value above £1 million, CEDR can suggest that a commercial mediation outside CAMS should be arranged, or (subject to court approval) that higher fees should be payable to the mediator if the case proceeds to mediation through CAMS.
- In all cases, parties of limited means who cannot obtain funding from the Legal Aid Agency, may be able to apply for pro bono assistance from LawWorks Mediation, as well as the provision of a mediator free of charge where the appeal involves Litigants in Person on both sides.

The West Midlands Family Mediation Scheme

18.26 This was set up in July 2009 and it aims to offer parties the chance to resolve their dispute by mediation rather than by recourse to the courts. Family mediation providers will operate in local courts, and work with judges to identify cases that are suitable for referral to the scheme.

County court local schemes

18.27 In some areas, mediators have formed a group to serve the county court in the local area. Mediators in the local area draw up a rota to serve the county court at a local centre, and the court usually makes a dedicated room available for the use of the mediator. The judges and the court ushers are pro-active in drawing the attention of the service to court users. The mediators will hold a MIAM (see 18.53–18.55) for the purposes of explaining the benefits and the cost of mediation and assessing whether it would be appropriate for the dispute. The parties will not pay for the MIAM in most cases. If the parties indicate that they are willing to attempt mediation, the court will stay proceedings for this to be done. It is always worth checking the position with the county court sitting in a particular area to see if a local mediation scheme is running in that court.

D CURRENT MEDIATION INFORMATION PILOT COURT SCHEMES

The Birmingham, Manchester, and Central London County Courts Mediation Information Pilot Schemes

18.28 The government has announced that it does not intend to introduce mandatory mediation information sessions for claims in the fast track or the multi-track at the present time.

However it has indicated that it intends to assess the effectiveness of mediation information sessions delivered by various means.

In 2011–12, mediation information pilot schemes have operated in the County Court at Birmingham, Manchester, and Central London. These pilots involved mediators being present at court to hold short meetings with parties in potentially suitable cases for the purposes of informing them of the benefits of mediation with a view to persuading them to mediate. These mediation information sessions operate in a similar way to the Mediation Information Assessment Meeting (MIAM) that currently takes place in family cases (see 18.53–18.55 for more details). The pilots have not yet been evaluated. **18.29**

The Court of Appeal Mediation Pilot Scheme

In March 2012, a new two-year mediation pilot scheme was launched in the Court of Appeal, commencing on 2 April 2012 and applying to all personal injury, clinical negligence, and contract claims where judgment was given for no more than £250,000, including interest but not costs, or where the appeal was against the dismissal of a claim which had a value of not more than £250,000 for which permission had been sought and obtained (or the application for permission had been adjourned). Such cases were automatically referred to CAMS for mediation unless the single judge considering the application for permission to appeal decided it inappropriate to do so. It should be noted that the parties were not coerced into mediation—but the automatic referral to mediation in these cases meant that the parties were mandated to consider it. A refusal to consider mediation ran the risk of a costs penalty (see Chapter 8). **18.30**

E THE CIVIL MEDIATION ONLINE DIRECTORY

This was set up on 1 October 2011 to replace the National Mediation Helpline (see 18.12–18.15). This Online Directory, which is maintained by the Ministry for Justice, can be used by parties to find an ADR provider organization operating in their local area that will carry out a time-limited, low-cost, fixed-fee mediation. The parties must explicitly specify that they found the provider using the Directory when they initially contact the provider for the fixed fees to apply. Only ADR provider organizations that are accredited by the CMC under its Provider Accreditation Scheme (see 14.88–14.91) are eligible to be registered on the Directory. **18.31**

The amount of the fixed fees depend on the value of the claim (which is calculated by adding together the sums claimed in the claim and any counterclaim). **18.32**

- Cases with a value of £5,000 or less will cost each party £50 + VAT for a one-hour mediation and £100 + VAT for a two-hour mediation.
- Cases between £5,000 and £15,000 cost £300 + VAT per party for a three-hour mediation appointment.
- Cases between £15,000 and £50,000 cost £425 + VAT per party for a four-hour mediation.

The fee will be individually negotiated between the parties and the selected provider where the case has a value over £50,000.

It is the parties who will take the initiative in making referrals to the provider of their choice using the Directory. The Online Directory therefore operates differently from the National Mediation Helpline (NMH) because a referral to the NMH could be made by the court. Unlike the NMH, no systems appear to have been agreed between the Ministry of Justice (who operates the Directory) and the Providers who are registered on the Directory in relation to response times and the standard procedure that should be applied by providers once a case is referred to them. The experience of users may therefore differ depending on which **18.33** provider they select. However, the Directory does offer advantages over the NMH in that the parties are able to choose the provider of their choice from amongst those registered on the Directory who operate in their local area.

F JUDICIAL MEDIATION SCHEMES

18.34 Judicial mediation (sometimes referred to as 'in-court mediation') is carried out in three main areas, each of which are considered in turn:

- the Technology and Construction Court (the Court Settlement Process);
- in family cases (by the Dispute Resolution Hearing);
- in the Employment Tribunal.

18.35 Mediation carried out by judges is not free from controversy and the debate is summarized in Brown and Marriott's *ADR Principles and Practice* (3rd edn, Sweet & Maxwell, 2011). Some commentators believe that it is not a proper exercise of the judicial function, which is to determine the rights and obligations of the parties according to the law based on a fair trial and the rules of natural justice. Judges are trained to be evaluative rather than facilitative and this may not necessarily be appropriate in the context of mediation. During mediation, a party will usually have private and confidential discussions with the judge as mediator and this is at odds with the concepts of impartiality and neutrality which are the cornerstones of the judicial system.

18.36 On the other hand, the neutrality, impartiality, clear analytical skills and familiarity with the underlying law which is relevant to the dispute could also be said to make judges excellent 'reality checkers' so as to facilitate effective negotiations between the parties. Judges are also likely to be highly effective evaluative mediators and any view they express as to the likely outcome of trial is likely to have a strong influence on the parties. There may also be a costs saving to the parties as they do not (usually) have to pay a fee to judges carrying out a mediation function and the mediation will also take place in the court premises.

The Court Settlement Process in the Technology and Construction Court

18.37 The Court Settlement Process (CSP) was initially operated as a pilot scheme but it is now set out in the Technology and Construction Court Guide (2nd edn, Second Revision, October 2010). The CSP is a form of mediation carried out by the assigned or another TCC judge with the consent of the parties. The process and the procedure will be regulated by the Court Settlement Order which will be made, with appropriate modifications, in the form set out in Appendix G of the Guide. Further information about this judicial mediation scheme can be found at www.tecsa.org.uk/mediation_adr-1328.htm.

18.38 The main features of the process are as follows:

- It is a private and confidential, without prejudice, voluntary, non-binding process.
- The Settlement Judge (in effect, the mediator) can conduct the CSP in any manner he or she considers appropriate, taking into account the wishes of the parties and the circumstances of the case and the overriding objective.
- A Preliminary Court Settlement Conference will take place to determine the procedure, the venue, duration, and disclosure to be made by the parties (and provided to the judge) in advance of the CSP.
- Unless the parties otherwise agree, during the CSP, the Settlement Judge may communicate with the parties together or separately, including private meetings at which the Settlement Judge can express views on the dispute. A party can request a private meeting with the Settlement Judge during the process.

- The Settlement Judge will not disclose information given to him or her in confidence by one party to the other party or to any other person at any time.
- If the CSP does not lead to settlement, the parties can ask the Settlement Judge to provide them with a written assessment on some or all of the issues in the dispute, the likely outcome of the case, and what would be an appropriate settlement.
- Nothing said during the CSP shall prejudice the position of the parties in the litigation or subsequent arbitration or adjudication.
- Parties shall bear their own costs and share equally in the court costs of the CSP, unless otherwise agreed.
- The Settlement Judge will perform no further 'judging' role in the litigation and nor can he or she be called as a witness in any proceedings arising out or connected with the CSP and also has the same immunity from suit as judges in court proceedings.

Research has been carried out on this judicial scheme by Nicholas Gould, Claire King and Phillip Britton—see 'Mediating Construction Disputes: An Evaluation of Existing Practice' (London, Kings College, Centre of Construction Law and Dispute Resolution, 2010). The report can be downloaded from www.fenwickelliott.com/mediating-construction-disputes-download. **18.39**

Judicial mediation in family cases

Judicial mediation in family cases currently takes place in two areas, disputes in relation to children and in applications for financial remedies following marriage breakdown. **18.40**

Where the Child Arrangements Programme applies in respect of disputes relating to children, under FPR, PD 12B (which came into effect on 22 April 2014), parents are expected to resolve their disputes out of court. The Legal Aid Agency will provide public funding for eligible parties to participate in family mediation. With very limited exceptions, an application to the court for determination of most issues involving a child can only be made after a MIAM has taken place, at which meeting mediation and other forms of dispute resolution will have been considered (see FPR, PD 12B, para 8.1). Where an application is made to the court, a First Hearing Dispute Resolution Appointment (FHDRA) will take place within four weeks following the issuing of the application. At the FHDRA, the judge working with the officer from Cafcass (the Children and Family Court Advisory and Support Service) will seek to assist the parties with the resolution of any disputes by discussing with them the nature of the dispute and whether it could be resolved by mediation or some other form of ADR (see PD 12B, para 14.11). **18.41**

Applications for financial remedies where couples are divorcing are dealt with in Part 9 of FPR 2010. This provides for a mandatory Financial Dispute Resolution (FDR) hearing at which a District Judge will facilitate and assist in open discussion and negotiations with a view to settlement of the dispute (see FPR, r 9.17(1) and PD 9A, para 6.1). The FDR hearing is a without prejudice, confidential process and the District Judge facilitating it will take no further part in the proceedings. During this hearing, the judge can in effect become an evaluative mediator, by offering an early view of the merits of the case (see *Rose v Rose* [2002] 1 FLR 978). If settlement is not reached, the district judge conducting the FDR hearing will exercise no further judicial role in the case. **18.42**

Judicial mediation in Employment Tribunals

A judicial mediation pilot was carried out in three regions of England—Newcastle, Central London, and Birmingham, by the Employment Tribunal Service in respect of all kinds of discrimination cases (age, sex, sexual orientation, disability, race, religion, or belief) in the **18.43**

Employment Tribunal between June 2006 and March 2007. The pilot was evaluated by Peter Urwin and others in the report 'Evaluating the use of judicial mediation in Employment Tribunals' (Ministry of Justice Research Series 7/10, March 2010). The evaluation showed that judicial mediation had no discernible, statistically significant effect on the rates of cases settled or avoidance of a hearing. Outcomes of judicial mediation were not significantly better than those of unmediated cases. Further, judicial mediation had an estimated cost to the Employment Tribunals Service of £908 per case.

18.44 Despite the conclusions drawn from the pilot, the Employment Tribunals Judicial Mediation Scheme is now available throughout England and Wales. Suitable cases for judicial mediation are selected by the judge at a Case Management Discussion. If both parties agree, the Regional Employment Judge will decide, bearing in mind the issues in the case and the Tribunal's resources, whether the case should be referred for judicial mediation. The judge will act as mediator and will assist the parties to resolve their dispute. The process is private and confidential, and nothing in the mediation can be used in subsequent court proceedings and the judge acting as mediator will have no further involvement with the case. It should be noted that judicial mediation is not an alternative to mandatory ACAS Early Conciliation (see 20.07) and it is possible for both processes to take place in relation to the same case.

18.45 Despite the existence of these judicial schemes in these courts, there is nothing to prevent the parties using a mediator of their own choice to help them to resolve their dispute.

G MEDIATION IN SPECIFIC CASES

Mediation in cases in the Commercial Court

18.46 The Commercial Court will usually make an ADR order, which strongly encourages the parties to attempt to resolve their dispute by ADR (usually mediation). The order usually requires the parties to co-operate with one another by exchanging lists each containing the names of three mediators who are able to conduct a mediation by the date fixed by the court. If the parties cannot agree, the court will usually select a mediator or provide that the mediator should be selected by an ADR organization. If the case does not settle, the parties are required to file a statement explaining what steps were taken to resolve the dispute by mediation, and why those steps failed.

18.47 An evaluation of the Commercial Court's practice of using ADR orders was undertaken by Professor Hazel Genn in 2002 (see DCA Research Paper, 'Court-based ADR initiatives for non-family civil disputes: The Commercial Court and the Court of Appeal'). This showed that ADR was attempted in a little over 50% of the cases in which an ADR order was made and, of those cases, 52% settled through ADR, 5% proceeded to trial and 20% settled some time after the conclusion of the ADR procedure. In cases in which ADR was not attempted following an ADR order, around 63% eventually settled, but 15% proceeded to trial.

Complex construction, engineering, and technology disputes

18.48 Construction, engineering, and technology disputes are very suitable for mediation because huge costs and a vast amount of time can be spent in litigating these cases. The parties can use the judicial mediation scheme (see 18.34–18.36) but more usually, the parties will want to have control over the selection of the mediator. When the parties choose to mediate outside the Court Settlement Process then the mediation will typically follow the general process set out in Chapters 15 and 16 but with some differences:

- There may be more than one pre-mediation meeting to discuss and agree the procedure for the mediation.
- The mediation meeting will be more formal and may take place over a number of days with the parties having the ability to make revised proposals as each stage takes place.
- It will usually involve the presentation of detailed expert or factual evidence.
- The mediator will usually be a lawyer, and may also be assisted in the resolution of the dispute by an expert in the relevant field.
- A formal evaluation of the party's case is likely to form part of the mediation.

Family cases

Use of mediation in family cases

18.49 In family cases, the general approach is that the courts should be used as a matter of last resort and mediation has been established as an ADR method since the introduction of the Family Law Act 1996. In publicly funded cases, there is a presumption that mediation should usually be tried before litigation. Since the implementation of the Children and Families Act 2014 came into force on 22 April 2014, the new ethos is that separating parties will be expected to make arrangements for the living arrangements for their children (a Parenting Plan), and also resolve their financial disputes without recourse to the courts. Legal aid is no longer available in the majority of private family law cases in relation to children or financial remedies. In such cases, parties will be expected to attend a MIAM (with very limited exceptions) before proceedings can be issued (see Parts 3, 9, and 12 of the Family Procedure Rules 2010 (as amended) and 7.27–7.31 and 18.40–18.42) with a view to the parties resolving any disputes between them by mediation.

18.50 Family mediation is more highly regulated than most other forms of mediation. Family mediators must be qualified and accredited. The Family Mediation Council, which was established in 2007, is responsible for setting and maintaining the professional standards for family mediators and for devising and implementing training standards with which all family mediators must comply.

18.51 Family mediations tend to be undertaken by specialist ADR providers, the main ones being National Family Mediation (NFM), which has a large number of affiliated providers in England and Wales, the Family Mediators Association (FMA), Resolution (which is the Solicitor's Family Law Association), the ADR Group, and, the College of Mediators (formerly known as the UK College of Family Mediators). These ADR providers, together with the Law Society, comprise the members of the Family Mediation Council (FMC) and their mediators will comply with the FMC's Code of Practice for Family Mediators (see www.familymediationcouncil.org.uk).

18.52 In family cases, the mediator will usually meet with the parties in advance to ensure that both parties are participating in mediation willingly and that they have not been influenced by threats of violence or other harm (see section 11 of the Law Society Code of Practice for Family Mediation and also the College of Mediators Code of Practice).

Mediation Information and Assessment Meetings (MIAM)

18.53 As explained in 7.29, the FPR 2010, Pre-Application Protocol for Mediation Information and Assessment (PD 3A) requires the parties to attend a mandatory meeting to consider mediation before making an application to the court in most private law cases relating to children or financial matters. Parties are expected to have followed the steps in the protocol before making an application to the court. The applicant, except in very limited specified circumstances, will be required to attend a MIAM with a family mediator and consider whether the dispute can be resolved by mediation. The court will expect a respondent to attend a MIAM, if invited to do so. The mediator will convene separate meetings with each party if the parties are unwilling to attend a joint meeting.

18.54 If court proceedings are issued, the applicant must, at the time of issue, file Form FM1 (which can be downloaded from www.direct.gov.uk) which must be completed and signed by the mediator, and countersigned by the applicant, which confirms whether the parties did or did not attend a MIAM, and that the mediator is satisfied that mediation is not suitable because the other party to the dispute is not willing to attend mediation or the case is not suitable for mediation. If they have not complied with the steps in the protocol or the court considers an exception for attending a MIAM does not apply, the court can refer the parties to a meeting with a mediator before the proceedings can continue further.

18.55 Although a MIAM is essential, it is important to note that this is not mandatory mediation, but rather mandatory pre-application consideration of mediation. At a MIAM the mediator will meet with the parties and explain the process and benefits of mediation and assess whether it is suitable in the circumstances of the case. It is not compulsory to undertake mediation, but it is compulsory to give consideration to using it. The requirement to have a MIAM only came into force on 1 April 2011 (and it is strengthened and put on a statutory footing by the Children and Families Act 2014 and the consequential amendments to the Family Procedure Rules), so it remains to be seen how the court will interpret these new provisions. The Family Mediation Council has issued guidance in relation to the competence of mediators carrying out MIAMs and also Agreed Minimum Requirements for Mediators carrying out MIAMs. These guidance documents can be downloaded from www.familymediationcouncil.org.uk. The Family Justice Council has also produced a 'Guide to family applications and mediation information and assessment meetings', which can be downloaded from its website.

An overview of the mediation process in family cases

18.56 If the parties do decide to take part in mediation before or after litigation is commenced, much of what is said in Chapters 15 and 16 will apply. However, during the main mediation meeting, the mediator will seldom conduct private meetings with the parties, in order to avoid any suggestion of bias. All parties will generally remain in the same room with the mediator throughout the process, although mediators in family cases are now more willing to hold private meetings with each party.

18.57 The parties must agree that all factual information material to financial issues must be provided on an open basis, so that it can be referred to in legal proceedings and all information or correspondence provided by either party should be shared openly (except for an address or telephone number). Privilege will also not apply if it appears that a child or other person is suffering or is likely to suffer significant harm (see FMC Code of Practice for Family Mediators, para 5.6.4).

18.58 The mediation may be conducted over several sessions, with revised proposals being made by the parties in between each session. Typically the mediation meetings will last for between three and six sessions, each lasting approximately 90 minutes, although in financial remedies cases, the meetings may last longer and fewer sessions may be required. There may be a gap of some weeks between each session. Normally lawyers will not be present in family mediations, although the mediator may invite them to participate if he considers this would be useful.

18.59 Mediators must not seek to impose their preferred outcome on the parties or to influence them to adopt it, whether by attempting to predict the outcome of court proceedings or otherwise. However, if the parties agree, a mediator can inform them that their proposals would fall outside the parameters that a court might approve or order and he or she can inform the parties of possible courses of action and assist them to explore these. However, any suggestions that the mediator puts forward are not binding on the parties (see para 5.3 of the FMC's Code of Practice).

The welfare, wishes, and feelings of each child of the family must be considered in appropriate cases in relation to any matter affecting them. Parents should be encouraged to focus on the needs of the children as well as their own needs and to consider the wishes and feelings of the children of the family. Mediators should discuss with the parties the extent to which the children should be consulted in the mediation, and no child should be consulted unless he or she agrees. Mediators should be specially trained in dealing with children and the child must be offered confidentiality in relation to any disclosure made by the child (see para 5.7 of FMC's Code of Practice). **18.60**

If settlement is reached at the mediation, it will usually be recorded in a privileged Memorandum of Understanding (MOU) and in financial cases, it will be accompanied by an Open statement of Financial Information. Parties must be given the opportunity to take legal advice on the proposed settlement before it is regarded as legally binding. The parties can waive privilege in the MOU for the purposes of obtaining a court order by consent. Unless the court orders or the parties agree, mediators should not provide the court with information about the discussions that took place in mediation. The FMC in conjunction with the Family Justice Council has produced guidance on appropriate dispute resolution, including guidance on MIAMs and also 'Independent Mediation—Information for Judges, Magistrates and Legal Advisors' and these can be downloaded from www.judiciary.gov.uk/about-the-judiciary/advisory-bodies/fjc. **18.61**

Public funding is available for family mediation, subject to satisfying eligibility requirements. Publicly funded mediation work can only be carried out by providers contracted to the Legal Services Commission. See the Legal Aid Agency Family Mediation Guidance Manual, which can be accessed at www.justice.gov.uk/legal-aid/civil/family-mediation-guidance-manual. **18.62**

Family mediation is regulated by the FMC. Parties can obtain information about mediation, be provided with details of mediation providers, and be given information about funding by contacting any of the member organizations of the FMC directly. An FMC registered mediator can also be found by using the 'Find a Mediation Service' on the Ministry of Justice's website at www.familymediationhelpline.co.uk. **18.63**

For research on MIAMs and mediation in private family law disputes, see the Ministry of Justice Analytical Series Research Paper 2014 by Anna Bloch, Rosie McLeod, and Ben Toombs (available from www.justice.gov.uk). **18.64**

Workplace mediation

This is a growing area of business in the mediation field and it concerns conflict avoidance and management in the workplace. The aim is to resolve internal complaints and disputes and grievances before they result in formal disciplinary or internal complaints investigation procedures and a loss in time and productivity. Workplace mediation can be used to resolve all forms of disputes between employees, or between employer and employee, ranging from relationship breakdown, bullying, harassment, performance and motivation issues, behavioural issues, or pay disputes. Mediation is particularly effective at resolving workplace disputes because of the need to maintain a continuing working relationship and perhaps to create a complex negotiated settlement which a win–lose outcome could not achieve. **18.65**

The 2009 ACAS Statutory Code of Practice on Discipline and Grievance recommends that disciplinary and grievance procedures should be resolved within the workplace if possible, **18.66** and, if necessary, independent third parties, such as an internal or external mediator, should be used to help resolve the problem. This is an expanding area of business for ADR providers. The Civil Mediation Council maintains a register of mediation providers who are accredited to provide workplace mediations. There are currently around 39 accredited workplace providers, some of whom are also accredited as civil and commercial mediation providers. ACAS and some other training providers also run training programmes in workplace mediation. ACAS has produced a guide, dated February 2013, entitled 'Mediation: An approach to resolving workplace issues', which can be accessed at www.acas.org.uk/media/pdf/m/f/Mediation-an-approaach-to-resolving-workplace-issues.

18.67 The employment tribunal system saw an increase of 44% in claims issued between 2008–9 and 2010–11 at an average cost to the taxpayer of £1,900 per claim. The government intends to do more to make businesses aware of the benefits of using mediation and other ways to resolve disputes without going to court. It published a consultation paper on Resolving Workplace Disputes. The consultation closed on 20 April 2011. The government's response to the consultation was published on 23 November 2011. Both the consultation and the response can be found at www.bis.gov.uk/Consultations/resolving-workplace-disputes. The Government's Response indicated that it intended, amongst other things:

- to make mediation more accessible and less costly for small businesses;
- to undertake more work to change attitudes to mediation and make it an accepted part of dispute resolution; and
- to undertake a fundamental review of the current rules of procedure for employment tribunals.

18.68 The Department for Business Innovation and Skills (BIS) has recently launched a regional mediation pilot scheme for small and medium-sized enterprises (SMEs) in Cambridge and Manchester. Under the 12-month pilot, BIS provides mediation training funding for employees from a group of 24 SMEs in each pilot area in 2012–13 in order to help to resolve workplace disputes before they reach the Employment Tribunal stage. If the pilots are successful, the government will consider introducing them into other areas of England, Scotland, and Wales.

Mediation in employment disputes

18.69 Mediation can be particularly useful for resolving employment disputes. The DTI consulted on the possibility of making it mandatory in all applications brought before the Employment Tribunal. Although the proposal had a lot of support, some commentators felt that it should not be mandatory for discrimination claims, which merit publicity in the public interest. Other commentators have pointed out that mediation is particularly effective in such cases, as part of the proposed solution can be an undertaking by the employer to change its procedures, provide relevant training, provide a written apology or reference to the employee and, in some cases, enable the relationship between the employer and employer to be preserved. Mediation can also be effective for resolving disputes arising out of a restrictive covenant in an employment contract, where part of the solution can be the redrafting of the covenant so that it meets the real needs of all parties concerned. See the useful chapter 'Mediation in Employment Disputes' by Michel Kallipetis QC in *Mediators on Mediation* (Tottel Publishing, 2005, ch 10) for some observations on the effectiveness of mediation in all types of claims arising out of the employment relationship.

18.70 Mediation and conciliation schemes have been offered by ACAS since 1984. ACAS mediation and conciliation schemes are regulated by statute, unlike most other mediation processes in the UK, which are regulated by the contract made between the parties.

The ACAS Conciliation Scheme

This is discussed in Chapter 20. It should be noted however that the term 'conciliation' is often used interchangeably with the term 'mediation'. ACAS conciliation is also a facilitative and non-evaluative mediation process. The only difference lies in the fact that ACAS state on their website that conciliation is the term used if an employee is making a specific complaint against their employer and where there is a potential or actual claim to the Employment Tribunal rather than more general employment matters. From the 6 May 2014, in most cases it has become mandatory for parties to attempt to resolve their dispute using the ACAS Early Conciliation service before they can bring a claim in the Employment Tribunal (see 20.07). In addition, fees have recently been introduced for issuing proceedings in the Employment Tribunal and claimants now have to pay a fee up to £950 if the claim is listed for a hearing (although fees can be waived in some cases for claimants who meet specified criteria). The government expects both of these measures to reduce the number of claims issued, and ensure that more employment disputes are settled by conciliation or mediation. **18.71**

The ACAS Mediation Scheme

Originally, this was an evaluative mediation scheme, but now, in common with the more widespread trend towards facilitative rather than evaluative mediation, the mediator will not make judgments or determine the outcome for the parties. If the complaint is about employment rights that could go to a tribunal, the service is offered free of charge. If the dispute is not about a statutory employment right, a charge is made for the mediation. It is generally used in workplace disputes and the key goal is the preservation of the employment relationship. It tends to be used in cases where proceedings have not been commenced in a tribunal and which are not likely to be commenced (if an application has been or is likely to be made to a tribunal, the early conciliation scheme must be used, which is free to the parties). Mediation can be used in individual disputes, as well as collective mediation where disputes about collective rights such as pay, workloads, holiday entitlement, job losses, or health and safety issues take place between representative groups such as trade unions or staff associations and employers. In collective mediation, the ACAS mediator may be more active in making non-binding recommendations for settlement of the dispute (see www.acas.gov.uk/index.aspx?articleid=2013). **18.72**

A particular feature of compromise agreements that result from the successful mediation of employment disputes is the need to ensure that they are drafted in a way that complies with s 203 of the Employment Rights Act 2003. Section 203 renders void any provision in an agreement that purports to preclude a person from bringing a claim under the Act before the Employment Tribunal, unless the agreement complies with the statutory conditions in s 203(3), the most important of which is that the employee receives independent legal advice from a person identified in the agreement who is covered by professional indemnity insurance. Any settlement reached at mediation in relation to a dispute that could be referred to an Employment Tribunal must therefore take the form of a statutory compromise agreement. The government has announced that it intends to reform the law to produce a standard form of text for compromise agreements and to make it easier to enter into a legally binding settlement in relation to existing and future claims without requiring long lists of causes of action. **18.73**

Mediation in personal injury cases

There was a perception by many lawyers and insurers that personal injury claims were not suitable for mediation. However, in recent years, there has been a growing awareness among personal injury practitioners that mediation is a more effective method for resolving those disputes than litigation, not least because: **18.74**

- the costs incurred in litigating personal injury claims of modest value are often disproportionate to the amount of the claim;
- mediation will often lessen the stress and trauma an injured claimant will face by attending a trial;
- mediation offers the parties the chance to build bridges by offering an explanation or an apology for the injury, and an acknowledgement of the effect that it has had on the claimant;
- mediation results in a high success rate, with some providers of personal injury mediation reporting settlement figures in excess of 80%.

18.75 A number of ADR providers have set up specialist personal injury mediation schemes, such as CEDR and Trust Mediation (www.trustmediation.org.uk). The Department of Energy and Climate Change also set up the British Coal Miners Mediation Scheme for Respiratory and Vibration White Finger to mediate claims for respiratory and vibration white finger in the coal mining industry. This scheme is administered by the ADR Group.

H MEDIATING MULTI-PARTY DISPUTES

18.76 Mediation has proved to be effective in multi-party disputes. Such disputes can take two forms:

- those involving large numbers of claimants or defendants, such as the Alder Hey retained organs claims and multiple holiday claims brought against a tour operator for food poisoning; and
- those cases where there are only a limited number of parties to the main dispute, but a large number of parties have been added to the dispute as additional parties. This is commonly the case in construction claims.

18.77 A team of mediators may need to be appointed to mediate multi-party claims. A number of things make them slightly different from mediation of other claims:

- crowd control;
- information management;
- time management while the mediator is having a private meeting with all of the various groups or parties.

18.78 In group litigation actions involving a very large number of claimants, it may be necessary to divide them into a number of sub-groups, each of whose claims raise issues similar to others in terms of liability or quantum, and then appoint parties to represent the interests of each group. Consideration also needs to be given to the effective management of the large volume of documents that such cases can generate and the use that will be made of those documents in the mediation.

18.79 During the mediation, the lawyers and the mediator will have to draw up strategies for management of the idle time that will inevitably occur as the mediator sees the parties or representatives of each sub-group in private meetings. The amount of idle time in such mediations can be significant. For example if there are ten parties or sub-groups and the mediator spends only 20 minutes with each party, it will be over three hours before the mediator will get back to the first party, and in fact the time usually spent with parties in the initial private meeting is likely to be longer than that. It is hard to keep the impetus and energy for settlement going within each of the teams where there are long periods of delay.

18.80 Mediating very complex claims involving multiple parties will often give rise to issues about the funding of the mediation, and issues of confidentiality, publicity, and neutrality of the mediator.

Mediation is a very flexible process, so it can be tailored to meet the needs of a multi-party dispute. The mediator will discuss with the lawyers the structure and form of the mediation, together with the order in which the issues will be discussed, and the time that the mediation is likely to take. Planning effectively for the substantive mediation is key, so a number of preliminary pre-mediation meetings are likely to be needed for this purpose to identify the interest groups, formulate and agree the issues, agree ground rules for the mediation process, determine how and by whom the mediation process should be funded, and resolve issues between different groups such as disclosure and information requests. Such disputes may need to involve a team of mediators. It is also useful to use the organizational and managerial skills that an ADR provider can provide. It is usually time efficient to deal with as many issues as possible in joint sessions in multi-party disputes, so such mediations tend to have extended joint sessions, with much of the exploration phase of the mediation taking place in those sessions. They may also involve post-mediation meetings to divide a global offer between a number of different parties. Mediating multi-party cases can take several months with various mediation meetings taking place during that time. **18.81**

Useful perspectives about mediating multi-party disputes and complex cases can be found in *Mediators on Mediation* (Tottel Publishing, 2005), ch 13 'Mediating Multi-party Disputes' by David Richbell, and ch 14 'The Impossible Takes a Little Longer—Mediating Really Complex Cases' by Eileen Carroll and Dr Karl Mackie. **18.82**

I OTHER SPECIALIST MEDIATION SCHEMES

There are many specific sector mediation schemes. This book cannot attempt to cover all of them, but this section notes a selection to give an indication of the range of cases in which mediation is available. **18.83**

- *The Financial Conduct Authority (FCA) Mediation Scheme.* The FCA has developed a successful mediation model for enforcement cases. For the types of case that can be mediated, and for the discount scheme that is offered in recognition of early settlement, see www.fca.org.uk. A very useful explanation of the practical operation of mediation in regulatory cases can be found in *Mediators on Mediation* (Tottel Publishing, 2005), ch 16, 'Mediation in the Regulatory Context' by Elizabeth Birch.
- *Banking and Investment Products Schemes.* Following the collapse of Lehman Brothers, the Hong Kong Monetary Authority appointed the Hong Kong International Arbitration Centre to administer the Lehman Brothers Related Investment Products Dispute Mediation and Arbitration Scheme. For details of the scheme, see www.hkiac.org.
- *Her Majesty's Custom and Revenue Mediation Schemes.* During 2011, HMRC operated two pilot schemes, one involving large businesses with complex tax affairs, and the other involving SMEs in order to evaluate whether tax disputes could be resolved by mediation. Following on from these pilot schemes it launched an Alternative Dispute Resolution Scheme in September 2013 to assist small and medium-sized enterprises and individuals with a cheaper and more cost-effective way of resolving tax disputes. For further detail see 'Analysis—Mediating Tax Disputes: HMRC's ADR Pilots' (2011) *Tax Journal* Issue 1986.
- *Mediation schemes in the healthcare sector.* The healthcare sector has now started to embrace mediation, and mediation schemes are being used by the National Health Service Litigation Authority, the Independent Healthcare Advisory Services, the Independent Doctor's Federation and by NHS Trusts.
- *International Trade Marks Association (INTA).* INTA has developed an ADR pledge for brand owners and law firms by which they commit to using ADR to resolve non-urgent non-counterfeiting trademark disputes and it accredits and maintains a Panel of Neutrals

who are experienced mediators and also specialists in trademark and unfair competition law who operate under INTA Mediation Guidelines and INTA Mediation Rules. See www.inta.org/MEDIATION for more information.

- *Trading Standards Institute.* There are many suppliers of goods and services in the fields of car repairs and servicing, debt management, energy, estate agents, home furnishings, the motor trade, removals, and will writers who are members of a trade association who operate under the Consumer Code Approval Scheme (CCAS), which has been approved by the Trading Standards Institute and which requires them to provide low-cost mediation and ADR services for resolving disputes. See www.tradingstandards.gov.uk/advice/ConsumerCodes.cfm.
- *Intellectual property cases.* Disputes involving unregistered copyright, registered patents, trademarks and registered designs and all other forms of intellectual property cases have their own specialized mediation scheme, which is operated by the Intellectual Property Office, using mediators accredited by mediation providers who are skilled in this type of work.
- *The London SEN Mediation Service.* This scheme aims to resolve disputes between local educational authorities (LEA) and parents about the provision of special educational needs (SEN). See www.kids.org.uk/mediation. An SEN mediation service operates in most regions of the UK.

J OTHER MEDIATION PROCESSES

Project mediation

18.84 This is useful for resolving problems that may arise during the currency of long-term contracts, or contracts involving a lengthy chain of parties such as contractors and sub-contractors on a large-scale building project. The aim of project mediation is to prevent problems escalating into entrenched disputes that may hinder or delay the project. The project mediator will usually be selected on the basis of his experience in the relevant industry. He will be available to the appointing parties during the currency of the project and he will have discussions with relevant parties involved in the project in relation to any matters of concern to prevent disputes arising that might impact on the performance of the contract. If needs be, the project mediator will also carry out a formal mediation, although the aim of project mediation is to solve problems before that becomes necessary. For an example of a project mediation scheme, visit www.cedr.com. CEDR has also devised a model mediation agreement, and a model mediation project protocol, which sets out the terms and conditions of its project mediation service, copies of which can be downloaded from the website.

18.85 A project mediation model was devised to help the Olympic Delivery Authority to identify and resolve disputes that arose during the construction of the Olympic Park for the London Olympics 2012 by setting up an Independent Dispute Avoidance Panel (IDAP) consisting of ten construction professionals. All parties still had the right to refer any dispute or difference to adjudication or arbitration.

The mini-trial or executive tribunal

18.86 This is a form of evaluative mediation, which can be employed as an alternative to the forms of mediation discussed in Chapter 16. It is particularly useful in corporate disputes. Each party to the dispute will make formal legal submissions to a panel, which is comprised of senior executives from each company and chaired by a neutral adviser. The executives, their lawyers, and the neutral adviser will then adjourn to discuss settlement of the issues in the case. The neutral adviser may act as a mediator to facilitate negotiations. If asked, the neutral adviser may also agree to assume an evaluative role by providing his opinion on the merits of the case and the likely outcome if it went to trial.

This process is advantageous because: **18.87**

- it can be arranged relatively speedily;
- it involves key executive officers of both companies at an early stage in the dispute, who have authority to settle the matter;
- it enables the parties themselves to have control over the outcome;
- it is cost effective and will represent a significant saving in the costs of a trial, particularly if it is carried out at an early stage of the litigation process;
- it enables the parties to create a more flexible settlement outcome than that which could be ordered by the court in litigation or arbitration;
- the procedure is flexible and can be created by the parties, in conjunction with the neutral chairperson, to best suit the needs of the parties and the subject-matter of the dispute.

However, the process itself is more formal and structured than a typical mediation. Each side will usually make detailed written submissions, supported with relevant documents. The parties control the information placed before the tribunal and can also put confidential documents before the tribunal, although these should be clearly marked as confidential. At the hearing, each party will make formal oral submissions to the tribunal. The parties may also agree to call evidence from witnesses and experts at the hearing. **18.88**

The process is useful for resolving disputes of a complex nature. Even if overall settlement is not reached at a mini-trial of this nature, often agreement can be reached on some issues, so narrowing the issues that need to be considered at trial. **18.89**

The parties can select and appoint the neutral person privately, or they may engage the services of an ADR provider to nominate a suitable person. If an ADR provider is used, they will probably also provide the venue and manage the process. Some ADR providers have model agreements and a model procedure for executive tribunals, which can be amended to suit the needs of any individual case (see eg CEDR Model Executive Tribunal Procedure at www.cedr.co.uk). **18.90**

Consensus-building mediation in environmental disputes or disputes that involve public policy issues

A variation in the mediation process can take place in cases involving environmental and other public policy issues that affect a number of different interest groups. A neutral third party will be appointed to identify and consult all of the interest groups and will promote consultation and negotiations between them with the aim of achieving a consensual outcome that satisfies the parties and all of the various interest groups. This approach historically has been more commonly employed in the USA and Australia, but a number of organizations in the United Kingdom have developed schemes to mediate disputes in cases involving environmental or public policy issues such as the Royal Institution of Chartered Surveyors (RICS) Planning and Environmental Mediation Service. **18.91**

A number of papers have been produced on the merits of using mediation in planning disputes, particularly major developments which affect a number of groups in the local community as well as wider interest groups (see, in particular, the 2008 report 'Review of Planning Applications' by Joanna Killian and David Pretty and more recently, 'Mediation in Planning: Report commissioned by the National Planning Forum and the Planning Inspectorate' by Leonora Rozee and Kay Powell, June 2010 (www.natplanforum.org.uk/ **18.92**

Final Report—Mediation in Planning—PDF.pdf), and the 'Short Guide to Mediation in Planning' (National Planning Forum, April 2011)).

Deal mediation

18.93 Mediation is not always about dispute resolution. Mediators can be used to broker deals between negotiating parties, particularly in relation to complex high-value, multi-national contracts in the energy, telecommunications, or intellectual property sectors. Using mediators to broker complex deals can reduce the risk of stalemate in negotiations and can help to create sound long-lasting contractual relations. See L Michael Hager and Robert Pritchard, 'Deal Mediation: How ADR techniques can help achieve durable agreements in the global markets' (1999) *ICSID Foreign Investment Law Journal*, reproduced at www.dundee.ac.uk/cepmlp/journal/html/vol6/article6–12.html). The International Mediation Institute has also collated a number of articles and webcasts on deal mediation which can be accessed from its website (http://imimediation.org/deal-mediation).

K RESTORATIVE JUSTICE

18.94 Mediation is also being used as part of the move towards restorative justice with the aim of achieving reconciliation between the victim and the wrongdoer and providing some form of reparation to the victim such as an apology or compensation. The Restorative Justice Council defines it as follows:

> In criminal justice, restorative processes give victims the chance to tell offenders the real impact of their crime, to get answers to their questions, and an apology. Restorative justice holds offenders to account for what they have done, helps them understand the real impact of what they've done, to take responsibility and make amends.

18.95 The Restorative Justice Council maintains a register of accredited mediators skilled in this area (see the Restorative Practitioner Register on www.restorativejustice.org.uk).

18.96 Restorative justice mediation involves a meeting between victim and offender and sometimes this may take place in prison if the offender is in custody, but it is most commonly used where the offender is below the age of 17. Both sides must agree to the process. The mediator will be provided with details of the offence in advance, and information about how this has impacted on the victim will be explored during the mediation. It is a growing area and in November 2013, the government announced that it was making at least £29 million available to Police and Crime Commissioners and charities to help them deliver restorative justice over the next three years. This, in part, will assist with the implementation of the Ministry of Justice Restorative Justice Action Plan for the Criminal Justice System which was published in November 2012. A National Forum of Restorative Practitioners was launched on 31 March 2014 to set a benchmark of competence for practitioners in this field.

L COMMUNITY MEDIATION

18.97 There are a large number of community mediation schemes in every area of the United Kingdom. They can be used to mediate a wide range of matters, including neighbour disputes, disputes about noise, litter, nuisance claims, parking, harassment, pets, some landlord and tenant disputes, and small debt claims. More recently, a number of community mediation schemes (eg the Centre for Conflict Transformation and the Asaha Gang Mediation

Project) have been set up in London and in the West Midlands to mediate disputes between gang members which can lead to violence and gang-related shootings.

Community mediators currently operate outside the terms of reference of the Civil Mediation Council. There is currently no umbrella group that draws together community mediation services (a company known as Mediation UK did fulfil that role, but it went into liquidation some years ago). It is relatively easy to find a number of community mediation groups local to any particular area by using the internet, and the local council should also be able to help. A fairly comprehensive (but by no means exhaustive) online directory of local community mediation providers can be found by searching the online Directory of UK Mediation on www.intermedial.org.uk. Local community mediation services are usually funded by community trusts or the local authority, many have charitable status and are usually run by volunteers, including volunteer mediators. **18.98**

The key characteristics of community mediation schemes are as follows: **18.99**

- They are usually free to the users.
- Lawyers are seldom instructed to attend community mediations.
- Referral is made by contacting the local service directly.
- An initial meeting (usually face-to-face, but contact may be made by telephone) will be made with the initiating party.
- If the dispute is suitable for mediation, the community service provider will usually contact the other party.
- If all parties agree, a mediation meeting is arranged to try to determine the dispute.
- The mediators are volunteers, but they will usually have received mediation training, in many cases by attending training courses organized by the local community mediation provider.
- Co-mediators are often assigned to a dispute.
- The mediation meeting can last from anything between one and three hours, depending on the type of dispute and the number of parties involved and the practice operated by the local organization.
- Each party will outline the nature of the dispute for the mediator and what they wish to achieve by the mediation. The parties will rarely provide position statements or a bundle of documents.
- The venue for the mediation will usually be a local community centre, or the offices of the community service provider.
- The dispute is usually resolved in a joint meeting, although separate meetings can take place if this is appropriate, with the mediator 'shuttling' between the two parties.
- If agreement is reached, it can be recorded in writing, or it may remain as a verbal agreement. In either case, it is unlikely to be legally binding on the parties.

The College of Mediators has recently set standards for community mediators and, to date, over 100 community mediators have met those standards. **18.100**

M PRO BONO MEDIATION AND LAWWORKS

LawWorks is an independent charity that operates throughout England and Wales. It has over 150 mediators who are willing to provide mediation services pro bono to those who cannot afford to pay the usual costs associated with mediation. It is free to both parties if one party qualifies. If a party is entitled to a fee remission in respect of the court fees, then they are also eligible for free mediation through LawWorks. In all other cases, LawWorks will assess whether a party qualifies, by ascertaining if that party's gross annual income is **18.101** below a prescribed amount or that person is in receipt of a means-tested benefit (see www.lawworks.org.uk).

18.102 More recently, the Society of Mediators was formed, with charitable status (see www.societyof mediators.org). It aims to promote mediation for the public benefit. Its approved objectives for 2013–2015 are to embark on a programme of education about mediation through the media and directly to institutions and in particular to deliver the Free Mediation Project, which will offer free mediation to individuals, businesses, or organizations that could not otherwise afford to buy mediation through conventional providers.

KEY POINTS SUMMARY

18.103
- Time-limited, fixed-cost mediations can take place through Court Mediation Schemes and the Civil Mediation Online Directory.
- Some courts also operate judicial mediation schemes.
- There are many industry and sector-specific schemes, and mediation is now being employed in some criminal cases to achieve restorative justice.
- Mediation can be used effectively in multi-party or complex disputes, although modifications may need to be made to the process to take account of the multiplicity of parties and/or issues.
- Mediation can also be used in public sector and regulatory disputes.
- There is a move towards mandatory information mediation assessment meetings at which the parties are required to consider but not undertake mediation.

19

INTERNATIONAL MEDIATION

A INTRODUCTION 19.01
B THE ADVANTAGES OF MEDIATION IN INTERNATIONAL DISPUTES 19.03
C PREPARATION FOR MEDIATION IN INTERNATIONAL DISPUTES 19.04
D THE PROCESS IN INTERNATIONAL MEDIATION 19.05
E THE GROWTH OF MEDIATION IN EUROPE 19.06
F A MOVE TOWARDS HARMONIZING PRACTICES IN INTERNATIONAL MEDIATION 19.09
G THE EU DIRECTIVE ON MEDIATION IN CIVIL AND COMMERCIAL CASES (DIRECTIVE 2008/52/EC) 19.12
H THE EUROPEAN CODE OF CONDUCT FOR MEDIATORS 19.60
I ENFORCEABILITY OF INTERNATIONAL MEDIATION SETTLEMENT AGREEMENTS 19.61
Key points summary 19.64

A INTRODUCTION

19.01 The USA was a key player in pioneering the use of mediation in civil disputes as an alterative to litigation. Mediation is now regarded as an important method of ADR in countries such as Canada, Australia, New Zealand, Hong Kong, Japan, China, and India, as well as being commonly used in most countries in the European Union. There has been a significant increase in the volume of mediations in international disputes in recent years in a wide range of cases such as the sale of goods, supply of services, intellectual property, insurance, international construction and engineering disputes, information technology, and pharmaceutical supply contracts.

19.02 In the EU, attempts have been made to standardize mediation procedures and promote mediation throughout member states by the introduction of the EU Directive on mediation in civil and commercial matters (Directive 2008/52/EC), and the development of the EU Code of Conduct for Mediators. On 25 October 2011 the European Parliament passed an ADR resolution which set out a wide range of proposals for the use and growth of ADR across a number of sectors and this was followed on 29 November 2011 with a proposal for a directive on the use of ADR for consumer/trader disputes and also a proposal for a regulation on online ADR. This chapter will concentrate on these developments and will also highlight some areas of practical importance to those wishing to undertake mediation in international disputes. In this chapter, an international dispute means a commercial dispute involving any subject-matter where the parties to the dispute are based in different countries, and which may require the performance of obligations in different countries.

B THE ADVANTAGES OF MEDIATION IN INTERNATIONAL DISPUTES

19.03 Mediation in international disputes offers all of the advantages that are described in Chapters 1 and 14 as well as the following additional advantages:

- The parties can determine where the mediation should take place, which need not necessarily be the place where the litigation would have to be commenced. The parties can select a neutral venue in a neutral country.
- It enables disputes in which there are multiple parties situated in different jurisdictions to avoid problems such as difficult jurisdiction and conflict of law issues that can arise in litigation in international cross-border cases.
- A complementary team of mediators can be appointed to take account of cultural differences between the parties and who have between them all the relevant expertise (and linguistic skills) necessary to facilitate a settlement with minimum delay and cost.
- Mediators can assist with communication problems that can arise in international disputes, despite modern communication techniques, because parties are in different geographical areas, many miles apart, in different time zones, with differences in language and culture.
- It enables facilitation of a speedy settlement in cases where there is an on-going valuable commercial relationship between the parties.
- The fact that mediation is a flexible process is particularly important in international disputes because it enables the parties to have a number of mediation meetings perhaps with each party in their own location, before the parties are all brought together at the main mediation meeting. The fact that the parties can decide the number and type of mediation meetings, the frequency and location of the meetings, and the issues that each meeting will deal with is particularly useful in complex disputes of this type.
- Mediation also enables the parties to the dispute to rely on local advisers in each relevant country to solve technical, practical, political, or legal issues that may arise and that would otherwise block a settlement agreement.
- It is particularly cost-effective compared to litigation and arbitration in such cases. Eileen Carroll and Karl Mackie in *International Mediation—The Art of Business Diplomacy* (2nd edn, Tottel Publishing, 2006) at p 69, give an example of clients in one case who made the choice to mediate before arbitration in a dispute involving US$20 million. The mediation took between 2 and 6 months, involved 100 hours of management time, the mediators cost $17,000, the legal costs were $90,000 and the outcome was an agreed commercial solution. Arbitrating the same case would have taken 24–36 months, involved 700 hours of management time and cost between $400,000–$600,000 in legal costs and the costs of the arbitrator panel would have been in the region of $350,000–$750,000 (on the assumption that the same hourly rates could be applied to mediators and arbitrators).

C PREPARATION FOR MEDIATION IN INTERNATIONAL DISPUTES

19.04 The preparatory steps for mediation in international disputes will follow the same general processes described in Chapters 14 and 15. However a number of factors deserve special mention:

- The selection of the mediator team will need to be undertaken with care in international disputes. Parties will need to ensure that the mediators they select have undergone appropriate training, have sufficient experience and expertise, and that they operate under a relevant and sufficient Code of Conduct. The parties may wish to use an organization such as the International Mediation Institute (IMI). IMI is a non-profit foundation and registered charity whose aim is to set high competency standards for mediation practice across all fields, worldwide (see www.imimediation.org). It has set up the Independent Standards Commission, which sets uniform standards for certification of mediators. Interested parties can use the search engine on the website to find the right IMI certified mediator for their particular international dispute. It has also published a useful document, *Guidelines for Lawyers Representing Clients in Mediation*, to assist them in the choice and selection of the right mediator with the necessary expertise and mediation style for their particular dispute. This document can be downloaded free of charge from the IMI's website. IMI-certified mediators operate under the IMI Code of Professional Conduct and the IMI Disciplinary Commission handles formal and informal complaints about IMI-certified mediators. Another useful source for selecting a mediator is the International Mediation and Arbitration Centre (www.imac-adr.com). Many domestic private mediators and those affiliated to ADR providers will also have expertise in international disputes. A number of other organizations that provide useful information in relation to mediation in international disputes are:

- Juris International (www.jurisint.org).
- The International Institute for Conflict Prevention and Resolution (CPR) (www.cpradr.org).
- The World Mediation Forum (www.worldmediationforum.org).
- The Arbitration and Mediation Centre of the World Intellectual Property Organisation (www.wipo.int/amc/en/).

- In international disputes, particular care needs to be given to consideration of how language and cultural differences between parties can be managed.
- The position statement is likely to be longer in international disputes than in most domestic mediations. As a general rule, the mediator will seek to confine each party's position statement to 15–20 pages, with the indexed bundle of other documents consisting of around 3–4 files (see Eileen Carroll and Karl Mackie in *International Mediation—The Art of Business Diplomacy* (2nd edn, Tottel Publishing, 2006)).
- More preparatory work will need to be undertaken by the mediator in relation to pre-mediation meetings with the parties by telephone or video conference link, or perhaps in person at each party's place of business (and this may mean travelling to several different countries).
- The mediation overall is likely to take longer, perhaps lasting several months.

D THE PROCESS IN INTERNATIONAL MEDIATION

The mediation process will follow a similar pattern to that described in Chapter 16, but the following factors should be borne in mind: **19.05**

- In the main mediation meetings, the mediator is more likely to encourage the parties to explore issues in joint meetings and there is likely to be an extended plenary session for that purpose.
- At an appropriate stage, the mediator team will convene private meetings of the parties to explore the issues, and commence the bargaining process by way of 'shuttle diplomacy' as described in Chapter 16.
- Expert evidence is likely to feature to a greater extent in an international mediation. The mediator may hold a meeting of experts or with a single expert on an issue and allow the parties to question them if this is likely to assist in the resolution of a particular issue.

- Time pressures may be more acute in international cases, particularly in the bargaining phase of the mediation due to practical matters such as the fact that the parties may come from different countries and time zones. A binding settlement agreement is not likely to be drawn up at the conclusion of the mediation, even if agreement is reached on all issues, as any final agreement is likely to be the subject of reflection, review and consultation, and require very detailed work by the lawyers before it can be signed off by the parties and become binding. If this is so, the mediation may be resumed at a different time, usually some weeks later, with a non-binding framework or heads of agreement being drawn up in the meantime to record areas of agreement. In international mediations it is not uncommon for the settlement phase of the negotiation to last several months.

E THE GROWTH OF MEDIATION IN EUROPE

19.06 Mediation has grown at a rapid rate across the EU in recent years, although it is has not developed at a uniform pace in each of the member states, and there are some differences in the process across member states.

19.07 Details of the historic state of development of mediation in each of the EU countries can be found in *The EU Mediation Atlas: Practice and Regulation* by Jayne Singer (LexisNexis, 2004). See also Chapter 19, 'Mediation in Continental Europe: A Meandering Path Toward Efficient Regulation' by Guiseppe De Palo and Sara Carmeli in *Mediators on Mediation, Leading Mediator Perspectives on the Practice of Commercial Mediation* by Newmark and Monaghan (eds)(Tottel Publishing, 2005) and Chapter 13 in Boulle and Nesic, *Mediator Skills and Techniques: Triangle of Influence* (Bloomsbury Professional, 2010).

19.08 The growth in mediation across Europe has revealed:

- differences in the training and accreditation of mediators between the 28 member states of the EU;
- the lack of a common code of conduct for mediators; and
- differences in the manner and frequency with which ADR in general, and mediation in particular, is promoted and employed in individual states.

F A MOVE TOWARDS HARMONIZING PRACTICES IN INTERNATIONAL MEDIATION

19.09 As mediation becomes more common in international disputes, there is a need for some aspects of mediation, such as confidentiality and the impartiality and neutrality of the mediator (see Chapter 14) to be standardized or harmonized.

19.10 To this end the United Nations Commission on International Trade Law (UNCITRAL) developed a Model Law on International Commercial Conciliation (although it is called conciliation, the process is, in effect, mediation) across international jurisdictions. This Model Law consists of detailed rules governing all aspects of the mediation (see www.uncitral.org).

19.11 The European Parliament and Council has also attempted to introduce standardization in EU cases with the *EU Directive on Mediation in Civil and Commercial cases* (Directive 2008/52/EC) and the *EU Code of Conduct for Mediators*. More recently, on 18 June 2013, a Directive on Consumer ADR was published (Directive 2013/11/EU). This aims to give EU consumers, regardless of the type of goods or services purchased, and whether online of offline, or the place of purchase (with some limited exceptions), the chance to resolve their dispute without the need for court proceedings. For the full text of the Directive, see http://eur-lex.europa.eu/LexUriServ/LexUriServ.do?uri=OJ:L:2013:165:0063:0079:EN:PDF. On 21 May 2013, a Regulation on Online Dispute Resolution (Regulation (EU) No 524/2013) was published (again following a draft Regulation in November 2011). The Regulation provides for the establishment of an Online Dispute Resolution (ODR) platform which offers consumers and traders a single point of entry for the resolution of disputes arising from online transactions, using ADR entities (ADR providers) linked to the platform. The intention is that all national ADR providers will serve the platform and the platform will also operate in all official EU languages. For the full text of the Regulation, see http://eur-lex.europa.eu/LexUriServ/LexUriServ.do?uri=OJ:L:2013:165:0001:0012:EN:PDF. For more information on both the ADR Directive and the ODR Regulation, see http://ec.europa.eu/consumers/redress_cons/adr_policy_work_en.htm. The UK government is currently consulting on both the ADR Directive and the ODR Regulation and is working towards implementation in 2015. The ODR platform established under the Regulation is due to commence operation in early 2016.

G THE EU DIRECTIVE ON MEDIATION IN CIVIL AND COMMERCIAL CASES (DIRECTIVE 2008/52/EC)

This Directive was preceded by a Green Paper presented by the European Commission in April 2002. This sought views from member states and interested parties on measures that could be taken to promote the use of mediation to aid the development of extra-judicial procedures for the settlement of disputes in civil and commercial cases and thus simplify and improve access to justice. The Commission recognized the benefits of mediation, the fact that those benefits were even more pronounced in cross-border cases, and wanted to encourage more use of mediation across the EU. The online consultation can be viewed at www.europarl.eu.int/comparl/juri/consultations/default_en.htm. **19.12**

The Directive was published in the Official Journal of the European Union on 24 May 2008 and came into force 20 days after that date (Art 13). Member states were required to implement the Directive into national law by 21 May 2011. **19.13**

The objective of the Directive

The objective of the Directive is to facilitate access to ADR and to promote the amicable settlement of disputes by encouraging the use of mediation and by ensuring a balanced relationship between mediation and judicial proceedings (Art 1). **19.14**

Mediation is comprehensively defined in Art 3(a) as meaning: **19.15**

> A structured process, however named or referred to, whereby two or more parties to a dispute attempt by themselves, on a voluntary basis, to reach an agreement on the settlement of their dispute with the assistance of the mediator. This process may be initiated by the parties or suggested or ordered by a court or prescribed by the law of the member state. It includes mediation conducted by a judge who is not responsible for any judicial proceedings concerning the dispute in question.

Article 5(1) makes it clear that national courts can invite parties to use mediation, and Art 5(2) provides that the Directive '... is without prejudice to national legislation making the use of mediation compulsory or subject to incentives or sanctions, whether before or after judicial proceedings have started, provided that such legislation does not prevent the parties from exercising their right of access to the judicial system'. **19.16**

19.17 The Directive makes it clear that court-ordered compulsory mediation (which exists in some member states) is still a voluntary process, despite the fact that parties are ordered to arrange and/or attend mediation, because the parties are not compelled to reach agreement in the process. Member states can promote mediation in whatever form they see fit, whether by a compulsory mediation referral by the court or by inviting the parties to use it. However, mediation should not be promoted so as to prevent the parties from litigating their dispute in court.

19.18 The Directive does not apply to any attempt made by a judge to settle a dispute acting in the course of judicial proceedings and therefore performing a 'judging' role, rather than a pure mediation role.

The application of the Directive

19.19 The provisions of the Directive apply only in cross-border disputes, in civil and commercial matters (Art 2). However nothing prevents member states from applying any provisions of the Directive to their own internal processes (Recital 8). A cross-border dispute is defined in Art 2(a) as a dispute in which at least one of the parties is domiciled or habitually resident in a member state (meaning any of the 28 states of the EU with the exception of Denmark) other than that of any other party on the date on which:

- the parties agree to use mediation;
- mediation is ordered by the court;
- an obligation to use mediation arises under national law; or
- the court invites the parties to use mediation.

19.20 The Directive is not intended to apply to:

- pre-contractual negotiations;
- processes of an adjudicatory nature such as judicial conciliation schemes, consumer complaint schemes, arbitration, and expert determination or to processes by which a formal recommendation is issued, whether or not it is to be legally binding as to the resolution of the dispute. It therefore will not apply to early neutral evaluation (Recital 11);
- revenue, customs or administrative matters or to the liability of the state for acts and omissions in the exercise of state authority (Art 2).

Implementation of the Directive by the United Kingdom

19.21 The EU Directive on mediation has been implemented by the UK by the Cross-Border Mediation (EU Directive) Regulations 2011 (SI 2011/1133) ('the Cross-Border Regulations') and the Civil Procedure (Amendment) Rules 2011 (SI 2011/88) which added a new section III to Part 78 of the CPR.

19.22 However, these new rules only apply to cross-border disputes where the mediation was commenced on or after 20 May 2011 (reg 3 of the Cross-Border Regulations). By reg 4 of the Cross-Border Regulations, the mediation starts on the date that the agreement to mediate has been entered into by the parties and the mediator.

The main provisions of the Directive and the implementation of these provisions by the United Kingdom

19.23 The Directive includes provisions directed at ensuring the quality of mediation, setting standards for the training of mediators, ensuring that mediation settlement agreements can be easily enforced, upholding the confidentiality of mediation, and ensuring that parties using mediation do not find themselves subsequently prevented from litigating their dispute by the operation of a limitation period. Details of these provisions and how they have been implemented in the UK by the Cross-Border Regulations and Part 78 Part III of the CPR are discussed in the following paragraphs.

Ensuring the quality of mediation

Member states are required '... to encourage, by any means which they consider appropriate, the development of, and adherence to, voluntary codes of conduct for mediators and organisations providing mediation services, as well as other effective quality control mechanisms concerning the provision of mediation services' (Art 4(1)). This is an area on which further work is needed in the United Kingdom, given the piecemeal system of regulation and accreditation that exists for mediators in civil and commercial disputes (see Chapter 14). **19.24**

Unfortunately, the Directive falls short of requiring member states to implement a uniform code of conduct for mediators. **19.25**

Training and continuous professional development of mediators

Member states are required to encourage the initial and further training of mediators in order to ensure that mediation is conducted in an effective, impartial, and competent way (Art 4(2)). **19.26**

The systems in place for the regulation and accreditation of mediators in England and Wales are described in 14.75–14.100. Although the UK government consulted on whether further regulation was required (see 14.95–14.100), it has not taken any specific measures to comply with Art 4 and it is likely that the measures currently in operation in the UK comply with Art 4. **19.27**

Recourse to mediation

Article 5(1) provides that: **19.28**

> A court before which an action is brought may, when appropriate and having regard to all the circumstances of the case, invite the parties to use mediation in order to settle the dispute. The court may also invite the parties to attend an information session on the use of mediation if such sessions are held and are easily available.

Article 5(2) provides that the Directive is without prejudice to national legislation making the use of mediation compulsory or subject to incentives or sanctions, whether before or after judicial proceedings have started, provided that these do not prevent the parties from exercising their right of access to the court. **19.29**

Chapter 7 describes the various ways in which the courts in England and Wales encourage parties to use ADR processes, including mediation, to resolve their disputes and Chapter 8 sets out the sanctions that can be imposed if a party unreasonably refuses to use ADR. Although the courts of England and Wales have not gone so far as to make the use of mediation compulsory, recent developments have required parties to undertake mandatory consideration of mediation (see Chapters 14 and 18). **19.30**

Enforceability of agreements resulting from mediation

Member states should ensure that the parties are able to request that a written agreement resulting from a mediation is made enforceable by a court, by a judgment or decision or other means in accordance with national law, unless the content of the agreement is contrary to national law (Art 6(1) and (2)). **19.31**

19.32 In the UK, if proceedings have already been issued (in relation to a domestic or a cross-border dispute), the parties can record their settlement agreement by way of a Tomlin order or a consent order in those proceedings (see Chapter 23).

19.33 In relation to cross-border disputes, CPR r 78.24 also provides that where the parties, or one of them with the explicit consent of the others, wish to apply for a mediation settlement to be made enforceable, an application can be made either under Part 23 (if proceedings have already been issued) or by using the Part 8 procedure (as modified by CPR r 78.24 and PD 78) for a Mediation Settlement Enforcement Order (MSEO) if no existing proceedings have been issued between the parties.

19.34 The party making the application for a MSEO must file the following documents with the Application Notice or the Part 8 Claim Form:

- The mediated settlement agreement (CPR r 78.24(3)).
- Evidence that the other parties to the mediation settlement agreement explicitly consent to the application for enforcement. However, this is not necessary if the application is made by all parties to the mediation settlement agreement, or the mediation settlement agreement provides that a MSEO should be made in respect of the agreement, or the other party or parties to the agreement have written to the court consenting to the application (CPR r 78.24(4) and (7)). In these circumstances the party is deemed to have given explicit consent to the application.

19.35 The court can only make an order making the mediation settlement agreement enforceable if it has evidence that each of the parties to the agreement explicitly consents to this (CPR r 78.24(5) and (6)).

19.36 Where an application is made under CPR Part 23 in existing proceedings, a copy of the application notice, mediation settlement agreement, and evidence of the explicit consent must be served on all parties to the agreement who are not parties to the application (PD 78, para 22.1).

19.37 If the Part 8 procedure applies, then CPR rr 8.3–8.8 do not apply to the proceedings (CPR r 78.24(2)). Furthermore, the Part 8 Claim Form can be issued without naming a defendant, although a copy of the Claim Form, the mediation settlement agreement, and evidence of explicit consent must be served on all parties to the settlement agreement who are not also parties to the application (PD 78, para 22.2).

19.38 Provided these requirements are satisfied, the court will usually make a MSEO without a hearing (CPR r 78.24(8)). In the event of default, the parties can then apply for this order to be enforced in the same way as any other judgment or order of the court.

19.39 If the conditions for obtaining a MSEO are not satisfied or the parties choose not to make an application for such an order, and they are not otherwise able to record their settlement agreement as a consent order in existing proceedings, the agreement reached in mediation can be enforced by suing for breach of the terms of the settlement agreement, obtaining judgment in that claim, and then enforcing the court order (see Chapter 32). However, using the procedure set out in CPR r 78.24 will enable the parties to proceed to enforcement by a more direct and speedy route.

19.40 Where a person applies to enforce a MSEO which is expressed in a foreign currency, the application must contain a certificate of the sterling equivalent of the sum remaining due under the order at the close of business on the day before the application (CPR r 78.25).

Confidentiality

The Directive recognizes that confidentiality in the mediation process is important and that there should be a minimum degree of compatibility of civil procedural rules with regard to how to protect the confidentiality of mediation in any subsequent civil or commercial judicial proceedings or arbitration (Recital 23). Article 7(1) provides that member states must ensure that neither mediators nor those involved in the administration of the mediation process shall be compelled to give evidence in civil or commercial judicial proceedings or arbitration regarding information arising out of or in connection with a mediation process, except in the following circumstances: **19.41**

- The parties agree otherwise.
- It is necessary for overriding considerations of public policy, in particular to ensure the protection of children or prevent physical or psychological harm to any person.
- Disclosure of the content of the agreement is necessary in order to implement or enforce that agreement.

Article 7(2) provides that nothing shall prevent a member state from enacting stricter measures to protect the confidentiality of mediation. **19.42**

The circumstances in which the confidentiality of mediation can be overridden are narrower under the Directive in relation to cross-border disputes than those that exist as a result of recent case law developments in the courts of England and Wales. As discussed in 14.135–14.145, confidentiality in mediation in domestic disputes can be overridden where the interests of justice require it. **19.43**

In cross-border disputes, reg 9 of the Cross-Border Regulations provides that, subject to reg 10, a mediator or a mediation administrator has the right to withhold mediation evidence in civil and commercial proceedings and in arbitration. Mediation evidence is defined by reg 8 and CPR r 78.23(2) as 'evidence arising out of or in connection with a mediation process'. **19.44**

Regulation 10 and CPR r 78.26–78.28 implement Art 7(1) of the Directive by providing that a court may order that a mediator or a mediation administrator must give or disclose mediation evidence where: **19.45**

(a) all the parties to the mediation agree;
(b) the evidence is necessary for overriding considerations of public policy; or
(c) the evidence relates to the mediation settlement, and disclosure is necessary to implement or enforce the mediation settlement agreement.

Where a person seeks disclosure or inspection of mediation evidence, an application is made by a Part 23 application if proceedings have already been issued or by Part 8 Claim Form if they have not. The mediator must be made a respondent to the Part 23 application or a party to the Part 8 Claim form (CPR r 78.26(2)). The evidence in support must establish one of the grounds set out in (a), (b), or (c) in 19.45. **19.46**

CPR r 78.27 provides that where a party wishes to obtain mediation evidence from a mediator by any of the following means then they must make an application to the court, providing evidence which establishes one of the grounds set out in (a), (b), or (c) in 19.45: **19.47**

- a witness summons;
- cross-examination with permission of the court under CPR r 32.7 or r 33.4;
- evidence by deposition by an order under CPR r 34.8;
- an order enforcing attendance of a witness by an order under CPR r 34.10;

- an order under CPR r 34.11(4) for a deponent's evidence to be given orally; or
- by an order under CPR r 34.13(1A) for the issue of a Letter of Request.

19.48 CPR r 78.27 and r 78.26 do not apply to proceedings that have been allocated to the Small Claims Track. If a party wishes to rely on mediation evidence in proceedings that are allocated to the Small Claims Track, that party must inform the court immediately (CPR r 78.28).

19.49 To ensure the privacy and confidentiality of mediation, PD 78, para 22.3 provides that no document relating to an application for a mediation settlement enforcement order may be inspected by a person who is not a party to the proceedings under CPR r 5.4C without the permission of the court.

Effect of mediation on limitation and prescription periods

19.50 Member states are required to ensure that parties who choose to attempt to settle their dispute by mediation are not subsequently prevented from initiating judicial proceedings or referring a dispute to arbitration by the expiry of limitation or prescription periods during the mediation process (Art 8).

19.51 The Cross-Border Regulations add a new provision to the Limitation Act 1980, namely s 33A. This provides that where a time limit under the Limitation Act applies, in whole or in part, to a cross-border dispute, and a mediation in relation to the dispute starts before the time limit expires and, if not extended by s 33A, the time limit would expire before the mediation ends or less than eight weeks after it ends, then for the purposes of initiating judicial proceedings or arbitration, the time limit expires instead at the end of eight weeks after the mediation ends. Section 33A(6) and (7) define when a mediation is deemed to start and end. It should be noted that these provisions are not a model of clarity.

19.52 Mediation starts on the date the agreement to mediate is entered into by the parties and the mediator (s 33A(6)).

19.53 Mediation ends on whichever one of the following dates occurs first:

- the parties reach an agreement in resolution of the dispute;
- one party notifies the other parties that it has withdrawn from the mediation;
- a party to whom a qualifying request is made (defined as a request to confirm to all parties that it is continuing with the mediation) fails to 'give a response reaching the other parties within 14 days of the request';
- the parties fail to agree to appoint a replacement mediator (in the event that the mediator's appointment has ended by death, resignation, or otherwise) within 14 days from the date the parties were notified that the mediator's appointment has ended. Although s 33A does not say this, presumably in a case where the parties were notified on different dates, the 14-day period will run from the latest date on which the last party was notified;
- the mediation otherwise comes to an end pursuant to the terms of the agreement to mediate.

19.54 By the operation of s 33A(4), if a time limit has been extended under s 33A, but a second mediation starts before that extended time limit expired, and if not extended by s 33A(2) and (3), the extended period would expire before the second mediation ends or less than eight weeks after it ends, then the time limit will expire instead at the end of eight weeks after the second mediation ends. There are no limits to the amount of times the limitation period could be extended by virtue of the operation of s 33A(2), (3) and (4).

19.55 Similar amendments are made to the limitation periods set out in the Prescription Act 1832, the Equal Pay Act 1970, the Sex Discrimination Act 1975, the Foreign Limitation Periods Act 1984, the Employment Rights Act 1996, the Land Registration Act 2002 and the Equality Act 2002 and also to specified secondary legislation made under some of those Acts.

Publicity

Member states should encourage the provision of information to the general public on how to contact mediators and organizations providing mediation services, in particular on the internet (Art 9). They should also encourage legal practitioners to inform their clients of the possibility of mediation (Recital 25).

The government has improved the level of information offered to the public about dispute resolution options and in particular mediation. New online information service is provided at www.direct.gov.uk. The Legal Services Commission has also published a booklet on 'Alternatives to Court' (www.communitylegaladvice.org.uk/media/808/FD/leaflet23e.pdf). **19.57**

Application of the Directive to domestic mediations

The Directive and CPR Part 78 Part III only apply to cross-border disputes as defined in Art 2 **19.58** of the EU Mediation Directive. These provisions have no application to domestic mediations, which continue to be governed by the law described in Chapters 14–16. The Ministry of Justice has consulted on the need to introduce similar measures for domestic mediations (*Solving Disputes in the County Courts: creating a simpler, quicker and more proportionate system*, Consultation Paper CP6/2011). The Civil Mediation Council's response to the consultation, which can be viewed on its website at www.civilmediation.org, showed that 84.6% of those surveyed agreed that provisions required by the EU Mediation Directive should be similarly provided for domestic cases. However, the government, in its Response to the Consultation, indicated that it intends to review the operation of the provisions implementing the Directive before deciding whether to introduce similar provisions for mediations in domestic disputes.

Implementation of the EU Mediation Directive in other member states

The Directive has now been implemented in almost all of the member states. Some states **19.59** (eg Belgium, Greece, and Italy) have implemented a system of compulsory referral to mediation. Other states, unlike the United Kingdom, have extended the scope of the Directive to domestic disputes. Other states (eg Bulgaria) have provided financial incentives to the parties to use mediation. For an overview of how the Directive has been implemented in other member states see the European Parliament's Resolution of 13 September 2011 on the implementation of the Directive on mediation in the member states, its impact on mediation, and its take-up by the courts (see www.europarl.europa.eu/oeil/FindByProcnum.do?lang=en&procnum=INI/2011/2026).

H THE EUROPEAN CODE OF CONDUCT FOR MEDIATORS

The European Code of Conduct for Mediators has been approved by the Justice Directorate **19.60** of the European Commission. It sets out a number of principles to which individual mediators can voluntarily decide to commit. It therefore falls far short of laying down a uniform set of principles which mediators across member states are obliged to follow. It sets out a range of principles covering matters such as competence, independence and impartiality, the procedure for the mediation, fairness of the process, confidentiality and the termination of the process. The CMC has endorsed the Code as laying down minimum standards which its members should observe. The Code of Conduct is discussed in more detail in 14.101–14.119.

·EABILITY OF INTERNATIONAL MEDIATION SETTLEMENT ·S

·ched in international mediation cannot be enforced in the same way as a · or an arbitration award in another jurisdiction. International arbitral · enforceable in almost every country in the world under the New York ·58 (see Chapter 32).

·ation or litigation proceedings have already been commenced, and a mediated set- ·ent is reached during the course of those proceedings, it could be reflected as a consent order in the litigation or an agreed award in the arbitration proceedings. For cross-border disputes, the parties may also be able to obtain a MSEO in the circumstances described in 19.34. Such orders could then be enforceable in the same way as a court order or arbitral award (see Chapters 23 and 32 for details).

19.63 If the consent order or MSEO is made in the courts of an EU state, reciprocal enforcement arrangements exist by virtue of the Jurisdiction and Judgments Regulation (Regulation (EC) No 44/2001). Consent orders of a court in an EU state which is a party to the Jurisdiction and Judgments Regulation can be registered for enforcement in the courts of England and Wales pursuant to CPR, Part 74. Reciprocal enforcement arrangements also exist in cross-border family cases by Council Regulation (EC) No 2201/2003 on the jurisdiction and recognition and enforcement of judgments in matrimonial matters and matters of parental responsibility.

KEY POINTS SUMMARY

19.64
- Mediation has grown globally at a rapid rate in the last ten years, particularly in EU countries.
- Mediation is particularly effective as an ADR process for resolving international disputes, because:
  - It enables linguistic and cultural differences to be managed and respected to a greater extent than is possible in court proceedings.
  - It avoids complex arguments about which court has jurisdiction to determine the dispute and which system of law applies to the dispute.
  - It can be speedy and cost-effective compared to the costs involved in arbitrating or litigating such disputes.
  - The flexibility of the process enables the parties to tailor it to their particular needs.
- A team of mediators will usually need to be appointed to mediate international disputes.
- A move to promote and set minimum standards for mediation in EU countries was created by the EU Directive on mediation in civil and commercial matters (Directive 2008/52/EC).
- EU member states were required to implement the Directive by 21 May 2011.
- The UK has implemented the Directive by, amongst other measures, adding s 33A of the Limitation Act 1980 to suspend the operation of the limitation period while the parties are attempting mediation in a cross-border dispute and providing for mediation settlement agreements in such disputes to be made orders of the court for ease of enforcement by enabling parties to apply for a MSEO.
- Other significant proposals have been made to harmonize mediation and other ADR processes across the EU in relation to consumer disputes and use of online ADR.
- A voluntary European Code of Conduct for Mediators has also been implemented.

PART IV

EVALUATION, CONCILIATION, AND OMBUDSMEN

20

CONCILIATION

A WHAT IS CONCILIATION? 20.01
B AN OUTLINE OF THE PROCESS 20.04
C ADVISORY, CONCILIATION AND ARBITRATION SERVICE 20.06
D CONCILIATION IN FAMILY CASES. 20.12
E OTHER CONCILIATION SCHEMES 20.15
Key points summary 20.17

A WHAT IS CONCILIATION?

Conciliation is a voluntary process whereby a neutral third party facilitates negotiations between the parties to a dispute and assists them to reach a settlement. The process is virtually identical to mediation. There is no international or national consistency over the terminology, so the terms 'conciliation' and 'mediation' can be used to describe the same process. Mediation is the term that is more commonly used now in the United Kingdom to describe ADR by third party facilitation in civil and commercial disputes. **20.01**

In some types of conciliation, the conciliator may express an opinion on the merits of the dispute and may, and usually will, suggest a solution if the parties cannot put forward proposals themselves to resolve the matter. In other types of conciliation processes, the conciliator will adopt a purely facilitative role. **20.02**

Conciliation is most commonly encountered in family and employment disputes (although mediation is also used in these cases—see Chapter 18). The role of conciliation in such disputes is therefore the primary focus of this chapter. **20.03**

B AN OUTLINE OF THE PROCESS

Conciliation is a confidential and 'without prejudice' voluntary process. Either party can withdraw from it at any time before settlement is reached. The conciliator has no power to impose a solution on the parties. Whether a settlement is reached and, if so, the terms of that settlement, lies within the control of the parties themselves. Factors influencing the choice of conciliation as an ADR process are set out in Chapter 3 and the advantages and disadvantages of ADR are set out in Chapter 1. **20.04**

The process is very similar to mediation (see Chapters 15 and 16). The only difference is that: **20.05**

- The parties will not usually select and appoint the conciliator themselves. If they are able to do so, the factors that are described in 15.03–15.19 will be relevant.
- The conciliator will hold private and joint meetings with the parties in much the same way as a mediator (see Chapter 16), although some conciliators will prefer to use joint meetings.

- The conciliator will perform the same function as a mediator in moving the parties towards settlement, although he or she may, in some cases, be more active in putting forward proposals for the consideration of the parties. In that sense the conciliator will perform a role similar to that of an evaluative mediator rather than a facilitative mediator (see 14.50–14.64).
- Like mediation, the parties do not have to agree to any solution that is recommended by the conciliator, although they can agree (usually in writing in advance of the conciliation) that any solution put forward is binding on them.
- An agreement reached in conciliation can be recorded and enforced in the same way as agreements reached in other ADR processes (see Chapters 17, 23, and 32).

C ADVISORY, CONCILIATION AND ARBITRATION SERVICE

20.06 The Advisory, Conciliation and Arbitration Service (ACAS) deals with all types of employment issues in the United Kingdom. It was founded in 1974 and is one of the most established ADR bodies in the United Kingdom. Full details of all services it provides can be found on its website: www.acas.org.uk. ACAS offer conciliation and mediation services. The only difference between the two ACAS processes is that conciliation is the term used to describe the ADR process if an employee has made or may make a claim to an employment tribunal. Mediation is used to resolve workplace disputes with the aim of restoring and maintaining the employment relationship between the parties.

Mandatory Early Conciliation

20.07 With effect from 6 May 2014, the Enterprise and Regulatory Reform Act 2013 introduced a mandatory requirement for prospective claimants to contact ACAS for Early Conciliation of the dispute before presenting a claim in the Employment Tribunal. There are a small number of exemptions to this requirement (see Reg 3 of the Employment Tribunals (Early Conciliation: Exemptions and Rules of Procedure) Regulations 2014. Claimants make a request for Early Conciliation by completing the Early Conciliation Notification form, which can be located on the ACAS website (see www.acas.org.uk/earlyconciliation). An ACAS conciliator will then contact the parties and explain what is involved in Early Conciliation and seek their agreement to the process. For a period up to one calendar month starting on the date of the request for conciliation, the conciliation officer must endeavour to promote a settlement between the parties. This period can be extended by agreement, although such an extension can only occur once and must not exceed 14 days. If during this period, the conciliation officer concludes that settlement is not possible, then ACAS must issue an Early Conciliation certificate, which bears a unique reference number, and this is sent to the parties. The claimant must provide this unique reference number when presenting a claim to the Employment Tribunal. If a settlement can be reached by Early Conciliation, then the agreement will be recorded on an ACAS form (known as a COT3), and this is signed by both parties as a record of the settlement agreement. This agreement will be legally binding on the parties. ACAS will then inform the tribunal that settlement has been reached. If the parties cannot reach a settlement, then the claimant can issue a claim in the Employment Tribunal. The limitation period for bringing such a claim is suspended during the period of Early Conciliation.

Post-claim conciliation

20.08 ACAS will also continue to offer conciliation to the parties after a claim has been made to the employment tribunal in respect of employment rights and this can occur up to the date of the Employment Tribunal hearing. Where possible, ACAS will seek to ensure that the same conciliator is involved in both Early Conciliation and any conciliation that takes place after the claim has been commenced. Both pre- and post-claim conciliation is free to the parties. ACAS conciliators are impartial and independent and they are not part of the Employment Tribunal Service. The conciliator will not impose a solution on the parties but will facilitate negotiations between the parties and assist them to reach their own solution. The parties can reach a settlement that a tribunal has no power to order (for example the provision of a reference, perhaps in agreed terms). ACAS conciliation is confidential and the tribunal will not be given details of what took place during the conciliation if settlement is not reached.

It is not the function of an ACAS conciliator to ensure that the terms of settlement are fair to the parties, nor should the conciliator advise the parties about the merits or likely outcome of the case (*Clarke v Redcar & Cleveland Borough Council* [2006] IRLR 324). **20.09**

ACAS reports that pre-claim conciliation has resulted in considerable costs savings to both employers and employees. For employers, the average cost of a tribunal case is £3,700, whereas pre-claim conciliation will cost around £475, for employees the cost of a tribunal case is £1,300 and pre-claim conciliation costs around £78. These estimates include staff time, administration, and legal costs. In 2010–11, around 17,781 disputes were referred for pre-claim conciliation and of these, 47.7% were settled or resolved, and in 73.7% of cases no subsequent claim was issued in the tribunal. The overall satisfaction rate with the service was reported to be around 83% (see ACAS Research Paper 07/2011 'The Dispute Resolution Regulations Two Years On: The Acas Experience' by Barbara Davey and Gill Dix on the operation of the conciliation schemes, and the ACAS Annual Report 2010–11, both of which can be accessed on www.acas.org.uk). Early claim conciliation evolved as a result of the success of the pre-existing ACAS pre-claim conciliation service. **20.10**

Collective conciliation

This is a term used to describe talks between representative groups such as trade unions and employers—which are facilitated by ACAS. **20.11**

D CONCILIATION IN FAMILY CASES

Conciliation is commonly employed in family disputes where the choice of process is driven by the court rather than the parties. In-court conciliation is offered in disputes by parents over children after the breakdown of a marriage. **20.12**

The process

In-court conciliation consists of a meeting at court, usually lasting around one hour, between the parents with the assistance of a neutral independent party from the Children and Family Court Advisory and Support Service (Cafcass) to help them to negotiate disputes relating to contact and residence arrangements for children following separation or divorce. The aim is to help them to resolve their dispute without the need for court intervention. In-court conciliation is delivered by Cafcass in the Family Court. **20.13**

In private law proceedings relating to children conciliation occurs in the following ways: **20.14**

- A First Hearing Dispute Resolution Appointment (FHDRA) will be arranged before the district judge or registrar where the court will consider the extent to which the parties can resolve some or all of the issues with the assistance of the Cafcass officer (and a mediator if available).

- At the FHDRA or a subsequent conciliation appointment, the parties will outline the nature of the application and the matters in dispute to the district judge and the Cafcass officer.
- The court in collaboration with the Cafcass officer (and sometimes a mediator) will seek to assist the parties in conciliation and resolution of the issues between them (see FPR 2010, PD 12B).
- All discussions at the conciliation appointment are privileged and will not be disclosed in any subsequent hearing other than a further conciliation appointment.
- If agreement is reached, the district judge will make the relevant orders by consent.
- If agreement is not reached, then the district judge will give directions for the hearing of the application. The Cafcass officer and the district judge will not be involved in any further applications between the parties other than further conciliation appointments.

E OTHER CONCILIATION SCHEMES

The Disability Conciliation Service

20.15 The Disability Conciliation Service offers individuals with a disability the opportunity to resolve disputes under the Equalities Act 2010 in relation to discrimination in the provision of goods, services, education, and employment instead of pursuing court or tribunal proceedings (see www.dcs-gb.net). A conciliator will assist the parties to help them resolve the dispute. The service is free to the parties as it is funded by the Disability Rights Commission (DRC). Referrals to the Scheme must be made by the DRC. For more details on the scheme see www.dcs-gb.net.

The Furniture Ombudsmen Conciliation Scheme

20.16 The Furniture Ombudsmen (TFO) is an independent organization offering ADR services for consumers of the furniture, home improvements, and floor coverings industry. It is overseen by Trading Standards and by representatives of retailers and manufacturers. The service is available to consumers who purchase goods or services from members of TFO. A list of organizations who are members is available at www.thefurnitureombudsman.org/services. The TFO conciliator will look at the matters in dispute, at no cost to the consumer, and put forward proposals to enable the matter to be resolved. Consumers must try to resolve the complaint with the member using any internal complaints procedure before using the scheme.

KEY POINTS SUMMARY

20.17
- Conciliation is very similar to mediation. The terms 'conciliation' and 'mediation' can be used interchangeably to describe the same process in some countries and by some commentators.
- In England and Wales, conciliation tends to be court-driven and it is most often used in family and employment cases.
- It is useful when the parties would benefit from the assistance of a neutral party to help them to settle their dispute.

- In employment cases, the parties must attempt mandatory Early Conciliation with ACAS before a claim is issued in the Employment Tribunal, and free conciliation can also be undertaken by ACAS after a claim has been lodged if Early Conciliation did not result in a settlement.
- In-court conciliation also takes place in family cases in disputes relating to children and money on the breakdown of the relationship between the parties.
- A number of independent conciliation schemes exists to help consumers solve disputes in relation to goods or services.

21

COMPLAINTS, GRIEVANCES, AND OMBUDSMEN

A INTRODUCTION 21.01
B COMPLAINTS AND GRIEVANCE PROCEDURES 21.02
C OMBUDSMEN 21.18
Key points summary 21.29

A INTRODUCTION

21.01 Grievance, complaints, and ombudsman schemes are designed to provide effective and speedy relief where problems arise between a customer and an organization. It is recognized that the customer often wants no more than an explanation or an apology (such as in relation to medical care). These schemes seek to provide a local or in-house solution when a problem arises. However, complaints procedures have themselves grown in sophistication, and increasingly they provide for 'appeals' to national bodies where a matter cannot be resolved by the local organization.

B COMPLAINTS AND GRIEVANCE PROCEDURES

21.02 It has become increasingly common for government agencies, companies and organizations that offer goods or services to the general public to have internal complaints and grievance procedures to look into and respond to any problems raised by their customers of a formal nature. It is seen to be good for customer relations for problems to be investigated by someone within the organization and for the problem to be resolved with the customer quickly and before it escalates into a contentious dispute. Efficient and effective complaints and grievance procedures also form part of an organization's quality control or quality assurance procedures, which are aimed at ensuring that high levels of service are maintained, with any weaknesses being addressed swiftly before other customers are affected by similar problems.

21.03 In many areas of activity, having a formal written complaints or grievance policy is simply a matter of good practice. In others, having these procedures may be:

- an effective requirement of a relevant code of professional conduct, such as the need to have a client complaints procedure for solicitors (SRA Code of Conduct 2011, Outcomes 1.10 and 1.11, and Indicative Behaviour 1.22) and barristers (Bar Code of Conduct, Outcome oC19 and Part 5, Enforcement Regulations);
- supported by legislation, as in the case of grievance and disciplinary procedures in employment law (Trade Union and Labour Relations (Consolidation) Act 1992 and Employment Act 2008).

Definitions

'Complaints' and 'grievances' are obviously related concepts. According to ACAS (the Advisory, Conciliation and Advisory Service in relation to employment matters), a grievance is a concern, problem, or complaint that an employee might raise with their employer, which would mean that complaints are subsumed within the general umbrella of 'grievances'. This is an area where there is a lack of generally agreed definitions, but for clarity: **21.04**

- a 'complaint' may be regarded as a problem raised in the context of a one-off transaction or incident. Examples may include a defective item that has been purchased, or misleading advice, or a bad service given on a particular occasion; and
- a 'grievance' arises in the context of a continuing relationship, particularly that between employees and employers.

'Complaints' are often divided into formal and informal complaints. Usually the difference is that a formal complaint has to be made in writing, or on a complaints form prescribed by the relevant policy of the organization. Most complaints procedures and policies only apply to formal, written, complaints. Informal complaints (those made orally, or not on the relevant form etc) may well be responded to, but not under the relevant complaints procedure, and probably without the investigation involved in a formal complaint. **21.05**

Complaints handling

Complaints are usually the first stage of resolution for many disagreements that members of the public have with companies or government departments. There is a guide issued by the Legal Ombudsman which says good complaints handling should be reasonable, fair and proportionate, as well as accessible and responsive to an individual's needs. Under many complaints schemes there is a fairly short time limit for lodging the complaint. In some schemes an official complaint form must be used, but others can be accessed by raising the complaint by letter or email. Many complaints procedures are handled at a local level, often informally. How the complaint will be dealt with depends on the procedures laid down by the relevant complaints policy and the circumstances of the particular case. **21.06**

The organization will typically acknowledge receipt of the complaint in writing, and indicate a period over which it is intended that the matter will be investigated and a decision reached. A person (the 'investigator'), or sometimes a panel, typically of three people, will be designated by the organization to investigate the matter. Some procedures give the investigation and decision-making responsibilities to a single person. Others designate one person to investigate, who reports to a more senior person who makes the decision on the basis of the report. A great many complaints are dealt with entirely on the basis of written materials. In others the complainant, and possibly employees of the organization, will be interviewed, followed by a decision. In others there will be a meeting where the facts relating to the complaint will be raised and considered. Most complaints and grievance policies say very little about the investigation process, leaving a great deal to the discretion and good sense of the investigator or panel. Where the policy sets out a specific procedure, that of course should be followed. **21.07**

Most investigators or panels will tailor the amount of time spent in investigating a matter and the degree of formality to the nature of the complaint and its seriousness. The guiding principles are the rules of natural justice. These mean that anyone who may have an adverse finding against them must be notified of the nature of the allegations being made, and be given a reasonable opportunity to respond to them. Most investigators will also want to **21.08** ensure that the real complaint is looked into, so will often communicate with the complainant to ensure they have fully understood what lies behind the complaint.

21.09 Meetings and hearings take a variety of different forms. They usually start with the person chairing the meeting getting each person to introduce themselves, and then explaining the nature of the investigation. The complainant is often asked to say what they are seeking from the investigation. The meeting can then take a number of different courses, from a general discussion to something more resembling a court hearing with questions being put to the different people in turn. Whatever form it takes, each person directly involved must be given a fair chance to state their case.

Complaints against solicitors

21.10 One of the most highly developed complaints systems is that operated by the legal profession. In relation to complaints against solicitors, initial complaints must be made to the firm. A template letter of complaint can be found on the Legal Ombudsman's website (www.legalombudsman.org.uk). Solicitors should deal with complaints in accordance with their firm's written complaints policy within eight weeks. If making a complaint to the firm fails to result in a resolution to the satisfaction of the client, the client can take the matter to either the Legal Ombudsman (see 21.23) or the Solicitors Regulation Authority (SRA) (see 21.11). The division of work between these two organizations is that complaints about poor service are made to the Legal Ombudsman, whereas reports of alleged failures to comply with the SRA Code of Conduct are made to the SRA. Poor service includes failure to communicate with the client, problems with fees, and loss of documents. Code of Conduct issues include breach of confidentiality, dishonesty, and discrimination.

21.11 Reports of professional misconduct to the SRA can be made by telephone or email, but there is also a report form that can be obtained from the SRA website (www.sra.org.uk). While reports are acknowledged by the SRA, in most cases there will be no further contact with the person making the report, unless they need to be approached for further information. The purpose behind SRA investigations is to ensure solicitors comply with their professional standards as set out in the Code of Conduct. If there is an adverse finding, the SRA has wide powers, which include taking formal enforcement action limiting or restricting the way the firm works, or even intervening and closing the firm. Unlike the Legal Ombudsman, the SRA has no power to require the firm to pay compensation to the client.

Employment grievances

21.12 A wide range of matters may be raised in employment grievances. These include:

- an employee's contractual terms and conditions;
- new working practices and organizational changes;
- health and safety issues;
- bullying and harassment;
- equal opportunities.

21.13 Most employment grievances should be capable of being resolved amicably and quickly through discussions between the employee and their line manager. Others are best resolved with the assistance of mediation (see Chapters 14–19). When a grievance affects several employees in a similar way it may be necessary to have the interests of the employees represented by the relevant trade union. Where an employment-related grievance cannot be resolved between the employee and employer, it may be necessary to refer the matter to ACAS, which has a range of conciliation (see Chapter 20), mediation, and other procedures available to it together with considerable experience in resolving employment disputes.

An example of an employment grievance is shown in Figure 21.1. This example is worded in a fairly formal way, typical of the drafting to be expected from a lawyer. Many formal complaints and grievances are written by the person affected, who will not be a lawyer and who cannot be expected to set the matter out in the structured way shown in Figure 21.1. It will be seen that in this case the written grievance makes specific reference to the company's relevant policy document, sets out the incidents complained about, and indicates that what has happened breaches the policy. It ends by setting out what the complainant wants to achieve if the grievance is upheld. A large number of complaints and grievances are based on anonymous information, and an example can be seen in para (c) of Figure 21.1. Most organizations rightly refuse to investigate anonymous complaints, particularly when they relate to the conduct of staff. This is because it is grossly unfair to the person identified in such a complaint, who cannot reasonably be expected to respond to an incident involving an unidentified person. Allegation (c) in this case would almost certainly be dismissed for this reason. **21.14**

Figure 21.1 Employment grievance

Grievance

This Grievance is being made because I feel that bullying, intimidation and drunkenness by [name of manager] have not been dealt with seriously enough by the company. The company's Harassment and Dignity at Work policy document states:

> 'The company takes the issue of harassment and bullying very seriously and is committed to a working environment that is free from discrimination and intimidation, and in which the dignity of the individual is paramount.'

The policy also states:

- Individuals should have confidence to complain about harassment and bullying should it arise (clause 2)
- Staff are required to make it clear they find such behaviour unacceptable (clause 4)
- The company will foster a climate that discourages the occurrence of harassment and bullying (clause 10)
- The company will act upon potential breaches of this policy and unacceptable behaviour despite the absence of a formal complaint (clause 11)

There are three related matters:

(a) On 16 July 2014 [*name of manager*] had been to the pub and was drunk. He exploded in anger over a batch of invoices which were a day late in being sent out. My supervisor wrote an email to him on 17 July saying: 'You cannot continue being so aggressive with members of staff. We all have to work together, and staff cannot cope with being bullied and belittled when due to pressures of work some things have to be slightly delayed.'

(b) [*Name of manager*] swore at me repeatedly in a meeting I had with him on 28 July 2014 about 3.30pm. He repeatedly used the word 'f...ing' to describe me and a report I had sent to him. He was shouting at me, and refused to listen and talked over me when I tried to give an explanation to him. His breath smelt of alcohol on this occasion too.

Figure 21.1 *Continued*

(c) These were not isolated incidents. I know of two occasions when [*name of manager*] was swearing and shouting at a female member of staff in the main office. This member of staff wants to remain anonymous, and has told me she will not make a formal complaint because, she says, it is far too dangerous to complain against [*name of manager*]. This shows that staff believe they will not be supported by the company if they make complaints about bullying.

The above falls within the definition of bullying set out in the company's policy, which includes:

- Using abusive language
- Shouting at or humiliating an individual in front of colleagues or in private

I raised these matters informally with [*name of senior manager*] on 28 July 2014.

What I would like is an assurance that the company's Harassment and Dignity at Work policy will be honoured. This should include taking these matters very seriously, and not tolerating conduct which creates an intimidating, hostile, degrading or humiliating environment. I would also like to know what if any disciplinary action is being taken against [*name of manager*].

Signed

Date 11 August 2014

Acting for a party in a complaint

21.15 When acting for either a complainant or the person against whom a complaint is raised, it is first necessary to get the full story, both from the person involved and from the relevant documents. This may involve some investigation of what documents are or should be available. It may also become clear that other people may need to be contacted to find out what they know. It is vital to obtain a copy of the relevant complaints procedure or policy, together with any of the company's written procedures or guidance notes that may be relevant. It may be that a meeting or hearing will have been already convened by the company or organization but, if not, consideration should be given to whether this would be helpful in conveying the case of the person who is being represented. Sometimes they will be best advised to have a matter considered on the papers, but in many cases, particularly serious matters, they will only have their side of events fully considered at a meeting or hearing.

Decisions in complaints and grievance investigations

21.16 The primary decision that needs to be made is whether to uphold or dismiss the complaint or grievance. This may be done at the meeting, or by letter shortly afterwards. It is best practice to give reasons for the decision, although these are usually short. Some complaints are dismissed after initial fact finding. Others are dealt with by conciliation between the client and organization (see Chapter 20). Organizations should keep records of successful and unsuccessful complaints, and good practice is to take appropriate action to rectify problems identified by the process for the benefit of future customers and employees. Typical outcomes that may be available in an individual matter under different complaints and grievance processes include:

- an explanation;
- an apology;
- compensation;

- reduction of a bill or a refund;
- disciplinary action.

Effectiveness of complaints and grievance procedures

Grievance and complaints procedures can be quick, may cost nothing to the complainant, and can produce helpful solutions. However, many complaints procedures are inefficient and may take a long time to complete. Objections are sometimes raised that complaints procedures are not independent, because they are operated by the organization against which the complaint is raised. If a complaints procedure does not produce the desired result, it may be necessary to take the matter further, such as through litigation, or with an ombudsman. **21.17**

C OMBUDSMEN

Ombudsmen act rather like umpires in complaints brought against public or private organizations. If an organization is a member of an ombudsman scheme, it should make this clear in a brochure or on its letterhead. Most ombudsmen belong to the Ombudsman Association, which can provide information about the available public and private sector ombudsman schemes. Its website is www.ombudsmanassociation.org.uk. **21.18**

Important ombudsman schemes include the Local Government Ombudsman (England), which deals with complaints about services provided by local authorities in England (see www.lgo.org.uk), and the Parliamentary and Health Service Ombudsman, which deals with complaints about services provided by government departments and the NHS in England (see www.ombudsman.org.uk). There are also ombudsman schemes for a range of different consumer services, including many professions, public utility companies such as energy, water, and telephones, and financial services such as banks and insurance companies. There is a statutory ombudsman scheme for the financial industry in the Financial Services and Markets Act 2000, ss 225–234A. **21.19**

Complaints handling by ombudsmen

Ombudsmen are independent from the organizations they investigate. Ombudsman schemes usually provide that reference to the ombudsman is only permitted after attempting to resolve the complaint through an organization's internal complaints procedure. Ombudsmen therefore frequently deal with the more difficult complaints that cannot be resolved by an organization's internal complaints system. How complaints are investigated under ombudsman schemes varies considerably, but good practice has been formulated in the Ombudsman Association's *Guide to Principles of Good Complaints Handling*. Two key goals are that: **21.20**

- complaints must be considered impartially and on their merits; and
- independent judgment must be brought to bear.

In order to achieve these aims, the *Guide to Principles of Good Complaints Handling* says that ombudsman schemes should be designed to comply with the following seven principles: **21.21**

- *clarity of purpose*, with a clear statement of the role of the ombudsman and the aims of the scheme;
- *accessibility*, so that the scheme is free and open to anyone who needs to use it;
- *flexible procedures*, which can be adjusted to meet the requirements of each case. The *Guide* makes the point that it is important that each complainant is made to feel they are being treated as an individual with their complaint being dealt with on its own merits;

- *transparency*, so that information is readily available;
- *proportionality*, so that the process used is appropriate to the complaint;
- *efficiency*; and
- *quality outcomes*, with the process leading to positive change.

Procedure on references to ombudsmen

21.22 Many schemes provide that there will be a governing body with a chair and members who oversee the scheme. Most schemes use a 'documents-only' process. They may be started by a letter or the completion of a complaints form. The depth of any particular investigation will depend on the nature and complexity of the complaint. In some cases the primary function of the ombudsman is to explain the decision-making process or to provide other information to the complainant because the complaint is essentially one where the complainant does not understand what has been done because it has not previously been clearly explained. In most other cases the ombudsman has to enter into detailed correspondence with the complainant and the organization in an attempt to identify exactly what lies behind the complaint, and to get the organization's explanation for what it has done. In seeking to do this the ombudsman has to abide by the rules of natural justice, and an obvious danger here is that it is possible for the correspondence to become unbalanced, with either the complainant or the organization appearing to be consulted more frequently than the other. There is no rule that there should be an equal number of letters to each party, but the ombudsman must be careful to ensure there is no appearance of favouring one side over the other.

21.23 An example is the legal ombudsman scheme. This was referred to at 21.10, and covers complaints of poor service against solicitors, barristers, and other legal professionals who carry out reserved legal activities within the meaning of the Legal Services Act 2007 s 129. In most cases the complainant must first use the lawyer's internal complaints procedure, although there are exceptions, such as where there has been an irretrievable breakdown in the relationship, or if the lawyer fails to resolve the complaint within eight weeks. Complaints to the Legal Ombudsman must ordinarily be made within a year from the relevant act or omission. There is a standard complaint form. The lawyer will be sent a copy of the complaint, and all parties are given an opportunity to make representations. Occasionally the ombudsman may refer the whole dispute or a legal question raised by the complaint to court. Otherwise, the ombudsman will resolve the complaint informally, or conduct an investigation. Investigations can include directions for the production of information or documents, but will only include a hearing if the complaint cannot be fairly determined without hearing the parties. Hearings can be conducted by any means considered appropriate, including by telephone.

Grounds on which ombudsmen make their decisions

21.24 Under the legal ombudsman and financial ombudsman schemes decisions are based on what the ombudsman considers to be fair and reasonable in all the circumstances of the case. This can include reference to how a court might have decided the case, the relevant code of conduct, and what the ombudsman considers to have been good practice at the time of the act or omission. Public sector ombudsmen normally only review how a decision was made, not whether it was right, and uphold a complaint if there was 'maladministration' that resulted in an injustice. Maladministration can include:

- a public body not following its own policies or procedures;
- rudeness;
- taking too long;
- failing to act;

- treating the complainant less fairly than other people; and
- giving wrong or misleading information.

Private sector ombudsmen may come to a decision against the organization on any of the above grounds, and also if it is felt that the organization's conduct was unfair or unreasonable when compared with industry standards of good practice. **21.25**

Effect of ombudsman's decision

Decisions made by ombudsmen may or may not be binding, depending on the terms of the particular scheme. Pensions Ombudsman decisions are binding, and those of the Financial Ombudsman are binding if they are accepted by the complainant (Financial Services and Markets Act 2000, s 228(5)). While a government department is not bound by the findings of the Parliamentary Ombudsman, it may only reject the Ombudsman's findings if doing so is not irrational (*R (Bradley) v Secretary of State for Work and Pensions* [2009] QB 114). **21.26**

Compensation is usually only available in private sector schemes. Compensation, interest, limitation on fees, and putting right specified errors are among the remedies available to the Legal Ombudsman. There is a £150,000 limit on the compensation that can be awarded by the Financial Ombudsman (Financial Services and Markets Act 2000, s 229(5)). The primary relief in public sector schemes is the review of a decision or act of a government department or local authority, with a changed decision being the ultimate goal of the complainant. There are a number of cases where an apology will be the primary relief given. **21.27**

An ombudsman's decision in a scheme providing for a binding decision can operate to prevent subsequent court proceedings on the same cause of action. This is so even if there is an artificial limit on the compensation awarded by the ombudsman (*Clark v In Focus Asset Management & Tax Solutions Ltd* [2014] EWCA Civ 118 (Financial Ombudsman)). In non-binding schemes complainants are able to bring court proceedings if they are not satisfied with the result. For the most part organizations will abide by ombudsmen's decisions, even though they are non-binding. A particular value of such schemes is that an impartial decision is obtained without the expense of litigation, which will be lost if the organization does not honour the decision. In some schemes the decision is published, which may act as an additional incentive to put right anything identified by the ombudsman's decision. **21.28**

KEY POINTS SUMMARY

- There is a large range of complaints, grievance, and ombudsman schemes. **21.29**
- Each one has its own procedure, which should be brought to the attention of customers and made available to them when asked for.
- These schemes usually seek an amicable resolution of the matter.
- If the procedure includes reaching a decision, in the absence of a contract to be bound it will only be binding on the professional person (through their professional code of conduct).
- These schemes can be quick and inexpensive. They can be time consuming, particularly if there is an appeal mechanism, and they can be ineffective.

22

EARLY NEUTRAL EVALUATION

A WHAT IS EARLY NEUTRAL EVALUATION? 22.01
B AT WHAT STAGE SHOULD IT BE EMPLOYED? 22.05
C WHEN SHOULD IT BE USED? 22.06
D WHO SHOULD BE APPOINTED TO CARRY OUT THE EVALUATION? 22.08
E THE PROCEDURE 22.10
F NEUTRAL FACT FINDING 22.14
G JUDICIAL EVALUATION 22.15
H EVALUATION IN PERSONAL INJURY CASES 22.26
Key points summary 22.30

A WHAT IS EARLY NEUTRAL EVALUATION?

22.01 Early neutral evaluation (ENE) is an assessment and evaluation of the facts, evidence and/or the legal merits of an issue in the case or of the case as a whole. It is usually undertaken by the parties jointly, although in some cases it can be undertaken at the request of one party only in relation to their own case. The parties will usually appoint a neutral third party to evaluate the facts, evidence, and law in relation to the issue or case and provide an opinion on the merits. This differs from mediation which is essentially a *facilitative* process. ENE is an *advisory* and *evaluative* process.

22.02 As discussed in Chapter 14 there is a close similarity between this and evaluative mediation. However, in this book, the term early neutral evaluation is used when a neutral third party is asked to evaluate a dispute, without themselves becoming involved in any way in the negotiations between the parties. It is this disengagement from the negotiation process that distinguishes early neutral evaluation from evaluative mediation.

22.03 ENE can take place within the court system, in which case the evaluation is usually carried out by a judge. ENE can also take place outside the litigation process, but parallel with it, and even before litigation has been commenced at all.

22.04 Like mediation, it is a private and confidential process, and the evaluator must be impartial. If the evaluator is appointed using an ADR provider, he or she will operate under a code of conduct that may be the same or similar to the code of conduct that governs the conduct of mediators.

B AT WHAT STAGE SHOULD IT BE EMPLOYED?

22.05 ENE is usually employed in the early stages of a dispute (hence its name), but in fact it could be utilized at any stage. Neutral evaluation employed at the early stages of a case can assist settlement by mediation, and can be carried out before or even during the mediation, and before or at any time during the process of litigation.

C WHEN SHOULD IT BE USED?

The rationale for ENE is that an unbiased evaluation of the case and the likely outcome by a neutral party, such as a judge or expert, will help the parties subsequently to settle the dispute by negotiation or even mediation. It can be particularly useful where the parties have taken an unrealistic and entrenched view of the claim and need a reality check and assessment of the case by an independent person. **22.06**

The process can be useful in that it enables each party to appreciate the strengths and weaknesses of their case and this in turn can encourage and lead to settlement, even if the parties do not agree to settle on the basis of the evaluation. **22.07**

D WHO SHOULD BE APPOINTED TO CARRY OUT THE EVALUATION?

The choice of evaluator will depend on the issues presented by the case. It may be that an expert is required, in which case the process will be an expert evaluation. Whether an expert is appointed to carry out the evaluation will depend on the underlying subject-matter of the dispute and whether issues of a technical nature are raised that require expertise to evaluate. **22.08**

The parties may privately appoint a neutral. This could be a solicitor, barrister, or an independent third party such as an expert. Alternatively they may enlist the assistance of an ADR provider (see Appendix 1 for a selection of providers) in order to help them select and appoint a suitable evaluator. For example, see CEDR's model ENE Agreement and Guidance Notes (at www.cedr.com), or the Chartered Institute of Arbitrators, but there are many other ADR providers who offer an ENE service. **22.09**

E THE PROCEDURE

The manner in which the evaluation is conducted will be primarily decided by the evaluator in most cases, although the evaluator will usually fix the procedure after consultation with the parties. The process is flexible and the parties can tailor it to meet the needs of their case. The parties can control the amount and form of the information that is placed before the evaluator, and they can identify the issues of fact or issues of law or both that they want the evaluator to evaluate. The evaluator will usually be instructed by both parties (although, as stated above, it is possible for one party only to seek an evaluation of some or all of the issues in their case), and they will agree the terms on which he or she is instructed and the ambit of the instructions. The parties can also agree that the evaluator should carry out his or her own investigations independently of the parties, and make a recommendation based on those investigations. The evaluator may wish to hold a preliminary meeting with the parties to agree the ground rules, the documentation to be provided, whether a hearing is required, and to set time limits for each stage of the process. **22.10**

Each party will usually make written submissions to the evaluator, together with such evidence and supporting documents as they see fit. It is also possible to agree that each party should present some or all of their case at an oral hearing. The evaluator may also wish to hold a meeting with the parties (instead of, or in addition to, a formal hearing) to obtain further information about the issues in dispute. **22.11**

The evaluator will evaluate the evidence (oral and/or written) and the law bearing in mind the submissions of each party and produce a recommendation based on the merits of the **22.12** dispute and the likely outcome of it. The recommendation may or may not contain detailed reasons for the decision depending on the agreement reached between the parties and the evaluator.

22.13 The evaluation is non-binding and the parties do not have to accept it, although they can agree subsequently to settle their dispute in accordance with the recommendations in it.

F NEUTRAL FACT FINDING

22.14 A variation in the process is to require the evaluator simply to investigate and evaluate the facts in dispute between the parties (but not the underlying issues of law or quantum) and reach a decision on those facts. It can be useful to appoint an expert to carry out a non-binding neutral fact-finding evaluation of one or more of the technical issues in the case to assist the parties to reach a settlement.

G JUDICIAL EVALUATION

22.15 The court may provide evaluation of a dispute, in which case the ENE is carried out by a judge.

Judicial evaluation in the Commercial Court

22.16 The Commercial Court may, with the agreement of the parties, in an appropriate case, provide ENE of a dispute or of some of the issues in the case. The approval of the judge in charge of the Commercial List must be obtained before an ENE is undertaken. If, after discussion with counsel, it appears to the judge that ENE will aid the resolution of the dispute, they will, with the agreement of the parties, refer the matter to the judge in charge of the list. The judge in charge of the list will, if the state of business in the list permits, nominate a judge to conduct the ENE. The judge conducting the ENE will then take no further part in the case, either for hearing applications or as trial judge, unless the parties agree otherwise.

Judicial evaluation in the Technology and Construction Court

22.17 Judicial evaluation can also take place in the Technology and Construction Court and in the Mercantile Court, although the parties must agree that a TCC Judge should evaluate the whole case or some of the issues in it, and if they do agree, they will usually seek an order at a Case Management Conference for an ENE to be carried out by the Court. The judge assigned to the case may carry out the evaluation himself, or it may be assigned to another TCC judge. The judge carrying out the evaluation will usually carry out no further judicial role in relation to the case. Paragraph 7.5.1 of the Technology and Construction Court Guide provides that the judge will produce a written report with conclusions and brief reasons. Unless the parties otherwise agree, the report will not be binding on them.

22.18 The judge will usually evaluate the case based on a summary of information provided to him. The judge undertaking the ENE will issue directions for the preparation and conduct of the ENE. These will usually include dates for the exchange of submissions and documents (which may include exchange of witness statements and expert evidence), a direction that the ENE will be conducted entirely on paper or alternatively the judge may direct that there be an oral hearing (with or without live evidence being called). If an oral hearing is required, it will usually only last one day. The judge may also require the parties to jointly instruct an expert to help him or her reach a determination of the technical issues in the case (if expert evidence has not already been obtained).

An example of an order providing for judicial neutral evaluation is Figure 22.1. **22.19**

Figure 22.1 An example of an order providing for judicial neutral evaluation

IN THE HIGH COURT OF JUSTICE 2014 Folio 2976
COMMERCIAL COURT

BETWEEN

MORROW TECHNOLOGY PLC

Claimant

and

BROWNSTONE HOLDINGS LIMITED

Defendant

ORDER

IT IS ORDERED BY CONSENT THAT:

1. The hearing of the early neutral evaluation shall take place at Room E300 on 22nd October 2014 at 2pm before Mr Justice James.
2. The claimant shall by 8th October 2014 lodge an agreed statement of issues, a chronology, a bundle containing statements of case, any relevant witness statements/summaries, any experts' reports and essential documents and correspondence.
3. Each party shall lodge at court and serve by no later than 4pm on 15th October 2014 a skeleton argument containing a brief outline of its case.
4. Each party shall have one hour to present its case.
5. Each party shall have 15 minutes to reply to the other party's case.
6. Each party shall have 15 minutes in which they may direct questions to the other party via the judge.
7. The judge will deliver an assessment orally or in writing.
8. Nothing said at the hearing will be used in court for any purpose.
9. The judge shall be disqualified from any further involvement in the case, unless the parties agree otherwise.
10. Representatives of the parties duly authorised to make decisions to resolve disputes between the parties shall be present at the hearing.
11. Each party shall bear its own costs of the evaluation.

Dated 24 September 2014

Judicial evaluation in Social Security and Child Support Tribunal ENE pilot scheme

From September 2007 until the end of January 2009, a pilot ENE scheme was operated in the Social Security and Child Support (SSCS) Tribunal in Sutton, Bristol, Cardiff, and Bexleyheath. The focus of the pilot was the use of ENE by a tribunal judge of the facts, evidence, or legal merits of appeal cases in the SSCS against decisions relating to the entitlement to or level of disability living allowance and attendance allowance. **22.20**

22.21 The aim of the pilot was to assess:

- the use of ENE as a cost-effective method of resolving administrative appeals without the need for a hearing;
- whether ENE provided a less formal and more convenient method of resolving the dispute;
- whether ENE produced a faster resolution of the dispute;
- whether ENE increased the operational efficiency of tribunals by reducing the number of hearings and speeding up case resolution; and
- what factors contribute to the success of ENE and therefore to understand where else in the Tribunals Service they could be applied.

22.22 The parties were given the option to have the dispute determined by ENE. If they elected to do so, stage one of the ADR process involved an ENE by a district tribunal judge (DTJ) within four weeks of receiving the appeal. If the DTJ assessed that one of the parties was likely to lose the appeal, then stage two involved a telephone call to that party. If the losing party was likely to be the Pension Disability and Carers Service, then they were invited to reconsider their decision and, if they did not do so, the matter proceeded to a hearing. If the appellant was likely to lose, they were contacted by the DTJ and this was explained to them, and they were invited to withdraw their appeal or alternatively submit further evidence in support of it and proceed to a hearing. If the DTJ was unable to make an initial assessment without a hearing, directions were given for a hearing. Where a hearing did take place, the DTJ undertaking the ENE did not chair the tribunal panel and the panel hearing the appeal was unaware that an ENE had taken place.

22.23 The pilot was evaluated by Carolyn Hay, Katherine McKenna, and Trevor Buck in January 2010 (Ministry of Justice Research Series 2/10, January 2010, www.justice.gov.uk). Key findings from their research are as follows:

- 78% of appellants opted for ENE;
- 42% of opt-in cases had directions (typically for further evidence) issued at the ENE stage and before the hearing compared to less than 1% of non-opt-in cases. ENE therefore resulted in cases being better prepared for the final hearing;
- The telephone calls that took place with the likely losing party at stage two of the process were largely positively received by the parties;
- 23% of opt-in cases were resolved without the need for a hearing, compared to 9% of non-opt-in cases;
- 77% of all opt-in cases were still resolved at a hearing, although opt-in cases had a lower rate of adjournment (9%) than non-opt in cases;
- Opt-in cases resulted in a slightly higher cost to the Tribunals Service (£222 per case for all opt-in cases and £202 for non-opt-in cases), although it also generated more savings in avoiding hearings or avoiding adjournments;
- ENE did not achieve swifter resolution of cases (an average of 46 working days for opt-in cases and 42 working days for non-opt-in cases);
- the pilot helped to build an effective working relationship between the Tribunals Service and the different stakeholder organizations.

22.24 The overall conclusion was that there should be a limited roll-out into a wider and geographically diverse set of areas and further monitoring should take place before the scheme was rolled out nationally.

Judicial evaluation in the Chancery Division

22.25 In the Chancery Modernisation Final Review: Final Report by Lord Justice Briggs, published in December 2013, he reports (at para 5.6), that in some chancery regional trial centres, a form of judicial ENE takes place in the context of inheritance, contested probate, and Trusts of Land and Appointment of Trustees Act 1996 (TOLATA) cases. District judges may convene a court hearing aimed specifically at exploring settlement, with the district judge expressing a preliminary evaluation of the merits or a range of likely outcomes at trial. He notes that this form of judicial ENE is not recognized in any rule, practice direction, or standard procedure in the Chancery Division at present. However, he recommends that judicial ENE would be a valuable tool for encouraging settlement in a range of chancery cases.

H EVALUATION IN PERSONAL INJURY CASES

Some ADR providers operate evaluation schemes for personal injury cases. For example, CEDR has created a range of ADR options for lower value personal injury cases through their dedicated Personal Injury Unit (PIU). PIU eValuate is described as '... A paper evaluation service which gives the parties early judicial insight into a Court outcome. Experienced evaluators with District Judge expertise provide a written evaluation steering the parties to a solution.' A key strength of the scheme is that the evaluator 'will have the same mindset, training and experience as the ultimate arbiter of the dispute'. **22.26**

This will enable the parties to have an indication of the likely outcome should the case proceed to trial. **22.27**

The scheme is designed for cases up to £50,000 in value (so personal injury cases that would be proceeding in the county court) and the fees start from £295 (this is taken from information on CEDR's website, which is updated regularly—so check www.cedr.com for the latest information about this scheme). **22.28**

The key features of this evaluation scheme are as follows: **22.29**

- An independent evaluator, who will have expertise as a district judge will be selected to evaluate the dispute (this could be the whole claim or an issue in it). The evaluations will usually be carried out by retired district judges who will have a great deal of experience in deciding similar cases.
- The parties will agree on the issues to be evaluated.
- The evaluation is not binding on the parties, unless they elect to be bound by it.
- Each of the parties will send written submissions to the evaluator together with any relevant documents. The submission should identify the issues that the evaluator is asked to assess and set out the party's case in relation to those issues.
- The evaluator will deliver a written evaluation within ten working days.
- The evaluation fee will usually be jointly split between the parties, although the costs of the process can be treated as 'costs in the case', meaning that the overall loser will pay the overall winner's costs of the evaluation.
- The whole process is confidential and without prejudice, so the parties cannot use the evaluation in any later court proceedings.
- The process is relatively cheap.

KEY POINTS SUMMARY

- ENE is useful if the parties would benefit from an independent assessment of the merits of the case or an issue in the case. **22.30**
- It can be undertaken at any stage of the case, even during mediation.

- ENE is not binding on the parties.
- It is a confidential process.
- If the ENE is carried out by a judge, they will have no further involvement in the case.
- ENE assists the parties to negotiate a settlement by direct negotiations or in mediation.
- Judicial evaluation may be an area for growth in ADR in the future.

PART V

RECORDING SETTLEMENT

23

RECORDING SETTLEMENT

A REACHING AGREEMENT 23.01
B FORMS OF RECORDED OUTCOME...... 23.07
C RECORDS MADE DURING THE ADR PROCESS 23.12
D WHO SHOULD PRODUCE A FORMAL RECORD 23.14
E ENFORCEABLE FORMS FOR RECORDING SETTLEMENT 23.16
F DRAFTING TERMS OF SETTLEMENT..... 23.23
G METHODS OF RECORDING SETTLEMENT AGREEMENTS 23.24
H TERMS AS REGARDS COSTS.......... 23.55
I INFORMING THE COURT OF SETTLEMENT....................... 23.60
Key points summary 23.61

A REACHING AGREEMENT

The purpose of an ADR process is to resolve a dispute. For the dispute to be effectively resolved there needs to be sufficient clarity about the outcome. If the basis for a resolution is not sufficiently clear, detailed, and comprehensive, there is a risk that the dispute will continue on some matters, or that a further dispute will arise over the outcome. In non-adjudicative processes there is a wide range of possible outcomes (see 13.122–13.126 for negotiated settlements and 16.52–16.57 in relation to mediation). In adjudicative processes, while the main focus will be on settling the dispute or difference, a settlement can still include terms going outside that dispute. Once a settlement has been agreed it needs to be recorded. **23.01**

The relative informality of some ADR processes compared to litigation can lead to difficulties as regards outcome. A focus on key issues can lead to less central issues being overlooked. Particularly where the agreement is essentially oral, as in negotiation or mediation, something may be left a little vague to achieve an agreement, or each party may have a slightly different understanding of what has been agreed. As a party's representative, you should address rather than ignore such problems as they may lead to a breakdown in the agreement. **23.02**

Recording a settlement is the final part of the ADR process, and the lawyer has several responsibilities in ensuring that the process is completed properly. They should ensure: **23.03**

- the terms are comprehensive. They should cover everything at issue;
- each term is clear and sufficiently detailed;
- the client understands the agreement. The lawyer should explain to the client what each side must do and not do under the agreement;
- the client accepts the agreement. Where the agreement is subject to client consent, the lawyer must provide the client with sufficient information and advice to ensure that the client takes an informed decision as to whether to accept the agreement;
- the terms are appropriately recorded. The options for this are given in this chapter;
- the terms are appropriately enforceable. The lawyer should explain to the client what steps may be taken if either side does not comply with the agreement: see Chapter 32.

23.04 It may not be easy to persuade your client to approve the terms of a compromise, especially following a difficult negotiation or mediation. The client may feel that the provisional agreement falls too far short of their objectives, especially if the client does not take a realistic view of the weaknesses of their case or the difficulties of obtaining certain concessions from the other side. It is important to prepare your client for the potential outcome in advance, and to do all you can to ensure your client is fully informed of the risks and benefits of the provisional settlement. Ultimately, it is the client's decision whether to accept a compromise, and the lawyer's role is to advise the client rather than impose their own views on the client. You will also have to review whether there are other options such as ongoing litigation, and perhaps whether you can continue to represent the client if the client refuses a provisional settlement. In such a case the other side must be informed of the client's decision.

23.05 Solicitors (under the SRA Code of Conduct 2011) and barristers (under the BSB Code of Conduct 2014) are under professional obligations to protect their client's interests when advising on a settlement, without regard to the lawyer's own interests or any consequences for the lawyer. It is important that funding arrangements with clients are clear about the impact of settlement decisions and continued representation. If there is a disagreement, the lawyer should consider very carefully whether they are entitled to withdraw from the case if the client will not approve the settlement. This may be appropriate if, for example, the client had misled the lawyer about the strength of the case. In publicly funded cases there is a duty on legal representatives to report to the Legal Aid Agency when a client refuses to accept an offer to settle or an offer to use ADR.

23.06 Where any of the parties is a child or if they lack mental capacity it will almost certainly be necessary to appoint a litigation friend under CPR Part 21, and for court approval to be sought for the compromise under r 21.10. Mental capacity for this purpose is the capacity to conduct the claim or cause of action the claimant in fact has (*Dunhill v Burgin (Nos 1 and 2)* [2014] 1 WLR 933 at [18]). Seeking approval of a consent judgment (see 23.39) is not the same as a proper application under r 21.10. This is because the underlying policy of r 21.10 is to protect persons under a disability from themselves and from their legal advisers, who through lack of skill or experience might otherwise settle their claims for far less than they are worth (*Dunhill v Burgin (Nos 1 and 2)* [2014] 1 WLR 933).

B FORMS OF RECORDED OUTCOME

23.07 The form used to record the outcome of an ADR process is often governed by the original agreement to enter ADR. For example, arbitration should result in an award, and a mediation agreement may include a statement that any compromise will only be binding if made in writing. In the absence of such a provision, the range of options is broadly as follows:

- An adjudicative process such as arbitration will lead to a written decision such as an agreed arbitration award (see Chapter 30). This decision should cover all relevant matters, such as interest and costs. An expert determination will also produce a written decision (see Chapter 24).
- A non-adjudicative process can also lead to a written report from a third party, as for example happens with early neutral evaluation (see Chapter 22). This report will not provide a final outcome, but will inform further discussion between the parties.
- Some processes lead to relatively simple or limited outcomes. For example an ombudsman will often produce a letter (see Chapter 21).
- The outcome of some processes is not always clear or set. For example a grievance resolution scheme or conciliation will not necessarily reach any definite outcome, so long as the concern raised is addressed (see Chapters 20 and 21).

- The major processes of mediation and negotiation normally result in an oral agreement. It is here that most potential issues arise with regard to ensuring that what is agreed is properly recorded, and this chapter deals largely with the outcomes of these processes.

Compromise agreements

A successful non-adjudicative ADR should result in a contract compromising the dispute. Agreeing not to litigate a valid claim is good consideration for the purposes of the law of contract, as is a promise not to litigate a claim that has no legal basis but which is honestly believed to be valid (*Cook v Wright* (1861) 1 B & S 559). It is best to state expressly that the right to litigate is being given up, but the court may be prepared to infer this if the circumstances are sufficiently clear (*Alliance Bank v Broom* (1864) 2 Dr & Sm 289). The compromise agreement will take effect and be interpreted in the same way as other contracts. For the approach to finding the parties' objective contractual intentions, see *Investors Compensation Scheme Ltd v West Bromich Building Society (No 1)* [1998] 1 WLR 896 and *Chartbrook Ltd v Persimmon Homes Ltd* [2009] 1 AC 1101. **23.08**

Full and final settlement

Where the whole dispute is settled the compromise agreement will normally be stated to be in 'full and final settlement' of the dispute. Care must be taken to ensure this is what the parties intend. It will mean the whole of the old dispute can no longer be litigated, and is replaced by the terms of the compromise. Use of the words makes it difficult to obtain a court order rectifying the agreement (*Ondhia v Ondhia* [2011] EWHC 3040 (Ch)). If the words are not used it may not be clear that the dispute has been fully settled, and one of the parties may then start proceedings. **23.09**

Two problems in using the phrase are that the settlement may affect related claims by other persons, or they may result in other disputes between the parties also being settled. For example, in *Jameson v Central Electricity Generating Board* [2000] 1 AC 455 a settlement of an asbestosis claim between the employee and his employer which was expressed to be in full and final settlement was held to bar a subsequent Fatal Accidents Act claim by the employee's widow brought after the employee died. If the words are used, whether other related claims between the parties will be barred on the basis they are included in the compromise depends on the proper construction of the compromise agreement (*Henley v Bloom* [2010] 1 WLR 1770). A party who wishes to preserve their right to sue on other causes of action should expressly reserve that right in the compromise agreement. **23.10**

Subject to contract

Where an offer is made 'subject to contract' there is no concluded agreement until a written contract is signed (Sir Thomas Bingham MR in *Pitt v PHH Asset Management Ltd* [1994] 1 WLR 327). In *Newbury v Sun Microsystems* [2013] EWHC 2180 (QB) the defendant wrote to the claimant offering a sum of money 'in full and final settlement' of the claim with 'such settlement to be recorded in a suitably worded agreement'. The claimant accepted by letter on the same day. A draft Tomlin order was sent by the claimant, but the defendant made some amendments to the draft which the claimant would not agree to. It was held that the claim had been settled in the terms of the letters. The offer had been stated to be in full and final settlement, and it had not stated that it was 'subject to contract'. Objectively, the claim was settled when the claimant accepted the offer. **23.11**

C RECORDS MADE DURING THE ADR PROCESS

23.12 It is vital to keep a clear record of what is being agreed or provisionally agreed during a negotiation or mediation. This may be needed for the purpose of reporting the settlement to the judge, or to form the basis of a written contract or consent order. It needs to be sufficiently detailed and accurate: it is easy to forget detailed points, and quickly written notes can be difficult to interpret later. It is also essential to check what is agreed—it is all too common for the lawyers to have a slightly different understanding of what is agreed. One lawyer can make a record and check the wording with the other. In a mediation, the mediator will normally assist with the recording process as proposals are raised and discussed.

23.13 At the end of a mediation or negotiation it is crucial to take time to agree a written version of the terms agreed, see 13.122–13.126 and 16.52–16.57. It is advisable to write this note of terms clearly on a fresh sheet of paper, to avoid any possible confusion from crossing out or amendment, and that the lawyers on both sides check the wording. Normally one lawyer will make a full note of the terms agreed, and check the words written down with the opponent. A copy of the note might be made and handed over straight away.

D WHO SHOULD PRODUCE A FORMAL RECORD?

23.14 You must agree who will draft the letter, contract, or order that will formally record the outcome. The lawyers for one side will produce a draft in the form agreed, and send it to the lawyers on the other side for agreement. There may be an advantage to the side that agrees to do the draft as they will have some control over the written detail, though note that the side drawing up the document will also bear the costs of doing so unless it has been agreed that the costs be shared.

23.15 In addition to agreeing who should produce the draft it should be agreed when the draft will be sent to the other parties and who should pay the costs. Note that the wording of a draft order is subject to the discretion of the judge, even if it is an agreed consent order.

E ENFORCEABLE FORMS FOR RECORDING SETTLEMENT

23.16 Any form of written or oral statement can set out the terms of a settlement. If the dispute is settled by an explanation, a clarification, or an apology then nothing further may be needed. However, when a dispute relating to legal rights is settled it will normally be in the interests of both parties to record the outcome in a form that is legally enforceable. It is important to understand what the options are, and to appreciate that some forms of ADR lead to more than one option, so that the most appropriate option needs to be chosen.

An oral contract

23.17 Non-adjudicative ADR processes often lead to an oral contract. Once both parties say they have reached agreement and the basic requirements of a contract exist (that is the terms are sufficiently certain, there is some form of consideration, etc) there will be an enforceable contract: see *Chanel v FW Woolworth* [1981] 1 All ER 745 and *Soulsbury v Soulsbury* (2007) Times, 14 November. Once a contract is made it may be difficult or impossible to vary it or to challenge it in court. If that agreement is conditional, for example on the approval of the client, that condition must be stated at the time, and will need to be fulfilled.

A written contract

Non-adjudicative ADR processes also commonly lead to a written contract, either because the process was wholly or partly conducted in writing, or because the oral agreement is reduced to a written contract. For example, an oral arrangement under which the parties state they will only be bound on signing a written agreement only becomes binding when the contemplated document is signed (*Investec Bank (UK) Ltd v Zulman* [2010] EWCA Civ 675). **23.18**

An award with statutory authority

Some awards carry statutory or other regulatory authority, because the ADR process is governed by statute or regulation (see Chapter 32). **23.19**

A court order

An ADR process can be wholly or partly incorporated into a court judgment, but only where proceedings have been issued. There are some restrictions in the CPR Part 2, over which judges have jurisdiction to make certain orders, and the judge may not be prepared to make an order in the terms sought. Settlements restricted to common law relief (money, delivery of goods), the stay or dismissal of the case and costs, can be made as consent orders without involving a judge (CPR r 40.6). Where no proceedings have been issued there will be no basis for a judge to make an order. If the terms of an interim order are agreed by negotiation a judge can be asked to make an interim order in the terms agreed. **23.20**

Other legal documents

The terms of an agreement can be wholly or partly incorporated into some other appropriate form, such as a deed or conveyance. It may be agreed to vary or amend an existing contract, if for example the parties agree to vary an existing commercial relationship. **23.21**

The main difference between these options is that where a court is involved the terms can normally be enforced by returning to court within the existing proceedings. If the court is not involved it may be necessary to issue new proceedings for breach of contract to enforce the settlement (see Chapter 32). The above options are not mutually exclusive—an agreed interim order might deal with some terms with others being put into a separate contract. **23.22**

F DRAFTING TERMS OF SETTLEMENT

Some points will apply to all forms of written settlement document. **23.23**

- The terms must be comprehensive and accurate—once the terms have been reduced to writing and agreed it will be difficult or impossible to argue that any additional oral term is part of the final agreement.
- All the essential terms of the agreement should be agreed, or machinery provided for establishing them. A failure to achieve this may mean the settlement will be unenforceable for lack of certainty. Providing that prices or dates are to be reasonable, or that details are to be resolved by arbitration or expert determination, may save an agreement from being struck down for uncertainty (see standard works on contract law, and *MRI Trading AG v Erdenet Mining Corp LLC* [2013] 1 Lloyd's Rep 638).
- All practical details should be included such as dates by which actions such as payment should be carried out.

- Court powers to award interest and make orders as to costs will only apply to a court order. Both matters should be dealt with specifically in an order or contract: *President of India v La Pintada Cia Navegacion* [1984] 2 All ER 773. If there is no mention of costs, each side will have to bear their own.
- Some expressions used in settlements make it difficult to avoid further proceedings, and should be used with care. For example, a term in a settlement agreement that one party would pay 'damages for trespass' to be determined by a chartered surveyor acting as an expert almost inevitably resulted in further court proceedings over what that expression meant, being something not within the professional expertise of a surveyor (*Thorne v Courtier* [2011] EWCA Civ 460).
- Some enforcement options can be built in—for example that a payment will carry interest if it is not made on time. In doing so, be careful to avoid the term amounting to a penalty clause (under contract law). Alternatively, one term can be made a pre-condition to another.
- As a general matter, ensure the terms are enforceable—for example they do not seek to affect third party rights, unless the third party agrees to be bound.
- Double check the draft to avoid any vagueness or ambiguity that may have been left at the end of the ADR process.
- The terms may usefully bear in mind any foreseeable future events that may affect them, so that the agreement covers and is not undermined by foreseeable change, if for example there will be a continuing relationship.

G METHODS OF RECORDING SETTLEMENT AGREEMENTS

Exchange of letters

23.24 It is common for the solicitor for one side to write a letter setting out terms of settlement, with the solicitors for the other side replying to indicate agreement. This is appropriate for a wide range of settlements in non-adjudicative ADR where there is no particular need for any more formal document. It is commonly used where proceedings have not been issued so a court order is not an option. It can also be used after proceedings have been issued if there is no particular need for a court order. An exchange of letters will normally be relatively cost effective. A typical exchange of letters settling a dispute can be seen in Figures 23.1 and 23.2.

23.25 An exchange of letters can form a contract in itself without any face-to-face ADR process where there is an appropriate offer and acceptance. A chain of letters on a single issue does not necessarily amount to a settlement: *Jackson v Tharker* [2007] EWHC 271 (TCC). If there has been a face-to-face process then the letters will evidence the oral agreement that was reached.

Contract or deed

Whether a contract is required or appropriate

23.26 Although there is no essential legal difference between a contract formed or evidenced in letters and a contract recorded in a separate document, there are circumstances where it may be preferable to have a separate signed contract or deed. Sometimes a specific form of contract may be needed to implement an agreement, for example matters which by law have to be evidenced or made in writing. Examples where writing is required include consumer credit agreements (Consumer Credit Act 1974 ss 60, 61, and 65), legal assignments (Law of Property Act 1925 s 136), and guarantees (Statute of Frauds 1677 s 4). Contracts for the sale or disposition of land also require writing (Law of Property (Miscellaneous Provisions) Act

Figure 23.1 Letter setting out terms of a negotiated settlement

17 September 2014

Dear Sir,

Groovy Music Ltd v Tracey Green

I am writing to you to record the terms of negotiated settlement of this case reached by counsel for the parties on 10 September 2014. These terms were subject to client approval, and we are pleased to inform you that our client, the claimant in these proceedings, has approved the terms. Please can you confirm in your reply that your client has also accepted the terms.

I am informed by counsel that the terms agreed are as follows:

1. There should be a new contract between the parties to commence on 3 November 2014. From that date this will replace the existing contract between the parties, which has been the subject of this dispute. The new contract will run for three years and be renewable. It will provide that the copyright of all songs written by the defendant within that period will vest in the claimant, and that the claimant will bear all costs of recording and publicising an album of twelve songs by the defendant, the album to be released within the contract period. All profits from merchandising will be shared equally by the parties. The defendant and a representative of the claimant will meet before 15 October 2014 to agree full detailed terms for this contract.
2. On the basis that the existing contract does not provide clearly for merchandising rights, but that income from existing merchandising sales is broadly equal to costs incurred by the claimant in producing merchandise, no payment will be made with regard to income from merchandising prior to the start of the new contract referred to above.
3. The defendant will pay to the claimant the sum of £16,759 in relation to income from her songs 'Climate Change' and 'Obama Rocks', which she released in contravention of her agreement with the claimant. This sum is to be paid within fourteen days of the date of this letter.
4. The position as regards the claimant's claim regarding income from the defendant's stall in Camden Market will be settled on the basis of a report from an agreed accountant. The accountant will be agreed by 3 November 2014, and the sum found due will be paid within 14 days of that accountant producing his or her report.
5. There will be no payment with regard to the defendant's alleged loss of profit from web-based downloads. However, the claimant and the defendant will discuss the possibility of developing a 'Green Gauge' blog, and the marketing options it may provide.
6. Each party will pay their own costs, save that the claimant will bear the costs of drawing up this agreement.

I look forward to hearing from you to confirm these terms, and your client's acceptance of them.

Yours faithfully
(Solicitor for the claimant)

Figure 23.2 Letter accepting the terms in Figure 23.1

22 September 2014

Dear Sir,

Groovy Music Ltd v Tracey Green

I am writing in reply to your letter of 17 September 2014 recording proposed terms of agreement for this case.

My client is prepared to accept these terms in full and final settlement of this case. She is sorry that the relationship between our clients deteriorated to this extent, and hopes that the new contract will prove beneficial to both parties.

I understand that it was also a term that your client would withdraw its claim on the basis of these terms. My client's acceptance is on the basis that your client will do this.

We are happy to nominate Ms Sophie Bennett to act as the accountant pursuant to term 4. Please can you let us know if this is acceptable to your client—I believe she is known to your client.

Yours faithfully,
(Solicitor for the defendant)

1989 s 2), but *Yeates v Line* [2013] Ch 363 held that s 2 only applies to agreements having a dispositive purpose, so does not apply to a settlement agreeing to demarcate an unclear land boundary.

23.27 A contract or deed may be appropriate where the terms are complex, or where the outcome is particularly important and the parties want a formal separate legal document for later reference. A contract may be particularly appropriate where there will be an ongoing commercial relationship. If there is already a contract between the parties it is necessary to decide whether that contract will be varied or replaced, and to make that clear. It may sometimes be appropriate for some of the terms agreed to be put into a contract and others separately recorded, for example in covering letters.

23.28 A deed may be more appropriate than a contract in relatively limited circumstances. Examples are where formality is important (for example as regards rights over land), or where it is not clear that one party is providing consideration, so there might otherwise be doubts over validity.

Drafting the contract or deed

23.29 The contract or deed will be a separately legally enforceable document, and all the normal rules for drafting such documents need to be followed. Normally the contract will be drawn up by the solicitor for one side and sent to the solicitor for the other for agreement as to terms. This option may well take more lawyer time than a simple exchange of letters. Depending on how much time is taken in drafting and negotiating the wording of the terms, potentially this is the most expensive method of recording a settlement.

23.30 It is common to include a preamble setting out that the contract is to resolve a dispute, summarizing the matters that were in dispute and are covered by the agreement. This is to ensure clarity over the issues that have been resolved, but it is not essential if it is not appropriate for the contract envisaged. This is followed by the agreed terms. An example can be seen in Figure 23.3.

Figure 23.3 Example of a contract settling a dispute

THIS AGREEMENT is made on 1 October 2014 between Jon Collins of the one part and Phabulous Phasions Ltd of the other part.

WHEREAS the aforesaid Jon Collins and Phabulous Phasions Ltd have been in dispute regarding alleged breaches of a contract for the supply of garments by the claimant to the defendant in a contract dated 14 January 2013.

NOW IT IS HEREBY AGREED by way of compromise of the said dispute as follows:

1. For the three years following the date of this agreement Jon Collins will produce for Phabulous Phasions 10 spring designs (to be produced by 10 January in each year) and 10 autumn designs (to be produced by 10 June each year). Each design will be for a dress, a suit or a coat, with a mix of designs in each category.
2. Phabulous Phasions will pay to Jon Collins the sum of £23,333 in respect of designs delivered up to the date of this agreement, and interest of £2,317. This sum is to be paid within twenty eight days of the date of this agreement, with interest at 5% pa if it is not paid when due.
3. Each party will pay their own costs, save that Phabulous Phasions will pay Jon Collins the costs he incurred with regard to an application for an interim injunction on a standard basis, such costs to be assessed if not agreed.

IN FURTHERANCE OF THIS AGREEMENT:

1. Jon Collins and a representative of Phabulous Phasions will meet within one month of the date of this agreement to vary the terms of their existing contract to reflect the terms of this agreement.
2. Phabulous Phasions will return to Jon Collins the five unique outfits that he created for the Brighton Bizarre show within 14 days of the date of this agreement.

Dated:

Signed Signed

In the presence of In the presence of

Settlements where there are existing court proceedings

Where there are existing court proceedings there are several different ways of recording a settlement, which are set out in Table 23.1. In addition to dealing with the terms of settlement, where there are court proceedings important issues to be agreed include how to dispose of the proceedings and the costs of the proceedings. **23.31**

Endorsement on briefs

When a barrister completes any task for which she or he is briefed, the brief is returned to their instructing solicitors with a written endorsement on the back sheet. The endorsement is primarily to confirm the nature of the work that has been done, but it is also commonly used **23.32**

Table 23.1 Different methods of recording settlements after proceedings have started

Method of recording settlement	Circumstances where it is appropriate
Judgment may be entered for immediate payment of the sum agreed together with costs.	Where settlement is for a sum of money (usually because the claim is for a debt or for damages). Often this form is used where a settlement is reached at the door of the court, with the judgment being pronounced when the case is called on before the judge. Immediate payment means within 14 days (CPR, r 40.11), so is not suitable if the defendant needs time to pay. Nor is this appropriate if the defendant wants to avoid an adverse judgment for credit-scoring purposes (because it will go onto the register of judgments if it is not paid immediately).
Judgment may be entered for the agreed sum (and costs), subject to a stay of execution pending payment by stated instalments.	Similar to the above, but provision is made for the principal sum to be paid by instalments, usually because the defendant cannot afford to pay the whole amount immediately. It has the disadvantage of having an adverse credit-scoring effect on the defendant.
The court may be informed that the case has been settled upon terms endorsed on counsel's briefs. This is the most informal compromise of a claim.	This is a long-established way of recording compromises at the door of the court. It can be used in a wide range of cases, from simple debt to family law to commercial claims. It is essential that counsel for both sides endorse their briefs in identical terms.
The court may be informed that the case has been settled, the terms being recorded in a contract.	Appropriate where the terms are detailed, or where signed writing is required. The outcome of the proceedings must still be dealt with.
Entry of a consent order setting out the agreement in the form of undertakings by both parties in a series of numbered paragraphs. There will also usually be a costs provision.	This is more suitable where the dispute is about non-monetary matters, such as a claim for injunctive relief, or specific performance. The undertakings will regulate the future relationship between the parties. For consent orders see 23.41.
Consent order staying all further proceedings upon the agreed terms. If the agreement is reached immediately before a hearing the terms will usually be endorsed on counsel's briefs and the court will be asked to make a consent order in those terms.	This is similar to the above, but goes further in that the court is asked to make a consent order as well. The consent order ensures all the parties leave court being confident everyone else has the same terms in mind. The stay of the court proceedings is intended to ensure that no further steps (which will mean incurring more costs) are needed (at least while the terms are being complied with).
Consent order providing for 'no order' save as to costs, but setting out the agreed terms in recitals.	This is more appropriate for non-money claims, and brings the proceedings to a conclusion other than quantifying costs. The terms of the compromise are recorded in the recitals, which means the parties can be confident each party will have the same terms in mind.
Recording the agreement in a Tomlin order.	Tomlin orders are dealt with at 23.46–23.53. They are particularly useful where either: • the agreed terms go outside the scope of the litigation; • the parties want to keep the agreed terms confidential.

to record the outcome of the case. When the barrister appears in court the endorsement will include the outcome, and a summary of what order has been made. If the barrister is briefed to appear in an ADR process and an agreement is reached, that is often endorsed on the backsheet.

Making the endorsement

If barristers negotiate and reach a relatively simple agreement the terms may be written onto the backsheet of the brief. If the settlement is very straightforward, for example an agreement for payment of a single figure, no additional written record of the agreement may be needed. If there will be no other document, make sure you set out what was agreed fully and accurately, including costs etc. It would be normal for the lawyer for each party to sign the other's endorsement signifying agreement. The parties may also sign to signify their agreement—useful if the client has been reluctant to agree. Make sure the same wording is used on both briefs. An example of an endorsement on counsel's brief in a case where the terms are relatively simple, and where the settlement is reached outside court, is shown in Figure 23.4. **23.33**

Figure 23.4 Example of an endorsement on a brief

JANE TURBOT

v

QUENTIN SMITH

It is hereby agreed that:

(1) The Claimant shall have ownership of the cocker spaniel dog known as 'Rufus'.
(2) The Defendant shall have ownership of the statue known as 'Life goes on'.
(3) The collection of twenty drawings accumulated by the parties shall be sold and the proceeds divided equally between the Claimant and the Defendant.
(4) The claim herein is dismissed.
(5) Each side to bear their own costs.

Signed (client) Signed (client)

Signed (barrister) Signed (barrister)

Dated

Effect of endorsements on briefs

The endorsement is evidence of an oral agreement. It is relatively quick and inexpensive, but it is only appropriate where the agreement is simple. It should only be used where the clients have confirmed the terms, for example where agreement is reached outside court. Endorsement is not appropriate where the terms are still subject to client approval as that means there is not yet a final outcome. A solicitor may write a letter to confirm the terms in the endorsement, but such a letter should not seek to add anything as the agreement is complete. The endorsement has no special form of enforcement, save that if the agreement relates to an interim matter it may be possible to go back to court if there is a change of circumstances, or it may be possible to ask that an undertaking be given to the judge as regards carrying out appropriate terms. In *Green v Rozen* [1955] 1 WLR 741 terms were endorsed on counsels' briefs with the words 'By consent all proceedings stayed on terms endorsed on briefs. Liberty to apply', but it was held that these words did not reserve a right to return to court and new proceedings would be required to enforce the terms. **23.34**

Interim order

23.35 An interim order will only be a possibility once proceedings have been issued, and if there has been an application for an interim order. Where an agreement is reached outside court on the terms of the application, these may be recorded as undertakings or in a consent order (see 23.38–23.45). A typical scenario would be where there is an application for an interim injunction and the terms of the injunction, or undertakings to be given by the respective parties, are negotiated outside court.

23.36 However, it is not uncommon for negotiations prior to interim applications to result in the settlement of the whole case rather than just the interim application. When the application is called on before the judge, an order may be made staying, adjourning, or dismissing the claim on the basis of the terms agreed by the parties. The terms may be recorded in the court's order, or as a schedule, or by a separate agreement such as a contract. An example of an interim order recording a settlement is shown in Figure 23.5.

Figure 23.5 Example of interim order

IN THE COUNTY COURT AT LANCASTER Claim No. 14LA3595

Before Her Honour Judge Jenkins

BETWEEN

Mr. MOHAMAD AZIZ

Claimant

and

Mrs. CLARISSA VANE

Defendant

ORDER

BY CONSENT it is ordered that the claim and counterclaim in these proceedings be adjourned generally upon the terms set out below:

1. That the Defendant pays to the Claimant the sum of £11,750 within 14 days of the date of this order.
2. That the Claimant returns to the Defendant her laptop computer within 28 days of the date of this order.

AND IT IS FURTHER ORDERED that in the event of the terms being carried out by the parties the claim and counterclaim be and are hereby dismissed with no order as to costs.

AND IT IS FURTHER ORDERED that in the event of any of the terms not being carried out, either party shall be at liberty to restore the claim for trial.

DATED: 13 October 2014

23.37 This option is only relevant in very limited circumstances—primarily where there has been an application to court for a specific order and one party is prepared to give an undertaking to the court governing their conduct rather than having an order made. For example, if there is an application for an interim injunction a negotiation outside court might result in a compromise under which one party gives an undertaking to the court and the application is not pursued (any failure to abide by the undertaking being contempt of court). This is most likely to happen if the party who has made the application for the interim order is sufficiently concerned about events and future compliance to want some form of protection, but is prepared to concede that a full order is not necessary. The undertaking must be carefully worded so that it is very clear what conduct will or will not breach the undertaking.

Consent order

A consent order can only be made where proceedings have been issued so that a court has jurisdiction over the case. The main benefit of having a consent order relates to enforcement, because a court order can be enforced with the full range of court enforcement powers without the need to start a new claim to enforce a separate contract made to compromise a dispute (see Chapter 32). The fact that a settlement is reached after proceedings have been issued does not mean that the terms have to be recorded in a consent order. Agreed terms can be recorded in an exchange of letters or a contract if appropriate. **23.38**

However, once proceedings have been commenced, those proceedings must be dealt with appropriately if a settlement is reached. The options, some of which are referred to in *Green v Rozen* [1955] 1 WLR 741, are as follows. **23.39**

- The judge may make an order in terms agreed through a consent order or a Tomlin order, in which case the order will bring the case to an end.
- The judge can make an order discontinuing the claim at the request of the claimant. This will bring the claim to an end with no formal court decision. If a claim is discontinued, the claimant is required to pay the defendant's costs unless specific provision is made to the contrary (CPR r 38.6). Also, the claimant is not necessarily barred from commencing fresh proceedings in respect of the same claim (see CPR r 38.7, which says that court permission is required for subsequent proceedings).
- The judge can make an order dismissing the claim at the request of the claimant. If the claim is dismissed, that will involve a formal court decision that the case should not proceed.
- The judge may stay proceedings. A stay is normally made for a set period, though it can be indefinite. This means that no further steps can be taken, but does not end the case. It may be appropriate where there is some concern that there may be problems in implementing the agreement.

Administrative consent orders

In limited circumstances a consent order can be entered by a purely administrative process, and sealed by a court officer without the need for the approval of a judge (CPR r 40.6). This can be done to order the payment of money, the delivery up of goods, the dismissal of all or part of the proceedings, an order to stay on agreed terms, and some other cases. The order should be drawn up and sent to the court together with letters expressing the consent of the parties (PD 23A, para 10). If there are any doubts or concerns, the draft consent order may be referred to a judge for consideration, which may be dealt with without a hearing. The judge has a discretion and does not have to accept the terms drafted by the parties if, for example, the terms are thought to be inappropriate or poorly drafted. **23.40**

Drafting of consent orders

A consent order is normally drafted using the wording agreed in the settlement. **23.41**

- It is important to note that the court can only make an order that is within its jurisdiction, that is an order that the court can normally make, such as an order for damages or costs, or a declaration: see *Hinde v Hinde* [1953] 1 All ER 171.

- The court cannot make an order it does not have the power to make, even if the terms are agreed by the parties.
- The court can only make an order based on the issues in the case, depending on the causes of action and claims for relief pleaded in the statements of case. If this is a problem you may ask for permission to amend the statements of case to provide a basis for the order you would like the court to make, though the judge may not allow a radical amendment.
- If the compromise includes matters outside the powers of the court and the issues in the case, the options are to use a Tomlin order or to record all or some of the terms in an alternative way.
- Consent judgments and orders must be expressed as being 'by consent' (CPR r 40.6(7)(b)) and must be signed by the legal representatives for each party.
- Care should be taken to ensure that the wording used reflects the parties' intentions, especially where the order is enshrining an existing oral contract.
- The terms should cover all costs, including for example any previous interim costs orders. If the order does not contain a provision as to costs then each side will bear their own.
- The order should state whether the claim is being stayed, discontinued etc (see above).

23.42 An example of a consent order is shown in Figure 23.6.

Figure 23.6 Consent order

IN THE HIGH COURT OF JUSTICE Claim No. HQ14 7564

QUEEN'S BENCH DIVISION

Before Mr Justice Maynard

BETWEEN

WEB WONDERS (a firm) Claimant

and

GREAT GRAPHICS PLC Defendant

DRAFT MINUTES OF ORDER

Upon hearing counsel for the Claimant and for the Defendant.

And upon the Defendant undertaking:

1. To continue to promote the services of the Claimant as agreed in the contract dated 4 March 2013.
2. Not to block or otherwise interfere with the access of the Defendant's customers to the Claimant's website.

By consent it is ordered:

1. The Defendant to pay to the Claimant damages of £33,700 within 14 days of the date of this order.
2. The Defendant to pay the Claimant's standard basis costs of this claim to be agreed, but if not agreed, to be subject to detailed assessment.

Dated

True consent orders and submission to agreed terms

A true consent order is based on a contract between the parties. As such, the court order is evidence of the contract arrived at by bargaining between the parties: *Wentworth v Bullen* (1840) 9 B & C 840. To be a true consent order there must be consideration passing from each side. Unlike other orders, a true consent order can only be set aside on grounds such as fraud, misrepresentation, or mistake, which would justify the setting aside of a contract: *Roult v North West Strategic Health Authority* [2010] 1 WLR 487 at [19]. **23.43**

There is a distinction between a consent order based on a real contract and a simple submission to an order. In *Siebe Gorman and Co Ltd v Pneupac Ltd* [1982] 1 WLR 185, Lord Denning MR said at 189: **23.44**

> It should be clearly understood by the profession that, when an order is expressed to be made 'by consent', it is ambiguous ... One meaning is this: the words 'by consent' may evidence a real contract between the parties. In such a case the court will only interfere with such an order on the same grounds as it would with any other contract. The other meaning is this: the words 'by consent' may mean 'the parties hereto not objecting'. In such a case there is no real contract between the parties. The order can be altered or varied by the court in the same circumstances as any other order that is made by the court without the consent of the parties.

Family consent orders

In family proceedings the court's jurisdiction over issues arising out of marriage or concerning the welfare and upbringing of children cannot be ousted by agreement (*Hyman v Hyman* [1929] AC 601). Consequently, the legal effect of a consent order derives from the order, not the agreement of the parties, so there is no jurisdiction to vary a matrimonial consent order: *Thwaite v Thwaite* [1982] Fam 1. Where such an order has been obtained by fraud, misrepresentation, or mistake, the remedy is to appeal or bring fresh proceedings: de *Lasala v de Lasala* [1980] AC 546 per Lord Diplock. It may also be possible to appeal out of time where there has been an unforeseeable event that invalidates a fundamental assumption on which the order was made, provided only a relatively short period of time has passed since the order (*Barder v Caluori* [1988] AC 20 at 43, although there is some controversy over the procedural mechanism to be used to bring the matter back to the court: see *Harris v Manahan* [1996] 4 All ER 454). **23.45**

Tomlin order

The Tomlin order is a form of consent order that offers particular advantages. The order is named after Tomlin J who created them (see *Practice Note* [1927] WN 290). **23.46**

Drafting Tomlin orders

A Tomlin order will provide that further proceedings in the claim be stayed, except for the purpose of carrying out the terms of the compromise, those terms being set out in a schedule to the order. The order will also provide for each party to have liberty to apply to the court if necessary to compel compliance with the terms. **23.47**

An example of a Tomlin order is shown in Figure 23.7. Note when you are drafting one that three things must be dealt with on the face of the order, with the other terms agreed normally being in the schedule: **23.48**

- further proceedings in the claim be stayed, except for the purpose of carrying out the terms of the compromise, those terms being set out in a schedule to the order;
- each party to have liberty to apply to the court if necessary to compel compliance with the terms;

- the payment of costs. By PD 40B, para 3.5, where a consent order is in the form of a Tomlin order any direction for the payment of money out of court or for the payment and assessment of costs must be contained in the body of the order and not the schedule. The reason is that these two forms of direction require the involvement of the court, and must therefore be included in the public part of the order and not concealed in the schedule. If the amount of costs has been agreed, this can be included in the schedule.

Figure 23.7 Tomlin order

IN THE HIGH COURT OF JUSTICE
CHANCERY DIVISION
Claim No 14HC9876

Before Mr Justice Allbright

BETWEEN

TAKOA LIGHT ENGINEERING CO LIMITED

Claimant

and

(1) Mr. DAVID WALLACE
(2) NUCOMPONENTS LIMITED

Defendants

ORDER

An application was made on 22 September 2014 by counsel for the Claimant and was attended by solicitors for the Defendants.
Mr. Justice Allbright approved the following terms of settlement and made them an Order of the Court.

BY CONSENT IT IS ORDERED that:—

1. The Claimant and the Defendants having agreed to the terms set forth in the schedule hereto, it is ordered that all further proceedings in this claim be stayed, except for the purpose of carrying such terms into effect.
2. Liberty to apply as to carrying the terms in the schedule to this Order into effect.
3. The Defendants do pay the Claimant's standard basis costs to be agreed and if not agreed to be assessed by a detailed assessment by the court.

Dated

SCHEDULE

The parties have agreed to compromise their dispute in these proceedings on the following terms:—

(a) The First Defendant shall sign and deliver to the Claimant's solicitors the annual accounts and directors' reports for the Claimant for the years ended 5 April 2013 and 5 April 2014 as prepared by Boswell Field & Co on 11 June 2014 by 4pm on 26 September 2014;
(b) The First Defendant shall co-operate with Mr. Brian Gunn, the other director of the Claimant, in holding a meeting of the directors of the Claimant by 4pm on 1 October

Figure 23.7 *(Continued)*

2014 and shall co-operate with Mr. Brian Gunn in taking all steps necessary to ensure the transfer of 10 ordinary shares in the share capital of the Claimant from Mr. Brian Gunn to Mrs. Jane Gunn at that meeting;

(c) The First Defendant shall sign and deliver to the Claimant's solicitors a duly completed form of resignation as a director of the Claimant by 4pm on 1 December 2014;

(d) The First and Second Defendants or either of them shall pay the sum of £150,000 to the Claimant by 4pm 1 December 2014;

(e) Until 31 December 2014, the Second Defendant will not accept any business from any person who placed an order with the Claimant in the period between 1 January 2011 and 5 April 2014; and

(f) The Claimant accepts these terms in full and final settlement of its claim in these proceedings.

Advantages and disadvantages of Tomlin orders

The first advantage of a Tomlin order is privacy. A court order is a public matter, because the order will normally be announced in court, and then becomes part of the court record, unless there is some specific justification for the order not to be dealt with in open court. However, a schedule does not have to be made public in court, and the court can direct that the schedule should not be released to anyone other than the parties or their advisers. This can be useful where, for example, the compromise includes the payment of money, and the defendant does not want it recorded in a court judgment that will become available for credit-scoring purposes, which may have adverse effects on its future ability to borrow money, or where the actual amount that may be agreed between the parties is of a sensitive nature (which is why in high-profile cases it is often reported in the news media only that a case has been settled for 'substantial damages'). **23.49**

The second advantage of a Tomlin order for an ADR process is that the schedule, unlike the order itself, is not limited to those orders that a judge has jurisdiction to make in the case. A schedule can therefore set out the terms agreed by the parties more fully, including matters that the judge could not order directly: see for example *EF Phillips and Sons Ltd v Clarke* [1970] Ch 322. **23.50**

A third advantage is that a Tomlin order is better suited to record long or complex terms, as the schedule can be worded in a more flexible way than the order itself. **23.51**

A possible drawback of a Tomlin order is that enforcement powers for the terms of the schedule are more limited than for the court order itself. If there is a difficulty with regard to the implementation of the terms of the schedule then the party seeking to enforce the terms must apply to court to have the matter brought back before the court, and seek an order requiring the other party to comply with the terms in the schedule. Any failure to comply with that order will be a contempt of court. **23.52**

Another consequence of using the Tomlin format is that any application to vary the terms of the provisions on the face of the order will be governed by the CPR, which means the court can vary those terms if there has been a material change of circumstances. The terms in the schedule, however, are contractual, so can only be impuned (such as for fraud, misrepresentation, or undue influence) or rectified on the same grounds as any other contract (*Community Care North East v Durham County Council* [2012] 1 WLR 338; *Lloyds TSB Bank plc v Crowborough Properties Ltd* [2013] EWCA Civ 107). **23.53**

Relitigating after settlement

23.54 An attempt to relitigate a dispute after a claim has been disposed of by a consent order is likely to be met by an application to strike out the new proceedings as an abuse of process under CPR r 3.4(2). Depending on the circumstances, the new claim may be barred by cause of action estoppel or issue estoppel, or on a more general basis as an abuse of process. There is some controversy over the doctrinal basis of the court's jurisdiction in this area, see *Zurich Insurance Co plc v Hayward* [2011] EWCA Civ 641, where it was said there could be no estoppel where the first proceedings were concluded by a Tomlin order, because the stay imposed by a Tomlin order is not a final decision. Whether the new proceedings are in fact an abuse of process depends on a range of factors, including the extent of any overlap with the issues in the old proceedings.

H TERMS AS REGARDS COSTS

23.55 It is very important to include a provision relating to costs in any settlement, whether a court order or a contract. If the case is a substantial one, or has gone on for some time, then the costs may be substantial, quite possibly exceeding the amount in the substantive claim. If there is no provision then each side will bear their own costs.

23.56 However, there can be significant difficulties in reaching a clear agreement about costs.

- The amount of costs incurred by each side will often not be known precisely when a claim is settled.
- If the agreement reached on costs is too vague it may not constitute an enforceable contractual term, which may in turn threaten the validity of the whole settlement.
- If agreement as to costs is simply deferred, the agreement reached could be undermined when costs are discussed.
- In litigation costs usually follow the event (CPR r 44.2(2)(a)), so that the unsuccessful party is ordered to pay the costs of the successful party. The default position in ADR is that each party will pay their own costs. If the claimant's costs are high this can be a difficult point to agree.
- If litigation has been commenced there may already be some interim orders as to costs to be picked up as part of the settlement.
- If there are no existing court proceedings and the parties cannot agree the amount of costs payable, special proceedings under CPR r 46.14, using the Part 8 procedure will have to be used to obtain an order for the court to assess the amount of costs that should be paid.

23.57 It is important to have the clearest and most up-to-date information about the costs in the case when you are involved in an ADR process so that a full and clear agreement can be reached. Terms as to costs should comply with the requirements of the CPR in order to ensure they are effective. This typically means the relevant term should provide for payment of costs on either the standard or indemnity basis, to be agreed (ie that the sum payable should be agreed between the parties if at all possible), but, if the parties cannot agree, with the amount of costs to be determined through a detailed assessment by the court. Possible agreements are therefore:

- each side to bear their own costs;
- one side to contribute a stated sum towards the costs of the other side;
- one side to pay a percentage of the other side's costs, or costs on specific issues, the precise sum to be agreed or subject to detailed assessment;
- one side to pay the costs of the other side, the precise sum to be agreed or subject to detailed assessment.

Poor drafting of the terms relating to costs can result in the whole compromise being void for uncertainty. The most common danger is in the use of the words 'reasonable costs', which are regularly used in settlements. To most litigators this term means standard basis costs (CPR r 44.3(2)), to be agreed, or failing agreement, to be assessed by the court in a detailed assessment (CPR Part 47). It is better to spell this out by saying 'standard basis' rather than relying on a vague term. Note that technically the standard basis only applies to contentious costs, which applies where litigation has commenced. Where ADR procedures have been used without the issue of a claim form the costs incurred by the parties are technically non-contentious costs. **23.58**

To illustrate the problems that can arise, in *Booker Belmont Wholesale Ltd v Ashford Developments Ltd* (2000) LTL 18/7/2000 a Tomlin order provided that 'the fourth party do pay such proportion of the claimant's costs of the action as the court shall determine'. The Court of Appeal commented that the order was not in a satisfactory form, but was plainly an order for costs as between the claimant and the fourth parties in a proportion to be fixed by the court. It required the court to consider, in light of the amount claimed by the claimant, the proportion of costs that it was right for the claimant to be awarded. **23.59**

I INFORMING THE COURT OF SETTLEMENT

Once proceedings have been issued, there is a duty to inform the court if settlement is reached, even if the court is not being asked to make a consent order. The solicitor will normally do this, unless the settlement is reached at the door of the court, in which case the advocate will inform the judge. Where a case is settled in advance of a hearing, each party has a responsibility to inform the court so that the time set aside for the hearing can be reallocated to other litigants. Any order giving effect to the settlement should be filed with the listing officer (PD 39, para 4.2). If the court is informed of a settlement at least seven days before the trial, all or part of the hearing fee is refunded (Civil Proceedings Fees Order 2008 (SI 2008/1053), fee 2.1: there is a 100% refund if more than 28 days' notice is given, 75% if 15–28 days and 50% if 7–14 days). **23.60**

KEY POINTS SUMMARY

- It is essential that all the issues between the parties are covered in a settlement agreement. **23.61**
- If particular issues are deliberately left out of the agreement, or are left for further agreement, this should be made clear.
- The normal rules of contract law must be adhered to, or the settlement will not be binding.
- While oral agreements are usually binding, the risk of misunderstandings means that it is invariably best practice to record the agreement in writing.
- Choosing the method of recording a settlement depends on:
  - whether there are existing proceedings;
  - whether the dispute has been referred to arbitration or adjudication;
  - the costs of different methods of recording the agreement;
  - whether the terms are to be kept confidential;
  - the ease with which different forms of agreement can be enforced. This is dealt with in Chapter 32.
- When drawing up the agreement it is important not to overlook how any existing proceedings are to be dealt with and on how the costs are to be paid.
- A Tomlin order can be used to keep terms confidential in a schedule.

PART VI

ADJUDICATIVE ADR

24

EXPERT OR NEUTRAL DETERMINATION

A INTRODUCTION 24.01
B WHEN SHOULD NEUTRAL OR EXPERT DETERMINATION BE USED? 24.07
C AGREEMENT TO USE EXPERT (OR NEUTRAL) DETERMINATION 24.10
D THE GENERAL APPROACH OF THE COURTS TO EXPERT DETERMINATION ... 24.11
E ADVANTAGES OF EXPERT DETERMINATION 24.15
F DIFFERENCES BETWEEN EXPERT DETERMINATION AND NEGOTIATION, MEDIATION, AND NEUTRAL EVALUATION 24.16
G SIMILARITIES WITH OTHER FORMS OF ADR 24.17
H SELECTION OF THE NEUTRAL OR EXPERT DETERMINER 24.18
I THE PROCESS 24.21
J CONFIDENTIAL INFORMATION 24.28
K THE NATURE OF THE DECISION 24.29
L REASONS FOR THE DECISION 24.32
M THE COURT IS THE FINAL DECISION MAKER AS TO WHETHER THE EXPERT HAS JURISDICTION 24.35
N OTHER GROUNDS FOR CHALLENGING A FINAL DECISION BY COURT PROCEEDINGS 24.39
O PROCEDURE FOR MAKING A CHALLENGE 24.60
P ENFORCING A DECISION 24.61
Q SUING THE EXPERT 24.63
R HOW NEUTRAL OR EXPERT DETERMINATION DIFFERS FROM ARBITRATION 24.66
S DISPUTES REVIEW PANELS 24.67
Key points summary 24.69

A INTRODUCTION

With most of the forms of ADR discussed so far, the parties themselves devise their own solution to the dispute, rather than the court imposing a solution at the conclusion of litigation and arbitration. **24.01**

Expert determination differs from early neutral or expert evaluation discussed in Chapter 22, because the parties will appoint an expert to make a decision or formal determination on the issues referred to the expert. The expert can only make a decision within the boundaries laid down by the parties. In this sense, expert determination is a determinative process, rather than a facilitative process (mediation) or an advisory evaluative process (neutral evaluation). Expert determination differs from evaluation because the expert is asked to do more than produce a non-binding evaluation, opinion, or recommendation in relation to the issues in dispute, but rather to determine those issues. **24.02**

Although the parties usually agree that the determination should be carried out by an appropriate expert such as a judge, lawyer, accountant, surveyor, or engineer, it is not always the case that an expert should be used. In appropriate cases, the parties can agree that the determination is carried out by an independent third party, or even by a panel consisting of a number of neutral third parties and a lawyer. **24.03**

24.04 Depending on the nature of the agreement made between the parties as to the terms on which the determiner is instructed, the determiner's decision can be:

- finally binding on the parties, although they must agree in advance that this is to be so. If they do agree that it is binding, there is no right of appeal, although the decision can be challenged in court on a limited number of grounds;
- binding on them, but only for a temporary or interim period.

24.05 Expert determination should not be confused with the rules relating to expert evidence that can be adduced under the CPR Part 35. In an expert determination, the expert is acting as the decision maker, not as a witness. In court proceedings, an expert acts as a witness, and the ultimate decision maker is the judge.

24.06 Expert determination is rooted in the law of contract. The relationship between the parties and the expert, the scope of the retainer, the obligations of the expert, whether the decision is final and binding on the parties, whether reasons need to be provided for the decision, and the circumstances in which the decision can be challenged will be primarily governed by the terms of the contract that the parties have agreed. There may be two contracts to be consulted, a contract between the parties containing the ADR clause to use Expert Determination (if applicable) and the contract that is entered into between the parties and the expert by which the expert is appointed. For further detail on all aspects of expert determination, see Kendall, Freedman and Farrell, *Expert Determination* (4th edn, Sweet & Maxwell, 2008).

B WHEN SHOULD NEUTRAL OR EXPERT DETERMINATION BE USED?

Stage at which the parties may agree to expert determination

24.07 Expert or neutral determination tends to be used in three main situations:

- where the parties contractually bind themselves, in advance of any dispute arising, to use this method of ADR in order to resolve disputes arising out of the contract between them; or
- where a case raises issues of a very technical nature and the parties decide, after the dispute has arisen, to use expert (or neutral) determination as the preferred method of ADR; or
- during the course of mediation, with the parties settling the remainder of the issues between them when that determination has been obtained.

24.08 In these cases, the parties will enter into a contract with the determiner to determine the dispute. The relationship between the parties and the determiner is primarily governed by the law of contract.

Cases where expert determination is particularly suitable

24.09 Expert determination is a very useful and cost-effective way of determining disputes of a highly technical nature. Examples of cases that are suitable for resolution using this form of ADR are:

- rent reviews where the determination will usually be by a surveyor acting as an expert;
- disputes as to causation, for example the cause of subsidence or a medical condition;
- valuation of a company or share valuations;
- construction disputes;
- real property disputes such as boundary disputes or land valuations;
- energy disputes.

C AGREEMENT TO USE EXPERT (OR NEUTRAL) DETERMINATION

If the parties agree to use expert or neutral determination to determine any disputes arising out of or in connection with the contract, care needs to be taken to ensure that these clauses are unambiguously drafted. They should make it clear which issues are to be referred to the determiner for determination and, where applicable, the area of expertise and qualifications of the expert that should be appointed to resolve the dispute. Some clauses will also spell out the procedure that must be followed to appoint the determiner, and even the procedure that should be followed by the determiner during the determination. An example of a standard clause is shown in Figure 24.1. **24.10**

Figure 24.1 Example of an expert determination clause

Any dispute arising out of this contract shall be referred to an independent chartered accountant or firm of chartered accountants ('the Expert') to be agreed between the Parties or, failing agreement, to be nominated by the president for the time being of the Institute of Chartered Accountants in England and Wales. The Expert shall act as an expert and not as an arbitrator. The Parties agree to provide the Expert with such information as may reasonably be required by him to enable him to determine the dispute. The Expert's determination shall be conclusive and binding on the Parties.

D THE GENERAL APPROACH OF THE COURTS TO EXPERT DETERMINATION

Contractual effect of expert determination clauses

Expert determination clauses, if clearly and unambiguously drafted, will be upheld by the courts, and such clauses will generally prevent the parties having recourse to the courts to resolve their dispute (*Harper v Interchange Group Ltd* [2007] EWHC 1834 (Comm)). See also 7.83–7.93. **24.11**

If one party refuses to comply with an expert determination clause in the contract, the other party will be entitled to damages for breach of contract if it has to issue proceedings to have the dispute determined (*Sunrock Aircraft Corporation v Scandinavian Airlines System* [2007] 2 Lloyd's Rep 612. See also *Union Discount v Zoller* [2002] 1 WLR 1517). **24.12**

Applications to stay court proceedings pending expert determination

The court also has discretion to stay court proceedings that have been issued by a party who failed to use the contractually agreed machinery to determine the dispute (*Channel Tunnel Group Ltd v Balfour Beatty Construction Ltd* [1993] AC 334). The burden will be on the party seeking to litigate the dispute to show grounds why the claim should not be stayed so that the parties can invoke the contractually agreed method of ADR (*Cott UK Ltd v FE Barber Ltd* [1997] 3 All ER 540). The action cannot be stayed if, as a matter of construction, the issues in dispute do not come within the ambit of the expert determination clause (*Guidance Investments Ltd v Guidance Hotel Investments Co BSC (Closed)* [2013] EWHC 3413 (Comm)). In exercising its discretion to enforce such clauses by staying proceedings commenced in breach of the clause, the court has considered the following factors: **24.13**

- the extent to which the parties have complied with the requirements in any pre-action protocol;
- whether the dispute is suitable for determination by the ADR process the parties have contractually agreed to use (*Cott UK Ltd v FR Barber Ltd* [1997] 3 All ER 540);
- the costs of that ADR process compared to the costs of litigation;

- whether the dispute could be resolved more quickly by court proceedings than by requiring the parties to use the contractually agreed ADR machinery (*Thames Valley Power Ltd v Total Gas & Power Ltd* [2006] 1 Lloyd's Rep 441);
- whether a stay would accord with the overriding objective (*DGT Steel and Cladding Ltd v Cubitt Building & Interiors Ltd* [2007] BLR 371);
- the extent to which there would have to be parallel proceedings in court in relation to matters not within the ambit of the expert determination clause (see *Abbas (t/a AH Design v Rotary (International) Ltd* [2012] NIQB 41; *Turville Health Inc v Chartis Insurance UK Ltd* [2012] EWHC 3019 (TCC)).

24.14 In *DGT Steel and Cladding Ltd v Cubitt Building & Interiors Ltd*, the court rejected an argument by the claimant that granting a stay would have the effect of debarring the claimant from pursuing its claim in court. The court held that a temporary stay of the proceedings, for a stated period, simply halts proceedings for a few weeks, until after the adjudication. If, following the adjudication, there is still a residual dispute, the court proceedings can be easily reactivated.

E ADVANTAGES OF EXPERT DETERMINATION

24.15 Expert determination has many advantages:

- It is cost effective.
- It provides for a speedy resolution of the dispute compared to litigation or arbitration.
- It removes the decision making from the parties themselves into the hands of an independent third party.
- It is relatively informal, as the strict rules of evidence and procedure will not apply.
- The parties can agree the procedure that the determiner will have to follow.
- It can be kept confidential and private to the parties.
- It gives the parties a final determination of their dispute where the parties agree that the process is binding on them, with no right of appeal.

F DIFFERENCES BETWEEN EXPERT DETERMINATION AND NEGOTIATION, MEDIATION, AND NEUTRAL EVALUATION

24.16 The main differences between expert determination and negotiation, mediation, and neutral evaluation are as follows:

- Expert determination has less flexibility than the other processes.
- The outcome is not within the parties' control in expert determination.
- In expert determination, the determination will be decided on a correct application of the law and the facts whereas negotiation and mediation enable the parties to move away from their strict legal position to obtain a more creative outcome.
- The decision of the determiner in expert determination will usually be binding on the parties, whereas in evaluation, the decision is not binding on them.

G SIMILARITIES WITH OTHER FORMS OF ADR

24.17 Expert determination also has a number of similarities with other forms of ADR:

- Selection of the process is within the parties' control.
- The selection of the expert is within the parties' control.

- It is a more timely and cost-effective way to resolve a dispute than litigation.
- Parties generally control the amount of information to put before the determiner (although, if required, the expert determiner can carry out an investigative role independently of the parties).
- It remains a confidential process. Unlike litigation, any hearing will take place in private and the determination will usually be private unless the parties agree otherwise.

H SELECTION OF THE NEUTRAL OR EXPERT DETERMINER

The parties may agree between themselves the identity of the expert they will appoint and may approach the expert directly. Alternatively, they may enlist the help of bodies such as the Academy of Experts, the Royal Institution of Chartered Surveyors, the Institute of Chartered Accountants in England and Wales, and the Law Society. **24.18**

Some ADR providers also offer an expert determination service (see for example CEDR at www.cedr.co.uk). An ADR provider will advise on the most appropriate type of expert to resolve the dispute and will offer a selection of experts for the consideration of the parties. The provider will also administer the process. Most ADR providers have their own standard rules for expert determination and a standard form of agreement that applies to the expert determination. For an example of this, see CEDR's Model Expert Determination Agreement and Rules of Conduct at www.cedr.com. **24.19**

When appointing the expert, the parties should give consideration to the following matters: **24.20**

- the nature of the expertise required;
- the procedure for appointing the expert;
- the issues to be referred to the expert;
- the procedure that the expert should employ to determine the dispute. In particular whether the expert should resolve the dispute from information supplied by the parties, conduct his own investigations and whether an oral hearing should take place. The parties may simply want to provide that, in the absence of agreement between them about the procedure, the relevant procedure should be determined by the expert;
- the information that should be provided to the expert;
- whether the determination is to be confidential;
- whether the determination is to be final and binding on the parties;
- whether the expert is to give reasons for the determination;
- the circumstances in which the parties can challenge the decision, for example for manifest error, fraud, or partiality;
- the time scale for the determination: this could include agreement on the date by which the determination should be provided;
- the dates for payment of the expert's fees and any monetary sum that the expert determines should be paid by one side to the other.

I THE PROCESS

If the parties have spelt out the procedure that should be followed in advance in the substantive contract, or in the contract appointing the determiner, then this procedure should be followed. However, it is more usual for the parties simply to agree in advance to refer disputes to an expert for determination, leaving the parties and the expert to agree on the appropriate procedure once the dispute has arisen and the referral to the expert has been made. **24.21**

24.22 The parties can retain a degree of control over the process and most experts will seek to agree any procedural directions with the parties. The parties can also tailor the process to suit their individual needs and requirements. There can be statements of case, disclosure, and a formal hearing with oral submissions and cross-examination of witnesses if the parties require this. If proceedings have not been issued, the determination can be done in a relatively informal way, with both parties simply making submissions on paper, and the expert providing his decision in writing.

24.23 The parties are under an implied duty to co-operate with each other and with the expert in relation to the determination (see *Yan Seng Pte Ltd v International Trade Corp Ltd* [2013] EWHC 111 (QB). Where an expert's proposed terms of engagement are reasonable and are consistent with the rights and obligations in the agreement between the parties, the implied duty to co-operate is likely to require the parties to accept the expert's appointment on those terms (*Cream Holdings Ltd v Davenport* [2011] EWCA Civ 1287).

24.24 If the parties agree on the procedure or machinery by which the determination is to be carried out, the court can intervene and provide its own machinery if the procedure agreed has broken down (*Sudbrook Trading Estate Ltd v Eggleton* [1983] 1 AC 444 and *Ursa Major Management Ltd v United Utilities Electricity plc* [2002] EWHC 3041 (Ch)). However, the court will not intervene to order that a particular party should be entitled to make representations to the expert, or that particular documents should be provided to the expert if the expert determination clause does not make provision for these matters, as these are procedural matters for the expert to decide (see *Vimercati v BV Trustco Ltd* [2012] EWHC 1410 (Ch)).

24.25 In the absence of any agreement between the parties and the expert about the procedure that should be followed, an expert determination cannot be set aside on the basis that the expert failed to follow a fair procedure in accordance with the notions of natural justice (*Bernard Schulte GmbH v Nile Holdings Ltd* [2004] 2 Lloyd's Rep 352).

24.26 The procedure that is typically agreed will provide for each party to send to the expert:

- written submissions setting out their case on each of the issues; and
- copies of all relevant documents (the parties should co-operate to produce an agreed bundle of documents if possible). If one party refuses to disclose relevant documents to the expert, having agreed to do so, the court may order him to do so (*Bruce v Carpenter* [2006] EWHC 3301 (Ch)).

24.27 In some cases, the parties may agree that the parties or their lawyers should make submissions at a meeting or hearing, or that live evidence should be called at a hearing before the expert, although this is usually not required. In some cases also, the parties may agree that the expert may conduct his own lines of inquiry.

J CONFIDENTIAL INFORMATION

24.28 The parties may agree that they can each provide information to the expert on a confidential basis. If they do so, and the expert is obliged to give reasons for his determination, he should summarize any information that has been provided to him but that is not known to the other party, so that both parties can ascertain what the expert took into account in reaching the determination (per Cresswell J in *Halifax Life Ltd v Equitable Life Assurance Society* [2007] 1 Lloyd's Rep 528). This is particularly important if the parties have agreed that the determination can be challenged on the grounds of manifest error. To avoid suggestions of bias in favour of one party, it is preferable if the parties openly exchange any information that is placed before the determiner, and that any hearings are held in the presence of all parties.

K THE NATURE OF THE DECISION

In expert determination the parties will usually agree that the decision will be binding on them and, where this is so, the court will uphold the decision unless there are grounds for setting it aside (see *Thames Valley Power Ltd v Total Gas & Power Ltd* [2005] EWHC 2208 (Comm)). **24.29**

The decision does not take the form of an award or an order, unlike arbitration. **24.30**

The agreement may also specify a time limit within which the determination may be challenged by court proceedings. Alternatively, the parties may agree to be bound by the determination with no right to challenge it in court or elsewhere. **24.31**

L REASONS FOR THE DECISION

The parties can agree whether written reasons should be provided for the determination. If the contract by which the expert is appointed does not require reasons for the determination, then the expert is not obliged to provide them. However, if the parties agree that the expert should give reasons for the decision, and the expert fails to do so, he will be ordered to do so by the court (*Halifax Life Ltd v Equitable Life Assurance Society* [2007] 1 Lloyd's Rep 528). Although in an expert determination (unlike arbitration) there is no statutory provision directing the expert to give reasons, where the contract provided for him to do so, the court can require him to give reasons by enforcing the contractual provisions, or under its inherent jurisdiction. **24.32**

Where reasons are to be given, they should be intelligible and adequate in all the circumstances. The reasons can be stated briefly, but they should explain the basis for the expert's conclusions on the issues he was asked to determine. **24.33**

If the parties have agreed that the decision will not be binding on them in the event of a 'manifest error' by the expert, it will be very difficult for them to show that a manifest error has been made if the written reasons contracted for have not been provided, or indeed to show that he departed from his instructions. **24.34**

M THE COURT IS THE FINAL DECISION MAKER AS TO WHETHER THE EXPERT HAS JURISDICTION

The underlying contract between the parties or the agreement appointing the expert may state that the court is to have exclusive jurisdiction to determine the extent of the expert's remit. However, some expert determination clauses may provide that the expert is to have exclusive jurisdiction to determine the extent of his own jurisdiction in the event of a dispute between the parties. **24.35**

In *Barclays Bank Plc v Nylon Capital LLP* [2011] EWCA Civ 826, the Court of Appeal held that where a dispute arises as to the jurisdiction of an expert, the court will be the final decision maker as to whether the expert has jurisdiction to determine the dispute, even **24.36** if a clause purports to confer that jurisdiction on the expert in a manner that is final and binding.

24.37 If a dispute arises between the parties as to whether an expert has jurisdiction, it may be in the interests of justice and convenience for the court to determine the jurisdiction of the expert before he or she makes a determination. Whatever the expert decided on jurisdiction would not be final and could be challenged, unlike a determination of a matter within his jurisdiction. If the expert found he had jurisdiction, but the court found that this was wrong, it would otherwise be wasteful of time and costs if the expert determined a dispute when he had no jurisdiction to do so (*Barclays Bank Plc v Nylon Capital LLP* [2011] EWCA Civ 826).

24.38 However, *Barclays Bank Plc v Nylon Capital LLP* should not be taken as laying down a prescriptive rule that it would always be wasteful for an expert to decide the issue first. The court has to determine whether it is faced with a dispute which is real and not hypothetical and if it is real, whether it is in the interests of justice and convenience for the court to determine the matter first. It may be that the obvious and convenient forum for arguments to be raised about jurisdiction is in the expert determination in the first instance and that can be done without prejudice to a party's contention that the expert had no jurisdiction (see *Wilky Property Holdings Plc v London & Surrey Investments Ltd* [2011] EWHC 2888 (Ch)).

N OTHER GROUNDS FOR CHALLENGING A FINAL DECISION BY COURT PROCEEDINGS

24.39 The court will give primary consideration to the contract in ascertaining whether the determination can be challenged. If the parties agree that their dispute should be resolved by expert determination and that the expert's decision is to be conclusive and binding for all purposes, then provided the expert has done exactly what he was instructed to do, and made the determination honestly and in good faith, the determination generally cannot be challenged by seeking to set it aside in court proceedings (*Jones v Sherwood Computer Services plc* [1992] 1 WLR 277).

24.40 However, the following grounds of challenge may exist as a matter of law, even in the absence of contractual grounds for challenge:

- material departure from instructions;
- fraud;
- partiality.

Material departure from instructions

24.41 The decision can be challenged if the expert has departed from his instructions in a material way. This could be established if, for instance, the expert was mistaken about the terms of his instructions, or did not do what he was appointed to do; if he valued the wrong number of shares, for example, or shares in the wrong company, or failed to carry out a test by a contractually stipulated method (*Veba Oil Supply and Trading GmbH v Petrotrade Inc* [2001] EWCA Civ 1832). In *Kollerich & Cie SA v The State Trading Corporation of India* [1980] 2 Lloyd's Rep 32 certificates of quality were set aside because they did not comply with the terms of the expert determination clause in the contract. Any decision reached on an issue that was not within the expert's terms of reference is also liable to be set aside. Any departure will be material unless it can be said to be trivial or *de minimis*. Once any departure is material, it is not necessary to show that it affected the result (*British Shipbuilders v VSEL Consortium plc* [1997] 1 Lloyd's Rep 106). However, doubt has recently been cast on this in *Ackerman v Ackerman* [2011] EWHC 2438 (Ch), where Vos J held that where a departure from instructions would have made no difference to the determination, the departure was not a material one and the determination was therefore binding on the parties. The Court of Appeal has granted leave to appeal on this single issue. Moore-Bick LJ, in granting leave to appeal considered that the decision of Vos J may have been wrong on this point (see [2012] EWCA Civ 768).

Fraud or collusion

If the expert is guilty of fraud or has colluded with one party in reaching his decision, then it can be set aside (*Campbell v Edwards* [1976] 1 WLR 403). In the case of partiality, it must be shown that the expert actually was biased. A mere possibility of bias will not suffice (*Marco v Thompson* (No 3) [1997] 2 BCLC 36). **24.42**

Moreover, one or more of the following *contractual* grounds for challenge may exist: **24.43**

- failing to provide reasons for the determination when the contract requires reasons to be given;
- manifest error;
- an error of law;
- lack of procedural fairness;
- the determination was not intended to be final and binding in relation to matters of construction.

No reasons for decision

If the expert fails to provide reasons for his decision (a decision for which reasons have to be given is sometimes known as a 'speaking decision'), despite having agreed to do so, then the decision can be challenged. However, the court is likely to order the expert to provide reasons, rather than set the decision aside (see 7.32). **24.44**

Manifest error

The parties may agree in their contract that the expert's decision will only be binding on them in the absence of manifest error. If there is such an error the decision may be set aside (*Veba Oil Supply and Trading GmbH v Petrotrade Inc* [2002] 1 Lloyd's Rep 295). However, even if a determiner has clearly erred in law or in fact, in the absence of any contractual term enabling the parties to challenge the decision on the grounds of a manifest error, the decision will be binding on the parties (*Jones v Sherwood Computer Services plc* [1992] 1 WLR 277). **24.45**

The meaning of 'manifest error' was considered in *Conoco (UK) Ltd v Phillips Petroleum Co UK Ltd* (unreported, 19 August 1996) to be '... oversights and blunders so obvious as to admit of no difference of opinion'. Mr Justice Lewison defined 'manifest error' slightly differently in *IIG Capital LLC v Van Der Merwe* [2008] 1 All ER (Comm) 1173 at para 52 as one which is 'obvious or easily demonstrable without extensive investigation', and this definition was upheld and approved on appeal (see [2008] 2 All ER (Comm) 1185 at para 35). In *Macdonald v Livingstone* [2012] CSOH 31, it was held that in order to show a manifest error, the challenging party had to demonstrate an error that was so obvious as to be beyond reasonable contradiction for it to be manifest. See also *Walton Homes Ltd v Staffordshire CC* [2013] EWHC 2554 (Ch). **24.46**

24.47 In *North Shire Ventures Ltd v Anstead Holdings Inc* [2011] EWCA Civ 230, the Court of Appeal held that the judge at first instance had been wrong to assume that for a party to rely on a manifest error, it had to be able to demonstrate the error immediately and conclusively. In that case, the certificate of indebtedness issued by an expert was based on the terms of the original contract between the parties. However, the contract was subsequently varied, and the certificate could be set aside on the grounds of manifest error because the amount certified was that due under the unvaried loan agreement instead of the amount due under the agreement as varied.

24.48 If the expert's reasoning is not apparent from the determination itself, the court can look at other material that was available to the expert to determine if a manifest error has been made and any subsequent reasons the expert may have given by way of clarification (*Homepace Ltd v Sita South East Ltd* [2008] EWCA Civ 1).

An error of law

24.49 At present, it is unclear whether an expert's decision could be set aside on the grounds that he made an error of law.

24.50 In *Nikko Hotels (UK) Ltd v MEPC plc* [1991] 2 EGLR 103 (Ch), Knox J held that if the parties do agree to refer to the final and conclusive judgment of the expert an issue that consists of a question of construction, the expert's decision will be final and conclusive and therefore not open to review by the courts on the ground that the expert's decision on construction was erroneous in law, unless it can be shown that the expert has not performed the task assigned to him. If he answered the right question in the wrong way, his decision will be binding on the parties.

24.51 The court in *Barclays Bank Plc v Nylon Capital LLP* [2011] EWCA Civ 826 did not have to decide this question on the facts of that case, but Lord Neuberger commented at paras 65–66 that an expert's decision might be able to be attacked if he made an error of law, which resulted in shares being valued on the wrong basis (eg he misinterpreted the company's articles), even if the valuation is agreed to be 'final and binding'. Accordingly, in his view, Knox J's observation at para 31 of *Nikko Hotels (UK) Ltd v MEPC Plc* [1991] 2 EGLR 103 could not be safely relied upon. Per Lord Neuberger at para 69:

> Accordingly, it seems to me that, where a contract requires an expert to effect a valuation which is to be binding between the parties, and there is an issue of law which divides the parties and needs to be resolved by the expert, it by no means follows that his resolution of the issue is incapable of being challenged in court by the party whose argument on the issue is rejected. As Hoffmann LJ said in *Mercury v The Director General* [1994] 1 WLR 48, 'The parties have agreed to a decision in accordance with this meaning and no other. Accordingly, if the decision-maker has acted upon what in the court's view was the wrong meaning, he has gone outside his decision-making authority', and it seems to me to follow that the court can review, and if appropriate, set aside or amend his decision. While certainty and clarity are highly desirable, it is, regrettably, inappropriate to consider that issue further in this case.
>
> I appreciate that, in cases of this sort, the advantage of leaving all points of law to the final determination of the expert is that it results in a relatively quick and cheap process for the parties. However, it must be questionable whether the parties would have intended an accountant, surveyor, or other professional with no legal qualification, to determine a point of law, without any recourse to the courts, even if it has a very substantial effect on their rights and obligations. It would, I suggest, be surprising if that were the effect of an expert determination agreement, when the Arbitration Act 1996 gives a right (albeit a limited and prescribed right) to the parties to refer points of law to the court. That Act applies where the parties have entered into an arbitration

agreement, which gives them a much greater ability, in law and in practice, to make representations and to involve lawyers in connection with the arbitration, than parties enjoy in connection with the great majority of contractual expert determinations.

Failure to act lawfully or fairly

If the procedure to be followed is set out in the contract, and the expert fails to follow it, it may be possible to challenge the determination on the basis that the expert has failed to act lawfully or fairly (*John Barker Construction Ltd v London Portman Hotel Ltd* [1996] 83 BLR 31). See 24.21 to 24.27. **24.52**

The decision is not intended to be final on matters of construction

Questions as to the role of the expert, the ambit of his instructions, and the nature of his instructions (namely whether he had exclusive jurisdiction to determine the matters referred to him or whether his jurisdiction was concurrent with that of the court) are to be determined as a matter of construction of the agreement. If the agreement confers on the expert the exclusive remit to determine the matter, then the jurisdiction of the court to determine that question is excluded. It is irrelevant whether the court would have reached a different conclusion or whether the court considers that the expert's decision is wrong, for the parties have, in either event, agreed to abide by the decision of the expert. (See *Mercury Communications Ltd v Director General of Telecommunications* [1996] 1 WLR 48, *British Shipbuilders v VSEL Consortium Plc* [1997] 1 Lloyd's Rep 106, and *National Grid Co Plc v M25 Group Ltd* [1998] EWCA Civ 1968.) **24.53**

However, if it can be said that, by the terms under which the expert was appointed, the expert's determination was not intended to oust the jurisdiction of the court in matters of interpretation of the terms of the underlying contract between the parties, then the court can intervene if the expert issues a determination based on an incorrect interpretation. See *Mercury Communications Ltd v Director General of Telecommunications* [1996] 1 WLR 48 and *Homepace Ltd v Sita South East Ltd* [2008] EWCA Civ 1. **24.54**

Recent decisions demonstrate that the courts will not readily accept that the parties intended an expert's decision to be final and conclusive in respect of the construction of the contract, even if the underlying contract, or the contract appointing the expert, provides that the expert's determination should be final and conclusive on matters of construction. **24.55**

In *Thorne v Courtier* [2011] EWCA Civ 460, the parties entered into a settlement agreement during the course of proceedings by which the claimant agreed to pay 'damages for trespass' determined by a rural chartered surveyor acting as an expert. A dispute arose between the parties as to whether the term 'damages for trespass' meant damages at large or damages for use and occupation. The Court of Appeal held that as a matter of construction of the agreement, in the absence of a clear indication that the parties intended the expert to determine the meaning of the phrase 'damages for trespass', it was difficult to believe that the parties intended the expert to determine the meaning of this term as he could not be expected to have professional expertise in determining matters of this kind. The court therefore had jurisdiction to determine the meaning of the agreement and the scope of the expert's instructions. **24.56**

The Court of Appeal in *Thorne v Courtier* also held that this fell into the category of exceptional cases in which the court should determine the meaning of that phrase before the expert made his determination. In this case, both parties reached different views on the meaning of the phrase. It was likely that one or other of them would seek to challenge the expert's interpretation of the meaning of the phrase, so this did fall within the category of exceptional **24.57** cases in which the court would construe the meaning of the phrase before the expert issued his valuation. Lord Justice Moore-Bick stated at para 22:

> Whether to determine the scope of the expert's instructions in advance of his determination is ultimately a matter of procedural convenience and as such the decision ultimately lies within the discretion of the judge. The accepted view, as appears clearly from the authorities to which I have referred, is that the court should not do so, save in exceptional cases, in order to avoid unnecessary litigation with its attendant waste of time and costs. However, there are some circumstances, of which the Mercury case provides an example, in which it is clear for one reason or another that it would be in the interests of the parties to define the position before the expert begins his task.

24.58 In *Menolly Investments 3 Sarl v Cerep Sarl* [2009] EWHC 516 (Ch), the court, following *National Grid Co Plc v M25 Group Ltd (No 1)* [1999] 1 EGLR 65, held that as a matter of interpretation of the building contract, the expert was not entitled to decide points of construction in a way which binds the parties as to what was or was not included in the scope of the contract works for the purposes of deciding whether there had been practical completion of those works. His expertise lay in project management and he had no particular expertise to bring to the interpretation of documents. Accordingly, he was not entitled to certify practical completion on the basis of his own view as to the meaning of the building contract as to what was included in the contract works. Accordingly, the expert's certificate could be set aside as it was invalid. However, it was not set aside on the facts as the claimant was estopped from contending that it was invalid or alternatively he had waived any defect in relation to the issue of the certificate.

24.59 In *Persimmon Homes Ltd v Woodford Land Ltd* [2011] EWHC 3109 (Ch), the court held that the parties had intended the court to decide questions of construction of the terms of an option agreement in rectification proceedings despite the existence of dispute resolution clauses which provided for any difference between the parties in relation to the interpretation of any part of the agreement shall be referred to an expert for determination and that his decision was to be final and binding on the parties save for manifest error.

O PROCEDURE FOR MAKING A CHALLENGE

24.60 A challenge to the decision in an expert determination will usually be made by issuing Part 8 proceedings. Part 8 proceedings may also be issued in advance of an expert determination to decide any disputes about the interpretation of the expert determination clause, or to resolve disagreement about matters that should be referred to the expert pursuant to the clause. If the decision is set aside, the court may, in some circumstances, make the determination itself, if necessary after considering expert evidence adduced by the parties, or it may direct a new expert to be instructed to determine the matter.

P ENFORCING A DECISION

24.61 A decision reached by expert or neutral determination cannot be enforced in the same way as if it were a court decision.

24.62 However, a failure by one side to honour the decision amounts to a breach of contract, and proceedings can be issued in relation to the breach. In those proceedings, the court can make an order giving effect to the decision of the expert. The court's decision can then be enforced in the same way as any other judgment. See Chapter 32 for more detail on enforcement proceedings. Winding-up or bankruptcy proceedings could also be brought against an individual or company or partnership that refused to pay a monetary sum awarded by an expert determination.

Q SUING THE EXPERT

An expert or neutral person carrying out a determination is not immune from suit in the same way as a member of the judiciary. An expert can be liable in negligence or breach of contract if he is negligent in the determination that he reaches or fails to act in accordance with the contract (*Sutcliffe v Thackrah* [1974] AC 727 and *Arenson v Casson Beckman Rutley and Co* [1977] AC 405). 24.63

Many experts seek to secure immunity by inserting clauses in the agreement by which the parties agree that they will not hold the expert liable in respect of the determination or call the expert as a witness in any proceedings. 24.64

These clauses may be unenforceable if they are unreasonable under the terms of the Unfair Contract Terms Act 1977. 24.65

R HOW NEUTRAL OR EXPERT DETERMINATION DIFFERS FROM ARBITRATION

Expert determination differs from arbitration in the following ways (see also Table 24.1): 24.66

- Unlike arbitration, the determiner has no power to make an order or an award.
- The determination does not take place within the formal scheme laid down in the Arbitration Act 1996, and that Act and the extensive body of common law that applies to arbitrations does not apply to neutral or expert determination.
- Unlike arbitration, there is no right of appeal, and the strict rules of evidence and natural justice do not apply, unless the contract so provides.
- Expert determination (unlike arbitration) is not subject to the supervision of the court. However, the court may be involved if a dispute arises as to the jurisdiction of the expert, or if one or both parties seek to challenge the determination.
- The parties retain a great deal of control over the timing and the procedure that applies to the determination.
- The parties retain a reasonable degree of control over the evidence that they place before the determiner.
- If it is an international dispute, it is not enforceable under the New York Convention 1958 (for which, see Chapter 32).
- An expert can be sued (unless the contract confers immunity from suit), unlike an arbitrator, who has judicial immunity from suit.
- An expert does not act in a judicial capacity, and so can use his or her own expertise to inform his or her decision.

S DISPUTES REVIEW PANELS

This can be a hybrid form of determination, which may or may not involve an expert. Disputes review panels can take a number of different forms, but typically they will allow for each party to appoint an independent party to the panel, and the independent parties will then choose a chairman. The chairman or the independent parties may or may not be experts, depending on the nature of the dispute that is being referred to the panel. Decisions made by the panel will be binding on the parties unless they agree that they will refer the decision to arbitration within a specified time limit. 24.67

Table 24.1 A comparison of early neutral evaluation (ENE), expert determination (ED), adjudication, and arbitration

Characteristic	ENE	ED	Adjudication	Arbitration
Neutral third party involved	Yes	Yes	Yes	Yes
Parties have control over selection of the neutral third party	Yes	Yes	Yes	Yes—to an extent
It is a *facilitative* dispute resolution process	No—unless evaluation is being done in the context of mediation (evaluative mediation)	No	No	No
Neutral third party's determination is legally binding on the parties	No	Yes	Yes—provided no challenge is made to it within a specified time limit	Yes—subject to any right of appeal
Parties have some control over the procedure and the evidence to be placed before the neutral third party	Yes	Yes	Yes—usually	Yes
The outcome is negotiated by the parties	Yes	No	No	No
The decision is made by the neutral third party	No	Yes	Yes	Yes
Private and confidential process	Yes	Yes	Yes	Yes
Process can be abandoned by the party at any time	Yes	No	No	No
The determiner is subject to control by the court	No	No	No	Yes
Right of appeal from the decision	No	No	No	Yes—in some circumstances
Determiner can be liable for negligence/breach of contract	Yes	Yes	No	No
Decision can be enforced as a court order without the need for fresh proceedings	No	No	No	Yes

24.68 A disputes review panel was used in the channel tunnel litigation (*Channel Tunnel Group Ltd v Balfour Beatty Ltd* [1993] AC 334).

KEY POINTS SUMMARY

- Expert determination is a speedy, cost-effective way of obtaining a determination on a case or an issue. **24.69**
- It is useful in cases raising technical issues that would require expert evidence to resolve in court proceedings.
- The parties can choose the determiner.
- The decision is usually final and binding on the parties.
- The parties may agree on a speaking decision, or one without reasons.
- The decision can only be challenged in court proceedings in very limited circumstances.

25

CONSTRUCTION INDUSTRY ADJUDICATION

A INTRODUCTION 25.01
B NATURE OF ADJUDICATION 25.04
C REQUIREMENTS 25.05
D EXPRESS CONTRACTUAL RIGHT TO ADJUDICATION 25.12
E DEFAULT PROVISIONS IN THE SCHEME FOR CONSTRUCTION CONTRACTS 25.15
F COMMENCEMENT OF THE ADJUDICATION 25.16
G PROCEDURE BEFORE THE HEARING 25.26
H ADJUDICATOR'S DECISION 25.36
I BINDING, BUT INTERIM EFFECT, OF DECISIONS 25.43
J OVERALL COST 25.46
K ADJUDICATION IN RESIDENTIAL BUILDING CONTRACTS 25.47
L COURT ENFORCEMENT OF SUM FOUND DUE ON ADJUDICATION 25.48
Key points summary 25.49

A INTRODUCTION

25.01 ADR has tended to develop through initiatives in particular organizations and industries, usually aimed at finding cost-effective and swift means of resolving disputes as alternatives to bringing proceedings in court. Different solutions, which have developed into the different ADR processes described in this book, have been adopted in different industries. One particular process is adjudication in construction industry disputes. Adjudication resembles arbitration (see Chapters 26–31), in that it produces a decision on the dispute, but one that is only of a temporary nature. The process involves an adjudicator reaching a decision very swiftly (only 28 days after appointment), with the idea being to get a decision on how much a contractor should be paid, potentially followed by a full-blown investigation through the courts or in a formal arbitration if either party does not agree with the adjudicator's decision. The underlying policy is 'pay now, argue later' (*RJT Consulting Engineers Ltd v DM Engineering (Northern Ireland) Ltd* [2002] 1 WLR 2344). An adjudication award is binding, but is not registrable as a judgment unlike an award in arbitration. Instead, enforcement is through suing on the adjudicator's decision, often followed by the entry of judgment in default or an application for summary judgment.

25.02 Adjudication procedures are laid down by the Housing Grants, Construction and Regeneration Act 1996 Part II, as amended by the Local Democracy, Economic Development and Construction Act 2009 ss 138–145. Before this legislation was enacted there was a serious problem in the late payment of sums due in construction industry contracts. Large construction projects will be ongoing for many months or even years. If contracting parties are not paid until the completion of the project they will often fall into financial difficulties, which then has an impact on the other parties and may jeopardize the successful completion of the project. In large projects there are also usually several contractors, each dealing with a particular aspect of the overall scheme (such as architects, main contractors, ground works, scaffolding, cement, brickwork, structural work, glazing, roofing, electrical, and other fitting out). If one of these stops work due to some dispute, it will have an adverse effect on all the other parties.

The Housing Grants, Construction and Regeneration Act 1996 Part II deals with these problems by laying down a scheme aimed at ensuring fair dealing in construction contracts. Adjudication of construction industry disputes, which is dealt with in s 108, is the key provision for the purposes of this chapter. Related provisions deal with matters such as stage payments (s 109), a right to suspend performance for non-payment, but only after giving notice of the grounds (s 112), and a general prohibition on making payment to a contractor conditional on the paying party itself being paid by someone else (s 113). The common theme of these provisions is that they provide mechanisms for ensuring contractors are paid the sums they are contractually entitled to at the time they are contractually due, or as soon as the law can practically achieve this. **25.03**

B NATURE OF ADJUDICATION

Adjudication is an interim dispute resolution process, under which an impartial adjudicator gives a decision on a dispute arising during the course of a construction contract (*Macob Civil Engineering Ltd v Morrison Construction Ltd* (1999) 64 Con LR 1). While a dispute seeking any type of relief may be referred to adjudication, an adjudicator simply makes a decision, and does not have any of the coercive powers available to a court. Adjudication is therefore not likely to be effective if relief in the form of specific performance or an injunction is sought. In practical terms, the vast majority of disputes referred to adjudication are about how much money is payable under the contract. **25.04**

C REQUIREMENTS

A party to a construction contract can refer a matter to adjudication if the following conditions are satisfied: **25.05**

(1) the underlying contract is a construction contract (Housing Grants, Construction and Regeneration Act 1996 ss 104 and 105);
(2) the underlying contract is a 'commercial' construction contract as opposed to a contract with a residential occupier (s 106). It is only contracts with the residential occupier that are excluded, so that contractor/sub-contractor and contractor/consultant contracts are covered if the other conditions are satisfied;
(3) the underlying commercial construction contract is required by s 108(2) to include terms providing a contractual right to refer disputes to adjudication. If it fails to do so, there is a default statutory right to refer disputes to adjudication;
(4) there is a dispute between the parties;
(5) the dispute is one relating to the underlying construction contract.

There are particular technical issues relating to requirements (1) and (4) that are discussed next, together with the now repealed requirement that the contract be in writing. They are followed by a discussion on express terms providing for adjudication, and the default statutory scheme (requirement (3)). **25.06**

Construction contract

25.07 A 'construction contract' is an agreement for the carrying out of construction operations, either directly or through others such as by sub-contracting, or by the provision of labour (Housing Grants, Construction and Regeneration Act 1996 s 104(1)). It includes architectural, design, and surveying work relating to construction operations (s 104(2)), but excludes contracts of employment (s 104(3)) and construction operations outside England, Wales, and Scotland (s 104(6)(b)). 'Construction operations' is widely defined in s 105(1) to cover the construction, alteration, repair, maintenance, extension, demolition, or dismantling of buildings or structures forming, or to form, part of land, and also various other activities, including:

- similar activities relating to walls, roads, power-lines, aircraft runways, harbours, pipelines, sewers, and reservoirs etc;
- installation of fittings for heating, lighting, air-conditioning, drainage, water supply etc;
- ground clearance, foundations, scaffolding, landscaping etc operations that are an integral part of construction operations;
- cleaning in the course of construction, restoration etc, and painting and decorating inside and outside any building or structure.

25.08 Extraction of oil and gas, mining for minerals, and building of nuclear power plants are excluded, as are artistic works (s 105(2)). Also excluded is the manufacture of building components, materials etc, unless the contract also provides for these items to be installed in a construction operation (s 105(2)(d)).

Dispute

25.09 The Housing Grants, Construction and Regeneration Act 1996 s 108(1) gives the parties a right to refer any 'dispute' to adjudication. This is defined to include any difference, and so has the same meaning as 'dispute' in relation to arbitration (Arbitration Act 1996 s 82; and see 26.21). Making a claim is therefore not enough. There will be a dispute if there is an express disagreement by the responding party or if it can be inferred that a claim is not admitted. Not much is needed for this purpose. It is far from unknown for a party to make a reference to adjudication just hours after lodging a claim. This may be enough provided it is considered that a reasonable time to consider and respond to the claim has been given. This will depend on the nature of the claim: only a short time for consideration is required for a simple claim for money contracted for, whereas claims for extensions of time, or additional costs due to site constraints, are likely to require more time before they can be considered to be disputed.

25.10 It is only the disputed claim that can be referred to adjudication. The basic guidance is that only a single dispute should be referred to adjudication in one reference. Where the parties try to wrap several disputes into a single reference, costs tend to escalate and keeping to the 28-day timetable becomes increasingly difficult. Once a reference is made, the referring party is not permitted to add further disputes at a later stage. An appearance of seeking to do just this is sometimes given where the referring party produces new documentation in the adjudication process that has not been seen by the responding party before the reference to adjudication. Experts' reports are particularly dangerous in this regard, because they often describe the dispute in more sophisticated ways than the terms used by the referring party. Practical advice is to ensure that all the evidence that will be used in the adjudication is sent to the responding party before making the formal reference to adjudication.

Former requirement for written agreement

25.11 Construction contracts entered into before 1 October 2011 were only covered by the adjudication scheme if they were in writing (Housing Grants, Construction and Regeneration Act 1996 s 107(1)). This requirement was repealed by the Local Democracy, Economic Development and Construction Act 2009 s 139. From 1 October 2011 construction contracts must include written terms dealing with adjudication (see 25.12), but if they do not, or if the whole contract is oral, the default provisions (see 25.15) apply.

D EXPRESS CONTRACTUAL RIGHT TO ADJUDICATION

25.12 Under the Housing Grants, Construction and Regeneration Act 1996 s 108(2), (3A), a construction contract must include written terms that:

- enable a party to give notice at any time of its intention to refer a dispute to adjudication;
- provide a timetable with the object of securing the appointment of the adjudicator and referral of the dispute to him within seven days of such notice;
- require the adjudicator to reach a decision within 28 days of referral or such longer period as is agreed by the parties after the dispute has been referred;
- allow the adjudicator to extend the period of 28 days by up to 14 days, with the consent of the party by whom the dispute was referred;
- impose a duty on the adjudicator to act impartially;
- enable the adjudicator to take the initiative in ascertaining the facts and the law; and
- permit the adjudicator to correct his decision to remove clerical or typographical errors.

25.13 Further, by s 108(3) the contract must provide in writing that the decision of the adjudicator is binding until the dispute is finally determined by legal proceedings, by arbitration (if the contract provides for arbitration or the parties otherwise agree to arbitration), or by agreement. However, the parties may agree to accept the decision of the adjudicator as finally determining the dispute.

25.14 It is important that all these matters are addressed in the clause, otherwise whatever provision is made will be void. A clause that provided that the adjudicator's decision was valid even if issued out of time has been held in *Aveat Heating Ltd v Jerram Falkus Construction Ltd* [2007] EWHC 131 (TCC) to fail to comply with s 108(2)(c), (d), and the clause was void. Typical, fairly basic, express terms dealing with references to adjudication are shown in Table 25.1. Standard form contracts in the construction industry are often far more sophisticated. The adjudication clause in the JCT standard form contract, local authority without quantities, for example, has 32 paragraphs laying down detailed procedures for adjudications.

Table 25.1 Contract clauses referring construction disputes to adjudication

Type of clause	Wording
Reference to construction adjudication	A party to this contract ('the referring party') may at any time give notice ('the notice') in writing to the other party of its intention to refer a dispute arising under the contract to adjudication.
Clauses dealing with procedure on the adjudication	The parties may agree the identity of the adjudicator. Where an adjudicator is not agreed within two days of the notice being given, the referring party shall immediately apply to [*name of adjudication provider*] for the nomination of an adjudicator, which nomination shall be communicated to the parties within five days of receipt of the application.

(Continued)

Table 25.1 *(Continued)*

Type of clause	Wording
	Within seven days of the notice the referring party shall refer the dispute to the adjudicator The adjudicator must act impartially and shall reach a decision within 28 days of referral or such longer period as is agreed by the parties after the dispute has been referred. The adjudicator may extend the period of 28 days by up to 14 days, with the consent of the party by whom the dispute was referred.
Clause to avoid conflict between enforcement of decision and any arbitration clause	The enforcement of any decision of an adjudicator is not a matter which may be referred to arbitration.

E DEFAULT PROVISIONS IN THE SCHEME FOR CONSTRUCTION CONTRACTS

25.15 To the extent that a construction contract does not make express provision for adjudication in accordance with the above requirements, the Housing Grants, Construction and Regeneration Act 1996 s 108(5), and the Scheme for Construction Contracts (England and Wales) Regulations 1998 (SI 1998/649) provide for disputes to be referred to adjudication under 'the Scheme for Construction Contracts'. This covers cases where the contract fails to say anything about adjudication, and also cases where a purported adjudication clause is void through failing to comply with s 108 (*Aveat Heating Ltd v Jerram Falkus Construction Ltd* [2007] EWHC 131 (TCC)). The Scheme for Construction Contracts makes the same provision on all the main features of adjudication as an express clause complying with s 108(2), (3), and (3A).

F COMMENCEMENT OF THE ADJUDICATION

25.16 In the case of express adjudication clauses, the contract may lay down a detailed set of procedures to be followed, but it is more likely to adopt the standard rules of a commercial dispute resolution service provider. In a similar way to arbitration, such providers publish rules for conducting adjudications that can be adopted by agreement between the parties. Examples are the CEDR Rules for Adjudication and the TeCSA Adjudication Rules. Institutional rules tend to follow the basic scheme in the default provisions in the Scheme for Construction Contracts. Figure 25.1 is a flow diagram showing how an adjudication develops from making a claim to notification of the decision.

Notice of adjudication: the commencement of adjudication

25.17 Under the Scheme for Construction Contracts, para 1, an adjudication is commenced by the referring party giving a notice of adjudication to all the other parties to the contract. This is a notice in writing stating the referring party's intention to refer a stated dispute arising out of the construction contract to adjudication. The notice needs to contain:

- the names and addresses of the parties;
- details to identify the contract (technically this is not one of the requirements in the Scheme for Construction Contracts, but in practical terms this is needed to show the dispute comes within the scheme and to provide a basis for explaining the nature of the dispute);
- brief details of the dispute to be referred to adjudication;

Figure 25.1 Stages in adjudication

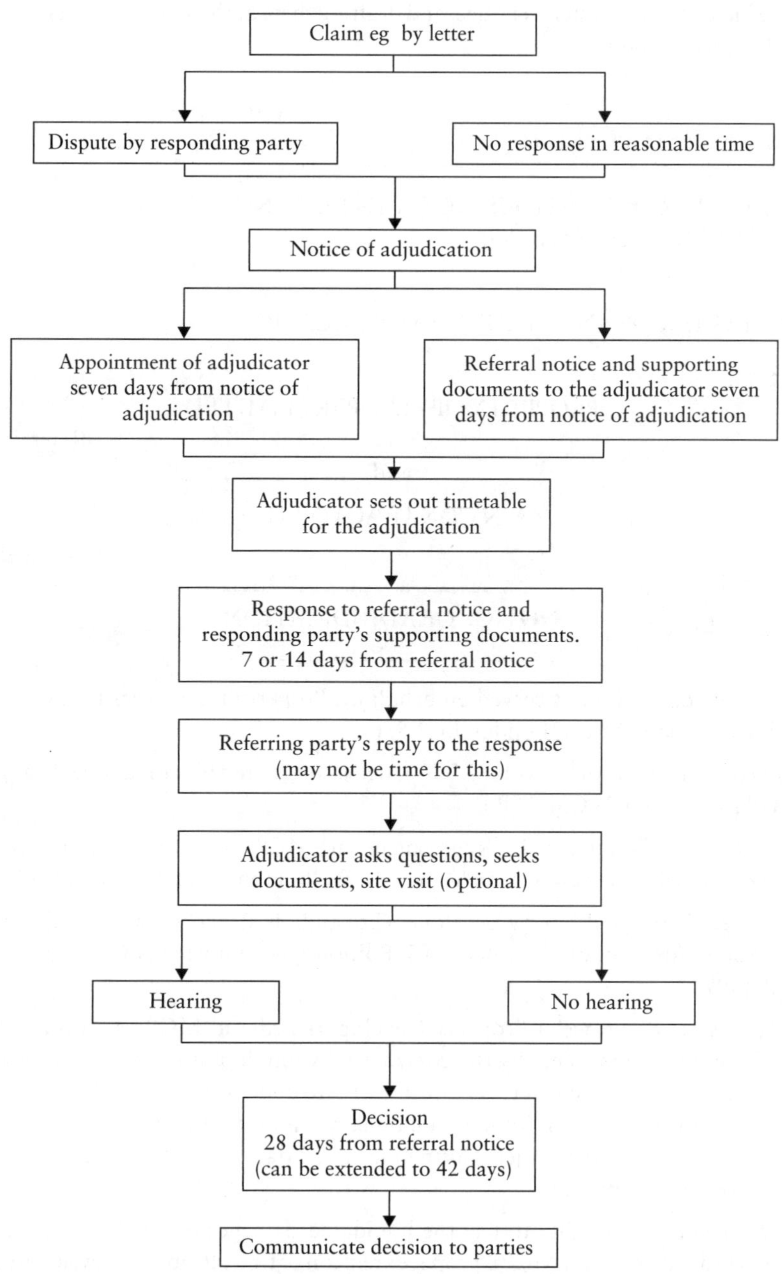

- details of where and when the dispute arose; and
- details of the remedy sought.

A notice of adjudication may be in a letter or a formal notice. An example is shown in Figure 25.2. It relates to a dispute between a property development company and the main contractor over whether the property development company is entitled to liquidated damages for delay in completion of a building project, or whether the main contractor is entitled to an extension of time. The notice of adjudication is often drafted at the same time as the referral **25.18** notice (see below), which has to be served within seven days of the notice of adjudication. In many ways a notice of adjudication is a summary of the key points from the details that have to be included in the referral notice, and drafting them at the same time ensures they are consistent with each other.

Figure 25.2 Notice of adjudication

IN THE MATTER OF THE HOUSING GRANTS, CONSTRUCTION AND REGENERATION ACT 1996

AND

IN THE MATTER OF AN INTENDED ADJUDICATION

BETWEEN

PROPERTY DEVELOPERS LIMITED

Referring party

and

MAIN CONTRACTORS PLC

Responding party

NOTICE OF ADJUDICATION

This notice of adjudication is served on behalf of: Property Developers Ltd, whose registered office is 47 Bank Street, London EC2 5SL.

It is served on Main Contractors plc ('MCP'), whose registered office is at Greyfriars House, Munton Place, London WC3J 7ZP.

We refer to Property Developers Ltd's agreement with MCP for the carrying out of refurbishment and remodelling work to Hardy Mansions, Wellington Road, Stafford ('the Project').

The Agreement between Property Developers Ltd and MCP incorporates the Construction Industry Standard Form of Contract 2007 Edition incorporating Amendments 1 and 2 ('CIS/1-2 2007').

A dispute has arisen between Property Developers Ltd and MCP as a result of MCPs failure to complete the Project by the contractual Completion Date pursuant to Clause 16 of the CIS/1-2 2007 contract. As a result of late completion of the Project Property Developers Ltd is entitled to liquidated damages amounting to £467,125.00 based on practical completion of the Project taking place 185 days after the contractual completion date of 6 February 2014.

MCP has disputed its liability to pay the liquidated damages on the basis that Property Developers Ltd did not grant MCP a proper extension of time. Property Developers Ltd dispute that MCP is entitled to the alleged extension of time, and its case is that the liquidated damages are properly payable by MCP.

We hereby give MCP notice, on behalf of Property Developers Ltd, of its intention to refer the above dispute to Adjudication under Clause 35 of the CIS/1-2 2007, which forms part of the contract between Property Developers Ltd and MCP.

The relief claimed comprises:

(a) An order that MCP should pay to Property Developers Ltd the sum of £467,125.00 (or such other sum as the Adjudicator may consider appropriate) in respect of the late

Figure 25.2 *(Continued)*

completion of the Project, plus interest pursuant to Clause 24 of the CIS/1-2 2007 contract (or such other Clause as may be relevant) within 7 days of the date of the Adjudicator's Decision.

(b) A declaration that, on the true construction of Clause 16 of the CIS/1-2 2007 contract and in the events that have happened in the execution of the works on the Project, MCP is not entitled to any extension of time to the Contractual Completion Date for the works of 6 February 2014 or, alternatively, that the Adjudicator declares that MCP is entitled to such extension as the Adjudicator considers appropriate.

DATED 22 September 2014

Signed: Wilkinson & Bradshaw, solicitors for Property Developers Ltd
Dunedin House, Victoria Road, London EC1H 5LD

Ambit of the reference

It is for the party making the reference to adjudication to define the issues to be adjudicated, and it is the notice of adjudication that achieves this. As the TeCSA Rules r 11 says, it is the notice of adjudication that identifies the scope of the adjudication. This means the adjudicator has no jurisdiction to decide matters outside these issues in the absence of agreement to vary by the parties (*McAlpine PPS Pipeline Systems Ltd v Transco plc* [2004] BLR 352 at [145]). The reason for including as relief in Figure 25.2 provision for substituting an extension period of such length as the adjudicator may consider appropriate (para (b) at the end of Figure 25.2) is to avoid an argument that the adjudicator can either decide there should be no extension or the full 185 days claimed by the main contractor, but nothing in between. Any dispute about the ambit of the reference is decided by the adjudicator (TeCSA Rules r 12). **25.19**

Nomination of adjudicator

An adjudicator needs to be appointed within seven days of the notice of adjudication. The adjudicator may be named in the construction contract, or else will have to be appointed in accordance with the machinery in the contract (which may adopt the institutional rules of a dispute resolution service provider) or the Scheme for Construction Contracts. These may provide for an adjudicator to be selected by a nominating body, such as the AICA, RIBA, RICS, or TeCSA. Most appointing bodies have a five-day turn-around time for making appointments and aim to make the appointment within the seven-day deadline (eg TeCSA Rules r 6). The Scheme for Construction Contracts has default provisions dealing with situations where the named adjudicator or nominating body is unable or unwilling to act. The adjudicator has two days to confirm whether they are available to act. **25.20**

A small fee is usually payable to the nominating body for making the nomination (it is £250 under the TeCSA Rules). The adjudicator will provide the parties with a copy of the terms on which they are prepared to act, including information regarding fees and expenses. **25.21**

An appointment fee (typically in four figures) is often charged by the adjudicator on accepting an appointment, and further work and any hearings will be charged on an hourly or daily fee basis. An adjudicator is not entitled to any fees if they produce an unenforceable decision (*PC Harrington Contractors Ltd v Systech International Ltd* [2013] Bus LR 970). **25.22**

Referral notice

25.23 A written referral notice needs to be sent by the referring party to the adjudicator not later than seven days from the date of the notice of adjudication (see Scheme for Construction Contracts para 7). These seven days run in parallel with the seven days for appointing the adjudicator. The adjudicator is required to inform the parties of the date of receipt of the referral notice. Referral notices are in effect formal statements of case, and are often set out in points of dispute format (rather like the points of claim in arbitration shown in Figure 28.3, but usually more discursive). For an example of this style, see Figure 25.3. As it is addressed to a particular adjudicator it takes a more personalized tone than court pleadings. Also, because there may be limited scope for oral argument, it seeks to explain and argue the referring party's case, unlike the more formal practice with court statements of case. Rule 4 of the CEDR Rules requires a referral notice to set out:

- the circumstances giving rise to the dispute;
- the reasons for entitlement to the remedy sought; and
- the evidence, including relevant documentation, in support of its case.

25.24 The referral notice should be consistent with the notice of adjudication, but will set out the full circumstances on each of these areas in some detail, and is the 'full version' of events rather than the summary as set out in the notice of adjudication. They can be very long.

Figure 25.3 Referral notice

IN THE MATTER OF THE HOUSING GRANTS, CONSTRUCTION AND REGENERATION ACT 1996

AND

IN THE MATTER OF AN INTENDED ADJUDICATION

BETWEEN

PROPERTY DEVELOPERS LIMITED

Referring party

and

MAIN CONTRACTORS PLC

Responding party

REFERRAL NOTICE

---

1. At all material times Property Developers Ltd has been the freehold owner of Hardy Tower, Wellington Road, Stafford, which is a 5-storey building divided into residential flats ('Hardy Mansions').
2. At all material times Main Contractors Plc ('MCP') were the main contractors on a project for the refurbishment and remodelling of Hardy Mansions ('the Project').
3. By a contract in writing dated 6 December 2013, MCP agreed with Property Developers Ltd to carry out the refurbishment and remodelling works on the Project ('the Contract').
4. The Contract incorporates the Construction Industry Standard Form of Contract 2007 Edition incorporating Amendments 1 and 2 ('CIS/1-2 2007').

Figure 25.3 (*Continued*)

5. The full contractual documentation between Property Developers Ltd and MCP relating to the Project can be found in File B.

6. It was an express term of the Contract that the parties must refer any dispute to Adjudication under Clause 35 of the CIS/1-2 2007.
7. A dispute has arisen between Property Developers Ltd and MCP as a result of MCP's refusal to pay liquidated damages in the sum of £467,125.00 to Property Developers Ltd. Property Developers Ltd's right to liquidated damages arises from MCP's failure to complete the Project by 6 February 2014, the contractual date for practical completion of the Project.
8. MCP has disputed its liability to pay the liquidated damages on the basis that Property Developers Ltd did not grant MCP a proper extension of time.
9. Notice of Adjudication was sent to MCP on 22 September 2014.
10. Property Developers Ltd do not believe there is any dispute that the contractual date for practical completion was 6 February 2014, or that there was a term in the Contract providing for liquidated damages at the daily rate of £2,525, or that practical completion was 185 days after 6 February 2014, or that no sum has been paid by MCP to Property Developers Ltd in respect of liquidated damages.
11. The dispute between the parties is as to whether MCP is entitled to an extension to the date for practical completion, and if so, for how long, with the result that the sum payable to Property Developers Ltd in respect of liquidated damages may be reduced or reduced to zero.
12. It was a further express term of the Contract that MCP should: 'Record progress on a copy of the programme kept on site. If any circumstances arise which may affect the progress of the works, put forward proposals or take other action as appropriate to minimize any delay and to recover any lost time' (clause 30.4).
13. In breach of the express term in paragraph 12 above MCP failed to record progress on any programme, on site or otherwise, and/or in breach of contract MCP failed to put forward proposals to minimize delay and/or to recover lost time. Property Developers Ltd submit that in consequence of the failure of MCP to comply with its contractual obligations it is now impossible with any degree of certainty to determine the date or duration that the various activities were undertaken by the various contractors on site, and also impossible to determine the impact or effect on other linked or non-linked activities. Property Developers Ltd submits that this being the case it is impossible to assess properly the true causes of the delay to the completion of the works, and the dates and durations of the delays claimed by MCP are therefore no more than speculation.
14. MCP has submitted the following as-built programmes (see file C, pages 1 to 231):

    FABP1: Critical Trade Activities
    FABP2: Stripping Out and Demolition Works
    FABP3: Brick and Block Works
    FABP4: Asphalt and Pitched Roofing Works
    FABP5: Carpentry Works
    FABP6: Window Installation Works
    FABP7: Decorating Works
    FABP8: Common Areas Works

15. Property Developers Ltd submits that the inadequate record keeping by MCP means that it can only report progress on a 'floor-by-floor' basis. Property Developers Ltd submits that such general records are hopelessly vague and inadequate. By way of example,

(*Continued*)

Figure 25.3 (*Continued*)

a variation in one flat on one floor (file C, page 147, for example) may have a delaying effect on that flat but it is submitted would have no impact or effect on the non-affected flats even on the same floor. The manner in which MCP has recorded progress makes it simply impossible to isolate any individual event. Thus an event in one trade in one flat on one floor is depicted by MCP as a delay to all flats on the entire floor (see file C, pages 232 to 278). This is simply not credible and calls into question the entire reliability of all the programmes.

16. MCP programmed the works on a flat type basis, without identifying the critical path. A critical path would have made it possible to compare the planned progress with the actual progress in a meaningful way. Instead, MCP's method (see file C, pages 232 to 278) produces an aggregate of all planned time, and compares that with all the actual time on a trade by trade basis. No attempt has been made by MCP to demonstrate any link between the trades.
17. It is Property Developers Ltd's case that the programme of MCP does not conform or comply with any of the recognized and accepted delays analysis methods used in the industry. It is observed that MCP has provided no explanation as to why it has not used any of the accepted delay analysis techniques. Property Developers Ltd submits that this is because none of the accepted methods would substantiate the delays claimed by MCP.
18. In the circumstances Property Developers Ltd submits that it is entitled to liquidated damages at the rate of £2,525 per day for 185 days amounting to £467,125.00.

Property Developers Ltd therefore claims:—

(a) An order that MCP should pay to Property Developers Ltd the sum of £467,125.00 (or such other sum as the Adjudicator may consider appropriate) in respect of the late completion of the Project, plus interest pursuant to Clause 24 of the CIS/1-2 2007 contract (or such other Clause as may be relevant) within 7 days of the date of the Adjudicator's Decision.

(b) A declaration that, on the true construction of Clause 16 of the CIS/1-2 2007 contract and in the events that have happened in the execution of the works on the Project, MCP is not entitled to any extension of time to the Contractual Completion Date for the works of 6 February 2014 or, alternatively, that the Adjudicator declares that MCP is entitled to such extension as the Adjudicator considers appropriate.

DATED 29 September 2014

Signed: Wilkinson & Bradshaw, solicitors for Property Developers Ltd

Dunedin House, Victoria Road, London EC1H 5LD

25.25 The referral notice should include the notice of adjudication and copies of, or extracts from, the construction contract and such other documents as the referring party intends to rely upon. Most adjudicators prefer to have documents in chronological order. There may or may not be a hearing, so the referring party has to ensure that everything the adjudicator will need to understand the dispute is included. As there may be little other opportunity to explain the significance of the documents, the referral notice may have to talk the adjudicator through the material. It is very unwise to think the documents will speak for themselves. Copies of the files containing the referral notice and supporting documents must be sent at the same time to the other parties.

G PROCEDURE BEFORE THE HEARING

The adjudicator is required to decide the procedure to be followed in the adjudication (Scheme for Construction Contracts para 13). This is often done through a telephone conference between the adjudicator and all the parties, shortly after the adjudicator is appointed. **25.26**

Response to referral notice

The adjudicator will consider whether the responding party should be allowed to put in a response to the referral notice, and when. Treating the parties fairly will mean that almost invariably a direction is given providing for the response within either 7 or 14 days of the referral notice. As the referring party will have had as long as they wanted to prepare before service of the notice of adjudication, it will often be fair to give as much as 14 days of the 28-day adjudication period for the response to the referral notice. The response often takes the form of points of response, and responds to the referral notice and sets out the responding party's case. **25.27**

Like a referral notice, the response should be supported by the relevant documentary evidence. The best practice is to include only such documentation as was not included with the referral notice, but it is not uncommon for a completely new set of documents, including duplicated documents, to be sent with the response. **25.28**

Subsequent statements of case

The short time before a decision has to be made may mean it is impractical to permit the referring party time to serve a reply, but the financial consequences of not doing so frequently compel the referring party to do so despite the lack of time. Likewise, particularly in large cases, further statements of case may be provided in response to the one before, in the sequence: rejoinder, rebutter, surrebutter. Provided each party has been given a fair opportunity to present its case and to respond to the allegations made by the other side, the adjudicator is entitled to decide (on giving fair notice to both sides) that no further submissions will be accepted after a set date. **25.29**

Timetable for procedural steps

The adjudicator is required to establish the timetable and procedure for the adjudication, which may include the consideration of any documentary or oral submission of the parties, site visits or inspections, and meeting the parties (CEDR Rules r 8). The adjudicator may seek expert advice (r 13). There is a general duty to avoid incurring unnecessary expense (Scheme for Construction Contracts, para 12(b)), and the need to make a decision within 28 days of referral means that the adjudication has to be conducted expeditiously. If a party fails to comply with a direction imposed by the adjudicator, the adjudicator may make a peremptory order, and ultimately the adjudicator (or a party with the consent of the adjudicator), can apply to the High Court for an order requiring compliance by the defaulting party (Arbitration Act 1996 s 42, as applied by the Scheme for Construction Contracts para 24). **25.30**

Documents, questions, and impartiality

Powers given to the adjudicator include the right to request any party to supply such documents as may be reasonably required, including any written statement from any party, and answers to questions. Questions are sometimes put to a party or witness in a separate meeting with the adjudicator as part of the fact-gathering process. **25.31**

25.32 All documents and information provided to the adjudicator must be made available to all the parties (Scheme for Construction Contracts para 17), which is part of a wider duty of impartiality (Housing Grants, Construction and Regeneration Act 1996 s 108(2)(e)). This means that the adjudicator must inform the other parties of any information or evidence provided by the other parties so they have a fair opportunity to comment on it. Failure to do so may invalidate the ultimate decision on the ground of a breach of the rules of natural justice.

Site visits

25.33 Subject to obtaining any necessary consent from third parties, the adjudicator may make such site visits and inspections as seem appropriate, and may do so whether accompanied by the parties or not (Scheme for Construction Contracts para 13(d)). The adjudicator may also carry out tests or experiments (para 13(e)), and particular rules may also make provision for opening up of work on site for the purpose of inspections or tests (an example is the JCT standard form contract adjudication clauses).

Related disputes

25.34 With the consent of all the parties, the adjudicator may adjudicate at the same time on more than one dispute, either under the same contract, or on related disputes under different contracts (Scheme for Construction Contracts para 8).

Confidentiality

25.35 All materials disclosed in an adjudication must be kept confidential except to the extent necessary for purposes in connection with the adjudication (Scheme for Construction Contracts para 18).

H ADJUDICATOR'S DECISION

Inquisitorial approach

25.36 The adjudicator may take the initiative in ascertaining the facts and the law necessary to decide the dispute (Housing Grants, Construction and Regeneration Act 1996 s 108(2)(f); Scheme for Construction Contracts para 13). This form of words, which can also be found in relation to arbitration in the Arbitration Act 1996 s 34(2)(g), means the adjudicator can (but is not obliged to) adopt an inquisitorial as opposed to an adversarial approach in the adjudication.

Hearing

25.37 There is no obligation to have a hearing, although the adjudicator may decide to hear oral evidence or representations (Scheme for Construction Contracts para 16(2)). A hearing will be more necessary or helpful where the case involves complex law or where there is conflicting evidence in any witness statements included in the parties' referral notice and subsequent statements of case on matters material to the decision. If there is a hearing the parties may be assisted or represented by legally qualified or other advisers. If there is no hearing, something similar is frequently achieved through communications by telephone, conference calls, email etc, which often come in quick succession as the deadline for the decision draws near.

The decision-making process

Adjudicators are required to act impartially in carrying out their duties, and must decide the dispute in accordance with the relevant terms of the contract and in accordance with the law applicable to the contract (Scheme for Construction Contracts para 12(a)). The adjudicator will consider any relevant information provided by the parties, but must not take into consideration any document or statement that has not been made available to the other parties for comment (CEDR Rules r 10). The adjudicator has the power to review any certificates etc made under the contract, unless precluded by the terms of the contract (Scheme for Construction Contracts para 20(a)). **25.38**

The adjudicator is required to reach a decision within 28 days of the referral notice (*Aveat Heating Ltd v Jerram Falkus Construction Ltd* [2007] EWHC 131 (TCC)), although this period may be extended by 14 days with the consent of the referring party or longer if agreed by all the parties (Housing Grants, Construction and Regeneration Act 1996 s 108(2)(c), (d)). This is recognized as being a very tight timetable, which might result in injustice, but one which Parliament must be taken to have been aware of (*Macob Civil Engineering Ltd v Morrison Construction Ltd* (1999) 64 Con LR 1). While the priority is to give effect to the rough and ready adjudication process, in an exceptional case the court can intervene by way of declaratory relief to prevent a breach of natural justice (*Dorchester Hotel Ltd v Vivid Interiors Ltd* [2009] Bus LR 1026). **25.39**

Communicating decision to the parties

Technically, it is the decision that has to be made within 28 days (or an agreed extended period) from the referral notice. This means actually communicating the decision to the parties may happen after this 28-day period without a breach of the Act. However, given immediate communications provided by email, there may be no excuse for any delay in sending the decision to the parties. **25.40**

Reasons, interest, and costs

Reasons must be given at the same time as delivering the decision unless the parties agree to the contrary under the CEDR Rules r 17, but under the Scheme for Construction Contracts reasons are only required if one of the parties makes a request (para 22). Giving reasons gives scope to arguments that the adjudication may have been flawed, which would undermine the quick and decisive purpose of the process. However, where parties have presented detailed cases to the adjudicator, they may feel they deserve to know the reasons for the decision. **25.41**

Interest may be awarded in addition to the principal sum if payable under the contract (para 20(c)). Any contractual provision in the construction contract allocating costs between the parties is ineffective unless it confers power on the adjudicator to allocate his fees and expenses between the parties (Housing Grants, Construction and Regeneration Act 1996 s 108A(2)(a)). Under the CEDR Rules each party bears its own costs (r 22). **25.42**

I BINDING, BUT INTERIM EFFECT, OF DECISIONS

By the Housing Grants, Construction and Regeneration Act 1996 s 108(3), the construction contract must provide in writing that the adjudicator's decision is binding until the dispute is finally determined by legal proceedings, by arbitration, or by agreement. An adjudicator's decision is binding in the sense that the losing party has an immediate obligation to pay the **25.43** sum decided upon. It also means that the adjudicator and the parties are bound by the decision in any subsequent adjudications between them (*Vertase Fli Ltd v Squibb Group Ltd* [2013] BLR 352). There is an implied term (see *Aspect Contracts (Asbestos) Ltd v Higgins Construction plc* [2014] BLR 79) that either party can reopen the dispute in the courts or through arbitration. The court or tribunal will not be bound by the adjudicator's decision, and can order any overpayment to be repaid. To avoid the expense of subsequent litigation, the parties may agree to accept the decision of the adjudicator as finally determining the dispute.

25.44 Any sum found to be payable by the adjudicator must be paid in full without any deduction by way of set-off, counterclaim, or abatement (CEDR Rules r 21). If there are multiple adjudications arising out of a single project, it is fundamental to the adjudication process that each decision must be complied with separately without set-offs (*Hart v Smith* [2009] EWHC (TCC) 2223).

25.45 To protect the adjudicator, the Housing Grants, Construction and Regeneration Act 1996 s 108(4) provides that the contract must provide in writing that the adjudicator shall not be liable for anything done or omitted in the discharge of his functions unless there is bad faith.

J OVERALL COST

25.46 Adjudication is not necessarily a cheap alternative. In *Amec Projects Ltd v Whitefriars City Estates Ltd* [2004] EWHC 393 (TCC) the costs of adjudication and enforcement were estimated at £277,000. In *AWG Construction Services Ltd v Rockingham Speedway Ltd* [2004] EWHC 888 (TCC) the costs came to over £1 million. In *McAlpine PPS Pipeline Systems Ltd v Transco plc* [2004] BLR 352 the adjudication costs were about £100,000 in relation to a claim for £45,000.

K ADJUDICATION IN RESIDENTIAL BUILDING CONTRACTS

25.47 While construction contracts with residential occupiers are excluded from the scheme in the Housing Grants, Construction and Regeneration Act 1996 Part II, by s 106 (see 25.05), this does not prevent the parties to such a contract including clauses in their contract making similar provision. There are even rules promulgated by the building industry specifically providing for the adjudication of disputes in building contracts with owner/occupiers. For example, the Joint Contracts Tribunal Limited (JCT) Rules for Adjudication are designed for use with the JCT building contract and the JCT consultancy agreement for home owner/occupiers.

L COURT ENFORCEMENT OF SUM FOUND DUE ON ADJUDICATION

25.48 A party with the benefit of an adjudicator's decision may bring enforcement proceedings in the courts by issuing a Part 8 claim form, and then applying for summary judgment. In most cases, summary judgment will be entered in accordance with the policy of the Housing Grants, Construction and Regeneration Act 1996. This is discussed in more detail in Chapter 32.

KEY POINTS SUMMARY

- The basic principle of adjudication is 'pay now, argue later'. 25.49
- Adjudication applies to commercial construction contracts.
- An adjudicator must be appointed within seven days of a notice referring a dispute to adjudication.
- The adjudicator must act impartially.
- The adjudicator's decision must be made within 28 days of referral (although this can be extended).
- The adjudication is binding until the dispute is decided by litigation, arbitration, or agreement.
- Normally the parties are required to comply with the adjudicator's decision immediately on delivery of the decision.
- Otherwise enforcement is normally through summary judgment of the adjudicator's decision.

26

ARBITRATION

A INTRODUCTION 26.01
B ARBITRATION AND LITIGATION 26.04
C FUNDAMENTAL CONCEPTS IN ARBITRATION 26.05
D HISTORY OF ARBITRATION 26.06
E INTERPRETATION OF THE ARBITRATION ACT 1996 ....26.08
F CONTRACTUAL FOUNDATION TO ARBITRATION 26.10
G REQUIREMENTS 26.19
H OVERVIEW OF ARBITRATION PROCEDURE 26.50
I GENERAL PRINCIPLES AND DUTIES 26.51
J FAIR RESOLUTION OF DISPUTES 26.52
K PARTY AUTONOMY 26.57
L COURT APPLICATIONS...............26.61
M DIFFERENT TYPES OF ARBITRATION 26.63
N MULTI-TIERED DISPUTE RESOLUTION.......................26.74
O ONE-STOP ADJUDICATION 26.75
P EUROPEAN CONVENTION ON HUMAN RIGHTS AND ARBITRATION 26.76
Q MAIN FEATURES OF ARBITRATION 26.78
Key points summary 26.80

A INTRODUCTION

26.01 Arbitration is an adjudicative dispute resolution process. It is based on an agreement between the parties to refer a dispute or difference between them to impartial arbitrators for a decision. There is no statutory definition of the term 'arbitration', probably because it can take a wide variety of forms and can arise in a wide variety of legal contexts. As a consequence of the contractual basis of arbitration, it is not every dispute that can go to arbitration. This chapter considers the requirements for an effective reference to arbitration, but it should be noted that the agreement to arbitrate may be made before or after the relevant dispute has arisen. This means that there may be a pre-existing arbitration agreement which, when a dispute arises, one of the parties wishes to evade. There is a strong public policy in favour of upholding arbitration agreements, which is supported by the idea that an arbitration clause in a contract is separable from the rest of the substantive contract (and so continues to apply even if the substantive contract is avoided), and by the jurisdiction to stay court proceedings that are commenced in breach of an arbitration agreement (see Chapter 31).

26.02 Arbitrations in England and Wales are governed by the Arbitration Act 1996 (which is set out in Appendix 3). A key philosophical question in arbitration law is the extent to which domestic law should prescribe how arbitrations should be conducted, and the extent to which the parties should be allowed to devise their own procedures. This is reflected in the distinction in the Arbitration Act 1996 between mandatory and non-mandatory provisions (discussed in this chapter). The intention is that the mandatory provisions cover only the matters that are essential to the effective resolution of matters referred to arbitration, with everything else covered by non-mandatory fall-back provisions, which the parties can change if they wish.

26.03 The Arbitration Act 1996 is also intended to lay down a highly developed set of procedures for arbitrations, in keeping with this country's status as a leading venue for international arbitrations. These include rules for how to start an arbitration, and how a panel of arbitrators is appointed, matters discussed in Chapter 27. A detailed consideration of how commercial arbitrations are conducted can be found in Chapter 28, which includes a number of precedents and also considers a number of sets of rules used by arbitral institutions dealing with the procedures that should be followed. Chapter 29 looks at a number of particular issues that arise in international arbitrations. These include jurisdictional issues, questions of the proper law to be applied, as well as the institutional rules for arbitrations published by the International Chamber of Commerce and the United Nations Commission on International Trade Law. Arbitral awards are considered in Chapter 30, and Chapter 31 deals with applications that can be made to the courts in support of arbitrations, and to review arbitral decisions that might be wrong. Enforcement of arbitral awards is considered in Chapter 32.

B ARBITRATION AND LITIGATION

Arbitration can be seen as a private version of litigation. It involves an independent arbitrator or tribunal considering both sides of the dispute and making a decision on the issues raised by the parties. Arbitration is an alternative to litigation. Where the parties have agreed to refer disputes to arbitration, that removes, for example, their right to apply to the court for pre-action disclosure (see 31.30). Arbitration differs from litigation in two main respects: **26.04**

- a dispute will only be referred to arbitration if that is the course agreed between the parties; and
- arbitrators are appointed by the parties (or through a mechanism agreed by the parties), whereas in litigation the judge will be appointed by the state.

C FUNDAMENTAL CONCEPTS IN ARBITRATION

Part of the object of arbitration is to obtain a fair resolution of a dispute by an impartial tribunal (Arbitration Act 1996, s 1(a)). A clause in *Turville Heath Inc v Chartis Insurance* [2012] EWHC 3019 (TCC) provided for independent appraisers to appraise a loss and to submit any differences to an arbitrator, and that a decision could be made by the two appraisers, or either appraiser and the arbitrator. This was not an agreement to arbitrate, because it is implicit in s1(a) that the decision has to be that of the arbitral tribunal alone, and not one made in conjunction with anyone else. Where the parties have agreed to refer their disputes to arbitration, Lord Hoffmann said in *Fili Shipping Co Ltd v Premium Nafta Products Ltd* [2007] Bus LR 1719 that this implies they want their disputes decided: **26.05**

- by a tribunal they have chosen (see Chapter 27);
- in a neutral location (this is of particular importance in international arbitration: see Chapter 29) and with neutral arbitrators;
- in privacy (see 28.06);
- by the arbitrators speedily and efficiently; and
- with light but efficient supervision by the courts (see Chapter 31).

D HISTORY OF ARBITRATION

Despite the modern feel to most of the procedures described in this book, arbitration in fact has an impressive history. It can be traced back to Ancient Greece, and in England at least as far back as 1468 (see *Anon* [1468] YB 8 Edw IV, fo 1, p 1, at which time it was **26.06** called arbitrament, a word still in use). For many years the Arbitration Act 1950 was the principal statute governing this area. It had a number of limitations, including giving excessive powers of review to the courts, and giving inadequate coverage of matters relating to procedure. It was amended by the Arbitration Act 1979 following a report by Lord Donaldson, and was replaced by the Arbitration Act 1996, which rectified these defects and provides a modern statement of the law that meets the needs of the international commercial community.

26.07 The Arbitration Act 1996 draws heavily on reports by the Departmental Advisory Committee (DAC) on arbitration set up by the Department of Trade and Industry. It also borrows from concepts to be found in the United Nations Commission on International Trade Law (UNCITRAL) Model Law on arbitration. It has been very successful in ensuring that English law on arbitration is consistent with international practice.

E INTERPRETATION OF THE ARBITRATION ACT 1996

26.08 The Arbitration Act 1996 restates and improves the law relating to arbitration. It was consciously drafted in accessible English, with the intention that it would be read and understood by non-lawyers who may be engaged in arbitrations either as parties or arbitrators. In a passage endorsed by Lord Steyn in *Lesotho Highlands Development Authority v Impregilo SpA* [2006] 1 AC 221 at [19], Thomas J in *Seabridge Shipping AB v AC Orssleff's Eft's A/S* [1999] 2 Lloyd's Rep 685, said:

> 'it would in my view be a retrograde step if when a point arose reference had to be made to pre-Act cases. Reference to such cases should only generally be necessary in cases where the Act does not cover some point—as, for example, in relation to confidentiality or where for some other reason it is necessary to refer to the earlier cases. A court should, in general, comply with the guidance given [in *Patel v Patel* [2000] QB 551] and rely on the language of the Act. International users of London arbitration should, in my view, be able to rely on the clear 'user-friendly language' of the Act and should not have to be put to the trouble or expense of having regard to the pre-1996 Act law on issues where the provisions of the Act set out the law. If international users of London arbitration are not able to act in that knowledge, then one of the main objectives of the reform will have been defeated.'

26.09 A large number of provisions in the Arbitration Act 1996 use the word 'shall' to describe matters to be done by the parties, arbitrators, or the courts. In 1996 'shall' was regarded by lawyers as connoting a mandatory requirement and as being synonymous with 'must'. That is the intention of the Arbitration Act 1996, and in this book the word 'shall' is used in a mandatory sense. In 2004 and 2006 two cases (*Metcalfe v Clipston* [2004] EWHC 9005 (Costs) and *Choudury v Kingston Hospital NHS Trust* [2006] EWHC 90057 (Costs)) decided that 'shall' is not mandatory. As a result, post-2006 legislation uses the word 'must' instead of shall, but this is not to be regarded as changing the legislative intent of the Arbitration Act 1996.

F CONTRACTUAL FOUNDATION TO ARBITRATION

26.10 Almost any type of dispute can be referred to arbitration, regardless of the legal classification of the underlying cause of action. That said, arbitration is most commonly used for resolving disputes arising out of a contract between the parties, frequently with the agreement to arbitrate being found in a clause in the substantive contract. Where such a dispute is referred to arbitration, from a technical legal point of view there will often be four contracts.

- the underlying substantive contract on which the dispute is based ('the substantive contract');
- the agreement to arbitrate. Even where the agreement to arbitrate is in point of form just one of many contractual clauses in the substantive contract, as a matter of arbitration law the clause is a separable contract, distinct from the substantive contract. See 26.11 below;
- the agreement between the parties and an arbitral institution referring the dispute to arbitration under the aegis of that institution. Often the institution's arbitration rules will apply to the arbitral proceedings;
- the agreement between the parties and/or the arbitral institution and the individuals who will act as arbitrators appointing those individuals to preside over the arbitration and make a decision on the dispute.

Separability of arbitration clause

The Arbitration Act 1996 s 7 provides: **26.11**

> Unless otherwise agreed by the parties, an arbitration agreement which forms or was intended to form part of another agreement (whether or not in writing) shall not be regarded as invalid, non-existent or ineffective because that other agreement is invalid, or did not come into existence or has become ineffective, and it shall for that purpose be treated as a distinct agreement.

This is an important principle, and prevents arbitral proceedings becoming frustrated in **26.12** cases where the arbitrators make a finding to the effect that the substantive agreement is invalid or discharged. Without s 7 such a finding would result in the arbitration clause also being ineffective, which would mean there is no decision on the substantive contract. If that was the position, a party who did not want a dispute referred to arbitration would always be tempted to argue for some invalidity in the substantive contract in order to undermine the jurisdiction of the arbitrators.

That this will not work was confirmed by *Fili Shipping Co Ltd v Premium Nafta Products* **26.13** *Ltd* [2007] Bus LR 1719 (this case is also known as *Fiona Trust & Holding Corporation v Privalov)*. Ship owners in this case had entered into charterparties (leases of ships) with the charterers. Each charterparty included a clause giving both parties the right to refer any dispute under the charter to arbitration. The owners alleged that the charterparties had been induced by bribery, and brought court proceedings in England seeking declarations that they were entitled to rescind the charterparties on the basis they had been procured by bribery, conspiracy, and breach of fiduciary duty. The charterers wanted the disputes to be referred to arbitration, and applied to have the court litigation stayed under the Arbitration Act 1996 s 9 (see 31.07). The owners sought an injunction to restrain the charterers referring the disputes to arbitration pursuant to s 72 (see Table 29.1). It was held by the House of Lords that an argument that the substantive contract (the charterparties) had been procured by bribery did not prevent the arbitrators ruling on whether the substantive contract was invalid. It is only if the alleged invalidity affects the arbitration clause itself that the arbitrators will be deprived of jurisdiction on this ground. As there were no grounds for challenging the validity of the separable arbitration clauses, the court proceedings were stayed under s 9.

Mandate of the arbitral tribunal

The jurisdiction given to an arbitral tribunal depends on the mandate given to it by the par- **26.14** ties. An arbitral tribunal will not have jurisdiction unless the dispute comes within the terms of the particular reference to arbitration. This will be limited by the terms of the arbitration agreement (which may be a standard clause in the substantive contract, or an agreement after the dispute has arisen to refer that dispute to arbitration), and the separate agreement between the tribunal and the parties appointing the tribunal. It means, for example, that the arbitrators cannot make a decision against a person who is not a party to the arbitration agreement, or on matters not covered by the arbitration agreement, or on matters not covered by the parties' agreement with the arbitrators. Restrictions based on the terms of the arbitration agreement are discussed at 26.44.

26.15 Further, the tribunal is only authorized to determine the dispute actually referred to it and on the terms of the agreement between the arbitrators and the parties. Once a dispute is referred to arbitration, the courts tend to give a wide interpretation to what is included in the tribunal's mandate. Partly this is in support of the 'one-stop' policy (see 26.75), that the parties usually intend that all their current disputes should be resolved at the same time by a single decision-making body. Partly this is a recognition that the precise scope of a dispute inevitably tends to evolve as it is investigated.

26.16 Restrictions imposed by a tribunal's mandate mean that the arbitrators have to comply with the agreement between the parties on the procedure to be followed. This is the agreement as at the time the tribunal is appointed, which may include a framework for further agreements between the parties on matters of procedure. This may include adhering to a set of arbitral institutional rules and, if so, the tribunal does not have the power to go behind what the parties have agreed.

26.17 By accepting their appointments, the arbitrators agree to consider the evidence and make decisions on the matters referred to them. They are obliged to make decisions on all the central issues of the dispute(s). In this connection, a purposive construction is placed on the 'issues' that are to be decided (*Checkpoint Ltd v Strathclyde Pension Fund* [2003] 1 EGLR 1). This means that decisions must be made on all the matters that are critical to the overall decision, and also such subsidiary issues that have to be decided en route to those central issues. It means that other matters, which may have appeared to be important at earlier stages of the arbitration, may fall away once certain decisions are made. Where a tribunal fails to reach a decision on a central issue in the dispute there is a serious irregularity for the purposes of the Arbitration Act 1996 s 68, which means the award may be challenged in court (*Ascot Commodities v Olam* [2002] CLC 277; and see 31.45).

26.18 These constraints do not necessarily prevent arbitrators making decisions on matters arising after their appointment. For example, in *Rederij Lalemant v Transportes Generales Navigacion SA* [1986] 1 Lloyd's Rep 45 it was held that the arbitrators were entitled to decide both the demurrage payable at the port of loading (arising from events before they were appointed) and demurrage payable at the port of discharge (which arose after they were appointed). What is covered depends on the terms of the appointment of the arbitrators.

G REQUIREMENTS

26.19 In order for there to be an effective reference to arbitration the following requirements must be met:

- there must be a dispute or difference (see 26.20);
- the dispute must be 'arbitrable' (see 26.24);
- there must be an agreement to arbitrate (see 26.27);

- for the Arbitration Act 1996 to apply, the agreement to arbitrate must be in writing (see 26.37);
- the nature of the dispute must come within the terms of the arbitration agreement (see 26.40);
- the parties must have had the capacity to enter into the arbitration agreement (see 26.45);
- any condition precedent to arbitration must be complied with (see 26.47);
- the parties must find an arbitral tribunal willing to act and decide the dispute (see Chapter 27); and
- the dispute must come within the terms of the particular reference to arbitration (the tribunal's mandate, see 26.14 above).

Dispute or difference

Arbitration is a dispute resolution process, and if there is no dispute there is nothing for the arbitrators to decide. The Arbitration Act 1996 s 6(1) defines an arbitration agreement as one to submit present or future disputes (whether they are contractual or not) to arbitration. What frequently happens in practice is that one of the parties will make a 'claim' against the other, such as for payment of the price due under a contract, or damages for non-performance. Such situations do not develop into disputes if the claim is admitted (or paid). Any other type of response, for example a denial of liability, or an assertion that the money is not yet payable, converts the claim into a dispute that may be referred to arbitration. **26.20**

'Dispute' is defined by s 82 to include any difference. A 'difference' was technically regarded as applying to a failure to agree, but the distinction between 'disputes' and 'differences' ceased being important when the Arbitration Act 1996 assimilated the two concepts. Both words must be given their natural meanings (*Cruden Construction Ltd v Commission for the New Towns* [1995] 2 Lloyd's Rep 387). They cover disputes of law or fact, and are intended to have a wide effect. They are even wide enough to cover a dispute whether there has been an effective compromise of a dispute arising out of the substantive contract (*Joseph Finney plc v Vickers* [2001] All ER (D) 235). **26.21**

Before the enactment of the Arbitration Act 1996 the courts were allowed to take over and grant summary judgment despite an arbitration clause where the grounds of defence to a claim were regarded as 'not disputable'. This is now regarded as too great an invasion by the courts, and the present position is that the courts cannot intervene to stop an arbitration even if the court thinks the defendant does not have an arguable defence (*Halki Shipping Corp v Sopex Oils Ltd* [1998] 1 WLR 726). **26.22**

Even under the modern law there will be no dispute if: **26.23**

- the defendant does not dispute liability; or
- the contention now being relied upon by the defendant was never put to the claimant (*Edmund Nuttall Ltd v RG Carter Ltd* [2002] BLR 312);
- the right to dispute the matter has been lost under the contract or by law (*Watkins Jones and Sons Ltd v Lidl UK GmbH* (2002) 86 Con LR 155).

Arbitrable dispute

While most arbitrations relate to contractual disputes, any private dispute or difference is amenable to arbitration, regardless of the nature of the underlying cause of action. The only restriction is that arbitration is available solely to resolve issues of a private law nature. This flows from the contractual basis of arbitration, which means that public law matters, and matters relating to legal status, cannot be determined by arbitration. **26.24**

26.25 This means that the following are all examples of disputes that are *not* arbitrable:

- marital status;
- care of children;
- validity of patents;
- status of a public right of way;
- bankruptcy;
- criminal liability; and
- judicial review of administrative decisions.

26.26 This does not mean that disputes that have a public element are entirely off-limits for arbitration. For example, arbitrators are obliged to respect EU competition law (*Nordsee Deutsche Hochseefischerei GmbH v Reederei Mond Hochseefischerei Nordstern AG & Co KG* Case 102/81 [1982] ECR 1095). Likewise, the provisions of the European Convention on Human Rights have to be given effect to in arbitrations, because these are directed at determining the civil rights and obligations of the parties (Art 6(1); but see 26.76).

Agreement to arbitrate

26.27 Arbitration stems from an agreement to refer a dispute to arbitration. As Lord Mance said in *Dallah Real Estate and Tourism Co v Ministry of Religious Affairs of the Government of Pakistan* [2011] 1 AC 763 at [24], 'Arbitration ... is consensual—the manifestation of the parties' choice to submit present or future issues between them to arbitration. Arbitrators ... cannot by their own decision ... create or extend the authority conferred on them'. An agreement to arbitrate can be made before or after the dispute has arisen. Where an arbitration clause is an express written term of the underlying contract there should be no problems other than construing what it requires. It is more difficult where the arbitration clause is in a connected contract, or a contract with someone else, or where a dispute covers a number of contracts each with different arbitration clauses (see 26.30–26.36).

Breach of an agreement to arbitrate

26.28 A party will be bound by its pre-dispute agreement to arbitrate if it subsequently changes its mind. If a party insists on ignoring an arbitration clause any litigation may be stayed under the Arbitration Act 1996 s 9 (see 31.07). Starting court proceedings to determine the dispute in breach of an arbitration clause may also be a repudiatory breach of the arbitration agreement (*Delta Reclamation Ltd v Premier Waste Management Ltd* [2008] EWHC 2579 (QB)). Correspondence denying the existence of the arbitration agreement may also be a repudiation (*Downing v Al Tameer Establishment* [2002] 2 All ER (Comm) 545). A party in breach of an arbitration agreement may be liable in damages (*Donohue v Armco* [2001] 1 Lloyd's Rep 425 (a jurisdiction clause case, and see *Russell on Arbitration* (23rd edn, Sweet & Maxwell, 2007), para 7–019).

Arbitration clauses

26.29 A selection of typical arbitration clauses, together with a post-dispute agreement to refer the dispute to arbitration, is shown in Table 26.1. The level of detail found in different arbitration clauses varies considerably. Such a clause can be very short and fully effective. Given the range of non-mandatory matters covered by the Arbitration Act 1996 (all or any of which may be addressed in an arbitration clause), and the range of solutions to just about every one of those elements, there is an almost infinite number of potential clauses that may be encountered. However, the clauses shown in Table 26.1 are fairly representative of clauses frequently found in standard form contracts.

Table 26.1 Arbitration contract clauses

Type of clause	Wording
Ad hoc arbitration, single arbitrator	Any dispute or difference arising out of or in connection with this contract shall be determined by the appointment of a single arbitrator to be agreed between the parties, or failing agreement within 14 days after either party has given to the other a written request to concur in the appointment of an arbitrator, by an arbitrator to be appointed by the President [*of a named arbitral institution or profession*]. The seat of the arbitration shall be England and Wales.
Ad hoc arbitration, clause referring dispute to two arbitrators	All disputes arising out of this contract shall be arbitrated at London and, unless the parties agree forthwith to a single arbitrator, be referred to the final arbitrament of two arbitrators, both to be commercial men, one to be appointed by each of the parties.
Rules for the arbitration	The arbitration shall be governed by both the Arbitration Act 1996 and the [*named Rules of an arbitral institution*] ('the Rules'), or any amendments to those provisions. The Rules are deemed to be incorporated by reference into this clause.
Facilitation of settlement in arbitration	The arbitral tribunal appointed under this agreement shall apply the [*name of arbitral institution*] Rules on the facilitation of settlement in arbitration.
Institutional arbitration, three arbitrators	Any dispute or difference arising out of or in connection with the present contract shall be administered by [*named arbitral institution*] and finally determined under the rules of the [*named Rules of the arbitral institution*] by three arbitrators appointed in accordance with those Rules.
Agreement to refer dispute to arbitration after dispute has arisen	A dispute having arisen between [*Party 1*] and [*Party 2*] concerning [*state the nature of the dispute*], the parties hereby refer that dispute to arbitration under the rules of the [*named Rules of an arbitral institution*]. Signed: Signed: Dated:

Two-contract cases

26.30 It is not unusual, particularly in shipping, reinsurance, and construction cases, for there to be an arbitration clause in the main agreement, and a clause in a subsidiary contract to adopt all or some of the terms of the main agreement, including the arbitration clause. Whether this is effective to make the subsidiary contract subject to the arbitration clause is a matter of construction.

26.31 There will often be good reasons for not being too quick to assume that an arbitration clause from the main contract is intended to apply to the subsidiary contract. These include the common occurrence that the main contract is quite different in its nature from the subsidiary contract (particularly if the subsidiary contract is a sub-sub-contract or even further removed from the main contract), or if the subsidiary contract is a transferable document of title (such as a bill of lading, the document evidencing a contract of carriage of goods by sea) issued under a charterparty (a lease of a ship). These considerations have resulted in a rule in construction and shipping cases that an arbitration clause in the main contract will only be imported into the subsidiary contract if there is a specific reference to the arbitration clause in the subsidiary contract. See *Aughton Ltd v MF Kent Services Ltd* [1991] 57 BLR 1 (construction contracts) and *Thomas and Co Ltd v Portsea SS Co Ltd* [1912] AC 1 (charterparty and bill of lading cases).

Contracts (Rights of Third Parties) Act 1999

26.32 Third parties may be subject to arbitration agreements in contracts between other parties in relation to contractual disputes over terms made for their benefit by virtue of the Contracts (Rights of Third Parties) Act 1999. Section 8(1) provides:

> Where—
>
> (a) a right under section 1 to enforce a term ('the substantive term') is subject to a term providing for the submission of disputes to arbitration ('the arbitration agreement'), and
> (b) the arbitration agreement is an agreement in writing for the purposes of Part I of the Arbitration Act 1996, the third party shall be treated for the purposes of that Act as a party to the arbitration agreement as regards disputes between himself and the promisor relating to the enforcement of the substantive term by the third party.

26.33 Under s 1(1), a third party may in his own right enforce a term of a contract if:

- the contract expressly provides that he may; or
- the term purports to confer a benefit on him. This is subject to s 1(2), which says this does not apply if on a proper construction of the contract it appears that the parties did not intend the term to be enforceable by the third party.

26.34 Section 8(1) operates against the principle that arbitration is a consensual process. The courts have therefore been reluctant to find that contractual rights relied upon by third parties come within arbitration clauses, with the result that it is difficult for third parties to establish that they are entitled to rely on s 8(1) (*Fortress Value Recovery Fund I LLC v Blue Skye Special Opportunities Fund LP* [2013] 1 WLR 3466). Where s 8(1) applies, not only is the third party able to rely on the arbitration clause, but the third party is also bound by it and can be required to refer any dispute covered by the clause to arbitration (*Nisshin Shipping Co Ltd v Cleaves and Co Ltd* [2004] 1 Lloyd's Rep 38).

26.35 Section 8(1) applies where a substantive term in the contract relied upon by the third party is subject to an arbitration clause. Section 8(2) deals with the rarer situation where the contracting parties have, for example, given a third party a unilateral right to arbitrate, or a situation where the contracting parties have given the third party a right to arbitrate a tort claim brought by one of the contracting parties. Under s 8(2), unlike s 8(1), the third party has the choice of whether to exercise the right to refer the dispute to arbitration.

Disputes covering several contracts

26.36 Where a single dispute raises issues based on a number of contracts each with different arbitration clauses, it is necessary to determine which clause takes precedence. It is best if this can be done by agreement between the parties. If this is not possible, the rule is that the arbitration clause in the contract at the commercial centre of the transaction is the one that applies (*UBS AG v HSH Nordbank AG* [2009] 2 Lloyd's Rep 272, a case on jurisdiction clauses).

The arbitration agreement

Written agreement

26.37 The provisions in the Arbitration Act 1996 apply only to arbitration agreements that are in writing (Arbitration Act 1996 s 5(1)). This is satisfied (s 5(2)) if the agreement is:

- made in writing, whether or not it is signed by the parties. This includes an agreement by reference to terms which are in writing (s 5(3)); or

- made by the exchange of communications in writing; or
- evidenced in writing. This applies where the agreement is recorded by one of the parties, or by a third party, with the authority of the parties to the agreement (s 5(4)).

References to writing include recording by any means (s 5(6)). If there is no consensus there can be no arbitration agreement, even if documents are exchanged containing an arbitration clause (*Hyundai Merchant Marine Co Ltd v Americas Bulk Transport Ltd* [2013] EWHC 470 (Comm)). On the other hand, where a charterparty with an arbitration clause had been signed by one party, both parties were held bound by the clause where the other party had on the evidence waived its entitlement to insist on a signature before being bound (*Oceanografia SA de CV v DSND Subsea AS* [2007] 1 Lloyd's Rep 37). **26.38**

Oral agreements to refer disputes to arbitration

Without a written agreement, even with the extended meaning given to writing by the Arbitration Act 1996 s 5, an agreement to refer a dispute to arbitration will not be governed by the Arbitration Act 1996. Despite this, an oral agreement to refer a matter to arbitration is effective (s 81(1)(b)), but the reference will be governed by the common law. Essentially this means that the matter should be arbitrated in accordance with the agreement between the parties. There are obvious problems in establishing such an oral agreement and in deciding what has been agreed, particularly where the parties are in acrimonious dispute. **26.39**

Dispute must come within the arbitration agreement

The range of disputes that will be covered by an arbitration agreement is a matter of contractual construction to determine what the parties intended. The underlying principle is that an arbitral tribunal can only have jurisdiction to determine matters that the parties have agreed should be referred to arbitration. The parties may agree to refer all disputes arising out of the substantive contract to arbitration, whether they are based on the law of contract, tort, unjust enrichment, or any other type of cause of action. Alternatively, the parties may agree that only certain types of dispute will go to arbitration. **26.40**

At one time a large number of technical distinctions were drawn by the courts over what disputes were and were not covered by different forms of words in arbitration clauses. The technicality of the rules left the law in some disrepute, and the modern approach is to give a broad and inclusive interpretation to most arbitration clauses. **26.41**

In *Fili Shipping Co Ltd v Premium Nafta Products Ltd* [2007] Bus LR 1719, the arbitration clause provided: 'Any dispute arising under this charter [lease of a ship] shall be decided' by arbitration. Lord Hoffmann pointed out that in construing such a clause regard must be had to the commercial background, and that businessmen are assumed to make agreements that achieve some rational commercial purpose. Agreeing with Longmore LJ in the Court of Appeal, Lord Hoffmann said that a new start was needed (see [12]). Rather than undertaking a semantic analysis of the clause and how similar clauses have been construed in the past, the court must start from the assumption that the parties, as rational businessmen, are likely to have intended that any dispute arising out of their relationship should be decided by the same tribunal. As a result, the clause in the case itself was wide enough to cover both: **26.42**

- disputes regarding the rights and obligations created by the charter of the ship itself; and
- disputes over matters said to invalidate the charter (on the facts these were allegations that the charter was vitiated through bribery).

26.43 Widely worded clauses may cover causes of action in contract, tort, restitution, breach of trust, and other non-contractual claims. Of course, ultimately the parties may agree to whatever restrictions on the nature of the disputes they intend to refer to arbitration, and the question remains one of contractual construction.

26.44 Thus, in *Food Corp of India v Achilles Halcoussis* [1988] 2 Lloyd's Rep 56, the arbitration clause said that disputes relating to demurrage and freight could be referred to arbitration. A dispute arose over a claim to elevator overtime, and Steyn J said that as it could not be inferred from the clause that it included elevator overtime, that was simply not a matter that had been entrusted to the arbitrators. In *Guidance Investments Ltd v Guidance Hotel Investment Co BSC* [2013] EWHC 3413 (Comm) a clause referring 'any dispute arising out of or in connection with an event of default' to arbitration did not cover a claim of gross negligence. In *Hillcrest Homes Ltd v Beresford & Curbishley Ltd* [2014] EWHC 280 (TCC) an arbitration clause covering 'any dispute or difference of any kind whatsoever' did not cover a misrepresentation claim because it did not arise 'under the contract'.

Capacity

26.45 There will be no valid reference to arbitration if either of the parties lacked the legal capacity to enter into the arbitration agreement. This is a matter of contract law, and means that in general children (those aged under 18) and persons suffering from mental incapacity within the meaning of the Mental Capacity Act 2005 cannot be parties to arbitrations. There may also be restrictions on the capacities of corporations that prevent them from entering into arbitration agreements, but the modern position is that registered companies under the Companies Acts have unlimited objects and therefore no restrictions on being parties to arbitrations (see Companies Act 2006 s 31).

26.46 Lack of capacity is a reason for not recognizing an arbitration agreement when a party seeks to enforce it through the court system (see Arbitration Act 1996 s 103(2)(a), and the New York Convention 1958, discussed in Chapter 32).

Conditions precedent to arbitration

Compliance with conditions precedent

26.47 Any condition precedent in the arbitration clause will need to be complied with. For example, it is not unusual for a clause to say that a dispute may be referred to arbitration 'at the request' of a party. In such a case a request must be made before arbitration becomes compulsory (*Secretary of State of the Environment, Transport and the Regions, ex p The Channel Group Ltd* [2001] EWCA Civ 1185). It has been known for other arbitration clauses to provide for arbitration 'after completion of the work' or 'after mediation', so that arbitration cannot be started until after these steps have been completed.

Scott v Avery clauses

26.48 A *Scott v Avery* clause (from *Scott v Avery* (1856) 25 LJ Ex 308) provides that court proceedings shall not be brought until after an arbitration award has been made. Its purpose is to ensure the parties arbitrate before they litigate. Such a clause is a condition precedent to litigation (as opposed to a condition precedent to arbitration). If the other side commences court proceedings without arbitrating, the *Scott v Avery* clause can be pleaded as a defence to the claim.

As the purpose of a *Scott v Avery* clause is to protect the right to arbitrate, it does not prevent a party applying for a court injunction for the purpose of enforcing the arbitration agreement (*Toepfer International GmbH v Societe Cargill France* [1998] 1 Lloyd's Rep 379). It will, however, prevent a party from seeking a freezing injunction in support of arbitral proceedings (*B v S* [2011] 2 Lloyd's Rep 18). **26.49**

H OVERVIEW OF ARBITRATION PROCEDURE

Figure 26.1 is an overall flow diagram showing the stages that many arbitrations go through from the initial formation of a dispute through the appointment of a tribunal to the hearing and enforcement. On the right-hand side of the flow diagram are indications of the types of application to the court that may be made at various stages of the process. As the actual procedures followed depends on the agreement of the parties, any arbitral institution rules that apply, and the approach of individual arbitrators, the steps taken in particular arbitrations may vary considerably from this basic model. **26.50**

I GENERAL PRINCIPLES AND DUTIES

Arbitrations governed by the Arbitration Act 1996 are subject to three general principles that are set out in s 1, as follows: **26.51**

(a) the object of arbitration is to obtain the fair resolution of disputes by an impartial tribunal without unnecessary delay or expense;
(b) the parties should be free to agree how their disputes are resolved, subject only to such safeguards as are necessary in the public interest; and
(c) the court should not intervene except as provided by the Arbitration Act 1996.

J FAIR RESOLUTION OF DISPUTES

The first of the general principles is in many respects similar to the overriding objective in normal litigation to be found in CPR r 1.1. There is a close affinity between obtaining the fair resolution of disputes in arbitration and dealing with litigation justly, and ensuring there is a fair trial pursuant to the European Convention on Human Rights (ECHR) Art 6. In most arbitrations the tribunal will seek to resolve the dispute by applying the appropriate law, but this is not always the case, as the parties are able to agree that the tribunal should apply some other system of rules or principles in deciding their dispute. It will be noticed that the Arbitration Act 1996 s 1(a) says that the dispute must be resolved by an 'impartial' tribunal, as opposed to an independent tribunal. This will be explored further in Chapter 27. **26.52**

Saving costs and expedition

In a similar way to litigation, the arbitral object of resolving the dispute fairly includes doing so without unnecessary delay or expense. To assist the tribunal in achieving this objective the parties are required to do all things necessary for the proper and expeditious conduct of the arbitral proceedings (s 40(1)). This includes complying without delay with any orders made by the tribunal on procedural or evidential matters and with any other orders and directions of the tribunal (s 40(2)). **26.53**

Figure 26.1 Stages in arbitration flow diagram, with possible applications to court

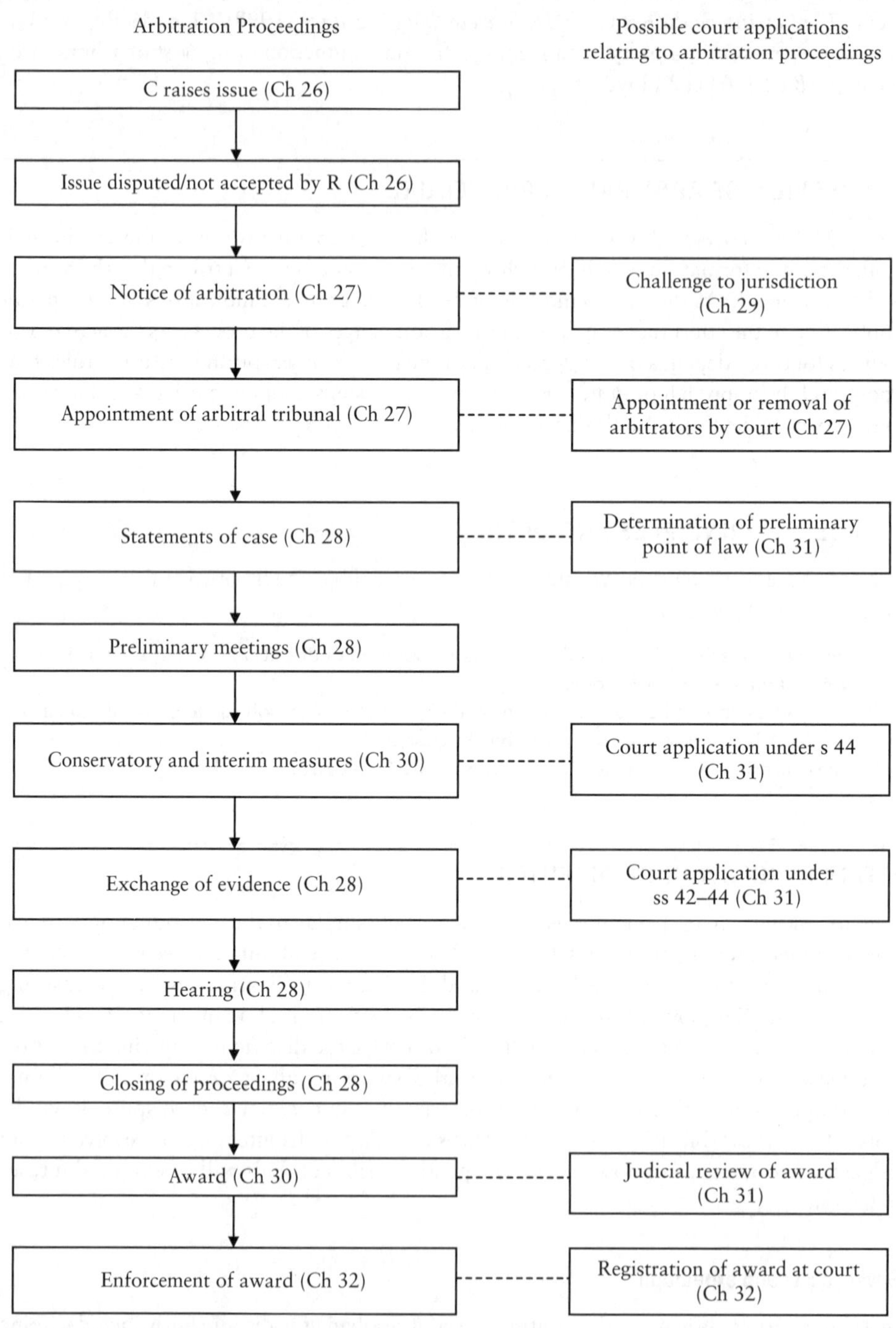

General duty of the tribunal

The first general principle in the Arbitration Act 1996 s 1(a) is supported by s 33(1), which imposes the following general duties on the arbitral tribunal: **26.54**

(a) to act fairly and impartially as between the parties, giving each party a reasonable opportunity of putting its case and dealing with that of its opponent; and
(b) to adopt procedures suitable to the circumstances of the particular case, avoiding unnecessary delay or expense, with a view to providing a fair means for the resolution of the matters falling to be determined.

Duty to follow the rules of natural justice

It follows from the Arbitration Act 1996 s 33(1) that the arbitral tribunal is required to follow the rules of natural justice. They will be breached if the arbitrators fail to give the parties an opportunity to deal with factors that the arbitrators intend to take into account in making a decision (*Gbangola v Smith & Sherriff Ltd* [1998] 3 All ER 730). Giving the parties a fair opportunity to present their case does not mean that the arbitrators are obliged to follow the strict procedures to be found in court procedure. An example is *Margulead Ltd v Exide Technologies* [2005] 1 Lloyd's Rep 324, where the arbitrator allowed both sides a closing speech, but refused to allow the claimant the last word, which is the usual position in litigation. **26.55**

Arbitration need not be adversarial

In fact arbitrators can go even further, and completely depart from the usual adversarial system found in the English courts. This follows from s 34(2)(e), which provides that, subject to the agreement of the parties, the arbitral tribunal can decide whether any and if so what questions should be put to and answered by the respective parties and when and in what form this should be done. This provision of course allows for minor variations on the adversarial system, for example the use of written questions. When s 34(2)(e) is read together with s 34(2)(g), which provides that the arbitral tribunal can decide whether and to what extent the tribunal should itself take the initiative in ascertaining the facts and the law, it is clear that arbitrators are able to adopt an inquisitorial rather than an adversarial system if that is preferred. **26.56**

K PARTY AUTONOMY

The second general principle in arbitration is that the parties should be free to decide how their dispute should be resolved. This flows from the entire concept of arbitration, in that it is a consensual process based on an agreement between the parties to refer their dispute to an impartial arbitral tribunal. The regime of the Arbitration Act 1996 is largely expressed in permissive terms (the 'non-mandatory' provisions) with an emphasis on party autonomy (*B v S* [2011] 2 Lloyd's Rep 18). **26.57**

Mandatory and non-mandatory provisions

Mandatory provisions

Table 26.2 sets out the mandatory provisions of the Arbitration Act 1996, which apply where there is a written arbitration agreement. They are listed in Sch 1 to the Act, and represent the essential minimum requirements that informed opinion would say are needed for an effective reference to arbitration. The mandatory provisions are aimed at supporting an **26.58**

Table 26.2 Mandatory provisions of the Arbitration Act 1996

Provision	Subject matter
ss 9–11	Stay of legal proceedings
s 12	Power of court to extend time limits for beginning arbitral proceedings
s 13	Application of the Limitation Acts to arbitration
s 24	Power of the court to remove an arbitrator if not impartial, or incapable etc
s 26(1)	Effect of death of an arbitrator
s 28	Liability of parties for the fees and expenses of arbitrators
s 29	Immunity of arbitrators
s 31	Objections to the substantive jurisdiction of arbitrators
s 32	Determination of preliminary point on jurisdiction
s 33	General duty of arbitral tribunals
s 37(2)	Items to be regarded as expenses of arbitrators
s 40	General duties of parties in arbitrations
s 43	Securing the attendance of witnesses
s 56	Power to withhold award on non-payment of arbitrators' fees
s 60	Agreements between the parties to pay costs in any event
s 66	Enforcement of the award
ss 67, 68, 70, 71	Challenging the award on the ground of lack of substantive jurisdiction or for serious irregularity
s 72	Parties not taking part in an arbitration
s 73	Loss of right to object
s 74	Immunity of arbitral institutions
s 75	Charge to secure payment of solicitors' costs

arbitration and ensuring it is effective, and provide machinery for limited court intervention to prevent substantial errors or arbitrators acting without jurisdiction.

Non-mandatory provisions

26.59 Anything not covered by the mandatory provisions listed in Table 26.2 can be agreed between the parties. One of the main things the Arbitration Act 1996 does is to lay down a detailed set of default provisions for just about everything else relating to an arbitration, which are subject to whatever other agreement may be reached between the parties. The areas covered by the non-mandatory provisions are set out in Table 26.3. The default provisions have been carefully crafted to provide a balanced and sensible set of rules for nearly all the non-mandatory issues that might arise, which will be adopted simply by not saying anything about the matter. However, if the parties do agree to a procedure that departs from the Arbitration Act 1996 scheme, the principle of party autonomy means that the parties' wishes will be respected.

Sources of party agreement

26.60 Party agreement departing from the non-mandatory provisions of the Arbitration Act 1996 may be reached in four distinct ways:

- before the dispute arises, where the contrary provisions will be found in the detailed wording of the arbitration agreement;

Table 26.3 Non-mandatory matters that may be agreed between the parties

Provision	Subject matter
s 3	Seat of the arbitration
s 4	Whether to adopt institution rules
s 7	Whether to agree the arbitration agreement is not a separable agreement
s 8	Effect of death of a party
s 14	When arbitral proceedings are to be regarded to commence
ss 15–22	Constitution etc of the arbitral tribunal
s 23	Circumstances in which the arbitrator's authority may be revoked
s 30	Whether the arbitral tribunal can rule on its own jurisdiction
s 35	Conferring power to consolidate
s 36	Rights to be represented in the arbitration
s 37	Tribunal's power to appoint experts
ss 38–41	Powers available to the tribunal
s 44	Exclusion of court's powers in support of arbitration
s 45	Exclusion of court's power to determine points of law
s 46	Which substantive law should apply
ss 47–49	Powers available to the tribunal when making its award
ss 52–58	Form, date etc of the final award
s 69	Excluding appeals to the court on a point of law
ss 76–79	Time limits and service of notices

- as a variation on this method, where the arbitration clause in the underlying contract adopts the rules of an arbitral institution (s 4(3)). This is discussed further in Chapter 28;
- after the dispute has arisen in a case where there is no pre-existing arbitration agreement, by a subsequent written agreement between the parties to refer the matter to arbitration. This may include provisions dealing with non-mandatory matters; or
- during the course of the arbitration. The principal example is the Arbitration Act 1996 s 34, which says that all procedural and evidential matters are for the tribunal to decide, but subject to the right of the parties to agree any matter. This in effect allows the parties to override the wishes of the arbitral tribunal on the procedure they wish to follow in resolving their dispute.

L COURT APPLICATIONS

The third principle is that the court should not intervene in an arbitration except as provided by the Arbitration Act 1996. The philosophy is that where parties have agreed that their dispute should be resolved by arbitration the court should not intervene except and to the extent that this is necessary. The two main reasons for court intervention are: **26.61**

- in order to give support to the arbitral proceedings; or
- in order to put right any serious injustice.

The principle of non-intervention is to support the implementation of the parties' decision to refer their dispute to arbitration. If the courts were too ready to intervene much of the **26.62** value in arbitrating as opposed to litigating would be lost. This topic is discussed further in Chapter 31.

M DIFFERENT TYPES OF ARBITRATION

Institutional arbitration

26.63 An institutional arbitration is where the arbitration itself is administered by an arbitral institution. This should be distinguished from an ad hoc arbitration (see 26.66–26.67). Very frequently an institutional arbitration will be conducted in accordance with the institution's own arbitration rules, although some institutions, such as CEDR, will apply the rules of another organization (CEDR uses the UNCITRAL Model Law).

26.64 In an institutional arbitration the institution may well provide a range of support services. These may include machinery for appointing the arbitrators, arranging facilities for hearings, and support in ensuring that the arbitration proceeds expeditiously and smoothly, and that awards are drawn up in a manner that makes them readily enforceable through the courts if they are not complied with (see Chapters 30 and 32). Some institutions even include an internal appeal process against the arbitrators' award. The additional services that will be provided by the institution depends on what is on offer from the institution, whether any of these are required by the institution's arbitration rules, and what the parties are prepared to pay for.

26.65 Almost inevitably there will be additional costs involved in making use of an institution's services, but doing so may be less expensive than trying to agree an equivalent with the other side, and the parties may well find that the benefits of using effective systems that are already established far outweigh the costs.

Ad hoc arbitration

26.66 Particularly in maritime disputes, the parties may enter into what is known as an ad hoc arbitration agreement. This simply means that the parties have agreed to arbitrate and not to use one of the arbitral institutions for the administration of the arbitration. This does not prevent the parties using such an institution as an appointing authority, but often the parties to an ad hoc arbitration will appoint the arbitrators themselves. It also does not stop the parties adopting the arbitration rules from an arbitral institution (this can be an effective short-hand way to agree the detailed procedures that will be adopted), but they may leave the details of the procedures to be followed to the arbitrators to decide (if these have not been prescribed by the arbitration agreement).

26.67 The net result is that in an ad hoc arbitration the parties save the fees that would be charged by an arbitral institution, and free themselves to choose arbitrators in any manner that may be agreed between them, and to agree to any procedures for the arbitration that they may choose. This level of freedom has many attractions while parties are on amicable terms, but can be a major source of difficulties if their relationship becomes less harmonious. Delays and additional expense can easily result if one party or the other decides to become obstructive. These problems can become particularly acute in arbitrations, because arbitrators have limited powers to force the parties into making progress in preparing the case. Ultimately, arbitrators may need to resort to the courts if one of the parties becomes deliberately obstructive (see Chapter 31).

Non-binding arbitration

Chapters 26–32 deal with traditional, binding, arbitration, which is intended to produce a final award on the issues in dispute. Binding arbitration may be contrasted with non-binding arbitration, which follows similar processes with an arbitrator making rulings on the issues between the parties, but which is not binding on the parties, and with no final award. Non-binding arbitration is similar to early neutral evaluation (Chapter 22) in that it produces an advisory decision which may be accepted or rejected by the parties. The underlying value in non-binding arbitration is that the decision may provide a basis for finding a negotiated settlement if it is not accepted. It is also said that non-binding arbitration gives the parties the opportunity of having a dry run on arguing their case, but without the risk of being bound by the decision. The arbitrator's decision will usually not be admissible in any subsequent litigation or binding arbitration, usually through suitable confidentiality and privacy clauses being inserted into the agreement for non-binding arbitration. **26.68**

Statutory arbitration

As an exception to the almost universal rule that arbitrations are based on agreement, the Arbitration Act 1996 ss 94–98 deal with statutory arbitrations. These occur where legislation requires certain types of dispute to be referred to arbitration. They are quite rare, but arise in some contexts in landlord and tenant and company law. The relevant legislation is treated for the purposes of the Arbitration Act 1996 as if it were an arbitration agreement between the parties. **26.69**

Consumer arbitration

There are restrictions, which can be found in the Arbitration Act 1996 ss 89–91, on the use of arbitration in consumer disputes. These give effect to Council Directive 93/13, and are aimed at ensuring that arbitration clauses are not used against consumers as a means of preventing them from seeking redress from the courts. **26.70**

Med-arb

Mediation-arbitration (med-arb) is a hybrid between mediation and arbitration. There are various different forms this can take. One version is for a single person to be nominated as a mediator, who will then become the arbitrator if the matter cannot be resolved in the mediation. A different version is for one individual to act as the mediator, and for a different person to be appointed as the arbitrator if the matter is not resolved in the mediation. **26.71**

While this combined approach may appear to give business people the best of both worlds, there are problems: **26.72**

- If the parties proceed first by referring the matter to mediation, and this is successful, the settlement will not be enforceable under the New York Convention 1958 or the Arbitration Act 1996 s 66 (see Chapter 32), because there is no 'dispute' as required by s 6. It is possible to ensure enforceability by starting with a formal reference to arbitration, then immediately referring the matter to mediation, and, if the matter is settled, recording the agreement in a consent award (see Chapter 31).
- There are obvious ethical problems in a person who has acted as a mediator changing roles and becoming an arbitrator (see Chapter 6).
- It is possible that important information may be disclosed in confidence in a mediation, which may influence the decision on the arbitration, and that private discussions with the

mediator in the absence of the other party may turn out to be entirely improper when the process converts over to arbitration. These considerations may also mean that the parties are more reticent in the mediation part of the process than would otherwise be the case, which may make settling the matter more difficult.

Family arbitration

26.73 An arbitration scheme for matrimonial financial and property disputes was set up in 2012 by the Institute of Family Law Arbitrators (IFLA). These arbitrations are governed by the Arbitration Act 1996, but with the important difference that the jurisdiction of the court cannot be ousted (see 23.45). The family courts seek to support IFLA arbitrations by providing a streamlined procedure for approving consent orders based on the IFLA award. It has been held that in the absence of some very compelling countervailing factor, the arbitral award should be determinative of the order made by the court (*S v S* [2014] Fam Law 448).

N MULTI-TIERED DISPUTE RESOLUTION

26.74 Some dispute resolution clauses are more complicated still, and provide for more than two levels or tiers of ADR. It is a matter of construction as to whether each of the tiers is a condition precedent to proceeding to the next tier. If they are not, a party can proceed directly to arbitration. Clauses will vary, but an example might be:

- to submit the dispute to designated officers of the respective parties to attempt to negotiate a settlement;
- followed by mediation if the matter remains unresolved;
- followed by arbitration.

O ONE-STOP ADJUDICATION

26.75 Where the parties have made a clear agreement for med-arb or multi-tiered dispute resolution, that will be upheld by the courts. However, there is a strong presumption that the parties will have intended that their dispute would be resolved through a single dispute resolution process (*Fili Shipping Co Ltd v Premium Nafta Products Ltd* [2007] Bus LR 1719). Reasonable businessmen are unlikely to have intended that their disputes should be looked into by both arbitrators and the courts. Consequently, the underlying purpose of the Arbitration Act 1996 is for one-stop adjudication (*Lesotho Highlands v Impreglio SpA* [2006] 1 AC 221 at [34]).

P EUROPEAN CONVENTION ON HUMAN RIGHTS AND ARBITRATION

26.76 While arbitrators cannot ignore the requirements of the ECHR, the courts have upheld the main features of arbitration in the face of a number of attacks based on ECHR arguments. In *Stretford v Football Association* [2007] Bus LR 1052 it was argued that an arbitration clause in the Football Association Rules infringed the ECHR Art 6. The appellant was a football players' agent who had to submit to the Rules in order to be licensed. It was held that arbitrations comply with much of Art 6 in that the Arbitration Act 1996 provides for a fair hearing by an impartial tribunal, and gives the High Court jurisdiction to review issues such as apparent bias and procedural unfairness. Two remaining issues, namely the right to a hearing in public and a hearing before a tribunal established by law, were waived by the appellant through the incorporation of the arbitration clause into the appellant's licence agreement.

In *Sumukan Ltd v Commonwealth Secretariat* [2007] Bus LR 1075 it was argued that Art 6 was infringed by the exclusion of the right to appeal to the courts against the decision of the arbitrators on a point of law under the Arbitration Act 1996 s 69. The exclusion was made by a clause in the contract, that referred to a statute, which set out the relevant rules for the arbitration and excluded the right to appeal. It was held that the exclusion did not infringe Art 6, being a common provision in arbitration rules, and it did not matter that the exclusion was in a document referred to in the substantive agreement, rather than being an express clause of that agreement. **26.77**

Q MAIN FEATURES OF ARBITRATION

Given the range of matters that can be agreed between the parties, and the range of options available on almost every matter of principle and procedure, it is perhaps not surprising that the Arbitration Act 1996 avoids seeking to define arbitration as a concept. The closest thing in the Act is the definition of an arbitration agreement given by s 6(1) (see 26.20). Nevertheless, a number of common features to most arbitrations can be identified; **26.78**

- Arbitrations are based on an agreement between the parties to have their dispute decided by impartial arbitrators.
- Arbitrators are frequently appointed by the parties, or through a mechanism agreed by the parties, rather than by the state (as happens in court proceedings). This should result in arbitrators being acceptable to the respective parties and who may have trade knowledge that will assist in coming to a decision. A disadvantage is that there is scope for a party who decides to be obstructive to delay the appointment of the arbitral tribunal, which can lead to the undesirable result of needing to go to court for the purpose of securing the appointment of the arbitrators (see Chapters 27 and 31). Another disadvantage is that it is difficult to find individuals better qualified than High Court judges, who are provided free as part of the service in High Court litigation, whereas arbitrators will charge fees at commercial rates, which can be expensive, particularly in tribunals of three arbitrators.
- Parties retain a measure of control over the procedures adopted by the tribunal (subject to their original agreement to arbitrate), whereas court procedures are controlled by the judge.
- Formality is often given to arbitrations by adopting institutional rules, but the parties can choose extremely informal procedures if they prefer.
- The level of formality adopted in an arbitration varies greatly between different arbitrators and different institutional arbitral rules, but are often less formal than court procedures.
- By choosing which set of institutional rules to adopt, or by entering into an ad hoc arbitration, the parties can decide between themselves the level of formality and the complexity of the procedures to be used in their arbitration. In court cases the procedures are largely laid down by the CPR and have to be followed.
- Most arbitrations are conducted in private, whereas court hearings have to be in public unless there are pressing countervailing considerations (ECHR Art 6(1)). Many business people do not want their disputes becoming widely known, so this is a major factor in deciding whether to arbitrate or litigate.
- Following on from its consensual nature, arbitration usually works best when there are only two parties. While it is possible to arbitrate where there are three or more parties, there are problems. These include agreeing on the arbitral rules, particularly where the substantive contracts between the different parties have inconsistent arbitration clauses. Further, unless express provision is made for this, arbitrators have no power to join additional

parties, or to consolidate two or more arbitrations. This can be useful to avoid irreconcilable decisions in related disputes, and is one of the advantages of litigation.

- Likewise, arbitrators have no powers against third parties. This is a drawback where documentation or property that needs to be inspected by an expert, is in the control of a third party.
- Arbitrators have relatively weak powers in relation to imposing sanctions on parties who do not comply with timetables and procedural orders. There is therefore more scope for parties to cause delays in arbitrations than in litigation, where judges impose a system of active case management.
- Unless the parties agree to confer such a power, arbitrators have no power to grant interim injunctions. They do have power to make final awards for injunctive relief (Arbitration Act 1996 s 48(5)), and there may be a limited power to grant interim injunctive relief under ss 38–39, but in any event arbitrators cannot enforce their orders by committal. Outside these provisions an application for an interim injunction has to be made to the court (Chapter 31).
- Similarly, arbitrators cannot grant orders equivalent to search orders and freezing injunctions.
- Generally, the decision of the arbitrators is final. There are exceptions, because some arbitral rules include an appeals process, and the courts have a limited power to review arbitral awards (Chapter 31). For business people finality is a great benefit. The CPR, however, have brought the English court system into a position that is fairly close to that in arbitration (almost all civil appeals require permission to appeal, and the grounds of appeal are quite limited), but it is generally regarded to be true that it is more difficult to overturn an arbitral award than a judgment of a court.
- In international arbitration there is a simple enforcement procedure through the New York Convention 1958 (see Chapter 32), which provides a huge advantage to arbitration compared with the more difficult overseas enforcement procedures that apply to court judgments. In cases where both parties are within the jurisdiction, enforcement will be more direct in litigation, because there is no need to go through the stage of registering the award as a judgment.

26.79 Whether it is cheaper to arbitrate than to go to court is an open question. It depends largely on the nature of the dispute and the approach taken by the parties. Often the balance is between the ability to save costs on simpler procedures in arbitration against the fees payable to the arbitrators (on a daily fee basis, and which may include international travel) and to the arbitral institution.

KEY POINTS SUMMARY

26.80

- The foundation of arbitration is the agreement to arbitrate, which is commonly found in an arbitration clause in the substantive contract between the parties.
- The arbitration agreement is separable from the substantive contract, which means that arbitrators can rule on the validity of the substantive contract without destroying their own jurisdiction.
- The three principles of arbitration law are:
  - the fair resolution of disputes by an impartial tribunal without unnecessary delay or expense;
  - party autonomy;
  - limited court interference.
- The Arbitration Act 1996 seeks to achieve a balance between these principles by setting out a relatively small number of mandatory provisions, which are those regarded as essential to

support effective arbitrations, and a wider range of non-mandatory provisions that the parties can choose whether to adopt.

- Party autonomy has resulted in a wide range of procedures that are adopted in arbitrations. Despite this, by agreeing to arbitration through an arbitral institution under the institution's rules a degree of certainty can be achieved.
- While the Arbitration Act 1996 contains quite a large number of provisions that allow applications to be made to the court, these are operated in accordance with the principle that the courts will honour the agreement between the parties that they want their disputes decided privately by an arbitral tribunal.
- By agreeing to arbitrate, the parties effectively waive their right to trial in the courts for the purposes of the ECHR Art 6.
- The main features of arbitration discussed in the final section of this chapter set out many of the pros and cons of arbitrating compared with litigating. Often the advantage enjoyed by one party will be balanced by a corresponding disadvantage for the other side.
- Often the balance boils down to having the dispute decided in private by a tribunal chosen by the parties, against having the dispute decided by a professional judge in public and with the coercive powers granted to the courts.

27

ARBITRAL TRIBUNALS

A INTRODUCTION 27.01
B COMMENCEMENT OF ARBITRATION 27.02
C NOTICE OF ARBITRATION 27.08
D APPOINTMENT OF ARBITRAL TRIBUNAL 27.10
E CONTRACTUAL BASIS OF THE ARBITRATORS' MANDATE 27.18
F TERMS OF REFERENCE..............27.23
G REMOVAL, RESIGNATION, AND VACANCIES........................27.24
H IMMUNITIES 27.33
I LIABILITY FOR ARBITRATORS' FEES 27.35
Key points summary 27.36

A INTRODUCTION

27.01 This chapter describes how arbitrations are commenced with a notice of arbitration and the appointment of arbitral tribunals. Typically arbitral tribunals will have either a sole arbitrator, or a panel of three arbitrators. There are a number of variations on this theme. Examples are tribunals with a chairperson or an umpire, and the use of judge-arbitrators. The chapter also describes the contractual basis of the appointment of arbitrators, and the procedures dealing with the removal, resignation, or death of an arbitrator.

B COMMENCEMENT OF ARBITRATION

Importance of the date of commencement of an arbitration

27.02 There are potentially two sets of time limits that may result in an arbitration being unsuccessful:

- any contractual restriction on bringing claims; and
- any limitation period.

Contractual time limits

27.03 The arbitration agreement, some other contractual provision, or the arbitral institution rules that apply to an arbitration, may include a requirement that any arbitration has to be commenced within a stated time limit. The wording of the clause will determine the effect of such a time limit. Unless the wording makes clear that compliance with the time limit is a condition of any claim, but does not limit the right to arbitrate, expiry of a contractual time limit will bar the commencement of the arbitration (*Metalfer Corp v Pan Ocean Shipping Co Ltd* [1998] 2 Lloyd's Rep 632).

Limitation periods

27.04 The normal limitation periods under the Limitation Act 1980 apply to arbitration: Arbitration Act s 13(1). In contract and most claims in tort the limitation period is six years (Limitation Act 1980 ss 2 and 5). Detailed consideration of limitation can be found in Sime, *A Practical Approach to Civil Procedure* (17th edn, OUP, 2014), ch 21. Limitation runs from the day after the cause of action accrues until the date a claim is brought.

Date of commencement of arbitration

27.05 In arbitration proceedings the parties are entitled to agree when the arbitration is to be regarded as having commenced for limitation purposes (Arbitration Act 1996 s 14(1)). If there is no such agreement s 14(3)–(5) sets out three rules for when the arbitration is to be regarded as having commenced, depending on how the arbitral tribunal is to be appointed. These are:

- where the arbitrator is named or designated in the arbitration agreement, arbitral proceedings are commenced when one party serves on the other party or parties a notice in writing requiring him or them to submit the dispute to the person so named or designated (s 14(3));
- where the arbitrator or arbitrators are to be appointed by the parties, arbitral proceedings are commenced when one party serves on the other party or parties notice in writing requiring him or them to appoint an arbitrator or to agree to the appointment of an arbitrator in respect of the dispute (s 14(4)); and
- where the arbitrator or arbitrators are to be appointed by a person other than a party to the proceedings, arbitral proceedings are commenced when one party gives notice in writing to that person requesting him to make the appointment in respect of the dispute (s 14(5)).

Avoiding the consequences of failing to comply with a time limit

27.06 In the case of a contractual time limit, there may be a provision in the arbitral institution's rules giving a discretion to the tribunal or institution to grant more time. Alternatively, the claimant may apply to the High Court under the Arbitration Act 1996 s 12 for an extension of time. Any arbitral process for extending time must be used before applying to court (s 12(2)). Successful applications to extend time are comparatively rare. In a further alternative, the respondent may simply decide not to raise the time bar by way of defence.

27.07 Other than the provisions in the Limitation Act 1980 (such as ss 14A and 14B on latent damage) that give the court some flexibility over certain limitation periods, there is no power to forgive a claimant who fails to comply with a Limitation Act time limit. However, as limitation is a procedural defence and is only effective if raised by the respondent, a time-barred arbitration will continue if limitation is not pleaded.

C NOTICE OF ARBITRATION

27.08 Under the Arbitration Act 1996 s 14(3)–(5) (see 27.05), a notice of arbitration (also known as a notice to arbitrate) has to be in writing and must comply with the requirements of the relevant subsection of s 14 on appointing the arbitral tribunal. These requirements can be met by a reasonably simple letter. In practice the letter tends to include various other details in order to comply with further requirements set out in any relevant institutional arbitral rules. Under the London Metal Exchange Ltd (LME) rules, for example, a notice to arbitrate must contain at least the following information:

- the address for service of the claimant;
- a brief statement of the nature and circumstances of the dispute including a brief description of any contract, sufficient to enable the respondent to identify it, to which the dispute relates;
- a brief statement of the relief claimed;
- the claimant's proposal with regard to the number of arbitrators to form the tribunal;
- the claimant's nomination of one arbitrator from the LME panel; and
- the name and address of the respondent to which the notice to arbitrate has been sent.

27.09 Often, the notice of arbitration is sent to the respondent. Where the arbitrators are appointed by an appointing institution, or where institutional rules so require, the notice needs to be sent to the institution as well. For example, under the LME rules a claimant commences an arbitration by serving the notice to arbitrate on the respondent, and by sending a copy of the notice to the secretary of the LME accompanied by the registration fee and deposit (reg 2.1). An example of a notice of arbitration in a carriage of goods by sea case can be seen in Figure 27.1.

Figure 27.1 Notice of arbitration under the Arbitration Act 1996 s 14(4)

Taylor, Andrews & Co.,
Solicitors
Tel 0121 847 4746 Fax 0121 857 8822

36 High Street,
Birmingham,
B4 8YD
Ref INA/863
Date: 24 April 2014

Dear Sirs,

M.V. ASIAN SUMMER

Bill of Lading KAY-3 of 6 January 2014

We are instructed on behalf of the subrogated underwriters, Seaborne Insurance plc, of a consignment of grapefruit carried from Seattle to Liverpool on board the M.V. 'Asian Summer', arriving at Liverpool on 1 February 2014. On arrival it was discovered that the consignment was subject to considerable physical damage. Our clients have suffered losses in the sum of US$210,563. We understand that the vessel is owned by Summer Navigation SA and is chartered by Ocean Shipping and Carriage plc. We further understand that the vessel is entered with the Bristol & Liverpool P & I Club.

We hereby notify you that we have appointed Mr James Morrison as arbitrator on behalf of our clients Seaborne Insurance plc and Midlands Fruit Importers plc in connection with all disputes and differences arising under the above mentioned bill of lading. We hereby require you to appoint a second arbitrator in accordance with clause 24 of the above mentioned bill of lading.

We look forward to receiving your acknowledgement of safe receipt of this letter within the next 14 days.

Yours faithfully,
Taylor, Andrews & Co

D APPOINTMENT OF ARBITRAL TRIBUNAL

Number of arbitrators

In accordance with the principle of party autonomy, the parties are given considerable scope on how their arbitral tribunal will be constituted. The Arbitration Act 1996, s 15(1), says the parties are free to agree on the number of arbitrators to form the tribunal and whether there is to be a chair or umpire. If there is no agreement as to the number of arbitrators, the tribunal shall consist of a sole arbitrator (s 15(3)). A clause that said disputes were to be decided 'by the arbitrators' (plural) without saying how many, failed to specify the 'number' of arbitrators, which meant the tribunal was to consist of a single arbitrator under s 15(3) (*Itochu Corp v Johann MK Blumenthal GmbH & Co KG* [2013] 1 All ER (Comm) 504). Having an even number of arbitrators risks deadlock. It will be recalled that the second arbitration clause in Table 26.1 provided for the appointment of two arbitrators. Unless otherwise agreed by the parties s 15(2) says that an agreement that the number of arbitrators shall be two or any other even number shall be understood as requiring the appointment of an additional arbitrator as chair of the tribunal. **27.10**

Appointing the arbitrators

The parties are free to agree on the procedure for appointing the arbitrator or arbitrators, including the procedure for appointing any chairperson or umpire (Arbitration Act 1996 s 16(1)). Arbitrators may be chosen because they are known professionally by, or recommended to, the appointing parties. Alternatively, an approach may be made to a professional body, with an arbitrator being nominated by (say) the President of that organization. Perhaps more frequently the parties will use an arbitral institution as a nominating authority. This usually involves completing a form applying for the necessary arbitral services, which will ask for details such as the nature of the dispute, whether there is an arbitration agreement, which institutional rules (if any) apply, and the seat, law, and language of the arbitration (see Chapter 29 for these concepts). **27.11**

In the absence of contrary agreement s 16 provides default for provisions for the main varieties of arbitral tribunal, as set out in Table 27.1. **27.12**

Chairperson

Where the arbitral tribunal has a chair, the parties are free to decide on the chairperson's functions and powers. In the absence of such an agreement, decisions, orders, and awards of the tribunal are made by all or a majority of the arbitrators (including the chair) (Arbitration Act 1996 s 20(3)). The view of the chairperson prevails in relation to a decision, order, or award where there is an evenly split decision (s 20(4)). **27.13**

Umpire

Arbitral tribunals with umpires are a peculiarly English idea. In the absence of contrary agreement, the umpire shall attend the proceedings and be supplied with the same documents and other materials as are supplied to the other arbitrators (Arbitration Act 1996 s 21(3)). Decisions, orders, and awards are made by the other arbitrators unless and until they cannot agree on a matter relating to the arbitration. In that event they must give notice in writing to the parties and the umpire, and the umpire then replaces them as the tribunal with power to make decisions, orders, and awards as if he were sole arbitrator (s 21(4)). Paying an umpire to wait in the wings until the party-appointed arbitrators fail to agree is not usually regarded as an efficient way of proceeding, so this arrangement is not all that common. **27.14**

Table 27.1 Default procedures for the appointment of arbitrators

Tribunal	Appointment procedure
Sole arbitrator	The parties jointly appoint the arbitrator not later than 28 days after service of a request in writing by either party to do so (s 16(3)). To prevent an appearance of unfairness, institutional arbitral rules often provide that where the parties are from different countries, a sole arbitrator should not be of the same nationality as any of the parties.
Two arbitrators (where this really is the intention of the parties)	Each party is required to appoint one arbitrator not later than 14 days after service of a request in writing by either party to do so (s 16(4)).
Three arbitrators	Each party is required to appoint one arbitrator not later than 14 days after service of a request in writing by either party to do so, and these arbitrators then forthwith appoint a third arbitrator as the chairman of the tribunal (s 16(5)). Again, to prevent an appearance of unfairness, institutional arbitral rules often provide that where the parties are from different countries, the chairperson should not be of the same nationality as any of the parties.
Two arbitrators and an umpire	Each party is required to appoint one arbitrator not later than 14 days after service of a request in writing by either party to do so, and these arbitrators may appoint an umpire at any time after they themselves are appointed and must do so before any substantive hearing or forthwith if they cannot agree on a matter relating to the arbitration (s 16(6)).

Judges as arbitrators

27.15 A judge of the Commercial Court or of the Technology and Construction Court may, if in all the circumstances he thinks fit, accept appointment as a sole arbitrator or as umpire under an arbitration agreement (Arbitration Act 1996 s 93(1)). Such an appointment requires the permission of the Lord Chief Justice having regard to the state of business in the relevant courts.

27.16 There is a £2,455 appointment fee for a judge arbitrator and daily fees, also of £2,455 (Civil Proceedings (Fees) Order 2008 (SI 2008/1053)), which are payable to the High Court. A judge arbitrator can exercise the jurisdiction of the High Court under various provisions of the Arbitration Act 1996 (s 93(6) and Sch 2), which may be attractive to the parties. However, pressure on court time makes such appointments very unusual.

Failure of appointment procedure

27.17 Where the above procedures break down, possibly because the other side does not make an appointment, there are default powers in the Arbitration Act 1996 ss 17–19. These may result in the claimant's nominee becoming the sole arbitrator, or may require an application to the High Court to resolve the problem (see Chapter 31).

E CONTRACTUAL BASIS OF THE ARBITRATORS' MANDATE

27.18 Where a person accepts an appointment as an arbitrator they enter into a contract with the parties in the terms that are agreed. These will usually include:

- the identification of the dispute or difference that has to be adjudicated upon;
- the terms on which the adjudicator is prepared to act, which will include the fees payable to the arbitrator;

- the basis on which the arbitration is to be conducted, which will usually be in accordance with the terms of the arbitration agreement between the parties and any institutional rules that have been incorporated or otherwise agreed between the parties;
- an agreement by the arbitrator to conduct the arbitration and to issue an award without undue delay (Arbitration Act 1996 s 33(1)(b)) or within any time frame agreed with the parties or in accordance with the relevant institutional rules.

Once appointed, the arbitrators are contractually bound to complete their mandate, which also has the effect of limiting the extent of their jurisdiction to the matters that have been referred to them in their mandate. **27.19**

Qualifications of arbitrators

While there are no requirements in the general law imposing minimum qualifications on arbitrators, it is not uncommon for arbitration agreements to specify such qualifications. These may specify minimum professional qualifications, or membership of an organization (such as membership of the Baltic Exchange), or status (such as being in business in the City of London). An arbitration clause that provided that disputes were to be resolved by three arbitrators who were each a respected member of the Ismaili Muslim community was held in *Hashwani v Jivaj* [2011] 1 WLR 1872 not to fall within the Employment Equality (Religion or Belief) Regulations 2003 reg 2(3), and so was perfectly lawful. Arbitrators appointed under the rules of arbitral institutions are invariably only on the relevant panel if they are suitably qualified. **27.20**

Impartiality and independence

Arbitrators, even those appointed by a particular party, must be impartial (Arbitration Act 1996 ss 1, 24, and 33). The word used in the Act is 'impartial' rather than 'independent', because, as stated in the report by the Departmental Advisory Committee on Arbitration (DAC), set up by the Department of Trade and Industry, whose reports formed the basis for the Arbitration Act 1996, it is possible to be impartial even if the arbitrator is not independent. An arbitrator is liable to be removed if their impartiality is compromised (s 24). This may happen if there is actual bias or a real possibility of bias. This is approached on the basis of whether a fair-minded and informed observer would conclude there is a real possibility of bias (*Porter v Magill* [2002] 2 AC 357). **27.21**

Some arbitral institution rules, such as the UNCITRAL Model Law Art 12, require arbitrators to be 'independent'. This has caused some controversy, but probably does not impose any substantially different standard than impartiality. **27.22**

F TERMS OF REFERENCE

Formal terms of reference are somewhat unusual, but do form part of the standard procedure in ICC arbitrations (ICC Rules Art 23). These are drawn up by the arbitral tribunal on the basis of the documents filed at the start of the arbitration or after an initial hearing with the parties. In addition to details of those involved, the place of the arbitration etc, this document summarizes the respective claims and counterclaims and the relief sought. Importantly, it also sets out a list of the issues to be determined. It therefore provides a clear definition of the limits of the arbitrators' mandate. **27.23**

G REMOVAL, RESIGNATION, AND VACANCIES

Removal

27.24 The parties are free to agree in what circumstances the authority of an arbitrator may be revoked (Arbitration Act 1996 s 23(1)). In the absence of such prior agreement, the authority of an arbitrator may not be revoked except by the parties acting jointly, or by an arbitral institution vested by the parties with such a power (s 23(3)). Revocation of the authority of an arbitrator by the parties acting jointly must be agreed in writing unless the parties also agree (whether or not in writing) to terminate the arbitration agreement (s 23(4)).

27.25 An early termination of an arbitrator's appointment is potentially a breach of contract that may lead to a claim of damages. It will not be a breach if the appointment contract has been discharged or if the termination of the appointment is for a reason permitted in the appointment contract. It may be discharged if the arbitrator is in fundamental breach of the agreement (which is accepted by the parties) or if it has become impossible for the arbitrator to continue.

27.26 In similar situations a party to arbitral proceedings may, provided avenues for the removal of the arbitrator under the arbitration agreement and any institutional rules have been exhausted, apply to the court for an order removing the arbitrator (s 24). Such an order can be made if:

- circumstances exist that give rise to justifiable doubts as to the arbitrator's impartiality;
- the arbitrator does not possess the qualifications required by the arbitration agreement;
- the arbitrator is physically or mentally incapable of conducting the proceedings or there are justifiable doubts as to his capacity to do so; or
- the arbitrator has refused or failed properly to conduct the proceedings, or to use all reasonable dispatch in conducting the proceedings or making an award, and substantial injustice has been or will be caused to the applicant.

27.27 Where the court removes an arbitrator, it may make such order as it thinks fit with respect to his entitlement (if any) to fees or expenses, or the repayment of any fees or expenses already paid (s 24(4)).

Resignation

27.28 Resignation by an arbitrator is also a potential breach of contract, so the Arbitration Act 1996 s 25(1) provides that the parties are free to agree with an arbitrator on:

- the consequences of his resignation;
- in particular, on the arbitrator's entitlement (if any) to fees or expenses; and
- any liability incurred by the arbitrator as a result of having resigned.

27.29 If agreement cannot be reached, the arbitrator can apply to the court for relief on the ground that resigning was reasonable in the circumstances (s 25(3), (4)).

Death

27.30 The authority of an arbitrator is personal and ceases on his death (Arbitration Act 1996 s 26(1)). This can have serious consequences for the parties, who may have to start all or part of the arbitration proceedings again. It is not uncommon for parties to insure against this eventuality.

Vacancies

Where an arbitrator ceases to hold office, the Arbitration Act 1996 s 27(1), says that the parties are free to agree: 27.31

- whether and if so how the vacancy is to be filled;
- whether and if so to what extent the previous proceedings should stand; and
- what effect (if any) his ceasing to hold office has on any appointment made by him (alone or jointly).

In the absence of agreement the same procedures apply as where there is a failure to make an initial appointment (s 27(2)–(3)). One possibility is that the vacancy will not be filled, which in a multi-member tribunal is called a truncated arbitral tribunal. The tribunal (when reconstituted) is required to determine whether and if so to what extent the previous proceedings should stand (s 27(4)). 27.32

H IMMUNITIES

Immunity of arbitrators

An arbitrator is not liable for anything done or omitted in the discharge or purported discharge of his functions as arbitrator unless the act or omission is shown to have been in bad faith (Arbitration Act 1996 s 29(1)). This immunity does not apply to any liability the arbitrator may have on account of resigning (s 29(3)). 27.33

Immunity of arbitral institutions

An arbitral institution which appoints or nominates an arbitrator at the request of the parties is not liable for anything done or omitted in the discharge or purported discharge of that function unless the act or omission is shown to have been in bad faith (Arbitration Act 1996 s 74(1)). Nor is such an arbitral institution liable, by reason of having appointed or nominated an arbitrator, for anything done or omitted by the arbitrator in the discharge or purported discharge of his functions as arbitrator (s 74(2)). These immunities do not cover every situation, and will not cover, for example, negligence in the way the institution administers an arbitration. 27.34

I LIABILITY FOR ARBITRATORS' FEES

The parties are jointly and severally liable to pay to the arbitrators such reasonable fees and expenses (if any) as are appropriate in the circumstances (Arbitration Act 1996 s 28(1)). This does not affect any liability of a party to any other party to pay all or any of the costs of the arbitration (see 30.28) or any contractual right of an arbitrator to payment of his fees and expenses (s 28(5)). The tribunal may refuse to deliver an award to the parties except upon full payment of the fees and expenses of the arbitrators (s 56(1)). Applications may be made to the court under these sections in the event of an impasse. 27.35

KEY POINTS SUMMARY

27.36
- It is most usual to have either one- or three-person arbitral tribunals.
- The procedure for having two party-appointed arbitrators, who then appoint a chairperson, is designed to ensure the parties have an equal involvement in choosing the tribunal.
- The appointment of an arbitrator creates a contract between the arbitrator and the parties.
- The contract(s) between the parties and the members of the tribunal creates the tribunal's mandate to make an award on the dispute or difference.
- The Arbitration Act 1996 seeks to give effect to the parties' agreements (between themselves or with the arbitrators) if it becomes necessary for an arbitrator to resign or be removed, but there are fall-back provisions allowing applications to the court because it is recognized that agreement may not be possible given the possibly contentious nature of these situations.

28

THE COMMERCIAL ARBITRATION PROCESS

A INTRODUCTION 28.01
B DEFINITION OF 'COMMERCIAL' 28.03
C PRIVACY AND CONFIDENTIALITY.......28.05
D RANGE OF PROCEDURAL APPROACHES IN ARBITRATION 28.10
E PROCEDURAL RULES GOVERNING THE ARBITRATION 28.12
F ROLE OF LEGAL REPRESENTATIVES IN ARBITRATION 28.16
G COMMENCEMENT 28.25
H 'LOOK-SNIFF' ARBITRATIONS 28.26
I SHORT-FORM ARBITRATIONS 28.28
J GENERAL PROCEDURE IN COMMERCIAL ARBITRATION 28.31
K EXAMPLE OF ARBITRAL RULES THAT CLOSELY FOLLOW COURT PROCEDURES 28.83
Key points summary 28.101

A INTRODUCTION

This chapter will describe the procedures followed in commercial arbitrations involving parties who are all located within England and Wales. The seat of the arbitration, its law, objections to the tribunal's jurisdiction, and the language to be used could, in theory, arise as issues in domestic commercial arbitration, but are far more frequently issues in international arbitration. These issues will therefore be considered in the next chapter on international arbitration. In most domestic arbitrations it will be obvious that the seat of the arbitration is England, that the dispute should be determined applying English law and that the language of the arbitration should be English. **28.01**

'Commercial' disputes and commercial law potentially cover a wide range of legal areas. For most purposes English law does not draw distinctions between different types of arbitration, with the two main areas where it does make a difference being: **28.02**

- there are restrictions in the use of arbitration in consumer disputes (Arbitration Act 1996 ss 89–91); and
- enforcement of international arbitration agreements under the New York Convention 1958 (see Chapter 32) is limited to commercial disputes where a country has entered into a commercial reservation. About a third of the states that are parties to the Convention have entered into such a reservation.

B DEFINITION OF 'COMMERCIAL'

In English law, the distinction between commercial and consumer arbitration is that there will be a consumer arbitration agreement where one of the parties is a legal or natural person (Arbitration Act 1996 s 90) who is acting for purposes outside those of a trade, business, **28.03** or profession (Unfair Terms in Consumer Contracts Regulations 1999 (SI 1999/2083) reg 3(1)). This covers an individual acting in their private capacity, and also a company (which is a legal person) provided it was acting for a purpose outside its business.

28.04 The most important definition of commercial arbitration is that set out in the UNCITRAL Model Law Art 1(1). This provides:

> The term 'commercial' should be given a wide interpretation so as to cover matters arising from all relationships of a commercial nature, whether contractual or not. Relationships of a commercial nature include, but are not limited to, the following transactions: any trade transaction for the supply or exchange of goods or services; distribution agreements; commercial representation or agency; factoring; leasing; construction of works; consulting, engineering; licensing; investment; financing; banking; insurance; exploitation agreements or concessions; joint venture; carriage of goods or passengers by air, sea, rail, or road.

C PRIVACY AND CONFIDENTIALITY

28.05 It is a long-established principle of arbitration law that arbitral proceedings are private and confidential. Interestingly, there are no express provisions enshrining these principles in the Arbitration Act 1996. This is because both principles have a large number of exceptions and were too unsettled to formulate suitable provisions for the Act (DAC report, paras 11–17).

Privacy

28.06 Privacy relates to holding hearings in places where the public have no access. Privacy in arbitration is based on the fact that the parties have agreed to submit their dispute to arbitration between themselves, and only between themselves (*Oxford Shipping Co Ltd v Nippon Yusen Kaisha* [1984] 3 All ER 835 at 842).

Confidentiality

28.07 Confidentiality relates to an obligation on those participating in an arbitration not to disclose details, documents, or information about the arbitration to anyone outside the arbitration. The duty of confidentiality arises as a corollary to the privacy of arbitration (*Ali Shipping Corp v Shipyard Trogir* [1999] 1 WLR 314). However, the deployment by a party of its own documents in an arbitration does not clothe those documents with any confidentiality that they did not already possess (*Milsom v Ablyazov* [2011] EWHC 955 (Ch)).

28.08 In *Michael Wilson & Partners Ltd v Emmott* [2008] Bus LR 1361 Lawrence Collins LJ pointed out that the limits of the duty of confidentiality in arbitration proceedings are still being developed, and will depend on the context and the nature of the documents or information at issue. As the law now stands the principal cases where disclosure may be permitted are:

- where there is consent; and
- where a court grants permission, which it has a discretion to grant, where:
  - disclosure is reasonably necessary for the protection of the legitimate interests of an arbitrating party;
  - the interests of justice require disclosure; or
  - possibly, the public interest requires disclosure.

28.09 It may be in the interests of justice to permit the use of documents disclosed in an arbitration where the party giving disclosure has advanced inconsistent cases in the arbitration and in related litigation, to avoid the tribunal dealing with the related litigation being mislead

(*Michael Wilson & Partners Ltd v Emmott*). It may also be in the interests of justice to allow arbitral materials to be used to bring to light wrongdoing, such as an unlawful means conspiracy (*Westwood Shipping Lines Inc v Universal Schiffahrtscgesellschaft mbH* [2013] 1 Lloyd's Rep 670).

D RANGE OF PROCEDURAL APPROACHES IN ARBITRATION

A wide range of procedures are possible in arbitrations. These include: **28.10**

- very simple procedures, which do not even include a hearing. An example is the 'look-sniff' arbitration (see 28.26);
- short-form arbitrations (see 28.28 for an example);
- arbitrations that adopt the default procedures in the Arbitration Act 1996;
- arbitrations that adopt the rules of an arbitral institution. Institutional rules vary in length and detail, but will be typically 6–30 pages long. There will often be gaps in institutional rules, which will be filled by the default provisions of the Arbitration Act 1996. Arbitrations broadly following the Arbitration Act 1996 and the format of most domestic commercial arbitration rules are considered at 28.31;
- arbitrations where the parties, often in consultation with the arbitrators, agree on a bespoke procedure;
- arbitrations where the procedure draws heavily on the procedures in the CPR (or even the pre-CPR rules of court). An example is discussed at 28.83. This may happen because the particular institutional rules adopt CPR procedures, or because these are specifically adopted by the arbitrators. The CPR are vastly more detailed than even the most highly developed of the institutional rules on arbitration. One of the reasons for choosing arbitration is to enable the dispute to be resolved with a simpler set of procedures than those laid down in the CPR, so for many people wholesale adoption of the CPR in an arbitration would be a retrograde step.

Arbitration proceedings are usually less formal than court proceedings, although what actually happens depends on the parties, their lawyers, the arbitrators, and the institutional rules (if any) that govern the arbitration. It is a common fallback in domestic commercial arbitrations to adopt the standard court procedures laid down in the CPR to fill in gaps in the relevant arbitral institution rules or as the basis for formulating the procedure in an ad hoc arbitration. **28.11**

E PROCEDURAL RULES GOVERNING THE ARBITRATION

Bespoke arbitration clause

As parties are allowed to agree anything not covered by the mandatory provisions (see Table 26.3 for the non-mandatory issues that may be included), the parties and their lawyers may decide to make detailed provision for the procedure to be followed in the event of any dispute being referred to arbitration. This is most likely to arise where a party contracts on terms drafted with this in mind by its lawyers. As a practical matter, it is when a contract is being negotiated that it is easiest to secure agreement to such matters. **28.12**

Arbitral institution rules

There are many commercial and international organizations, trade associations, and professions, as well specialist dispute resolution organizations that publish their own rules **28.13** for arbitrations in their areas of interest. Examples of arbitral institutions are given in Table 28.1. Most institutional rules of arbitral institutions located in England and Wales have been written or redrafted in order to be consistent with the scheme of the Arbitration Act 1996. Obviously, the same cannot be said of international organizations, the rules of which are intended for use in a wide range of jurisdictions, including non-common-law countries.

28.14 The arbitral institutions listed in Table 28.1 are just examples, and with a very large number of different sets of rules there are inevitably differences in style, coverage and detail. Most rules cover:

- appointment of the arbitrators;
- pleadings;
- procedure and exchange of information and evidence;
- decision-making by the arbitrators;
- awards; and
- payment of fees and costs.

Table 28.1 Arbitral institutions

Institution	Full name	Area covered by rules
AAA	American Arbitration Association	Wide range of domestic and international arbitrations
CEDR	Centre for Effective Dispute Resolution	Commercial. It acts as an appointing and administering institution, applying the UNCITRAL rules
CIA	Chartered Institute of Arbitrators	Arbitration schemes for trade associations and professional bodies
CIETAC	China International Economic and Trade Arbitration Commission	International commercial arbitration
FOSFA	Federation of Oils, Seeds and Fats Association	Commodity disputes
GAFTA	Grain and Feed Trade Association	Commodity disputes
HKIAC	Hong Kong International Arbitration Centre	International commercial arbitration
ICC	International Chamber of Commerce	International commercial, financial, and technical disputes
ICE	Institute of Civil Engineers	Civil engineering disputes
ICSID	International Centre for Settlement of Investment Disputes	Investment disputes between states and nationals of other states
JCT	Joint Contracts Tribunal Ltd	Building disputes
LCIA	London Court of International Arbitration	International commercial arbitration
LMAA	London Maritime Arbitrators Association	Shipping arbitration
LME	London Metal Exchange Ltd	Metals trade etc disputes
PCA	Permanent Court of Arbitration	Differences between states
SIAC	Singapore International Arbitration Centre	Shipping, banking, insurance, construction
UNCITRAL	United Nations Commission on International Trade Law	International commercial contracts

Silence in institutional rules

Where the rules of an arbitral institution apply to an arbitration, but are silent on a non-mandatory matter covered by the Arbitration Act 1996, the relevant provision of the Arbitration Act 1996 applies. This follows from s 4(3), which allows the parties to make use of institutional rules, read together with s 4(2). This provides that while the parties can make their own arrangements by agreement, the non-mandatory provisions lay down rules 'which apply in the absence of such agreement'. **28.15**

F ROLE OF LEGAL REPRESENTATIVES IN ARBITRATION

Being an adjudicative process, solicitors and barristers representing clients in arbitrations need to be adept at all the traditional lawyering skills, from legal analysis to drafting, advising, and advocacy. **28.16**

Advice on the arbitration clause

A lawyer's input starts from the time a client is being advised on the drafting of the terms and conditions to be included in its standard terms of trading. Decisions have to be made on whether to include an arbitration clause (or indeed, some other dispute resolution clause) in those terms and conditions, and on the nature of the clause to be included. Key questions include: **28.17**

- the composition of the arbitral panel;
- whether to include use of a named set of rules from an arbitral institution;
- whether the arbitration should be administered by a named arbitral institution;
- the seat of the arbitration (see 29.11);
- the governing law (see 29.21);
- whether, and how, any non-mandatory provisions in the Arbitration Act 1996 should be adjusted;
- whether to require or dispense with reasons for the arbitrators' decision;
- the extent to which appeals to the courts should be allowed.

Often this involves a consideration of the client's priorities and business needs, as well as a good understanding of the relative merits and drawbacks of the various different sets of institutional rules governing arbitrations. **28.18**

Reference of a dispute to arbitration

When a dispute arises, the lawyer needs to come to a view on which documents constitute the substantive contract, and assess whether there is any arbitration clause and its effect. A clause may require reference of disputes to arbitration, or may permit such reference. Consideration is also needed on whether the actual dispute comes within the arbitration clause. Consideration is then required of the options available to the client, and tactically what is in the best interests of the client. This often depends on the nature of the dispute and what is needed in order to succeed. It may be that the strength of the case is primarily legal, which would make litigation attractive. On the other hand, privacy or obtaining a fair result may point towards arbitration. If there is a binding arbitration clause there will be no choice. **28.19**

Proper case analysis is required in formulating the nature of the dispute and the remedies that should be sought, or in formulating a response to a claim brought by the other side. **28.20**

This requires obtaining as full a picture as possible of the background facts and evidence as early as possible, because it is important to ensure that the dispute identified in the early correspondence accurately reflects the real problem so that the correct matter can be referred to arbitration, and that costs are not wasted in investigating a mistaken version of events.

Defining the issues

28.21 A clear statement of the client's case is required in the early stages of an arbitration, both in the initial reference to arbitration and in the statements of case that are usually required shortly after the tribunal is appointed. Lawyers play a key role in identifying the right issues, ensuring the correct causes of action are relied upon, and sustainable relief is sought. When acting for the respondent, each allegation made in the points of claim has to be responded to, so detailed instructions are required from the client both on whether these allegations are disputed, and on the nature of any affirmative case that should be advanced by the respondent. For both sides, this involves having conferences and meetings with the clients and their witnesses, and ensuring that all the relevant documentation is identified and provided for use in the arbitration.

Putting together the case

28.22 In most arbitrations a great deal of time has to be taken in collating the relevant documentation and in taking evidence from potential witnesses for the purpose of drafting their witness statements. Likewise, identifying expert witnesses on matters requiring expertise, putting together the necessary documents for the experts, instructing them, and finalizing their reports, requires a high level of expertise on the part of solicitors acting in arbitrations. Perhaps of even greater importance is deciding how to deal with the expert and other evidence provided by the other parties. Matters to consider include whether written questions should be put to the other side's experts, and whether a without prejudice meeting of the experts from both sides would be an advantage.

28.23 Considerable care is required over the disclosure of documents and the compilation of bundles of documents for any hearings before the tribunal. This may involve considering the scope of disclosure and privilege in a number of jurisdictions, particularly in international arbitrations. An accurate appreciation of the issues is needed to ensure that the documentation used, whether in the disclosure process or included in the bundles for the tribunal, covers the issues that are relevant to the dispute. Translations may also be required, with care needing to be taken that these are accurate.

Hearings

28.24 While it is possible to have decisions in arbitrations on the papers, it is more usual to have one or a number of hearings both for the tribunal to hear from the witnesses and for the parties to make submissions. Usually, English arbitrations follow an adversarial approach, but this is not an absolute requirement, and less formal approaches are encountered. Typically, counsel will be briefed, and counsel will produce written skeleton arguments or written submissions on how the facts and evidence should be analysed within the framework of the relevant legal principles. If witnesses are to be heard, the usual approach is to take their witness statements as their testimony on behalf of the party calling them (their evidence-in-chief), but they will be cross-examined by counsel for the other party, as well as being questioned by the tribunal. Legal representatives therefore need the full range of forensic skills in preparing for and appearing at arbitral hearings, which are often conducted with a similar level of formality as court hearings.

G COMMENCEMENT

Arbitrations are commenced by sending a notice of arbitration (see 27.08) and then appointing the members of the arbitral tribunal (see 27.10–27.17). It is relatively unusual for terms of reference to be drawn up, but see 27.23. **28.25**

H 'LOOK-SNIFF' ARBITRATIONS

'Look-sniff' arbitrations are most commonly met in disputes over the quality of goods in import-export transactions. If the dispute boils down to whether the goods match the contract specification or description, it may be that all that is needed is for an expert in the field to go to the warehouse or storage tank, have a look at the goods, do other tests (such as sniffing them, but nowadays also more scientific tests), and to express a view on the quality of the goods (such as the appropriate grade of fruit, or the fineness of textiles or flour etc). In these cases delay is to be avoided, because of possible market fluctuations and the risk of deterioration. The procedure is largely aimed at agreeing on a suitably qualified arbitrator, with a minimum of documents, and a minimum of argument (even on paper) from the parties, because all that is needed is a decision on the quality of the goods as seen by the arbitrator. **28.26**

There is not a great deal of distinction between this type of arbitration and the process of expert evaluation (see Chapter 22). **28.27**

I SHORT-FORM ARBITRATIONS

It is recognized that the full-blown procedure under the Arbitration Act 1996 and the full arbitration rules of many arbitral institutions are too expensive and unnecessary for disputes of a simple nature or where the monetary value of the dispute is relatively low. A number of arbitral institutions have therefore promulgated short-form procedures to deal with these cases on a cost-efficient basis. An example is the ICE Short Procedure. **28.28**

Under the ICE Short Procedure, r 14.2, within two working days after the appointment of the arbitrator the claimant is required to deliver a file setting out its case to the arbitrator and the respondent, which must contain: **28.29**

- a statement of the orders or awards sought;
- a statement of the reasons for being entitled to those orders or awards; and
- copies of all the documents relied upon, including any witness statements relied upon.

The respondent must deliver its defence in the same format within 14 days of receiving the claimant's file. No counterclaim is permitted. If the respondent has a cross-claim it has to be brought as a separate reference (r 14.4). Following delivery of the respondent's file there is a 14-day period during which the parties may comment on the other side's case, and in which they may add to or remove documents from their file. Normally there is no formal hearing (r 14.9) and the arbitrator makes an award on considering the papers within 14 days of the close of the parties' files (r 14.6). There is a power to extend this period, and the arbitrator may hold a site visit, require either or both parties to submit further documents or information, or to attend a meeting for the purpose of answering questions (r 14.8). The arbitrator **28.30** also has a discretion to hold a hearing with cross-examination of witnesses (r 14.9), although doing so rather detracts from the procedure being 'short'. The normal rule under the ICE Short Procedure rules is that each side bears its own costs (r 14.7).

J GENERAL PROCEDURE IN COMMERCIAL ARBITRATION

28.31 Figure 28.1 is a flow diagram showing the main stages followed in an arbitration, which broadly adopts the procedures in the Arbitration Act 1996 and most domestic commercial arbitration rules. These are aimed at ensuring the fair resolution of the dispute without unnecessary delay

Figure 28.1 Typical steps in arbitration proceedings

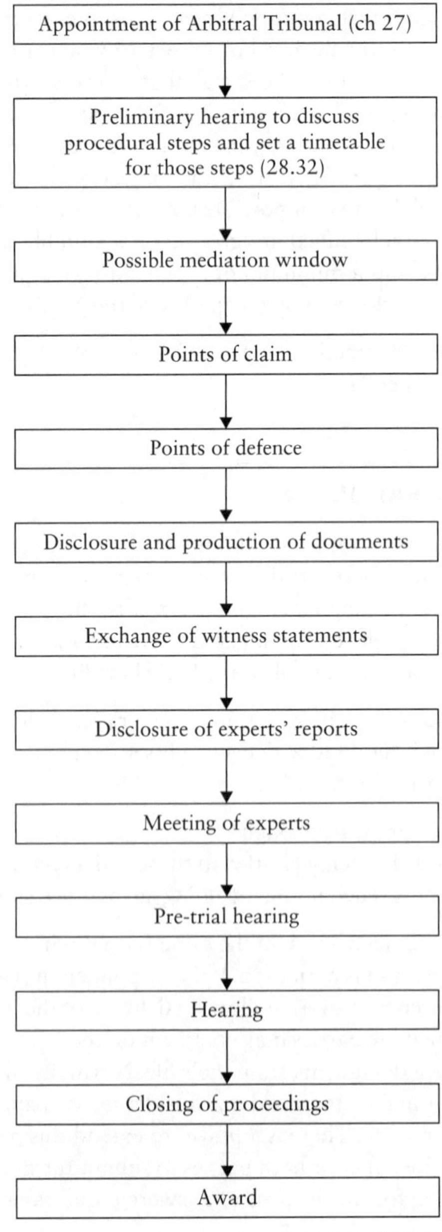

or expense (Arbitration Act 1996 s 1(a)). This is achieved by adopting procedures suitable for the circumstances of the particular case (s 33(1)(b)). Different stages in the process may be heavily prescribed by the rules of an arbitral institution as chosen by the parties. In the absence of agreement the default provisions of the Arbitration Act 1996 will apply.

Preliminary meeting

A preliminary meeting will often be convened shortly after the tribunal is appointed. Its actual timing is a matter for the arbitrators, and there is no absolute requirement to hold such a meeting. It is an opportunity for the parties and arbitrators to see each other, but its main purpose is as a forum for the tribunal to discuss jurisdictional matters and to make procedural directions for the preparation of the evidence needed for deciding the reference. There is no set agenda for preliminary meetings. It may well be possible for directions to be agreed between the parties, which will make a preliminary meeting less necessary. It is becoming increasingly common to hold preliminary meetings by conference telephone calls or through video-conferencing. **28.32**

Procedural orders

In accordance with the principle that the parties are free to agree how their dispute should be resolved (Arbitration Act 1996 s 1(b)), the following discussion on the powers of arbitrators to make provisional orders is subject to any contrary agreement between the parties. **28.33**

Interim payments, security for costs, etc

The Arbitration Act 1996 s 39, gives an arbitral tribunal the power to make orders on a provisional basis on any relief which it had the power to grant in a final award. This includes, for example, making a provisional order for an interim payment, or for the disposition of property between the parties (s 39(2)), and to provide security for costs (s 38(3)). These subjects are considered in Sime, *A Practical Approach to Civil Procedure* (17th edn, OUP, 2014, chs 25 and 26). A provisional award for an interim payment, of course, has to be taken into account in the arbitral tribunal's final award (s 39(3)). **28.34**

Directions on procedure and evidence

More generally, it is for the arbitration tribunal to decide all procedural and evidential matters that have been referred to it, subject to the right of the parties to agree such matters between themselves (Arbitration Act 1996 s 34(1)). By s 34(2), procedural and evidential matters include: **28.35**

- when and where any part of the proceedings is to be held;
- the language or languages to be used in the proceedings and whether translations of any relevant documents are to be supplied;
- whether any and if so what form of written statements of claim and defence are to be used, when these should be supplied and the extent to which such statements can be later amended;
- whether any and if so which documents or classes of documents should be disclosed between and produced by the parties and at what stage;
- whether any and if so what questions should be put to and answered by the respective parties and when and in what form this should be done;
- whether to apply strict rules of evidence (or any other rules) as to the admissibility, relevance, or weight of any material (oral, written, or other) sought to be tendered on any matters of fact or opinion, and the time, manner, and form in which such material should be exchanged and presented;

- whether and to what extent the tribunal should itself take the initiative in ascertaining the facts and the law; and
- whether and to what extent there should be oral or written evidence or submissions.

28.36 The tribunal may fix the time within which any directions given by it are to be complied with, and may if it thinks fit extend the time so fixed (whether or not it has expired) (s 34(3)).

Conservatory measures

28.37 There will be some cases where it is important to preserve the subject-matter of a dispute, or to allow an expert retained by the other side to have access to land, goods, or vehicles relevant to the dispute. In these cases the Arbitration Act 1996 s 38(4), provides:

> The tribunal may give directions in relation to any property which is the subject of the proceedings or as to which any question arises in the proceedings, and which is owned by or is in the possession of a party to the proceedings—
>
> (a) for the inspection, photographing, preservation, custody or detention of the property by the tribunal, an expert or a party, or
> (b) ordering that samples be taken from, or any observation be made of or experiment conducted upon, the property.

28.38 It is to be noted that these powers may be exercised for the benefit of the arbitrators, an expert, or another party. Such directions only extend to property in the possession of another party to the proceedings. If the property belongs to a non-party, it may be possible to get a court order permitting inspection etc under s 44(2)(c) (see Chapter 31).

Procedural matters typically considered

28.39 The matters that need to be decided once the tribunal has been appointed, either at the preliminary meeting or in correspondence, depends on the nature of the dispute, the terms of the agreement to arbitrate, any institutional rules, and the preferences of the parties and arbitrators. Typical matters that might be considered are included in the directions that are set out in Figure 28.2, a set of interim directions in an arbitration to resolve a dispute relating to a contract alleged to have been tainted by bribery.

Figure 28.2 Interim directions in an arbitration

IN THE MATTER OF THE ARBITRATION ACT 1996

AND

IN THE MATTER OF AN ARBITRATION

BETWEEN

CHIPOKA AIRWAYS LIMITED

Claimant

and

RUNWAY AIRCRAFT MAINTENANCE LIMITED

Respondent

INTERIM DIRECTIONS

Upon hearing the solicitors for the parties the following directions are given:

1. That there be statements of case in this arbitration as follows:

1.1 Points of Claim to be delivered within 21 days from this date.

Figure 28.2 Interim directions in an arbitration (*Continued*)

1.2 Points of Defence (and Counterclaim if any) to be delivered within 21 days from delivery of the Points of Claim.
1.3 Points of Reply (and Defence to Counterclaim if any) to be delivered within 21 days from delivery of the Points of Defence (and Counterclaim).
2. That the Claimant and the Respondent do each deliver to the other a list of the documents on which it relies within 14 days of delivery of the Points of Reply (and Defence to Counterclaim if any) together with copies of all the listed documents.
3. That the Claimant and Respondent mutually exchange written witness statements for each factual witness they intend to call at the hearing within 28 days after disclosure of documents.
4. That expert witnesses be limited to one forensic accountant for each party, and limited to an expert whose written report has been delivered to the other party within 56 days after the exchange of witness statements.
5. Within 14 days after the delivery of experts' reports the parties shall deliver to the Arbitrators their estimates for the length of the hearing and their and their witnesses' dates of availability.
6. There be a without prejudice discussion between the experts not less than 28 days before the hearing, and a statement of the areas of agreement and disagreement must be signed by both experts not less than 14 days before the hearing.
7. Any communication with the Arbitrators shall also be copied to the other party by the party writing to the Arbitrators.
8. The parties are to agree any financial loss and other financial figures if possible.
9. Not less than 14 days before the hearing each party shall deliver a written summary of their submissions on each of the matters to be decided.
10. Not less than 14 days before the hearing the Claimant shall deliver to the Arbitrators all the documents relevant to the hearing in ring binders with all the pages copied legibly and page numbered. Identical files shall be provided by the Claimant for both parties and a further copy must be available at the hearing for the use of witnesses.
11. The Claimant shall be responsible for hiring of suitable rooms for the hearing. The hire costs shall be costs in the arbitration.
12. The costs of the preliminary hearing shall be costs in the arbitration.
13. The dates for the hearing shall be notified to the parties after the Arbitrators have had the opportunity to consider the respective parties' and witnesses' availability.
14. Permission to apply for further or other directions.

DATED 3 March 2014
Signed: (1)
(2)
(3)
Arbitrators

Peremptory orders

While the parties are free to agree on the powers of the arbitral tribunal to deal with procedural default (Arbitration Act 1996 s 41(1)), unless otherwise agreed the powers in s 41(5)–(7) will apply. They apply where an order requires a step to be taken within a prescribed time, and one or other of the parties fails to comply within the time limit. These subsections give the tribunal a range of powers so that any default can be dealt with in a proportionate manner. **28.40**

28.41 By s 41(5), the tribunal may make a peremptory order requiring the same steps to be taken as an existing order where a party fails to comply with the previous order or direction without showing sufficient cause. These peremptory orders operate in much the same way as 'unless' orders in normal litigation (see Sime, *A Practical Approach to Civil Procedure* (17th edn, OUP, 2014), ch 37). The wording of s 41(5) means that a peremptory order may only be made if an ordinary order has been made first (*Wicketts v Brine Builders* [2001] CILL 1805).

28.42 If a party fails to comply with a peremptory order, by s 41(7) the arbitral tribunal may do any of the following:

- direct that the defaulting party shall not be entitled to rely on any allegation or material that was the subject-matter of the order;
- draw such adverse inferences from the act of non-compliance as the circumstances justify;
- proceed to an award on the basis of such materials as have been properly provided to it; or
- make such order as it thinks fit as to the payment of costs of the arbitration incurred in consequence of the non-compliance.

28.43 What the arbitrators cannot do is impose penal sanctions for default (committal to prison or a fine), these being powers only exercisable by a court. Where the innocent party has exhausted all the available arbitral processes to seek compliance with an arbitral tribunal order, unless otherwise agreed by the parties the innocent party may apply to the High Court for an order requiring the defaulting party to comply with the peremptory order (s 42), which may include committal for non-compliance. Section 42 confers a discretion on the court, which does not act as a rubber stamp on orders made by the tribunal (*Patley Wood Farm LLP v Brake* [2013] EWHC 4035 (Ch)). However, it will be inconsistent with the general principle in s 1(c) (see 26.51) for the court to be too ready to review the decision made by the tribunal, the primary question for the court being whether a court order is required in the interests of justice to assist with the proper functioning of the arbitral process (*Emmott v Michael Wilson & Partners Ltd* [2009] 1 Lloyd's Rep 233).

Dismissal for inordinate and inexcusable delay

28.44 Where the claimant in an arbitration is guilty of inordinate and inexcusable delay that:

- gives rise, or is likely to give rise, to a substantial risk that it is not possible to have a fair resolution of the issues in the arbitration; or
- has caused or is likely to cause, serious prejudice to the respondent,

the tribunal may make an award dismissing the claim (Arbitration Act 1996 s 41(3)).

28.45 Dismissal for inordinate and inexcusable delay is the equivalent of a former procedure by the same name under the pre-CPR High Court procedural rules. There was a great deal of reported case law on this concept in relation to ordinary litigation, all of which is now redundant. The leading case was *Birkett v James* [1978] AC 297, but it is these principles that are enshrined in s 41(3). It is a restrictive concept, and there are not many cases where there is both the protracted delay contemplated by the subsection and the substantial risk that it is no longer possible to deal fairly with the arbitration or where there is serious prejudice to the respondent. An example where dismissal was upheld is *TAG Wealth Management v West* [2008] 2 Lloyd's Rep 699 where the claimant was responsible for five years of delay in dealing with disclosure of documents in the arbitration. Dismissal under s 41(3) is only possible if the limitation period has expired (*Lazenby (James) & Co v McNicholas Construction Co Ltd* [1999] 3 All ER 820).

Statements of case

Statements of case are intended to set out the respective contentions on the dispute by the parties. The Arbitration Act 1996 s 34(1) says it is for the tribunal to decide all procedural and evidential matters, subject to the right of the parties to agree any matter. Procedural matters by s 34(2)(d) include whether any and if so what form of written statements of claim and defence are to be used, when these should be supplied and the extent to which such statements can be later amended. It follows that the tribunal may decide against the use of formal pleadings, and this may be sensible where the dispute is reasonably straightforward. In some cases the tribunal may decide that the issues can best be defined by requiring the parties to provide lists of issues. In most other cases statements of case will be used. Like pleadings in court proceedings, these are intended: **28.46**

- to set out what happened;
- to set out each side's case;
- to define the issues (through the responses to each allegation in subsequent statements of case); and
- to set out the relief sought and the respondent's response on whether that relief is available.

There are no set rules on what the statements of case should be called, or indeed on whether they should be called statements of case, pleadings, or case summaries. Typically the claimant will start with its points of claim, with the respondent's case being set out in its points of defence. If the respondent has a cross-claim, the response is called the points of defence and counterclaim. The tribunal may allow further statements of case, which would continue with a claimant's points of reply (and defence to counterclaim). Examples of points of claim and points of defence in the same bribery case as the interim directions in Figure 28.2 can be seen in Figures 28.3 and 28.4. **28.47**

Figures 28.3 and 28.4 broadly follow the approach in English court proceedings, but in a slightly less formal way. The technical rules of pleading in CPR Part 16, do not apply in arbitrations. It is good practice to set out the facts and legal consequences in a statement of case, while avoiding setting out evidence and legal arguments. However, a wide range of practice is encountered, particularly in international arbitrations where the lawyers may practise in jurisdictions with very different traditions on setting out a client's statement of case. **28.48**

Figure 28.3 Points of claim

IN THE MATTER OF THE ARBITRATION ACT 1996

AND

IN THE MATTER OF AN ARBITRATION

BETWEEN

CHIPOKA AIRWAYS LIMITED

<u>Claimant</u>

and

RUNWAY AIRCRAFT MAINTENANCE LIMITED

<u>Respondent</u>

POINTS OF CLAIM

---

1. The Claimant is a limited company incorporated and registered under the Companies Act 1985 and at all material times ran an international airline service operating from Chipoka Airport in Malawi, Africa.

(Continued)

Figure 28.3 (*Continued*)

2. The Respondent was at all material times a company providing aircraft maintenance and repair services.
3. In about October 2009 Aircraft Service Agencies plc approached the Claimant with a proposal that the Respondent was a suitable company to service the Claimant's fleet of four Boeing 737-800 jet airliners ('the four aircraft').
4. By a contract in writing dated 12 March 2010 ('the Contract') the Respondent agreed to provide aircraft maintenance services for the Claimant in respect of the four aircraft for a period of five years from 6 April 2010 to 5 April 2015.
5. The Claimant will rely on the Contract for its full terms, meaning and effect.
6. There were express terms of the Contract that:
   (a) the Claimant would pay sums to the Respondent on a power-by-the-hour basis under which specified sums would be paid in respect of each of the four aircraft for every hour it was in flight;
   (b) any work done on the four aircraft not covered by the power-by-the-hour clause would be charged by the Respondent to the Claimant at US $40.00 per hour;
   (c) the Respondent would undertake all maintenance and inspection work required on the four aircraft for the duration of the Contract; and
   (d) any dispute or difference arising out of or in connection with the Contract shall be administered by the London Court of International Arbitration and finally determined under the Rules of the London Court of International Arbitration by three arbitrators appointed in accordance with those Rules.
7. Unknown to the Claimant the Respondent paid certain sums to Aircraft Service Agencies plc which were used by Aircraft Service Agencies plc to pay bribes to the directors of the Claimant for the purpose of obtaining the Claimant's agreement to enter into the Contract.
8. The Claimant discovered the matters set out in paragraph 7 above on hearing of proceedings between Aircraft Service Agencies plc and the Respondent in which Aircraft Service Agencies plc sought to recover its commission from the Respondent, in which the Respondent set up the illegality of the commission payments on the basis of the bribes which the Respondent alleged were paid to the Claimant's directors.
9. As a result of the matters set out in paragraph 7 above the Claimant is entitled to and does treat the Contract as vitiated for fraud and/or corruption.
10. By a letter from the Claimant's solicitors to the Respondent dated 25 October 2013 the Claimant sought to recover the sums it had paid to the Respondent under the Contract. By a letter dated 22 November 2013 the Respondent accepted that the Contract was vitiated for fraud and/or corruption, but disputed the amount that is payable to the Claimant.
11. It is common ground between the Claimant and the Respondent that the total amount paid by the Claimant to the Respondent pursuant to the Contract was the sum of US $55,553,886.03.
12. Of the sum of US $55,553,886.03 paid by the Claimant to the Respondent the amount paid by the Claimant to the Respondent as represented the provision for commissions payable to Aircraft Service Agencies plc in excess of the Respondent's selling price was the sum of US $9,887,480.38.
13. In the circumstances, the Claimant is entitled to repayment of the sum of US $55,553,886.03. Alternatively the Claimant, in the bona fide and reasonable, but mistaken, belief that the amounts were payable to the Respondent, effected payments totalling US $55,553,886.03 to the Respondent and the Respondent was unjustly enriched at the Claimant's expense in that amount.

Figure 28.3 *(Continued)*

14. Alternatively to paragraph 13, the Claimant is entitled to repayment of the sum of US \$9,887,430,38, alternatively the Claimant, in the bona fide and reasonable, but mistaken, belief that the amounts were payable to the Respondent, effected payments totalling US \$9,887,430,38 to the Respondent and the Respondent was unjustly enriched at the Claimant's expense in that amount.
15. The Claimant has demanded payment of the above sums and the Respondent has refused to make payment of all or any part of the sums so demanded.

AND the Claimant therefore seeks an award against the Respondent as follows:

(a) Payment of the sum of US \$55,553,886.03, alternatively
(b) Payment of the sum of US \$9,887,480.38;
(c) Interest pursuant to the Arbitration Act 1996, section 49, on the amount found to be due to the Claimant at such rate and for such period as the arbitral tribunal considers appropriate.
(d) Costs.

I believe that the facts stated in these Points of Claim are true.

SERVED this 24 day of March 2014 by Taylor, Andrews & Co., Solicitors, of 36 High Street, Birmingham, B4 8YD

Signed:
Dated: 24 March 2014

Evidence

An arbitral tribunal has a wide discretion on whether to apply the strict rules of evidence (or any other rules) as to the admissibility, relevance or weight of any material (oral, written, or other) sought to be tendered on any matters of fact or opinion (Arbitration Act 1996 s 34(2)(f)).The discretion has to be exercised in ways that are consistent with the fair resolution of the dispute (s 1(a)). **28.49**

Figure 28.4 Points of defence and counterclaim

IN THE MATTER OF THE ARBITRATION ACT 1996

AND

IN THE MATTER OF AN ARBITRATION

BETWEEN

CHIPOKA AIRWAYS LIMITED

Claimant

and

RUNWAY AIRCRAFT MAINTENANCE LIMITED

Respondent

POINTS OF DEFENCE
AND COUNTERCLAIM

1. The Respondent adopts the definitions used in the Points of Claim.
2. The allegations in paragraphs 1 to 6 of the Points of Claim are admitted.

(Continued)

Figure 28.4 *(Continued)*

3. Except that the Respondent is unable to admit or deny and requires the Claimant to prove that the payment of the bribes was unknown to the Claimant or when the Claimant discovered the matters set out in paragraph 7 of the Points of Claim, paragraphs 7 and 8 of the Points of Claim are admitted.
4. The allegations in paragraphs 9 to 11 of the Points of Claim are admitted.
5. The Respondent denies each and every allegation contained in paragraphs 12 and 13 of the Points of Claim as if specifically traversed and puts the Claimant to the proof of those allegations.
6. The Respondent denies each and every allegation contained in paragraph 14 of the Points of Claim as if specifically traversed and the Claimant is put to the proof of those allegations.
7. Without derogating from the generality of the denials in paragraphs 5 and 6, Respondent pleads that:
   7.1. it performed all its obligations under the Contract and gave good and proper value by way of its services and inspections provided under the Contract to the Claimant;
   7.2. it has not been unjustly enriched nor has the Claimant been prejudiced;
   7.3. the Claimant has received the services and inspections it required and for which it had contracted at a fair cost.
8. The Respondent:
   8.1. avers that if the Claimant were to succeed in these proceedings, it would receive the full value in respect of the services rendered by the Respondent without giving credit for the value of those services, and taking such benefit without giving credit would, in all the circumstances, be inequitable and not in accordance with the law;
   8.2 relies upon the Counterclaim set out below.
9. The allegations in paragraph 15 of the Points of Claim are admitted.
10. In the event of it being found that the Contract entered into by the Claimant and the Respondent was tainted by bribery and/or corruption and that, as a result, the Claimant is entitled to the relief sought in this arbitration, then and in that event the Respondent proceeds with the Counterclaim set out below.

POINTS OF COUNTERCLAIM

11. The Respondent repeats its Points of Defence.
12. The Respondent performed all its obligations under the Contract and gave good and proper value by way of its services under the Contract, in accordance with the provisions of the Claimant's approved maintenance schedule, and further, in accordance with such instructions as were given to the Respondent by the Claimant from time to time, the Respondent rendered technical services, in the form of, among other things, special inspections and/or replacement of parts on the four aircraft.
13. At the time it entered into the Contract, the Respondent was not aware of the possible illegality of the Contract and/or the possible illegality of the performance of the Contract.
14. The Respondent has performed under the Contract and has, in terms of the Contract, received payment in respect of the maintenance and inspection services rendered and the parts replaced on the four aircraft. In the circumstances an award to the effect that the Respondent should repay to the Claimant the amount of US $55,553,866.03 or any part of that sum would have the effect of enriching the Claimant at the expense of the Respondent in that sum of money, the Claimant having received the benefit of the

Figure 28.4 *(Continued)*

servicing, parts and inspections in respect of the four aircraft under the alleged illegal Contract.

15. The retention by the Respondent of the amount of US $55,553,866.03 or any part of that sum would not be contrary to public policy, and/or would not be unjust and inequitable, in the circumstances.

AND the Respondent Counterclaims:

That the Respondent is entitled to a declaration to the effect that it is entitled to the retention of the amount of US $55,553,866.03 or such other sum as the arbitral tribunal shall decide.

I believe that the facts stated in these Points of Defence and Counterclaim are true.

SERVED this 15th day of April 2014 by Scott & Avery LLP., Solicitors, of 16-24 Archway Road, London WC2H 6SP

Signed:

Dated: 15th April 2014

By the Arbitration Act 1996 s 34(2)(d), the tribunal must consider whether any, and if so which, documents or classes of documents should be disclosed between and produced by the parties and at what stage. From the use of the word 'any' it is clear the tribunal may decide against any form of disclosure of documents. Far more frequently, the tribunal will make a direction requiring the parties to disclose to the tribunal and to each other the documents that will assist the arbitrator in deciding the dispute. There is no requirement to import the concept of 'standard disclosure' from the CPR r 31.6. Disclosure may be limited to specified categories of documents, or to the documents on which each side relies. There are cases where disclosure of adverse documents in the possession of each side, or documents that support the other side's case, may also be required by the arbitrators' directions. **28.50**

Method of disclosure

The form in which disclosure is given does not have to follow court procedures. This may be done simply by providing copies to the other side and the tribunal. Sometimes a list is specified in the arbitrators' directions, but it need not have the formalities laid down in CPR Part 31, unless that is specified too. A particular form used in arbitration is what is called a 'Redfern Schedule' (after one of the authors of *Redfern and Hunter on International Arbitration* by Redfern, Hunter, and Blackaby (6th edn, OUP, 2014)). An example is shown in Figure 28.5. **28.51**

Figure 28.5 Redfern schedule

IN THE MATTER OF THE ARBITRATION ACT 1996

AND

IN THE MATTER OF AN ARBITRATION

BETWEEN

CHIPOKA AIRWAYS LIMITED

Claimant

and

RUNWAY AIRCRAFT MAINTENANCE LIMITED

Respondent

(Continued)

Figure 28.5 *(Continued)*

REDFERN SCHEDULE

Description of document	Respondent's objection	Claimant's response	Arbitrators' ruling
Draft statement of James Morris	Protected by legal professional privilege	Agreed	Not required
Invoice 54546	Not relevant to the issues in this reference	Relevant to issue of how much the Respondent paid to Aircraft Service Agencies plc	Relevant and disclosable
Respondent's list of aircraft maintenance service parts and labour costs 2010	This document is a trade secret as it sets out cost prices for the Respondent's services which would undermine its business if disclosed to competitors or customers	Highly relevant to the issues in this reference. The confidentiality of the list can be maintained by the privacy of these proceedings and a suitable undertaking on behalf of the Claimant	To be disclosed on an undertaking on behalf of the Claimant and its lawyers

Implied obligation of confidentiality

28.52 Parties to an arbitration are under an implied obligation not to use or disclose any documents provided to them by the other parties for any purpose outside the scope of the reference (*Dolling-Baker v Merrett* [1991] 2 All ER 891). This is very similar to the implied undertaking relating to disclosed documents in litigation (CPR r 31.22). A significant difference is that in litigation the undertaking is lifted once documents are used in open court, whereas the obligation in arbitration continues after a hearing because of the privacy of arbitration proceedings.

Witness statements

28.53 It is common for arbitrators to make directions for the exchange of witness statements from factual witnesses intended to be relied upon at the hearing.

Experts

Party-appointed experts

28.54 As with court proceedings, there are concerns in arbitrations over the cost of expert evidence. Directions frequently impose limits on the expert evidence that each party may rely upon, typically restricting the parties to one expert in each relevant field of expertise. Usually the directions will require the parties to deliver copies of their experts' written reports to each other and the tribunal by a specified date. It is also common for further directions to cover things like putting written questions to the other side's experts, which must be answered in writing, and for the experts in a particular field to have a without prejudice discussion for the purpose of seeking agreement and identifying where they disagree.

Tribunal-appointed experts

Under the Arbitration Act 1996 s 37(1), unless otherwise agreed by the parties the tribunal may appoint experts or legal advisers to report to it and the parties, or appoint assessors to assist it on technical matters. The parties must be given a reasonable opportunity to comment on any information, opinion, or advice offered by an expert appointed by the tribunal, and the tribunal may allow the expert, legal adviser, or assessor to attend the proceedings. The fees of a tribunal-appointed expert need to be provided for. Usually they are paid by the parties. **28.55**

Pre-trial hearing/conference

If the arbitration is of some complexity it may be sensible to hold a pre-trial hearing or conference. This will usually take place a number of weeks before the expected start of the hearing. Frequently the tribunal will want the advocates who will be representing the parties at the final hearing to attend so that matters relating to the management of the hearing can be discussed with the lawyers who will be there. The main purpose is to review what has been done in preparation for the hearing, to assess whether the parties are going to be ready for the hearing (so there is no need to adjourn), to make any directions that will assist in ensuring both parties are ready for the hearing, and to agree how the hearing can be conducted in the most efficient manner. For example, it may be that costs will be saved by having the experts for both sides dealt with on specified days of the hearing, to avoid having to pay retainers when they are not needed. A procedural hearing at this stage can also be a catalyst for either settling the dispute or narrowing the issues. **28.56**

No right to an oral hearing

Before the Arbitration Act 1996 the parties to an arbitration had the right to demand an oral hearing. Under the Arbitration Act 1996 s 34(2)(h), subject to contrary agreement between the parties, the tribunal can decide whether and to what extent there should be oral or written evidence or submissions. In deciding whether to deal with the dispute on the documents or after an oral hearing the tribunal must bear in mind the need to act fairly, giving every party a reasonable opportunity of putting its case and dealing with that of the other side, and the need to avoid unnecessary expense and delay (s 33(1)). In *Boulos Gad Tourism and Hotels Ltd v Uniground Shipping Co Ltd* (2001) LTL 21/2/2002 Tomlinson J said it was unwise of the tribunal to have proceeded without a hearing on an arbitration where a substantial amount of money was at stake, although the arbitrators were acting within their powers in doing so. **28.57**

While the Arbitration Act 1996 therefore allows a tribunal to make an award without an oral hearing, a number of institutional rules reverse this and give the parties the right to insist on an oral hearing. **28.58**

Bundles

Directions are usually made for the compilation of bundles for the hearing. This task is usually given to the claimant. Bundles will be needed for all members of the tribunal, each of the parties, and for the use of witnesses. Bundles should be paginated and identical. **28.59**

Bundles are usually compiled in consultation between the parties. They will usually contain the documents dealing with the reference to the arbitration and the appointment of the tribunal. They will then usually have the statements of case, in order (points of claim, then defence, then reply), with any amendments standing in place of the original, and any answers **28.60** to requests for clarification of a statement of case coming immediately after the relevant statement of case. Procedural orders and directions usually come next.

28.61 It may well be that separate bundles will be required for the evidence. These files should be divided into the contemporaneous documentation, the witness statements of the factual witnesses, and the expert evidence. Care is needed in organizing the files of evidence where this is voluminous. It is usual to group similar documents together, and to maintain chronological order within sections of these files. There may also be a need for a correspondence file dealing with correspondence since the dispute arose.

28.62 A further file is likely to be needed to contain the written opening submissions or skeleton arguments (and in due course the closing submissions or skeleton arguments), together with the legal authorities relevant to the dispute. Unless there is something unusual, all the authorities that the legal representatives wish to refer to will feature in the written submissions or skeleton arguments.

Arrangements for the hearing

28.63 Fixing dates for a hearing can be difficult, particularly where a number of witnesses and experts will need to attend, and where there is a multi-member tribunal. Directions are often made that the claimant must book the necessary rooms for the hearing (in addition to the main room for the hearing, other rooms are usually necessary for each of the parties and the tribunal). Hearings often take place in hotels or rooms provided by the arbitral institution. Arrangements may also be needed for the appointment of a secretary to the tribunal, and for the recording or transcription of the evidence and submissions given at the hearing. It is increasingly common for the evidence of some of the witnesses to be given through video-conferencing or similar means and, if so, arrangements will need to be in place for the hearing.

The hearing

Adversarial or inquisitorial

28.64 It is clear from the Arbitration Act 1996 s 34(2)(e) and (g), which provide that the arbitral tribunal can decide whether and to what extent it should take the initiative in ascertaining the facts and the law, that arbitrators can choose to adopt either an adversarial (the traditional English court method of conducting hearings) or inquisitorial (civil law system) approach to the hearing. In English arbitrations the adversarial system remains dominant.

Written submissions and skeleton arguments

28.65 The modern approach is for the opening and closing submissions by the advocates for the parties in an arbitration to be by or supported by written submissions or skeleton arguments. Written submissions tend to be reasonably full, and at their extreme completely replace oral submissions. They can be very long (it is not unknown for them to exceed 100 pages in complex cases). They perhaps merge with 'written briefs' that originated in other jurisdictions, which often contain a large amount of documentary evidence as well as written submissions on the law and how the party would like it applied to the facts.

28.66 Skeleton arguments are intended to summarize the main submissions that will be made, and include some of the detailed information or law that would otherwise have to delivered at dictation pace at the hearing. In *Raja v Van Hoogstraten (No 9)* [2009] 1 WLR 1143 Mummery LJ said that skeleton arguments should not be prepared as verbatim scripts to be read out in public or as footnoted theses to be read in private. Good skeleton arguments are tools with practical uses: an agenda for the hearing, a summary of the main points, propositions and arguments to be developed orally, a useful way of noting citations and references, a convenient place for making cross-references, a time-saving means of avoiding unnecessary dictation to the court, and laborious and pointless note-taking by the court. They are aids to oral advocacy, not substitutes for oral argument.

It is usually necessary to prepare these documents (or at least prepare the substance of them) well in advance of the hearing. There will usually be a direction for the exchange and delivery to the tribunal of opening written submissions or opening skeleton arguments a stated period in advance of the hearing. **28.67**

Witnesses

Witnesses in arbitrations usually attend voluntarily, because the tribunal has no power to issue witness summonses (which compel attendance). If a witness summons is needed for an unwilling witness, it is possible to obtain one by making an application to the High Court (Arbitration Act 1996 s 43). **28.68**

Witnesses are rarely sworn in arbitrations. Their witness statements are usually taken as their evidence-in-chief, so the party relying on their evidence will usually ask only a few questions to establish the witness's identity, involvement in the dispute, and to deal with any relevant documents or corrections to their statements. Unless the expected answer is not controversial, the usual rule is that questions during examination-in-chief should be non-leading (see 28.70 for leading questions). It is intended that everything that the witness knows that is relevant to establishing the case of the party calling them should be in the exchanged witness statement. By verifying their statement the witness adopts it, which is why there should be no need to ask further questions in-chief. **28.69**

Witnesses are then tendered for cross-examination, which often follows the same format as in court proceedings. In cross-examination the advocate is allowed to use leading questions (broadly, these are questions that suggest the intended answer, or that give the witness a choice of answering 'yes' or 'no'). The purpose of cross-examination is to advance the case of the cross-examining party. It may be that some witnesses who are cross-examined can help the cross-examining party on certain issues and, if so, the opportunity should not be lost in obtaining this helpful evidence. Otherwise, the cross-examining party may seek to undermine or limit the potential effect of the witness by asking questions designed to show the witness may be mistaken, or not to have understood what they think they saw, or that their memory may have faded, or to point out inconsistencies between their witness statement and other evidence in the case. **28.70**

After being cross-examined each witness may be re-examined by the party who called them. Strictly, questions in re-examination should be put in non-leading form, and should be restricted to points raised in cross-examination. **28.71**

The tribunal is able to ask its own questions of witnesses at any point while they are giving evidence. **28.72**

Witness conferencing

An alternative to having witnesses called in sequence is to have a number of witnesses give evidence simultaneously. This process is sometimes called witness conferencing, or colloquially as 'hot tubbing'. Precise mechanics vary, but fairly typically the tribunal will consult with the parties over which witnesses will be dealt with in this way, and to formulate a list of questions for the witnesses. Each witness will then be asked the same questions from the list. The process was adopted by the courts in 2013 (PD 35, para 11). **28.73**

Expert evidence at the hearing

28.74 The experts who should attend the hearing will be stated in the directions previously given by the tribunal. Often the arbitrators will be minded to have the expert evidence presented in the form of the experts' reports, supplemented by any written answers to questions and any note produced following a without prejudice meeting of the experts. In other cases experts will appear at the hearing, either as witnesses for the parties or on behalf of the tribunal. Their reports are usually taken as their evidence-in-chief (perhaps with some supplementary questions), and they will be cross-examined and re-examined in a similar way to factual witnesses.

Views and site visits

28.75 In a number of arbitrations, such as rent review and construction disputes, the tribunal may well decide to include a view or site visit as part of the evidence it takes into account in making its decision.

Closing submissions

28.76 When the evidence is complete, the advocates for both sides make their closing submissions. These may be oral, but are increasingly given by written submissions, or in conjunction with a skeleton argument. Usually the respondent makes the first closing submission, followed by the claimant.

Closing of proceedings

28.77 The arbitrators will include a mechanism for closing the proceedings. This may be a date designated in the tribunal's directions, or a set period after a stage in the process, or after the last closing submission at the hearing. After the closure of proceedings the usual rule is that no further evidence or submissions can be given to the tribunal (although sometimes tribunals give permission for further material to be advanced even after the close of proceedings).

The decision

28.78 The arbitrators will need to confer to discuss the evidence and the submissions made by the parties, and make a decision. Arbitrators must act judicially, even if they are appointed on the basis of qualifications or experience that they possess (this follows from the duty to decide the reference fairly as stated by the Arbitration Act 1996 s 33). Appointing arbitrators with relevant experience means the parties must be taken to have agreed that such arbitrators will bring their own knowledge to bear in making their decisions (*Hawk Shipping Ltd v Cron Navigation* [2003 EWHC 1828 (Comm)). From *Checkpoint Ltd v Strathclyde Pension Fund* [2003] 1 EGLR 1, the dividing line is that:

- it is permissible for the arbitrator to use his technical knowledge and experience in evaluating the evidence presented by the parties, provided it is knowledge that the parties could reasonably expect the arbitrator to have; but
- it is impermissible for the arbitrator to supply evidence from his own knowledge without disclosing that knowledge to the parties so they can put in an answer either through submissions or with additional evidence.

28.79 *Checkpoint Ltd v Strathclyde Pension Fund* was a rent review arbitration that provided for the appointment of an arbitrator experienced in the letting and/or valuation of similar properties. The landlord's expert surveyor gave evidence of six similar properties. The tenant's surveyor's evidence was to the effect that only one of the landlord's comparables was in fact relevant. The Court of Appeal held that the arbitrator had not strayed over the line mentioned above in using his knowledge and experience in evaluating the evidence of the two experts. For example, he had not introduced any comparables of his own into the equation. There was therefore no need for the arbitrator to disclose anything to the parties, as all he did was to do what the parties should have expected given he was appointed on account of his experience.

Usually decisions are valid if made by a majority, although arbitrators usually seek to reach a unanimous decision. They also need to consider their reasons for their decision, which should be included in the award (unless there has been an agreement that no reasons will be stated for the award). **28.80**

Ex aequo et bono/amiable compositeur (equity clauses)

Normally, arbitrators in England and Wales will be expected to reach a decision in accordance with English substantive law. Obviously judges in the courts are best placed to apply substantive law to a dispute. By choosing arbitration the parties may also intend that their dispute should be decided on principles other than the strict application of law. This is perfectly permissible given the provision in the Arbitration Act 1996 s 46(1), which says the arbitral tribunal shall decide the dispute either in accordance with the law chosen by the parties as applicable to the substance of the dispute, or, if the parties so agree, in accordance with such other considerations as are agreed by them or determined by the tribunal. One possibility is that the substantive dispute will be decided *ex aequo et bono*, or with the tribunal acting as an *amiable compositeur*. These concepts, together with deciding on the proper law of an arbitration, are considered in Chapter 29. **28.81**

The award and appeals

Chapter 31 deals with the practice relating to the delivery of the tribunal's award. Appeals to the High Court are dealt with in Chapter 32. **28.82**

K EXAMPLE OF ARBITRAL RULES THAT CLOSELY FOLLOW COURT PROCEDURES

This section will describe a system of commercial arbitration run by the London Metal Exchange Ltd (LME). The LME's arbitration service is in fact used by a large number of enterprises that have no direct involvement in the metals trade. The parties will have agreed to refer their dispute to LME arbitration under the LME arbitration regulations ('the LME regulations'). Arbitrations under the LME regulations are conducted in accordance with the provisions of the Arbitration Act 1996 as amended from time to time (reg 16). **28.83**

Commencement of arbitration

Under the LME regulations a claimant commences an arbitration by serving a notice to arbitrate on the respondent, and by sending a copy of the notice to the secretary of the LME accompanied by the registration fee and deposit (reg 2.1). The date of receipt by the respondent of a valid notice to arbitrate is deemed to be the date on which the arbitration commenced (reg 2.4). The notice to arbitrate must contain at least the following information: **28.84**

- the address for service of the claimant;
- a brief statement of the nature and circumstances of the dispute including a brief description of any contract, sufficient to enable the respondent to identify it, to which the dispute relates;

- a brief statement of the relief claimed;
- the claimant's proposal with regard to the number of arbitrators to form the tribunal;
- the claimant's nomination of one arbitrator from the LME panel; and
- the person and address of the respondent to which the notice to arbitrate has been sent.

Counter-notice

28.85 Within 21 days of receipt of the notice to arbitrate, the respondent is required to send to the claimant, with a copy to the secretary, a counter-notice (reg 2.5). A counter-notice must contain:

- the address for service of the respondent;
- confirmation that the respondent agrees to the number of arbitrators proposed by the claimant, or the respondent's counter-proposal; and
- if relevant, the respondent's nomination of one arbitrator from the LME panel.

28.86 If the respondent fails to serve a counter-notice the secretary of the LME will appoint the tribunal on receipt of a written application from the claimant.

Appointment of tribunal

28.87 LME tribunals consist of one, two, or three arbitrators. Arbitrators are only admitted to the LME panel if they have a broad experience of trading in metals. They are also required to have a legal or arbitration background.

28.88 Usually the tribunal has two arbitrators unless the parties agree to a tribunal of either one or three arbitrators (reg 3.1). If the tribunal is to consist of three arbitrators, the two arbitrators appointed by the parties nominate the third or inform the secretary that they are unable to agree. In this event the secretary appoints the third arbitrator (reg 3.3). The third arbitrator is the chairperson of the tribunal (reg 3.6, and see 27.13). A challenge to the appointment of an arbitrator must be made within 28 days of the appointment of that arbitrator or within 28 days of the party becoming aware of the facts and circumstances on which the challenge is based. It is made by sending a written statement of the reasons for the challenge to the secretary (reg 3.12). Challenges can be made on grounds of non-independence, partiality, unfitness, or inability to act. Unless the other party agrees to the challenge or the arbitrator withdraws within seven days, the secretary refers the matter to the LME panel committee for a decision on whether the challenge should be sustained.

Procedure

28.89 The tribunal is by reg 4 given the widest discretion permitted by law to determine the procedure to be adopted, and to ensure the just, expeditious, economical, and final determination of the dispute.

Statements of case

28.90 Within 21 days of the appointment of the tribunal, the claimant is required to send to the tribunal and to the respondent written points of claim that set out any facts or contentions of law on which it relies, and the relief claimed (reg 6.2). The claimant may serve the points of claim at the same time as the notice to arbitrate. If so, the information required by reg 2.2(b) and (c) need not be contained in the notice to arbitrate, and no further copies of the points of claim need be served.

Within 21 days of receipt of the points of claim, or of the appointment of the tribunal if later, the respondent must send to the tribunal and to the claimant written points of defence (reg 6.4). Points of defence must state in sufficient detail which of the facts and contentions of law in the points of claim the respondent admits or not, or denies, on what grounds, and on what other facts and contentions of law it relies. Any counterclaims must be included in the points of defence in the same manner as claims are set out in the points of claim. **28.91**

Within 21 days of receipt of the points of defence, the claimant may send to the tribunal and to the respondent written points of reply which, where there are counterclaims, should include points of defence to counterclaims (reg 6.5). If the points of reply contain points of defence to counterclaims, the respondent may, within 21 days of receipt, send to the tribunal and to the claimant written points of reply regarding counterclaims (reg 6.6). **28.92**

Documents and samples

All statements of case must be accompanied by legible copies, or if they are especially voluminous, lists of all essential documents on which the party concerned relies and, where appropriate, by any relevant samples (reg 6.8). Any document not in English must be accompanied by a translation into English and a note explaining who prepared the translation and the translator's qualifications, if any, to do so. The authority to be accorded to any translation is a matter for the tribunal (reg 6.9). **28.93**

Directions

Within seven days of close of pleadings the tribunal is required to give directions for the subsequent procedure of the arbitration and may convene a hearing for this purpose (reg 6.10). The tribunal fixes the date, time, and place of any meetings and hearings in the arbitration, and must give the parties reasonable notice (reg 7.2). Before any hearing, the tribunal may require either party to give notice of the identity and qualification of witnesses it wishes to call and may require the parties to exchange statements of evidence to be given by the witnesses a specified time in advance of the hearing (reg 9.1). The tribunal has the power either on its own motion or on the application of either party to order either party to take specified steps within a specified time (reg 10.1(a)). Among the powers given to the tribunal are those: **28.94**

- to order either party to produce and to supply copies of, any documents in that party's possession, custody, or power, which, in the event of dispute, the tribunal determines to be relevant;
- to order either party to answer interrogatories (these are rather like requests for further information under CPR Part 18);
- to require the parties to provide a written statement of their respective cases in relation to particular issues, to provide a written answer, and to give reasons for any disagreement;
- to order the inspection, preservation, storage, interim custody, sale, or other disposal of any property or thing relevant to the arbitration under the control of either party;
- to make orders authorizing any samples to be taken, or any observation to be made, or experiment to be tried which may, in the tribunal's discretion, be necessary or expedient for the purposes of obtaining full information or evidence; and
- to appoint one or more investigators or experts to report to the tribunal on specified issues.

The tribunal can also make orders for interim payments and security for costs. In other words, by agreeing to arbitration under the LME rules the parties confer on the tribunal almost all the powers of a court of law. **28.95**

Hearings

28.96 Either party has the right to be heard before the tribunal, unless the parties have agreed to a documents-only arbitration (reg 7.1). The tribunal has a discretion to direct hearings to be conducted without the physical presence of every participant in the same room, but with participants linked through an audio or audio-visual telecommunication system (reg 7.4). The tribunal may submit to the parties a list of questions in advance of a hearing that it wishes them to treat with special attention (reg 7.5). Neither party may be represented at any hearing by a legal practitioner without the consent of the tribunal, such consent to be requested not later than close of pleadings (reg 8.1). Any consent has to be given on a reciprocal basis. Regulation 8.1 does not preclude either party from otherwise seeking legal advice.

28.97 The tribunal may allow, refuse, or limit the appearance of witnesses, whether witnesses of fact or expert witnesses (reg 9.2). Any witness who gives oral evidence may be questioned by each of the parties or their representative, under the control of the tribunal. The tribunal may put questions at any stage of the examination of the witnesses (reg 9.3). The tribunal may allow the evidence of a witness to be presented in written form either as a signed statement or by a duly sworn affidavit (reg 9.4). Either party may request that such a witness should attend for oral examination at a hearing. If the witness fails to attend, the tribunal may place such weight on the written evidence as it thinks fit, or exclude it altogether.

28.98 Everything that occurs in the arbitration is confidential save to the extent that disclosure may be required by a legal duty or to protect a legal right (reg 6.11).

Awards

28.99 The tribunal is required to make its award in writing and give reasons for the award (reg 12.1). If the tribunal consists of two arbitrators and they fail to agree on any issue, they shall request the secretary to appoint a third arbitrator (reg 12.2.1). If the tribunal consists of three arbitrators and they fail to agree on any issue, they shall decide by a majority. If an arbitrator refuses or fails to sign the award, the signatures of the majority are sufficient, provided that the reason for the omitted signature is stated (reg 12.2.2). In addition to the statutory power to award interest, the tribunal has the power to award interest on any monetary award at such rate and for such period as it considers fit on any sum after its due date but before commencement of the arbitration (reg 12.5). The award can also apportion costs between the parties (reg 13.2). Awards are final and binding on the parties as from the date they are made (reg 12.8). The award of the arbitrators is deposited with the secretary who notifies each party (reg 12.10). Either party may then take up the award upon payment by that party of the costs and expenses of the arbitration as specified in the award (including the remuneration of the arbitrators). Until the award is taken up by one of the parties it confers no rights upon either party.

Appeals

28.100 While there is the possibility of appeals on points of law to the High Court, the parties in LME arbitrations may exclude this possibility by agreement after the arbitration has commenced.

KEY POINTS SUMMARY

- Arbitration is intended to be private and confidential, concepts that flow from the private agreement of the parties to refer the matter to arbitration rather than the courts. **28.101**
- Privacy and confidentiality are not absolute, and there are exceptions.
- There are many arbitral institutions, which may have their own institutional rules for arbitration, and they may also administer arbitrations.
- There are speedy, streamlined arbitration procedures for the simpler types of dispute. These often dispense with hearings, and often have tight timetables for the delivery of written documentation to the tribunal.
- The procedural rules in the Arbitration Act 1996 are subject to contrary agreement by the parties.
- If institutional rules are silent on a procedural matter, the default provisions in the Arbitration Act 1996 apply.
- It is common in commercial arbitration for the process to follow the stages set out in Figure 28.1.
- The LME regulations described towards the end of this chapter are an example of institutional rules that follow a system similar to the CPR. They adopt court procedures in a more overt way than the Arbitration Act 1996, but their general scheme is in fact very similar to that laid down by the Act.

29

INTERNATIONAL ARBITRATION

A INTRODUCTION 29.01
B MEANING OF 'INTERNATIONAL' IN ARBITRATION 29.06
C ADVISING THE CLIENT. 29.08
D SEAT 29.11
E PROBLEMS CAUSED BY DIFFERENT SYSTEMS OF LAW 29.18
F APPLICABLE LAW 29.21
G OBJECTIONS TO JURISDICTION. 29.45
H PROCEDURAL MATTERS RELEVANT TO INTERNATIONAL ARBITRATION 29.59
I ICC RULES OF ARBITRATION. 29.68
J UNCITRAL MODEL LAW ON INTERNATIONAL COMMERCIAL ARBITRATION 29.79
Key points summary 29.92

A INTRODUCTION

29.01 International arbitration broadly covers any reference to arbitration involving parties in different states. A fuller definition is provided in the United Nations Commission on International Trade Law Model Law of 1985 (as subsequently amended) (UNCITRAL Model Law) (see 29.06). So far as English law is concerned there is no fundamental difference between domestic commercial arbitration and international arbitration. There are provisions in the Arbitration Act 1996 (ss 85–88) that were intended to make special provision on a number of aspects of arbitration law for domestic arbitrations. These sections have not been brought into force (Arbitration Act 1996 (Commencement No 1) Order 1996 (SI 1996/3146)), and never will be (Department of Trade and Industry press release 30 January 1997).

29.02 International arbitration is most frequently met in the shipping, construction and engineering, oil and gas industries, and also in disputes involving insurance, banking, and financial services.

29.03 A significant factor encouraging parties to use arbitration as their dispute resolution process in international disputes is that the New York Convention 1958 (see Chapter 32) makes it easy to enforce the award made in an arbitration almost anywhere in the world. Another factor particularly of importance in international cases where the parties are in different states is that neither party may want the matter dealt with in the other side's country. By choosing arbitration the parties are able to find a neutral jurisdiction that is satisfactory to both sides. The parties may also agree to the tribunal applying a neutral system of law when making a decision on the dispute. In other cases the parties achieve a balance between themselves by agreeing on the arbitration being located in one jurisdiction but applying the law of another jurisdiction.

29.04 This chapter will consider a number of issues, such as the seat of the arbitration, the law governing the arbitration, and disputes over jurisdiction, which often arise as important issues in international arbitrations. These issues apply to domestic arbitrations as much as to those of an international character, but in domestic arbitrations the answers are often uncontentious.

29.05 There are a number of arbitral institutions that deal with international arbitration. Examples can be seen in Table 28.1. There are two well-known sets of institutional rules specifically aimed at international arbitration, namely the ICC arbitration and ADR rules (ICC rules) and the UNCITRAL Model Law. These will be considered towards the end of this chapter, as well as being referred to where appropriate in other parts of this chapter. It will be recalled from Chapter 26 that the Arbitration Act 1996 drew quite extensively from the UNCITRAL Model Law, so there is a large degree of affinity between these instruments. The ICC rules take a significantly different approach on a number of matters, as explained at the end of this chapter.

B MEANING OF 'INTERNATIONAL' IN ARBITRATION

29.06 The UNCITRAL Model Law Art 1(3) provides that an arbitration is international if:

(a) the parties to an arbitration agreement have, at the time of the conclusion of that agreement, their places of business in different states; or
(b) one of the following places is situated outside the state in which the parties have their places of business:
  (i) the place of arbitration if determined in, or pursuant to, the arbitration agreement;
  (ii) any place where a substantial part of the obligations of the commercial relationship is to be performed or the place with which the subject-matter of the dispute is most closely connected; or
(c) the parties have expressly agreed that the subject-matter of the arbitration relates to more than one country.

29.07 For the purposes of the UNCITRAL definition, if a party has more than one place of business, the relevant place of business is the one with the closest relationship to the arbitration agreement (Art 1(4)(a)). Also, if a party does not have a place of business, the relevant place is his place of residence rather than his place of business (Art 1(4)(b)).

C ADVISING THE CLIENT

29.08 Advising the client on the best venue for an arbitration, and on how to approach questions of the proper system of law or other rules to be applied in determining the dispute, is one of the most important responsibilities of solicitors retained in international arbitrations. There are obvious advantages in having the arbitration conducted in the client's home jurisdiction, but balanced against that are the costs and litigation risks in a full-blown dispute over jurisdiction, or over the proper law of the contract, with the other party. Assessing those risks, which will depend largely on how clearly the arbitration agreement is worded, is central in giving this advice.

29.09 Where an arbitration is to be conducted in England and Wales, but with a foreign system of law applying to the substantive contract, consideration has to be given to how that system differs from English law, whether to take a point on any such differences, and how to prove those differences. As discussed at 29.35, there is a presumption that foreign law is the same as English law, so if neither party takes a point, the tribunal simply applies English law. Advice invariably has to be taken from a law firm in the overseas jurisdiction, and if a point is to be taken, a lawyer from that jurisdiction has to give factual evidence of the relevant provisions of the foreign law.

29.10 Where the seat of the arbitration (see 29.11) is overseas, particularly where this is combined with hearings taking place in an overseas country, it is often best to advise the client to instruct local lawyers, sometimes instead of the English firm, sometimes in addition. The actual decision is usually based on questions of cost, expertise, and convenience.

D SEAT

29.11 The 'seat' and the 'place' of an arbitration are interchangeable terms. The Arbitration Act 1996 s 3, provides:

> 'the seat of the arbitration' means the juridical seat of the arbitration designated—
> (a) by the parties to the arbitration agreement, or
> (b) by any arbitral or other institution or person vested by the parties with powers in that regard, or
> (c) by the arbitral tribunal if so authorised by the parties,
>
> or determined, in the absence of any such designation, having regard to the parties' agreement and all the relevant circumstances.

29.12 Being the juridical seat means this is about the system of law that governs the arbitration. This implies there must be a country whose duty it is to administer, control, or decide what control there should be over an arbitration (*Braes of Doune Wind Farm (Scotland) Ltd v Alfred McAlpine Business Services Ltd* [2008] 2 All ER (Comm) 493). If England is the seat of an arbitration, this means it is the Arbitration Act 1996 and English law that provide the framework for the procedural steps to be followed in the arbitration. It also means that the level of judicial intervention prescribed by the Arbitration Act 1996 applies.

29.13 The seat need not be the place where the arbitration hearings take place. In the modern world with digital communications and easy air travel, this produces very sensible results. If the seat of an arbitration was fixed by some other rule, such as where the tribunal conducted its hearings, or where the award is signed, bizarre results would be produced. For example, an arbitration conducted entirely in London would have its seat in France if the chairperson of the tribunal took the draft award on holiday to France and signed it in Paris.

Designation of seat

29.14 The seat of an arbitration is decided on the basis of the intentions of the parties, either directly or through a body they have chosen for the purpose (Arbitration Act 1996 s 3). An arbitration clause that provided for arbitration to be conducted in accordance with the rules of the ICC in Paris, and that included a provision that the venue of the arbitration was to be London, was held in *Shashoua v Sharma* [2009] 2 Lloyd's Rep 376 to be a designation of London as the juridical seat for the purposes of the Arbitration Act 1996 s 3. In *U & M Mining Zambia Ltd v Konkola Copper Mines plc* [2013] 2 Lloyd's Rep 218 a dispute between two Zambian companies where the contract provided for LCIA arbitration in London was held to have its seat in England. A surprising case is *Braes of Doune Wind Farm (Scotland) Ltd v Alfred McAlpine Business Services Ltd* [2008] 2 All ER (Comm) 493. In this case the arbitration clause provided that the seat of the arbitration was to be Glasgow, Scotland, but the High Court decided that England was the designated seat of the arbitration. Another clause of the contract provided that the courts of England and Wales had exclusive jurisdiction to settle disputes under the contract. It was held that the English jurisdiction clause had the effect that English law was the curial law of the arbitration, so England was the seat of the arbitration, whereas the Scottish 'seat' clause just meant that the arbitration hearings would take place in Scotland.

29.15 Where there is no express designation of the seat, important factors among the relevant circumstances include whether the parties have agreed to arbitration administered by an institution located in a particular country (*Whitworth Street Estates (Manchester) Ltd v James Miller and Partners Ltd* [1970] AC 583) or whether a particular system of law has been agreed as the proper law of the substantive contract or as being the procedural law of the arbitration (*Egon Oldendorff v Liberia Corporation (No 2)* [1996] 1 Lloyd's Rep 380).

Supervisory jurisdiction

The courts of the seat of an arbitration have supervisory jurisdiction over the arbitration (*C v D* [2008] Bus LR 843). This means that any challenge to an interim or final award made by the arbitrators may be made only in the courts of the place designated as the seat of the arbitration. Most applications to the courts in support of an arbitration (such as applications dealing with the appointment of arbitrators where there are problems in appointing a tribunal) are also brought in the country of the seat of the arbitration. It is recognized that the courts of the seat of an arbitration will not always have an effective jurisdiction over some matters, so that certain applications in a practical sense have to be brought in the courts of the country where an order will be effective. Examples are applications to secure the attendance of witnesses to attend the arbitration hearing and applications for injunctions in support of an arbitration (Arbitration Act 1996 s 2(3)). The need to give effect to the parties' agreement to arbitrate a dispute means that an English court will grant a stay of English litigation under s 9 whether or not the seat of the arbitration is in England and Wales (s 2(2)(a)). For similar practical reasons, applications relating to the enforcement of arbitral awards are made in the country where enforcement is to take place, rather than the seat of the arbitration (s 2(2)(b)). **29.16**

Place of award

The seat of the arbitration is also, unless otherwise agreed by the parties, the place where any award is treated as having been made (Arbitration Act 1996 s 53). This is important because certain of the grounds for refusing to recognize arbitral awards in the New York Convention 1958 Art 5 apply to matters arising in the place of the award. Examples include if any of the parties was under an incapacity under the law of the place of the award, or if the award has been set aside by a court in the country in which the award was made. **29.17**

E PROBLEMS CAUSED BY DIFFERENT SYSTEMS OF LAW

Where the parties to a dispute are based in different countries they may well be totally unfamiliar with the system of law and the methods of resolving disputes that apply in the country of the other side to the dispute. International commerce covers every country on the globe, and the differences in the legal systems that may be met are far wider than those between different common law systems or that between common and civil law. **29.18**

Prior to 1985, there were numerous recurrent problems faced by parties involved in international arbitrations. Most countries had developed laws that focused on domestic arbitrations, which meant they were ill suited to international disputes. Different countries dealt with the procedures to be followed in different levels of detail. It was most common for local laws to deal with procedure on a fragmentary basis, so there were a great many gaps that could lead to expensive litigation in resolving how to fill them. The range of mandatory and non-mandatory provisions in local laws varied widely (for the position in England and Wales, see 26.58), and was a source of considerable difficulty, with parties regularly falling victim of technical local laws that they were not expecting. While most systems provide for some form of supervision of arbitration by their courts, the degree of intervention, when it may be resorted to, and the grounds on which the courts may act have the potential for **29.19** wide variations. Avoiding these problems invariably meant parties had to spend considerable sums in obtaining appropriate legal advice.

29.20 That said, there is a measure of consensus between different legal systems on the general nature of arbitration law and the procedures to be followed in arbitrations. It has also been recognized that it is desirable that states should work towards the harmonization of their domestic arbitration laws, so that the business community can resort to arbitration in the reasonable expectation that the laws and procedures that will be followed will comply with internationally recognized principles that are acceptable to parties from a wide range of legal traditions. The most important development in achieving this goal was the promulgation of the UNCITRAL Model Law. This is intended to provide a framework to be adopted by states when they codify or revise their local arbitration laws, with the consequence that as more countries do this, local arbitration laws will have a large measure of consistency around the world.

F APPLICABLE LAW

29.21 The substantive contract, the arbitration clause, the contracts with the arbitrators, and each part of the arbitration process potentially has its own applicable system of law. There may therefore be systems of law from different countries dealing with:

- the substantive contract ('the proper law of the contract');
- the arbitration agreement (the law governing the obligation to refer the dispute to arbitration);
- the curial law (also known as the *lex arbitri*), which is the procedural law governing how the arbitration should be conducted;
- the law relating to the contracts with any arbitral institution and the individual arbitrators;
- the law of any place where actual hearings take place;
- the law relating to any agreement to compromise the dispute; and
- the law of the place or places where it is sought to register and enforce any arbitral award.

29.22 This can create unseemly complexities. It will be assumed, in the absence of an indication to the contrary, that the parties intended the whole of their relationship to be governed by the same system of law (*Sulamerica Cia Nacional de Seguros SA v Enesa Engelharia SA* [2013] 1 WLR 102).

Proper law of the contract

29.23 The Arbitration Act 1996 s 46(1) provides that the arbitral tribunal shall decide the dispute:

- in accordance with the law chosen by the parties as applicable to the substance of the dispute; or
- if the parties so agree, in accordance with such other considerations as are agreed by them or determined by the tribunal.

29.24 For this purpose the choice of the laws of a country by the parties shall be understood to refer to the substantive laws of that country and not its conflict of laws rules (s 46(2)). If or to the extent that there is no such choice or agreement, the tribunal must apply the law determined by the conflict of laws rules that it considers applicable (s 46(3)). It is usually the conflict of laws rules from the country where the arbitration has its seat that are applied (*CGU International Insurance plc v Astrazeneca Insurance Co Ltd* [2007] Bus LR 162).

Law, or other rules

Usually, the proper law of the substantive dispute will be the system of law of a state. It can be seen from the Arbitration Act 1996 s 46(1)(b) that it is open to the parties to agree that the substantive dispute is be decided in accordance with 'such other considerations' as they might agree or that may be determined by the arbitrators. One of the options available is that the tribunal could be authorized to decide the dispute as *amiable compositeur* or *ex aequo et bono* (see 29.27–29.30). Another possibility is that the dispute may be determined by a system of rules that have not have been incorporated into the law of any particular state, for example the United Nations Convention on Contracts for the International Sale of Goods. **29.25**

Use of a system of rules that are not the laws of a named state is possible where the parties so agree, or where the parties agree that the tribunal has this level of choice. If there is no such agreement, the default position is that the tribunal must apply a system of national law (s 46(3)) as determined by the conflict of laws rules that the tribunal considers applicable. **29.26**

Amiable compositeur *or* ex aequo et bono *(equity clauses)*

The terms *amiable compositeur* and *ex aequo et bono* ('equity clauses') probably mean the same thing, although there may be a slight though ill-defined difference between them. Different legal systems recognize or do not recognize these concepts, and some provide definitions (which are not the same in every jurisdiction). Acting as an *amiable compositeur* allows the tribunal to decide the arbitration in according with the principles the arbitrators believe to be just rather than those that the law would technically apply. Deciding a matter *ex aequo et bono* means in justice and good faith. Equity clauses are not intended to give the tribunal complete scope to do whatever it wants, but they are intended to give the tribunal the flexibility to decide the dispute in accordance with notions of justice and equity. **29.27**

Broadly, the idea is that by appointing arbitrators who are sensible and practical commercial people, the parties trust them to decide the dispute fairly and in accordance with the expectations and business ethics of reasonable people in the relevant trade. The risk is that by adopting such an ill-defined basis for deciding the matter, what may seem reasonable to one person may be wholly unacceptable to another, but there are limited means for saying one is to be preferred over the other. **29.28**

Anticipating this problem, the UNCITRAL Model Law says at Art 28(4) that even in these cases the tribunal must decide the dispute in accordance with the terms of the contract, and must take into account the usages of the trade applicable to the transaction. This provision is not included in the Arbitration Act 1996, the view taken by the DAC report being that if the applicable law allows account to be taken of trade usages etc, the provision is unnecessary, whereas if it does not, the provision overrides the law. This misses the point that the clause is most aimed at providing minimum requirements when the tribunal is acting under an equity clause. **29.29**

One particular effect of having a dispute decided under an equity clause is that doing so excludes the possibility of an appeal to the courts as there is no possibility of a 'question of law'. **29.30**

Determination of the proper law

Where England is the seat of the arbitration (see 29.11), the proper law is determined: **29.31**

- for contracts entered into before 17 December 2009 by applying the rules in the Contracts (Applicable Law) Act 1990, which gives effect to the Rome Convention 1980;
- for contracts entered into after 17 December 2009 by applying the rules in Regulation (EC) No 593/2008 ('Rome I'); and

- for non-contractual obligations from 11 January 2009 by applying the rules in Council Regulation (EC) No 864/2007 ('Rome II').

29.32 Under Rome I, the guiding principle is one of party autonomy on the choice of law. By Art 3(1), a contract shall be governed by the law chosen by the parties. The choice has to be made expressly or clearly demonstrated by the terms of the contract or the circumstances of the case. By their choice the parties can select the law applicable to the whole or to part only of the contract. The parties can subsequently agree to change their initial choice (Art 3(2)). Articles 4–8 deal with cases where there is no agreement, and provide special rules for consumer, employment, and insurance contracts. Among the particular situations provided for, the following are important in the context of international arbitration:

- contracts for the sale of goods are governed by the law of the country where the seller is habitually resident (Art 4(1)(a));
- contracts for the provision of services are governed by the law of the country where the service provider is habitually resident (Art 4(1)(b));
- contracts for the carriage of goods are governed by the law of the country where the carrier is habitually resident, provided that the place of receipt or the place of delivery or the habitual residence of the consignor is also situated in that country. If those requirements are not met, the contract is governed by the law of the country where the place of delivery as agreed by the parties is situated (Art 5(1)).

29.33 Where it is clear from all the circumstances of the case that the contract is manifestly more closely connected with a country other than that indicated in these provisions, the law of that other country applies instead (Arts 4(3) and 5(3)).

29.34 Under the Contracts (Applicable Law) Act 1990 it was held that a choice of seat in an arbitration agreement meant that the applicable law was that of the seat. Choosing a seat demonstrated a choice for that system of law with reasonable certainty (*Egon Oldendorff v Liberia Corporation (No 2)* [1996] 1 Lloyd's Rep 380). Although other circumstances may point in another direction, a choice of seat is also likely to be a sufficiently clear demonstration of the parties' choice for the purposes of Rome I Art 3(1)).

Presumption that the applicable law is the same as English law

29.35 In arbitrations, as much as in litigation, there is a presumption that any system of law that is the proper law of a dispute is the same as the law of England and Wales (*Hussman (Europe) Ltd v Al Almeen Development and Trade Co* [2000] 2 Lloyd's Rep 83). As Thomas J said in this case, 'to hold otherwise would mean that international arbitrations held in London would be encumbered with the considerable extra expense of obtaining general evidence of foreign law relevant to the matters in issue in every case where the proper law of the contract was not the law of England and Wales'. What tends to happen is that the presumption is the starting point, but it is open to any of the parties to suggest that the applicable law is different on any specific issues. Where they do so, expert evidence from suitably qualified lawyers in the relevant jurisdiction will be required.

Law of the arbitration agreement

29.36 The law of the arbitration agreement governs matters such as the meaning and effect of the agreement to arbitrate, the validity of any unusual provisions in the arbitration agreement (*Weissfisch v Julius* [2006] 1 Lloyd's Rep 716), and whether the dispute in question falls within the terms of the arbitration agreement (*Nova (Jersey) Knit Ltd v Kammgarn Spinnerei* [1977] 1 WLR 713).

Often the law of the arbitration agreement will be the same as the proper law of the contract, particularly where the reference to arbitration is based on an arbitration clause in the substantive contract. There are cases where even in this situation the parties agree to different systems of law to govern the substantive contract and the arbitration agreement. It will be recalled that the agreement to arbitrate is separable from the substantive contract (see 26.11), so there is no objection in principle to having different systems of law for the two purposes. The possibility of having different systems of law for the two purposes is increased where the arbitration agreement is in a separate contract from the substantive contract. **29.37**

Arbitration agreements are expressly excluded from the choice of law rules in Rome I (Art 1(2)(e)), so different conflicts of laws rules apply in determining the applicable law of the arbitration agreement than apply in relation to the substantive contract. There is a three-stage inquiry into (i) express choice; (ii) implied choice; and (iii) closest and most real connection (*Sulamerica Cia Nacional de Seguros SA v Enesa Engelharia SA* [2013] 1 WLR 102). Where there is no express statement of the applicable law, the court must consider all the circumstances, including the proper law of the substantive contract, the place of performance of the contract, and whether the parties agreed to a neutral forum for the arbitration (*Deutsche Schachtbau-und Tiefbohrgesellschaft mbH v Ras Al Khaimah National Oil Co* [1987] 2 All ER 769). Powerful indicators are the applicable law of the substantive contract and the location of the seat of the arbitration (*Sonatrach Petroleum Corp v Ferrell International Ltd* [2002] 1 All ER (Comm) 627). **29.38**

Jurisdiction Regulation (Brussels Convention)

Regarding court proceedings, jurisdiction between member states of the EU is governed by Council Regulation (EC) No 44/2001 ('the Jurisdiction Regulation', which will be replaced by Regulation (EU) No 1215/2012 on 10 January 2015), which replaced the Brussels Convention on Jurisdiction and Enforcement of Judgments in Civil and Commercial Matters 1968. The Jurisdiction Regulation covers litigation involving civil and commercial matters, but does not apply to arbitration (Art 1(2)(d)). **29.39**

Proceedings relating to the incorporation or validity of an arbitration clause come within Art 1(2)(d), with the result that they are outside the scope of the Jurisdiction Regulation (*National Navigation Co v Endesa Generación SA* [2009] 1 Lloyd's Rep 666). The mere fact that a contract includes an arbitration clause does not mean the proceedings are outside the Jurisdiction Regulation (*Youell v La Réunion Aérienne* [2009] Bus LR 1504). It is the nature of the claim that is crucial. If any arbitration point is merely incidental to the proceedings, the claim is not excluded on this ground. **29.40**

Procedural law of the arbitration (curial law)

The procedural law of an arbitration covers matters such as the appointment of the tribunal, the tribunal's powers and duties, defining the issues and preparation of the evidence, making interim and final awards, and the degree to which the courts can intervene to support the arbitral process or to review decisions made by the arbitrators. The detailed framework of procedural law set out in the Arbitration Act 1996 ss 1–84 applies to any arbitration seat of which is in England or Wales (s 2(1)). Institutional arbitral rules only apply to the extent that the procedural law permits agreement between the parties on matters of procedure. Under the Arbitration Act 1996 in fact a great deal of scope is given to the parties in this regard, but the parties cannot override the mandatory provisions of the Act (for which, see Table 26.2). **29.41**

29.42 An agreement between the parties that a particular country will be the seat of an arbitration operates as an agreement that the law of that country is the procedural law of the arbitration (*Shashoua v Sharma* [2009] 2 Lloyd's Rep 376).

Law of the place of enforcement

29.43 Enforcement of arbitral awards is considered in Chapter 32. As a practical matter, the parties to an arbitration ought to have in mind in the early stages of the process the likely countries where they might wish to enforce an award, to make sure they comply with any local requirements as to procedure or the form of the award if it is to be enforceable in the countries where the other side are likely to have assets.

Stateless arbitrations

29.44 Academic lawyers, particularly from civil law jurisdictions, have argued for the recognition of 'stateless' arbitrations, free from the law of any particular state. The appearance that this may have some validity comes from the contractual basis of arbitration (rather than state provided litigation) conducted in accordance with arbitration rules chosen by the parties. It is perfectly possible for such an arbitration to be conducted with the arbitrators deciding the dispute *ex aequo et bono* rather than under the laws of any particular country and without any involvement of any court. Like many aspects of business life, the appearance that there is no need for any system of law only survives as long as no one needs to seek the assistance of a court. Stateless arbitration, 'delocalized' from any national system of law, is simply not recognized in English law (*Bank Mellat v Helliniki Techniki SA* [1984] 1 QB 291). Ultimately, every arbitration (other than arbitration under the ICSID rules) is required to have a seat (Arbitration Act 1996 s 3), which means that the law of the state of the seat is the procedural law of the arbitration.

G OBJECTIONS TO JURISDICTION

29.45 The jurisdiction of an arbitral tribunal depends on it being appointed in accordance with the terms of an agreement between the parties to refer the relevant dispute to arbitration. This means that the tribunal may not have jurisdiction for a number of reasons, which include:

- there was no effective arbitration agreement;
- the arbitration agreement was between parties that are different to the parties to the dispute;
- the dispute does not come within the terms of the arbitration agreement;
- the arbitrators have not been appointed in accordance with the terms of the arbitration agreement;
- the arbitrators are purporting to decide matters that have not been referred to them.

29.46 Objections to the jurisdiction of arbitrators can be used to cause delays and can be very expensive. They are an obvious means of making life difficult for a claimant at the hands of a respondent who has no real grounds of defence. On the other hand, if the arbitrators have no jurisdiction they have no right to pronounce on a dispute.

Procedures available for raising an objection to jurisdiction

29.47 A person who is named in existing arbitration proceedings, or who may be named in a future arbitration, has a number of procedural routes for registering any jurisdictional objection they may have. The main options are set out in Table 29.1.

Table 29.1 Jurisdictional objections

Procedure	Description	Advantages/disadvantages
Ignore the arbitration, and challenge the award by seeking either: (a) an injunction; or (b) a declaration	A person who takes no part in an arbitration is allowed by the Arbitration Act 1996 s 72(1), to question: (a) whether there was a valid arbitration agreement; (b) whether the tribunal was properly constituted; or (c) whether the submission to arbitration was in accordance with the arbitration agreement	Taking no part in the arbitration avoids the costs involved in participation. It runs the risk, however, that the tribunal will make an adverse finding which, unless challenged successfully, will be enforceable. An application under s 72 made after an award therefore involves the loss of the right to defend the arbitration. There is no need to await the tribunal's decision, and it may be better to make an application early in the arbitration to see whether the challenge is successful. The applicant, however, can take no part in the arbitration while the challenge is being resolved.
Ignore the arbitration, and challenge enforcement of the award	Permission to enforce an award under s 66 will be refused where it is shown that the tribunal lacked substantive jurisdiction to make the award (s 66(2)).	As with the previous method, this is a high-risk strategy. Section 66 deals with domestic enforcement. There are different grounds for refusing to recognize an international award under the New York Convention 1958 (see s 103(2)).
Oppose the appointment of the arbitrators	By not agreeing to the appointment of a tribunal, the effect may be that the claimant is forced into applying to the court for the appointment of the necessary arbitrators under s 18.	This may not work at all because the arbitration agreement may contain sufficient machinery for the appointment of the tribunal. Even if the matter comes before the court under s 18, the objection may not be regarded as sufficient to warrant not appointing any tribunal at all.
Make an objection to the substantive jurisdiction of the arbitrators to the tribunal under s 31	The objection must be made no later than the time the party making the objection takes the first step to contest the merits (s 31(1)).	While the tribunal may well have jurisdiction to determine its own jurisdiction (s 30), its decision may be just the first step in the process, with a review by the courts.
Apply to the court to determine a question as to the substantive jurisdiction of the arbitrators under s 32	Requires the written agreement of the other parties or the permission of the tribunal (and other conditions set out in s 32(2)).	There are restrictions on the right to apply to the court (ss 32(2) and 73). The arbitration may continue (and costs continue being incurred) while the application to the court is pending (s 32(4)). These costs may be wasted if the court decides the tribunal does not have jurisdiction.
Apply for an anti-suit injunction to restrain the arbitration	Interim application to the High Court supported by written evidence under CPR Parts 23 and 25.	While there technically may be jurisdiction to grant such an injunction under the Senior Courts Act 1981 s 37, the principle that the court has no supervisory jurisdiction over arbitrations beyond those set out in the Arbitration Act 1996 (see s 1(c)) means the court should rarely if ever exercise this power.

(Continued)

Table 29.1 Jurisdictional objections *(Continued)*

Procedure	Description	Advantages/disadvantages
Start normal court proceedings relating to the substantive dispute	Normal Part 7 claim form followed by the CPR procedures for litigation.	The other side may apply for a stay of the court proceedings under s 9. The dispute over the jurisdiction to arbitrate may be argued on the s 9 application.
Challenge the tribunal's award as to its substantive jurisdiction under s 67	This is only available if the applicant has exhausted any available arbitral process of appeal or review (s 70(2)). The challenge is brought as an arbitration claim under CPR, Part 62. There are detailed procedures in PD 62 that have to be followed.	There are restrictions on the right to apply to the court (ss 70(2), (3) and 73). The arbitration may continue (and costs continue being incurred) while the application to the court is pending (s 67(2)). These costs may be wasted if the court decides the tribunal does not have jurisdiction.

Substantive jurisdiction

29.48 Objections to a tribunal's substantive jurisdiction cover (Arbitration Act 1996 s 82(1)):

- whether there is a valid arbitration agreement;
- whether the tribunal is properly constituted; and
- what matters have been submitted to arbitration in accordance with the arbitration agreement.

Time when an objection to jurisdiction should be taken

29.49 Although there are numerous different procedures that can be used in raising a jurisdictional objection, unless the party making the objection takes no part in the arbitration, the objection must be made at the time it arises or when it was first discovered. Further, a party is not allowed to contest an arbitration on its merits, and then raise a jurisdictional objection for the first time if the award is unfavourable. As was stated by Thomas J in *Hussmann (Europe) Ltd v Al Ameen Development and Trade Co* [2000] 2 Lloyd's Rep 83, a party is not allowed to 'keep a point "up his sleeve" and wait and see what happens while considerable expense is incurred. A party cannot be allowed to take part in proceedings and then challenge the award if he is dissatisfied with it on the basis of a point about which he knows or ought with reasonable diligence to have discovered'. A party who brings an arbitration claim in the High Court (see 31.82) to challenge the jurisdiction of the arbitrators relying on one of the provisions in the Arbitration Act 1996 referred to in Table 29.1, but does not take the High Court challenge through to a final determination, is not permitted to bring any further challenge to the arbitrators' award (*Sheltam Rail Co (Proprietary) Ltd v Mirambo Holdings Ltd* [2009] Bus LR 302).

29.50 In *Dallah Real Estate and Tourism Co v Ministry of Religious Affairs of the Government of Pakistan* [2011] 1 AC 763 the substantive contract was between Dallah and Awami Hajj Trust (the 'Trust') and contained an arbitration clause. Dallah made a claim for money alleged to be due under the contract against the Government of Pakistan, which was referred to ICC arbitration in Paris. The Government of Pakistan denied it was a party to the contract, and refused to take part in the arbitration. The arbitrators ruled they had jurisdiction, and made an award of US$20 million against the Government of Pakistan. It was held by the Supreme Court on an objection to the arbitrators' jurisdiction on an application to enforce the award that an arbitral tribunal's decision as to the existence of its own jurisdiction cannot bind a party who has not submitted the question of arbitrability to the tribunal. Such a person could challenge the enforcement of the final award on the basis they were not a party to the arbitration agreement, which would be decided anew rather than as a review of the arbitrators' decision.

Reserving client's position

Solicitors not infrequently seek to avoid the problems mentioned at 29.49 by raising an objection at an early stage in correspondence, stating that they are reserving their client's rights in relation to the objection, and then proceeding with contesting the arbitration on the merits. Such an attempt to reserve the right to raise the objection later in the process was held to be ineffective in *ASM Shipping Ltd of India v TTMI Ltd of England* [2006] 1 Lloyd's Rep 375 (a case under the Arbitration Act 1996, s 68). Instead, the arbitral tribunal should be invited to rule that it will deal with the matter in its final award under s 31(4)(b), if a party wants to take part in the arbitration, but leave the determination of the jurisdictional issue to the end. Where all the parties agree this is the best course, the tribunal has to comply with the parties' wishes (s 31(4)). **29.51**

Taking a step in the arbitration

The right to challenge the arbitral tribunal's jurisdiction under the Arbitration Act 1996 s 72 (the first entry in Table 29.1) will be lost if the applicant takes any part in the arbitration (s 72(1)). **29.52**

By s 31(1), any objection to the substantive jurisdiction of the tribunal must be raised no later than the time the applicant takes the first step in the arbitration proceedings to contest the merits of the matter relating to the jurisdictional challenge. Further, by s 73(1) any objection that: **29.53**

- the tribunal lacks substantive jurisdiction;
- the proceedings have been improperly conducted;
- there has been a failure to comply with the arbitration agreement or with any provision of the Arbitration Act 1996 ss 1–84; or
- there has been any other irregularity affecting the tribunal or the proceedings,

can only be raised if the applicant shows that, at the time he took part or continued to take part in the arbitral proceedings, he did not know and could not with reasonable diligence have discovered the grounds for the objection.

Appointing, or participating in the appointment, of the arbitrators by a party does not preclude a challenge to the substantive jurisdiction of the tribunal (s 31(1)). This is because it is legitimate to appoint a tribunal to decide a dispute over its own jurisdiction (see *Kompetenz-Kompetenz* at 29.55–29.57). Almost any other action in the arbitration, and sometimes doing nothing, will operate as a bar to later objecting to the tribunal's jurisdiction by virtue of ss 31 and 73. Contesting the merits will amount to taking a step, as will taking up an award (*Thyssen Canada Ltd v Mariana Maritime SA* [2005] 1 Lloyd's Rep 640). It is clear from *Rustal Trading Ltd v Gill and Duffas SA* [2000] 1 Lloyd's Rep 14 that simple inaction may amount to taking a step. Moore-Bick J said: **29.54** 'there might well be periods in the arbitration during which no formal step is required of one or other party but, during these periods, the parties will be taking part in the proceedings'.

Kompetenz-Kompetenz

29.55 Purists will say that it is impossible to allow a tribunal to decide a dispute over its own jurisdiction. If it decides it has no jurisdiction, what is the status of that decision? Intellectual difficulties of this kind find no home in the modern law of arbitration, which is firmly rooted in providing practical justice. However, this can be pushed too far, particularly when married to the idea that there should be limited or no court review of decisions made by arbitrators. At its extreme is the German concept of *Kompetenz-Kompetenz*. This meant that not only was an arbitral tribunal empowered to decide on its own jurisdiction, but also that its decision was not amenable to review by the courts. Such an extreme position no longer applies in Germany, and does not apply in England either. However, the expression *Kompetenz-Kompetenz* is still commonly used to describe any system that provides for a tribunal ruling on its own jurisdiction (even if that decision is reviewable by the courts).

29.56 The Arbitration Act 1996 s 30(1) provides that unless otherwise agreed by the parties, the arbitral tribunal may rule on its own substantive jurisdiction. In construing any arbitration agreement, the presumption is that the parties will have intended that any dispute arising out of their relationship is to be decided by the same tribunal rather than having some matters decided by the courts, and others by the arbitrators (*Fili Shipping Co Ltd v Premium Nafta Products Ltd* [2007] Bus LR 1719). This, together with s 30, means that where the parties have included an arbitration clause, the arbitrator can decide any objection to his jurisdiction, even if there is a dispute over the validity of the substantive contract.

29.57 It is not uncommon for arbitrators to be called upon to consider submissions that they are not competent to act by reason of bias. An arbitrator's decision on jurisdiction is not final, provided the seat of the arbitration was in a country, such as England, where the courts exercise a supervisory jurisdiction over arbitration (*Weissfisch v Julius* [2006] 1 Lloyd's Rep 716; and see Chapter 31).

Anti-suit injunctions

29.58 Anti-suit injunctions to restrain proceedings in another state which would be in breach of an agreement to arbitrate may be granted by the High Court under the Senior Courts Act 1981, s 37(1). This is so even if arbitration proceedings have not been commenced or even contemplated (*AES Ust-Kamenogorsk Hydropower Plant LLP v Ust-Kamenogorsk Hydropower Plant JSC* [2013] 1 WLR 1889). Anti-suit injunctions are only available where it is necessary to restrain the breach of the arbitration agreement (*Compagnie Europeenne de Cereals SA v Tradax Export SA* [1986] 2 Lloyd's Rep 301). Anti-suit injunctions can be made in the opposite direction under the Senior Courts Act 1981 s 37, to restrain the bringing of arbitration proceedings which ought not to be commenced (*Excalibur Ventures LLC v Texas Keystone Inc* [2011] EWHC 1624 (Comm)). Anti-suit injunctions are, however, not available where the legal proceedings are in another EU member state, because in such cases granting the injunction would be incompatible with the Jurisdiction Regulation (see 29.39) (*West Tankers Inc v Riunione Adriatica di Sicurtà SpA* (Case C-185/07) [2009] 1 AC 1138). At present, within the EU it is exclusively for the courts of the member state seised of the original proceedings to determine any objection to its jurisdiction.

H PROCEDURAL MATTERS RELEVANT TO INTERNATIONAL ARBITRATION

Language of the arbitration

Having an arbitration conducted in a party's first language is a significant advantage both at a practical level and in ensuring that the party's case is conveyed as effectively as is possible. While there are translation services available, even the best translations are never as effective as being able to address a tribunal directly in a shared language. **29.59**

The parties will not infrequently make express provision for the language to be used in any arbitration in the substantive contract. If they do the tribunal is obliged to adopt what the parties have agreed. **29.60**

If there is no express agreement on the language of the arbitration, the Arbitration Act 1996 s 34(2)(b) provides that it is for the tribunal to decide the language or languages to be used in the proceedings and whether translations of any relevant documents are to be supplied. Institutional rules often deal with these matters, and will often deal with translations of the statements of case and documentary evidence. Directions will, as a practical matter, also have to cover the translation services required for the final hearing (both for the parties and witnesses). **29.61**

Under the ICC rules, in the absence of an agreement by the parties, the tribunal is required to determine the language or languages of the arbitration (Art 20). In making this decision the tribunal is to have due regard to all relevant circumstances, including the language of the substantive contract. The UNCITRAL Model Law is similar (Art 22(1)), but this also says that the language of the arbitration shall apply, unless otherwise provided, to any written statement by a party, as well as to the hearing, the award, and any other communication by the tribunal. Article 22(2) gives the tribunal the power to order that any documentary evidence must be accompanied by a translation into the language or languages of the arbitration. **29.62**

Meetings and hearings

Considerations of cost and distance mean that greater thought is required of how and where meetings and hearings should take place in international arbitrations. In addition to the parties and their witnesses, who are likely to be based in different countries, there may also be a panel of (say) three arbitrators all based in different countries. Telephone conferences and video-conferences may be effective ways of conducting at least certain meetings at reasonable cost. Where actual hearings and meetings take place, consideration has to be given to where these can take place with the least inconvenience to those who need to attend, which is why on occasions hearings take place in countries otherwise unconnected with the dispute but which are the most easily accessible to those who need to attend. **29.63**

Privilege

A particular issue in international arbitration is that there is a distinct possibility that the scope of the rules relating to privilege and the right not to disclose documents to other parties often differ between different countries. It is obviously unfair if one side gives the other side wider access to its documents than it receives in return. Further, there can be difficulties in requiring a party to an arbitration to disclose documents that would be protected from production under the law where it conducts its business. If it had known that certain categories of documents that would be protected under its domestic law might be disclosable in a dispute with a party from another jurisdiction, those documents may never have been written or compiled in the first place. **29.64**

29.65 It ought to be that the procedural law of the arbitration (the curial law) should govern the scope of disclosure to be given by all the parties in an arbitration. Disclosure is traditionally regarded as a procedural issue, so the procedural law should prevail. The contrary argument is that privilege has become established as a substantive right (see *McE v Prison Service of Northern Ireland* [2009] 1 AC 908), and that therefore the scope of privilege should be decided in accordance with the law of the state where the documents were created.

Security for costs

29.66 One of the powers given to arbitral tribunals (unless the parties agree otherwise) is a power to order the claimant to provide security for costs (Arbitration Act 1996 s 38). Unlike CPR r 25.13, which specifies the grounds on which security for costs may be ordered in court proceedings, an arbitral tribunal is given a general discretion untrammeled by any conditions. However, s 38(3) prohibits an arbitral tribunal from ordering security for costs on the ground that the claimant is incorporated or ordinarily resident outside the United Kingdom. This is to avoid the power to order security for costs acting as a disincentive to overseas parties using England and Wales as the seat for their arbitrations.

29.67 This means that security for costs will typically be ordered where the claimant is a corporation (whether or not it is a registered company) and there is reason to believe it will be unable to pay the respondent's costs, or if the claimant fails to give an address, or changes its address to avoid having to pay costs, or if the claimant is acting in a nominal capacity, or if it has taken steps to make it difficult to enforce a costs award (compare CPR r 25.13, which English arbitrators normally apply by analogy).

I ICC RULES OF ARBITRATION

29.68 The International Chamber of Commerce (ICC) is based in Paris, and has published an internationally recognized set of arbitration and ADR rules (2012). The ICC has established the International Court of Arbitration (ICA), which oversees arbitrations conducted under the ICC rules and scrutinizes ICC awards. The ICA is not a court of law, and its members are not permitted to act as arbitrators or counsel in cases submitted to ICC arbitration (Internal Rules of the ICA Art 2(1)). The ICA secretariat has various delegated functions, and may issue notes and guidance for parties and arbitrators involved in ICC arbitrations. All documents in ICC arbitrations are provided to the secretariat as well as the parties and arbitrators (Art 3(1)).

Request for arbitration

29.69 An ICC arbitration is commenced by the submission of a request for arbitration to the secretariat (ICC rules Art 4(1)). This must include:

- the names, description, and address for each party;
- a description of the nature and circumstances of the dispute;
- a statement of the relief sought;
- copies of all relevant contracts, including the arbitration agreement;
- the number of arbitrators required by the arbitration agreement, and details of any nominations; and
- any comments on the place of arbitration, applicable law, and the language of the arbitration.

By submitting their dispute to arbitration under the ICC rules, the parties undertake to carry out any award without delay (Art 34(6)). After receipt of the request the ICC can request the claimant to pay a provisional advance to cover the costs of the arbitration until the terms of reference have been drawn up (Art 36(1)). 29.70

Answer to the request

The request for arbitration is sent to the respondent by the secretariat (Art 4(5)). Within 30 days of receipt of the request the respondent is required to file an answer, which sets out the respondent's comments on the dispute, the relief claimed, and matters relating to the arbitration (Art 5(1)). At the same time the respondent may file a counterclaim (Art 5(5)). A copy of the answer and any counterclaim is sent to the claimant by the secretariat (Art 5(4)). The claimant is required to respond to any counterclaim within 30 days of receipt (Art 5(6)). 29.71

ICC arbitral tribunals

ICC arbitral tribunals have either one or three arbitrators (Art 12(1)). Where there are to be three arbitrators, each party nominates one arbitrator, subject to confirmation by the ICA, with the third arbitrator being appointed by the ICA (Art 12(4)). There are default provisions to deal with cases where a party fails to make a nomination, where the ICA refuses to confirm a nomination, and where there are challenges to arbitrators (for example, for alleged lack of independence). Each arbitrator has to sign a statement of acceptance, availability, impartiality, and independence before they are appointed (Art 11(2)). 29.72

Seat of the arbitration

The seat of the arbitration is fixed by the ICA (Art 18(1)). 29.73

Terms of reference

Once the tribunal is constituted the secretariat will provide it with a copy of the secretariat's file. The tribunal then draws up, on the basis of the documents or in the presence of the parties and on considering their representations, a document defining the tribunal's terms of reference (Art 23). This will include the following particulars: 29.74

- the names and descriptions of the parties;
- their addresses;
- a summary of the respective claims and relief sought by the parties;
- a list of issues (which may be dispensed with);
- names and addresses of the arbitrators;
- the place (seat) of the arbitration; and
- details of the applicable law, and whether the tribunal is to act as *amiable compositeur* or to decide *ex aequo et bono*.

The terms of reference have to be signed by the parties and the arbitral tribunal, and filed with the ICA within two months of transmission of the file to the tribunal (Art 23(2)). 29.75

Procedure prior to the hearing

At the same time as considering its terms of reference, or as soon as possible thereafter, the tribunal will convene a case management conference to consult the parties on the procedural steps needed to prepare for the final disposal of the matter. A procedural timetable for these 29.76

steps is sent to the ICA and the parties, and may be modified to ensure continuing effective case management (Art 24).

Hearings and the decision

29.77 ICC tribunals are required to establish the facts within as short a time as possible, and by using all appropriate means (Art 25(1)). These are likely to include contemporaneous documents provided by the parties, written submissions, and may include hearings with witnesses being called to give evidence (Art 25(2), (3)). Decisions may be made without a hearing, but a hearing must be held if requested by any of the parties (Art 25(6)). Expert evidence may be necessary, and the tribunal may appoint its own experts (with their own terms of reference (Art 25(4)). Actual meetings and hearings can be held anywhere as decided by the tribunal in consultation with the parties (Art 18(2)). Hearings are held in private (Art 26(3)), and parties may be legally represented (Art 26(4)).

29.78 As soon as possible after the last hearing, or the filing of the last authorized submissions by the parties, the tribunal will declare the proceedings closed (Art 27). Once the proceedings are closed, no further submissions or evidence will be admitted without the authorization of the tribunal. The tribunal indicates to the secretariat when the draft award will be submitted. There is a time limit of six months from the signing of the terms of reference until the final award (Art 30(1)). This time limit may be extended by the ICA (Art 30(2)). ICC awards give reasons as well as the decision (Art 31(2)). A final award will fix the costs of the arbitration, and will include a decision on which of the parties will bear the costs (Art 37(4)). Before the award is signed, a draft is provided to the ICA for scrutiny. The ICA may lay down modifications, and no ICC award can be finalized until it has been approved by the ICA (Art 33).

J UNCITRAL MODEL LAW ON INTERNATIONAL COMMERCIAL ARBITRATION

29.79 The UNCITRAL Model Law is published by United Nations Commission on International Trade Law, whose secretariat is based in Vienna. UNCITRAL is a subsidiary body of the General Assembly of the United Nations. A particular function of UNCITRAL is in promoting the harmonization and modernization of international trade law. The Model Law is just one of many publications dealing with different aspects of international trade published by UNCITRAL. Unlike the ICC, UNCITRAL is not an arbitral institution, and neither is it an appointing institution. Its Model Law has, however, been used as the basis of arbitration law reform in many countries, including England and Wales. While the primary purpose of the Model Law was to provide a framework for law reform, it contains a detailed set of rules which (with one or two minor exceptions) provide a comprehensive set of rules that can be adopted by parties as the rules for ad hoc arbitrations. Some arbitral institutions, such as CEDR in England, adopt the Model Law as their standard rules for international arbitrations.

Interpretation of the Model Law

29.80 When interpreting the Model Law regard is to be had to its international origin, and the need to promote uniformity in its application and the observance of good faith (Art 2A(1)). To assist in the interpretation of the Model Law the secretariat of UNCITRAL has published an explanatory note, which is technically for information purposes only. UNCITRAL also publishes a series of decisions from around the world on the Model Law and other UNCITRAL texts (Case Law on UNCITRAL Texts).

Commencement of Model Law arbitration

Unless the parties otherwise agree, an arbitration under the Model Law commences on the date a request for a particular dispute to be referred to arbitration is received by the respondent (Art 21). **29.81**

Model Law arbitral tribunals

The Model Law allows the parties to determine the number of arbitrators on their tribunal (Art 10(1)). In the absence of agreement, there are three arbitrators in Model Law arbitrations (Art 10(2)). In these cases, each party appoints one arbitrator, and the two party-appointed arbitrators appoint the third arbitrator (Art 11(3)(a)). One of the abuses the Model Law seeks to address is that of a party delaying matters by not co-operating in the appointment of the tribunal. It therefore lays down strict 30-day time limits for the appointment of arbitrators, and provides for a right to apply to the courts of the seat of the arbitration to make the necessary orders to ensure the tribunal is properly constituted in the case of default (Art 11(4)).There are express provisions in Art 16 stating that the arbitration agreement is separable from the substantive contract and that the arbitrators have power to rule on their own jurisdiction (matching the position in English law: see 26.11 and 29.56). **29.82**

Interim measures

There are detailed provisions in the Model Law, in Arts 17 to 17J, dealing with preliminary orders and interim measures. A preliminary order resembles a without notice application in English civil litigation (see Sime, *A Practical Approach to Civil Procedure* (17th edn, OUP, 2014), ch 23). Preliminary orders are available unless otherwise agreed by the parties (Art 17B(1)). They are made without notice to the respondent, and usually last for up to 20 days, when there should be a decision by the tribunal on whether to adopt or modify the preliminary order as an interim measure (Art 17C(4)). They are available where there is a risk that giving advance notice to the respondent will frustrate the purpose of the measure (Art 17B(2)). **29.83**

Interim measures under the Model Law are broadly equivalent to conservatory measures and procedural orders in English law (see 28.37 and 30.04). They are any temporary measure, whether or not in the form of an award, which orders a party to maintain the status quo pending determination of the dispute, or to take action to prevent imminent harm, or to preserve assets (a freezing order) or evidence (Art 17(2)). Under the Model Law a tribunal has the power to grant interim measures unless otherwise agreed by the parties (Art 17(1)). **29.84**

Article 17A says that an interim measure in the form of an interim injunction is only available if the arbitral tribunal is satisfied that: **29.85**

- it is likely there will be harm that is not adequately reparable in damages without the measure;
- such harm substantially outweighs the harm that the respondent is likely to suffer if the measure is granted; and
- there is a reasonable possibility that the requesting party will succeed on the merits of the arbitration.

The arbitral tribunal can require the party seeking an interim measure to provide security, and will usually do so if it grants a preliminary order (Art 17E). There is a continuing duty on the requesting party to disclose any material change in the circumstances (Art 17F). The requesting party is under an obligation to pay any costs and damages caused by the measure if it later transpires it should not have been granted (Art 17G). One of the drawbacks in **29.86** arbitration is that arbitrators themselves have no coercive powers, and the parties have to resort to the courts for enforcement if arbitrators' decisions are not complied with. To make this as easy as possible, Arts 17H and 17I say that interim measures are enforceable in the courts on the same basis as final awards (ie with limited grounds for objecting to recognition or enforcement by the courts). Preliminary orders, however, are not recognized or enforceable in the courts.

Statements of case under the Model Law

29.87 Either the parties may agree, or the tribunal may direct, the times when the parties must provide their statements of case (Art 23). The claimant's statement of claim must state the facts supporting the claim, the points at issue, and the relief or remedies sought. The respondent responds in a statement of defence, which must answer the particulars set out in the statement of claim. Article 23(1) says that the parties may provide supporting documents with their statements of case, or they may choose to make references to the relevant documents or other evidence that they say support their version of events.

Subsequent procedure

29.88 In accordance with the principle of party autonomy, the parties are free to agree on the procedure to be followed in the conduct of proceedings under the Model Law (Art 19(1)). In the absence of agreement, the tribunal may conduct the arbitration in such manner as it considers appropriate (Art 19(2)). It will usually make directions for the steps to be taken by the parties to prepare for the final determination of the reference. All statements, documents, or other information supplied to the arbitral tribunal must be communicated to all the parties (Art 24(3)). Procedural matters can be decided by a presiding arbitrator (Art 29).

29.89 The tribunal has the power (unless otherwise agreed by the parties) to appoint one or more experts to report on specific issues (Art 26(1)(a)), and may direct any of the parties to provide access to any relevant documents, goods or other property for inspection (Art 26(1)(b)). All experts' reports must be communicated to all the parties (Art 24(3)). A tribunal-appointed expert should attend any hearing for the purpose of answering questions from the parties (Art 26(2)). The parties must be given sufficient notice of any hearing (Art 24(2)).

Hearings

29.90 Where the tribunal feels it appropriate, and provided there is no objection from the parties, the tribunal can decide to determine the reference without a hearing. In such a case the tribunal decides the dispute on the basis of the documents and any other materials available to it (Art 24(1)). However, unless the parties have previously agreed there will be no hearings, any party may request a hearing, in which event a hearing will take place at an appropriate stage of the proceedings (Art 24(1)). There is nothing in this provision laying down any minimum requirements on the length, number, or timings of any hearings. However, Art 18 says the parties must be treated with equality, and each party must be given a full opportunity of presenting its case.

29.91 Article 19(2) gives the tribunal an express power to determine the admissibility, relevance, materiality, and weight of any evidence submitted to it. Decisions are made in accordance with the proper law of the dispute (Art 28). Where there is a tribunal with more than one member, any decision may be made by a majority of its members (Art 29). Reasons must be stated, unless the parties have agreed that no reasons be given (Art 31(2)). The proceedings, and the tribunal's mandate, terminate with the signing of the final award (Art 32).

KEY POINTS SUMMARY

- In English law, there are no differences in the Arbitration Act 1996 between domestic and international commercial arbitrations. **29.92**
- Other jurisdictions often draw a distinction between domestic and international arbitrations.
- The seat of an arbitration is its juridical location.
- Different systems of law may govern the substantive contract, the agreement to arbitrate, and the procedural law of an arbitration.
- Ideally the parties will have reached express agreement on the system(s) of law governing each of these areas.
- If there is no express agreement on the system of law, it will be determined from all the circumstances. There are particular rules, for example Rome I, that provide a framework for determining the proper law of contracts etc.
- There is a range of possible challenges to the jurisdiction of a tribunal.
- There are also several different ways in which a challenge to the tribunal's jurisdiction can be brought.
- These include the tribunal deciding its own jurisdiction (*Kompetenz-Kompetenz*) and challenges being made to the court.
- International arbitrations give rise to issues such as the language to be used in the process, and possibly different concepts on matters such as the scope of the law of privilege, which present difficulties in ensuring the process is fair to all sides.
- The UNCITRAL Model Law and ICC arbitration rules are widely used across the globe in international arbitration.

30

ARBITRATION AWARDS AND ORDERS

A INTRODUCTION 30.01
B PROCEDURAL ORDERS 30.04
C INTERIM AWARDS AND AWARDS ON DIFFERENT ISSUES 30.06
D SETTLEMENT 30.09
E MAIN AWARDS 30.10
F AWARD OF COSTS 30.28
Key points summary 30.31

A INTRODUCTION

30.01 Making awards, which are binding decisions, is what distinguishes arbitration from the non-adjudicatory methods of ADR. These other ADR processes are aimed at facilitating the parties in coming to a consensual arrangement between themselves. Arbitration, on the other hand, is designed to ensure the final disposal of a dispute by an impartial arbitral tribunal agreed upon by the parties.

30.02 There are four different types of awards and orders that are available to arbitrators, namely:

- *procedural orders*, which provide procedural directions and measures designed to preserve evidence or the subject-matter of the dispute ('conservatory measures') while an arbitration is proceeding;
- *interim awards and awards on different issues*, which finally dispose of one or more of the substantive issues in the arbitration, leaving the other issues to be decided later;
- *main awards*, finally disposing of the arbitration; and
- *costs awards*, which provide for the payment of the costs incurred in the arbitration between the parties.

30.03 Usually, once an order or award is made it is binding on the parties. Most sets of institutional arbitral rules include provision for parties making suggestions for the correction of clerical mistakes in orders and awards. In addition to making such checks, lawyers need to advise their clients on the meaning and effect of the tribunal's decision, and where there is further work to be done, to take the client's instructions on the next steps. If it is a procedural order these will be the further steps needed in preparing the matter for the final decision. If it is a final award, and if the decision is adverse to the client, consideration needs to be given to whether there are grounds for challenging the award, for which see Chapter 31.

B PROCEDURAL ORDERS

30.04 Arbitrators have the power to make a range of orders and to give directions in the period between the time they are appointed and when they make their final award. The various types of order available are considered in Chapter 28, and fall into the following categories:

- *procedural directions*, which will set out a timetable for the parties to follow in preparing for the hearing (see 28.33);

- *interim remedies*, such as security for costs and interim payments on account of the sum that may eventually be awarded (see 28.34);
- *conservatory measures*, which are designed to preserve the subject-matter of the dispute, or give one side access to property in the control of the other party (see 28.37);
- *peremptory orders*, which are usually backed by sanctions in default, which are used where a party fails to comply with earlier orders of the tribunal (see 28.40); and
- *orders dismissing the arbitration*, which is the ultimate sanction for non-compliance with the timetable laid down by the arbitrators (see 28.44).

An example of a tribunal's order for directions can be seen at Figure 28.2. **30.05**

C INTERIM AWARDS AND AWARDS ON DIFFERENT ISSUES

Unless otherwise agreed by the parties, arbitrators have powers to make interim awards and awards on different issues under the Arbitration Act 1996 s 47. Interim awards are to be distinguished from provisional orders in that they are final and binding (*Sucafina SA v Rotenberg* [2013] Bus LR 158), but only on part of the dispute, whereas provisional orders regulate the position of the parties during the interim stages of an arbitration, but do not finally dispose of any of the issues in the arbitration. **30.06**

Particular powers given by s 47(2) include: **30.07**

- making an award relating to an issue affecting the whole claim; and
- making an award relating to a part only of the claims or cross-claims remitted to the arbitrators.

These powers may be useful, for example, where it is possible to identify a single issue that may be capable of being disposed of swiftly, and once there is a final decision on that issue the parties may be enabled to settle the rest of their dispute. Alternatively, it may be that resolution of part of a claim, for example liability, may avoid the need to investigate and determine other issues, such as those relating to remedies, thereby saving costs. **30.08**

D SETTLEMENT

If the parties settle their dispute before the arbitrators make their final decision, unless otherwise agreed by the parties, the arbitral tribunal will terminate the substantive proceedings and will record the settlement in the form of an agreed award (Arbitration Act 1996 s 51(1), (2)). An agreed award must state that it is an award of the arbitration tribunal, and has the same status and effect as any other award on the merits of the case (s 51(3)). A duly authenticated original award of a settlement makes it possible to effect enforcement overseas under the New York Convention 1958 (see Chapter 32). **30.09**

E MAIN AWARDS

Again in accordance with the principle that the parties are free to agree on the way in which their dispute is determined (Arbitration Act 1996 s 1(b)), the parties can agree on the form of their award in an arbitration (s 52(1)). However, the default provisions in the Arbitration Act 1996 are usually adopted because they provide a sensible and practical regime for ensuring that awards are properly recorded and enforceable. Section 52(3) provides that the award shall be in writing signed by all the arbitrators or all those assenting to the award. The award must also **30.10** contain the reasons for the decision (see 30.15) unless it is an agreed award or the parties have agreed to dispense with reasons (s 52(4)). Dispensing with reasons will mean that it is impossible to appeal the decision to the High Court on a point of law under s 69 (see Chapter 31), and also excludes the jurisdiction of the court to determine preliminary points of law (s 45(1)).

30.11 The award must state the seat of the arbitration (see 30.16), and the date when the award is made (see 30.17) (s 52(5)).

30.12 An example of a final award based on the bribery case in Chapter 28 is shown in Figure 30.1. After the heading the award has a number of recitals (under the word 'whereas'). There then follow three procedural issues dealing with the seat of the arbitration and the applicable law. The substantive provisions of the award then follow. The short para 1 means that the claimant won on liability, with the other paragraphs dealing with costs (which are to be decided later in a separate award on costs).

Figure 30.1 Final award in an arbitration

IN THE MATTER OF THE ARBITRATION ACT 1996

AND

IN THE MATTER OF AN ARBITRATION

BETWEEN

CHIPOKA AIRWAYS LIMITED

Claimant

and

RUNWAY AIRCRAFT MAINTENANCE LIMITED

Respondent

FINAL AWARD

WHEREAS:

(1) By a contract in writing dated 12 March 2010 ('the Contract') the Respondent agreed to provide aircraft maintenance services for the Claimant in respect of four aircraft for a period of five years from 6 April 2010 to 5 April 2015.

(2) The Contract provided that any dispute or difference arising out of or in connection with the Contract shall be administered by the London Court of International Arbitration and finally determined under the Rules of the London Court of International Arbitration ('the Rules') by three arbitrators appointed in accordance with the Rules.

(3) By a letter dated 17 January 2014 the Claimant appointed James Benson to act as an arbitrator for the determination of such disputes and differences who accepted his appointment by a letter dated 30 January 2014.

(4) By a letter dated 27 January 2014 the Respondent appointed Margaret Swaledale to act as an arbitrator for the determination of such disputes and differences who accepted her appointment by a letter dated 3 February 2014.

(5) By an instrument in writing dated 10 February 2014 the arbitrators appointed Philip Wilson to be the third arbitrator and chairman in the matter of this arbitration.

(6) Formal statements of case having been exchanged, an oral hearing took place opening on 24 November 2014 and closing on 28 November 2014.

(7) The oral hearing was attended by the parties and their legal representatives, and oral evidence was heard from witnesses called by both parties.

Figure 30.1 Final award in an arbitration (*Continued*)

PROCEDURAL ISSUES

1. In accordance with article 16.1 of the Rules the parties agreed that the place of the arbitration should be London.
2. The seat of the arbitration is accordingly London, England.
3. By clause 26 of the Contract the parties agreed that the proper law of the Contract was the law of England and Wales.

THE AWARD

Having considered the oral and written evidence, and the oral and written submissions by the legal representatives of both parties, and for the reasons set out in the annex to this award, we hereby award and direct as follows:

1. The Respondent shall pay to the Claimant the sum of US$ 8,421,765 being the sum we award in respect of the matters arising for decision on the disputes in this reference.
2. This award is final on all matters except costs.
3. The arbitrators' award as to costs and the fees of the arbitrators is reserved.
4. If either party wishes to make oral submissions regarding costs they must give notice in writing to the arbitrators at the address set out in the covering letter to this award within 14 days of the date of this award.
5. If no such written notice is received within the time limited in paragraph 4 above, the parties are at liberty to deliver to the arbitrators at the same address written submissions on costs no later than 28 days after the date of this award.

DATED 14 January 2015

Signed: (1)
(2)
(3)
Arbitrators

Witnessed by:

ANNEX

[The reasons for the award will be set out in an annex, unless the parties have agreed that no reasons should be given.]

Majority decisions

An obvious reason for having an odd number of arbitrators is to avoid the risk of stalemate. If the arbitral tribunal has more than one member, the usual rule is that decisions are made by a majority. In accordance with the principle of party autonomy, the parties may agree some other method of decision making (such as unanimous decisions), but the risks of having to start again with a new tribunal are such that such arrangements are rare. **30.13**

Where the arbitral tribunal includes a chairperson (see 27.13), decisions, orders, and awards are made by all or a majority of the arbitrators, including the chairperson (Arbitration Act 1996 s 20(3)). The view of the chairperson prevails where there is neither unanimity nor a majority (s 20(4)). Where the arbitral tribunal has an umpire (see 27.14), decisions, orders, and awards shall be made by the other arbitrators unless and until they cannot agree on a matter relating to the arbitration (s 21(4)). Where there is stalemate between the other arbitrators, they are required to give notice in writing to the parties and the umpire, whereupon **30.14** the umpire replaces them as the tribunal with power to make decisions, orders, and awards as if he or she were the sole arbitrator. Where the parties agree that there shall be two or more arbitrators with no chair or umpire, in the absence of contrary agreement between the parties, decisions, orders, and awards are made by all or a majority of the arbitrators (s 22).

Reasons

30.15 Reasons, where they are to be given for an award, need to be adequate and capable of being understood by the parties. There is no requirement for the tribunal to deal with every possible argument in the case, nor is there any duty to explain why greater weight was given to some items of evidence rather than others (*World Trade Corporation v Czarnikow Sugar Ltd* [2005] 1 Lloyd's Rep 422). The arbitral tribunal does however need to deal with each of the essential issues to be decided in the case. What these are depends in part on the statements of case of the parties and in part on the nature of the decision that has to be made (*Hussmann (Europe) Ltd v Al Ameen Development and Trade Co* [2000] 2 Lloyd's Rep 83; *Checkpoint Ltd v Strathclyde Pension Fund* [2003] 1 EGLR 1).

Seat of the arbitration

30.16 The need to include the seat of the arbitration in an award is important for enforcement in other jurisdictions. Establishing the seat of an arbitration is considered at 29.14. Failing to state the seat of the arbitration in an award will not prevent enforcement of the award within England and Wales (see for example *Ranko Group v Antarctic Maritime SA* (1998) LMLN 492). Ultimately, where a failure to state the seat of the arbitration does cause a problem, it may be cured by an application to the High Court under the Arbitration Act 1996 s 68, as an irregularity causing substantial injustice (see Chapter 31).

Date of award

30.17 Unless otherwise agreed by the parties, the arbitration tribunal may decide what is to be taken to be the date on which the award is made (Arbitration Act 1996 s 54(1)). In the absence of such a decision the award shall be taken to be dated when it is signed by the arbitrator, or where there is more than one arbitrator, when it is signed by the last of them (s 54(2)).

30.18 Institution rules may provide machinery for dealing with difficulties, such as the death or lack of co-operation of one of the arbitrators after a decision has been reached. The LME regulations provide that if an arbitrator refuses or fails to sign the award, the signatures of the majority are sufficient, provided that the reason for the omitted signature is stated (reg 12.2.2).

30.19 The date of the award is important for the purposes of any challenge or appeal. By s 70(3) any application or appeal must be brought within 28 days of the date of the award (see Chapter 31). The date of the award is also important for the purposes of calculating interest (see 30.23).

Place where award is made

30.20 Unless otherwise agreed by the parties, where the seat of the arbitration is in England and Wales, the award is treated as being made here (Arbitration Act 1996 s 53). This is regardless of where the award was signed, dispatched, or delivered. This section reverses the decision in *Hiscox v Outhwaite* [1992] 1 AC 562, where an English arbitration happened to have been signed in Paris. Section 53 makes clear that the accident of where an arbitration award happens to have been signed does not affect where it is treated as a matter of law to have been made. Section 53 is consistent with the rule relating to enforcement under the New York Convention 1958 (see s 100(2)(b), and see Chapter 32).

Remedies

The parties are free to agree on the remedies available to the arbitral tribunal (Arbitration Act 1996 s 48(1)). Unless otherwise agreed by the parties, the arbitrators have the following powers: **30.21**

- to make declarations (s 48(3));
- to order payment of a sum of money in any currency (s 48(4));
- the same powers as a court to order a party to do or be refrained from doing anything (s 48(5));
- to order specific performance of a contract other than a contract relating to land, if and so far as it relates to land (s 48(5)(b) and *Tilia Sonera Ab v Hilcourt (Docklands) Ltd* [2003] EWHC 3540 (Ch), where it was held that specific performance could be ordered in respect of remedial works on land); and
- to order the rectification, setting aside, or cancellation of a deed or other document (s 48 (5)(c)).

Injunctions

While the Arbitration Act 1996 s 48(5)(a) gives arbitrators a power equivalent to granting mandatory and prohibitory injunctions, this is restricted to final awards and does not give arbitrators the power to make the equivalent of interim injunctions (*Kastner v Jason* [2004] 2 Lloyd's Rep 233 and see the further discussion at 31.25). **30.22**

Interest

Unless otherwise agreed by the parties, arbitrators may award simple or compound interest from such dates and at such rates and with such rests as are considered to meet the justice of the case (Arbitration Act 1996 s 49). Interest may be awarded both up to the date of the award and also for the period after the award until the date of payment (s 49(3), (4)). Interest is usually awarded at a rate equivalent to the rate that the successful party would have had to pay on money borrowed from its bank. **30.23**

Notification of award

Subject to the agreement of the parties, the award shall be notified to them by service of copies of the award, which must be done without delay (Arbitration Act 1996 s 55(2)). This provision does not affect the power of the arbitrators to withhold their award in the case of non-payment of their fees (ss 55(3) and 56). **30.24**

Binding effect

Unless otherwise agreed by the parties a final award is both final and binding upon the parties and any persons claiming through or under them (Arbitration Act 1996 s 58(1)). This does not affect the right of a party to challenge the award either by an internal appeal under the arbitration provider's institutional rules, or through an appeal to the High Court (for which see Chapter 31). **30.25**

Different arbitration institutions either do or do not provide for an appeal mechanism within their institutional rules. A challenge to the arbitrators' award is not permitted to the High **30.26**

Court before the appellant has first exhausted any available arbitral process of appeal or review (s 70(2)), but the 28-day period for making the application to the High Court does not run until the internal appeal or review process has been completed (s 70(3)).

30.27 Different institutional rules make various different provisions for the mechanics for finalizing an award. Awards of the arbitrators in commercial arbitration under the LME regulations are deposited with the secretary to the LME, who notifies each party (reg 12.10). Either party may then take up the award upon payment by that party of the costs and expenses of the arbitration as specified in the award (including the remuneration of the arbitrators). Until the award is taken up by one of the parties it confers no rights upon either party.

F AWARD OF COSTS

30.28 An arbitral tribunal may make an award allocating costs of the arbitration between the parties, this power being subject to any agreement between parties (Arbitration Act 1996 s 61(1)). It will be seen from paras 2–5 in the final award shown in Figure 30.1 that the tribunal reserved the question of costs when making its award on liability and quantum. The outstanding matters cover whether the losing party (in this instance the respondent) should pay the successful party's costs, how much should be payable under the award of costs, and also payment of the arbitrators' fees.

30.29 Arbitration costs awards are made on similar principles to those applicable in court litigation (see Sime, *A Practical Approach to Civil Procedure* (17th edn, OUP 2014), ch 46). The main principle is that the arbitrators shall award costs in favour of the successful party (s 61(2)), except where this appears to be inappropriate. Similar factors to those affecting the usual principle in court litigation apply also to arbitrations. Arbitrators will therefore take into account factors such as the conduct of the parties in the arbitration, whether the claim has been exaggerated, and the degree, if any, to which the successful party was only partially successful.

30.30 In the example shown in Figure 30.1 it would be very difficult for the respondent to mount a successful argument avoiding paying all the claimant's costs. From the statements of case, the respondent did not dispute liability, but argued on how much should be paid to the claimant. While the claimant made a claim for US$55 million odd, and recovered only US$8.5 million odd, the claim was put forward in alternative ways. The US$55 million claim was based on the whole amount the claimant had paid to the respondent under the contract, and while this is considerably more than the sum recovered, the alternative claim based on what the claimant thought was either the total amount of the bribes or the amount by which the respondent was unjustly enriched by the transaction, namely US$9.9 million odd, was clearly set out in the points of claim. It is not therefore an exaggeration case. All the respondent can reasonably point to is that the claimant sought US$9.9 million on the alternative case, and recovered 'only' US$8.5 million. Therefore, to some extent, the claimant was not totally successful in the reference, both because the respondent defeated the total amount paid (US$55 million) basis of the claim, and by paring off US$1.4 million on the alternative way of quantifying the claim. Whether these points have any effect on the costs award depends on the view taken by the arbitrators of how important these two areas of partial success by the respondent were in the overall picture of the reference. If, for example, the main issue was whether the sum awarded should be based on the total outlay (US$55 million) or the amount by which the respondent was unjustly enriched (US$8.5 million), a substantial deduction from the claimant's award of costs would be likely. If the US$55 million basis of quantification was not a major issue (because the claimant recognized early that it was unlikely to be awarded), suffering a US$1.4 million reduction on the sum set out in the points of claim is unlikely to be regarded as a sufficiently clear partial success on the part of the respondent to justify any departure from the usual rule that the losing party pays the whole costs of the successful party. If the tribunal does decide there was partial success, this is likely to be reflected by ordering the respondent to pay only a percentage of the claimant's costs.

KEY POINTS SUMMARY

- The provisions in the Arbitration Act 1996 on awards are all subject to the agreement of the parties. **30.31**
- Arbitrators have wide powers to make procedural orders enabling them to lay down timetables for the steps to be taken by the parties to prepare for the arbitration hearing and to preserve property pending the final award.
- Interim awards are final decisions on aspects of the whole dispute, but are not all that common. They can be a useful method of saving expense.
- Final awards finally determine the dispute between the parties.
- Final awards must be in writing and comply with certain formalities.
- The normal position is that the final award should also state reasons, but the parties may agree to dispense with reasons, in which case it will not be possible to mount an appeal on a point of law.
- Although there are some restrictions, arbitrators have wide-ranging powers on remedies and interest.
- The purpose of the formalities on awards is to ensure that they are enforceable, for example under the New York Convention 1958.

31

HIGH COURT JURISDICTION IN ARBITRATION CLAIMS

A INTRODUCTION .31.01
B ORDERS TO PREVENT PARTIES BREACHING AGREEMENTS TO ARBITRATE 31.05
C APPOINTMENT, REMOVAL, AND REPLACEMENT OF ARBITRATORS 31.15
D PROCEDURAL ORDERS TO ASSIST IN THE DETERMINATION OF ARBITRAL PROCEEDINGS .31.23
E JUDICIAL REVIEW OF ARBITRAL PROCEEDINGS .31.40
F PRELIMINARY POINTS OF LAW 31.41
G SERIOUS IRREGULARITY. 31.45
H APPEAL ON A POINT OF LAW 31.61
I PROCEDURE IN ARBITRATION CLAIMS. 31.82
J APPEALS TO THE COURT OF APPEAL. . . .31.91
Key points summary 31.95

A INTRODUCTION

31.01 Achieving a balance between the autonomy of arbitration proceedings and judicial intervention to ensure arbitral proceedings are conducted fairly and in accordance with the rights of the parties is a difficult issue. Different solutions have been advanced in different jurisdictions and at different times. In England they are largely summarized by two of the general principles in the Arbitration Act 1996 s 1, namely:

- the parties are free to agree how their disputes are resolved, subject only to such safeguards as are necessary in the public interest (s 1(b)); and
- the court should not intervene except as provided by the Arbitration Act 1996 (s 1(c)).

31.02 There is a significant public interest in preserving the binding effect of decisions made by arbitrators. If these are readily overturned by the courts, arbitration would be little more than a precursor to the 'real' litigation in the courts, which would be expensive for the parties and would drive arbitration business away from this country. Balanced against this is the need to ensure the parties in arbitration proceedings are treated fairly, have a proper chance to present their version of events, and are able to put right any burning injustices that may occur in an arbitration. Despite being founded on an agreement to arbitrate between the parties, with the passing of time there are cases where one side loses its enthusiasm for arbitration. Witnesses of course were not parties to the agreement to arbitrate, so are not under a contractual obligation to assist the parties to an arbitration.

31.03 To deal with these situations, the Arbitration Act 1996 gives the civil courts a number of powers to support or intervene in arbitrations. These powers fall into five broad categories:

- court orders to prevent parties breaching agreements to arbitrate;
- court assistance in the appointment of arbitrators where there has been a problem in making the necessary appointments;

- court orders over procedural steps that the arbitral tribunal either cannot make or cannot enforce;
- interim remedies granted by the court to preserve the status quo; and
- judicial review and enforcement of arbitral awards to ensure arbitral decisions have the effect intended when the arbitral agreement was entered into.

In this context, arbitration lawyers use the expression 'judicial review' (see 31.40) to describe going to court to challenge an award for want of jurisdiction or for serious irregularity, or to appeal to the court on a point of law. This is not to be confused with the High Court's jurisdiction of judicial review of administrative decisions of local and central government decisions under the Senior Courts Act 1981 s 31. **31.04**

B ORDERS TO PREVENT PARTIES BREACHING AGREEMENTS TO ARBITRATE

A party may bring court proceedings in breach of an existing arbitration agreement for a number of reasons. It may be that the existence of the arbitration clause is simply overlooked, or it may be that the party bringing the court proceedings hopes that the other side will not object to the matter being dealt with by the courts rather than through arbitration. In some cases the question of arbitrating or litigating has already been canvassed in correspondence, and the claimant may take the view that the other side has also stated a preference for going to court rather than arbitration. Rather more difficult issues may be raised where there is a disagreement between the parties over whether an arbitration clause applies to the current dispute, or whether there is a valid arbitration clause at all. See Chapter 28 for a number of the issues that might arise. **31.05**

Where court proceedings have already been started, the appropriate application to make is for a stay of those proceedings. If successful, such an application prevents the court proceedings being taken any further. Where it is feared that proceedings are about to be commenced, it may be possible to apply for an anti-suit injunction (see 29.58). **31.06**

Stay of legal proceedings

To prevent a party from breaching an agreement to arbitrate by bringing court proceedings, the Arbitration Act 1996 s 9(1) allows the other side to apply for a stay of those court proceedings. A stay can be sought whether the legal proceedings said to breach the arbitration agreement are brought by way of claim or counterclaim (s 9(1)), and include unfair prejudice petitions under the Companies Act 2006 s 996, as well as ordinary Part 7 claims (*Fulham Football Club (1987) Ltd v Richards* [2012] Bus LR 606). A stay imposes a halt on the legal proceedings, apart from taking any steps allowed by the terms of the stay. While in technical terms the proceedings can be continued if the stay is lifted (see the glossary to the CPR), in practical terms stays under s 9 are usually permanent, because the usual consequence is that the dispute will be referred for final determination by arbitration. **31.07**

Procedure for seeking a stay

Applications for stays under the Arbitration Act 1996 s 9 are made in the court in which the claim is proceeding (s 9(1)). The party seeking the stay is required to file an acknowledgement of service (Form N9) in the court proceedings before making the application (s 9(3)), and will tick the box on the form stating an intention to contest the court's jurisdiction. The application for the stay is made by issuing an application notice in Form N244 (CPR r 62.3(3)). A witness statement in support will need to set out all the relevant circumstances, including the arbitration agreement as an exhibit, and explain why the dispute comes within that **31.08** agreement. The application has to be served on all the other parties to the litigation (CPR r 62.8(1), (2)).

Determination of the application for a stay

31.09 The main question under the Arbitration Act 1996 s 9 is whether the dispute raised in the litigation is a matter 'which under the [arbitration] agreement is to be referred to arbitration...' (s 9(1)). If it is s 9(4) says the court 'shall' grant a stay (so this is mandatory rather than discretionary), unless the court is satisfied that the arbitration agreement is null and void, inoperative, or incapable of being performed.

Taking a step in the proceedings

31.10 An application for a stay under the Arbitration Act 1996 s 9 must be made before the applicant takes any step in the proceedings to answer the substantive claim (s 9(3)). It is not every step in the court proceedings that will deprive the applicant of the right to a stay. The question is whether the step impliedly affirmed the applicant's willingness to go along with the court proceedings (*Eagle Star Insurance Co Ltd v Yuval Insurance Co* [1978] 1 Lloyd's Rep 357). Acknowledging service or applying for a stay will not be 'steps' for this purpose. Filing a defence or agreeing case management directions would be (*Nokia Corp v HTC Corp* [2012] EWHC 3199 (Pat)).

Whether the dispute comes within arbitration agreement

31.11 It sometimes happens that the claimant in the court proceedings raises a question as to:

- whether there was a concluded arbitration agreement; or
- whether the dispute in the court proceedings falls within the terms of the arbitration agreement.

31.12 The court cannot grant a stay under the Arbitration Act 1996 s 9 if the parties to the court proceedings are not the parties, or persons claiming through or under a party, to the arbitration agreement (*City of London v Sancheti* [2009] Bus LR 996). For a stay to be granted, both parties in the litigation have to be parties to the arbitration agreement. It is not enough if one or other of the parties to the litigation has a mere commercial connection with one of the parties to the arbitration agreement.

31.13 In cases where there is a dispute over whether the dispute comes within the arbitration agreement, the court may by CPR r 62.8(3), either:

- decide that question on the hearing of the application for the stay; or
- give directions as how that question is to be decided and, if so, consider granting a stay of the proceedings pending that decision.

Anti-suit injunctions

31.14 The jurisdiction to grant anti-suit injunctions was considered at 29.58. They will typically be brought in the Commercial Court of the High Court, by an application notice supported by evidence in witness statements. The application will need to be served on the other party to the arbitration agreement, and will have to comply with the additional requirements in CPR Part 58, PD 58, and the *Commercial Court Guide*. These impose time limits for the filing of witness statements by the applicant and respondents (PD 58, paras 13.1–13.4), and various requirements for the compilation and filing of bundles of papers for the hearing (*Commercial Court Guide*, paras F5.4 and F11), skeleton arguments (paras F5.5 and F6.5), and authorities (para F13).

C APPOINTMENT, REMOVAL, AND REPLACEMENT OF ARBITRATORS

The usual position is that arbitrators are appointed by the parties or through mechanisms agreed by the parties without any involvement of the courts (see Chapter 27). Where there are problems in securing the appointment of the tribunal, or in the continuation of an arbitration caused by problems with members of the panel, there are a number of provisions in the Arbitration Act 1996 that give the courts power to make orders that may be exercised to provide solutions to the problems. **31.15**

Extending time for beginning arbitral proceedings

Arbitration clauses sometimes provide that claims will be barred, or the claimant's rights will be extinguished, unless specified steps to begin the arbitration are taken within some fixed time limit. The Arbitration Act 1996 s 12(1) provides that in these cases the court has power to extend the time for beginning the arbitration. An extension can be granted either before or after the time limit has elapsed (s 12(4)) on the grounds either that there has been a change of circumstances that was not contemplated by the parties, or the conduct of the other side makes it unjust to hold the applicant to the strict terms of the time limit (s 12(3)). **31.16**

Setting aside appointment of sole arbitrator

Where an arbitration agreement provides for both sides to appoint one arbitrator each, and one side refuses to do so, the party not in default can give notice under the Arbitration Act 1996 s 17(1) appointing its arbitrator as a sole arbitrator. Where this happens, the defaulting party is given a right to apply to the court to set aside the appointment of the sole arbitrator (s 17(3)). **31.17**

Failure of the appointment procedure

Where there is a failure in the procedure agreed by the parties for the appointment of the tribunal, either party may apply to the court for directions or other orders under the Arbitration Act 1996 s 18(3). An order may be made where there is a good arguable case for the arbitration agreement (*Noble Denton Middle East v Noble Denton International Ltd* [2011] 1 Lloyd's Rep 387). Powers in s 18(3) include the court making any necessary appointments itself. The courts have similar powers where a vacancy arises during the course of an arbitration (s 27(3)). **31.18**

Removal of arbitrators

A party to an arbitration is permitted to apply to the court under the Arbitration Act 1996 s 24 for the removal of an arbitrator. Grounds for removal set out in s 24(1) are: **31.19**

- justifiable doubts over the arbitrator's impartiality;
- the arbitrator does not have the qualifications required by the arbitration agreement;
- mental or physical incapacity; and
- refusal or failure to conduct the arbitration properly or with all reasonable dispatch.

Bias, or a lack of impartiality, is a recurrent issue in arbitrations. This is often caused by there being a limited pool of qualified people in the relevant field, so that it becomes difficult to find someone who has not had dealings (whether these be business dealings, or previous arbitrations) with one or other of the parties. To reduce the risks of such dealings only becoming known to both sides after substantial progress has been made in the arbitration, **31.20** it is good practice for arbitrators both to conduct a 'conflicts of interest' check and to communicate the results to both sides before their appointment is confirmed. Institutional arbitration rules on occasions make express provision for this. The UNCITRAL Model Law Art 12(1) provides that when approached in connection with possibly being appointed as an arbitrator, a person is under an obligation to disclose any circumstances likely to give rise to justifiable doubts as to his impartiality or independence. This duty continues after an appointment is made.

31.21 A doubt about partiality is only justifiable if a fair-minded and informed observer would conclude there was a real possibility that the arbitrator was biased, or if there was a reasonable appearance of bias (*Porter v Magill* [2002] 2 AC 357). The guidance given in *Locabail (UK) Ltd v Bayfield Properties Ltd* [2000] QB 451 (see Sime, *A Practical Approach to Civil Procedure* (17th edn, OUP, 2014), ch 39) is of general application and is just as relevant in arbitration as in litigation. It is not any appearance of bias that will justify the removal of an arbitrator. In *Andrews v Bradshaw* [2000] BLR 6 both parties were supposed to contribute to the arbitrator's fees, but only one had done so, and the arbitrator wrote a number of angry letters about the non-payment of his fees. While accepting the appointment with this one-sided payment arrangement and the tone of the letters was clearly unwise, neither was regarded by the Court of Appeal as sufficient to call into question the arbitrator's impartiality.

Relief from liability after resignation of an arbitrator

31.22 After resigning from his appointment, an arbitrator may apply to the court for relief from any liability for breaking his contract to conduct the arbitration, and for an order relating to his entitlement to any fees or expenses (Arbitration Act 1996 s 25(3)). Whether any relief is granted depends on whether in all the circumstances it was reasonable to resign (s 25(4)).

D PROCEDURAL ORDERS TO ASSIST IN THE DETERMINATION OF ARBITRAL PROCEEDINGS

Powers to secure evidence etc available to tribunals

31.23 The powers available to an arbitral tribunal depend primarily on what the parties have chosen to confer on their tribunal. These may be set out in the arbitration agreement, or in any institutional rules adopted by the parties. In the absence of contrary agreement by the parties, arbitral tribunals have various powers by virtue of the Arbitration Act 1996 for:

- appointing experts (s 37);
- inspecting, preserving, and ordering samples and experiments of the subject-matter of the arbitration if it is in the possession of a party (s 38(4));
- preserving evidence in the custody or control of a party (s 38(6)); and
- giving permission to a party to apply to the court for a witness summons to secure the attendance of a witness at the tribunal's hearings if the witness is in the United Kingdom (s 43).

31.24 There are limitations on these powers, which stem from the contractual basis of arbitration. Tribunals can only make orders about inspection of property or the preservation of evidence between the parties, so these orders are only available where the property is in the control of a party to the arbitration. While in many cases the tribunal will give permission to apply for a witness summons (s 43 also applies where all the parties agree), there will be cases where one party wants a witness summons, but the tribunal and other parties disagree.

There is an unresolved issue over whether the Arbitration Act 1996 permits an arbitral tribunal to make an order for an interim injunction. There is no express provision giving such a power. It is often thought that such a power can be seen in s 48. This provides in s 48(5)(a) that the tribunal has the same powers as the court to order a party to do or refrain from doing anything. The problem is that s 48 is located within ss 46–58, which deal with the final award. Cases like *Econet Wireless Ltd v Vee Networks Ltd* [2006] 2 Lloyd's Rep 428 assume that tribunals do have such a power. The doubt over this may be dispelled by the institutional rules that may be adopted by the parties. The clearest rules are those in the UNCITRAL Model Law Arts 17–17J (see Chapter 29), which contain detailed provisions for interim injunctions granted by arbitral tribunals. **31.25**

Court jurisdiction on procedural matters

Given the gaps and limitations on the powers available to arbitrators, the Arbitration Act 1996 s 44 makes the following provision in support of arbitral proceedings: **31.26**

(1) Unless otherwise agreed by the parties, the court has for the purposes of and in relation to arbitral proceedings the same power of making orders about the matters listed below as it has for the purposes of and in relation to legal proceedings.
(2) These matters are—
 (a) the taking of the evidence of witnesses;
 (b) the preservation of evidence;
 (c) making orders relating to property which is the subject of the proceedings or as to which any question arises in the proceedings [...];
 (d) the sale of any goods the subject of the proceedings;
 (e) the granting of an interim injunction or the appointment of a receiver.

Under these provisions the courts may make orders for recording the evidence of witnesses in depositions, orders for the preservation of evidence, or for the inspection, sampling etc of property that is the subject-matter of the arbitration, which may be in the possession of someone who is not a party to the arbitration. **31.27**

The purpose of s 44 is to give the court powers to be used when the arbitral tribunal is unable to act effectively. In *Belair LLC v Basel LLC* [2009] EWHC 725 (Comm) this was satisfied because the tribunal had not been constituted. An order was made to enable a party to deal with certain property, which was the only asset in the case, in the period until the tribunal could be constituted. Once this had happened it was for the tribunal to decide whether steps were required to preserve the property. **31.28**

Disclosure in aid of arbitration

Norwich Pharmacal *orders*

Where a dispute is referred to arbitration, the Arbitration Act 1996 s 43 provides that court procedures to procure documents or other material evidence may only be used with the permission of the arbitral tribunal or the agreement of the other parties. This provision does not prevent a court making a *Norwich Pharmacal* order (see Sime, *A Practical Approach to Civil Procedure* (17th edn, OUP, 2014), ch 30) in the period before a dispute has been referred to arbitration, where the power is used for preserving assets or remedies (*Glidepath Holding BV v Thompson* [2005] 1 All ER (Comm) 434). **31.29**

Pre-action disclosure

31.30 It has been held that the Senior Courts Act 1981 s 33(2) is limited to likely court proceedings, and does not confer jurisdiction to order pre-action disclosure in aid of arbitration (*EDO Corporation v Ultra Electronics Ltd* [2009] Bus LR 1306).

Non-party disclosure

31.31 The five powers specified under the Arbitration Act 1996 s 44(2) do not include orders for non-party disclosure under the Senior Courts Act 1981 s 34(3) and CPR r 31.17. Where there is a risk that documents may cease to exist or become unavailable, it may be possible to obtain an order for their preservation, such as by copying, under s 44(2)(b): see *Assimina Maritime Ltd v Pakistan National Shipping Corporation* [2005] 1 All ER (Comm) 460.

Interim injunctions

31.32 Courts are given jurisdiction to grant interim injunctions to preserve the status quo in support of arbitral proceedings by the Arbitration Act 1996 s 44(2)(e). The purpose of this power is to provide protection for the period before an arbitrator can be appointed (*Econet Wireless Ltd v Vee Networks Ltd* [2006] 2 Lloyd's Rep 428). In *Econet Wireless Ltd v Vee Networks Ltd* it was held to be inappropriate to seek an interim injunction in England under s 44 when the arbitration is to take place in another jurisdiction. Such an application should be made in the courts for the seat of the arbitration.

31.33 In *Cetelem SA v Roust Holdings Ltd* [2005] 1 WLR 3555 a dispute arose between parties to a share sale contract containing a London arbitration clause. A condition precedent under the contract was that approval had to be given by the Russian Central Bank. Five weeks before the expiry of the time for obtaining approval, no action had been taken by the defendant, so the claimant applied for an urgent mandatory interim injunction requiring the defendant to lodge the necessary papers in Russia. It was held that such an order could only be made if it was necessary for the preservation of evidence or assets, and there was no jurisdiction to make the order on any wider basis. Nevertheless the injunction satisfied the test. 'Assets' to be preserved under s 44(3) could include things in action. In this case the injunction was necessary to preserve the claimant's contractual right to purchase the shares, because the right to purchase them would be lost if no application was made for Russian Central Bank approval.

31.34 An application to the court for a freezing injunction in support of arbitration proceedings under the Arbitration Act 1996 s 44 has the advantages that the court's order will bind third parties and is buttressed by sanctions (*Pacific Maritime (Asia) Ltd v Holystone Overseas Ltd* [2008] 1 Lloyd's Rep 371).

Applications for procedural orders

On-notice applications

31.35 Applications for interim remedies under the Arbitration Act 1996 s 44 are usually made on notice to the other parties to the arbitration, using the arbitration claim form (Form N8: see PD 62, para 8.1, and discussed at 31.82). A Part 8 claim form is used because the dispute is being dealt with by arbitration, which means there will be no existing court proceedings.

Urgent applications

31.36 If an application for a procedural order is urgent, the Arbitration Act 1996 s 44(3) provides that the court may, on the application of a party or proposed party to the arbitral proceedings, make such orders as it thinks necessary for the purpose of preserving evidence or assets. These are usually made without notice to the other party, which in technical terms means without giving the usual three clear days' notice of the hearing to the other side (CPR r 23.7(1)).

Even in urgent cases, such notice as can be given must be attempted (such as by telephone or email informing the other party of the nature of the application and when it will be considered by the court). It is only if secrecy is essential (such as in applications for freezing injunctions), or where the urgency makes it impossible to give even informal notice, that giving no notice at all can be justified (*National Bank of Jamaica Ltd v Olint* [2009] 1 WLR 1405). **31.37**

Procedure for seeking interim injunctions

As with other procedural orders in support of arbitration, applications for interim injunctions under the Arbitration Act 1996 s 44(2)(e) are brought using the arbitration claim form. As the power under s 44(2)(e) is to preserve the position pending the appointment of the tribunal, it is necessary to set out the steps being taken to appoint an arbitrator in the evidence in support, and there must be an undertaking to appoint an arbitrator without delay. **31.38**

Exclusion of section 44

In accordance with the principle of party autonomy (see Chapter 26), the opening words of the Arbitration Act 1996 s 44 say it applies unless otherwise agreed by the parties. The powers given by s 44 are designed to support the effectiveness of arbitral proceedings, and are regarded as being highly beneficial. Accordingly, any purported exclusion of the section requires clear words, and the courts are not prone to finding the section has been excluded by reference to allegedly inconsistent provisions in the arbitration agreement (*SAB Miller Africa v East African Breweries* [2010] EWCA Civ 1564). Clauses that make equivalent provision to s 44 will not be taken to have excluded the section. It was held in *SAB Miller Africa v East African Breweries* that if the parties want to agree that interim relief is to be granted under the Senior Courts Act 1981 s 37 (for which, see Sime, *A Practical Approach to Civil Procedure* (17th edn, OUP, 2014), ch 42) free from the provisions of the Arbitration Act 1996 s 44, very clear provision would have to be made to that effect. **31.39**

E JUDICIAL REVIEW OF ARBITRAL PROCEEDINGS

Judicial review of arbitral proceedings takes four forms: **31.40**

- challenges to the jurisdiction of arbitrators (see 29.45);
- preliminary points of law (see 31.41);
- challenges to decisions for serious irregularity (see 31.45); and
- appeals on a point of law (see 31.61).

F PRELIMINARY POINTS OF LAW

Unless otherwise agreed by the parties, a party to arbitral proceedings may apply to the court for the determination of any question of law arising in the course of the arbitral proceedings (Arbitration Act 1996 s 45(1)). If such an application is made the tribunal may continue with the arbitration while the application to the court is pending (s 45(4)). **31.41**

Conditions to be satisfied

31.42 An application to the court for the determination of a preliminary question of law may only be brought if:

- the application is made with the agreement of all the other parties to the arbitration or with the permission of the tribunal (Arbitration Act 1996 s 45(2)). The agreement should ideally be in writing. Where reliance is placed on the permission of the tribunal rather than the consent of the parties, the court must be satisfied that:
  - the determination of the question is likely to produce substantial savings in costs; and
  - the application has been made without delay;
- there is no agreement to dispense with reasons for the tribunal's award (s 45(1)). Dispensing with reasons means the tribunal cannot make an error of law; and
- the court is satisfied that the point substantially affects the rights of one or more of the parties (s 45(1)). This is primarily directed at how important the point is in determining the rights of the parties. There is some authority that the value of the claim may be a factor in deciding whether a party's rights are substantially affected (*Retla Steamship Co v Gryphon Shipping Co SA* [1982] 1 Lloyd's Rep 55).

Procedure on applications on preliminary points of law

31.43 The application is an arbitration claim, and follows the procedure in CPR Part 62 (see 31.89–31.90). The arbitration claim form must identify the question of law to be determined (Arbitration Act 1996 s 45(3)). The witness statement in support should state whether the application is made with the consent of the parties or with the tribunal's permission, exhibiting the relevant documents. If the application is brought with the tribunal's permission, the witness statement must state the grounds on which it is alleged the question should be determined by the court (s 45(3) and PD 62, para 9.2).

31.44 In an application made with the tribunal's permission, as soon as practical after the written evidence of all the parties has been filed, the court will decide whether or not it should consider the application. Unless the court otherwise directs, the court will make its decision under s 45(2)(b) on whether to allow the application to proceed without a hearing (PD 62, paras 9.3 and 10.1).

G SERIOUS IRREGULARITY

31.45 Challenges to an arbitral award may be made under the Arbitration Act 1996 s 68 on the ground of serious irregularity. A challenge on this ground will only be successful if the claimant establishes both that:

- there was a serious irregularity affecting the tribunal, the proceedings, or the award; and
- it caused or will cause substantial injustice (s 68(1) and *Commercial Court Guide*, para O8.6(a)).

Meaning of 'serious irregularity'

31.46 The meaning of 'serious irregularity' is set out in the Arbitration Act 1996 s 68(2). This provides that a serious irregularity is one involving either:

- a failure by the tribunal to comply with the general duty to act fairly and impartially between the parties, giving each party a reasonable opportunity to put its case, as set out in s 33 (see Chapter 26);
- the tribunal exceeding its powers;

- a failure by the tribunal to conduct the arbitration in accordance with the procedure agreed by the parties;
- a failure by the tribunal to deal with the issues put before it;
- an arbitral institution exceeding its powers;
- uncertainty or ambiguity as to the effect of the award;
- obtaining the award by fraud or by means contrary to public policy;
- a failure to comply with the requirements as to the form of the award (see Chapter 30); or
- any irregularity in the conduct of the proceedings or in the award that is admitted by the tribunal or arbitral institution.

In considering these grounds, the court must be astute not to impose the standards that would be expected of judges and the courts in civil litigation. Having chosen to refer their dispute to arbitration, the parties must be taken to have accepted that the process adopted by the arbitrators may well lack the formality found in court proceedings. It is only if the complaint discloses a defect that cannot on any view be justified as an acceptable consequence of having chosen to arbitrate that s 68 may be engaged (*Petroships Pte Ltd v Petec Trading and Investment Corporation* [2001] 2 Lloyd's Rep 348). **31.47**

General duty to act fairly and impartially

Matters that have been held to come within the Arbitration Act 1996 s 68(2)(a) include an arbitrator failing to recuse himself where there was a real possibility of bias (*ASM Shipping Ltd v TTMI Ltd* [2006] 1 Lloyd's Rep 375) and delegating decision-making to an expert witness (*Brandeis Brokers Ltd v Black* [2001] 2 Lloyd's Rep 359). Deciding the case by overriding common ground between the parties without giving the parties the opportunity to address the contrary view on that matter taken by the arbitrator comes within s 68(2)(a) (*Omnibridge Consulting Ltd v Clearsprings (Management) Ltd* [2004] EWHC 2276 (Comm)). Failing to follow court practice, such as not giving the claimant's representative the final speech at the hearing, would not of itself come within s 68(2)(a) (*Margulead Ltd v Exide Technologies* [2005] 1 Lloyd's Rep 324). **31.48**

Exceeding powers

A tribunal will exceed its powers within the meaning of the Arbitration Act 1996 s 68(2)(b) where it exercises a power it does not have. Section 68(2)(b) is not engaged by merely wrongly exercising a power it does have (*Lesotho Highlands Development Authority v Impregilo SpA* [2006] 1 AC 221). One of the complaints in this case was that the arbitrators had exceeded their powers by expressing their award in favour of the contractors for payments due under a contract for the construction of a dam in European currencies rather than in Lesotho malotis. The significance was that in the period between the date the payments should have been made under the contract and the award the maloti had fallen dramatically against the European currencies. The majority view in the House of Lords was that the arbitrators had made an error of law in either misinterpreting the substantive contract or in misinterpreting s 48(4) (on making awards in any currency) by making the award in the European currencies. **31.49**

Lord Steyn at [32] said that in deciding whether s 68(2)(b) is engaged it is necessary to focus intensely on the particular power under the arbitration agreement, the terms of reference, or the Arbitration Act 1996, in the context of all the circumstances of the case. The mere 'erroneous exercise of an available power cannot by itself amount to an excess of power. A mere error of law will not amount to an excess of power under s 68(2)(b))'. Accordingly, the court could not intervene under s 68 despite the error of the tribunal. Being an error of law it would have been possible to mount a challenge under s 69, but that was not available on the facts because the parties had excluded rights of appeal on points of law under s 69. **31.50**

Failing to deal with all the issues

31.51 The Arbitration Act 1996 s 68(2)(d) provides for situations where there has been a 'failure by the tribunal to deal with all the issues that were put to it'. Morison J in *Fidelity Management SA v Myriad International Holdings BV* [2005] EWHC 1193 (Comm) at [9] said that s 68(2)(d):

- is designed to cover the essential issues in the arbitration. These are the issues that it is essential for the tribunal to determine in coming to a decision on the claims or defences raised in the course of the arbitration;
- is concerned with cases where the arbitral tribunal has not dealt at all with the case of a party. Examples are where a claim has been overlooked or where the decision cannot be justified as a particular key issue that is crucial to the result has not been decided;
- does not require arbitrators to deal with every argument on every point that is raised;
- is not to be used as a means of launching a detailed enquiry into the manner in which the tribunal considered the various issues, or with whether there has been a failure to come to the right answer on an issue; and
- is not concerned with the reasons given by the arbitrators on the issues. Deficiency of reasons is dealt with separately in s 70(4).

Fraud and public policy

31.52 In order to amount to fraud within the Arbitration Act 1996 s 68(2)(g) the alleged conduct must amount to serious impropriety, and requires cogent evidence (*Cuflet Chartering v Carousel Shipping Ltd* [2001] 1 Lloyd's Rep 707).

Substantial injustice

31.53 It is clear from the second requirement under the Arbitration Act 1996 s 68(2), that any irregularity either must have caused, or will cause, substantial injustice to the applicant, and that the section imposes a high hurdle. The DAC report (Departmental Advisory Committee on Arbitration, set up by the Department of Trade and Industry, whose reports formed the basis for the Arbitration Act 1996) at para 280 commented that s 68 'is really designed as a long stop only available in extreme cases where the tribunal has gone so wrong in its conduct of the arbitration that justice calls out for it to be corrected'. This passage has been cited with approval in a number of cases, including *Lesotho Highlands Development Authority v Impreglio SpA* [2006] 1 AC 221 (Lord Steyn).

31.54 Where the decision would clearly have been different if the irregularity had not occurred, there will almost certainly have been a substantial injustice (*Newfield Construction Ltd v Tomlinson* (2004) 97 Con LR 148); likewise where the irregularity results in the denial of a fair hearing (*Checkpoint Ltd v Strathclyde Pension Fund* [2003] 1 EGLR 1). An arbitrator's failure to recuse himself in circumstances where the court found there was a real possibility of bias was regarded as of itself a substantial injustice in *ASM Shipping Ltd v TTMI Ltd* [2006] 1 Lloyd's Rep 375.

31.55 In deciding whether an injustice is substantial, all the circumstances must be taken into account. The monetary value of the claim may be a factor in this assessment (*Groundshire v VHE Construction* [2001] 1 Lloyd's Rep 395).

31.56 It is to be noted that substantial injustice is not the sole test, but the second limb of the test. The mere fact something has or has not occurred in an arbitration that may have caused a substantial injustice is not sufficient to satisfy the test in s 68. In addition, one of the specific irregularities set out in s 68(2) must be established.

Where an irregularity has been remedied, no relief should be given under s 68. For example, where reasons have not been given, the availability of applying for reasons or further reasons under s 70(4) would make it impossible to contend there was any substantial injustice (*Fidelity Management SA v Myriad International Holdings BV* [2005] EWHC 1193 (Comm)). **31.57**

Loss of right to object

The right to object under the Arbitration Act 1996 s 68, that the proceedings have been improperly conducted or that there has been a failure to comply with the arbitration agreement or with the provisions of the Arbitration Act 1996, or that there has been any other irregularity affecting the tribunal or the proceedings, is lost if it is not taken at the time (s 73). This arises if the party making the complaint takes part, or continues to take part, in the arbitral proceedings without making the objection either forthwith or within such time as is allowed by the arbitration agreement or the tribunal or by any provision of the Arbitration Act 1996 (s 73(1)). **31.58**

Powers available to deal with a serious irregularity

Where the court finds there has been a serious irregularity that causes a substantial injustice, the Arbitration Act 1996 s 68(3), says the court may: **31.59**

- remit the award to the tribunal, in whole or in part, for reconsideration;
- set aside the award in whole or in part; or
- declare the award to be of no effect, in whole or in part.

The choice between these powers will depend on the nature of the problem. Most problems within s 68 will be dealt with by setting aside, although remitting to the tribunal may be appropriate if the tribunal failed to deal with the issues, if the award is ambiguous, or if there is a formal defect in the award. The proviso to the subsection says that setting aside and declarations under sub-paras 3(b) and (c) cannot be made unless the court is satisfied that it would be inappropriate to remit the matters in question to the tribunal for reconsideration. **31.60**

H APPEAL ON A POINT OF LAW

Unless otherwise agreed by the parties, a party to arbitral proceedings may appeal to the court on a question of law arising out of an award (Arbitration Act 1996 s 69(1)). This is a controversial provision, because many arbitration lawyers believe it goes too far in allowing a court to interfere with decisions made by arbitrators. It is a commonly held view that as the parties have agreed to have their dispute decided by arbitration, it is inconsistent to have that decision reviewed by a court. The contrary view, which s 69 seeks to promote, is that where the parties have agreed to have their dispute decided in accordance with a system of law, it is right that the courts should be able to review decisions if they were not in the event decided in a way consistent with that law. **31.61**

There are a large number of restrictions on appeals under s 69, which are discussed below, which mean that successful appeals under s 69 are comparatively rare. **31.62**

Question of law

The Arbitration Act 1996 s 69 only applies to questions of law. The courts are vigilant in preventing the parties from seeking to dress up questions of fact as questions of law (*Demco Investments and Commercial SA v SE Banken Forsakring Holding Aktiebolag* [2005] **31.63**

EWHC 1398 (Comm)). On an appeal under s 69 the parties must take the arbitrator's findings of fact as the starting point. The appellant must then identify the question of law arising from those facts, and explain why the arbitrator's decision on that question was in error. Questions of law include disputes over the legal principles to be applied, the meaning of statutory provisions, and questions of construction of contracts.

31.64 For this purpose, 'law' means the law of England and Wales (s 82(1)). Questions of foreign law, where this is the proper law of the dispute, are questions of fact. As such, errors of foreign law do not come within s 69. They are still questions of fact if the foreign law is presumed to be, or if it is in fact, the same as English law. In *Reliance Industries Ltd v Enron Oil and Gas India Ltd* [2002] 1 All ER (Comm) 59, the parties had agreed that the proper law of the substantive contract was Indian law, which applies the same rules of contractual construction as English law. An appeal against the arbitrators' decision on the construction of the contract was not possible under s 69 because this was a matter of Indian law and therefore a question of fact.

No contrary agreement

31.65 The opening words of the Arbitration Act 1996 s 69(1) expressly say that its provisions apply unless otherwise agreed by the parties. It is therefore open to the parties to oust judicial review on points of law by agreement. Such agreement may be included in the arbitration clause in the substantive contract, or subsequently. Clear wording is required for a clause to have the effect of excluding the court's jurisdiction (*Essex CC v Premier Recycling Ltd* [2007] BLR 233). In *Shell Egypt West Manzala Gmbh v Dana Gas Egypt Ltd* [2010] 1 Lloyd's Rep 109 the phrase 'final, conclusive and binding' in the parties' arbitration agreement was not construed as an exclusion agreement. It was no more than a fairly standard governing law and arbitration clause. 'Final and binding' traditionally means simply that the arbitrators' award creates a res judicata between the parties.

31.66 Adoption of institutional arbitral rules may have the result of ousting the court's jurisdiction under s 69 if those rules prohibit appeals on points of law. For example, by adopting the ICC rules (see Chapter 29) the parties waive their right to any form of recourse in so far as such waiver can validly be made (ICC rules Art 34(6)). This amounts to a contrary agreement, ousting s 69 (see *Lesotho Highlands Development Authority v Impregilo SpA* [2006] 1 AC 221 at [3]).

No agreement to dispense with reasons

31.67 A written agreement to dispense with reasons for the tribunal's decision excludes the court's jurisdiction over points of law (the proviso to the Arbitration Act 1996 s 69(1), and s 5). Without reasons for the award, it is impossible to identify any error of law.

Tribunal asked to determine the point

31.68 Permission to appeal under the Arbitration Act 1996 s 69 cannot be granted unless the arbitral tribunal was asked to determine the question (s 69(3)(b)).

Exhaustion of arbitral appeals and reviews

31.69 An appeal under the Arbitration Act 1996 s 69 can only be made once all arbitral appeal and review opportunities have been exhausted (ss 57 and 70(2)).

Point must arise from an award

Appeals under the Arbitration Act 1996 s 69 can only be made on points arising from awards. They are not available from procedural orders that do not amount to awards. See Chapter 30 for the distinction between awards and orders. **31.70**

Appeal must be made within 28 days

By virtue of the Arbitration Act 1996 s 70(3), an appeal on a point of law must be made within 28 days of the award (see 31.84). **31.71**

Agreement or permission to appeal

An appeal under the Arbitration Act 1996 s 69 can only be made with the agreement of the other parties to the arbitration or with the permission of the court (s 69(2)). Agreements to enable appeals on points of law are the reverse of agreements to exclude such appeals. Their effect is to remove the need to obtain the court's permission for an appeal under s 69. **31.72**

Applications for permission to appeal are dealt with in a summary way. Usually they are dealt with on the papers. If they are dealt with orally, the practice is that they should be disposed of in half an hour or so, and the applicant has to show a clear-cut case that the statutory criteria are satisfied (*CMA CGM SA v Beteiligungs-KG MS 'Northern Pioneer' Schiffahrtsgesellschaft mbH and Co* [2003] 1 WLR 1015). **31.73**

Permission of the court

When seeking permission to appeal, the appellant must issue an arbitration claim form supported by a witness statement, which must address the requirement for seeking permission as set out in s 69(3) (see PD 62, para 12.2). Permission will not be granted (see s 69(3)) unless the court is satisfied that: **31.74**

(a) the determination of the question will substantially affect the rights of one or more parties;
(b) the question was raised with the tribunal (see 31.68);
(c) on the basis of the findings of fact in the award either:
  (i) the decision of the tribunal on the question is obviously wrong; or
  (ii) the question is one of general public importance and the decision of the tribunal is at least open to serious doubt; and
(c) despite the agreement of the parties to resolve the matter by arbitration, it is just and proper in all the circumstances for the court to determine the question.

As these are statutory criteria for granting permission, there is no scope for the courts to amplify or adapt them to changing circumstances (*CMA CGM SA v Beteiligungs-KG MS 'Northern Pioneer' Schiffahrtgesellschaft mbH and Co* [2003] 1 WLR 1015). They are based on the criteria laid down by Lord Diplock in *The Nema* [1982] AC 724, but sub-para (b) is new and sub-para (c)(ii) is a little wider than the guidance given in *The Nema*. **31.75**

Substantially affect the rights of the parties

In criterion (a), 'substantially' means of major importance (*International Sea Tankers Inc v Hemisphere Shipping Co Ltd* [1982] 1 Lloyd's Rep 128). 'Rights' means the issues in dispute in the arbitration (*CMA CGM SA v Beteiligungs-Kg MS 'Northern Pioneer' Schiffahrtgesellschaft mbH and Co* [2003] 1 WLR 1015). Permission therefore will not be granted on technical points. In the *Northern Pioneer* case the claimant raised an issue over whether its right to withdraw from a charterparty within a reasonable time under a war **31.76** clause arose from an implied term or through the principles of waiver, election, or estoppel. While this was an arguable point of law, it had no substantial impact on either party's rights because whatever the juridical basis of the right to withdraw, it had to be exercised within a reasonable time, and the arbitrators' decision that the claimant was too late to raise it was not open to serious doubt.

Obviously wrong

31.77 If the point of law is not of general public importance, it is necessary to show that the arbitrators' decision is obviously wrong. In *HMV UK Ltd v Propinvest Friar Ltd Partnership* [2011] EWCA Civ 1708 it was said the error has to be so obvious that it can be classified as a major intellectual aberration. If the arbitrator might be right, permission has to be refused.

General public importance

31.78 If the point of law is of general public importance, rather than having to show the arbitrators' decision was obviously wrong, it is only necessary to show that the decision is open to serious doubt (Arbitration Act 1996 s 69(3(c)(ii)). The distinction is often between points of law arising from one-off clauses (which do not raise questions of general public importance), and those arising from standard form contracts in common use (which do): see *The Nema* [1982] AC 724. Additional factors suggested by *Geogas Ltd v Trammo Gas Ltd* [1991] 1 Lloyd's Rep 349 are whether the point raises a matter of general legal principle, and whether it is likely to arise often in other cases. Events operating outside standard form contracts, such as whether the closure of a sea lane or shipping canal is a frustrating event, or whether the conflict in Kosovo amounted to a war for the purpose of shipping and insurance contracts (*The Northern Pioneer*), can therefore be of general public importance.

31.79 Showing a decision is open to serious doubt is plainly a lower test than showing it is obviously wrong. It may be satisfied, for example, where there is a split decision by the arbitrators (*The Northern Pioneer*) or where there are conflicting decisions in the courts or in previous arbitrations.

Overall discretion

31.80 Even if the three main conditions in sub-paras (a)–(c) of the Arbitration Act 1996 s 69(3), are satisfied, permission to bring an arbitration claim on a point of law will only be granted if it is just and proper for the court to determine the matter in all the circumstances of the case. The fact the parties have agreed to arbitrate rather than litigate is an important and powerful factor (DAC report, para 290).

Powers available to deal with points of law

31.81 On an appeal on a point of law, the Arbitration Act 1996 s 69(7), says the court may:

- confirm the award;
- vary the award;
- remit the award to the tribunal, in whole or in part, for reconsideration; or
- set aside the award in whole or in part.

I PROCEDURE IN ARBITRATION CLAIMS

Application or Part 8 claim

31.82 Arbitration claims are commenced using the arbitration claim form (Form N8), and follow the procedure for Part 8 as amended by Part 62 (CPR r 62.3(1); and see Sime, *A Practical*

Approach to Civil Procedure (17th edn, OUP, 2014), ch 8). An application to stay legal proceedings (which have already started) is made by making an interim application within those proceedings (CPR r 62.3(2)).

An example of an arbitration claim form is shown in Figure 31.1. It is a claim seeking permission to appeal on a point of law under the Arbitration Act 1996 s 69. The question of law is one of the proper construction of a term in a standard form shipping contract, and is identified in para (a). As it arises in a standard form contract the claimant takes the view that the lower test in s 69(3)(c)(ii) applies on the merits of the application. The statutory criteria for granting permission to appeal are dealt with in paras 1–12, with paras 5–11 dealing with why it is said the arbitrator's decision is open to serious doubt. Paragraph 13 deals with the no alternative review requirement in s 70(2), and para 14 with the need to bring the claim within 28 days of the award (s 70(3)). **31.83**

Time limit

An application to challenge an award under the Arbitration Act 1996 s 67 or 68, or to appeal under s 69, must be brought within 28 days of the date of the award (s 70(3)). The 28-day time limit in s 70(3) may be extended, either under s 79 (the view favoured by the DAC) or s 80(5) (which seems more consistent with the scheme of the Arbitration Act 1996). An application to extend time is made by issuing an application notice if the time limit has not expired, or in a separately identified part of the arbitration claim form if the 28 days have expired (CPR r 62.9 and PD 62, para 11.1). Respondents are permitted to file witness statement evidence in opposition to an application to extend time (CPR, r 62.9(3)). On applications to extend time, according to *Nagusina Naviera v Allied Maritime Inc* [2003] 2 CLC 1 the three most important considerations are: **31.84**

- the length of the delay;
- whether, in allowing the time limit to expire and the subsequent delay to occur, the defaulting party nevertheless acted reasonably in the circumstances; and
- whether the respondent to the application or the arbitrator contributed to the delay.

A number of other factors were also identified in *AOOT Kalmneft v Glencore* [2001] 1 Lloyd's Rep 128, such as any irremediable prejudice that may be suffered by the respondent (which may in some circumstances outweigh all other factors), the strength of the application, and any unfairness to the applicant. **31.85**

Defendants to the arbitration claim

Where a provision of the Arbitration Act 1996 requires notice to be given of a court application, that requirement is fulfilled by making the relevant person a defendant to the arbitration claim (CPR r 62.6). Thus, the arbitrator must be made a defendant in the following cases: **31.86**

- applications to remove an arbitrator (Arbitration Act 1996 s 24);
- applications to consider and adjust the arbitrator's fees and expenses (s 28); and
- applications to determine the arbitrator's fees and expenses where the award has been withheld pending payment (s 56).

Courts having jurisdiction over arbitration claims

The courts that can deal with arbitration claims are listed in PD 62, para 2.3(1), and include the Admiralty and Commercial Registry, the TCC, and the Mercantile Courts. Arbitration claims involving landlord and tenant matters are dealt with in the Chancery Division (para 2.3(2)). **31.87**

Figure 31.1 Arbitration claim form

Claim Form (arbitration)

In the	
HIGH COURT OF JUSTICE QUEEN'S BENCH DIVISION, COMMERCIAL COURT	
	for court use only
Claim No.	
Issue date	

In an arbitration claim between

Claimant

ANTAIOS COMPANIA NAVIERA SA

Defendant(s)

SALEN REDERIERNA AB

In the matter of an [intended] arbitration between

Claimant

ANTAIOS COMPANIA NAVIERA SA
30 AFENTOULI STR.
158 27, PIRAEUS
GREECE

Respondent(s) *Set out the names and addresses of persons to be served with the claim form stating their role in the arbitration and whether they are defendants.*

SALEN REDERIERNA AB (DEFENDANT)

MR. JONATHAN HODSON (ARBITRATOR)

Defendant's name and address

SALEN REDERIERNA AB (DEFENDANT)
SYDATLANTEN 7
SKANDIAHAMMEN,
GOTHENBURG 411 72
SWEDEN

☐ This claim will be heard on:

at am/pm

☐ This claim is made without notice.

The court office at

When corresponding with the court, please address forms or letters to the Court Manager and quote the case number.

N8 Claim form (arbitration)

Figure 31.1 Arbitration claim form *(Continued)*

Claim No.	

Remedy claimed and grounds on which claim is made

The Claimant seeks orders pursuant to the Arbitration Act 1996, section 69:
(a) granting permission to appeal from the award of Mr Jonathan Hodson ('the Arbitrator') dated 13 September 2012 ('the Award') in an arbitration between the Claimant and the Defendant on the following question of law ('the question'), namely: Whether clause 5 of the New York Produce Exchange standard form time charterparty ('the New York charterparty') applies to any breach of the New York charterparty, or to any serious breach of the New York charterparty, or only to repudiatory breaches of the New York charterparty; and
(b) that if permission to appeal is granted by this Court that the Award be:
(i) varied;
(ii) remitted in whole or in part for reconsideration in the light of this Court's determination in this claim; or
(iii) set aside in whole or in part; and
(c) that the costs of the application for permission to appeal be costs in the appeal.

The grounds for the application for permission to appeal are that:
1. Determination of the question will substantially affect the rights of the Claimant and/or the Defendant.
2. The question is one that the Arbitrator was asked to determine.
3. On the basis of the findings of fact of the Arbitrator, the question is one of general public importance in that:
(a) the question is one of the construction of the New York charterparty which is a standard form contract in common use in the shipping industry;
(b) there have been numerous conflicting court and arbitral decisions on the question; and
(c) determination of the question by this Court is necessary to promote legal certainty.
4. On the basis of the findings of fact of the Arbitrator, the decision of the Arbitrator on the question is open to serious doubt for the reasons set out in paragraphs 5 to 11.
5. Clause 5 of the New York charterparty confers a right on the owner of the vessel to withdraw the vessel from the charterparty failing punctual and regular payment of the hire "or for any breach of this charterparty".
6. There is a dispute between the Claimant and the Defendant on the question whether clause 5 of the New York charterparty applies to any breach of the New York charterparty, or to any serious breach of the New York charterparty, or only to repudiatory breaches of the New York charterparty.
7. The Arbitrator found as facts that sub-charterers of a vessel chartered from the Claimant by the Defendant had procured false bills of lading, which were false in that they were antedated, issued in respect of cargo not yet shipped, or unclaused despite defects in the condition of the goods shipped. The Arbitrator also found that the Defendant was responsible for the bills of lading procured by the sub-charterers.
8. The Arbitrator found that clause 5 of the New York charterparty only applies to repudiatory breaches.
9. The Arbitrator also found that the breaches referred to in paragraph 7 above were not repudiatory breaches.
10. The Arbitrator's decision referred to in paragraph 8 above was wrong in that it is inconsistent with the decisions in The Tropwind [1977] 1 Lloyd's Rep 397, and The Athos [1981] 2 Lloyd's Rep 74 and [1983] 1 Lloyd's Rep 127.
11. The Arbitrator should have held that the words "any breach" in clause 5 of the New York charterparty include the breaches of the kind referred to in paragraph 7 above, which are breaches, alternatively serious breaches, of the New York charterparty.
12. In the circumstances it is just and proper for this Court to determine the question.
13. There is no arbitral process of appeal or review available to the Claimant.
14. This application is brought within 28 days of the date of the Award.

Figure 31.1 Arbitration claim form *(Continued)*

Claim No.	

The claimant seeks an order for costs against
SALEN REDERIERNA AB

Statement of Truth
*(I believe)(The Claimant believes) that the facts stated in these particulars of claim are true.
* I am duly authorised by the claimant to sign this statement

Full name ______________________

Name of claimant's solicitor's firm ______________________

signed______________________ position or office held ______________________
*(Claimant)(Claimant's solicitor) (if signing on behalf of firm or company)

**delete as appropriate*

Scott and Avery LLP, solicitors,
16-24 Archway Road,
London
WC2H 6SP

Claimant's or claimant's solicitor's address to which documents should be sent if different from overleaf. If you are prepared to accept service by DX, fax or e-mail, please add details.

Procedure on arbitration claims

An arbitration claim form must be served within one month of issue (CPR r 62.4(2)). The court may grant permission for service outside the jurisdiction (CPR r 62.5). A defendant must acknowledge service within 14 days of service by filing Form N15 or Form N210(CC) (CPR, r 10.3(1)(b)). All arbitration claims are allocated to the multi-track, and there is no requirement to file allocation questionnaires (CPR r 62.7). Automatic directions apply, unless the court orders otherwise, as set out in Table 31.1 (PD 62, paras 6.1–6.7). An application for alternative directions is made using the procedure in CPR Part 23 (see Sime, *A Practical Approach to Civil Procedure* (17th edn, OUP, 2014), ch 23). The claimant should apply for a hearing date as soon as possible after issuing the claim (*Commercial Court Guide*, para O6.2). **31.88**

Table 31.1 Automatic directions in arbitration claims

Step	Time limit
Defendant files and serves witness statements	21 days after acknowledgement of service
Claimant files witness statements in reply	Seven days after service of defendant's evidence
Agreed, indexed, and paginated bundles (prepared by claimant)	Five days before the hearing
Time estimates and complete documentation to be filed	Five days before the hearing
Chronology, list of persons involved (if necessary), skeleton argument filed by claimant	Two days before the hearing
Skeleton argument filed by defendant	Day before the hearing

Hearings in arbitration claims under Part 62

Arbitration hearings are usually held in private, although preliminary determinations of points of law under the Arbitration Act 1996 s 45, and appeals under s 69, are usually heard in public (CPR r 62.10). **31.89**

The following questions in applications in arbitration claims are usually made without hearings: **31.90**

- decisions in preliminary points of jurisdiction and preliminary points of law as to whether determining the question is likely to produce substantial savings in costs and whether the application is made without delay (ss 32(2)(b) and 45(2)(b); see PD 62, para 10.1);
- whether to grant permission to appeal on a point of law (s 69(5)); and
- whether to extend the 28-day time limit prescribed by s 70(3) (PD 62, para 10.2).

J APPEALS TO THE COURT OF APPEAL

As mentioned at the start of this chapter, any scope for making applications to court where a matter has been referred to arbitration derogates from the principle of one-stop dispute resolution. The various situations discussed in this chapter where it is seen as appropriate to allow recourse to the courts are aimed at supporting the arbitral process, and to put right the most serious kinds of injustices that may occur from time to time. Allowing parties to go further, and to bring appeals against the decisions of the High Court judges dealing with matters dealt with in this chapter, is seen as being contrary to the ethos of the Arbitration Act 1996, as this risks the parties being tied up in the courts for years, with costs escalating out **31.91** of control. Consequently, almost all the provisions in the Arbitration Act 1996 that allow applications to the courts also contain restrictions on appeals.

31.92 A fairly typical provision is s 68(4) (in the context of challenges for serious irregularity), which says: 'The leave of the court is required for any appeal from a decision of the court under this section.' In this context, 'the court' is the High Court judge dealing with the arbitration claim (s 105(1)). This means that an appeal to the Court of Appeal can only be made if the High Court judge grants permission to appeal. If the judge refuses permission, the Court of Appeal has no jurisdiction to overrule that decision (*Athletic Union of Constantinople v National Basketball Association* [2002] 1 WLR 2863). The effect is that decisions of the judges in the High Court are usually final in arbitration claims.

31.93 A first instance judge should apply the same test for granting permission to appeal as the appeal court. A non-arbitration appeal can only be made if the court considers the appeal would have a real prospect of success or if there is some other compelling reason why the appeal should be heard (CPR r 52.3(6)). In arbitration appeals there may be an additional element of whether the appeal warrants the consideration of the Court of Appeal (*Geogas SA v Trammo Gas Ltd* [1991] 1 Lloyd's Rep 349). There is some doubt whether there is such an additional requirement. Leggatt LJ, who was in the majority in that case, expressly said that, given the restrictions on appeals from arbitrators to the court at first instance, there was no apparent justification for making arbitration appeals more difficult to maintain than other appeals to the Court of Appeal.

31.94 While usually a refusal of permission to appeal by the judge at first instance means no appeal can be brought to the Court of Appeal, there are authorities that the Court of Appeal can review such a refusal if either:

- the first instance judge had no jurisdiction to make the order under appeal (*Cetelem SA v Roust Holdings Ltd* [2005] 1 WLR 3555). A very restricted approach is taken to finding matters over which the judge had no jurisdiction as opposed to merely cases where the judge made an error in exercising his jurisdiction (see 31.49); or
- the refusal of permission at first instance was unfair or arbitrary (*CGU International Insurance plc v Astrazeneca Insurance Co Ltd* [2007] Bus LR 162). These will be exceptionally rare cases where there has been a failure of intellectual engagement with the arguments, or where there has been an absence of a decision on the issue.

KEY POINTS SUMMARY

31.95
- Intervention by the courts in arbitrations is restricted to those situations allowed by the Arbitration Act 1996 (s 1(c)).
- The situations where the courts have a role in arbitration are those where the judicial system can offer support to the arbitral process to make it effective and to correct obvious injustices.
- Applications in support of the arbitral process include applications relating to the appointment of arbitrators and procedural orders to secure evidence for use in arbitrations.
- Judicial review of arbitral awards is strictly restricted. The main provisions deal with serious irregularities (s 68) and appeals on points of law (s 69).
- Rights to object are in general lost if the objection is not raised forthwith (s 73).
- Challenges and appeals under ss 67–69 must be brought within 28 days of the award (s 70(3)).
- Applications to stay court proceedings under s 9 are made within the existing litigation.

- All the other types of application are made by issuing an arbitration claim form under CPR Part 62.
- Arbitration claims are brought by a special form of Part 8 claim form, and must be brought in designated specialist courts within the High Court.
- Arbitration claims are automatically allocated to the multi-track.
- Appeals to the Court of Appeal are (with minor exceptions) only available with the permission of the High Court judge.

32

ENFORCEMENT OF SETTLEMENTS AND AWARDS

A INTRODUCTION 32.01
B BASIC METHODS OF ENFORCING COMPROMISE AGREEMENTS 32.04
C MERGER OR DISCHARGE OF ORIGINAL OBLIGATION BY COMPROMISE 32.05
D MAKING A CHOICE ON ENFORCEMENT OPTIONS 32.09
E ENFORCEMENT OF COMPROMISES RECORDED AS A CONTRACT 32.12
F CHALLENGING A SETTLEMENT RECORDED AS A CONTRACT 32.18
G ENFORCEMENT OF COURT ORDERS 32.19
H COSTS ONLY PROCEEDINGS 32.20
I ENFORCEMENT OF CONSTRUCTION INDUSTRY ADJUDICATION DECISIONS 32.22
J ARBITRATION SETTLEMENTS AND AWARDS 32.26
Key points summary 32.36

A INTRODUCTION

32.01 Entering into a compromise agreement as a result of negotiation or mediation, or obtaining an award through arbitration or adjudication, produces a solution to the underlying difference or dispute between the parties. In most cases, the fact that the parties have agreed to use an ADR process, and that they will have agreed to the terms of the settlement in a non-adjudicative process, will hopefully mean that there are no difficulties as regards enforcement, and the parties will willingly honour the terms of settlement and what they have agreed to do.

32.02 Unfortunately, there are many cases where there are difficulties with enforcement. This may happen where a party is not happy with the outcome of an adjudicative process, where a party realizes that the terms agreed are not as attractive as they seemed, or when practical problems arise. Obligations may not be honoured on time, or in the correct form, or at all. In these cases the party with the benefit of the compromise or award will need to consider how to enforce compliance by the other side.

32.03 Some methods are simpler and less expensive than others. The importance of choosing an appropriate form in which to record a settlement where there is a choice was dealt with in Chapter 23, and the point was made there that any concern about enforcement is a relevant criterion. The enforcement methods available to a large extent depend on the form taken by the compromise agreement. It is therefore important that the legal advisers for the parties take into account how the agreement can be enforced when formulating the compromise agreement, to minimize the risks and difficulties that may arise at a later stage.

B BASIC METHODS OF ENFORCING COMPROMISE AGREEMENTS

The approach taken to enforcement of compromises in large measure depends on the nature of the process used to resolve the original dispute. Essentially: **32.04**

- in adjudicative procedures, the tribunal will make an award. Enforcement will often be through registering the award with the courts of the state where enforcement is to take place, and then enforcing the award as a civil judgment (see 32.27–32.35);
- an exception is construction industry adjudications (Chapter 25), where the decision is not itself registrable. Instead it may be enforced through bringing court proceedings and entering judgment (see 32.22);
- in non-adjudicative procedures, if the parties have resolved their dispute, they will have entered into a contract of compromise. Enforcement is through suing on that contract;
- alternatively, in a non-adjudicative procedure the parties may convert the compromise agreement into a court judgment or order, and then enforce that judgment or order.

C MERGER OR DISCHARGE OF ORIGINAL OBLIGATION BY COMPROMISE

In each of the situations set out in the previous paragraph it will be seen that enforcement is of the compromise, decision, or award, rather than the original dispute. In other words, by settling the original claim or having it adjudicated, the original cause of action is merged or converted into a contract of compromise or an adjudicative award. In fact, as a result it is no longer open to either party to sue on the original cause of action, and their rights and obligations are now defined by the compromise or adjudicative award. **32.05**

There are three apparent exceptions to this rule, namely where:

- there is an express term reviving old obligations in the event of non-performance;
- compromise is based on performance of the agreed terms;
- the compromise is ineffective.

Express term reviving old obligations in the event of non-performance

It is not uncommon for a compromise of a money claim to provide for payment by instalments and also that in the event of default of an instalment the whole amount then outstanding shall become due and payable immediately. If there is a default, the old obligations revive, subject to deduction of any instalments paid under the compromise. An express term to this effect in the compromise agreement is required if this is to be the consequence of non-performance (*Smith v Shirley and Bayliss* (1875) 32 LT 234). **32.06**

Compromise based on performance of the agreed terms

Most compromises take effect from the time the parties reach agreement (sometimes referred to as an accord). The old dispute then immediately merges into the new compromise (*Jameson v Central Electricity Generating Board* [1998] QB 323). However, as a matter of construction it is possible for the parties to agree that their compromise will only become effective when one of the parties performs its obligations under the compromise (*British Russian Gazette and Trade Outlook Ltd v Associated Newspapers Ltd* [1933] 2 KB 616). In such a case the party who has agreed to perform on the compromise agreement remains liable on the old cause of action until performance is completed. **32.07**

Compromise ineffective

32.08 It sometimes happens that an apparent compromise agreement does not comply with the requirements for the formation of a valid contract. This ought not to happen, but there are occasions where, for example, lax language in the compromise agreement leads to such uncertainty of terms that the alleged compromise is held to be ineffective. In such a case, as there is no valid compromise, the parties revert back to the original position with the underlying cause of action (although with the passing of time there may be limitation or other difficulties).

D MAKING A CHOICE ON ENFORCEMENT OPTIONS

32.09 In giving professional advice to a client, you should not ignore enforcement until some problem with enforcement arises. It should be a relevant consideration from the time you first advise on the case. If there are likely to be enforcement problems, this should be built in to earlier decisions so that enforcement can be as efficient as possible in terms of what can be done, in what time frame, and at what cost.

32.10 If it is envisaged that enforcement may be a significant issue, because of what is at stake, the complexity of the case, or the attitudes of the parties, then enforcement possibilities will be an important issue from the time the lawyer is first consulted. The factors relevant to selecting an ADR option were dealt with in Chapters 2–3. The use of litigation or an adjudicative option will bring with it specific recording and enforcement options. If arbitration is used an arbitration award should be the outcome. The availability of the full enforcement powers of the court may be a reason for selecting litigation.

32.11 Some ADR processes leave options on enforcement open to a later stage. The factors relevant to recording a settlement are dealt with in Chapter 23, and the client may need to be advised as to which form for recording the settlement will give the best enforcement options. The main distinction is between some form of contract, which will need to be enforced by starting new court proceedings, or a consent order, which can be enforced through appropriate court enforcement powers without the need for separate proceedings.

E ENFORCEMENT OF COMPROMISES RECORDED AS A CONTRACT

Enforcement by civil proceedings

32.12 As mentioned above, where a compromise or full and final settlement is reached in a dispute at a time when no proceedings have been started, the old dispute is merged with the compromise agreement, and the parties can then sue on the compromise if it is breached. 'No proceedings' includes both litigation in the courts and references to arbitration. If a party fails to comply with the agreed terms, in most cases there will be an obvious breach of the compromise contract. A civil claim based on that breach should be reasonably straightforward. In most cases there will be no defence, and it would be expected that entering judgment should be a matter of either:

- entering judgment in default if the defendant does not respond to the particulars of claim within 14 days of the deemed date of service; or
- applying for summary judgment if there is a response, on the basis that the defendant has no real prospect of defending the claim.

Once judgment has been entered, the claimant can use the normal court enforcement processes. These include taking control of goods, warrants of delivery and of possession, charging orders, third-party debt orders, attachment of earnings orders and receivership orders. **32.13**

If the contract is repudiated, is invalid, or a dispute arises outside the matters covered by the agreement, proceedings can be started on the original subject-matter of the dispute, so long as the limitation period has not expired. **32.14**

Defences to claims for breach of compromise agreements

Exceptionally, a party who is sued for breach of a compromise agreement may be able to defend the claim by relying on one of the usual defences to claims in contract. The difficulty is in persuading the court that the defence is available on the facts. What cannot be done is to rely on an argument to the effect that there was no merit in the underlying dispute. Two exceptions to this rule are: **32.15**

- where the original claim was not made in good faith; and
- where an undisputed claim for a liquidated amount is compromised by an agreement to pay a smaller sum (the rule in *Pinnel's Case* (1602) 5 Co Rep 117a, although there are restrictions on this principle: see *Chitty on Contracts* (31st edn, Sweet & Maxwell, 2012)).

General defences under contract law that may be available include: **32.16**

- no offer or acceptance in relation to the alleged compromise agreement;
- the terms of the compromise being too uncertain;
- consideration being past or there being no consideration;
- incapacity of a party to the compromise (unless the compromise is approved by the court under CPR, r 21.10);
- lack of writing where that is required by contract law;
- mistake;
- misrepresentation;
- duress;
- undue influence;
- lack of authority if the compromise was apparently entered into by an agent;
- illegality;
- frustration;
- performance;
- renunciation;
- impossibility;
- fundamental breach which has been accepted; or
- discharge of the compromise by a further agreement.

Bankruptcy and winding up

Insolvency is often an alternative to enforcement by proceedings in the civil courts. Breach of a compromise agreement may well be evidence that the other party is unable to pay its debts as they fall due (or any of the other grounds set out in the Insolvency Act 1986), which may make use of bankruptcy or winding-up procedures attractive. Bankruptcy is used in the case of individuals, and winding up for companies. They are not inexpensive alternatives to litigation, and operate as relief on behalf of all the creditors of the individual or company rather than specifically for the person bringing the proceedings. These insolvency procedures are swift, and can be very effective in obtaining payment from a reluctant payer. However, **32.17** if the individual is made bankrupt or the company is wound up, the petitioning creditor is extremely unlikely to see any of their money, so these can be risky procedures to use.

F CHALLENGING A SETTLEMENT RECORDED AS A CONTRACT

32.18 As regards challenging the terms of a settlement:

- A settlement can only be set aside in limited circumstances, for example if it was obtained by fraud or misrepresentation (*Detz v Lennig* [1969] 1 AC 170), mutual mistake, unilateral mistake encouraged by the other side (*Huddersfield Banking Co Ltd v Henry Lister & Son Ltd* [1895] 2 Ch 273), mutual mistake of law (*Brennan v Bolt Burden (a firm)*) Times, 7 November 2003), or for economic duress or undue influence (*D & C Builders v Rees* [1966] 2 QB 107). It is unlikely that it can be argued that the agreement should be rectified if it was drawn up by lawyers.
- It is not normally possible to appeal against a consent order, or to apply to court to vary its terms: *Peacock v Peacock* [1991] Fam Law 139. It might be possible to get the agreement rectified, but this is unlikely where it has been drawn up by lawyers.
- The court may decline to enforce a compromise if there is an equitable reason for not doing so, or if it can be argued that the terms of compromise have been frustrated. One side may not be bound by the terms of a settlement if they can argue that the other side has breached or repudiated it.
- A court may refuse to enforce a consent order for someone who is not abiding by its terms: *Thwaite v Thwaite* [1982] Fam 1.

G ENFORCEMENT OF COURT ORDERS

32.19 Where a compromise is reached in a case where there are existing court proceedings, it is likely that the compromise will be recorded in a court order or a Tomlin order as set out in Chapter 23. Normally the terms will be complied with but, if they are not, a key question is whether the party with the benefit of the compromise can immediately use the court's enforcement processes, or whether it is first necessary to take some other step. Table 32.1 sets out for each of the processes whether enforcement is either a one-stage or two-stage process, and the nature of the procedure to be followed.

Table 32.1 Enforcement of the different methods of recording settlements

Method of recording settlement	Enforcement procedure
Judgment entered for immediate payment of the sum agreed together with costs.	Enforcement proceedings (by taking control of goods, charging order etc) can be taken on such a judgment immediately (which means 14 days after judgment). The practical disadvantages for a defendant in having a judgment entered against them means that settlements rarely take this form.
Judgment entered for the agreed sum (and costs), subject to a stay of execution pending payment by stated instalments.	If the instalments fall into arrears, the stay will be lifted, and the judgment creditor can immediately bring enforcement proceedings.
Consent order setting out the agreement in the form of undertakings by both parties in a series of numbered paragraphs.	If any of the terms are not complied with, enforcement may be possible immediately or on application to the court depending on the nature of the term in question.

(Continued)

Table 32.1 Enforcement of the different methods of recording settlements *(Continued)*

Method of recording settlement	Enforcement procedure
Tomlin order.	• Substantive terms in a Tomlin order take effect and are enforceable as they stand without the need for any further court order. Figure 23.7 is a fairly typical Tomlin order. If there is no agreement on the amount of costs to be paid under para 3 of Figure 23.7, the claimant can proceed directly to a detailed assessment of its costs under CPR, Part 47. • In the event of the scheduled terms being breached, enforcement is a two-stage process. First, the claim must be restored under the 'liberty to apply' clause, and an order obtained to compel compliance with the term breached. Secondly, if that order is itself breached, enforcement can follow in the usual way.
Settlement upon terms endorsed on counsel's briefs.	The effect of this type of arrangement is to supersede the original claim with the compromise. Any breach can only be enforced by issuing fresh proceedings.
Consent order staying all further proceedings upon agreed terms.	The courts are very unwilling to remove the stay imposed by this type of order, so enforcement can usually be effected only by bringing fresh proceedings for breach of the contract embodied in the compromise (see *Rofa Sport Management AG v DHL International (UK) Ltd* [1989] 1 WLR 902).
Consent order providing for 'no order' save as to costs, but setting out the agreed terms in recitals.	*Atkinson v Castan* (1991) *Times*, 17 April, held that the recitals in the consent order could be enforced without the need to bring a fresh claim.

H COSTS ONLY PROCEEDINGS

In cases where costs have to be assessed, but there are no existing substantive proceedings between the parties, the claimant may use the procedure in CPR r 46.14 to obtain an order for a detailed assessment of its costs pursuant to the compromise agreement. This rule is intended to provide a solution to the problem that, as a technical matter, in the absence of court proceedings between the parties there was no mechanism for the court to conduct a detailed assessment of costs. CPR r 46.14 sets out a procedure which may be followed where: **32.20**

- the parties to a dispute have reached an agreement on all issues (including which party is to pay the costs), which is made or confirmed in writing; but
- they have failed to agree the amount of those costs; and
- no proceedings have been started.

In such a case either party may commence proceedings using the CPR Part 8 procedure (CPR r 46.14(3)) seeking an order that the compromised costs be determined by the court by assessment or for fixed costs. What CPR r 46.14 does not do is to provide a means of resolving what the parties meant by an unclear term as to costs in a compromise agreement (see 23.58). **32.21**

I ENFORCEMENT OF CONSTRUCTION INDUSTRY ADJUDICATION DECISIONS

32.22 A party with the benefit of an adjudicator's decision under the Housing Grants, Construction and Regeneration Act 1996 s 108 (Chapter 25) may bring enforcement proceedings in the courts by issuing a Part 8 claim form, and then entering default judgment (*Coventry Scaffolding Co (London) Ltd v Lancsville Construction Ltd* [2009] EWHC 3295 (TCC)) if there is no acknowledgement of service, or otherwise applying for summary judgment. In most cases summary judgment will be entered in accordance with the policy of the Act (see Chapter 25).

32.23 Summary judgment will be refused, however, if the defendant advances a properly arguable jurisdictional objection. A dispute as to whether the defendant was a party to the relevant contract (*Estor Ltd v Multifit (UK) Ltd* (2009) 126 Con LR 40), or whether the agreement has been replaced (*Lead Technical Services Ltd v CMS Medical Ltd* [2007] BLR 251), may be effective objections.

32.24 A number of other situations where a valid objection to the adjudicator's decision may be mounted include cases where:

- the adjudicator was not the person nominated by the contract, or was not appointed in accordance with the agreed procedure (*Amec Projects Ltd v Whitefriars City Estates Ltd* [2004] EWHC (TCC) 393);
- there is a real risk the adjudicator was biased (*Glencott Development v Barrett* [2001] BLR 207);
- the decision was not responsive to the issues referred to adjudication (*Ballast plc v The Burrell Company* [2001] BLR 529);
- there is no dispute, because the matter was not previously brought to the attention of the other party (*Fastrack v Morrison* [2000] BLR 168); and
- the adjudicator acted unfairly, resulting in significant prejudice, such as where the adjudicator allowed new claims to be added without giving the defendant an opportunity to respond (*Project Services v Opek Prime Development Ltd* [2000] BLR 402).

32.25 If the defendant has agreed that the adjudicator can rule on the issue of jurisdiction and that they will be bound by the adjudicator's decision, summary judgment will be entered even if the adjudicator is wrong (*Thomas-Fredric's (Construction) Ltd v Wilson* [2004] BLR 23 at [20]). Summary judgment may also be entered if the defendant has not submitted to the adjudicator's jurisdiction, provided the adjudicator's decision is plainly right (*Thomas-Fredric's (Construction) Ltd v Wilson*).

J ARBITRATION SETTLEMENTS AND AWARDS

Negotiated settlements in arbitration proceedings

32.26 Where the parties settle their dispute after referring the matter to arbitration, it will be necessary to bring the arbitration to an end, and also to deal with the costs of the arbitration and the arbitrator's fees. As with litigation, the form of the settlement may have itself effected an end of the dispute, or the settlement may be conditional on performance by one of the parties, or it may require the entry of an award in the agreed terms. One great advantage in recording the agreed terms in an arbitrator's award is that it will then be enforceable, such as under the New York Convention 1958, in the same way as other arbitral awards (see 32.29).

Enforcement of domestic arbitral awards

A domestic arbitral award may be enforced either by bringing an ordinary action on the award in the High Court, or by using the summary procedure under the Arbitration Act 1996 s 66(1). This section allows the court to grant permission to enforce an award of an arbitral tribunal in the same manner as a judgment or order of the court. Permission is sought by issuing an arbitration claim form in the High Court, which is considered without notice (CPR r 62.18). Permission to enforce an award will not be given where, or to the extent that, the person against whom it is sought to be enforced shows that the tribunal lacked substantive jurisdiction to make the award (s 66(3), which is considered at 29.48). Enforcement under s 66 may also be prevented if the court grants a freezing injunction in favour of the debtor party (*CMA CGM Marseille v Petro Broker International* [2011] EWCA Civ 461). Otherwise, there are very strong policy reasons in favour of granting permission, and unless there are grounds for impeaching the award, permission is usually granted (*Tongyuan (USA) International Trading Group v Uni-Clan Ltd* (unreported, 19 January 2001). **32.27**

After permission to enforce an award as a judgment of the court has been granted, the award will attract statutory interest under the Judgments Act 1838, s 17 at 8 per cent per annum. This is because s 66 operates by merging the award into a judgment debt (*La Société Pour La Recherche, La Production, Le Transport, La Transformation et La Commercialisation des Hydrocarbures SPA v Statoil Natural Gas LLC* [2014] EWHC 875 (Comm)). **32.28**

Recognition and enforcement of New York Convention arbitration awards

The New York Convention 1958 on the recognition and enforcement of arbitral awards is one of the most successful international treaties of its kind, having been ratified by no less than 144 countries (at the last count only 51, mostly quite small, countries had not ratified it). In practical terms it means that arbitral awards are enforceable almost all over the world, and this alone is one of the major advantages of using arbitration over most other ways of resolving disputes. Enforcement of an arbitration award under the New York Convention is in addition to seeking permission to enforce under the Arbitration Act 1996 s 66 (see ss 66(4) and 104). **32.29**

The New York Convention applies to arbitral awards made in the territory of a state other than the state where the recognition and enforcement of such awards are sought, and arising out of differences between persons, whether physical or legal (Art I). It also applies to arbitral awards not considered as domestic awards in the state where their recognition and enforcement are sought. In deciding whether the Convention applies, an award shall be treated as made at the seat of the arbitration, regardless of where it was signed, dispatched, or delivered to any of the parties (Arbitration Act 1996 s 100(2)). **32.30**

A New York Convention award may be relied on by way of defence or set-off in any legal proceedings, or, with the permission of the court, be enforced in the same manner as a judgment or order of the court (s 101). Where permission is given, judgment may be entered in terms of the award (s 101(3)). Technically, there are two procedures that may be used: **32.31**

- to apply for permission to enforce the award as if it were a High Court judgment, but without entering the award as a judgment in the court; or
- to apply for permission to enter the award as a High Court judgment. It then has the status of a High Court judgment, and can be enforced as such.

32.32 A party seeking the recognition or enforcement of a New York Convention award must by s 102(1) produce:

- the duly authenticated original award or a duly certified copy; and
- the original arbitration agreement or a duly certified copy.

32.33 If the award or agreement is in a foreign language, the party seeking recognition must also produce a translation certified by an official or sworn translator or by a diplomatic or consular agent (s 102(2)).

Grounds for refusing recognition or enforcement of a New York Convention award

32.34 Recognition or enforcement of a New York Convention award may be refused (see the Arbitration Act 1996 s 103) only if the person against whom it was made proves that:

- a party to the arbitration agreement was under some incapacity;
- the arbitration agreement was not valid under the law to which the parties subjected it or, failing any indication on the award itself, under the law of the country where the award was made;
- he was not given proper notice of the appointment of the arbitrator or of the arbitration proceedings or was otherwise unable to present his case;
- the award deals with a difference not contemplated by or not falling within the terms of the submission to arbitration or contains decisions on matters beyond the scope of the submission to arbitration;
- the composition of the arbitral tribunal or the arbitral procedure was not in accordance with the agreement of the parties or, failing such agreement, with the law of the country in which the arbitration took place;
- the award has not yet become binding on the parties, or has been set aside or suspended by a competent authority of the country in which, or under the law of which, it was made;
- the award is in respect of a matter that is not capable of settlement by arbitration; or
- it would be contrary to public policy to recognize or enforce the award.

Enforcement of Geneva Convention awards

32.35 The Arbitration Act 1996 s 99 provides for the continuing effect of the UK's obligations under the Geneva Convention on the execution of foreign arbitral awards that are not also New York Convention awards. While there are 49 countries that are signatories to the Geneva Convention (Arbitration (Foreign Awards) Order 1984 (SI 1984/1168)), there is a great deal of overlap with countries that are parties to the New York Convention. As the latter takes precedence over the Geneva Convention, the Geneva Convention has relatively limited practical application.

KEY POINTS SUMMARY

32.36
- Most compromises operate as contracts, and can be enforced by suing on the compromise agreement.
- There are some exceptions, such as where a compromise agreement is conditional on the performance by one side of the compromise terms (in which case the original cause of action revives).
- Construction adjudication awards can be enforced by suing on the award and entering default or summary judgment. Judgment is usually entered in accordance with the policy of 'pay now, argue later'.

- Where there are existing court proceedings, a compromise is often incorporated into a consent order or Tomlin order.
- Compromises recorded in court orders and judgments can usually be enforced directly using the court's enforcement procedures.
- Sometimes, for example terms included in the schedule to a Tomlin order, enforcement follows a two-stage process.
- Where there is a compromise of a dispute on terms that one side will pay the other's costs, but there are no existing proceedings, CPR r 46.14 provides a special procedure commenced by a Part 8 claim form to get a court order for the assessment of those costs.
- Domestic arbitration awards can be enforced as a court judgment with the leave of the court under the Arbitration Act 1996 s 66.
- International arbitration awards can be enforced and recognized cheaply and easily under the New York Convention.

APPENDICES

APPENDIX 1

| CEDR's Dispute Resolution Service | www.cedrsolve.com

CEDR Model Mediation Agreement 13th Edition

THIS AGREEMENT dated IS MADE BETWEEN

Party A

....*of*..

Party B

....*of*..

(together referred to as **"the Parties"**)

The Mediator

....*of*..

(a term which includes any agreed **Assistant Mediator**)

and

CEDR Solve of IDRC, 70 Fleet Street, London EC4Y IEU

in relation to a mediation to be held

on ....

at ....

(**"the Mediation"**)

IT IS AGREED by those signing this Agreement THAT:

The Mediation

1 The Parties agree to attempt in good faith to settle their dispute at the Mediation and to conduct the Mediation in accordance with this Agreement and consistent with the CEDR Solve Model Mediation Procedure and the CEDR Code of Conduct for Mediators current at the date of this Agreement.

Authority and status

2 The person signing this Agreement on behalf of each Party warrants having authority to bind that Party and all other persons present on that Party's behalf at the Mediation to observe the terms of this Agreement, and also having authority to bind that Party to the terms of any settlement.

3 Neither the Mediator nor CEDR Solve shall be liable to the Parties for any act or omission in relation to the Mediation unless the act or omission is proved to have been fraudulent or involved wilful misconduct.

Confidentiality and without prejudice status

4 Every person involved in the Mediation:

4.1 will keep confidential all information arising out of or in connection with the Mediation, including the fact and terms of any settlement, but not including the fact that the Mediation is to take place or has taken place or where disclosure is required by law to implement or to enforce terms of settlement or to notify their insurers, insurance brokers and/or accountants; and

4.2 acknowledges that all such information passing between the Parties, the Mediator and/or CEDR Solve, however communicated, is agreed to be without prejudice to any Party's legal position and may not be produced as evidence or disclosed to any judge, arbitrator or other decision-maker in any legal or other formal process, except where otherwise disclosable in law.

5 Where a Party privately discloses to the Mediator any information in confidence before, during or after the Mediation, the Mediator will not disclose that information to any other Party or person without the consent of the Party disclosing it, unless required by law to make disclosure.

6 The Parties will not call the Mediator or any employee or consultant of CEDR Solve as a witness, nor require them to produce in evidence any records or notes relating to the Mediation, in any litigation, arbitration or other formal process arising from or in connection with their dispute and the Mediation; nor will the Mediator nor any CEDR Solve employee or consultant act or agree to act as a witness, expert, arbitrator or consultant in any such process. If any Party does make such an application, that Party will fully indemnify the Mediator or the employee or consultant of CEDR Solve in respect of any costs any of them incur in resisting and/or responding to such an application, including reimbursement at the Mediator's standard hourly rate for the Mediator's time spent in resisting and/or responding to such application.

Settlement formalities

7 No terms of settlement reached at the Mediation will be legally binding until set out in writing and signed by or on behalf of each of the Parties.

Fees and costs of the Mediation

8 The Parties will be responsible for the fees and expenses of CEDR Solve and the Mediator (**"the Mediation Fees"**) in accordance with CEDR Solve's Terms and Conditions of Business current at the date of this Agreement (including any provision for additional hours if the mediation process extends beyond the allocated hours).

9 Unless otherwise agreed by the Parties and CEDR Solve in writing, each Party agrees to share the Mediation Fees equally and also to bear its own legal and other costs and expenses of preparing for and attending the Mediation (**"each Party's Legal Costs"**) prior to the Mediation. However, each Party further agrees that any court or tribunal may treat both the Mediation Fees and each Party's Legal Costs as costs in the case in relation to any litigation or arbitration where that court or tribunal has power to assess or make orders as to costs, whether or not the Mediation results in settlement of their dispute.

Legal status and effect of the Mediation

10 This Agreement is governed by the law of [England and Wales] and the courts of [England and Wales] shall have exclusive jurisdiction to decide any matters arising out of or in connection with this Agreement and the Mediation.

11 The referral of the dispute to the Mediation does not affect any rights that exist under Article 6 of the European Convention of Human Rights, and if their dispute does not settle through the Mediation, the Parties' right to a fair trial remains unaffected.

Changes to this Agreement

12 All agreed changes to this Agreement and/or the Model Procedure are set out as follows:

Signed

Party A ____________________

Party B ____________________

Mediator ____________________

CEDR Solve ____________________

APPENDIX 2

Arbitration Act 1996

PART I ARBITRATION PURSUANT TO AN ARBITRATION AGREEMENT 535

INTRODUCTORY 535

1. General principles 535
2. Scope of application of provisions 535
3. The seat of the arbitration 536
4. Mandatory and non-mandatory provisions 536
5. Agreements to be in writing 536

THE ARBITRATION AGREEMENT 537

6. Definition of arbitration agreement 537
7. Separability of arbitration agreement. . . 537
8. Whether agreement discharged by death of a party 537

STAY OF LEGAL PROCEEDINGS 537

9. Stay of legal proceedings 537
10. Reference of interpleader issue to arbitration 538
11. Retention of security where Admiralty proceedings stayed 538

COMMENCEMENT OF ARBITRAL PROCEEDINGS 538

12. Power of court to extend time for beginning arbitral proceedings, &c 538
13. Application of Limitation Acts. 539
14. Commencement of arbitral proceedings 539

THE ARBITRAL TRIBUNAL 540

15. The arbitral tribunal 540
16. Procedure for appointment of arbitrators 540
17. Power in case of default to appoint sole arbitrator 540
18. Failure of appointment procedure 541
19. Court to have regard to agreed qualifications 541
20. Chairman. 541
21. Umpire 541
22. Decision-making where no chairman or umpire 542
23. Revocation of arbitrator's authority. . . . 542
24. Power of court to remove arbitrator 542
25. Resignation of arbitrator 542
26. Death of arbitrator or person appointing him. 543
27. Filling of vacancy, &c. 543
28. Joint and several liability of parties to arbitrators for fees and expenses 543
29. Immunity of arbitrator. 544

JURISDICTION OF THE ARBITRAL TRIBUNAL 544

30. Competence of tribunal to rule on its own jurisdiction. 544
31. Objection to substantive jurisdiction of tribunal 544
32. Determination of preliminary point of jurisdiction 544

THE ARBITRAL PROCEEDINGS 545

33. General duty of the tribunal. 545
34. Procedural and evidential matters 545
35. Consolidation of proceedings and concurrent hearings. 546
36. Legal or other representation. 546
37. Power to appoint experts, legal advisers or assessors 546
38. General powers exercisable by the tribunal 546
39. Power to make provisional awards. 547
40. General duty of parties. 547
41. Powers of tribunal in case of party's default 547

POWERS OF COURT IN RELATION TO ARBITRAL PROCEEDINGS 548

42. Enforcement of peremptory orders of tribunal 548
43. Securing the attendance of witnesses . . . 548
44. Court powers exercisable in support of arbitral proceedings. 548
45. Determination of preliminary point of law. 549

THE AWARD 549

46. Rules applicable to substance of dispute 549
47. Awards on different issues, &c. 550
48. Remedies 550
49. Interest. 550
50. Extension of time for making award . . . 550
51. Settlement 551

52. Form of award 551
53. Place where award treated as made 551
54. Date of award 551
55. Notification of award 551
56. Power to withhold award in case of non-payment 552
57. Correction of award or additional award 552
58. Effect of award 553

COSTS OF THE ARBITRATION 553

59. Costs of the arbitration 553
60. Agreement to pay costs in any event 553
61. Award of costs 553
62. Effect of agreement or award about costs 553
63. The recoverable costs of the arbitration 553
64. Recoverable fees and expenses of arbitrators 554
65. Power to limit recoverable costs 554

POWERS OF THE COURT IN RELATION TO AWARD 554

66. Enforcement of the award 554
67. Challenging the award: substantive jurisdiction 554
68. Challenging the award: serious irregularity 555
69. Appeal on point of law 555
70. Challenge or appeal: supplementary provisions 556
71. Challenge or appeal: effect of order of court 557

MISCELLANEOUS 557

72. Saving for rights of person who takes no part in proceedings 557
73. Loss of right to object 558
74. Immunity of arbitral institutions, &c. 558
75. Charge to secure payment of solicitors' costs 558

SUPPLEMENTARY 558

76. Service of notices, &c. 558
77. Powers of court in relation to service of documents 559
78. Reckoning periods of time 559
79. Power of court to extend time limits relating to arbitral proceedings 559
80. Notice and other requirements in connection with legal proceedings 560
81. Saving for certain matters governed by common law 560
82. Minor definitions 560
83. Index of defined expressions: Part I 561
84. Transitional provisions 561

PART II OTHER PROVISIONS RELATING TO ARBITRATION 562

DOMESTIC ARBITRATION AGREEMENTS 562

85. Modification of Part I in relation to domestic arbitration agreement 562
86. Staying of legal proceedings 562
87. Effectiveness of agreement to exclude court's jurisdiction 562
88. Power to repeal or amend sections 85 to 87 563

CONSUMER ARBITRATION AGREEMENTS 563

89. Application of unfair terms regulations to consumer arbitration agreements 563
90. Regulations apply where consumer is a legal person 563
91. Arbitration agreement unfair where modest amount sought 563

SMALL CLAIMS ARBITRATION IN THE COUNTY COURT 564

92. Exclusion of Part I in relation to small claims arbitration in the county court 564
93. Appointment of judges as arbitrators 564

STATUTORY ARBITRATIONS 564

94. Application of Part I to statutory arbitrations 564
95. General adaptation of provisions in relation to statutory arbitrations 564
96. Specific adaptations of provisions in relation to statutory arbitrations 565
97. Provisions excluded from applying to statutory arbitrations 565
98. Power to make further provision by regulations 565

PART III RECOGNITION AND ENFORCEMENT OF CERTAIN FOREIGN AWARDS 565

ENFORCEMENT OF GENEVA CONVENTION AWARDS 565

99. Continuation of Part II of the Arbitration Act 1950 565

RECOGNITION AND ENFORCEMENT OF NEW YORK CONVENTION AWARDS 565

100. New York Convention awards 565
101. Recognition and enforcement of awards 566
102. Evidence to be produced by party seeking recognition or enforcement 566
103. Refusal of recognition or enforcement 566

104. Saving for other bases of recognition or enforcement 567

PART IV GENERAL PROVISIONS 567

105. Meaning of 'the court': jurisdiction of High Court and county court. 567
106. Crown application 568
107. Consequential amendments and repeals 568
108. Extent 568
109. Commencement 568
110. Short title 568

SCHEDULE 1 569

Mandatory provisions of Part I........... 569

SCHEDULE 2 569

Modifications of Part I in relation to judge-arbitrators 569
Introductory 569
General............................. 569
Arbitrator's fees 570
Exercise of court powers in support of arbitration 570
Extension of time for making award....... 570
Withholding award in case of non-payment 570
Correction of award or additional award . . . 571
Costs............................... 571
Enforcement of award.................. 571
Solicitors' costs 571
Powers of court in relation to service of documents 571
Powers of court to extend time limits relating to arbitral proceedings 571

SCHEDULE 3

Consequential amendments [not reproduced here]

SCHEDULE 4

Repeals [not reproduced here]

An Act to restate and improve the law relating to arbitration pursuant to an arbitration agreement; to make other provision relating to arbitration and arbitration awards; and for connected purposes.

[17th June 1996]

BE IT ENACTED BY THE QUEEN'S MOST EXCELLENT MAJESTY, BY AND WITH THE ADVICE AND CONSENT OF THE LORDS SPIRITUAL AND TEMPORAL, AND COMMONS, IN THIS PRESENT PARLIAMENT ASSEMBLED, AND BY THE AUTHORITY OF THE SAME, AS FOLLOWS:—

PART I ARBITRATION PURSUANT TO AN ARBITRATION AGREEMENT

INTRODUCTORY

1 General principles

The provisions of this Part are founded on the following principles, and shall be construed accordingly—

(a) the object of arbitration is to obtain the fair resolution of disputes by an impartial tribunal without unnecessary delay or expense;
(b) the parties should be free to agree how their disputes are resolved, subject only to such safeguards as are necessary in the public interest;
(c) in matters governed by this Part the court should not intervene except as provided by this Part.

2 Scope of application of provisions

(1) The provisions of this Part apply where the seat of the arbitration is in England and Wales or Northern Ireland.
(2) The following sections apply even if the seat of the arbitration is outside England and Wales or Northern Ireland or no seat has been designated or determined—
 (a) sections 9 to 11 (stay of legal proceedings, &c.), and
 (b) section 66 (enforcement of arbitral awards).

(3) The powers conferred by the following sections apply even if the seat of the arbitration is outside England and Wales or Northern Ireland or no seat has been designated or determined—
   (a) section 43 (securing the attendance of witnesses), and
   (b) section 44 (court powers exercisable in support of arbitral proceedings);
   but the court may refuse to exercise any such power if, in the opinion of the court, the fact that the seat of the arbitration is outside England and Wales or Northern Ireland, or that when designated or determined the seat is likely to be outside England and Wales or Northern Ireland, makes it inappropriate to do so.

(4) The court may exercise a power conferred by any provision of this Part not mentioned in subsection (2) or (3) for the purpose of supporting the arbitral process where—
   (a) no seat of the arbitration has been designated or determined, and
   (b) by reason of a connection with England and Wales or Northern Ireland the court is satisfied that it is appropriate to do so.

(5) Section 7 (separability of arbitration agreement) and section 8 (death of a party) apply where the law applicable to the arbitration agreement is the law of England and Wales or Northern Ireland even if the seat of the arbitration is outside England and Wales or Northern Ireland or has not been designated or determined.

3 The seat of the arbitration

In this Part 'the seat of the arbitration' means the juridical seat of the arbitration designated—
   (a) by the parties to the arbitration agreement, or
   (b) by any arbitral or other institution or person vested by the parties with powers in that regard, or
   (c) by the arbitral tribunal if so authorised by the parties,
   or determined, in the absence of any such designation, having regard to the parties' agreement and all the relevant circumstances.

4 Mandatory and non-mandatory provisions

(1) The mandatory provisions of this Part are listed in Schedule 1 and have effect notwithstanding any agreement to the contrary.

(2) The other provisions of this Part (the 'non-mandatory provisions') allow the parties to make their own arrangements by agreement but provide rules which apply in the absence of such agreement.

(3) The parties may make such arrangements by agreeing to the application of institutional rules or providing any other means by which a matter may be decided.

(4) It is immaterial whether or not the law applicable to the parties' agreement is the law of England and Wales or, as the case may be, Northern Ireland.

(5) The choice of a law other than the law of England and Wales or Northern Ireland as the applicable law in respect of a matter provided for by a non-mandatory provision of this Part is equivalent to an agreement making provision about that matter.

   For this purpose an applicable law determined in accordance with the parties' agreement, or which is objectively determined in the absence of any express or implied choice, shall be treated as chosen by the parties.

5 Agreements to be in writing

(1) The provisions of this Part apply only where the arbitration agreement is in writing, and any other agreement between the parties as to any matter is effective for the purposes of this Part only if in writing.

The expressions 'agreement', 'agree' and 'agreed' shall be construed accordingly.

(2) There is an agreement in writing—

(a) if the agreement is made in writing (whether or not it is signed by the parties),
(b) if the agreement is made by exchange of communications in writing, or
(c) if the agreement is evidenced in writing.

(3) Where parties agree otherwise than in writing by reference to terms which are in writing, they make an agreement in writing.

(4) An agreement is evidenced in writing if an agreement made otherwise than in writing is recorded by one of the parties, or by a third party, with the authority of the parties to the agreement.

(5) An exchange of written submissions in arbitral or legal proceedings in which the existence of an agreement otherwise than in writing is alleged by one party against another party and not denied by the other party in his response constitutes as between those parties an agreement in writing to the effect alleged.

(6) References in this Part to anything being written or in writing include its being recorded by any means.

THE ARBITRATION AGREEMENT

6 Definition of arbitration agreement

(1) In this Part an 'arbitration agreement' means an agreement to submit to arbitration present or future disputes (whether they are contractual or not).

(2) The reference in an agreement to a written form of arbitration clause or to a document containing an arbitration clause constitutes an arbitration agreement if the reference is such as to make that clause part of the agreement.

7 Separability of arbitration agreement

Unless otherwise agreed by the parties, an arbitration agreement which forms or was intended to form part of another agreement (whether or not in writing) shall not be regarded as invalid, non-existent or ineffective because that other agreement is invalid, or did not come into existence or has become ineffective, and it shall for that purpose be treated as a distinct agreement.

8 Whether agreement discharged by death of a party

(1) Unless otherwise agreed by the parties, an arbitration agreement is not discharged by the death of a party and may be enforced by or against the personal representatives of that party.

(2) Subsection (1) does not affect the operation of any enactment or rule of law by virtue of which a substantive right or obligation is extinguished by death.

STAY OF LEGAL PROCEEDINGS

9 Stay of legal proceedings

(1) A party to an arbitration agreement against whom legal proceedings are brought (whether by way of claim or counterclaim) in respect of a matter which under the agreement is to be referred to arbitration may (upon notice to the other parties to the proceedings) apply to the court in which the proceedings have been brought to stay the proceedings so far as they concern that matter.

(2) An application may be made notwithstanding that the matter is to be referred to arbitration only after the exhaustion of other dispute resolution procedures.

(3) An application may not be made by a person before taking the appropriate procedural step (if any) to acknowledge the legal proceedings against him or after he has taken any step in those proceedings to answer the substantive claim.

(4) On an application under this section the court shall grant a stay unless satisfied that the arbitration agreement is null and void, inoperative, or incapable of being performed.

(5) If the court refuses to stay the legal proceedings, any provision that an award is a condition precedent to the bringing of legal proceedings in respect of any matter is of no effect in relation to those proceedings.

10 Reference of interpleader issue to arbitration

(1) Where in legal proceedings relief by way of interpleader is granted and any issue between the claimants is one in respect of which there is an arbitration agreement between them, the court granting the relief shall direct that the issue be determined in accordance with the agreement unless the circumstances are such that proceedings brought by a claimant in respect of the matter would not be stayed.

(2) Where subsection (1) applies but the court does not direct that the issue be determined in accordance with the arbitration agreement, any provision that an award is a condition precedent to the bringing of legal proceedings in respect of any matter shall not affect the determination of that issue by the court.

11 Retention of security where Admiralty proceedings stayed

(1) Where Admiralty proceedings are stayed on the ground that the dispute in question should be submitted to arbitration, the court granting the stay may, if in those proceedings property has been arrested or bail or other security has been given to prevent or obtain release from arrest—
   (a) order that the property arrested be retained as security for the satisfaction of any award given in the arbitration in respect of that dispute, or
   (b) order that the stay of those proceedings be conditional on the provision of equivalent security for the satisfaction of any such award.

(2) Subject to any provision made by rules of court and to any necessary modifications, the same law and practice shall apply in relation to property retained in pursuance of an order as would apply if it were held for the purposes of proceedings in the court making the order.

COMMENCEMENT OF ARBITRAL PROCEEDINGS

12 Power of court to extend time for beginning arbitral proceedings, &c

(1) Where an arbitration agreement to refer future disputes to arbitration provides that a claim shall be barred, or the claimant's right extinguished, unless the claimant takes within a time fixed by the agreement some step—
   (a) to begin arbitral proceedings, or
   (b) to begin other dispute resolution procedures which must be exhausted before arbitral proceedings can be begun,

the court may by order extend the time for taking that step.

(2) Any party to the arbitration agreement may apply for such an order (upon notice to the other parties), but only after a claim has arisen and after exhausting any available arbitral process for obtaining an extension of time.

(3) The court shall make an order only if satisfied—
   (a) that the circumstances are such as were outside the reasonable contemplation of the parties when they agreed the provision in question, and that it would be just to extend the time, or

(b) that the conduct of one party makes it unjust to hold the other party to the strict terms of the provision in question.

(4) The court may extend the time for such period and on such terms as it thinks fit, and may do so whether or not the time previously fixed (by agreement or by a previous order) has expired.

(5) An order under this section does not affect the operation of the Limitation Acts (see section 13).

(6) The leave of the court is required for any appeal from a decision of the court under this section.

13 Application of Limitation Acts

(1) The Limitation Acts apply to arbitral proceedings as they apply to legal proceedings.

(2) The court may order that in computing the time prescribed by the Limitation Acts for the commencement of proceedings (including arbitral proceedings) in respect of a dispute which was the subject matter—

(a) of an award which the court orders to be set aside or declares to be of no effect, or

(b) of the affected part of an award which the court orders to be set aside in part, or declares to be in part of no effect,

the period between the commencement of the arbitration and the date of the order referred to in paragraph (a) or (b) shall be excluded.

(3) In determining for the purposes of the Limitation Acts when a cause of action accrued, any provision that an award is a condition precedent to the bringing of legal proceedings in respect of a matter to which an arbitration agreement applies shall be disregarded.

(4) In this Part 'the Limitation Acts' means—

(a) in England and Wales, the Limitation Act 1980, the Foreign Limitation Periods Act 1984 and any other enactment (whenever passed) relating to the limitation of actions;

(b) in Northern Ireland, the Limitation (Northern Ireland) Order 1989, the Foreign Limitation Periods (Northern Ireland) Order 1985 and any other enactment (whenever passed) relating to the limitation of actions.

14 Commencement of arbitral proceedings

(1) The parties are free to agree when arbitral proceedings are to be regarded as commenced for the purposes of this Part and for the purposes of the Limitation Acts.

(2) If there is no such agreement the following provisions apply.

(3) Where the arbitrator is named or designated in the arbitration agreement, arbitral proceedings are commenced in respect of a matter when one party serves on the other party or parties a notice in writing requiring him or them to submit that matter to the person so named or designated.

(4) Where the arbitrator or arbitrators are to be appointed by the parties, arbitral proceedings are commenced in respect of a matter when one party serves on the other party or parties notice in writing requiring him or them to appoint an arbitrator or to agree to the appointment of an arbitrator in respect of that matter.

(5) Where the arbitrator or arbitrators are to be appointed by a person other than a party to the proceedings, arbitral proceedings are commenced in respect of a matter when one party gives notice in writing to that person requesting him to make the appointment in respect of that matter.

THE ARBITRAL TRIBUNAL

15 The arbitral tribunal

(1) The parties are free to agree on the number of arbitrators to form the tribunal and whether there is to be a chairman or umpire.

(2) Unless otherwise agreed by the parties, an agreement that the number of arbitrators shall be two or any other even number shall be understood as requiring the appointment of an additional arbitrator as chairman of the tribunal.

(3) If there is no agreement as to the number of arbitrators, the tribunal shall consist of a sole arbitrator.

16 Procedure for appointment of arbitrators

(1) The parties are free to agree on the procedure for appointing the arbitrator or arbitrators, including the procedure for appointing any chairman or umpire.

(2) If or to the extent that there is no such agreement, the following provisions apply.

(3) If the tribunal is to consist of a sole arbitrator, the parties shall jointly appoint the arbitrator not later than 28 days after service of a request in writing by either party to do so.

(4) If the tribunal is to consist of two arbitrators, each party shall appoint one arbitrator not later than 14 days after service of a request in writing by either party to do so.

(5) If the tribunal is to consist of three arbitrators—

(a) each party shall appoint one arbitrator not later than 14 days after service of a request in writing by either party to do so, and

(b) the two so appointed shall forthwith appoint a third arbitrator as the chairman of the tribunal.

(6) If the tribunal is to consist of two arbitrators and an umpire—

(a) each party shall appoint one arbitrator not later than 14 days after service of a request in writing by either party to do so, and

(b) the two so appointed may appoint an umpire at any time after they themselves are appointed and shall do so before any substantive hearing or forthwith if they cannot agree on a matter relating to the arbitration.

(7) In any other case (in particular, if there are more than two parties) section 18 applies as in the case of a failure of the agreed appointment procedure.

17 Power in case of default to appoint sole arbitrator

(1) Unless the parties otherwise agree, where each of two parties to an arbitration agreement is to appoint an arbitrator and one party ('the party in default') refuses to do so, or fails to do so within the time specified, the other party, having duly appointed his arbitrator, may give notice in writing to the party in default that he proposes to appoint his arbitrator to act as sole arbitrator.

(2) If the party in default does not within 7 clear days of that notice being given—

(a) make the required appointment, and

(b) notify the other party that he has done so,

the other party may appoint his arbitrator as sole arbitrator whose award shall be binding on both parties as if he had been so appointed by agreement.

(3) Where a sole arbitrator has been appointed under subsection (2), the party in default may (upon notice to the appointing party) apply to the court which may set aside the appointment.

(4) The leave of the court is required for any appeal from a decision of the court under this section.

18 Failure of appointment procedure

(1) The parties are free to agree what is to happen in the event of a failure of the procedure for the appointment of the arbitral tribunal.
There is no failure if an appointment is duly made under section 17 (power in case of default to appoint sole arbitrator), unless that appointment is set aside.

(2) If or to the extent that there is no such agreement any party to the arbitration agreement may (upon notice to the other parties) apply to the court to exercise its powers under this section.

(3) Those powers are—
(a) to give directions as to the making of any necessary appointments;
(b) to direct that the tribunal shall be constituted by such appointments (or any one or more of them) as have been made;
(c) to revoke any appointments already made;
(d) to make any necessary appointments itself.

(4) An appointment made by the court under this section has effect as if made with the agreement of the parties.

(5) The leave of the court is required for any appeal from a decision of the court under this section.

19 Court to have regard to agreed qualifications

In deciding whether to exercise, and in considering how to exercise, any of its powers under section 16 (procedure for appointment of arbitrators) or section 18 (failure of appointment procedure), the court shall have due regard to any agreement of the parties as to the qualifications required of the arbitrators.

20 Chairman

(1) Where the parties have agreed that there is to be a chairman, they are free to agree what the functions of the chairman are to be in relation to the making of decisions, orders and awards.

(2) If or to the extent that there is no such agreement, the following provisions apply.

(3) Decisions, orders and awards shall be made by all or a majority of the arbitrators (including the chairman).

(4) The view of the chairman shall prevail in relation to a decision, order or award in respect of which there is neither unanimity nor a majority under subsection (3).

21 Umpire

(1) Where the parties have agreed that there is to be an umpire, they are free to agree what the functions of the umpire are to be, and in particular—
(a) whether he is to attend the proceedings, and
(b) when he is to replace the other arbitrators as the tribunal with power to make decisions, orders and awards.

(2) If or to the extent that there is no such agreement, the following provisions apply.

(3) The umpire shall attend the proceedings and be supplied with the same documents and other materials as are supplied to the other arbitrators.

(4) Decisions, orders and awards shall be made by the other arbitrators unless and until they cannot agree on a matter relating to the arbitration.
In that event they shall forthwith give notice in writing to the parties and the umpire, whereupon the umpire shall replace them as the tribunal with power to make decisions, orders and awards as if he were sole arbitrator.

(5) If the arbitrators cannot agree but fail to give notice of that fact, or if any of them fails to join in the giving of notice, any party to the arbitral proceedings may (upon notice to the other parties and to the tribunal) apply to the court which may order that the umpire shall replace the other arbitrators as the tribunal with power to make decisions, orders and awards as if he were sole arbitrator.

(6) The leave of the court is required for any appeal from a decision of the court under this section.

22 Decision-making where no chairman or umpire

(1) Where the parties agree that there shall be two or more arbitrators with no chairman or umpire, the parties are free to agree how the tribunal is to make decisions, orders and awards.

(2) If there is no such agreement, decisions, orders and awards shall be made by all or a majority of the arbitrators.

23 Revocation of arbitrator's authority

(1) The parties are free to agree in what circumstances the authority of an arbitrator may be revoked.

(2) If or to the extent that there is no such agreement the following provisions apply.

(3) The authority of an arbitrator may not be revoked except—
   (a) by the parties acting jointly, or
   (b) by an arbitral or other institution or person vested by the parties with powers in that regard.

(4) Revocation of the authority of an arbitrator by the parties acting jointly must be agreed in writing unless the parties also agree (whether or not in writing) to terminate the arbitration agreement.

(5) Nothing in this section affects the power of the court—
   (a) to revoke an appointment under section 18 (powers exercisable in case of failure of appointment procedure), or
   (b) to remove an arbitrator on the grounds specified in section 24.

24 Power of court to remove arbitrator

(1) A party to arbitral proceedings may (upon notice to the other parties, to the arbitrator concerned and to any other arbitrator) apply to the court to remove an arbitrator on any of the following grounds—
   (a) that circumstances exist that give rise to justifiable doubts as to his impartiality;
   (b) that he does not possess the qualifications required by the arbitration agreement;
   (c) that he is physically or mentally incapable of conducting the proceedings or there are justifiable doubts as to his capacity to do so;
   (d) that he has refused or failed—
      (i) properly to conduct the proceedings, or
      (ii) to use all reasonable despatch in conducting the proceedings or making an award,
   and that substantial injustice has been or will be caused to the applicant.

(2) If there is an arbitral or other institution or person vested by the parties with power to remove an arbitrator, the court shall not exercise its power of removal unless satisfied that the applicant has first exhausted any available recourse to that institution or person.

(3) The arbitral tribunal may continue the arbitral proceedings and make an award while an application to the court under this section is pending.

(4) Where the court removes an arbitrator, it may make such order as it thinks fit with respect to his entitlement (if any) to fees or expenses, or the repayment of any fees or expenses already paid.

(5) The arbitrator concerned is entitled to appear and be heard by the court before it makes any order under this section.

(6) The leave of the court is required for any appeal from a decision of the court under this section.

25 Resignation of arbitrator

(1) The parties are free to agree with an arbitrator as to the consequences of his resignation as regards—
   (a) his entitlement (if any) to fees or expenses, and
   (b) any liability thereby incurred by him.

(2) If or to the extent that there is no such agreement the following provisions apply.

(3) An arbitrator who resigns his appointment may (upon notice to the parties) apply to the court—

(a) to grant him relief from any liability thereby incurred by him, and

(b) to make such order as it thinks fit with respect to his entitlement (if any) to fees or expenses or the repayment of any fees or expenses already paid.

(4) If the court is satisfied that in all the circumstances it was reasonable for the arbitrator to resign, it may grant such relief as is mentioned in subsection (3)(a) on such terms as it thinks fit.

(5) The leave of the court is required for any appeal from a decision of the court under this section.

26 Death of arbitrator or person appointing him

(1) The authority of an arbitrator is personal and ceases on his death.

(2) Unless otherwise agreed by the parties, the death of the person by whom an arbitrator was appointed does not revoke the arbitrator's authority.

27 Filling of vacancy, &c

(1) Where an arbitrator ceases to hold office, the parties are free to agree—

(a) whether and if so how the vacancy is to be filled,

(b) whether and if so to what extent the previous proceedings should stand, and

(c) what effect (if any) his ceasing to hold office has on any appointment made by him (alone or jointly).

(2) If or to the extent that there is no such agreement, the following provisions apply.

(3) The provisions of sections 16 (procedure for appointment of arbitrators) and 18 (failure of appointment procedure) apply in relation to the filling of the vacancy as in relation to an original appointment.

(4) The tribunal (when reconstituted) shall determine whether and if so to what extent the previous proceedings should stand.

This does not affect any right of a party to challenge those proceedings on any ground which had arisen before the arbitrator ceased to hold office.

(5) His ceasing to hold office does not affect any appointment by him (alone or jointly) of another arbitrator, in particular any appointment of a chairman or umpire.

28 Joint and several liability of parties to arbitrators for fees and expenses

(1) The parties are jointly and severally liable to pay to the arbitrators such reasonable fees and expenses (if any) as are appropriate in the circumstances.

(2) Any party may apply to the court (upon notice to the other parties and to the arbitrators) which may order that the amount of the arbitrators' fees and expenses shall be considered and adjusted by such means and upon such terms as it may direct.

(3) If the application is made after any amount has been paid to the arbitrators by way of fees or expenses, the court may order the repayment of such amount (if any) as is shown to be excessive, but shall not do so unless it is shown that it is reasonable in the circumstances to order repayment.

(4) The above provisions have effect subject to any order of the court under section 24(4) or 25(3)(b) (order as to entitlement to fees or expenses in case of removal or resignation of arbitrator).

(5) Nothing in this section affects any liability of a party to any other party to pay all or any of the costs of the arbitration (see sections 59 to 65) or any contractual right of an arbitrator to payment of his fees and expenses.

(6) In this section references to arbitrators include an arbitrator who has ceased to act and an umpire who has not replaced the other arbitrators.

29 Immunity of arbitrator

(1) An arbitrator is not liable for anything done or omitted in the discharge or purported discharge of his functions as arbitrator unless the act or omission is shown to have been in bad faith.

(2) Subsection (1) applies to an employee or agent of an arbitrator as it applies to the arbitrator himself.

(3) This section does not affect any liability incurred by an arbitrator by reason of his resigning (but see section 25).

JURISDICTION OF THE ARBITRAL TRIBUNAL

30 Competence of tribunal to rule on its own jurisdiction

(1) Unless otherwise agreed by the parties, the arbitral tribunal may rule on its own substantive jurisdiction, that is, as to—

(a) whether there is a valid arbitration agreement,

(b) whether the tribunal is properly constituted, and

(c) what matters have been submitted to arbitration in accordance with the arbitration agreement.

(2) Any such ruling may be challenged by any available arbitral process of appeal or review or in accordance with the provisions of this Part.

31 Objection to substantive jurisdiction of tribunal

(1) An objection that the arbitral tribunal lacks substantive jurisdiction at the outset of the proceedings must be raised by a party not later than the time he takes the first step in the proceedings to contest the merits of any matter in relation to which he challenges the tribunal's jurisdiction.

A party is not precluded from raising such an objection by the fact that he has appointed or participated in the appointment of an arbitrator.

(2) Any objection during the course of the arbitral proceedings that the arbitral tribunal is exceeding its substantive jurisdiction must be made as soon as possible after the matter alleged to be beyond its jurisdiction is raised.

(3) The arbitral tribunal may admit an objection later than the time specified in subsection (1) or (2) if it considers the delay justified.

(4) Where an objection is duly taken to the tribunal's substantive jurisdiction and the tribunal has power to rule on its own jurisdiction, it may—

(a) rule on the matter in an award as to jurisdiction, or

(b) deal with the objection in its award on the merits.

If the parties agree which of these courses the tribunal should take, the tribunal shall proceed accordingly.

(5) The tribunal may in any case, and shall if the parties so agree, stay proceedings whilst an application is made to the court under section 32 (determination of preliminary point of jurisdiction).

32 Determination of preliminary point of jurisdiction

(1) The court may, on the application of a party to arbitral proceedings (upon notice to the other parties), determine any question as to the substantive jurisdiction of the tribunal.

A party may lose the right to object (see section 73).

(2) An application under this section shall not be considered unless—
(a) it is made with the agreement in writing of all the other parties to the proceedings, or
(b) it is made with the permission of the tribunal and the court is satisfied—
(i) that the determination of the question is likely to produce substantial savings in costs,
(ii) that the application was made without delay, and
(iii) that there is good reason why the matter should be decided by the court.

(3) An application under this section, unless made with the agreement of all the other parties to the proceedings, shall state the grounds on which it is said that the matter should be decided by the court.

(4) Unless otherwise agreed by the parties, the arbitral tribunal may continue the arbitral proceedings and make an award while an application to the court under this section is pending.

(5) Unless the court gives leave, no appeal lies from a decision of the court whether the conditions specified in subsection (2) are met.

(6) The decision of the court on the question of jurisdiction shall be treated as a judgment of the court for the purposes of an appeal.
But no appeal lies without the leave of the court which shall not be given unless the court considers that the question involves a point of law which is one of general importance or is one which for some other special reason should be considered by the Court of Appeal.

THE ARBITRAL PROCEEDINGS

33 General duty of the tribunal

(1) The tribunal shall—
(a) act fairly and impartially as between the parties, giving each party a reasonable opportunity of putting his case and dealing with that of his opponent, and
(b) adopt procedures suitable to the circumstances of the particular case, avoiding unnecessary delay or expense, so as to provide a fair means for the resolution of the matters falling to be determined.

(2) The tribunal shall comply with that general duty in conducting the arbitral proceedings, in its decisions on matters of procedure and evidence and in the exercise of all other powers conferred on it.

34 Procedural and evidential matters

(1) It shall be for the tribunal to decide all procedural and evidential matters, subject to the right of the parties to agree any matter.

(2) Procedural and evidential matters include—
(a) when and where any part of the proceedings is to be held;
(b) the language or languages to be used in the proceedings and whether translations of any relevant documents are to be supplied;
(c) whether any and if so what form of written statements of claim and defence are to be used, when these should be supplied and the extent to which such statements can be later amended;
(d) whether any and if so which documents or classes of documents should be disclosed between and produced by the parties and at what stage;
(e) whether any and if so what questions should be put to and answered by the respective parties and when and in what form this should be done;
(f) whether to apply strict rules of evidence (or any other rules) as to the admissibility, relevance or weight of any material (oral, written or other) sought to be tendered on any matters of fact or opinion, and the time, manner and form in which such material should be exchanged and presented;

(g) whether and to what extent the tribunal should itself take the initiative in ascertaining the facts and the law;

(h) whether and to what extent there should be oral or written evidence or submissions.

(3) The tribunal may fix the time within which any directions given by it are to be complied with, and may if it thinks fit extend the time so fixed (whether or not it has expired).

35 Consolidation of proceedings and concurrent hearings

(1) The parties are free to agree—

(a) that the arbitral proceedings shall be consolidated with other arbitral proceedings, or

(b) that concurrent hearings shall be held,

on such terms as may be agreed.

(2) Unless the parties agree to confer such power on the tribunal, the tribunal has no power to order consolidation of proceedings or concurrent hearings.

36 Legal or other representation

Unless otherwise agreed by the parties, a party to arbitral proceedings may be represented in the proceedings by a lawyer or other person chosen by him.

37 Power to appoint experts, legal advisers or assessors

(1) Unless otherwise agreed by the parties—

(a) the tribunal may—

(i) appoint experts or legal advisers to report to it and the parties, or

(ii) appoint assessors to assist it on technical matters,

and may allow any such expert, legal adviser or assessor to attend the proceedings; and

(b) the parties shall be given a reasonable opportunity to comment on any information, opinion or advice offered by any such person.

(2) The fees and expenses of an expert, legal adviser or assessor appointed by the tribunal for which the arbitrators are liable are expenses of the arbitrators for the purposes of this Part.

38 General powers exercisable by the tribunal

(1) The parties are free to agree on the powers exercisable by the arbitral tribunal for the purposes of and in relation to the proceedings.

(2) Unless otherwise agreed by the parties the tribunal has the following powers.

(3) The tribunal may order a claimant to provide security for the costs of the arbitration.

This power shall not be exercised on the ground that the claimant is—

(a) an individual ordinarily resident outside the United Kingdom, or

(b) a corporation or association incorporated or formed under the law of a country outside the United Kingdom, or whose central management and control is exercised outside the United Kingdom.

(4) The tribunal may give directions in relation to any property which is the subject of the proceedings or as to which any question arises in the proceedings, and which is owned by or is in the possession of a party to the proceedings—

(a) for the inspection, photographing, preservation, custody or detention of the property by the tribunal, an expert or a party, or

(b) ordering that samples be taken from, or any observation be made of or experiment conducted upon, the property.

(5) The tribunal may direct that a party or witness shall be examined on oath or affirmation, and may for that purpose administer any necessary oath or take any necessary affirmation.

(6) The tribunal may give directions to a party for the preservation for the purposes of the proceedings of any evidence in his custody or control.

39 Power to make provisional awards

(1) The parties are free to agree that the tribunal shall have power to order on a provisional basis any relief which it would have power to grant in a final award.

(2) This includes, for instance, making—

(a) a provisional order for the payment of money or the disposition of property as between the parties, or

(b) an order to make an interim payment on account of the costs of the arbitration.

(3) Any such order shall be subject to the tribunal's final adjudication; and the tribunal's final award, on the merits or as to costs, shall take account of any such order.

(4) Unless the parties agree to confer such power on the tribunal, the tribunal has no such power. This does not affect its powers under section 47 (awards on different issues, &c.).

40 General duty of parties

(1) The parties shall do all things necessary for the proper and expeditious conduct of the arbitral proceedings.

(2) This includes—

(a) complying without delay with any determination of the tribunal as to procedural or evidential matters, or with any order or directions of the tribunal, and

(b) where appropriate, taking without delay any necessary steps to obtain a decision of the court on a preliminary question of jurisdiction or law (see sections 32 and 45).

41 Powers of tribunal in case of party's default

(1) The parties are free to agree on the powers of the tribunal in case of a party's failure to do something necessary for the proper and expeditious conduct of the arbitration.

(2) Unless otherwise agreed by the parties, the following provisions apply.

(3) If the tribunal is satisfied that there has been inordinate and inexcusable delay on the part of the claimant in pursuing his claim and that the delay—

(a) gives rise, or is likely to give rise, to a substantial risk that it is not possible to have a fair resolution of the issues in that claim, or

(b) has caused, or is likely to cause, serious prejudice to the respondent,

the tribunal may make an award dismissing the claim.

(4) If without showing sufficient cause a party—

(a) fails to attend or be represented at an oral hearing of which due notice was given, or

(b) where matters are to be dealt with in writing, fails after due notice to submit written evidence or make written submissions,

the tribunal may continue the proceedings in the absence of that party or, as the case may be, without any written evidence or submissions on his behalf, and may make an award on the basis of the evidence before it.

(5) If without showing sufficient cause a party fails to comply with any order or directions of the tribunal, the tribunal may make a peremptory order to the same effect, prescribing such time for compliance with it as the tribunal considers appropriate.

(6) If a claimant fails to comply with a peremptory order of the tribunal to provide security for costs, the tribunal may make an award dismissing his claim.

(7) If a party fails to comply with any other kind of peremptory order, then, without prejudice to section 42 (enforcement by court of tribunal's peremptory orders), the tribunal may do any of the following—

(a) direct that the party in default shall not be entitled to rely upon any allegation or material which was the subject matter of the order;

(b) draw such adverse inferences from the act of non-compliance as the circumstances justify;

(c) proceed to an award on the basis of such materials as have been properly provided to it;

(d) make such order as it thinks fit as to the payment of costs of the arbitration incurred in consequence of the non-compliance.

POWERS OF COURT IN RELATION TO ARBITRAL PROCEEDINGS

42 Enforcement of peremptory orders of tribunal

(1) Unless otherwise agreed by the parties, the court may make an order requiring a party to comply with a peremptory order made by the tribunal.

(2) An application for an order under this section may be made—
   (a) by the tribunal (upon notice to the parties),
   (b) by a party to the arbitral proceedings with the permission of the tribunal (and upon notice to the other parties), or
   (c) where the parties have agreed that the powers of the court under this section shall be available.

(3) The court shall not act unless it is satisfied that the applicant has exhausted any available arbitral process in respect of failure to comply with the tribunal's order.

(4) No order shall be made under this section unless the court is satisfied that the person to whom the tribunal's order was directed has failed to comply with it within the time prescribed in the order or, if no time was prescribed, within a reasonable time.

(5) The leave of the court is required for any appeal from a decision of the court under this section.

43 Securing the attendance of witnesses

(1) A party to arbitral proceedings may use the same court procedures as are available in relation to legal proceedings to secure the attendance before the tribunal of a witness in order to give oral testimony or to produce documents or other material evidence.

(2) This may only be done with the permission of the tribunal or the agreement of the other parties.

(3) The court procedures may only be used if—
   (a) the witness is in the United Kingdom, and
   (b) the arbitral proceedings are being conducted in England and Wales or, as the case may be, Northern Ireland.

(4) A person shall not be compelled by virtue of this section to produce any document or other material evidence which he could not be compelled to produce in legal proceedings.

44 Court powers exercisable in support of arbitral proceedings

(1) Unless otherwise agreed by the parties, the court has for the purposes of and in relation to arbitral proceedings the same power of making orders about the matters listed below as it has for the purposes of and in relation to legal proceedings.

(2) Those matters are—
   (a) the taking of the evidence of witnesses;
   (b) the preservation of evidence;
   (c) making orders relating to property which is the subject of the proceedings or as to which any question arises in the proceedings—
      (i) for the inspection, photographing, preservation, custody or detention of the property, or
      (ii) ordering that samples be taken from, or any observation be made of or experiment conducted upon, the property;

and for that purpose authorising any person to enter any premises in the possession or control of a party to the arbitration;

(d) the sale of any goods the subject of the proceedings;

(e) the granting of an interim injunction or the appointment of a receiver.

(3) If the case is one of urgency, the court may, on the application of a party or proposed party to the arbitral proceedings, make such orders as it thinks necessary for the purpose of preserving evidence or assets.

(4) If the case is not one of urgency, the court shall act only on the application of a party to the arbitral proceedings (upon notice to the other parties and to the tribunal) made with the permission of the tribunal or the agreement in writing of the other parties.

(5) In any case the court shall act only if or to the extent that the arbitral tribunal, and any arbitral or other institution or person vested by the parties with power in that regard, has no power or is unable for the time being to act effectively.

(6) If the court so orders, an order made by it under this section shall cease to have effect in whole or in part on the order of the tribunal or of any such arbitral or other institution or person having power to act in relation to the subject-matter of the order.

(7) The leave of the court is required for any appeal from a decision of the court under this section.

45 Determination of preliminary point of law

(1) Unless otherwise agreed by the parties, the court may on the application of a party to arbitral proceedings (upon notice to the other parties) determine any question of law arising in the course of the proceedings which the court is satisfied substantially affects the rights of one or more of the parties.

An agreement to dispense with reasons for the tribunal's award shall be considered an agreement to exclude the court's jurisdiction under this section.

(2) An application under this section shall not be considered unless—

(a) it is made with the agreement of all the other parties to the proceedings, or

(b) it is made with the permission of the tribunal and the court is satisfied—

(i) that the determination of the question is likely to produce substantial savings in costs, and

(ii) that the application was made without delay.

(3) The application shall identify the question of law to be determined and, unless made with the agreement of all the other parties to the proceedings, shall state the grounds on which it is said that the question should be decided by the court.

(4) Unless otherwise agreed by the parties, the arbitral tribunal may continue the arbitral proceedings and make an award while an application to the court under this section is pending.

(5) Unless the court gives leave, no appeal lies from a decision of the court whether the conditions specified in subsection (2) are met.

(6) The decision of the court on the question of law shall be treated as a judgment of the court for the purposes of an appeal.

But no appeal lies without the leave of the court which shall not be given unless the court considers that the question is one of general importance, or is one which for some other special reason should be considered by the Court of Appeal.

THE AWARD

46 Rules applicable to substance of dispute

(1) The arbitral tribunal shall decide the dispute—

(a) in accordance with the law chosen by the parties as applicable to the substance of the dispute, or
(b) if the parties so agree, in accordance with such other considerations as are agreed by them or determined by the tribunal.

(2) For this purpose the choice of the laws of a country shall be understood to refer to the substantive laws of that country and not its conflict of laws rules.

(3) If or to the extent that there is no such choice or agreement, the tribunal shall apply the law determined by the conflict of laws rules which it considers applicable.

47 Awards on different issues, &c

(1) Unless otherwise agreed by the parties, the tribunal may make more than one award at different times on different aspects of the matters to be determined.

(2) The tribunal may, in particular, make an award relating—
(a) to an issue affecting the whole claim, or
(b) to a part only of the claims or cross-claims submitted to it for decision.

(3) If the tribunal does so, it shall specify in its award the issue, or the claim or part of a claim, which is the subject matter of the award.

48 Remedies

(1) The parties are free to agree on the powers exercisable by the arbitral tribunal as regards remedies.

(2) Unless otherwise agreed by the parties, the tribunal has the following powers.

(3) The tribunal may make a declaration as to any matter to be determined in the proceedings.

(4) The tribunal may order the payment of a sum of money, in any currency.

(5) The tribunal has the same powers as the court—
(a) to order a party to do or refrain from doing anything;
(b) to order specific performance of a contract (other than a contract relating to land);
(c) to order the rectification, setting aside or cancellation of a deed or other document.

49 Interest

(1) The parties are free to agree on the powers of the tribunal as regards the award of interest.

(2) Unless otherwise agreed by the parties the following provisions apply.

(3) The tribunal may award simple or compound interest from such dates, at such rates and with such rests as it considers meets the justice of the case—
(a) on the whole or part of any amount awarded by the tribunal, in respect of any period up to the date of the award;
(b) on the whole or part of any amount claimed in the arbitration and outstanding at the commencement of the arbitral proceedings but paid before the award was made, in respect of any period up to the date of payment.

(4) The tribunal may award simple or compound interest from the date of the award (or any later date) until payment, at such rates and with such rests as it considers meets the justice of the case, on the outstanding amount of any award (including any award of interest under subsection (3) and any award as to costs).

(5) References in this section to an amount awarded by the tribunal include an amount payable in consequence of a declaratory award by the tribunal.

(6) The above provisions do not affect any other power of the tribunal to award interest.

50 Extension of time for making award

(1) Where the time for making an award is limited by or in pursuance of the arbitration agreement, then, unless otherwise agreed by the parties, the court may in accordance with the following provisions by order extend that time.

(2) An application for an order under this section may be made—
(a) by the tribunal (upon notice to the parties), or
(b) by any party to the proceedings (upon notice to the tribunal and the other parties),
but only after exhausting any available arbitral process for obtaining an extension of time.

(3) The court shall only make an order if satisfied that a substantial injustice would otherwise be done.

(4) The court may extend the time for such period and on such terms as it thinks fit, and may do so whether or not the time previously fixed (by or under the agreement or by a previous order) has expired.

(5) The leave of the court is required for any appeal from a decision of the court under this section.

51 Settlement

(1) If during arbitral proceedings the parties settle the dispute, the following provisions apply unless otherwise agreed by the parties.

(2) The tribunal shall terminate the substantive proceedings and, if so requested by the parties and not objected to by the tribunal, shall record the settlement in the form of an agreed award.

(3) An agreed award shall state that it is an award of the tribunal and shall have the same status and effect as any other award on the merits of the case.

(4) The following provisions of this Part relating to awards (sections 52 to 58) apply to an agreed award.

(5) Unless the parties have also settled the matter of the payment of the costs of the arbitration, the provisions of this Part relating to costs (sections 59 to 65) continue to apply.

52 Form of award

(1) The parties are free to agree on the form of an award.

(2) If or to the extent that there is no such agreement, the following provisions apply.

(3) The award shall be in writing signed by all the arbitrators or all those assenting to the award.

(4) The award shall contain the reasons for the award unless it is an agreed award or the parties have agreed to dispense with reasons.

(5) The award shall state the seat of the arbitration and the date when the award is made.

53 Place where award treated as made

Unless otherwise agreed by the parties, where the seat of the arbitration is in England and Wales or Northern Ireland, any award in the proceedings shall be treated as made there, regardless of where it was signed, despatched or delivered to any of the parties.

54 Date of award

(1) Unless otherwise agreed by the parties, the tribunal may decide what is to be taken to be the date on which the award was made.

(2) In the absence of any such decision, the date of the award shall be taken to be the date on which it is signed by the arbitrator or, where more than one arbitrator signs the award, by the last of them.

55 Notification of award

(1) The parties are free to agree on the requirements as to notification of the award to the parties.

(2) If there is no such agreement, the award shall be notified to the parties by service on them of copies of the award, which shall be done without delay after the award is made.

(3) Nothing in this section affects section 56 (power to withhold award in case of non-payment).

56 Power to withhold award in case of non-payment

(1) The tribunal may refuse to deliver an award to the parties except upon full payment of the fees and expenses of the arbitrators.

(2) If the tribunal refuses on that ground to deliver an award, a party to the arbitral proceedings may (upon notice to the other parties and the tribunal) apply to the court, which may order that—

(a) the tribunal shall deliver the award on the payment into court by the applicant of the fees and expenses demanded, or such lesser amount as the court may specify,

(b) the amount of the fees and expenses properly payable shall be determined by such means and upon such terms as the court may direct, and

(c) out of the money paid into court there shall be paid out such fees and expenses as may be found to be properly payable and the balance of the money (if any) shall be paid out to the applicant.

(3) For this purpose the amount of fees and expenses properly payable is the amount the applicant is liable to pay under section 28 or any agreement relating to the payment of the arbitrators.

(4) No application to the court may be made where there is any available arbitral process for appeal or review of the amount of the fees or expenses demanded.

(5) References in this section to arbitrators include an arbitrator who has ceased to act and an umpire who has not replaced the other arbitrators.

(6) The above provisions of this section also apply in relation to any arbitral or other institution or person vested by the parties with powers in relation to the delivery of the tribunal's award.

As they so apply, the references to the fees and expenses of the arbitrators shall be construed as including the fees and expenses of that institution or person.

(7) The leave of the court is required for any appeal from a decision of the court under this section.

(8) Nothing in this section shall be construed as excluding an application under section 28 where payment has been made to the arbitrators in order to obtain the award.

57 Correction of award or additional award

(1) The parties are free to agree on the powers of the tribunal to correct an award or make an additional award.

(2) If or to the extent there is no such agreement, the following provisions apply.

(3) The tribunal may on its own initiative or on the application of a party—

(a) correct an award so as to remove any clerical mistake or error arising from an accidental slip or omission or clarify or remove any ambiguity in the award, or

(b) make an additional award in respect of any claim (including a claim for interest or costs) which was presented to the tribunal but was not dealt with in the award.

These powers shall not be exercised without first affording the other parties a reasonable opportunity to make representations to the tribunal.

(4) Any application for the exercise of those powers must be made within 28 days of the date of the award or such longer period as the parties may agree.

(5) Any correction of an award shall be made within 28 days of the date the application was received by the tribunal or, where the correction is made by the tribunal on its own initiative, within 28 days of the date of the award or, in either case, such longer period as the parties may agree.

(6) Any additional award shall be made within 56 days of the date of the original award or such longer period as the parties may agree.

(7) Any correction of an award shall form part of the award.

58 Effect of award

(1) Unless otherwise agreed by the parties, an award made by the tribunal pursuant to an arbitration agreement is final and binding both on the parties and on any persons claiming through or under them.

(2) This does not affect the right of a person to challenge the award by any available arbitral process of appeal or review or in accordance with the provisions of this Part.

COSTS OF THE ARBITRATION

59 Costs of the arbitration

(1) References in this Part to the costs of the arbitration are to—
  (a) the arbitrators' fees and expenses,
  (b) the fees and expenses of any arbitral institution concerned, and
  (c) the legal or other costs of the parties.

(2) Any such reference includes the costs of or incidental to any proceedings to determine the amount of the recoverable costs of the arbitration (see section 63).

60 Agreement to pay costs in any event

An agreement which has the effect that a party is to pay the whole or part of the costs of the arbitration in any event is only valid if made after the dispute in question has arisen.

61 Award of costs

(1) The tribunal may make an award allocating the costs of the arbitration as between the parties, subject to any agreement of the parties.

(2) Unless the parties otherwise agree, the tribunal shall award costs on the general principle that costs should follow the event except where it appears to the tribunal that in the circumstances this is not appropriate in relation to the whole or part of the costs.

62 Effect of agreement or award about costs

Unless the parties otherwise agree, any obligation under an agreement between them as to how the costs of the arbitration are to be borne, or under an award allocating the costs of the arbitration, extends only to such costs as are recoverable.

63 The recoverable costs of the arbitration

(1) The parties are free to agree what costs of the arbitration are recoverable.

(2) If or to the extent there is no such agreement, the following provisions apply.

(3) The tribunal may determine by award the recoverable costs of the arbitration on such basis as it thinks fit.
  If it does so, it shall specify—
  (a) the basis on which it has acted, and
  (b) the items of recoverable costs and the amount referable to each.

(4) If the tribunal does not determine the recoverable costs of the arbitration, any party to the arbitral proceedings may apply to the court (upon notice to the other parties) which may—
  (a) determine the recoverable costs of the arbitration on such basis as it thinks fit, or
  (b) order that they shall be determined by such means and upon such terms as it may specify.

(5) Unless the tribunal or the court determines otherwise—
  (a) the recoverable costs of the arbitration shall be determined on the basis that there shall be allowed a reasonable amount in respect of all costs reasonably incurred, and
  (b) any doubt as to whether costs were reasonably incurred or were reasonable in amount shall be resolved in favour of the paying party.

(6) The above provisions have effect subject to section 64 (recoverable fees and expenses of arbitrators).

(7) Nothing in this section affects any right of the arbitrators, any expert, legal adviser or assessor appointed by the tribunal, or any arbitral institution, to payment of their fees and expenses.

64 Recoverable fees and expenses of arbitrators

(1) Unless otherwise agreed by the parties, the recoverable costs of the arbitration shall include in respect of the fees and expenses of the arbitrators only such reasonable fees and expenses as are appropriate in the circumstances.

(2) If there is any question as to what reasonable fees and expenses are appropriate in the circumstances, and the matter is not already before the court on an application under section 63(4), the court may on the application of any party (upon notice to the other parties)—
   (a) determine the matter, or
   (b) order that it be determined by such means and upon such terms as the court may specify.

(3) Subsection (1) has effect subject to any order of the court under section 24(4) or 25(3)(b) (order as to entitlement to fees or expenses in case of removal or resignation of arbitrator).

(4) Nothing in this section affects any right of the arbitrator to payment of his fees and expenses.

65 Power to limit recoverable costs

(1) Unless otherwise agreed by the parties, the tribunal may direct that the recoverable costs of the arbitration, or of any part of the arbitral proceedings, shall be limited to a specified amount.

(2) Any direction may be made or varied at any stage, but this must be done sufficiently in advance of the incurring of costs to which it relates, or the taking of any steps in the proceedings which may be affected by it, for the limit to be taken into account.

POWERS OF THE COURT IN RELATION TO AWARD

66 Enforcement of the award

(1) An award made by the tribunal pursuant to an arbitration agreement may, by leave of the court, be enforced in the same manner as a judgment or order of the court to the same effect.

(2) Where leave is so given, judgment may be entered in terms of the award.

(3) Leave to enforce an award shall not be given where, or to the extent that, the person against whom it is sought to be enforced shows that the tribunal lacked substantive jurisdiction to make the award.
   The right to raise such an objection may have been lost (see section 73).

(4) Nothing in this section affects the recognition or enforcement of an award under any other enactment or rule of law, in particular under Part II of the Arbitration Act 1950 (enforcement of awards under Geneva Convention) or the provisions of Part III of this Act relating to the recognition and enforcement of awards under the New York Convention or by an action on the award.

67 Challenging the award: substantive jurisdiction

(1) A party to arbitral proceedings may (upon notice to the other parties and to the tribunal) apply to the court—
   (a) challenging any award of the arbitral tribunal as to its substantive jurisdiction; or
   (b) for an order declaring an award made by the tribunal on the merits to be of no effect, in whole or in part, because the tribunal did not have substantive jurisdiction.
   A party may lose the right to object (see section 73) and the right to apply is subject to the restrictions in section 70(2) and (3).

(2) The arbitral tribunal may continue the arbitral proceedings and make a further award while an application to the court under this section is pending in relation to an award as to jurisdiction.

(3) On an application under this section challenging an award of the arbitral tribunal as to its substantive jurisdiction, the court may by order—

(a) confirm the award,

(b) vary the award, or

(c) set aside the award in whole or in part.

(4) The leave of the court is required for any appeal from a decision of the court under this section.

68 Challenging the award: serious irregularity

(1) A party to arbitral proceedings may (upon notice to the other parties and to the tribunal) apply to the court challenging an award in the proceedings on the ground of serious irregularity affecting the tribunal, the proceedings or the award.

A party may lose the right to object (see section 73) and the right to apply is subject to the restrictions in section 70(2) and (3).

(2) Serious irregularity means an irregularity of one or more of the following kinds which the court considers has caused or will cause substantial injustice to the applicant—

(a) failure by the tribunal to comply with section 33 (general duty of tribunal);

(b) the tribunal exceeding its powers (otherwise than by exceeding its substantive jurisdiction: see section 67);

(c) failure by the tribunal to conduct the proceedings in accordance with the procedure agreed by the parties;

(d) failure by the tribunal to deal with all the issues that were put to it;

(e) any arbitral or other institution or person vested by the parties with powers in relation to the proceedings or the award exceeding its powers;

(f) uncertainty or ambiguity as to the effect of the award;

(g) the award being obtained by fraud or the award or the way in which it was procured being contrary to public policy;

(h) failure to comply with the requirements as to the form of the award; or

(i) any irregularity in the conduct of the proceedings or in the award which is admitted by the tribunal or by any arbitral or other institution or person vested by the parties with powers in relation to the proceedings or the award.

(3) If there is shown to be serious irregularity affecting the tribunal, the proceedings or the award, the court may—

(a) remit the award to the tribunal, in whole or in part, for reconsideration,

(b) set the award aside in whole or in part, or

(c) declare the award to be of no effect, in whole or in part.

The court shall not exercise its power to set aside or to declare an award to be of no effect, in whole or in part, unless it is satisfied that it would be inappropriate to remit the matters in question to the tribunal for reconsideration.

(4) The leave of the court is required for any appeal from a decision of the court under this section.

69 Appeal on point of law

(1) Unless otherwise agreed by the parties, a party to arbitral proceedings may (upon notice to the other parties and to the tribunal) appeal to the court on a question of law arising out of an award made in the proceedings.

An agreement to dispense with reasons for the tribunal's award shall be considered an agreement to exclude the court's jurisdiction under this section.

(2) An appeal shall not be brought under this section except—
  (a) with the agreement of all the other parties to the proceedings, or
  (b) with the leave of the court.

  The right to appeal is also subject to the restrictions in section 70(2) and (3).

(3) Leave to appeal shall be given only if the court is satisfied—
  (a) that the determination of the question will substantially affect the rights of one or more of the parties,
  (b) that the question is one which the tribunal was asked to determine,
  (c) that, on the basis of the findings of fact in the award—
    (i) the decision of the tribunal on the question is obviously wrong, or
    (ii) the question is one of general public importance and the decision of the tribunal is at least open to serious doubt, and
  (d) that, despite the agreement of the parties to resolve the matter by arbitration, it is just and proper in all the circumstances for the court to determine the question.

(4) An application for leave to appeal under this section shall identify the question of law to be determined and state the grounds on which it is alleged that leave to appeal should be granted.

(5) The court shall determine an application for leave to appeal under this section without a hearing unless it appears to the court that a hearing is required.

(6) The leave of the court is required for any appeal from a decision of the court under this section to grant or refuse leave to appeal.

(7) On an appeal under this section the court may by order—
  (a) confirm the award,
  (b) vary the award,
  (c) remit the award to the tribunal, in whole or in part, for reconsideration in the light of the court's determination, or
  (d) set aside the award in whole or in part.

  The court shall not exercise its power to set aside an award, in whole or in part, unless it is satisfied that it would be inappropriate to remit the matters in question to the tribunal for reconsideration.

(8) The decision of the court on an appeal under this section shall be treated as a judgment of the court for the purposes of a further appeal.

  But no such appeal lies without the leave of the court which shall not be given unless the court considers that the question is one of general importance or is one which for some other special reason should be considered by the Court of Appeal.

70 Challenge or appeal: supplementary provisions

(1) The following provisions apply to an application or appeal under section 67, 68 or 69.

(2) An application or appeal may not be brought if the applicant or appellant has not first exhausted—
  (a) any available arbitral process of appeal or review, and
  (b) any available recourse under section 57 (correction of award or additional award).

(3) Any application or appeal must be brought within 28 days of the date of the award or, if there has been any arbitral process of appeal or review, of the date when the applicant or appellant was notified of the result of that process.

(4) If on an application or appeal it appears to the court that the award—
  (a) does not contain the tribunal's reasons, or
  (b) does not set out the tribunal's reasons in sufficient detail to enable the court properly to consider the application or appeal,

  the court may order the tribunal to state the reasons for its award in sufficient detail for that purpose.

(5) Where the court makes an order under subsection (4), it may make such further order as it thinks fit with respect to any additional costs of the arbitration resulting from its order.

(6) The court may order the applicant or appellant to provide security for the costs of the application or appeal, and may direct that the application or appeal be dismissed if the order is not complied with.
The power to order security for costs shall not be exercised on the ground that the applicant or appellant is—
(a) an individual ordinarily resident outside the United Kingdom, or
(b) a corporation or association incorporated or formed under the law of a country outside the United Kingdom, or whose central management and control is exercised outside the United Kingdom.

(7) The court may order that any money payable under the award shall be brought into court or otherwise secured pending the determination of the application or appeal, and may direct that the application or appeal be dismissed if the order is not complied with.

(8) The court may grant leave to appeal subject to conditions to the same or similar effect as an order under subsection (6) or (7).
This does not affect the general discretion of the court to grant leave subject to conditions.

71 Challenge or appeal: effect of order of court

(1) The following provisions have effect where the court makes an order under section 67, 68 or 69 with respect to an award.

(2) Where the award is varied, the variation has effect as part of the tribunal's award.

(3) Where the award is remitted to the tribunal, in whole or in part, for reconsideration, the tribunal shall make a fresh award in respect of the matters remitted within three months of the date of the order for remission or such longer or shorter period as the court may direct.

(4) Where the award is set aside or declared to be of no effect, in whole or in part, the court may also order that any provision that an award is a condition precedent to the bringing of legal proceedings in respect of a matter to which the arbitration agreement applies, is of no effect as regards the subject matter of the award or, as the case may be, the relevant part of the award.

MISCELLANEOUS

72 Saving for rights of person who takes no part in proceedings

(1) A person alleged to be a party to arbitral proceedings but who takes no part in the proceedings may question—
(a) whether there is a valid arbitration agreement,
(b) whether the tribunal is properly constituted, or
(c) what matters have been submitted to arbitration in accordance with the arbitration agreement,
by proceedings in the court for a declaration or injunction or other appropriate relief.

(2) He also has the same right as a party to the arbitral proceedings to challenge an award—
(a) by an application under section 67 on the ground of lack of substantive jurisdiction in relation to him, or
(b) by an application under section 68 on the ground of serious irregularity (within the meaning of that section) affecting him;
and section 70(2) (duty to exhaust arbitral procedures) does not apply in his case.

73 Loss of right to object

(1) If a party to arbitral proceedings takes part, or continues to take part, in the proceedings without making, either forthwith or within such time as is allowed by the arbitration agreement or the tribunal or by any provision of this Part, any objection—
  (a) that the tribunal lacks substantive jurisdiction,
  (b) that the proceedings have been improperly conducted,
  (c) that there has been a failure to comply with the arbitration agreement or with any provision of this Part, or
  (d) that there has been any other irregularity affecting the tribunal or the proceedings,

he may not raise that objection later, before the tribunal or the court, unless he shows that, at the time he took part or continued to take part in the proceedings, he did not know and could not with reasonable diligence have discovered the grounds for the objection.

(2) Where the arbitral tribunal rules that it has substantive jurisdiction and a party to arbitral proceedings who could have questioned that ruling—
  (a) by any available arbitral process of appeal or review, or
  (b) by challenging the award,

does not do so, or does not do so within the time allowed by the arbitration agreement or any provision of this Part, he may not object later to the tribunal's substantive jurisdiction on any ground which was the subject of that ruling.

74 Immunity of arbitral institutions, &c

(1) An arbitral or other institution or person designated or requested by the parties to appoint or nominate an arbitrator is not liable for anything done or omitted in the discharge or purported discharge of that function unless the act or omission is shown to have been in bad faith.

(2) An arbitral or other institution or person by whom an arbitrator is appointed or nominated is not liable, by reason of having appointed or nominated him, for anything done or omitted by the arbitrator (or his employees or agents) in the discharge or purported discharge of his functions as arbitrator.

(3) The above provisions apply to an employee or agent of an arbitral or other institution or person as they apply to the institution or person himself.

75 Charge to secure payment of solicitors' costs

The powers of the court to make declarations and orders under section 73 of the Solicitors Act 1974 or Article 71H of the Solicitors (Northern Ireland) Order 1976 (power to charge property recovered in the proceedings with the payment of solicitors' costs) may be exercised in relation to arbitral proceedings as if those proceedings were proceedings in the court.

SUPPLEMENTARY

76 Service of notices, &c

(1) The parties are free to agree on the manner of service of any notice or other document required or authorised to be given or served in pursuance of the arbitration agreement or for the purposes of the arbitral proceedings.

(2) If or to the extent that there is no such agreement the following provisions apply.

(3) A notice or other document may be served on a person by any effective means.

(4) If a notice or other document is addressed, pre-paid and delivered by post—
  (a) to the addressee's last known principal residence or, if he is or has been carrying on a trade, profession or business, his last known principal business address, or
  (b) where the addressee is a body corporate, to the body's registered or principal office,

it shall be treated as effectively served.

(5) This section does not apply to the service of documents for the purposes of legal proceedings, for which provision is made by rules of court.

(6) References in this Part to a notice or other document include any form of communication in writing and references to giving or serving a notice or other document shall be construed accordingly.

77 Powers of court in relation to service of documents

(1) This section applies where service of a document on a person in the manner agreed by the parties, or in accordance with provisions of section 76 having effect in default of agreement, is not reasonably practicable.

(2) Unless otherwise agreed by the parties, the court may make such order as it thinks fit—
   (a) for service in such manner as the court may direct, or
   (b) dispensing with service of the document.

(3) Any party to the arbitration agreement may apply for an order, but only after exhausting any available arbitral process for resolving the matter.

(4) The leave of the court is required for any appeal from a decision of the court under this section.

78 Reckoning periods of time

(1) The parties are free to agree on the method of reckoning periods of time for the purposes of any provision agreed by them or any provision of this Part having effect in default of such agreement.

(2) If or to the extent there is no such agreement, periods of time shall be reckoned in accordance with the following provisions.

(3) Where the act is required to be done within a specified period after or from a specified date, the period begins immediately after that date.

(4) Where the act is required to be done a specified number of clear days after a specified date, at least that number of days must intervene between the day on which the act is done and that date.

(5) Where the period is a period of seven days or less which would include a Saturday, Sunday or a public holiday in the place where anything which has to be done within the period falls to be done, that day shall be excluded.
In relation to England and Wales or Northern Ireland, a 'public holiday' means Christmas Day, Good Friday or a day which under the Banking and Financial Dealings Act 1971 is a bank holiday.

79 Power of court to extend time limits relating to arbitral proceedings

(1) Unless the parties otherwise agree, the court may by order extend any time limit agreed by them in relation to any matter relating to the arbitral proceedings or specified in any provision of this Part having effect in default of such agreement.
This section does not apply to a time limit to which section 12 applies (power of court to extend time for beginning arbitral proceedings, &c.).

(2) An application for an order may be made—
   (a) by any party to the arbitral proceedings (upon notice to the other parties and to the tribunal), or
   (b) by the arbitral tribunal (upon notice to the parties).

(3) The court shall not exercise its power to extend a time limit unless it is satisfied—
   (a) that any available recourse to the tribunal, or to any arbitral or other institution or person vested by the parties with power in that regard, has first been exhausted, and
   (b) that a substantial injustice would otherwise be done.

(4) The court's power under this section may be exercised whether or not the time has already expired.

(5) An order under this section may be made on such terms as the court thinks fit.

(6) The leave of the court is required for any appeal from a decision of the court under this section.

80 Notice and other requirements in connection with legal proceedings

(1) References in this Part to an application, appeal or other step in relation to legal proceedings being taken 'upon notice' to the other parties to the arbitral proceedings, or to the tribunal, are to such notice of the originating process as is required by rules of court and do not impose any separate requirement.

(2) Rules of court shall be made—
  (a) requiring such notice to be given as indicated by any provision of this Part, and
  (b) as to the manner, form and content of any such notice.

(3) Subject to any provision made by rules of court, a requirement to give notice to the tribunal of legal proceedings shall be construed—
  (a) if there is more than one arbitrator, as a requirement to give notice to each of them; and
  (b) if the tribunal is not fully constituted, as a requirement to give notice to any arbitrator who has been appointed.

(4) References in this Part to making an application or appeal to the court within a specified period are to the issue within that period of the appropriate originating process in accordance with rules of court.

(5) Where any provision of this Part requires an application or appeal to be made to the court within a specified time, the rules of court relating to the reckoning of periods, the extending or abridging of periods, and the consequences of not taking a step within the period prescribed by the rules, apply in relation to that requirement.

(6) Provision may be made by rules of court amending the provisions of this Part—
  (a) with respect to the time within which any application or appeal to the court must be made,
  (b) so as to keep any provision made by this Part in relation to arbitral proceedings in step with the corresponding provision of rules of court applying in relation to proceedings in the court, or
  (c) so as to keep any provision made by this Part in relation to legal proceedings in step with the corresponding provision of rules of court applying generally in relation to proceedings in the court.

(7) Nothing in this section affects the generality of the power to make rules of court.

81 Saving for certain matters governed by common law

(1) Nothing in this Part shall be construed as excluding the operation of any rule of law consistent with the provisions of this Part, in particular, any rule of law as to—
  (a) matters which are not capable of settlement by arbitration;
  (b) the effect of an oral arbitration agreement; or
  (c) the refusal of recognition or enforcement of an arbitral award on grounds of public policy.

(2) Nothing in this Act shall be construed as reviving any jurisdiction of the court to set aside or remit an award on the ground of errors of fact or law on the face of the award.

82 Minor definitions

(1) In this Part—

'arbitrator', unless the context otherwise requires, includes an umpire;

'available arbitral process', in relation to any matter, includes any process of appeal to or review by an arbitral or other institution or person vested by the parties with powers in relation to that matter;

'claimant', unless the context otherwise requires, includes a counterclaimant, and related expressions shall be construed accordingly;

'dispute' includes any difference;

'enactment' includes an enactment contained in Northern Ireland legislation;

'legal proceedings' means civil proceedings in England and Wales in the High Court or the county court or in Northern Ireland in the High Court or a county court;

'peremptory order' means an order made under section 41(5) or made in exercise of any corresponding power conferred by the parties;

'premises' includes land, buildings, moveable structures, vehicles, vessels, aircraft and hovercraft;

'question of law' means—

(a) for a court in England and Wales, a question of the law of England and Wales, and

(b) for a court in Northern Ireland, a question of the law of Northern Ireland;

'substantive jurisdiction', in relation to an arbitral tribunal, refers to the matters specified in section 30(1)(a) to (c), and references to the tribunal exceeding its substantive jurisdiction shall be construed accordingly.

(2) References in this Part to a party to an arbitration agreement include any person claiming under or through a party to the agreement.

83 Index of defined expressions: Part I

In this Part the expressions listed below are defined or otherwise explained by the provisions indicated—

agreement, agree and agreed	section 5(1)
agreement in writing	section 5(2) to (5)
arbitration agreement	sections 6 and 5(1)
arbitrator	section 82(1)
available arbitral process	section 82(1)
claimant	section 82(1)
commencement (in relation to arbitral proceedings)	section 14
costs of the arbitration	section 59
the court	section 105
dispute	section 82(1)
enactment	section 82(1)
legal proceedings	section 82(1)
Limitation Acts	section 13(4)
notice (or other document)	section 76(6)
party—	
—in relation to an arbitration agreement	section 82(2)
—where section 106(2) or (3) applies	section 106(4)
peremptory order	section 82(1) (and see section 41(5))
premises	section 82(1)
question of law	section 82(1)
recoverable costs	sections 63 and 64
seat of the arbitration	section 3
serve and service (of notice or other document)	section 76(6)
substantive jurisdiction (in relation to an arbitral tribunal)	section 82(1) (and see section 30(1)(a) to (c))
upon notice (to the parties or the tribunal)	section 80
written and in writing	section 5(6)

84 Transitional provisions

(1) The provisions of this Part do not apply to arbitral proceedings commenced before the date on which this Part comes into force.

(2) They apply to arbitral proceedings commenced on or after that date under an arbitration agreement whenever made.

(3) The above provisions have effect subject to any transitional provision made by an order under section 109(2) (power to include transitional provisions in commencement order).

PART II OTHER PROVISIONS RELATING TO ARBITRATION

DOMESTIC ARBITRATION AGREEMENTS

85 Modification of Part I in relation to domestic arbitration agreement

(1) In the case of a domestic arbitration agreement the provisions of Part I are modified in accordance with the following sections.

(2) For this purpose a 'domestic arbitration agreement' means an arbitration agreement to which none of the parties is—

(a) an individual who is a national of, or habitually resident in, a state other than the United Kingdom, or

(b) a body corporate which is incorporated in, or whose central control and management is exercised in, a state other than the United Kingdom,

and under which the seat of the arbitration (if the seat has been designated or determined) is in the United Kingdom.

(3) In subsection (2) 'arbitration agreement' and 'seat of the arbitration' have the same meaning as in Part I (see sections 3, 5(1) and 6).

86 Staying of legal proceedings

(1) In section 9 (stay of legal proceedings), subsection (4) (stay unless the arbitration agreement is null and void, inoperative, or incapable of being performed) does not apply to a domestic arbitration agreement.

(2) On an application under that section in relation to a domestic arbitration agreement the court shall grant a stay unless satisfied—

(a) that the arbitration agreement is null and void, inoperative, or incapable of being performed, or

(b) that there are other sufficient grounds for not requiring the parties to abide by the arbitration agreement.

(3) The court may treat as a sufficient ground under subsection (2)(b) the fact that the applicant is or was at any material time not ready and willing to do all things necessary for the proper conduct of the arbitration or of any other dispute resolution procedures required to be exhausted before resorting to arbitration.

(4) For the purposes of this section the question whether an arbitration agreement is a domestic arbitration agreement shall be determined by reference to the facts at the time the legal proceedings are commenced.

87 Effectiveness of agreement to exclude court's jurisdiction

(1) In the case of a domestic arbitration agreement any agreement to exclude the jurisdiction of the court under—

(a) section 45 (determination of preliminary point of law), or

(b) section 69 (challenging the award: appeal on point of law),

is not effective unless entered into after the commencement of the arbitral proceedings in which the question arises or the award is made.

(2) For this purpose the commencement of the arbitral proceedings has the same meaning as in Part I (see section 14).

(3) For the purposes of this section the question whether an arbitration agreement is a domestic arbitration agreement shall be determined by reference to the facts at the time the agreement is entered into.

88 Power to repeal or amend sections 85 to 87

(1) The Secretary of State may by order repeal or amend the provisions of sections 85 to 87.

(2) An order under this section may contain such supplementary, incidental and transitional provisions as appear to the Secretary of State to be appropriate.

(3) An order under this section shall be made by statutory instrument and no such order shall be made unless a draft of it has been laid before and approved by a resolution of each House of Parliament.

CONSUMER ARBITRATION AGREEMENTS

89 Application of unfair terms regulations to consumer arbitration agreements

(1) The following sections extend the application of the Unfair Terms in Consumer Contracts Regulations 1994 in relation to a term which constitutes an arbitration agreement.

For this purpose 'arbitration agreement' means an agreement to submit to arbitration present or future disputes or differences (whether or not contractual).

(2) In those sections 'the Regulations' means those regulations and includes any regulations amending or replacing those regulations.

(3) Those sections apply whatever the law applicable to the arbitration agreement.

90 Regulations apply where consumer is a legal person

The Regulations apply where the consumer is a legal person as they apply where the consumer is a natural person.

91 Arbitration agreement unfair where modest amount sought

(1) A term which constitutes an arbitration agreement is unfair for the purposes of the Regulations so far as it relates to a claim for a pecuniary remedy which does not exceed the amount specified by order for the purposes of this section.

(2) Orders under this section may make different provision for different cases and for different purposes.

(3) The power to make orders under this section is exercisable—

- (a) for England and Wales, by the Secretary of State with the concurrence of the Lord Chancellor,
- (b) for Scotland, by the Secretary of State, and
- (c) for Northern Ireland, by the Department of Economic Development for Northern Ireland with the concurrence of the Lord Chancellor.

(4) Any such order for England and Wales or Scotland shall be made by statutory instrument which shall be subject to annulment in pursuance of a resolution of either House of Parliament.

(5) Any such order for Northern Ireland shall be a statutory rule for the purposes of the Statutory Rules (Northern Ireland) Order 1979 and shall be subject to negative resolution, within the meaning of section 41(6) of the Interpretation Act (Northern Ireland) 1954.

SMALL CLAIMS ARBITRATION IN THE COUNTY COURT

92 Exclusion of Part I in relation to small claims arbitration in the county court

Nothing in Part I of this Act applies to arbitration under section 64 of the County Courts Act 1984.

93 Appointment of judges as arbitrators

(1) A judge of the Commercial Court or an official referee may, if in all the circumstances he thinks fit, accept appointment as a sole arbitrator or as umpire by or by virtue of an arbitration agreement.

(2) A judge of the Commercial Court shall not do so unless the Lord Chief Justice has informed him that, having regard to the state of business in the High Court and the Crown Court, he can be made available.

(3) An official referee shall not do so unless the Lord Chief Justice has informed him that, having regard to the state of official referees' business, he can be made available.

(4) The fees payable for the services of a judge of the Commercial Court or official referee as arbitrator or umpire shall be taken in the High Court.

(5) In this section—

'arbitration agreement' has the same meaning as in Part I; and

'official referee' means a person nominated under section 68(1)(a) of the Senior Courts Act 1981 to deal with official referees' business.

(6) The provisions of Part I of this Act apply to arbitration before a person appointed under this section with the modifications specified in Schedule 2.

STATUTORY ARBITRATIONS

94 Application of Part I to statutory arbitrations

(1) The provisions of Part I apply to every arbitration under an enactment (a 'statutory arbitration'), whether the enactment was passed or made before or after the commencement of this Act, subject to the adaptations and exclusions specified in sections 95 to 98.

(2) The provisions of Part I do not apply to a statutory arbitration if or to the extent that their application—

(a) is inconsistent with the provisions of the enactment concerned, with any rules or procedure authorised or recognised by it, or

(b) is excluded by any other enactment.

(3) In this section and the following provisions of this Part 'enactment'—

(a) in England and Wales, includes an enactment contained in subordinate legislation within the meaning of the Interpretation Act 1978;

(b) in Northern Ireland, means a statutory provision within the meaning of section 1(f) of the Interpretation Act (Northern Ireland) 1954.

95 General adaptation of provisions in relation to statutory arbitrations

(1) The provisions of Part I apply to a statutory arbitration—

(a) as if the arbitration were pursuant to an arbitration agreement and as if the enactment were that agreement, and

(b) as if the persons by and against whom a claim subject to arbitration in pursuance of the enactment may be or has been made were parties to that agreement.

(2) Every statutory arbitration shall be taken to have its seat in England and Wales or, as the case may be, in Northern Ireland.

96 Specific adaptations of provisions in relation to statutory arbitrations

(1) The following provisions of Part I apply to a statutory arbitration with the following adaptations.

(2) In section 30(1) (competence of tribunal to rule on its own jurisdiction), the reference in paragraph (a) to whether there is a valid arbitration agreement shall be construed as a reference to whether the enactment applies to the dispute or difference in question.

(3) Section 35 (consolidation of proceedings and concurrent hearings) applies only so as to authorise the consolidation of proceedings, or concurrent hearings in proceedings, under the same enactment.

(4) Section 46 (rules applicable to substance of dispute) applies with the omission of subsection (1)(b) (determination in accordance with considerations agreed by parties).

97 Provisions excluded from applying to statutory arbitrations

The following provisions of Part I do not apply in relation to a statutory arbitration—

(a) section 8 (whether agreement discharged by death of a party);

(b) section 12 (power of court to extend agreed time limits);

(c) sections 9(5), 10(2) and 71(4) (restrictions on effect of provision that award condition precedent to right to bring legal proceedings).

98 Power to make further provision by regulations

(1) The Secretary of State may make provision by regulations for adapting or excluding any provision of Part I in relation to statutory arbitrations in general or statutory arbitrations of any particular description.

(2) The power is exercisable whether the enactment concerned is passed or made before or after the commencement of this Act.

(3) Regulations under this section shall be made by statutory instrument which shall be subject to annulment in pursuance of a resolution of either House of Parliament.

PART III RECOGNITION AND ENFORCEMENT OF CERTAIN FOREIGN AWARDS

ENFORCEMENT OF GENEVA CONVENTION AWARDS

99 Continuation of Part II of the Arbitration Act 1950

Part II of the Arbitration Act 1950 (enforcement of certain foreign awards) continues to apply in relation to foreign awards within the meaning of that Part which are not also New York Convention awards.

RECOGNITION AND ENFORCEMENT OF NEW YORK CONVENTION AWARDS

100 New York Convention awards

(1) In this Part a 'New York Convention award' means an award made, in pursuance of an arbitration agreement, in the territory of a state (other than the United Kingdom) which is a party to the New York Convention.

(2) For the purposes of subsection (1) and of the provisions of this Part relating to such awards—

(a) 'arbitration agreement' means an arbitration agreement in writing, and

(b) an award shall be treated as made at the seat of the arbitration, regardless of where it was signed, despatched or delivered to any of the parties.

In this subsection 'agreement in writing' and 'seat of the arbitration' have the same meaning as in Part I.

(3) If Her Majesty by Order in Council declares that a state specified in the Order is a party to the New York Convention, or is a party in respect of any territory so specified, the Order shall, while in force, be conclusive evidence of that fact.

(4) In this section 'the New York Convention' means the Convention on the Recognition and Enforcement of Foreign Arbitral Awards adopted by the United Nations Conference on International Commercial Arbitration on 10th June 1958.

101 Recognition and enforcement of awards

(1) A New York Convention award shall be recognised as binding on the persons as between whom it was made, and may accordingly be relied on by those persons by way of defence, set-off or otherwise in any legal proceedings in England and Wales or Northern Ireland.

(2) A New York Convention award may, by leave of the court, be enforced in the same manner as a judgment or order of the court to the same effect.

As to the meaning of 'the court' see section 105.

(3) Where leave is so given, judgment may be entered in terms of the award.

102 Evidence to be produced by party seeking recognition or enforcement

(1) A party seeking the recognition or enforcement of a New York Convention award must produce—

(a) the duly authenticated original award or a duly certified copy of it, and

(b) the original arbitration agreement or a duly certified copy of it.

(2) If the award or agreement is in a foreign language, the party must also produce a translation of it certified by an official or sworn translator or by a diplomatic or consular agent.

103 Refusal of recognition or enforcement

(1) Recognition or enforcement of a New York Convention award shall not be refused except in the following cases.

(2) Recognition or enforcement of the award may be refused if the person against whom it is invoked proves—

(a) that a party to the arbitration agreement was (under the law applicable to him) under some incapacity;

(b) that the arbitration agreement was not valid under the law to which the parties subjected it or, failing any indication thereon, under the law of the country where the award was made;

(c) that he was not given proper notice of the appointment of the arbitrator or of the arbitration proceedings or was otherwise unable to present his case;

(d) that the award deals with a difference not contemplated by or not falling within the terms of the submission to arbitration or contains decisions on matters beyond the scope of the submission to arbitration (but see subsection (4));

(e) that the composition of the arbitral tribunal or the arbitral procedure was not in accordance with the agreement of the parties or, failing such agreement, with the law of the country in which the arbitration took place;

(f) that the award has not yet become binding on the parties, or has been set aside or suspended by a competent authority of the country in which, or under the law of which, it was made.

(3) Recognition or enforcement of the award may also be refused if the award is in respect of a matter which is not capable of settlement by arbitration, or if it would be contrary to public policy to recognise or enforce the award.

(4) An award which contains decisions on matters not submitted to arbitration may be recognised or enforced to the extent that it contains decisions on matters submitted to arbitration which can be separated from those on matters not so submitted.

(5) Where an application for the setting aside or suspension of the award has been made to such a competent authority as is mentioned in subsection (2)(f), the court before which the award is sought to be relied upon may, if it considers it proper, adjourn the decision on the recognition or enforcement of the award.

It may also on the application of the party claiming recognition or enforcement of the award order the other party to give suitable security.

104 Saving for other bases of recognition or enforcement

Nothing in the preceding provisions of this Part affects any right to rely upon or enforce a New York Convention award at common law or under section 66.

PART IV GENERAL PROVISIONS

105 Meaning of 'the court': jurisdiction of High Court and county court

(1) In this Act 'the court' in relation to England and Wales means the High Court or the county court and in relation to Northern Ireland means the High Court or a county court, subject to the following provisions.

(2) The Lord Chancellor may by order make provision—

(za) allocating proceedings under this Act in England and Wales to the High Court or the county court;

(a) allocating proceedings under this Act in Northern Ireland to the High Court or to county courts; or

(b) specifying proceedings under this Act which may be commenced or taken only in the High Court or in the county court or (as the case may be) a county court.

(3) The Lord Chancellor may by order make provision requiring proceedings of any specified description under this Act in relation to which a county court in Northern Ireland has jurisdiction to be commenced or taken in one or more specified county courts.

Any jurisdiction so exercisable by a specified county court is exercisable throughout Northern Ireland.

(3A) The Lord Chancellor must consult the Lord Chief Justice of England and Wales or the Lord Chief Justice of Northern Ireland (as the case may be) before making an order under this section.

(3B) The Lord Chief Justice of England and Wales may nominate a judicial office holder (as defined in section 109(4) of the Constitutional Reform Act 2005) to exercise his functions under this section.

(3C) The Lord Chief Justice of Northern Ireland may nominate any of the following to exercise his functions under this section—

(a) the holder of one of the offices listed in Schedule 1 to the Justice (Northern Ireland) Act 2002;

(b) a Lord Justice of Appeal (as defined in section 88 of that Act).

(4) An order under this section—

(a) may differentiate between categories of proceedings by reference to such criteria as the Lord Chancellor sees fit to specify, and

(b) may make such incidental or transitional provision as the Lord Chancellor considers necessary or expedient.

(5) An order under this section for England and Wales shall be made by statutory instrument which shall be subject to annulment in pursuance of a resolution of either House of Parliament.

(6) An order under this section for Northern Ireland shall be a statutory rule for the purposes of the Statutory Rules (Northern Ireland) Order 1979 which shall be subject to negative resolution (within the meaning of section 41(6) of the Interpretation Act (Northern Ireland) 1954).

106 Crown application

(1) Part I of this Act applies to any arbitration agreement to which Her Majesty, either in right of the Crown or of the Duchy of Lancaster or otherwise, or the Duke of Cornwall, is a party.

(2) Where Her Majesty is party to an arbitration agreement otherwise than in right of the Crown, Her Majesty shall be represented for the purposes of any arbitral proceedings—

(a) where the agreement was entered into by Her Majesty in right of the Duchy of Lancaster, by the Chancellor of the Duchy or such person as he may appoint, and

(b) in any other case, by such person as Her Majesty may appoint in writing under the Royal Sign Manual.

(3) Where the Duke of Cornwall is party to an arbitration agreement, he shall be represented for the purposes of any arbitral proceedings by such person as he may appoint.

(4) References in Part I to a party or the parties to the arbitration agreement or to arbitral proceedings shall be construed, where subsection (2) or (3) applies, as references to the person representing Her Majesty or the Duke of Cornwall.

107 Consequential amendments and repeals

(1) The enactments specified in Schedule 3 are amended in accordance with that Schedule, the amendments being consequential on the provisions of this Act.

(2) The enactments specified in Schedule 4 are repealed to the extent specified.

108 Extent

(1) The provisions of this Act extend to England and Wales and, except as mentioned below, to Northern Ireland.

(2) The following provisions of Part II do not extend to Northern Ireland—

section 92 (exclusion of Part I in relation to small claims arbitration in the county court), and

section 93 and Schedule 2 (appointment of judges as arbitrators).

(3) Sections 89, 90 and 91 (consumer arbitration agreements) extend to Scotland and the provisions of Schedules 3 and 4 (consequential amendments and repeals) extend to Scotland so far as they relate to enactments which so extend, subject as follows.

(4) The repeal of the Arbitration Act 1975 extends only to England and Wales and Northern Ireland.

109 Commencement

(1) The provisions of this Act come into force on such day as the Secretary of State may appoint by order made by statutory instrument, and different days may be appointed for different purposes.

(2) An order under subsection (1) may contain such transitional provisions as appear to the Secretary of State to be appropriate.

110 Short title

This Act may be cited as the Arbitration Act 1996.

SCHEDULE

Section 4(1)

SCHEDULE 1

MANDATORY PROVISIONS OF PART I

sections 9 to 11 (stay of legal proceedings);
section 12 (power of court to extend agreed time limits);
section 13 (application of Limitation Acts);
section 24 (power of court to remove arbitrator);
section 26(1) (effect of death of arbitrator);
section 28 (liability of parties for fees and expenses of arbitrators);
section 29 (immunity of arbitrator);
section 31 (objection to substantive jurisdiction of tribunal);
section 32 (determination of preliminary point of jurisdiction);
section 33 (general duty of tribunal);
section 37(2) (items to be treated as expenses of arbitrators);
section 40 (general duty of parties);
section 43 (securing the attendance of witnesses);
section 56 (power to withhold award in case of non-payment);
section 60 (effectiveness of agreement for payment of costs in any event);
section 66 (enforcement of award);
sections 67 and 68 (challenging the award: substantive jurisdiction and serious irregularity), and sections 70 and 71 (supplementary provisions; effect of order of court) so far as relating to those sections;
section 72 (saving for rights of person who takes no part in proceedings);
section 73 (loss of right to object);
section 74 (immunity of arbitral institutions, &c.);
section 75 (charge to secure payment of solicitors' costs).

Section 93(6).

SCHEDULE 2

MODIFICATIONS OF PART I IN RELATION TO JUDGE-ARBITRATORS

Introductory

1 In this Schedule 'judge-arbitrator' means a judge of the Commercial Court or official referee appointed as arbitrator or umpire under section 93.

General

2(1) Subject to the following provisions of this Schedule, references in Part I to the court shall be construed in relation to a judge-arbitrator, or in relation to the appointment of a judge-arbitrator, as references to the Court of Appeal.

(2) The references in sections 32(6), 45(6) and 69(8) to the Court of Appeal shall in such a case be construed as references to the Supreme Court.

Arbitrator's fees

3(1) The power of the court in section 28(2) to order consideration and adjustment of the liability of a party for the fees of an arbitrator may be exercised by a judge-arbitrator.

(2) Any such exercise of the power is subject to the powers of the Court of Appeal under sections 24(4) and 25(3)(b) (directions as to entitlement to fees or expenses in case of removal or resignation).

Exercise of court powers in support of arbitration

4(1) Where the arbitral tribunal consists of or includes a judge-arbitrator the powers of the court under sections 42 to 44 (enforcement of peremptory orders, summoning witnesses, and other court powers) are exercisable by the High Court and also by the judge-arbitrator himself.

(2) Anything done by a judge-arbitrator in the exercise of those powers shall be regarded as done by him in his capacity as judge of the High Court and have effect as if done by that court.

Nothing in this sub-paragraph prejudices any power vested in him as arbitrator or umpire.

Extension of time for making award

5(1) The power conferred by section 50 (extension of time for making award) is exercisable by the judge-arbitrator himself.

(2) Any appeal from a decision of a judge-arbitrator under that section lies to the Court of Appeal with the leave of that court.

Withholding award in case of non-payment

6(1) The provisions of paragraph 7 apply in place of the provisions of section 56 (power to withhold award in the case of non-payment) in relation to the withholding of an award for non-payment of the fees and expenses of a judge-arbitrator.

(2) This does not affect the application of section 56 in relation to the delivery of such an award by an arbitral or other institution or person vested by the parties with powers in relation to the delivery of the award.

7(1) A judge-arbitrator may refuse to deliver an award except upon payment of the fees and expenses mentioned in section 56(1).

(2) The judge-arbitrator may, on an application by a party to the arbitral proceedings, order that if he pays into the High Court the fees and expenses demanded, or such lesser amount as the judge-arbitrator may specify—

(a) the award shall be delivered,

(b) the amount of the fees and expenses properly payable shall be determined by such means and upon such terms as he may direct, and

(c) out of the money paid into court there shall be paid out such fees and expenses as may be found to be properly payable and the balance of the money (if any) shall be paid out to the applicant.

(3) For this purpose the amount of fees and expenses properly payable is the amount the applicant is liable to pay under section 28 or any agreement relating to the payment of the arbitrator.

(4) No application to the judge-arbitrator under this paragraph may be made where there is any available arbitral process for appeal or review of the amount of the fees or expenses demanded.

(5) Any appeal from a decision of a judge-arbitrator under this paragraph lies to the Court of Appeal with the leave of that court.

(6) Where a party to arbitral proceedings appeals under sub-paragraph (5), an arbitrator is entitled to appear and be heard.

Correction of award or additional award

8 Subsections (4) to (6) of section 57 (correction of award or additional award: time limit for application or exercise of power) do not apply to a judge-arbitrator.

Costs

9 Where the arbitral tribunal consists of or includes a judge-arbitrator the powers of the court under section 63(4) (determination of recoverable costs) shall be exercised by the High Court.

10(1) The power of the court under section 64 to determine an arbitrator's reasonable fees and expenses may be exercised by a judge-arbitrator.

(2) Any such exercise of the power is subject to the powers of the Court of Appeal under sections 24(4) and 25(3)(b) (directions as to entitlement to fees or expenses in case of removal or resignation).

Enforcement of award

11 The leave of the court required by section 66 (enforcement of award) may in the case of an award of a judge-arbitrator be given by the judge-arbitrator himself.

Solicitors' costs

12 The powers of the court to make declarations and orders under the provisions applied by section 75 (power to charge property recovered in arbitral proceedings with the payment of solicitors' costs) may be exercised by the judge-arbitrator.

Powers of court in relation to service of documents

13(1) The power of the court under section 77(2) (powers of court in relation to service of documents) is exercisable by the judge-arbitrator.

(2) Any appeal from a decision of a judge-arbitrator under that section lies to the Court of Appeal with the leave of that court.

Powers of court to extend time limits relating to arbitral proceedings

14(1) The power conferred by section 79 (power of court to extend time limits relating to arbitral proceedings) is exercisable by the judge-arbitrator himself.

(2) Any appeal from a decision of a judge-arbitrator under that section lies to the Court of Appeal with the leave of that court.

INDEX

abruptness 171
Academy of Experts 381
ACAS *see* Advisory, Conciliation and Arbitration Service
Access to Justice Report (1996) 95
accreditation
  arbitrators 20–1
  mediation 234–6, 254
Accredited Mediation Provider 238
acrimonious disputes 69, 284
ad hoc arbitration 424
additional outcomes, proposing 170
adjournment of mediation 283
adjudication 33
  confidentiality 85–6
  disclosure of information 90
  and expert determination, comparison with 390
  see also construction and industry adjudication
Adjudication Rules 396
adjudicative ADR options 31–4
  see also adjudication; arbitration; expert determination
adjudicative processes and confidentiality 85–6
adjudicator nomination 399
Admiralty and Commercial Courts Guide, The 101–2, 139, 151
Admiralty and Commercial Registry 509
ADR Group 21, 307, 312
ADR Principles and Practice 240–1
advancing client's case 81–2
adversarial hearing 458
adverse costs orders 127–39
  extent to which other settlement methods have been attempted 130–7
  merits of the case 129–30
  nature of the dispute 129
  whether ADR had reasonable prospect of success 138–9
  whether any delay in setting up and attending ADR would be prejudicial 137
  whether costs of ADR would be disproportionately high 137
adverse information 90
adverse precedent, avoidance of 220
advice, professional duty to give 37–8
advice-giving, pre-trial 39
Advisory, Conciliation and Arbitration Service (ACAS) 7
  collective conciliation 334
  complaints and grievance procedures 339
  conciliation 30, 334
  Conciliation Scheme 311
  Early Conciliation 306, 311
  employment grievances 340–1
  form (COT3) 334
  mandatory early conciliation 334
  mediation 256
  Mediation Scheme 311
  post-claim conciliation 334
  Statutory Code of Practice on Discipline and Grievance 309–10
advocacy skills in mediation 287–8
advocates, role of in mediation 287–91
after the event (ATE) insurance 60, 96, 265
agenda setting for negotiation 197–8
aggression in negotiation 172
agreed bundle in mediation 263–4
Agreed Minimum Requirements for Mediators 308
agreed terms, submission to 369
agreements
  for ADR 49–50
  arbitration 414–18, 470, 472–3
  costs of ADR 151–2, 153
  mediation 256–7, 258
  see also damages-based agreements
allocation hearings 112, 149
alternative dispute resolution (ADR)
  acknowledged by Civil Procedure Rules (CPR) 3
  advantages 13–15
  choice of forum 14
  civil litigation costs 9–10
  clear and public finding, lack of 16
  client satisfaction 15
  confidentiality 14
  confusion of process 16–17
  control of process 13
  cost 13
  court judgment 15–16
  court recognition 8–9
  definition 5–6
  delays 15
  disadvantages 15–17
  evidence 14
  evidential rules 16
  expense 15
  flexibility of process 14
  growth of 7–8
  international context 11–12
  issues with 12–13, 14
  options, advising on 4, 17, 38–9, 50, 77–8
  outcomes 14, 15–16
  pledge 313
  problem-solving approach 15
  procedural regulation developments 10–11
  procedural steps 16
  process, backing out of agreed 144
  provider's fee 57–8

alternative dispute resolution (ADR) (*cont.*)
  psychology of dispute escalation 17–18
  reasons for 6–7
  regulatory frameworks 19–20
  risk 15
  settlement, speed of 13
  specific benefits 49
  success 18–19
  training and accreditation overview 20–1
alternative dispute resolution (ADR) order 306
  Chancery Division 104
  Commercial Court 103
  made by the court 139–40
  multi-track standard direction 109
Alternative Dispute Resolution Scheme 313
Alternatives to Court 329
ambiguity 179–80
American Arbitration Association (AAA) 442
amiable compositeur 461, 471
animosity 41–2
Annual Pledge Report 301
anti-suit injunctions 475, 478, 496
apology 45, 338, 345
appeals
  arbitration 505–8, 513–14
  commercial arbitration 461, 464
  exhaustion of 506
  High Court jurisdiction in arbitration claims 505–8
  rejection of ADR before hearing 142–3
  see also Court of Appeal
applicable law in international arbitration 472
application notice 326, 496
appointment
  arbitral tribunals 433–4
  arbitrators 475, 497
  commercial arbitration 462
  fee 399
Apportionment Agreement 154–5
appropriateness of ADR 41–2
ARB-MED 34, 285–6
arbitrable disputes 413–14
arbitral awards 330, 523
arbitral institutions 437, 441–2
arbitral proceedings
  judicial review 501
  procedural orders
    to assist in determination 498–501
  time extension for commencement 497
arbitral reviews, exhaustion of 506
arbitral rules closely following court procedures 461–4
arbitral tribunals 430–8, 498
  appointment of 433–4, 462
  asked to determine the point 506
  chairperson 433
  commencement of arbitration 430–1
  contractual time limits 430
  duty to follow rules of natural justice 421
  general duty of 421
  International Chamber of Commerce (ICC) 481
  limitation periods 431
  mandate of 411–12
  notice of arbitration 431–2
  powers to secure evidence available to 498–9
  terms of reference 435
  umpire 433, 434
  UNCITRAL Model Law 483
arbitration 31–3, 408–29
  ad hoc 424
  agreement to arbitrate 414–16
  capacity for 418
  claim form 500, 508
  claims *see* High Court jurisdiction in arbitration claims
  conditions precedent to 418–19
  confidentiality 85–6
  consumer 425
  contractual foundation to 410–12
  cost savings 419
  court applications 423–4
  disclosure of information 90
  dispute or difference 413
  disputes covering several contracts 416
  duty to follow rules of natural justice 421
  and expert determination 389, 390
  fair resolution of disputes 419–21
  family 426
  fundamental concepts 409
  funding 59–60
  general principles and duties 419
  High Court jurisdiction *see* High Court jurisdiction in arbitration claims
  history of 409–10
  human rights and 426–7
  institutional 424
  and litigation compared 409
  main features of 427–8
  MED-ARB 425–6
  multi-tiered dispute resolution 426
  need not be adversarial 421
  non-binding 425
  non-party disclosure 500
  one-stop 426
  overview of procedure 419
  party agreement 422–3
  party autonomy 421–3
  request for 480–1
  requirements for 412–19
  s 44 exclusion 501
  settlements and awards 522–4
  short-form 445–6
  stages 420
  statutory 410, 416, 425
  two-contract cases 415–16
  types of 424–6
  see also commercial arbitration; international arbitration
arbitration agreements 416–18, 470, 472–3
arbitration awards and orders 486–93
  binding effect 491–2
  conservatory measures 487
  costs awards 486, 492–3
  date of award 490
  dismissal orders 487

final award 488–9
injunctions 491
interest 491
interim awards and awards on different issues 486, 487
main awards 486, 487–92
majority decisions 489–90
notification of award 491
peremptory orders 487
place where award is made 490–1
procedural directions/ orders 486–7
reasons 490
remedies 491
seat of arbitration 490
settlement 487
arbitration clauses 414–15
bespoke 441
commercial arbitration 443
separability of 411
Arbitration and Mediation Centre of the World Intellectual Property Organisation 321
arbitrators
appointment 433, 434, 497
death 436
fees 437
immunity 437
impartiality and independence 435
judges as 434
mandate 434–5
number of 433
qualifications 435
removal 436, 497–8
resignation 436, 498
sole 434, 497
two and an umpire 434
two or three 434
vacancies 437
arguments 182–3
oral 204–5
Asaha Gang Mediation Project 316–17
Assessed Professionally Competent Mediator (APCM) 235
assessment
costs 65, 111, 152, 370, 521
damages 44
Assessment of Professional Competence Scheme 235
Association of Independent Construction Adjudicators (AICA) 116, 118, 399
Association of Litigation Funders of England and Wales 62
attendance 137
mediation 258–60
Australia 315, 319
authority
clarification in negotiation 188–9
limitation on 200–1
to settle 90–1, 169, 259
'automated mediation' 72
'automated negotiation' 72
autonomy of parties in arbitration 421–3
avatars 74
awards
arbitral 330, 523
commercial arbitration 461, 464
costs in arbitration 492–3
domestic 523
final 488–9
interim 486, 487
main 486, 487–92
with statutory authority 359
see also arbitration awards and orders; enforcement of settlements and awards

Banking and Investment Products Schemes 313
bankruptcy 519–20
Bar Council 236
Bar Pro Bono Unit 259
Bar Professional Training Course 20
Bar Standards Board (BSB) 20, 76
Code of Conduct 37, 240, 356
Core Duties 76, 79, 80
Guidance 77
Handbook 76
Outcomes 77, 80
Rules 77, 78, 79, 80
bargaining tactics 209–10
bargaining/negotiation stage 269, 270, 278–80
barristers
fees 56, 61
and professional clients, relationship between 91–2
professional ethics 76–7, 78–9, 80–1
benefit cases 62
bespoke arbitration clauses 441
best alternative to a negotiated agreement (BATNA)
mediation 234, 265
negotiation 165, 186–8, 205
'best endeavours' 47
best interests, acting within client's 37, 79–80
Beyond Right and Wrong: The Power of Effective Decision Making for Attorney and Clients 18
bias 497–8, 503, 522
binding decisions 486
binding effect
arbitration awards and orders 491–2
construction and industry adjudication 405–6
Birmingham, Manchester, and Central London County Courts Mediation Information Pilot Schemes 302–3
Blackstone's Civil Practice 54, 63
Bleak House 3
'blind-bidding' software 72
bluffing 171–2
body language 194
breakdown in settlement 213–14
brief fees 58, 59, 60
briefs, endorsement on 295, 363–5
Briggs, Sir Michael 102
British Coal Miners Mediation Scheme for Respiratory and Vibration White Finger 312
Britton, Philip 227, 305
Buck, Trevor 350
bundles 263–4, 457–8, 496
Business Innovation and Skills (BIS) 310

Cafcass (Children and Family Court Advisory and Support Service) 305, 335–6
Calderbank letters 132, 135
Canada 122, 319
capacity, mental 356, 418
Carroll, Eileen 320
case analysis (advocates) 287
case law 178
case management 105–9
  hearing 38
  orders 108–9, 264
Case Management Conference for ENE 348
Case Management Discussion 306
case preparation 177
case reviews 38
CEDR Commission on Settlement in International Arbitration, The 285
CEDR Rules for the Facilitation of Settlement in International Arbitration 285
Central London County Court 8, 298–9
Central London County Court Pilot Mediation Scheme, The: Evaluation Report 221
Centre for Conflict Transformation 316
Centre for Effective Dispute Resolution (CEDR) 7, 21, 39, 57, 312
  Code of Conduct for Mediators 19, 529
  commercial arbitration 442
  ENE Agreement and Guidance Notes 347
  Fourth Mediation Audit (2010) 239
  institutional
    arbitration 424
  mediation 215
  Mediation Audit 221, 239, 242, 329
  Model Executive Tribunal Procedure 315
  Model Expert Determination Agreement and Rules of Conduct 381
  Model Mediation Agreement 256, 529–31
  personal injury cases 351
  project mediation 314
  Rules for Adjudication 396, 400, 403, 405, 406
  Sector award 301
  Solve Model Mediation Procedure 153, 301, 302, 529–31
  Third Mediation Audit Report (2007) 242, 329
  UNCITRAL Model Law 482
chairperson 433, 489
challenge, expert determination 388
Chancery Court 102
Chancery Division 350–1, 509
Chancery Guide, The 102–4
Chancery Modernisation Review: Final Report 102, 350–1
charitable donation 280
Chartered Institute of Arbitrators 21, 347, 442
checking coverage and detail of settlement 293–4
Child Arrangements Programme 305
children, disputes involving 305, 356
Children and Family Court Advisory and Support Service (Cafcass) 305, 335–6
China 319
China International Economic and Trade Arbitration Commission (CIETAC) 442
choice of forum in ADR 14
chronology, position statements 263
City Disputes Panel 299
Civil Appeals Office 301
civil litigation
  costs 9–10
  courts' approach to ADR 96
  rules compliance 38
Civil Mediation Council (CMC) 9, 21, 22, 222, 239
  Accreditation Committee 237
  Accreditation Scheme 237–8
  Accredited Mediation Provider 238
  Board 237
  'CMC and Accreditation, The' 239
  Code of Good Practice for Mediators 242
  Conference 301
  confidentiality exceptions 248
  court mediation schemes 310
  enforceability of agreements resulting from 325–6
  ethical considerations for mediators 240
  Guidance Note No 1 'Mediation Confidentiality' 249
  Individual Membership Scheme 236, 238
  international mediation 329
  mediation 236–9
  Mediation, CFAs and conflicts of interest 229
  Members' Complaints Resolution Service 237
  National Mediation Helpline 9, 221, 298, 299, 303, 304
  online ADR and ODR 71
  Provider Accreditation Scheme 235, 236, 303
  Registered Workplace Mediation Organisation Scheme 238
Civil Mediation Online Directory 97, 137, 221, 223, 235–6, 303–4
  court mediation schemes 297, 298
  mediator's fee 228
  position statements 261
civil proceedings, enforcement by 518–19
claim form 98
claims
  money 175
  possession 99
client satisfaction 15
client's best interests 37, 79–80

clinical negligence 62, 303
close-settlement 213–14
closed meetings in mediation 270
closing joint meeting in mediation 283
closing of proceedings in commercial arbitration 460
closing submissions in commercial arbitration 460
closing/settlement stage of mediation 269, 270, 281–3
co-operative negotiation 161–2, 208
Code of Conduct for the Bar 37, 240, 356
Code of Conduct for Litigation Funders 61–2
Code of Conduct for Mediators 19, 529
 see also European Union
Code of Practice for Civil and Commercial Mediation 231–2
Code of Practice for Family Mediators 307
codes of conduct 20, 254
 international mediation 320
 professional ethics 76, 77, 84, 240
codes of practice in mediation 231–2, 257
collaborative law 12
collaborative negotiation 163–5, 166, 208
collective conciliation 335
College of Mediators 307
collusion 385
commencement
 ADR, delay in 137
 arbitration 430–1
 commercial arbitration 445, 461–2
 mediation 268–9
commercial agreements 22
commercial arbitration
 appeals 461, 464
 appointment of tribunal 462
 arbitral rules closely following court procedures 461–4
 awards 461, 464
 bundles 457–8
 case, putting together 444
 closing of proceedings 460
 closing submissions 460
 commencement 445, 461–2
 confidentiality 440–1, 456
 conservatory measures 448
 counter-notice 462
 counterclaim 453–5
 decisions 460–1
 defence 453–5
 defining issues 444
 directions 447–8, 463
 disclosure 455–6
 dismissal for delay 450
 documents 463
 equity clauses 461
 evidence 453–6
 expert evidence 460
 experts 456–7
 hearings 444–5, 458–60, 464
 interim directions 448–9
 interim payments 447
 legal representatives, role of 443–5
 'look-sniff' arbitrations 445
 oral hearing, no right to 457
 peremptory orders 449–50
 points of claim 451–3
 pre-trial hearing/conference 457
 preliminary meeting 447
 privacy 440
 procedural approaches 441
 procedural matters considered 448
 procedural orders 447–9
 procedural rules 441–3
 procedure 446–61, 462
 process of 439–65
 reference of dispute to 443–4
 samples 463
 security for costs 447
 short-form arbitrations 445–6
 silence in institutional rules 443
 site visits 460
 statements of case 451–3, 462–3
 views 460
 witness conferencing 459
 witness statements 456
 witnesses 459
commercial contract 33, 39
Commercial Court 95, 102, 121, 123
 ADR order 103, 261
 anti-suit injunctions 496
 early neutral and/or expert evaluation 31
 judge 434
 judicial evaluation 348
 mediation 306
 order 108, 120–1
 'Practice Note: Commercial Court; Alternative Dispute Resolution' (1994) 8
Commercial Court Guide 496, 502, 513
'commercial', definition of 439–40
commercial disputes in mediation 28, 221
commercial law, training and accreditation for 20
common commercial market 73
common law relief 359
communication
 construction and industry adjudication 405
 negotiation 194–7
 non-verbal 194
 not protected by without prejudice rule 244–6
 without prejudice 86–9
Communication on Alternative Dispute Resolution for consumer disputes in the Single Market (EU) 73–4
community mediation 316–17
compensation 345
competence 81, 240
competitive negotiation/negotiator 161, 162–3, 166, 208
competitive opponent 212
complaints and grievance procedures 19, 338–43
 acting for party in complaint 342
 against solicitors 340
 decisions in 342–3

complaints and grievance procedures (*cont.*)
  definitions 339
  effectiveness of 343
  employment grievances 340–2
  handling 339–40
  ombudsmen 343–4
complexity 41, 74, 306–7, 313
compliance with core professional duties 79–82
compliance, failure of *see* sanctions
compromise 517–18
  agreements 357, 517, 519
compulsory ADR schemes, failure to use 139
compulsory court mediation schemes 298–9
Compulsory Mediation Pilot Scheme 298–9
compulsory mediation processes 121–2
compulsory use of ADR 12
concealment of information 136
concentration, importance of 197
concerns, addressing 47–9, 50
concessions
  gaining 206
  implementing 205–6
  linking 186, 207–8
  making 207
  multiple 209
  negotiation 183–6
conciliation 30, 333–7
  definition 333
  Disability Conciliation Service 336
  early 224, 334, 335
  family cases 335–6
  outline of process 333–4
  The Furniture Ombudsmen (TFO) Conciliation Scheme 336
  see also Advisory, Conciliation and Arbitration Service
conditional fee agreements (CFAs) 60–1, 80
  funding 50–1, 229
  mediation 265
  settlement 293
conduct, unreasonable 144–5
Confederation of British Industry 7
conference call mediation 70
conferences
  giving advice 38
  see also pre-trial hearing/conference
confidential bundles in mediation 264
confidential information and expert determination 382–3
confidentiality 14, 50–1
  adjudication 85–6
  arbitration 85–6
  commercial arbitration 440–1
  construction and industry adjudication 404
  court overriding in interests of justice 248
  duties 83–6
  early neutral evaluation (ENE) 85
  exceptions 248–9
  expert determination 85
  implied obligation 456
  importance 43
  mediation/mediators 84–5, 242, 247–9, 327–8
confidentiality clauses 85, 247–8
Conflict Prevention and Resolution (CPR) 321
'conflicts of interests' check 498
confrontational style 161, 168
confusion of process 16–17
consensual nature of arbitration 427
consensus-building mediation 315–16
consent orders 47, 369, 520, 521
  administrative 367
  challenging settlement recorded as a contract 520
  drafting 367–8
  example 368
  family 369
  international mediation 326, 330
  recording settlement 295, 367–9
  true 369
conservatory measures 448, 487
construction contracts 394, 396
construction disputes 22, 33, 312
Construction and Engineering Disputes Pre-action Protocol 99–100, 152
construction, engineering, and technology disputes 306–7
construction and industry
  adjudication 392–407
  adjudicator's decision 404–5
  ambit of reference 399
  commencement of 396–402
  communicating decision to parties 405
  confidentiality 404
  costs 406
  court enforcement of sum found due on 406
  decision-making process 405–6
  documents, questions and impartiality 403–4
  enforcement of settlements and awards 522
  expert determination 387–8
  express contractual right to 395–6
  hearing 404
  inquisitorial approach 404
  nature of 393
  nomination of adjudicator 399
  notice of 398–9
  procedure before hearing 403–4
  reasons, interest and costs 405
  referral notice 400–2, 403
  related disputes 404
  requirements for 393–5
  residential building contracts 406
  site visits 404
  stages of 397
  statements of case 403

timetable for 403
see also Technology and Construction Court
Construction and Technology Court Guide 304
consumer arbitration 425
Consumer Code Approval Scheme (CCAS) 314
consumer disputes 11, 72–3
international mediation 319
online ADR and ODR 68
continuing professional development (CPD) 237, 238, 240
mediators 325
online ADR and ODR 71
contract claims 303
contract clauses 395–6
contracts
recording settlement 295, 360–3
settling a dispute 363
substantive 411, 470
written 359
contractual issues
ADR clauses 116–20
arbitration 410–12
arbitrators' mandate 434–5
construction and industry adjudication 395–6
expert determination clauses 379
settlement 296
contributory negligence 66
control
ADR 13
client's 43–4
cooperative strategy 166
costs
ADR 13, 56–60, 153
agreement between the parties determining liability 151–2
budget in settlement/ADR 110
cap on solicitor–client costs 146
considerations for the parties 64
construction and industry adjudication 405, 406
disproportionately high 137
failed ADR as part of costs of litigation 150–1
financial analysis and risk assessment 65
interim applications 149–50
liability may shift 55
litigation 175
management 109–11
may be recovered 55
mediation 227–9
non-agreement of parties 152–3
penalty 78
recovery 149–55
reforms 96
relative 43
saving 48, 419
security for 447, 480
settlement 372–3
solicitor–client 146
costs awards 486, 492–3
costs only proceedings 521
costs orders
adverse 127–8, 138–9
courts' general powers to make 126–7
financial analysis and risk assessment 66
indemnity 145–6
Legal Aid Agency funding 62
costs shifting 55, 96
Council of Europe 301
counterclaim in commercial arbitration 453–5
counter-notice in commercial arbitration 462
County Courts
local schemes 302
Money Claims Centre 11
reluctant parties in mediation 224
Small Claims Scheme 228
Court of Appeal 8, 224
Court of Appeal Mediation Scheme. Court-based initiatives for non-family civil disputes 19, 221
court applications for arbitration 423–4
court enforcement of sum found due in construction and industry adjudication 406
court guides 101–5
court judgment needed as precedent 41
court mediation
schemes 299–302, 309
voluntary 298–9
court orders 42, 359, 520–1
court proceedings
arbitral rules closely following 461–4
challenging final decision by an expert determination 384–8
recording settlement 363
Court Settlement Order 304
Court Settlement Process (CSP) 105, 304–5, 307
court system 3, 6
Court-Based ADR Initiatives for Non-Family Civil Disputes: The Commercial Court and the Court of Appeal 19, 221
courts
approach to ADR 95–124
attitude of 46–7
case management 105–9
contractual clauses 116–20
costs management 109–11
court guides 101–5
as decision maker in expert determination jurisdiction 383–4
directions questionnaires 112–13
judicial encouragement 114–16
overriding confidentiality provisions in interests of justice 248
overriding objective 105
powers of 41
powers to make costs orders 126–7
stay of proceedings 113–14
whether can compel parties to use ADR 120–3
see also pre-action protocols
cross-border disputes and confidentiality 85
cultural considerations 255, 321
see also language
curial law and international arbitration 470, 473–4

custody 62
Cybersettle 71

damages, recovery of costs as 154–5
damages-based agreements (DBAs)
  courts' approach to ADR 96
  funding 61
  mediation 265
  professional ethics 80
  settlement 293
date, awards 490
'day in court', client's desire for 45
deadlock 214, 282–3, 295–6, 506
  avoidance of 171
  mediator devising strategies to help parties work through 279–80
  reaching 211
deal mediation 316
Deal Mediation: How ADR techniques can help achieve durable agreements in the global markets 316
deals, reaching in negotiation 208
death of arbitrator 436, 490
decision-making in construction and industry adjudication 405
decisions
  commercial arbitration 460–1
  no reasons for in expert determination 385
  not intended to be final 387–8
deed in recording settlement 295, 360–3
defamation 97
defences
  commercial arbitration 453–5
  to claims for breach of compromise agreements 519
defendants in arbitration claims 509
DEFRA 246
delay
  additional in ADR 15
  in consent to mediation 143
  inordinate and inexcusable, dismissal for 450
  in setting up and attending ADR may be prejudicial 137
delaying tactic, ADR used as 49
demands
  escalating 209
  extreme 209
  making 206–7
  negotiation 183–6
  tactics relating to 169–70
Department of Energy and Climate Change 312
Department of Trade and Industry (DTI) 310, 410, 435, 504
Department of Work and Pensions 99
Departmental Advisory Committee (DAC) on arbitration 410, 435, 471
  commercial arbitration 440
  permission of the court 508
  substantial injustice 504
  time limits 509
Dickens, Charles 3
difficulties, dealing with in negotiation 210–13
Dilapidations Protocol 97
directions 447–9, 463
Directions Questionnaires 112–13
Directory of UK Mediation 317
Disability Conciliation Service 336
Disability Rights Commission 336
disbursements 56, 60, 62
disciplinary action 342
disciplinary procedures 251, 309–10
disclosure
  arbitration 499–500
  commercial arbitration 455–6
  duty of 84
  giving advice 38
  of information 89–90
  non-party 500
  of position statements and documents 264–5
  pre-action 500
discretion 508
discrimination cases 305, 310
disease and illness claims 97
dismissal for inordinate and inexcusable delay 450
Dispute Doctor 70
Dispute Resolution Commitment 11
Dispute Resolution Hearing 304
Dispute Resolution Regulations Two Years On: The Acas Experience 335
disputes
  arbitrable 413–14
  escalation 17–18
  management systems 35
  review panels 389–90
District Judge 305, 351
district tribunal judge (DTJ) 350
divorce 19, 62, 69, 305
Djanogly, Jonathan 301
documents
  commercial arbitration 463
  construction and industry adjudication 403–4
  drafting 81–2
  mediation 264–5
  pro-forma 68
'double blind-bidding' 72
draft preparation 171
drafting documents 81–2
duties
  confidentiality 83–6
  mediation 82
  negotiation 82–3
  professional 37–8, 79–82
  to act fairly and impartially 503
  when advancing client's case and drafting documents 81–2

e-commerce 69, 70, 73
e-Justice portal 74
e-mediation 70, 286–7
  see also online dispute resolution (ODR)
E-Mediator 70
Early Conciliation 224, 335
  certificate 334

Notification form 334
early neutral evaluation (ENE) 30–1, 346–52
Agreement and Guidance Notes 347
choice of evaluator 347
confidentiality 85
definition 346
and expert determination, comparison with 390
judicial evaluation 348–51
neutral fact finding 348
order 102
personal injury cases 351
procedure for 347–8
stage at which it should be employed 346
when it should be used 347
easily agreed issues 200
economic duress 85, 520
effectiveness of mediation 216–18
emotional factors 17–18, 42, 44–5, 69, 74, 212
see also acrimonious disputes
Employers' Liability and Public Liability Claims 69
employment disputes 22, 62, 87
mediation 256, 310–11
employment grievances 340–2
Employment Tribunals 224, 304, 310, 311
conciliation 334, 335
court mediation schemes 297, 310
Judicial Mediation Scheme 305–6
Service 306, 335
endorsement on briefs 295, 363–5
enforcement
of agreements resulting from mediation 325–6
as an issue 47
expert determination 388
see also enforcement of settlements and awards
enforcement of settlements and awards 358–9, 516–25
agreements 296
arbitration 522–4
challenging 475, 520
choice of enforcement options 518
compromise agreements 517–20
consent order 520, 521
construction industry adjudication 522
costs only proceedings 521
court orders 520–1
method of recording settlement 520–1
payment of agreed sum and costs 520
settlement upon terms endorsed on counsel's briefs 521
Tomlin order 521
engineering disputes 306–7
environmental disputes 42, 284, 315–16
Equity, ADR, Arbitration and the Law: Different Dimensions of Justice 116
equity clauses 461, 471
error of law 385–7
escalating demands 209–10
ethical issues 37, 61, 240–3
see also professional ethics
EU Mediation Atlas: Practice and Regulation 322
Europe 322
European Court of Human Rights 120
European Crystal Scales of Justice Award 301
European e-Justice portal 74
European Small Claims Procedure (ESCP) 73
European Union (EU) 11, 12, 122, 330
anti-suit injunctions 478
arbitration 414, 473
Code of Conduct for Mediators 238, 240, 242, 319, 322, 329
development of ADR 73–4
mediation 47, 121–2, 238, 319, 322–3
Model of Conduct for Mediation 237
online dispute resolution (ODR) 69, 70, 73–4
regulatory frameworks 19
Evaluating the use of judicial mediation in Employment Tribunals 306
Evaluation of the Effectiveness of Court-based Mediation Processes in Non-Family Civil Proceedings at Exeter and Guildford County Courts, An 221
evaluative mediation 229–30, 231–2, 284
and facilitative mediation compared 230
evaluator, choice of 347
evasion 171
evidence 204
client's view of 178–9
commercial arbitration 453–6
dealing with 178–80
flexibility of 14
funding 56
further 140–1
inspection of 38
orders relating to 46
powers to secure, available to arbitral tribunals 498–9
evidential rules 16
ex aequo et bono 461, 471
exaggerated claims 132, 136
exceeding powers in arbitration 503
exchange of letters and recording settlement 360
executive tribunal in mediation 314–15
expense 15, 54–6
Expert Determination 378
expert determination 33–4, 377–91
advantages of 380
agreement to use 379
approach of courts to 379–80, 383–4
arbitration, differing from 389
cases suitable for 378
challenging final decision by court proceedings 384–8
confidentiality 85, 382–3
differences between negotiation, mediation and neutral evaluation 380

expert determination (*cont.*)
  disclosure of information 89–90
  disputes review panels 389–90
  early neutral evaluation (ENE), adjudication and arbitration, comparison of 390
  enforcing decisions 388
  nature of decision 383
  procedure for making challenge 388
  process of 381–2
  reasons for decision 383
  selection of neutral or expert determiner 381
  similarities with other forms of ADR 380–1
  stage at which parties may agree to 378
  stay of proceedings, pending 379–80
expert determination clauses and contractual effect 379
expert determiner 381
expert evaluation 30–1
expert evidence 39, 275, 460
expert fees 61
expert knowledge, importance of 43
expert reports 264
expertise 253–4
experts
  commercial arbitration 456–7
  independent 34
  joint meetings of 281
  mediation 260, 275
  party-appointed 456
  suing 389
  tribunal-appointed 457
explanation
  as decision in complaints and grievance procedure 338, 358
  as objective 45
exploration/information stage in mediation 269, 270, 277–8, 281
extreme demands 209
eye contact 273, 289

facilitative mediation 229–31
  and evaluative mediation compared 230
facilitators, mediators as 74, 233–4
facts 178–80
  arguments based on 182
  finding, neutral 348
  position statements 262
failed ADR and costs 150–1
failure
  of proceedings by claimant 135–7
  to act lawfully or fairly 387
  to consider/pursue ADR 145–6
  to deal with all issues 504
fair and public hearing, right to 12
fair resolution of disputes 419–21
fairness 81, 241
faith, lack of in case 48
false issues 209
family arbitration 426
family cases
  conciliation 335–6
  Court of Appeal Mediation Scheme 301
  court mediation schemes 297
  courts' approach to ADR 96
  judicial mediation 304, 305
  mediation 59, 307–9
  Mediation Information Assessment Meetings (MIAMs) 123, 224
  without prejudice communications 87
Family and Civil and Commercial Mediation Accreditation Schemes 236
family consent orders 369
Family Courts 10, 100
  conciliation 335
  court mediation schemes 297
family disputes 11, 22, 28
Family Justice Council 308, 309
family law 12, 62
  training and accreditation 20
Family Law Arbitration Scheme 11
Family Mediation Council (FMC) 235, 307, 308, 309
Family Mediation Panel 301
family mediators 235, 307
Family Mediators Association (FMA) 307
family proceedings 100–1, 284
fast-track 7, 10, 299
fault of both parties 141–2
Federation of Oils, Seeds and Fats Association (FOSFA) 442
fees
  ADR provider's 57–8
  arbitrators 437
  barristers 56, 61
  brief 58, 59, 60
  daily 228
  expert 61
  fixed 228, 303
  hourly 57, 59, 60, 228
  mediation 221
  mediator's 228
  normal 60
  offer to pay 50
  process 56
  solicitor 56
  success 60–1, 96
  see also conditional fee agreements
Fenn, Paul 298
figures 205
  preparing to deal with 180–1
'final and binding' 506
financial analysis 64–6
Financial Conduct Authority (FCA) Mediation Scheme 313
financial considerations 66–7
  see also costs; funding
Financial Dispute Resolution (FDR) 103, 305
Financial Ombudsman 345
financial remedies cases 87, 101
Financial Services Authority (FSA) 139
'Find a Civil Mediation Provider' 235
'Find a Mediation Service' 309
First Hearing Dispute Resolution Appointment (FHDRA) 305, 335–6
Fisher, Roger 164
fixed fees 228, 303

fixed-cost online claims procedure for road traffic accidents 58
flexibility of process 14
foreseeability 182
formalities (position statements) 262
formality 427
fraud 42, 520
 arbitration 504
 expert determination 385
Free Mediation Project 318
freezing injunctions 500, 501, 523
freezing orders 483
frustration 212
full and final settlement 357
funding
 ADR procedures 52–67
 basis for 60–2
 conditional fee agreements (CFAs) 60–1, 229
 context 52–3
 general considerations 53–5
 Legal Aid Agency 62
 mediation 229
 public 80, 265, 309
 third party 53–4, 61–2, 76, 80, 293
Funding Code 62, 229
Funding Code, The: Decision Making Guidance 229
Furniture Ombudsmen Conciliation Scheme 336
future relationships, importance of 44, 175

gangs, mediating disputes between 316–17
gaps 179–80
 in conversation 197
 in information 210–11
Geneva Convention awards, enforcement of 524
Genn, Hazel 221, 298, 306
Getting Past No: Negotiating Your Way from Confrontation to Cooperation 212
Getting to Yes: Negotiating Agreement Without Giving In 164, 165
global payment 58
good faith 47
goods and services cases 69, 74
Gould, Nicholas 227, 305
Grain and Feed Trade Association (GAFTA) 442
grievance procedures 34, 251, 309–10
 see also complaints and grievance procedures
group disputes *see* multi-party disputes
Guardian Public Service Awards: Innovation category 301
Guide to family applications and mediation information and assessment meetings 308
Guide to Principles of Good Complaints Handling 343
Guidelines for Lawyers Representing Clients in Mediation 321

harmonization in international mediation 322–3
Harvard Negotiation Project 164, 167
Hay, Carolyn 350
heading (position statements) 261–2
'heads of agreement' 259, 282, 295, 322
healthcare sector mediation schemes 297, 313
hearings
 adversarial 458
 allocation 112, 149
 in arbitration claims under Part 62 513
 commercial arbitration 444–5, 458–60, 464
 construction and industry adjudication 404
 fee refunds 96
 inquisitorial 458
 international arbitration 479
 oral 457
 pre-trial 457
 skeleton arguments 458–9
 UNCITRAL Model Law 484
 written submissions 458–9
Her Majesty's Courts and Tribunals Services (HMCTS) 300–1
Her Majesty's Revenue and Customs (HMRC) 248, 313
High Court 95
 anti-suit injunctions 478
 appeals 464, 513–14
 arbitral tribunals 431
 arbitration 427
 binding effect 491–2
 construction industry adjudication 403
 enforcement of domestic arbitral awards 523
 family proceedings 100
 judges as arbitrators 434
 New York Convention arbitration awards 523
 seat of arbitration 490
 see also High Court jurisdiction in arbitration claims
High Court jurisdiction in arbitration claims 494–515
 anti-suit injunctions 496
 appeals on point of law 505–8
 appeals to Court of Appeal 513–14
 application or Part 8 claim 508–9
 appointment procedure, failure of 497
 arbitration claim form 510–12
 arbitrators, appointment, removal and replacement of 497–8
 automatic directions 513
 conditions to be satisfied 502
 courts having jurisdiction over arbitration claims 509
 defendants to arbitration claim 509
 disclosure 499–500
 exhaustion of arbitral appeals and reviews 506
 extending time for beginning of proceedings 497
 hearings under Part 62 513
 interim injunctions 500
 judicial review of arbitral proceedings 501

High Court jurisdiction in arbitration claims (*cont.*)
  loss of right to object 505
  no agreement to dispense with reasons 506
  no contrary agreement 506
  orders to prevent parties breaching agreements to arbitrate 495–6
  permission of the court 507–8
  point must arise from award 507
  points of law 501–2, 508
  powers to secure evidence available to tribunals 498–9
  procedural orders 498–501
  procedure 508–13
  question of law 505–6
  resignation of arbitrator 498
  s 44 exclusion 501
  serious irregularity 502–5
  setting aside appointment of sole arbitrator 497
  stay of legal proceedings 495–6
  substantial injustice 504–5
  taking a step in the proceedings 496
  time limits 509
  tribunal asked to determine the point 506
  witnesses 459
High Court Practice Note: Civil Litigation: Case Management (1995) 8
Hong Kong 319
Hong Kong International Arbitration Centre (HKIAC) 313, 442
Hong Kong Monetary Authority 313
'hot tubbing' (witness conferencing) 459
hourly fees/rates 57, 59, 60, 228
housing disputes 28, 62, 97, 99
human rights 12, 426–7
Hybrid Dispute Resolution Processes - Getting the Best while Avoiding the Worst of Both Worlds? 286
hybrids 34
immigration cases 62
immunity of arbitrators 437
impartiality 497–8
  arbitrators 435
  construction and industry adjudication 403–4
  mediators 241
implied terms, wording of 177
Impossible Takes a Little Longer, The - Mediating Really Complex Cases 313
in-court mediation *see* judicial mediation
indemnity costs orders 145–6
independence
  arbitrators 435
  mediators 240–1
  solicitors 80–1
Independent Dispute Avoidance Panel (IDAP) 314
Independent Doctor's Federation 313
independent expert 34
Independent Healthcare Advisory Services 313
Independent Mediation - Information for Judges, Magistrates and Legal Advisors 309
Independent Standards Commission 321
independent third parties 310
India 319
Individual Membership Registration Scheme 236, 238
industry adjudication *see* construction and industry adjudication
inexperience, concern about 212–13
information
  about ADR options 50
  concealing as a tactic 168–9
  disclosure 89–90
  funding 56
  further, request for before using ADR 140–1
  given to mediator 247
  negotiation 180, 201–3
  position statements 262
  tactics relating to 168–9
information and communication technology (ICT) 34–5, 57, 68
  online dispute resolution (ODR) 70–1
information stage in mediation 269, 270, 277–8, 281
initial advice 38
initiation and failure of proceedings 135–7
injunctions
  anti-suit 475, 478, 496
  arbitration awards and orders 491
  interim 500, 501
  jurisdictional objections 475
injustice, substantive 504–5
inquisitorial approach in construction and industry adjudication 404
Institute of Chartered Accountants 381
Institute of Civil Engineers (ICE) 442
  Short Procedure 445–6
Institute of Family Law Arbitrators (IFLA) 426
institutional arbitration 424
institutional rules, silence in 443
instructions
  clarification of in negotiation 188–9
  material departure from 384–5
insurance 72
  funding 61
insurers and attendance at mediation 260
integrity 81
intellectual property disputes 297, 314
Intellectual Property Office 314
inter-client discussion 25
interest 523
  arbitration awards and orders 491
  construction and industry adjudication 405
interest groups and attendance at mediation 260
interim applications 149–50

interim awards in arbitration 486, 487
interim directions
in commercial arbitration 448–9
interim injunctions in arbitration 500, 501
interim measures and UNCITRAL Model Law 483–4
interim orders 41, 46
recording settlement 295, 366–7
interim payments and commercial arbitration 447
interim remedies and arbitration 487
intermediary, mediator as 234
internal market clause 73
international arbitration 11–12, 31–2, 40, 60, 466–85
advising client 467
amiable compositeur 471
answer to request for arbitration 481
anti-suit injunctions 478
applicable law 470–4
award, place of 469
definition of 'international' in arbitration 467
EU 473
ex aequo et bono 471
hearings 479
ICC arbitral tribunals 481
ICC Rules of Arbitration 480–2
jurisdictional issues 473, 474–8
Kompetenz-Kompetenz 478
language 479
law of arbitration agreement 472–3
law, or other rules 471
law, problems caused by different systems of 469–70
meetings 479
online ADR and ODR 69
privilege 479–80
procedural law 473–4
procedural matters 479–80
procedure prior to hearing 481–2
proper law of contract 470–2
request for arbitration 480–1
reserving client's position 477
seat or place of 468–9, 474, 481
security for costs 480
stateless arbitrations 474
supervisory jurisdiction 469
terms of reference 481
timing of objection to jurisdiction in 476–7
see also United Nations Commission on International Trade (UNCITRAL) Model Law
International Centre for Settlement of Investment Disputes (ICSID) 442
International Chamber of Commerce (ICC) 409
arbitral tribunals 481
commercial arbitration 442
jurisdictional objections 476
seat of arbitration 468
tribunals 482
see also International Chamber of Commerce (ICC) Rules of Arbitration
International Chamber of Commerce (ICC) Rules of Arbitration 467
answer to the request 481
arbitral tribunals 481
arbitration 480–1
hearings and decision 482
international arbitration 480–2
language of arbitration 479
no contrary agreement 506
procedure prior to hearing 481–2
request for arbitration 480–1
seat of arbitration 481
terms of reference 435, 481
International Corporation for the Assignment of Names and Numbers (ICANN) 71
International Court of Arbitration (ICA) 480, 481, 482
International Dispute Resolution Centre 299–300
international disputes 69, 122
International Institute for Conflict Prevention and Resolution (CPR) 321
international law 506
international mediation 40, 319–30
advantages 320
enforceability of settlement agreements 330
EU Directive on Mediation in Civil and Commercial Cases 323–9
European Code of Conduct for Mediators 329
growth of in Europe 322
harmonization 322–3
preparation for 320–1
process of 321–2
International Mediation - The Art of Business Diplomacy 320, 321
International Mediation and Arbitration Centre 321
International Mediation Institute (IMI) 21, 255, 316, 321
Code of Professional Conduct 321
Disciplinary Commission 321
International Trade Marks Association (INTA) 297, 313–14
Mediation Guidelines 314
Mediation Rules 314
Internet Dispute Resolution (iDR) 69
internet use 37, 68
see also information and communications technology; online dispute resolution
interviews, mediators 254
introductions in mediation 269, 271
irregularity
powers to deal with 490
serious 487–9
issue of proceedings, after 176

issues
  identification of 177
  making case on 203–5
  position statements 262
  underlying, probing 277–8
IT-based arbitration 57
IT-based options 34–5

Jackson ADR Handbook 139
Jackson, Lord Justice Rupert Matthew 10
Jackson Review 4, 9, 11, 24, 47, 107
  active case management 106
  compulsory ADR 122
  courts' approach to ADR 96
  funding 52–3
  mediation 216, 222
  Part 36 offers to settle 63, 106
  sanctions 126
Jackson's Recommendations: The Government Response 10
Jacob, Sir Jack 116
Japan 319
Jarndyce v Jarndyce 3
Joint Contracts Tribunal (JCT) 442
  Rules for Adjudication 406
  standard form contract adjudication clauses 404
joint meetings 271–3, 281
joint position statement 263
judges as arbitrators 434
judgment, rejection of ADR after 142–3
judicial encouragement of ADR 114–16
judicial endorsement in negotiation 218–19
judicial evaluation
  Chancery Division 350–1
  Commercial Court 348
  early neutral evaluation (ENE) 103, 105, 348–51
  Social Security and Child Support (SSCS) Tribunal ENE pilot scheme 349–50
  Technology and Construction Court 348–9
judicial mediation in in-court Civil Mediation Council schemes 297, 304–6
judicial review of arbitral proceedings 501–8
  appeal on a point of law 505–8
  High Court jurisdiction 495
  objections to jurisdiction 474–8
  preliminary points of law 501–2
  serious irregularity 502–5
Juris International 321
jurisdiction
  High Court *see* High Court
  international arbitration 469, 473, 474–8
  selection of ADR 40
  substantive 475–6
  supervisory 469
Justice Directorate of the European Commission 329

Katsh, Ethan 70
key questions, asking 199
King, Claire 227, 305
Kiser, Randall 18
Kompetenz-Kompetenz 478

LAA Mediation Quality Mark Standard (MQMS) 229
language
  affecting mediator selection 255
  EU 323
  interactive multilingual system 74
  international arbitration 479
  international mediation 321
law 205
  of arbitration agreement 472–3
  international arbitration 471, 474
  tactics relating to 172–3
Law Reform Commission of the Republic of Ireland 250
Law Society 236, 307, 381
  Code of Practice for Civil and Commercial Mediation 231–2
  Family Mediation Panel 301
LawWorks 57, 71
  mediation 259, 302, 317–18
lawyers
  control of case, ADR undermining 48
  expertise gained as (mediators) 254
  mediation 259
  providing ADR service 78–9
  role of 24
  settlement 292
lay clients, joint meetings between 281
lay witnesses 275
legal advice and dispute resolution problems 36–9
legal advice privilege in mediation 246
Legal Aid Agency (LAA) 62, 229
  mediation 265, 302, 305
  recording settlement 356
legal aid scheme 96
Legal Negotiation and Settlement 167
Legal Ombudsman 339–40, 344–5
legal professional privilege 86
legal representatives
  role of in commercial arbitration 443–5
  see also barristers; lawyers; solicitors
legal research in ADR 14, 173
legal rights 175
legal service providers, competition between 45
Legal Services Commission (LSC) 80, 229, 309, 329
Legal Services Complaints Commissioner 19
legal terminology and tests 172–3
legislation: full text of Arbitration Act 1996 533–71
Lehman Brothers Related Investment Products Dispute Mediation and Arbitration Scheme 313
letters and negotiated settlement 361–2

liability 69
  arbitrators' fees 437
  in respect of costs 55, 151–2
libel 42
limitation periods
  arbitral tribunals 431
  mediation 328
listening 196–7
Litigants in Person 96, 302
litigation
  ADR undermining 47
  and arbitration compared 409
  costs 150–1, 175
  main stages 38–9
  mediation prior to 225–7
  recovery of costs 149–55
Litigation Funding Agreement (LFA) 62
local education authorities (LEAs) 314
Local Government Ombudsman 343
London Court of International Arbitration (LCIA) 442, 468
London Maritime Arbitrators Association (LMAA) 442
London Metal Exchange (LME) 431–2, 442, 461
  appeals 464
  binding effect 492
  date of award 490
  panel 462
  rules 463
London SEN Mediation Service 314
'look-sniff' arbitrations 445

McKenna, Katherine 350
Mackie, Karl 320
majority decisions in arbitration 489–90
mandatory provisions in arbitration 421–2
manifest error 385–6
marriage breakdown and mediation 305
Mayor's and City of London County Court Mediation Scheme 297, 299–300
MED-ARB 34, 285, 425–6
Mediating Construction Disputes: An Evaluation of Existing Practice 227, 305
Mediation: An approach to resolving workplace issues 310
mediation 28–30, 215–51
  accreditation 234–6
  adjournment 283
  advantages 220, 226
  advocates, role of 287–91
  after litigation begins 226
  agreed bundle 263–4
  agreement to mediate 256–7
  attendees 258–60
  'automated' 72
  before issue 226
  Civil Mediation Online Directory 303–4
  closed meetings 270
  closing joint meeting 283
  commencement 268–9
  communications not protected by without prejudice rule 244–6
  community 316–17
  confidential bundles 264
  confidentiality 84–5, 247–9, 327–8
  consensus-building in environmental disputes or public policy issues 315–16
  costs 227–9
  court mediation schemes 299–302
  deal 316
  definition 215–16
  delay in consent to 143
  disadvantages 226
  disclosure of position statements and documents 264–5
  disputes suitable for 219–20
  domestic 329
  duration of 255
  duties 82
  effectiveness 216–18
  encouraging use 223–5
  evaluative 229–30
  expenses 228–9
  and expert determination, differences between 380
  experts 260
  exploration/information stage 269, 270, 277–8
  facilitative 229–30
  file 28
  funding 58–9, 229
  healthcare sector schemes 313
  historic schemes 298–9
  insurers 260
  interest groups 260
  international 319–30
  joint open meetings in exploration or bargaining stage 281
  judicial mediation schemes 304–6
  key stages in preparation for 266
  LawWorks 317–18
  lawyers 259
  legal advice privilege 246
  limitation periods 328
  litigation, prior to 225–7
  mini-trial or executive tribunal 314–15
  multi-party disputes 312–13
  and negotiation, differences between 217
  negotiation/bargaining stage 269, 270, 278–80
  open joint meeting 270
  opening stage 269, 270, 271–7
  organizing process 233
  other documents that parties may wish to bring 265
  other steps that may need to be taken for preparation 265–6
  overview 159
  person with authority to settle 259
  pilot schemes 298–9, 302–3
  position statements 261–3, 264–5
  practice administration 242–3
  pre-mediation meeting/contact 258
  preparing for 252–67
  prescription periods 328
  privilege 244
  pro bono 317–18
  procedure 241
  process of 268–91
  project 314

mediation (*cont.*)
  quality of 325
  reasons for using 222–3
  recourse to 325
  regulation 234–6, 238–9
  repeat instructions 242
  representatives of the parties 259
  restorative justice 316
  settlement/closing stage 269, 270, 281–3
  specialist schemes 313–14
  specific cases 306–12
  stages of 269–71
  styles of 229–32, 254
  success of 221–2
  supporting documents 263–4
  termination 242, 283
  timing 225–7
  training 235–6
  unreasonable conduct 144–5
  venue selection 255–6
  whether law should be reformed 250
  without prejudice rule 243–6
  witnesses of fact 260
Mediation Advocacy 275, 288
mediation advocacy 287–8
Mediation Agreement 28, 29, 85, 242
Mediation Audits 221, 239
mediation awareness session 11
Mediation, CFAs and conflicts of interest 229
Mediation Directory 236
Mediation Information Assessment Meetings (MIAMs) 11, 224–5
  court mediation schemes 297, 302
  family proceedings 100–1, 123, 307–8
  judicial mediation 305
  pilot court schemes 11, 303
  pre-mediation meeting/contact 258
Mediation in Planning 315
Mediation Quality Mark Standard (MQMS) 229
Mediation Room 70
Mediation Scheme (CAMS) 142, 221, 225, 228, 297, 301–2, 303
Mediation Scheme (FCA) 313
mediation services, lack of oversight in 21–2
Mediation Settlement Enforcement Order (MSEO) 326, 330
Mediation Standards Board 239
Mediation UK 317
mediation-arbitration (MED-ARB) 34, 285, 425–6
Mediator Skills and Techniques: Triangle of Influence 255, 275, 284, 322
mediators
  accreditation 254
  competence 240
  confidentiality 242, 247–8
  continuous professional development 325
  disciplinary proceedings against 251
  ethical considerations 240–3
  expertise 253–4
  factors influencing selection 253–5
  fairness 241
  fees 228
  impartiality 241
  independence 240–1
  information given to 247
  interviewing 254
  language and cultural considerations affecting selection of 255
  neutrality 240–1
  opening statement 271–3
  other information from parties prior to mediation 265
  personal recommendation assisting selection 253
  personality 253
  practical experience as 254
  qualities required 253
  role 232–4, 283–4
  selecting 252–5
  shuttle-diplomat, acting as 279
  strategies to help parties work through deadlock 279–80
  team of 255
  training 325
  whether can be sued 250–1
  and without prejudice rule 246
  as witness 249–50
Mediators on Mediation 253, 310, 313, 322
medical negligence 62, 303
meetings
  giving advice 38
  international arbitration 479
  joint 271–3, 281
member states 329
Members' Complaints Resolution Service 237
memorandum of agreement 29
Memorandum of Understanding (MOU) 309
Menkel-Meadow, Carrie 164
Mercantile Court 348, 509
merits of case
  adverse costs orders 129–30
  evaluation requested by both parties 284–5
  negotiation 203
miners 312
mini-trial in mediation 314–15
Ministry of Justice 215
  Annual Pledge Report 221
  civil court fees reform 96
  Consultation on the Civil Court Reforms 239
  court mediation schemes 297
  Find a Civil Mediation Provider 235
  Find a Mediation Service 309
'mirroring' behaviour 195
misconduct 85
misrepresentation 520
mistake 520
Model Code of Conduct for Mediations in the EU 237
Model Executive Tribunal Procedure 315

Model Expert Determination Agreement 381
monetary offers 280
money claims 175
moving on in negotiation 170
multi-party disputes 35, 41, 312–13
multi-tiered dispute resolution in arbitration 426
multi-track 10, 96, 109, 513
multilingual system, interactive 74
multiple concession 209

National Center for Technology and Dispute Resolution (NCTDR) 70, 71
National Family Mediation (NFM) 21, 307
National Forum of Restorative Practitioners 316
National Health Service (NHS) Litigation Authority 313
National Health Service (NHS) Trusts 313
National Mediation Helpline (NMH) 9, 221, 298, 299, 303, 304
National Planning Forum 315–16
natural justice 421
negligence 85
  clinical 62, 303
  contributory 66
negotiation 25–8
  'automated' 72
  competitive 208
  duties 82–3
  and expert determination, differences between 380
  funding 58
  judicial endorsement 218–19
  and mediation, differences between 217
  overview 159
  position statements 262
  preparing for 174–91
  pro-forma plan 190–1
  process of 192–214
  strategies 160, 161–7
  styles 160
  tactics 160, 167–73
  when, how, where and who 192–4
negotiation/bargaining stage 269, 270, 278–80
Neuberger, Lord David Edmond 116, 386
neutral assistance 45
neutral determination *see* expert determination
neutral evaluation
  and expert determination, differences between 380
  see also early neutral evaluation (ENE)
neutral fact finding 348
neutrality 58, 59, 240–1
New Law Journal 250
New York Convention
  arbitration awards 522–4
  capacity 418
  commercial arbitration 439
  international arbitration 466
  international mediation 330
  jurisdictional objections 475
  MED-ARB 425
  seat/place of arbitration 469, 491
  settlement 487
New Zealand 319
no agreement *see* deadlock
non-adjudicative options 25–31
  disclosure of information 89–90
  expert evaluation 30–1
  inter-client discussion 25
  written offers 25
  see also conciliation; early neutral evaluation; mediation; negotiation
non-binding arbitration 425
non-binding findings 23
non-lawyers 410
non-mandatory provisions in arbitration 422, 423
non-party disclosure in arbitration 500
non-performance 413, 517
non-verbal communication 194
Norwich Pharmacal orders 499
notice of adjudication 396–9
notice of arbitration 431–2
notification of awards 491

objective standards 165, 169
objectives
  client's 44
  identifying 174–5
objectivity 45
offender, meeting between victim and 316
offers
  best reasonable 211
  negotiation 183–6, 208
  tactics relating to 169–70
  timely 131–2
  to pay reasonable fees 50
  to settle 8
  written 25
  see also Part 36 offers
Office for the Legal Services Complaints Commissioner 19
old obligations 517
Olympic Delivery Authority 314
Ombudsman Association 343
ombudsmen 7, 22, 34, 339–40, 343–5
on-notice applications in arbitration 500
one-stop arbitration 426
online dispute resolution (ODR) 11, 35, 68–75
  background to 69
  cross-jurisdictional 71
  development within the EU 73–4
  ICT, current role of 70–1
  international mediation 319, 323
  main bodies concerned with 70
  software options 68, 69, 71–3, 74
  terminology 69
online mediation (e-Mediation) 70, 286–7
Online Resource Centre 237, 239
Open statement of Financial Information 309

opening
  by agreeing on an agenda 198
  negotiation 198–201
  problems 201
  with a statement or proposal 198–9
opening joint meeting
  closing 275
  mediation 270
  seating plan 272
opening stage of mediation 269, 270, 271–7
opening statement in mediation 271–5, 289
opponent
  case, weaknesses in 204
  competitive, dealing with 212
  inviting to open 199–200
  poorly prepared, dealing with 211
  view of facts and evidence 179
options
  adjudicative 31–4
  key elements 23
  non-adjudicative 25–31
  weighing up 17
oral agreements 292, 417
oral arguments 204–5
oral contract 213, 358
oral hearing in arbitration 457
orders
  case management 108–9
  court 42, 359, 520–1
  granting a stay 114
  interim 41, 46, 295, 366–7
  peremptory 449–50, 487
  preliminary 483–4
  to prevent parties breaching agreements to arbitrate 495–6
  Ungley 108, 121, 122
  see also alternative dispute resolution (ADR) order; arbitration awards and orders; consent orders; costs orders
outcomes
  ADR 15–16
  proposing 204
  recording 213
overriding objective in ADR 105
oversight, lack of in mediation services 22

Panel of Neutrals 313–14
parameters setting 169
parking issues 170
Parliamentary Health Service Ombudsman 343
Parliamentary Ombudsman 345
Part 7 claims 496
Part 8 claims 326, 327, 500, 508–9, 521
Part 23 applications 326, 327
Part 26 offers 134
Part 36 offers 25, 38, 46, 50, 51
  adverse costs orders 132
  advice-giving 39
  both parties at fault 141
  case management 106–7
  considerations for the parties 64
  financial analysis and risk assessment 65–6, 67
  funding 53, 63–4
  impact on refusal to use ADR 132–5
  Legal Aid Agency funding 62
  mediation 264
  negotiation 21
  position statements 262
  rejecting ADR after judgment and before hearing of appeal 142
  unreasonable conduct in mediation 144
partiality 381, 385, 462, 498
  see also impartiality
parties
  compelled by court to use ADR 120–3
  considerations for 64
  opening statements 273–5
  own costs of preparing for mediation 227
  position statements 262
party agreement in arbitration 422–3
party autonomy in arbitration 421–3
party-appointed experts 456
Pension Disability and Carers Service 350
Pensions Ombudsman 345
people, separating from problem 165
peremptory orders in arbitration 449–50, 487
performance, compromise based on of agreed terms 517
Permanent Court of Arbitration (PCA) 442
personal injury cases
  Court of Appeal Mediation Pilot Scheme 303
  courts' approach to ADR 96
  early neutral evaluation (ENE) 351
  mediation 311–12
  online ADR and ODR 69
personal injury claims 58
  online dispute resolution (ODR) 68, 72
Personal Injury Unit (PIU) 351
personal objectives 175
personal recommendation in mediation 253
personality affecting selection of mediator 253
persuasive arguments, identifying 181–3
Picking up the Pieces: Marriage and divorce two years after Information Provision. A study of the pilot scheme for the use of mediation as a part of the divorce process 19
pilot schemes 11, 221, 298–9, 300, 302–3, 349–50
place *see* seat/place in arbitration
planning 184–6, 205
Planning and Environmental Mediation Service 315
Planning Inspectorate 315
plenary session 271–3, 276
point of law, preliminary 501–2
points of claim in commercial arbitration 451–3
Police and Crime Commissioners 316
poorly prepared opponent 211

position statements
aims of 261
content of 261–3
disclosure 264–5
joint 263
mediation 261–3
positional strategy 162–3, 168
possession claims 99
post-claim conciliation 334
post-mediation role 234
Practical Approach to Civil Procedure, A 54, 63, 498, 499, 501, 508–9, 513
Practical Approach to Effective Litigation, A 64
practical experience of mediators 254
practice administration in mediation 242–3
practitioner texts 178
pragmatic strategy in negotiation 165
Pre-Action Conduct Practice Direction 97–8, 223
pre-action disclosure in arbitration 500
Pre-Action Protocol for Claims for Damages in Relation to the Physical State of Commercial Property at Terminations of a Tenancy (Dilapidations Protocol) 97
Pre-Action Protocol for Construction and Engineering Disputes 99–100, 152
Pre-Action Protocol for Low Value Personal Injury Claims in Road Traffic Accidents 69
pre-action protocols 97–101, 176
adverse costs orders 127–8
construction and engineering disputes 99–100, 152
financial remedies cases 101
general position 98–9
giving advice 38
possession claims 99
Pre-Application Protocol for Mediation Information and Assessment 100, 307
pre-conditions 169, 209
pre-mediation meeting/contact 258
pre-trial hearing/conference in commercial arbitration 457
pre-trial reviews 108, 131
precedent 418–19
Preliminary Court Settlement Conference 304
preliminary meeting in commercial arbitration 447
preparation
mediation 252–67, 287
negotiation 174–91
prescription periods in mediation 328
presentation
effective 195–6
tactics relating to 171–2
Pride comes before a Claim - The Psychology of Dispute Resolution 17
pride, personal 17
'principled strategy' 164–5
priorities, understanding client's 183–4
privacy 50, 83, 440
private (closed) meetings
mediation 289–90
separate 276–7
privilege 43, 86
international arbitration 479–80
negotiation 201
privileged material and sanctions 147–8
pro bono mediation 317–18
problem solving approach/strategy 15, 36–7, 163–5
procedural directions
arbitration 441, 473–4, 486
international arbitration 479–80
procedural orders
arbitration 486–7, 498–501
commercial arbitration 447–9
procedural regulation 10–11
procedural rules
in commercial arbitration 441–3
procedural stage 175–7
procedural steps, strategic use of 16
procedure in commercial arbitration 446–61, 462
process fees 56
process, variations in during mediation 284–7
Professional Conduct Rules 243
professional duties
compliance with core 79–82
to give advice 37–8
professional ethics 76–92
advice about ADR options 77–8
authority to settle 90–1
compliance with professional duties 79–82
confidentiality 83–6
disclosure 89–90
lawyers providing ADR service 78–9
legal professional privilege 86
mediation 82
negotiation 82–3
practical considerations 89
relationship with clients 91–2
without prejudice communications 86–9
professional misconduct 340
professional negligence 19–20, 78
progress in negotiation 210
Promise of Mediation, The: The Transformative Approach to Conflict 232
proper law, contract in international arbitration 470–2
proportionality 53, 54
proposal, opening 198–9
Provider Accreditation Scheme 235, 236, 303
provider's fee 57–8
Psychological Barriers to Litigation Settlement: An Experimental Approach 17
psychological factors 17–18, 194
Psychological Principles in Negotiating Civil Settlements 17

public bodies, complaints against 22
public funding 80, 265, 309
public importance 507, 508
public interest 16
  disclosure 86
public policy 42, 284, 315–16, 504
publicity 329

qualifications of arbitrators 435
Qualified One Way Costs Shifting (QOCS) 96
quality in mediation 325
quasi-criminal allegations 42
Queen's Bench Guide, The 104
question of law in arbitration 505–6
questions/questioning
  construction and industry adjudication 403–4
  effective 196
  key 199
  as tactic 168

reactive devaluation 216
'reality test' 277
'reasonable costs' 373
reasons 405, 490
reciprocal behaviour 195
recognition (New York Convention arbitration awards) 523–4
record-keeping 358
recording settlement 355–73
  compromise agreements 357
  consent order 367–9
  contract or deed 360–3
  different methods after proceedings have commenced 364
  drafting terms 359–60
  endorsements on briefs 363–5
  enforceable forms 358–9
  exchange of letters 360
  existing court proceedings 363
  forms of recorded outcome 356–7
  full and final 357
  informing court of settlement 373
  interim order 366–7
  methods of recording settlement agreements 360–72
  options for 295
  outcome, recording 213, 294–5
  reaching agreement 355–6
  records made during ADR process 358
  relitigating after settlement 372
  subject to contract 357
  terms as regards costs 372–3
  Tomlin order 369–71
  who should produce a formal record 358
recovery of costs 149–55
  as damages 154–5
  unsuccessful processes 150–4
Redfern schedule 455–6
reduction of bill 343
referral notice in construction and industry adjudication 400–2, 403
Reform of Civil Cases 301
reframing 169
refugee status 115
refund 96, 343, 373
refusal to use ADR *see* sanctions
Regional Employment Judge 306
Registration Scheme 236, 239
regulation 19–20, 234–6, 238–9
rejection of ADR after judgment and before hearing of an appeal 142–3
related disputes 238, 404, 428
relationships, preserving 220, 226, 262
relitigation after settlement 372
reluctance to engage in mediation 220
remedies 491
  financial 87, 101
  interim 487
removal of arbitrators 436, 497–8
removal industry 34
rent arrears claims 97
reopening issues 170
repeat referrals 242
replacement of arbitrators 497–8
Report on Alternative Dispute Resolution: Mediation and Conciliation 250
representatives of parties 259, 281
research 173
reserving client's position in international arbitration 477
residential building contracts and adjudication 406
resignation of arbitrators 436
Resolute Systems 71
Resolution 307
resolution of disputes *see* fair resolution of disputes
Resolution group 12
Resolving Workplace Disputes 310
respect for private and family life 115
response in negotiation 196
restorative justice 316
Restorative Justice Action Plan for the Criminal Justice System 316
Restorative Justice Council 316
Restorative Practitioner Register 316
Review of Planning Applications 315
reviews, exhaustion of 506
Rifkin, Janet 70
right to object, loss of 505
rights of the parties, substantially affecting 507–8
risk assessment 64–6
risk reduction 15
road traffic accidents 58, 69
  see also personal injury
Roberts, Simon 300
robustness 49
Royal Institute of British Architects (RIBA) 399
Royal Institution of Chartered Surveyors (RICS) 315, 381, 399
Rules of Conduct 381

samples in commercial arbitration 463
sanctions 46–7, 125–48
avoidance of 146–7
backing out of agreed process 144
both parties at fault 141–2
costs cap on solicitor–client costs 145
costs orders 126–7
delay in consent to mediation 143
indemnity costs orders 145–6
information or evidence, requests for 140–1
practical steps for avoidance of 146–7
privileged material 147–8
rejection of ADR after judgment and before hearing of appeal 142–3
treatment of privileged material when seeking to impose 147–8
unreasonable conduct 144–5
whether ADR order made by court 139–40
see also adverse costs orders
'scatter-gun' approach 140
Scheme for Construction Contracts 396, 399, 403, 404, 405
Scott v Avery clause 418–19
seat/place in arbitration 468–9, 481, 490–1
seating plan in joint meetings for mediation 272
security for costs 447, 480
selection
ADR 40–7
mediators 252–5
neutral or expert determiner 381
sensitive information 46, 240
'serious irregularity' (definition) 502–5
settlement
advising on 79–80
advocate's role in mediation 290–1
on all issues apart from costs 154
alternative methods 130–7
arbitration 487
authority to settle 90–1, 169, 259
checking coverage and detail 293–4
contractual principles 296
full and final 357
informing court of 373
lawyer, role of 292
negotiated 361, 362, 522
no agreement reached 295–6
options for 278
oral agreement 292
pressure to reach 49
reaching 292–6
terms, drafting 359–60
see also enforcement of settlements and awards; recording settlement
settlement agreements 330
Settlement Judge 304–5
settlement/closing stage of mediation 269, 270, 281–3
Short Guide to Mediation in Planning 316
short-form arbitrations 445–6
shuttle-diplomat, mediator acting as 234, 279, 281
Side Letter 154
silence 139, 171, 443
Sime, Stuart 54, 63, 64, 431, 447, 450, 483, 492, 498, 499, 501, 508, 513
Singapore International Arbitration Centre (SIAC) 442
site visits 404, 460
skeleton arguments 458–9, 460, 496
Skype 70
small claims cases 4, 255, 299
Small Claims County Court Scheme 297, 299
Small Claims Court Mediation Scheme 286
Small Claims Mediation. A collection of 4 research reports on pilot schemes in County Courts 18
Small Claims Mediation Pilot Scheme 300
Small Claims Mediation Scheme 299, 300–1
Small Claims Mediation Service 300
small claims track 57–8, 224, 328
Social Security and Child Support (SSCS) Tribunal ENE pilot scheme 349–50
Society of Mediators 318
software for ODR 68, 69, 71–3, 74
sole arbitrators 434
setting aside appointment of 497
solicitor fees 56
solicitors
complaints against 340
professional ethics 76, 78–9, 80–1
Solicitors' Family Law Association 301, 307
Solicitors Regulation Authority (SRA) 20, 76
Code of Conduct 37, 76, 78, 240, 340, 356
Handbook 76
Indicative Behaviours 76
Outcomes 76
Principles 76, 77–9, 80, 240
Solving Disputes in the county courts: creating a simpler, quicker and more proportionate system 238, 329
special educational needs (SEN) 314
specialist systems 34
speed of ADR 13
'splitting the difference' 209–10
standard basis for costs 373
standardization 322
Standing Council of Mediation Advocates (SCMA) 287–8
stateless arbitrations 474
Statement of Truth 237–8
statements 198–9
as tactic 168
statements of case 264
commercial arbitration 451–3, 462–3
construction and industry adjudication 403
UNCITRAL Model Law 484

statutory arbitration 425
Statutory Code of Practice
  on Discipline and
  Grievance 309–10
stay of proceedings 47,
  113–14
  High Court
    jurisdiction 495–6
  pending 379–80
  persuading judge to
    order 50
strategies in negotiation
  161–7
stress, inducing 209
strong case 41
structure
  negotiation 197–8
  tactics relating to 170–1
style
  choice of 161, 254
  mediation 229–32
  negotiation 161
subject to contract
  settlement 357
subsequent procedure under
  UNCITRAL Model
  Law 484
substantial injustice in
  arbitration 504–5
substantive contract
  411, 470
substantive dispute 476
substantive jurisdiction
  475–6
success
  assessment 18–19
  chances of 44–5, 55
  government department
    involvement 222
  mediation 221–2
  reasonable prospect
    of 138–9
success fees 60–1, 96
summary judgment 522
supervisory jurisdiction
  in international
  arbitration 469
supporting documents in
  mediation 263–4
surprise 170, 174, 176, 202,
  213
  avoidance of in negotiation
    178–9, 196
systems of law 469–70
tactics
  bargaining 209–10
  law 172–3
  negotiation 167–73
  offers and demands
    169–70
  presentation 171–2
  structure 170–1
'take it or leave it' 209
Tax Journal 313
*Technology and Construction
  Court Guide, The* 104–5,
  348
Technology and Construction
  Court (TCC)
  arbitration 509
  court mediation
    schemes 297
  Court Settlement Process
    (CSP) 304–5
  early neutral and/or expert
    evaluation 31
  early neutral evaluation
    (ENE) 348–9
  judge 348, 434
  Pre-action Protocol 104
Technology and Construction
  Solicitors' Association
  (TeCSA) 399
  Adjudication Rules 396
technology disputes 306–7
telephone mediations 70, 71,
  286
termination of mediation 242,
  283
terms of reference 435, 481
The Furniture Ombudsmen
  (TFO) Conciliation
  Scheme 336
third parties 74, 137, 147
third party funding 53–4,
  61–2, 76, 80, 293
threats in negotiation 172
time to think 171
time limits
  arbitration 430, 509
  mediations 297
timing 51
  construction and industry
    adjudication 403
  mediation 225–7
Tomlin orders 43, 369–71, 521
  advantages 371
  disadvantages 371
  drafting 357, 369–71
  enforcement of court
    orders 520
  example 370–1
  funding 53
  international
    mediation 326
  mediation 257, 282
  professional ethics 80
  recovery of ADR
    costs 151–2
  subject to contract 357
  terms as regards costs 373
*Toward another View of
  Legal Negotiation: The
  Structure of Problem
  Solving* 164
track allocation stage 38
  see also fast-track; multi-
    track; small claims
trade association mediation
  schemes 297
Trading Standards
  Institute 314
training
  ADR 20–1
  mediation 235–6, 325
  online ADR and ODR 71
travel expenses 57
trial, case being prepared
  for 177
tribunal-appointed
  experts 457
tribunals 7
  see also arbitral tribunals;
    employment tribunals
Tribunals Service 350
Trust Mediation 312
*Twisting Arms: Court referred
  and court linked mediation
  under judicial pressure.
  A review of the Central
  London County Court
  Scheme* 18, 221, 298–9
two-contract cases in
  arbitration 415–16

UK College of Mediators 301
ultimatums 169
umpire 433–4, 489–90
underlying issues 277–8
undue influence 520
unfair prejudice petitions 496
Ungley Order 108, 121, 122

Uniform Domain Name Dispute Resolution Policy (UDRP) 71
United Nations Commission on International Trade Law (UNCITRAL) 69, 70, 71, 409, 442
Model Law on International Commercial Arbitration 410, 482–4
applicable law 471
arbitral tribunals 483
commencement of arbitration 483
commercial arbitration 440
different systems of law 470
hearings 484
impartiality and independence 435
institutional arbitration 424
interim measures 483–4
international arbitration 466, 467
international mediation 322
interpretation 482
language of arbitration 479
powers to secure evidence available to tribunals 499
removal of arbitrators 498
statements of case 484
subsequent procedure 484
United States 12, 18, 19, 122, 319
consensus-building mediation 315
mediation 250
online ADR and ODR 72
unreasonable conduct in mediation 144–5
unreasonable refusal to consider ADR *see* adverse costs orders
unsuccessful processes in recovery of costs 150–4
urgent applications in arbitration 500–1
Urwin, Peter 306
Ury, William 164, 212

vacancies for arbitrators 437
venue selection in mediation 255–6
victim, meeting between offender and 316
video-conferencing 68
views in commercial arbitration 460
virtual collaborative workspaces (e-rooms) 74
virtual meetings 70, 287
virtual reality 74
'visual blind-bidding' 72
Voluntary Mediation Pilot Scheme 298

wasted costs order 19, 66, 78
WATNA *see* worst alternative to a negotiated agreement
weak cases 48, 203–4
weaknesses in strategies 162–8
webcam conferencing 70, 287
West Midlands Family Mediation Scheme 302
Williams, G. 167
winding up 519–20
withdrawal from mediation 152
without prejudice communications 86–9
without prejudice discussion 131, 449, 456
without prejudice matters 144
without prejudice rule in mediation 243–6
witness conferencing in commercial arbitration 459
witness statements 38, 264, 456
witnesses
commercial arbitration 459
of fact in mediation 260
lay 275
mediation 249–50, 275
Woolf, Lord Harry Kenneth 95
Woolf reforms 8, 95–6, 114
Working Group on Online Dispute Resolution 70
workplace mediation 309–10
Workplace Mediation Provider Registration Scheme 236
World Intellectual Property Organisation Arbitration and Mediation Centre (WIPO) 321
World Mediation Forum 321
worst alternative to a negotiated agreement (WATNA) 188, 205, 234, 265
written agreement
arbitration agreement 416–17
construction contracts 395
written communications 83, 147, 243
written contract as settlement 359
written offers 25
written submissions in commercial arbitration 458–9